D0848962

f**P**

FREE PRESS   *New York London Toronto Sydney Singapore*

The Beginning of Wisdom

READING GENESIS

Leon R. Kass

FREE PRESS
A Division of Simon & Schuster, Inc.
1230 Avenue of the Americas
New York, NY 10020

Copyright © 2003 by Leon R. Kass, M.D.
All rights reserved,
including the right of reproduction
in whole or in part in any form.

FREE PRESS and colophon are trademarks
of Simon & Schuster, Inc.

For information regarding special discounts for bulk purchases,
please contact Simon & Schuster Special Sales at
1-800-456-6798 or business@simonandschuster.com

Designed by Jeanette Olender
Manufactured in the United States of America

1   3   5   7   9   10   8   6   4   2

Library of Congress Cataloging-in-Publication Data
Kass, Leon.
The beginning of wisdom : reading Genesis / Leon R. Kass.
p.   cm.
Includes bibliographical references (p.   ) and index.
1. Bible. O.T. Genesis—Commentaries.   I. Title.
BS1235.53.K37   2003
222'.1106—dc21   2002045593
ISBN 0-7432-4299-8

For Zayda's treasures—

Polly, Hannah, Naomi, and *Abigail*

—and, God willing, also for theirs:

Engage the text. Hold it close. Hand it down.

Contents

X   Contents

PREFACE

THE PROFESSOR AND THE FOSSIL

How does a man of medicine and science, raised in a strictly secular home without contact with Scripture, come to write a book on the Bible? It is a mystery, even to the author. My scientific training leads me to suspect that it all comes from a late-onset, dominant—and, I fear, lethal—rabbinic gene, one that, like Huntington's chorea, gave no evidence of its existence during my first forty years. But such a hereditary cause would require for its expression some appropriate environmental stimulus. About this stimulus I am quite certain. For I remember exactly when and how I came to study Genesis. It was all because of Darwin.

In autumn 1978, I gave a lecture on Darwin's *Origin of Species* at St. John's College in Santa Fe, New Mexico. The following morning—it was Saturday, the Jewish Sabbath, when my observant coreligionists were in synagogues reading from the book of Genesis—and still in a Darwinian mood, I persuaded my host and friend, Robert Sacks, to drive me to a nearby rock quarry where I might hunt for fossils. As I sat upon the ground in that barren excavation, splitting open rocks to no avail, I discovered something far more precious than fossils. For my friend Sacks, who had just completed a full commentary on the book of Genesis, was regaling me with one after another of his discoveries in the text. I had, the previous year, taught Genesis in a new common-core course my colleagues and I had designed at the University of Chicago, but it had not then seemed to me a book carefully constructed or worth studying as closely as the works of the great philosophers or poets. It was, so I then thought, an edifying book that spoke only to believers. But as I listened to Sacks point out and interpret strange juxtapositions in the text—what is the point of the long and boring genealogical chapter of "begat's," detailing the generations from Adam to Noah, and how is it related to the global violence that follows immediately thereafter? why does God say that the imagination of man's heart is evil from his youth right after Noah's sacrifice? why do the Noahide law and covenant come right after Noah's sacrifice and God's comment?—I realized that I had badly underestimated the subtlety of the book and that I had yet to learn how to read it. I returned to Chicago eager to have another look.

For the next two years my wife and I, along with a faculty colleague (Ralph Lerner) and some of our students (Adam Schulman, David Sher, Karen Kapner, and Sidney Keith), met weekly at our house to discuss the weekly portion of the Pentateuch that is read aloud in synagogues on the Sabbath. I read the chapters in Genesis with the aid of Sacks's commentary, a copy of which he had been kind enough to give me even before it was published.[1] The stories of Genesis took hold of me. Though the characters seemed larger than life, the troubles they faced were clearly not so different from our own. I brought the stories to the family dinner table, where conversation was keen but closure was never reached about their meaning. There was, it seemed evident, deep wisdom to be found here, but it would not be available without great effort. I knew I had to persist.

At the University of Chicago, disciplinary boundaries have long been fluid, and my own appointment gave me great latitude in teaching. Although I had been brought to Chicago because of my interest in science and morals and my work in biomedical ethics, I had begun teaching courses on classic texts— Plato's *Symposium*, Aristotle's *Nicomachean Ethics* and *De Anima*, Lucretius's *On the Nature of Things*, Descartes's *Discourse on Method*, Bacon's *New Atlantis*, Rousseau's *Discourse on the Origin of Inequality Among Men*, Darwin's *Origin of Species* and *The Descent of Man*—with a view to the question of the nature of man and its bearing on how we are to live. It was now becoming clear to me that the Bible also had an "anthropology," an account of the human being, embedded in its account of the good life. The Bible belonged in conversation with these philosophical texts, where, I began to suspect, it could more than hold its own.

Yet it did not seem proper for me to offer courses at the university on the Hebrew Bible. Public teachers of the book, I then thought and still think, should be either biblical scholars or knowledgeable and religiously observant keepers of the tradition—preferably both—and I was neither. But adhering to these strictures led to a difficulty. As I soon learned, biblical scholars, preoccupied with determining the sources of the text or comparing it with the writings of other traditions, now rarely read and teach the Bible in a wisdom-seeking spirit. And the traditional readers of the text often read too narrowly, resolving textual difficulties in the most pious direction. After a while, I persuaded myself that I would do my students no harm if I convened a not-for-credit course on Genesis in which we would read philosophically, solely for meaning and understanding, in search of wisdom.

---

1. Sources for all quotations except those from the Bible, as well as other citations, can be found by looking up the appropriate page and the last few words of each phrase in the backmatter Endnotes.

In autumn 1980, ten handpicked students joined me one evening a week, over ten weeks, for a three-hour session on Genesis. The discussions were exhilarating. Everyone had good things to say. Everyone saw the power of the stories and the value of reading them philosophically. My intuitions were vindicated.

It would take five more years before I got up my nerve to publicly offer an official course on Genesis, for credit and open to all. Since then, I have taught eight seminars (now lasting two quarters, since we cannot finish in one) on Genesis, for both undergraduate and graduate students; these have provided the most enjoyable and successful experiences in nearly thirty years in the classroom. The classes, devoted solely to expounding and interpreting this single text, proceed entirely by discussion. As a result, I have learned enormously from my students, benefiting both from their original insights and from the objections they raise to my suggested interpretations. While I am indebted to many, I would like to acknowledge here the special help I have received from Rachel Airmet, Kristen Dietrich Balisi, Monty Brown, Adam Davis, Daniel Doneson, Craig Hanoch, Hannah Hintze, Ward Jacobs, Eric Lavoie, Yuval Levin, Margaret Litvin, Paul Ludwig, Anna Dannhauser Marks, Dan Meron, Chris Nadon, Reeghan Raffals, Richard Resnick, Eric Schwarze, Dan Sofaer, Bret Stephens, Andrew Varcoe, and Kirstin Wilcox. Where possible, I will acknowledge their particular contributions as I proceed.

Invitations to lecture have enabled me to put my thoughts in order on some topics and stories in Genesis. Thanks are due to the Institute of Religion and Public Life, the Theology Department at Boston College, Cornell College, St. John's College (both Annapolis and Santa Fe campuses), and the Basic Program of Liberal Education for Adults and the "Human Being and Citizen" course at the University of Chicago. In the spring of 2000, I was privileged to serve as Joseph McCarthy visiting professor of philosophy at the Gregorian University in Rome, where, in a course on the first eleven chapters of Genesis, I learned much from trying out my approach with Roman Catholic priests and seminarians. Father Paul Mankowski, professor of biblical Hebrew at the Pontifical Biblical Institute, sat in on my class and made marvelous contributions, both philological and philosophical, in every session. Fittingly, the journey that began looking for fossils in New Mexico brought me to Jerusalem in May 2000, where three of my chapters were subjected to a most spirited and instructive critique by the scholars at the Shalem Center. Special thanks are owed to Dan Polisar, Josh Weinstein, Rabbi Yitzhak Lifschitz, Gabriel Danzig, David Hazony, and Asaph Sagiv.

Over the years, I found occasion to publish some ten articles on various subjects in Genesis, always aiming to bring this ancient text to bear on some enduring question of human existence. These essays have appeared since 1987 in *Commentary, The American Scholar,* and *First Things.* At some point it occurred to me to attempt an interpretation of the book as a whole, read in a wisdom-seeking spirit, in the hope that others might be able to follow my own journey from fossil hunting in New Mexico to biblical discussions in Jerusalem. (I give a fuller account of my rationale and a substantive account of my special approach in the Introduction.) A wonderful year (1998–99) as the William H. Brady Jr. visiting scholar at the American Enterprise Institute, courtesy of Christopher De-Muth (president of AEI) and Elizabeth Lurie (the Brady Foundation), enabled me to get most of the chapters drafted.

Two people have read the entire manuscript. Yuval Levin read the penultimate draft and made many valuable substantive and rhetorical suggestions, drawing on his broad knowledge of Hebrew, the Bible, and political philosophy and his great good sense about the many subjects under discussion. Amy Apfel Kass, my wife and dialectic partner of forty years, has for more than half those years conversed with me regularly and deeply about the text and its meanings. She has read and commented on multiple drafts of every chapter, saving me from error and self-indulgence and always enriching my understanding. So often have I made her insights and questions my own that I no longer know where any one of those written here—or at least the good ones—originated.

At the Free Press, I have been blessed to have Bill Rosen as my editor. His knowledge of and love for the biblical text, his immediate sympathy for my approach to reading it, and his excellent substantive advice and stylistic suggestions have made the editorial process simply a delight. I am deeply grateful for his thoughtful ways and skillful touch.

The reader may well wonder how these studies have affected my own outlook on life, morals, and religion. I wish I could give a definitive answer, but I am still in the middle of my journey. There are truths that I think I have discovered only with the Bible's help, and I know that my sympathies have shifted toward the biblical pole of the age-old tension between Athens and Jerusalem. I am no longer confident of the sufficiency of unaided human reason. I find congenial the moral sensibilities and demands of the Torah, though I must confess that my practice is still wanting. And I am frankly filled with wonder at the fact that I have been led to this spiritual point, God knows how. For the rest, I will let the book speak for me. If the reader finds here insights true and helpful for himself, that, more than my personal religious professions, should justify my efforts to share the search.

When I was an undergraduate at the University of Chicago in the mid-1950s, headed for a career in medicine and science, Maurice Samuel, a Jewish man of letters, published a book entitled *The Professor and the Fossil*. It was Samuel's spirited defense of Judaism, offered in rebuttal of the famous historian Arnold Toynbee, who in his magnum opus, *A Study of History*, had referred to Judaism as a "fossil religion." At the time, though I was impressed with Samuel's nerve, I had little opinion and less concern about the controversy, for I was then inclined to think all religions were fossils, superstitious leftovers from before the Age of Enlightenment. Little did I then imagine that I would someday be a professor myself. Little did I then imagine that I would later come to see the insufficiency of the scientific understanding of human life and the Enlightenment's view of the world. It would have been inconceivable to me that I would later find a most compelling kind of wisdom in the oldest of the still living religions—by the way, with the help of another book by Maurice Samuel, *Certain People of the Book*. Who is to say that the Lord does not work in mysterious ways?

A NOTE ON TRANSLATIONS

In studying Genesis and in preparing this book, I have consulted many translations of the Hebrew text. I have most frequently used those provided by Robert Alter, Umberto Cassuto, Dr. J. H. Hertz, the Reverend M. Rosenblum and Dr. A. M. Silberman (translators of the edition containing Rashi's commentary), Robert Sacks, and Nahum M. Sarna. Occasionally I have looked also at the King James Version and the Revised Standard Version. The translated excerpts of Genesis that appear throughout this book are often composites of versions found in different sources, selected and modified according to my own sense of what seems most fitting. As far as possible, I have sought the most literal translation compatible with readable English. The Hebrew original makes no distinction between what some editions treat as prose and as poetry: in layout everything looks the same. For my own exegetical purposes, I have often elected to have the biblical passages set off in verse format, the better to visualize certain patterns or to make evident the recurrence of terms or themes.

THE BEGINNING OF WISDOM

INTRODUCTION

THE BEGINNING OF WISDOM

This book offers a philosophic reading of the book of Genesis. Addressed to believers and nonbelievers alike, it should be of special interest to thoughtful children of skeptics, people who (like the author) now have good reason to want to see for themselves and to learn firsthand what it was and is that their parents or grandparents rejected. For though we are knowledgeable, powerful, and privileged with opportunities beyond our ancestors' wildest dreams, many of us remain psychically, morally, and spiritually adrift. This introduction aims both to clarify these claims and to invite the reader to take up a philosophic reading of the Bible.

QUESTS FOR WISDOM

What, you may well ask, do I mean by "philosophic" and "philosophic reading"? By "philosophic" I mean wisdom-seeking and wisdom-loving, after the literal meaning of the ancient Greek term *philosophia*, the love and pursuit of wisdom. Philosophy in this original sense refers not to some specialized academic subject matter (the field of philosophy) or to some finished doctrine (my philosophy of life) or to some method of reasoning and questioning practiced by card-carrying professional philosophers (the discipline of philosophy). Rather it denotes the activity of Socrates, Plato, Aristotle and any of their descendants who single-mindedly and wholeheartedly—yet thoughtfully and self-critically—seek to discover the truth about the world and our place within it and to find thereby guidance for how we are to live. This book results from my efforts to read the book of Genesis in this spirit, the same spirit in which I read Plato's *Republic* or Aristotle's *Nicomachean Ethics*—indeed, any great book—seeking wisdom regarding human life lived well in relation to the whole.

It is, I am well aware, unusual to read the Bible in this manner and with these aspirations, especially today. Contemporary academic prejudices tend to

1

deny that the Bible can still serve as a vital source of human understanding and moral instruction. Since the nineteenth century most biblical scholars, interested less in the meaning and more in the sources of the text, have seen the Hebrew Bible not as a unified literary whole but as an aggregate of separate documents derived from diverse sources. They read it not as a possible source of wisdom regarding enduring human questions but as documentary evidence of the sensibilities and prejudices of an ancient people. In their view, the truths to be learned from the book are not universal and enduring truths about God and man, but merely parochial and historical truths about the beliefs of the ancient children of Israel whose book it once was. This view of the source critics is perfectly compatible with the more recent approach of many literary critics who read the Bible as literature but who do not regard literature as an aid to wisdom. They tend to be interested, for example, in finding cross-cultural comparisons between the biblical myths of the ancient Hebrews and the myths of *Gilgamesh* and other literary works of the ancient world, but they rarely ponder which, if any, might be closer to the truth of things. Most recently, self-proclaimed politicized scholars, distressed over the continuing authority of the book in some quarters of American society, have not been content just to historicize and relativize the text. Instead, reading it under the influence of, say, Marxist or feminist or environmentalist ideologies, they attack its apparent teachings as racist, sexist, and anthropocentric. In their view the Bible, if taken seriously, turns out to be a source not of wisdom but of dangerous error and folly.

There are, of course, serious readers of Scripture who still see it as a font of wisdom, there for the taking. I have in mind, among others, those fundamentalist Protestants and Orthodox Jews who approach the text piously and who study it reverently. Many of them engage in the hard work of exegesis and interpretation, but they usually do so not in what I am calling the reflective or philosophic spirit. They believe from the start that the text is Holy Writ and that it speaks truly. Often they brush aside textual ambiguity—say, about creation ex nihilo or about the goodness of sacrifice—and they incline to the most pious reading of any difficult passage and assign the most pious motives to all of their biblical heroes. Though they gain much of worth from their biblical study, their piety places certain obstacles in the way of a disinterested and philosophic pursuit of the truth, both about the meaning of the text and about the world the text illuminates. Such readers, too, will be suspicious of my approach, and, I hasten to add, for good reason.

The Bible, I freely acknowledge, is not a work of philosophy, ordinarily understood. Neither its manner nor its manifest purposes are philosophical. Indeed, there is even good reason for saying that they are *anti*philosophical, and deliberately so.[1] Religion and piety are one thing, philosophy and inquiry another. The latter seek wisdom looking to nature and relying on unaided human reason; the former offer wisdom based on divine revelation and relying on prophecy. There is, I readily admit, a reason to be suspicious of a philosophical approach to the Bible.

According to Plato and Aristotle, philosophy begins in wonder and seeks understanding for its own sake:

> For it is through wondering that human beings both now begin and at first began to philosophize, wondering in the first place at nearby perplexities, then progressing gradually to raising difficulties also about greater matters, for example, about the occurrences [or changes] of the moon, and those of the sun and stars, and about the coming-into-being of the whole. But the one who is perplexed and who wonders supposes himself to be ignorant (thus the lover of myth [*philomythos*] is somehow a lover of wisdom [*philosophos*]; for myths are composed of wonders); so that if it was in order to escape ignorance that men philosophized, it is clear that they pursued knowledge for the sake of understanding, and not for anything useful.

Wonder at perplexity provokes thought, for "all human beings by nature desire understanding." It is especially those natural wonders manifest to sight— for example, the changing phases of the moon or the wandering motions of the sun and planets through the zodiac—that prompt the search for wisdom: "for of all the senses, sight most of all makes us know something and reveals many distinctions." Philosophy, born of wonder, seeks ultimately to know the nature and being of things, as well as the reasons or causes why things are the way they are.

For the Bible, in contrast, the beginning of wisdom comes not from wonder but from awe and reverence, and the goal is not understanding for its own sake but rather a righteous and holy life. True, the Psalmist sings that "the heavens declare the glory of God and the sky proclaims His handiwork." But "the beginning of wisdom is the fear [awe; reverence] of the Lord, and good understanding comes to all who practice it." The path to wisdom and happiness lies not through wondrous sights seen by the eye but through awesome command heard by the ear:

---

1. I will myself make the argument in my first two chapters.

The works of His hands are truth and justice; all his precepts are enduring. They are established for ever and ever, they are done in truth and rectitude. . . . He has commanded His covenant for ever; holy and awful is
His Name. . . . Happy is the man that fears [reveres] the Lord, that delights greatly in His commandments.

Not the attractive, beautiful, ceaselessly circling, and seemingly imperishable
heavenly bodies, but the awe-inspiring, sublime, ceaselessly demanding, and imperishable divine covenant and commandments provide the core of biblical wisdom. The wisdom of Jerusalem is not the wisdom of Athens.

SCIENCE IN PLACE OF WISDOM

Wisdom, whether biblical or philosophical, has always been in short supply, today probably more than ever. For the dominant modes of modern thought are
frankly inhospitable to the pursuit of wisdom—indeed, are profoundly skeptical about the very possibility of wisdom of the sort pursued in premodern
times. For this reason, the differences between the wisdom of Athens and the
wisdom of Jerusalem pale by comparison with the difference between both of
them and the "antiwisdoms" of modern thought. I am not speaking only or
even mainly about the postmodern prejudice that there is no such thing as
truth and that what we call truth is at best only cultural construction. I refer especially to the fact that even our most honored form of gaining knowledge,
modern science, is profoundly skeptical about the possibility of wisdom. The
doubts about the *possibility* of wisdom that begin with the emergence of modern science in the seventeenth century have resulted, after three centuries that
saw the spread of the scientific outlook and its technological fruit, in a growing
need for wisdom

Modern science emerged uniquely in the West, in important respects a recognized child of the marriage between the rational spirit of Athens and the
moral spirit of Jerusalem. On the one side, in its rationalist approach—
methodically to describe and predict physical change through the quantifica-
tion of nature and her lawful regularities—science arose by a transformation of
Greek mathematics and the ancient philosophical efforts to capture change by
using numbers and figures. On the other side, in its philanthropic intent—
to relieve man's estate through mastery of nature—science borrowed its hu-
manitarian moral force from a secularized transformation of Christian charity.
Modern science would use a newly constructed tree of methodical knowledge
to restore to humankind the tree of life and to create on earth through tech-

nology the easy and blessed way of life associated with the mythic Garden of Eden.[2]

Yet modern science, from the start, also broke with both its philosophic and religious ancestors, especially in abandoning the large metaphysical-theological questions and spiritual-moral concerns that preoccupied them—philosophical questions about the being or essence or causes of things, philosophical and religious concerns about the meaning of human life and how it should be lived. Indeed, science's success in describing the world depended—and still depends—precisely on its deliberate decision to avoid those big questions or, for that matter, any other question that cannot be turned into a problem admitting of methodical resolution. Precisely by eschewing the search for wisdom about what things are and mean in favor of securing knowledge of how things move and work, science has made glorious progress in uncovering some of nature's secrets and offered bounteous contributions to reducing human toil and sickness. Yet modern science and its intellectual and cultural companions have increasingly troubled the hearts of wisdom seekers, both philosophical and religious.

On the philosophical side, the findings of modern science have surely created grave difficulties for the ancient philosophical quest to live life solely by the light of reason, exercised on the natural world. For according to our science, the universe is not a cosmos, is not an integral and finite whole. The splendid heavenly bodies are not ensouled or divine, but are, like us, limited and perishable. Moreover, nature is not teleological or purposive. Beneath the surface of things, everything obeys the laws of nature, but in the world of our experience all is flux, and chance and necessity rule, indifferent to our concerns or even to our sur-

---

2. The classical statement of this vision for the new science was offered by one of its philosophical founders, René Descartes, in the *Discourse on Method:*

So soon as I had acquired some general notions concerning Physics . . . I believed that I could not keep them concealed *without greatly sinning again the law which obliges us to procure, as much as in us lies, the general good of all mankind.* For they caused me to see that it is possible to attain knowledge *which is very useful in life,* and that, instead of that speculative philosophy which is taught in the Schools, we may find a practical philosophy by means of which, knowing the force and action of fire, water, air, the stars, heaven and all the other bodies that environ us, as distinctly as we know the different crafts of our artisans, we can in the same way employ them in all those uses to which they are adapted, and *thus render ourselves as the masters and possessors of nature.* This is not merely to be desired with a view to the invention of an infinity of arts and crafts that enable us to enjoy *without any trouble the fruits of the earth* and all the good things which are to be found there, but also principally because it brings about the preservation of health, which is without doubt the chief blessing and the foundation of all other blessings in this life. For the mind depends so much on the temperament and disposition of the bodily organs that, if it is possible to find a means of rendering men wiser and cleverer

vival. On the earth, not only beings but also species come and (mostly) go, while the vast emptiness of space preserves its icy silence. For these reasons especially, nature as understood by science has nothing to teach us about human good: the descriptive laws of nature do not issue in normative Natural Law or Natural Right. In this respect above all, nature by herself does not provide us a true home. As subject to the flux as is everything else, we human beings have no fixed nature or special dignity. True, thanks to the peculiar arrangement of our cosmic dust, we have longings for truth and goodness. And unlike other beings, we can come to know our cosmic insignificance. But the truths that might make us free are beyond our reach, and the Good—or even only the *human* good—if there is one, cannot be known by scientific reason.

In some respects, these teachings of modern science seem not to be at variance with Scripture. The Bible might be said to share science's beliefs in the importance of history, the noneternity of the earth and the human species, and the nondivinity of nature. The Bible also recognizes the silence of the heavens and the earth regarding the human good and, therefore, emphasizes the incompetence of human reason, thinking only about nature, to find a decent and righteous way to live. These deficiencies of nature and human reason the Bible supplies by what is traditionally called revelation—a teaching for human life that, though *accessible* to human reason, is apparently not *available* to unaided human reason as it ponders the natural world. Yet, to state the obvious, modern science, according to conventional wisdom, is no friend of biblical religion. The very possibility of a natural science requires denying the possibility of "miracles," of events—like the parting of the Red Sea or the sun's standing still—that defy or suspend the iron necessity of the laws of nature.[3] And science's specific

---

than they have hitherto been, I believe that it is in medicine that it must be sought. . . . [W]e could be free of an infinitude of maladies both of body and of mind, *and even also possibly of the infirmities of age,* if we had sufficient knowledge of their causes, and of all the remedies with which nature has provided us.

Striking are the appeal to the Golden Rule (the moral law), the practical and philanthropic intention of a nonspeculative philosophy (or science) of nature, and the not very veiled references to the expulsion from Eden and the promise, through science and mastery of nature, of both wisdom and enduring life.

3. To address this difficulty, a quasi-scientific spirit has foolishly led some pious readers to read the Bible "scientifically," scouring it for physical evidence or testable hypotheses that might help support and explain a literal and historical reading of extraordinary happenings (for example, the origin of life on earth, the burning bush, or the splitting of the Red Sea). These readers do not consider that such an approach might actually blind them to the lessons of the text as the text itself wants to present them. This scientific reading would be especially misleading if, as we shall argue, the text deliberately sets itself up in opposition to those who take their human bearings from nature and natural happenings.

findings have challenged numerous biblical teachings, including the account of creation, the divine origins of man, the special place of man and the earth in the universe, and the rulership of the one God as biblically described. As a consequence, many of the moral teachings of the Bible are also put in doubt—to be sure, not primarily by science or scientists but by a science-based culture whose trust in the veracity of Scripture has been undermined by the triumph of the scientific worldview. The wisdom offered by the followers of Jerusalem, no less than the wisdom sought by the descendants of Athens, appears to be increasingly out of date and irrelevant.

ENLIGHTENMENT AND ITS DISCONTENTS

None of this is exactly news. We are often told that we live in secular, even postmodern, times. The old pieties, not only about God or morality but even about truth itself, no longer command our unqualified allegiance. We are too sophisticated to believe in the existence of absolute right and wrong or to make confident moral judgments. We are too worldly to submit to the genius of tradition. We are too enamored of our rights to take our bearings from what were once thought to be our duties. With science and technology pointing the way, the race for health, pleasure, and prosperity is rapidly becoming the only successful game in town.

Such, at least, is the conventional wisdom about life in the modern world, at least in the liberal democracies of the West. But this view of contemporary life must contend with certain inconvenient facts, both about our culture as a whole and about individual private life. Yes, science and technology have unquestionably yielded vast improvements in human life and will no doubt continue to do so. And modern freedom-loving political regimes friendly to scientific inquiry and technological innovation have liberated large parts of the globe from despotism and enabled a growing fraction of the human race to feel secure in life and liberty and to enjoy the pursuit of happiness. Yet we have lost our naïveté regarding the moral innocence and neutrality of technology. More important, the *cultural* victory of a science-based Enlightenment has proved to be but a partial success. For it has in practice and in principle weakened the moral ground—both philosophical and biblical—upon which progress was to be made. We have been increasingly deprived of firm confidence in *any* moral standard by which we could judge whether change was for the better or for the worse. The prominence of agnosticism, moral relativism, cynicism, and nihilism is only the most visible intellectual sign of our cultural moral predicament, a predicament made all the more worrisome given our ever-expanding technological powers to transform the globe, our own hearts and minds included. As we stand on the threshold of a new biotechnological age, armed with powers for genetic, somatic, and psychic human engineering, we feel—or should feel—the deep cultural weakness beneath our superficial technical strength. From where, precisely, are we to seek—never mind find—the wisdom we so badly need, if we are to use well and for good our awesome Promethean powers?

Few people, I admit, are personally concerned with such abstract and global concerns. But many people—including many young people, often the children of skeptics—are existentially unwilling to let science or postmodernity have the last word about the kind of world this is. For their own private existential reasons, they are looking for wisdom in their personal lives. Paradoxically, our secular society seems to be stimulating a reawakening of religious sensibilities and aspirations. In recent years, interest in religion has increased greatly in American society, and not only among evangelical Protestants, traditional Roman Catholics, Orthodox Jews, practicing Muslims, and similar denominations whose traditions continue to remain strong. Unaffiliated students on college campuses are flocking to courses on religious themes and texts, looking for meaning and "spirituality." Sometimes they are led to so-called New Age religions, but often they return to examine or practice the venerable traditions of their ancestors. Adult Bible study groups are springing up across the country even among the previously indifferent, and new English translations of, and commentaries on, the Bible are produced seemingly every year. Not long ago public television aired a ten-part series of serious discussions of the book of Genesis. More and more Americans are owning up to the fact that something is missing in their lives. More and more of us are looking for spiritual direction and guidance. It seems like only yesterday that the Enlightenment overthrew the rule of religious orthodoxy, promising an earthly paradise of human fulfillment based solely on scientific reason. Yet today, the enlightened children of skeptics are discovering for themselves that man does not live—or live *well*—by bread alone, not even by bread and circuses, and that science's account of human life and the world is neither adequate to the subject nor satisfying to the longings of the soul.

Both the moral crisis of modern thought and the public and personal need for wisdom make urgent a reconsideration of our present beliefs and opinions and recommend a reexamination of seemingly rejected or abandoned alternatives—to be sure, considered afresh in the light of modern thought and its challenges. Friends of wisdom today must be willing to seek help from wherever it may be found. This includes, too, undertaking a serious reexamination of the Bible, considered in the light of modern science. How much damage does science—and modern thought generally—really do to the biblical teachings about human life and the human good? Can a thoughtful person today still accept or affirm the teachings of the Bible? The answer to these questions depends, of course, on what the Bible in fact says and means. On a matter of such importance, we dare not rely on hearsay. We must read it and think about it for ourselves.

BEGINNING(S)

The best place to start is at the beginning, with the first book of the Bible. This book, known to us as Genesis, is famously a book about beginnings: the beginning of the heavens and the earth; the beginning of human life on earth; the beginning of the Children of Israel, beginning with Father Abraham; and before, behind, and above all these temporal beginnings, the tireless and enduring beginning that is God—Creator of the world, maker of man in His own image, covenant maker with Abraham and with Israel. In addition, as a book among kindred books, Genesis is itself the beginning of the Torah, of the biblical teaching about how human beings are to live. Though it contains very little prescription and propounds very few commandments, Genesis serves as a prelude to the laws (given mainly in Exodus and Leviticus, and repeated in Deuteronomy). This it does primarily by making clear through its stories why the laws might be needed and for what sorts of human weaknesses and difficulties. For this reason especially the book of Genesis lends itself to philosophical reading, at least at the start.

True, once Abraham appears on the scene in Genesis 12, the Bible's account of "human history" acquires a unique and singular particularity, with a portion of the human race living in a special relationship with the biblical God. Such a teaching could neither be discovered nor even be countenanced by unaided philosophic reason. But the so-called universal human history of the first eleven chapters—from the creation to the tower of Babel—is different. To be sure, these stories also describe singular figures and unique events, for example, Adam and Eve, Cain and Abel, Noah and the flood. But read philosophically, they convey a universal teaching about "human nature," an anthropology in the original meaning of the term: a *logos* (account) of *anthropos* (the human being). Without using argument or philosophical language—there is no biblical Hebrew word for "nature"—the stories of these first eleven chapters nevertheless offer (among other things) a coherent anthropology that rivals anything produced by the great philosophers.[4] To see this, we must learn to read the beginning of Genesis as offering a more than historical sense of "beginning."

On the face of it, the early chapters of Genesis appear to give an account of humankind's *temporal beginnings,* a history that tells the sequence of what happened at the start: first the creation of the world and humankind; then the expulsion of man and woman from Eden; then Cain and Abel; then events leading up to the flood, and so on. But these seemingly historical stories are in fact (also and especially) vehicles for conveying the timeless psychic and social elements or principles—the *anthropological beginnings* or roots—of human life, and in all their moral ambiguity. The stories cast powerful light, for example, on the problematic character of human reason, speech, freedom, sexual desire, the love of the beautiful, shame, guilt, anger, and man's response to mortality. The stories cast equally powerful light on the naturally vexed relations between man and woman, brother and brother, father and son, neighbor and neighbor, stranger and stranger, man and God. Adam and Eve are not just the first but also the paradigmatic man and woman. Cain and Abel are paradigmatic brothers. Babel is the quintessential city. By means of such paradigmatic stories, the beginning of Genesis shows us not so much what happened as what *always* happens. And by holding up a mirror in which we readers can discover in ourselves the reasons why human life is so bittersweet and why uninstructed human beings generally get it wrong, Genesis reflectively read also provides a powerful *pedagogical beginning* for the moral and spiritual education of the reader. As a result of what we learn from this early education, when God calls Abraham in Genesis 12 *we* will also be inclined to pay attention.

The educational lessons of the beginning are supplemented by the rest of the book. After the first eleven chapters expose some of the enduring psychic and social obstacles to decent and righteous living, the rest of Genesis presents beginning efforts to overcome these obstacles in the lives of the Israelite founders Abraham, Isaac, and Jacob and their families. These national beginnings are fraught with difficulties and success is hard to come by. Yet remarkably, a new human way of acting and standing in the world is established and transmitted for several generations through the education of the patriarchs, an education in which we readers may vicariously and reflectively participate.

Genesis is thus in many different ways about "what is first." It *tells* of the tem-

---

4. Indeed, both Rousseau and Kant, among others, were careful philosophical students of Genesis and wrote important anthropological essays that were (in Kant's case) explicitly or (in Rousseau's case) implicitly commentaries on the early chapters in Genesis. See Rousseau's *Discourse on the Origin of Inequality Among Men* and Kant's *Conjectural Beginning of Human History.* I will later make use of these works in expounding the text.

porally first men ("history"). But more important, it *shows* us what is first *in* man, what is primordial, elemental, principal, and essential ("anthropology"). It also *invites reflection* on what is cosmically first and how human beings stand in relation to the whole ("ontology'), as well as on who acts well and who acts badly, who is worthy of praise and who of blame, and why ("ethics"). It introduces us to the seeds of a new nation, following a new and God-fearing way, a way that will eventually be codified in law and transmitted through political institutions and religious-cultural traditions ("politics"). And by confronting us with all these firsts, in the form of stories told with very little commentary, it begins the education of the reader who is seeking wisdom not only about what is first but also and especially about *how first or best to live* ("philosophy"). What I am suggesting is that Genesis is a coherent narrative that conveys a moral whole, in which the opening part prepares the philosophic reader to take seriously, when it comes, the arrival of God's new way for humankind, while the rest enables him to learn along with the patriarchs what it might offer and require of him.

A full defense of this unusual claim cannot be provided in advance; evidence regarding Genesis's narrative, moral, and pedagogical integrity can be obtained only through careful scrutiny of the entire text. But I hope that it will not spoil the reader's pleasure of discovery if I provide here a few suggestions about the overall structure and direction of the narrative, indicating also what I take to be its central concerns.[5]

Genesis begins with a comprehensive and universal panorama of the entire cosmic whole (chapter 1), moves to naturalistic and universal portraits of human life (chapters 2–11), and concludes with the emergence of a tiny and distinctive people, bearing a new and distinctive human way on earth (chapters 12–50). Throughout, the text is concerned with this question: Is it possible to *find, institute,* and *preserve* a way of life, responsive to both the promise and the peril of the human creature, that *accords with man's true standing in the world* and that serves to *perfect his god-like possibilities?*

In the opening chapter of Genesis, we learn how cosmic order is produced out of primordial chaos by means of a progressive process of separation and dis-

---

5. No great book worthy of study in a wisdom-seeking manner can be adequately summarized in a few pages, and any attempt to do so must cast aside most of what makes it worth pondering. Genesis is no exception. If Genesis had a single distillable teaching—which it does not—and if its most important insights could be simply captured in PowerPoint presentations—which they cannot—there would be no point in reading it whole and experiencing for oneself its rich and (as I will argue) deliberately perplexing character. Yet a reader standing on the threshold of this unusual approach to that venerable and endlessly commented-on text is entitled to a few preliminary suggestions regarding my view of the shape of the whole and its guiding nerve.

tinction. At the peak of creation stands man, the one god-like creature, alone capable, thanks to his reason, of recognizing the distinctive articulated order of things. But as we learn, beginning in Genesis 2, man is also the creature—again, thanks to his reason and freedom—who is most capable of disturbing and destroying order, especially as pride in his own powers distorts his perception of the world. In a series of tales—from the primordial couple in the Garden of Eden, through the fratricide of Cain and the warring Age of Heroes leading to the Flood, to the ambitious building of the universal city of Babel—readers are shown the dangerous natural tendencies of humankind: on the one hand, toward order-destroying wildness and violence, on the other hand, toward order-transforming efforts at self-sufficiency and mastery of the given world. Against the aspiration toward man-made unity and re-creation, with its proud illusion of human autonomy, the text begins (in chapter 12) to recount a new human alternative, carried by a separated small portion of humankind yet ordered in pursuit of wholeness and holiness. The new way accepts as given the heterogeneous world of distinctive peoples but seeks to cultivate attitudes that will treat strangers justly, generously, and, ultimately, as one would treat oneself. And it recognizes human dependence on powers not of our own making and the need to align human life with the highest principle of Being. In a word, the new human way—the way of the Children of Israel, launched as a light unto the nations—is to be built on two related principles: the practice of *righteousness* in relations toward others, informed by the pursuit of *holiness* in relation to the divine. Both are grounded not in human reason or freedom but in the peculiarly human experience of awe and reverence, elicited by the mysteries of the world's order and power and especially by the voice of commanding moral authority.

Beginning with the call of Abraham (Genesis 12), the text enables us to experience the struggles to embody the ideals of righteousness and holiness in the way of life of a nascent people—beginning with one man, the founder (Abraham), moving to one household of perpetuation (Isaac and Rebekah), and flowering into one clan or tribe, on the threshold of nationhood (Jacob and his sons). Each generation faces and solves the perennial threats to survival and decency, including the intrafamilial dangers of patricide, fratricide, and incest, the international dangers of conquest, injustice, and assimilation, and the spiritual danger of idolatry. Through their trials—domestic, political, and spiritual—Abraham (the founder) and Isaac, Jacob, and Judah (the perpetuators) are educated to the work of proper patriarchy, all in the service of advancing the cause of righteousness and holiness in the world. ("The Education of the Fathers" would be a most appropriate subtitle for the book of Genesis; it was, in fact, the working title under which I first began this book.)

Yet although the focus of Genesis often centers on the household, its most important implications are cultural and political. For the new way is set off against, and can best be seen as an alternative to, important competing cultural alternatives: the heaven-gazing and heaven-worshiping Babylonians, the earth-worshiping and licentious Canaanites, and the technologically sophisticated and masterful Egyptians. As Abraham must emerge out of and against the ways of Babylonia, so the nation of Israel must emerge out of and against the ways of Egypt. Accordingly, Genesis culminates in an encounter between nascent Israel and civilized Egypt, exemplified especially in the contrast between Judah, the prudent and reverent statesman, and Joseph, the brilliant and cosmopolitan administrator. Although the full picture will not emerge until the book of Exodus, which follows next, Genesis leaves us with these clear alternatives, which represent in fact a permanent human choice: a world in which the rational mastery of nature and the pursuit of immortality leads ultimately to the enslavement of mankind under the despotic rule of one man worshiped as a god, versus a way of life in which all human beings, mindful of their limitations and standing in awe-and-fear of the Lord, can be treated as equal creatures, equally servants of the one God toward whose perfection we may strive to align our lives.

READING IN A PHILOSOPHICAL SPIRIT

This book on Genesis, addressed to serious and thoughtful readers of whatever kind or degree of religious knowledge and practice, has three major purposes: First, to demonstrate by example a wisdom-seeking approach to the Bible that attempts to understand the text in its own terms yet tries to show how such an understanding may address us in our current situation of moral and spiritual neediness. Second, to recover in their full power the stories of Genesis as tales to live with, as stories illuminating some of the most important and enduring questions of human existence. Third, to make at least plausible the power of the Biblical approach and response to these questions, with its emphasis on righteousness, holiness, and reverence for the divine.

Great difficulties face anyone who proposes such a philosophic approach to the Bible. For it is far from clear that the Bible is a book like any other, or enough like any other, to be read and interpreted in the usual ways. Because of its place in our religious traditions, few people are prepared to approach it impartially. Even before they read it some people know—or think they know—that the Bible speaks truly, being the word of God; others know—or think they know—that, claiming to be the word of God, it in fact speaks falsely. In addition, as already noted, the academic study of the Bible has raised major methodological questions, not least about whether the Bible—and even the single book of Genesis—is in fact a coherent and integral whole. The so-called documentary hypothesis argues that what we call the Bible is in fact a latter-day compilation of disparate materials, written by different authors at different times, having different outlooks and intentions, even employing different concepts of and names for God. But even granting that the material compiled in Genesis came, to begin with, from different sources, one must still consider what intention or idea of wholeness governed the act of compilation that produced the present text. Must one assume that the redactor was some pious fool who slavishly stitched together all the available disparate stories without rhyme or reason, heedless of the contradictions between them? Or should we not rather give the redactor the benefit of the doubt and assume that he knew precisely what he was about? Could he perhaps have deliberately juxtaposed contradictory stories to enable us to discover certain contradictory aspects of the world thereby made plain? True, finding a coherent interpretation of the whole does not guarantee that one has found the biblical author's (or redactor's) own intention. But it should give pause to those who claim that the text could have no such unity. Besides, knowing the historical origins or sources of the text is no substitute for learning its meaning; to discover the meaning, a text must be studied in its own terms.

An equally severe difficulty comes from the other side, from those who regard the Bible as the revealed word of God. For them it is definitely a book, but *not* a book that can be read and interrogated like any other. It seems rather to demand a certain prior commitment to the truth of the account, even in order to understand it. Faith, it is sometimes said, is the prerequisite to understanding. But the Hebrew Bible in fact suggests the contrary. In Deuteronomy, Moses asserts that observing the statutes and ordinances that God has commanded is Israel's "wisdom and understanding in the eyes of the people, that when they hear all these statutes shall say, 'Surely this great nation is a wise and understanding people' " (4:6). The wisdom of the Torah is said *by* the Torah to be accessible to everyone, at least in part.

Be this as it may, the biblical text, whether revealed or not, whether read by believers or atheists, is not self-interpreting. To understand its meaning, the hard work of exegesis and interpretation is required. The task of interpretation is complicated by the fact that the Bible, like most great books, does not explicitly provide rules for how to read it. As with the content, so with the approach, the philosophical reader is forced to find his own way. As a result of many readings and rereadings, I now make the following "methodological" assumptions in my efforts at interpretation: First, there is a coherent order and plan to the whole, and the order of the stories is of more than chronological significance. Second, every word counts. Third, juxtapositions are important; what precedes or what follows a given sentence or story may be crucial for discovering its meaning. (It matters, for example, that the Noahide code and covenant appear as the immediate sequel to Noah's animal sacrifice tendered at the end of the Flood. It matters, too, that there are two juxtaposed and very different stories of the creation of man or of the multiplication of nations and languages.) Fourth and finally, the teachings of the text are not utterly opaque to human reason, even if God and other matters remain veiled in mystery. Though, as we shall see, the text takes a dim view of the sufficiency of human reason, it presents this critical view *to* human reason in a most intelligible and powerful way. One can approach the text in a spirit of inquiry, even if one comes as a result to learn the limitations of such philosophic activity.

I am well aware that this suggestion, though allowed for by the Bible, still appears to be at odds with the way *recommended* by the Bible. As I noted near the start, the beginning of biblical wisdom is said to be fear (awe-reverence) for the Lord, not open inquiry spurred by wonder. In addition, there is the great danger that hangs over all efforts at interpretation: I will find in the text not what the author intended but only what I have put there myself (usually unwittingly). For these reasons, a philosophic reading of Genesis must proceed with great modesty and caution, not to say fear and trembling. If I sometimes forget myself and seem too bold, it is only out of zeal for understanding. Moreover, I make no claim to a final or definitive reading. On the contrary, the stories are too rich, too complex, and too deep to be captured fully, once and for all.[6] It is therefore possible, as I hope to demonstrate, that one can approach the book in a spirit and manner that is simultaneously naïve, philosophic, and reverent. The pursuit of wisdom, through the direct and unmediated encountering of the text, can proceed even as one is humbly mindful of the inexhaustible depths and mysteries of the text and the world it describes. As the example of Socrates reminds us, humility before mystery and knowledge of one's own ignorance are hardly at odds with a philosophic spirit.

Let me try to make these remarks about reading philosophically yet humbly a bit more concrete. When we set out to read the book of Genesis, we begin, quite properly, at the beginning. But getting started is not as easy as it seems. For though we know where to start, we do not yet know how to proceed. To begin properly, it seems, we need prior knowledge. What kind of book are we reading? In what spirit and manner should we read? For the beginning reader, answers to these questions cannot be had in advance. They can be acquired, if at all, only as a result of reading. We are in difficulty from the start.

The opening of the book only adds to our difficulty, even before we get to the

---

6. Indeed, as a result of my own frequent teaching of the text, I am regularly compelled by my students to reassess my understanding, and in many important respects the interpretations I advance in this book differ from those that I have offered previously in print.

first chapter. Unlike most books, it declares no title and identifies no author. The name we call it in English, Genesis, meaning "origin" or "coming into being," is simply the Greek mistranslation of the book's first, Hebrew word, *ber'eshith*, "in beginning," by which Hebrew name the book is known in Jewish tradition.[7] That tradition ascribes authorship to Moses—the first five books of the Hebrew Bible are also known as the Five Books of Moses—yet nowhere in Genesis is such a claim made or even supported. We do not know whose words we are reading, and we also do not know whether it matters that we do not know whose words we are reading.

When we begin to read—"In beginning God created the heavens and the earth"—we discover that the internal voice or speaker of the text—what literary critics would call "the narrator" but what I will simply call "the text"—is also nameless. Someone is addressing us in a commanding voice, speaking about grand themes, speaking with seeming authority. But who is talking? We are not told. The voice of the text is apparently not the direct voice of God: God's speeches the text identifies and reports using the third person ("And the Lord said"). But if it is not God who is speaking, our perplexity only increases; for the text begins by talking confidently about things that no human being could possibly have known from direct experience: the prehuman world and its coming into being, or creation. How, we wonder, does the speaker know what he is talking about? Why should we believe him? Is this a divinely inspired account? Is this the revealed word of God, passed to us through the prophetic voice of the text? How can we know? On the basis of what other than prejudice—prejudgment—can we decide whether the text is speaking truly?

In the face of our ignorance before these questions, many skeptical readers will be tempted to quit right here, absent some outside evidence for the veracity of the biblical account. On the other side, some pious readers, responding to the skeptic's challenges, will argue that the text is accessible only to the faithful, those who trust that the text is indeed the revealed word of God. Let me propose a third alternative, an attitude between doubt, demanding proof in advance, and faith, comfortable that proof is unnecessary: the attitude of thoughtful engagement, of suspended disbelief, eager to learn. I offer a biblical example of what I mean.

At the beginning of the twelfth chapter of the book of Genesis, we readers are called to witness a crucial turning point in human history. Out of the blue,

---

7. In that tradition, each of the first five books of the Bible is known simply by its first word—for example, the book of Exodus is known by the nondescript title "Names" *(shemoth)*. Such a name, unlike a title devised by an author, tells us very little about the substance of the book or about its author's intention.

with no advance warning, a mysterious and awesome voice calls to Abraham, commanding him to take a journey—"to the land I will show you"—and promising him great rewards should he do so. Abraham, without so much as a question or a comment, immediately hearkens to the call: he promptly sets off as commanded. If we wish to imagine ourselves in Abraham's place as he hears the commanding voice, we must forget that we know, because the biblical text explicitly tells *us,* that the voice calling Abraham was the voice of the Lord: "And the Lord said to Abram . . ." (12:1). Abraham himself is not told who is calling him; the voice that calls does not identify itself. Although he is, for reasons we shall explore in a later chapter, open to such a call, Abraham at this moment cannot know with certainty who is speaking to him or whether the voice can deliver on its great promises. Nevertheless, trustingly and courageously, Abraham decides to take a walk with this voice. Putting aside any possible doubts and suspicions, he embarks on a path that enables him eventually to discover just who had spoken to him and why.

Readers who take up the book of Genesis without presuppositions or intermediaries find themselves in a position not unlike Abraham's: a commanding but unidentified voice is addressing us from out of the text, without warning or preparation, speaking to us right away about things (for openers, the creation of the world) that we human beings could not by ourselves know anything about. To be sure, the opening words of Genesis do not command us to act. Neither can we compare ourselves to Abraham in setting, stature, or virtue. Nonetheless, we readers are being invited, as was Abraham, to proceed trustingly and courageously, without knowing yet who is speaking to us, what he might want from us, and whether or not he speaks truly.

How then shall we respond? What does the call of the author of Genesis require of us readers? Not, as some might insist, a leap of faith or a commitment in advance to the truth of the biblical story, but rather, only a suspension of disbelief. Being awake and thoughtful, we cannot help but note the difficult questions regarding both our beginning and *the* beginning, but we will, at least for now, put them aside and plunge right in. We will suspend our doubts and suspicions and accept the book's invitation to take a walk with the biblical author keeping our eyes and ears open and our judgment keen, to be sure. We will proceed in the hope that we might have our doubts addressed and our uncertainties resolved. If we allow ourselves to travel its narrative journey, the book may reward our openness and gain our trust. Who knows, we may even learn who (or Who) is speaking to us, and why.

In adopting such an attitude, we are self-consciously deciding now to decide only later, after reading and pondering, whether we think the book and its author speak truly. In making such a decision, we are according the Bible the same courtesy that we give to other books that place large obstacles before our credulity, for example, the *Iliad,* in which we are told, in the very first sentence, that we will hear how "the will of Zeus was accomplished." As with other books, to judge the veracity of the text we shall have to find out what kind of a text, teaching or pointing to what kind of truth, we have before us. As with other books, we shall have to read and reread many times if we are to learn from the Bible how it wants to be read.[8]

As a result of many readings and rereadings of Genesis, I am increasingly impressed by the leanness of the text and the lacunae in the stories. Little of what we readers might like to know about an event or a character is told to us. Much of what we are told admits of a wide variety of interpretations. Rarely does the text tell us the inner thoughts and feelings of a character. Rarely does the text tell us the meaning of an event. And almost never does the text pronounce judgment on the words or deeds of any protagonist. Why this reticence? What purpose could it possibly serve?

Let me suggest that these formal features of the text are responsible for its enduring vitality and the success of its timeless pedagogical power. The book has been read by several hundred generations of readers, with each reader located in a particular time and place. Yet the compiled text remains the same, letter for letter, now as then, here as there. How can a static age-old text continue to speak to changing and always more modern readers? How can seemingly time-bound characters and stories that may possibly carry timeless insights retain their power in differing times and places and for differing types of readers? How can the text allow for every reader's historical and cultural particularity, while bringing him into contact with what might be a transhistorical and universal wisdom? It is precisely the text's sparseness, lacunae, ambiguity, reticence, and lack of editorial judgment that both permit and require the engagement of the

---

8. People who have already encountered the Bible within their own religious traditions will most likely already have formed some notion of how the book should be read. In traditional Judaism, for example, beginning students do not confront the text entirely on their own but rather with the aid of rabbinic commentaries, most notably that of Rashi, the famous eleventh-century exegete. Roman Catholic readers first become familiar with some portions of the Bible as presented and integrated into the catechism of the Catholic Church, while Protestant readers have in the past been influenced by Luther's commentaries or Milton's *Paradise Lost.* Though acutely mindful of what I am sacrificing in doing so, I have aimed in my interpretive work to rely as little as possible on intermediaries and to try instead to face the text as immediately and directly as possible (though I will from time to time cite one or another previous commentary when it seems to be especially useful to do so). Commentators, even great ones, often read according to their own purposes, which may or may not be identical to the purposes of the text. Though a fully naïve and unmediated reading is, of course, impossible, it remains a desired objective for anyone who wants to be as open as possible to the original text itself.

reader. The difficulties of exegesis and interpretation force us to grapple with the text and to attempt and weigh alternative readings and judgments, always testing our opinions against the textual evidence as well as the differing interpretations and judgments of fellow readers of our own and earlier times. As a result of these efforts, the venerable stories and characters of Genesis become again and again ever young and ever fresh, taking up residence in the hearts and minds of all serious readers. By this means, each reader's imagination is furnished and enlivened and his thinking is enlarged and deepened. In the end, the concerns of the text and its characters become the concerns also of the reader. The education of the patriarchs and matriarchs can become the way to our own education.

All of us necessarily come at the text beginning from where we are, in our own time and place, equipped—but also limited—by our particular experiences of the world around us. Yet the mysteries and perplexities of the text disturb our complacent attachment to our own parochial situation and invite our active participation in a world larger than our own. We are drawn into the stories only to discover there a profundity not hitherto available to us. When we analyze, ponder, and discuss the text and when we live with its stories, the enduring text comes alive, here and now. We who live here and now are offered a chance to catch a glimpse of possibly timeless and transcendent truth about, say, man and woman, kin and strangers, man and God, or whatever matter the text has under consideration. At the same time, our need to continue grappling with the abiding ambiguities of the text teaches us, by performative experience, another timeless truth about ourselves: the truth of our own ignorance and the impossibility of ever resting comfortably with what we think we have understood. The open form of the text and its recalcitrance to final and indubitable interpretation are absolutely perfect instruments for cultivating the openness, thoughtfulness, and modesty about one's own understanding that is the hallmark of the pursuit of wisdom.

THE SEEDS OF WISDOM

Not only in form and spirit but also in substance will seekers for wisdom be easily drawn into the world of Genesis. Despite the great distance between the nomadic culture of the ancient Promised Land and the promise-filled technological civilization of third-millennium America, we will find that Genesis takes up and considers themes and questions of paramount concern also to us—one might even say, to human beings always and everywhere. Human beings now as ever need wisdom regarding family and private life, regarding public and civic affairs, and regarding their place in and relation to the whole and their relation to the powers that be.

As were the protagonists in the world of Genesis, so are we today troubled by vexing questions of family life. Not only do we face often irreconcilable struggles between man and woman, parent and child, or sibling and sibling. We are also increasingly uncertain about the proper organization of family life, especially with regard to providing well for the rearing of children. Our inherited cultural forms in these matters are in a state of flux—evolving, if you approve, or breaking down, if you don't, into God only knows what new patterns. Reading Genesis reveals that this is hardly a new dilemma. Not only does it offer for reflection its famous tales of family struggle; read philosophically, the stories of Genesis reveal the deepest roots of these conflicts and show us why it is so hard to organize and sustain a flourishing human household.

The topics of sex and the relation between the sexes are, not surprisingly, amply considered in Genesis. Women figure prominently in many of the stories, often playing vital and even heroic roles. But Genesis is mainly about the adventures of men, and especially of the Israelite patriarchs and their male offspring. More precisely, much of Genesis is devoted to efforts at educating men in the work of fatherhood: the task of transmitting to their descendants not just life but a worthy way of life, devoted to justice and holiness and looking up to the divine. Why this emphasis? Does it represent (as current fashion believes) the sexist or patriarchal mentality of ancient Israel? Or does it reflect something closer to the reverse: a belief that men are by nature much more than women in need of education if they are to live responsibly, righteously, and well? Are men naturally drawn to domestic life and the care of those who will someday replace them? Or will they, if left to their own devices, pursue ways of life devoted to heroic quests for personal honor and glory, to power and domination, and to wealth and pleasure? Reflection about such questions is open in every time and place to prospective fathers—and mothers—who can learn vicariously along with, and through the stories of, the patriarchs.

In addition to examining private life, Genesis also explores the life of cities and civilizations, shedding light on the problems of crime and injustice, the dangers of xenophobia and abuse of strangers, and the meaning of the political aspiration to independence and self-sufficiency. Contemporary concerns over unbridled technology are anticipated in the story of Babel. Our worries about civic licentiousness are taken up in the story of Sodom. Our wish neatly to disentangle justice from revenge is challenged by the story of the rape of Dinah. Most important, the text gets us thinking about competing *cultural* and *political* visions of the best human life. For Genesis presents the emergence of nascent Israel, bearer of God's new way, in the context of three major cultural alternatives, the Babylonians, the Canaanites, and the Egyptians, each characterized by different ruling ideas, each looking up to different gods. Much can be learned about the distinctive character of the Judeo-Christian way—then and now—by thinking through the meaning of these quasi-polar alternatives. For though these ancient civilizations are long gone, their animating principles survive. Indeed, they find expression in cultural alternatives competing today for our attention and allegiance.

Biblical Egypt should be of special interest for modern Americans. For Egypt was the peak of ancient civilization, a civilization characterized by agricultural plenty, high levels of science and technology, advanced bureaucracy and public administration, and—perhaps most relevant for us—a passion for longevity and the pursuit of bodily immortality through the conquest of decay and death. Yet Egypt was also the place where women were rounded up for the ruler's harem, foreigners were held in contempt, a man was worshiped as a god, and in the end, the people's preoccupation with survival and material well-being led to their enslavement. Is Egypt, perhaps, a permanent human possibility and temptation? Is something like Egypt in *our* future?

Finally, the stories in Genesis address our current concern with man's relation to nature and the earth, to the other animals, and to the divine—ultimate questions in any pursuit of wisdom. For a variety of reasons—including our belief in evolution, our interest in animal welfare, and our concern for the environment—we find ourselves once again agitating the question of the difference of man and the difference it makes. Modern biology, from molecular genetics to evolutionary psychology, has raised a large challenge to the traditional belief in human distinctiveness. Deep ecologists speak with reverent awe about Gaia, our Mother Earth, almost as if she were a goddess. What does all this nature worship mean for human self-understanding and the belief that man was made in the image of God? And what follows for human life and the way we should live it? Can a "pan-naturalism" that glorifies nature and makes light of the human difference provide the ground for standards of human justice and decency? These seemingly contemporary concerns, the careful reader will find, are not foreign to the book of Genesis. To the contrary, who we are and how we stand in the world is of the utmost importance to the biblical author. Indeed, these are the questions addressed at the very beginning of the beginning, in the story of creation, to which we are now ready to turn.

PART ONE

DANGEROUS BEGINNINGS:
THE UNINSTRUCTED WAYS
(GENESIS 1–11)

CHAPTER ONE

AWESOME BEGINNINGS: MAN, HEAVEN,
AND THE CREATED ORDER

*T*he fifty chapters of the book of Genesis tell a continuous story, beginning from the beginning of our world and ending with the children of Israel settled in the land of Egypt and with the death and mummification of Israel's favorite son, Joseph. After the opening chapter, we will have what looks like a historical narrative of early human life. In chapters 2–11, with stories from the Garden of Eden (through Cain and Abel and Noah and the Flood) to the tower of Babel, we will be shown the beginnings of human life in general, as human beings live largely on their own and without instruction, prior to the election of Abraham and the founding of God's new way. In chapters 12–50 (the so-called patriarchal narratives), we will be shown the beginnings of Israel's life in particular, as Abraham, Isaac, and Jacob struggle to establish God's new way, despite—or perhaps by means of—trials and tribulations with their families, their neighbors, and with God. But the story told in chapter 1 (completed by the first three verses of chapter 2) is different. It is not an account of human life or even of human beginnings, but rather an account of the whole world and its creation. Man is included, to be sure, but neither he nor his world is seen from the ordinary human point of view.

The uniqueness of the first chapter—the so-called *first creation story*—is shown in many ways: in its elevated and majestic tone, in its repetitive and paratactic style, and above all in its content. Here, the big cosmological and metaphysical questions—about the status of the lofty heavens, the being of the whole, and its ultimate origins and first causes—are answered without even being asked, seemingly disposed of once and for all. With these matters apparently settled in the beginning, we readers can hereafter devote ourselves instead to more urgent human concerns: the character of human life and the question of how to live.[1]

---

1. There is a midrash that explains why the Bible opens with the letter bet (ב): "Just as *bet* is closed on three sides and open only in front [that is, to the left, in the direction of the ensuing text, Hebrew

Yet if the text were simply interested in getting us started on ethical and polit-ical subjects, it could have begun in the Garden of Eden and skipped the first chapter entirely. But here it is, right at the start, with its endlessly fascinating cos-mological suggestions and assertions. Moreover, whether it intends to or not, the account gives rise to almost as many speculative questions as it answers—for example, about creation ex nihilo, a constant theme of latter-day theological speculation.

Why, then, this kind of beginning? Is it logically or pedagogically necessary for what comes next? How is the cosmological or metaphysical related to the ethical or political? Does the acceptability of God's later commandments de-pend on first recognizing God's power as creator? Regarding speculation, if the story of creation is really intended to close off cosmic wonder and inquiry, why does it in fact provide such speculation with a partial license by putting cosmo-logical matters first? Finally, regarding pedagogy, does either the content or the manner of this beginning account gain the reader's trust and persuade him to keep reading? Do the content and manner of the story of creation initiate us into the proper spirit and manner of reading? Regarding all these questions, we have no alternative but to read and ponder, thoughtfully.

If we are to read in the spirit of thoughtful engagement, suspending disbelief and seeking reasons to trust, the text's pedagogic way, perhaps more than its substance, must draw us in. Perhaps even more than with most books, the be-ginning of this text must gain the interest and goodwill of the reader and dispose him to pay attention, to learn, and to care. How might it do so? Partly, of course, by making plausible to him its teachings about the world and his own place in it. But the text can also inspire trust to the extent that it addresses not only the reader's mind but also his desires, passions, and concerns: for example, his cu-riosity and wonder about the world, as well as his anxiety and restlessness about his own existence within it. Should it succeed in providing a mirror for his own reflection, the text may lead the reader to heightened self-awareness. Finally, the reader's own experience of *reading and considering the story* might itself provide testimony in support of the text's teaching about man's special place in the world order. Should this occur, the reader's perspective on the world might be altered. His focus may even be moved from what is first for him to what might be first in itself.

---

being written from right to left], so you are not permitted to investigate what is above [the heavens] and what is below [the deep], what is before [the six days of creation] and what is [to happen] after [the world's existence]—you are permitted only from the time the world was created and thereafter [the world we live in]." *Genesis Rabbah* 1:10, from *The Book of Legends: Sefer Ha-Aggadah,* ed. Hayim Nahman Bialik and Yehoshua Hana Ravnitzky, trans. William G. Braude (New York: Schocken Books, 1992), 6.

To interpret the first chapter of Genesis, open to such progress of understanding, we will need at least three readings. The first and most naïve reading
stays right on the surface and attempts imaginatively to visualize the unfolding
events of creation in their seemingly temporal order.

AT FIRST GLANCE: THE VISIBLE CAST OF CREATURES
(IN ORDER OF APPEARANCE)

Unfortunately for those who demand clear pictures, the text's account of the
very beginning is shrouded in mystery:

In beginning, God [*'elohim*] created the heavens and the earth.[2]

The first sentence of Genesis majestically summarizes the entire story and states
its main theme and thesis: *creation, by God, and creation by God.* The heavens
and the earth, the high and the low, were *created,* and created *by God.* Yet there is
much in this verse that is hard to understand: in beginning[3] of what? (Of time?
Of everything? Of God's creative activities?) What is "creating"? And who or
what is this creating being, God? To some of these difficulties—especially creation—we shall return. But even now, with our incomplete understanding, we
grasp a major point: the assertion of creation by God emphatically denies important competing alternatives. Right from its beginning, Genesis, by speaking
about the origins of heaven and earth, denies the eternity and, a fortiori, the divinity of the visible universe: neither the heavens—the lofty celestial vault with
its sun, moon, stars—nor the earth, the fertile, teeming source of life, are gods.
They are, rather, creatures, creations of God. Perhaps more important, Genesis
denies the alternative of *generative* beginnings: the sky did not beget upon the
earth; our world is not the result of sexual (or warring) activities of gods and
goddesses. In denying that the world comes to be through giving birth—that is,
in rejecting cosmogony and, all the more so, theogony—Genesis begins by rejecting the necessity of polytheism. The coming into being of our world does
not imply or demand more than one god.

The Bible does not polemicize against these alternatives. As Umberto Cassuto
remarks, "the controversial note is heard indirectly, as it were, through the delib-

2. The translations here and throughout this chapter are my own.
3. The Hebrew lacks the definite article; thus, the popular translation, "In the beginning," is incor-
rect. In his splendid new translation, Robert Alter treats the first (and second) verse not as a declara-
tive sentence but as a subordinate clause: "When God began to create heaven and earth, and the
earth was welter and waste and darkness over the deep and God's breath hovering over the waters,
God said. . . ." Robert Alter, *Genesis: Translation and Commentary* (New York: W. W. Norton, 1996), 3.

erate, quiet utterances of Scripture, which sets the opposing views at naught by silence or by subtle hint." Still, one cannot exaggerate the importance the Bible attaches to rejecting these alternatives.[4] Numerous peoples of the ancient Near East—and elsewhere—regarded the heavenly bodies as divine. In the course of Genesis, we shall meet—as alternative and rejected ways of life—the Babylonians, who looked up to the heavens, and the Egyptians, who worshiped the sun and other nature gods. Because every people (and also every person) is defined ultimately by what it (or he or she) admires and reveres, the Bible wastes no time in denying the standing of other peoples' candidates for the divine. The reason for this urgent rejection is a matter to which we shall return.

The second verse is even more mysterious than the first:

> And the earth was unformed and void and darkness [was] over the face of the deep, and the spirit of God hovered over the face of the waters.

The terms here translated "unformed and void"—*tohu vavohu*—are notoriously hard to translate and understand.[5] Mysterious too are the meanings of "the deep," "the spirit [*or* breath] of God," and His hovering. Yet some impressions are conveyed.

Apparently describing the situation before the first creative act, this verse focuses on a primordial earth—to be distinguished from the Earth that is the dry land and that appears later, on Day Three—above which were only darkness and the spirit (*ruach:* literally, "wind" or "breath") of God. The primordial earth was, to begin with, watery, formless, chaotic, mobile but lifeless, undifferentiated stuff; out of this, everything (or nearly everything) else will come to be, through a process of demarcation, distinction, separation. God, the separator and distinguisher, appears Himself to be separate from the watery stuff. But the origin of the primordial chaos is absolutely unclear; there is no explicit assertion of its creation out of nothing. The *ultimate* beginnings—and even the status quo ante, before God's creative acts—are shrouded in mystery.[6] And well

4. Curiously, these alternatives are rejected also by modern cosmology: the cosmos is not eternal; the sun is not a god, and neither is the cosmos; the coming to be of the universe is not by sexual generation. Whatever their differences on "creation," Genesis and modern science agree on these most significant matters.

5. Alter, who translates them as "welter and waste," points out that this pair of words "occurs only here and in two later biblical texts that are clearly alluding to this one.... *Tohu* by itself means emptiness or futility, and in some cases is associated with the trackless vacancy of the desert." (*Genesis*, 3).

6. About this, too, modern cosmology cannot help but agree: "What was there before the big bang?" "God only knows." Despite all our sophistications, the utter mysteriousness of the *ultimate* beginning and its source or cause cannot be eradicated.

they should be, for neither of the two options—"came from nothing" and "it was there always"—can we human beings picture to ourselves. We may be disappointed in the text's lack of clarity, but we are at the same time grateful that the account leaves mysterious what cannot help but be mysterious. In this sense, at least, we believe that the text tells the truth: we already suspect that there is no way for us human beings to visualize clearly or to understand fully the awesome coming into being of the world. We begin to trust the text.

Happily, the accessibility of the account improves in the sequel (starting in verse 3), once we are introduced to the cast of particular creatures, beginning with light and ending with man. Here they are, in their familiar order of appearance:

DAY ONE: light, and the separation of light and dark, named Day and Night (1:3–5)

DAY TWO: the firmament, that vault of the sky, named Heavens, which separates the waters above and the waters below (1:6–8)

DAY THREE: (a) the separation of gathered terrestrial waters from the emerging dry land, respectively named Seas and Earth, and (b) vegetation—grass, herbs, and trees, each after its kind—put forth by the Earth (1:9–13)

DAY FOUR: the lights in the Heavens—the greater, the lesser, and the stars (1:14–19)

DAY FIVE: the fish of the sea and the birds of the open sky, after their kinds (1:20–23)

DAY SIX: (a) the terrestrial animals, after their kinds, and (b) man, made in God's image, male and female (1:24–30)

The account, though comprehensive, has an earth-centered focus. Though it speaks about what we call, in nonbiblical language, the universe or the cosmos, it addresses *us,* as terrestrial beings and as seeing beings, looking around and about and, especially, up. It begins with what we recognize and trust: the visible world we see above and about us. It shows us the articulated world of our native experience, as it manifests itself to sight.

All the beings mentioned are known to us in ordinary experience: There are no mythical beasts and no gods and goddesses. The main regions of our world are present—land, sea, and air—with their appropriate inhabitants, divided into recognizable kinds or species. And the overarching, star-studded, watery blue vault of heaven that beckons our gaze is present almost from the start, preceded only by light, in the absence of which nothing at all could be distinguished or gazed upon. By addressing human beings exactly as *they* experience the world, especially through sight, Genesis begins with what is both familiar and first for us, and for all mankind at all times.

But in the course of appealing first to our familiar point of view, the story in fact calls that viewpoint into question. Although addressed to our experience, the account of Genesis 1 does not simply *accord* with our experience; indeed, some of the peculiarities of the account induce perplexities about the way we ordinarily encounter the world.

First, there are peculiarities related to time: the creatures do not just come in order, they come sharply separated in a day-by-day sequence. But what does this mean? As early as the Middle Ages, Christian scholars pondering this matter debated whether creation was largely instantaneous (a mere six days) or whether it was gradual (it took time); in this debate, everything depends on the nature and meaning of time—a subject that we shall, mercifully, not entangle ourselves with. But our ordinarily sure sense of temporality—tied to the daily "motions" of the sun—is called into question by this simple fact: we have day and night, and the marking of what appears to be time, on Day One, well before we have the sun, which is created only on Day Four. The forced explanation that creation days are not solar days merely avoids the difficulty and prevents us from recognizing the risks of trusting too much our notions of temporality.

The order of creatures poses other challenges to our ordinary perceptions of things: there is light in the absence of the sun or of any other light-giving heavenly bodies; and there is terrestrial vegetation (Day Three) before the sun (Day Four). In short, although all the beings are familiar, the *order* of their appearance does not square perfectly with facts of ordinary experience.

What are we to make of these difficulties? We could try to rationalize them away. For example, we know at least one source of light that does not require a luminous body, namely, lightning (though it does require clouds, earth, and so forth). Also, the appearance of plants with the earth and before the sun might be due to the fact that the earthbound and earthborn character of vegetation is more impressive to the naïve observer than is its dependence on sunlight. But what if these incongruities should *not* be rationalized away? What if they were *intentionally* arranged incongruously, out of the expected order? What if the text intends, in this way, to challenge, or at least correct, certain aspects of our naïve, untutored perception of our world, a perception that relies mainly on sight and that tacitly holds that seeing is believing?

This suggestion gains force when we notice that the sun is the common feature of all the peculiarities: light without the sun, days or time without the sun, earth and vegetation without the sun. In keeping with its rejection of the belief in cosmic gods, Genesis depreciates the importance of *the* primary being in the world of our common visible experience: the sun, source of light, warmth, and sustenance, that luminously beautiful, seemingly everlasting being, which moves with perfect regularity in perfect circular motion.

This striking demotion of the status of the sun leads us to suspect that the author of Genesis is engaged in teaching something besides what came first and what came next, that the sequence of creatures may not be primarily an effort to tell a *historical* or temporal story. Instead, the apparently temporal order could be an image for the ontological order; the temporal sequence of comings into being could be a vivid literary vehicle for conveying the *intelligible* and *hierarchic* order of the beings that have come to be and *are*. We need a second, and different, kind of look at the biblical sequence.[7]

LOOKING WITH THE MIND'S EYE: INTELLIGIBLE HIERARCHY

We begin our second glance at the order of creatures with the following observation: the six days of creation are organized quite clearly into two *parallel* groups of three: Days One to Three and Days Four to Six (see Table 1). Day One brings light; Day Four, the heavenly lights. Day Two brings heaven, separating waters above from the waters below; Day Five, the living creatures—fish and fowl—that live in the waters below and that fly before the blue heaven. Days Three and Six have, in parallel, double creations, giving them preeminence in their respective triads. Day Three: first, the earth or dry land; and second, the plants, put forth by the earth. Day Six: first, the land animals; second, man.

TABLE 1
The Creatures, Day by Day

1. light	4. lights (heavenly)
2. heaven* (separating space between waters below and waters above)	5. fish and fowl
3. *(a)* earth (dry land)	6. *(a)* land animals
(b) including plants (makers of fruits)	*(b)* including man*

* Not said to be "good."

7. I owe this new way of reading Genesis 1 largely to the writings of Umberto Cassuto and Leo Strauss, on which the next section of this essay heavily depends. See Cassuto, ibid., 7–70, and Leo Strauss, "On the Interpretation of Genesis," *L'Homme XXI*, no. 1 (Jan.-Mar. 1981), 5–20. This remarkable essay informs my entire reading of Genesis 1. It has been recently collected in a posthumous volume of essays by Leo Strauss, *Jewish Philosophy and the Crisis of Modernity: Essays and Lectures in Modern Jewish Thought*, ed. Kenneth Hart Green (Albany: State University of New York Press, 1997), 359–76.

This observation prepares the next: the second three days bring creatures that all have locomotion: the heavenly bodies, the fish and fowl, the land animals and man all move. None of the creatures of the first three days can move. Moreover, the mobile creatures are arranged in order of progressively greater freedom of movement: the heavenly bodies move in fixed orbits and cannot change their paths; all living things—fish, fowl, beasts—can change their paths, though they move in set and prescribed ways, governed, as we would say, by largely fixed instincts; man alone moves in paths and ways that he can set for himself (at least in part).

Having begun to attend not to the temporality but to the logic—or intelligibility—of the sequence, we are in a position to discern the utterly logical and intelligible structure of the entire account.

The main principles at work in the creation are *place, separation, motion,* and *life,* but especially *separation* and *motion.* Places are regions necessary for the placement of separated kinds of beings and backgrounds for the detection of their motion, whereas life may be looked at—at least at a first glance—as a higher and more independent kind of motion. Further, one can treat locomotion as a more advanced kind of separation, in which a distinct being already separated from others also separates itself from place. Thus, we could say that *the* fundamental principle through which the world is created is *separation.* Creation is the bringing of order out of chaos largely through acts of separation, division, distinction.

This view is strongly encouraged by the language of the text: the word "divide" or "separate" (from the root *b-d-l*) occurs explicitly five times in the first chapter (verses 4, 6, 7, 14, 18). And the idea is implicitly present ten more times in the expression "after its kind" (verses 11, 12 twice, 21 twice, 24 twice, 25 thrice), which implies the separation of plants and animals into distinct and separable kinds or species. Separating or dividing is the means of addressing and holding at bay the twin unruly conditions of the beginning-before-the-beginning: darkness and the watery chaos. In verse 4, God divides the light from the primordial darkness; in verses 14 and 18, it is the heavenly lights that divide day from night, light from darkness. The firmament, or vault of heaven, that great separator, divides the waters above from the waters below (verses 6 and 7); it keeps back the chaotic waters above heaven and prevents them from restoring the original chaos through flooding. In contrast to the divisions produced by such intervening deeds of separation, the division that exists "after its kind" refers to the higher and more stable sort of distinctiveness that is embodied in plant and animal species. These creatures manage, by themselves and without the aid of external dividers, to maintain their own distinctness through species-preserving reproduction, each after its kind.

Here is how Leo Strauss summarizes the sequence of creation in the first chapter, showing the principle of separation at work:

[F]rom the principle of separation, light [which allows discernment and distinction]; via something which separates, heaven; to something which is separated, earth and sea; to things which are productive of separated things, trees, for example; then things which can separate themselves from their places, heavenly bodies; then things which can separate themselves from their courses, brutes; and finally a being which can separate itself from its way, the right way. . . . [T]he created world is conceived to be characterized by a fundamental dualism: things which are different from each other without having the capacity of local motion and things which in addition to being different from each other do have the capacity of local motion. This means the first chapter seems to be based on the assumption that the fundamental dualism is that of distinctness, otherness, as Plato would say, and of local motion. . . . The dualism chosen by the Bible, the dualism as distinguished from the dualism of male and female, is not sensual but intellectual, noetic, and this may help to explain the paradox that plants precede the sun.

In short: we have an *intelligible* account of a cosmic order based on noetic or intelligible principles, not mythic or sensual ones. Like the experience- or sense-based view of the world that it corrects, this account is accessible to *all* human beings as *human,* that is, as rational. Granted, the intelligible principles of being (such as separation and motion) are less immediately evident than are the visible beings (such as fish and fowl). But once they are presented to the mind's eye, by means of carefully wrought speech, any human being can appreciate them. When we grasp the intelligible order, the text that bespeaks and reveals that order gains our trust.

The creation of the world, in accordance with these intelligible principles, proceeds through divine acts of intelligible speech. Creation through speech fits creation by separation, for speech implies the making and recognition of distinctions. To name something presupposes (mentally) seeing it distinctly, both as the same with itself and as other than everything else. To predicate or combine words in speech is to put together what mind has first seen as separate. Separation, otherness, distinction—or if you prefer, the principle of contradiction, that A is other than not-A—is the very foundation of the possibility both of speech and of an articulated world.

With this in mind, we look again at the order of creation, as it is called into being through acts of speech. I again quote Strauss (see Figure 1):

[T]he first thing created is light, something which does not have a place. All later creatures have a place. . . . [T]he things which have a place either do not have a definite place but rather fill a whole region, or [are] something to be filled—heaven, earth, seas; or else . . . they do not fill a whole region but [fill] a place within a region, within the sea, within heaven, on earth. The things which fill a place within a region either lack local motion—the plants; or they possess local motion. Those which possess local motion either lack life, the heavenly bodies; or they possess life. The living beings are either non-terrestrial, water animals and birds, or they are terrestrial. The terrestrial living beings are either not created in the image of God, brutes; or in the image of God—man. In brief, the first chapter of Genesis is based on a division by two, or what Plato calls *diaresis*.

FIGURE 1. Creation by Division

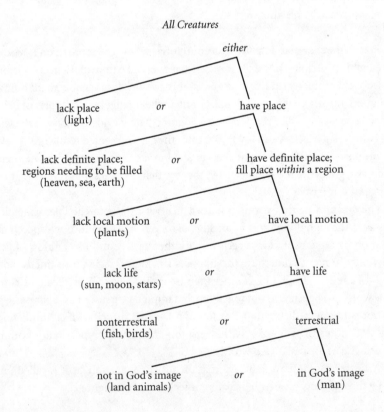

It should not escape our notice that this highly intelligible account of the world, though presented in a religious text, is in substantial agreement with the world as we experience it and as we reflect on it. Our world is indeed an articulate world, with distinctly different kinds of beings occupying different kinds of places, and moving with varying degrees of freedom—some in fixed courses, some in fixed ways, and some (human beings) in ways partly of their own devising. A formed world is necessarily a world of distinction, a world of forms ordered along intelligible lines, a world whose ordered divisions can be made articulate in intelligible speech, a world that is fittingly founded upon intelligibly articulate speech. Wonder of wonders, the text's articulate speech, reporting to us God's creative speeches, makes it possible for us *intellectually* to participate, long after the fact, in God's creation of the world. Through our understanding, we are, in a sense, present at the creation.[8]

The order of the cosmos is not only supremely intelligible; it also appears to be *hierarchic*. The work of creation is completed by living things, created on Days Five (fish and fowl) and Six (land animals and man).[9] Living things are higher than the heavenly bodies, by virtue of having greater freedom of motion, man most of all. Like the heavenly bodies, every animal has its *proper place*—in the waters, above the earth before the firmament, or on the earth—as well as a form of *motion appropriate to its place* (freer on land). Unlike the heavenly bodies (but like the plants), animals are formed according to their *kinds,* with powers to reproduce themselves (to "be fruitful and multiply") according to their *kinds* (or species). Significantly, unlike the heavenly lights, living things also have *powers of awareness*—especially hearing—which are implied in the receipt of God's blessings; they can recognize the distinctions that are manifest in the world, and ultimately, at least one of them—man—can convey and understand these and other distinctions as they are conveyed in speech. Finally, living things are character-

8. We are present at, or participate in, the creation only by way of understanding, not by way of deed. For the divine speech, as reported to us, is not merely intelligible: it is active, it is performative, it is creative. It goes beyond recognizing and appreciating already distinctive kinds; it brings them into being. It is not theoretic speech, in which "letting be" means an appreciative "Leave it alone to be what it is," but a *performative* speech, in which "letting be" means a formative "Call it into being so that it may reveal itself." We shall later in this chapter take up the subject of creation; in the next, we shall consider the difference between divine and human speech. For now, we simply wonder about the words we are reading, and their relation to the acts of divine speech that they describe: is the text of Genesis 1 itself performative and revelatory, an instance of the kind of speech that lets things appear and reveal themselves?

9. In this account, the plants (created on Day Three, before even the heavenly bodies) do not count among the living things, because they are not the *lively* things, the beings that move around on their own. In Hebrew, as in many other languages, the words for "life" (*chay*) and "animal" (*chayah*) are cognate (compare Latin *anima,* "soul" or "life," and *animalia,* "animals").

ized also by *neediness and vulnerability*—indicated by the remarks about food (1:29–30)—which may be what makes them in need of God's blessing. But if animals have needs, they also have *appetites*, that is, inward and felt awareness of their lack coupled with an impetus to act in order to remedy the lack. From this germ of appetition, present even in lower animals, eventually emerge desire, feeling, and a rich inner life, a badge of distinction for the higher animals and man. Life, precisely because it is perishable, has aspiration for what is eternal.

The phenomenological characterization of life implicit in Genesis 1 is remarkably rich and remarkably apt: need and appetite for food from the world, openness to the world through sensory and intellectual awareness, power to move in the world and to alter it through action, activated by desire, passion, and will. Living things are higher than nonliving things; and among living things, some are more alive than others—that is, their powers of awareness, action, and desire are more fully developed. Who could disagree? [10] The special powers of human beings make the case most boldly.

THE HIGHEST CREATURE AND HIS PLACE IN THE WHOLE

In the cosmology of Genesis, human beings clearly stand at the peak of the creatures. To dramatize the point, the text announces their appearance on the scene in high, poetic style:

> And God created the human being [*ha'adam*] [11] in His image [*betsalmo*],
> in the image of God [*betselem 'elohim*] He created him,
> male and female He created them. (1:27)

10. Evolutionary theorists might disagree. Or rather, they would resist entering into the argument about hierarchy altogether. In his notebooks, Darwin wrote an exhortatory note to himself, "Never use higher or lower," but he could not keep himself from doing so; the terms are all over *Origin of Species.* Insofar as evolutionary theory offers any standard for higher and lower, that standard could only be a standard of success, namely, most surviving offspring—in which case, at least in Chicago, the cockroach would be the highest being. Because evolutionary theory does not deal with the *beings* and the *character* of their *lives,* but only with their coming into being, it can in principle never fully appreciate theoretically the different degrees and grades of *being present* that are manifestly here on earth.

But one point bears emphasis: the biblical assertion—I would say the *fact*—of hierarchy is not incompatible with the fact of evolution, or even with evolution by natural selection. It is only incompatible with orthodox evolutionary theory, which refuses to notice it *as hierarchy* and which cannot at present explain it. This ought to make us wonder about the hierarchy-blind character of present evolutionary theory.

11. The Hebrew word is *'adam,* often translated "man," denoting a member of the human species. Though the noun is male in gender (a grammatical fact, merely), its meaning is sex neutral, like *anthropos* in Greek.

Man is the ultimate work of creation: he is the last of the creatures listed in hier-archic order, and once he appears, the work of creation is complete. Man himself is not said by God to be good—a point to which we shall return. But once man is present (and blessed), "God saw *all* that He had made and behold, it was *very good*" (1:31), by which, I take it, is meant that the all or the whole was now com-plete, lacking in nothing. Blessed with dominion or rule over the other animals, man is the most godlike or godly of the creatures: man alone is said to be in the image of God.

This teaching about the place and special dignity of man is today on the defensive. It has been attacked as both false and dangerous. Some say it ex-presses merely an anthropocentric prejudice, vulgarly called "speciesism" by some advocates of animal rights. Others, appealing to evolutionary theory, al-lege that far from being godly, man does not even differ fundamentally from other animals: since all life is in the same business—survival and reproduc-tion—man's apparent difference is merely superficial, a difference not of kind but only of degree. Still others, with moralistic purposes, blame this allegedly self-promoting thesis of man's special place for man's ruthless and smug ex-ploitation of his planet and his animal relations, and even, indirectly, for the smugness that leads—so they argue—directly from self-preference and hier-archic thinking to racism and sexism.

I believe these charges are all mistaken and that the text, properly read, can answer them. Human beings really are different from and higher than the other animals; and only the human animal could be called god-like. To make the case, one needs to understand the meaning of "image of God," no small task. It is probably safest to begin with the term "image" itself and to consider its meaning in the local context provided by the text.

The Hebrew word translated "image" is *tselem,* from a root meaning "to cut off," "to chisel"; *tselem,* something cut or chiseled out—in the first instance, a statue—becomes, derivatively, any image or likeness or resemblance. Any image, insofar as it is an image, has a most peculiar manner of being: it both *is* and *is not* what it resembles. The image of my granddaughter that smiles at me out of the picture frame on my desk *is* my granddaughter—not yours. But it is *not* re-ally she—just a *mere* image. Although being merely a likeness, an image not only resembles but also points to, and is dependent for its very being on, that of which it is an image. Man, like any other creature, is simply what he is. But ac-cording to the text, he is—in addition—also something more insofar as he re-sembles the divine. What could this possibly mean?

To see how man might be godlike, we look at the text to see what God is like. In the course of recounting His creation, Genesis 1 introduces us to God's *activities and powers:* (1) God speaks, commands, names, blesses, and hallows;

(2) God makes, and makes freely; (3) God looks at and beholds the world; (4) God is concerned with the goodness or perfection of things; (5) God addresses solicitously other living creatures and provides for their sustenance.

In short: God exercises speech and reason, freedom in doing and making, and the powers of contemplation, judgment, and care.

Doubters may wonder whether this is truly the case about God—after all, it is only on biblical authority that we regard God as possessing these powers and activities. But it is indubitably clear—even to atheists—that we human beings have them, and that they lift us above the plane of a merely animal existence. Human beings, alone among the creatures, speak, plan, create, contemplate, and judge. Human beings, alone among the creatures, can articulate a future goal and use that articulation to guide them in bringing it into being by their own purposive conduct. Human beings, alone among the creatures, can think about the whole, marvel at its many-splendored forms and articulated order, wonder about its beginning, and feel awe in beholding its grandeur and in pondering the mystery of its source.

These self-evident truths do *not* rest on biblical authority. Rather, the biblical text enables us to confirm them by an act of self-reflection. Our reading of this text, addressable and intelligible only to us human beings, and our responses to it, possible only for us human beings, provide all the proof we need to confirm the text's assertion of our special being. *Reading* Genesis 1 *performatively* demonstrates the truth of its claims about the superior ontological standing of the human. This is not anthropocentric prejudice, but cosmological truth. And nothing we shall ever learn about *how* we came to be this way could ever make it false.[12]

But the text does not exaggerate our standing. Man may be, of all the creatures, the most intelligent, resourceful, conscious, and free—and in these respects the most godlike—but he is also the most questionable. In fact, Genesis 1, read with an eye for the fine print, provides this teaching as well. Man may have powers that resemble divinity, but he is also at most merely an image; man, who quite on his own is prone to think of himself as a god on earth and to lord it over the animals, is reminded by the biblical text that he is, like the other creatures, not divine. Though brought into being by a special creative act, man appears on

---

12. Once again, modern science should have no real difficulty with this conclusion. The sempiternal heavenly bodies may outlast and outshine us and move in beautiful circular paths; or if you prefer a modern equivalent, matter-energy may be virtually indestructible. But only we, not they, can know these facts. Not until there are human beings does the universe become conscious of itself—a remarkable achievement, well appreciated by first-rate scientists. I was once present when the Nobel laureate physicist James Cronin was asked by a skeptical high school student whether he believed in miracles. "Yes," said Cronin, as the student's jaw dropped. "That there should be physics is a miracle."

the same day as the terrestrial animals; though in some respects godlike, man belongs emphatically to the world of animals, whose protective ruler he is told to be. As the later verses about food remind us, we are, like the animals, needy and vulnerable. Man is the ambiguous being, in between, more than an animal, less than a god. This fact—and it is a fact—makes man a problem, as the Bible, even in this celebratory chapter, subtly teaches.

After nearly every act of creation, God looked at the creature and "saw that it was good." There are two striking exceptions: neither the firmament (or heavens), on Day Two, nor man, on Day Six, is said to be good. What bearing, if any, might these omissions have on the place and status of human beings?

Now, one might say that there is no need to see or say that man is good; after all, he is made in God's image and that might make man "better" than good. Moreover, once human beings are present, the whole is said to be *very* good: does this not imply that each part—man especially included—is good? Perhaps. But what if the omission were intended and meaningful? What if it were very good that the creation contain a creature that is himself *not*—or not *yet*—good?

"Good" as used throughout Genesis 1 cannot mean *morally* good; when "God saw the light that it was good," He could not have seen that the light was honest or just or law-abiding. The meaning of "good" seems rather to embrace notions like the following: (1) fit to the intention; (2) fit to itself and its work, that is, able to function for itself and in relation to the unfolding whole; and especially (3) complete, perfect, fully formed, clear and distinct, and fully what it is. A being is good insofar as it is fully formed and fully fit to do its proper work.

A moment's reflection shows that man as he comes into the world is not yet good. Precisely because he is the free being, he is also the incomplete or indeterminate being; what he becomes depends always (in part) on what he freely will choose to be. Let me put it more pointedly: precisely in the sense that man is in the image of God, man is not good—not determinate, finished, complete, or perfect. It remains to be seen whether man will *become* good, whether he will be able to complete himself (or to be completed).

Man's lack of obvious goodness or completeness, metaphysically identical with his freedom, is, of course, the basis also of man's *moral* ambiguity. As the being with the greatest freedom of motion, able to change not only his path but also his way, man is capable of deviating widely from the way for which he is most suited or through which he—and the world around him—will most flourish.

The rest of the biblical narrative elaborates man's moral ambiguity and God's efforts to address it, all in the service of making man "good"—complete, whole, holy. That account does not really begin in earnest until the tale of the Garden of

Eden in the next chapter; Genesis 1 does not dwell on man's work or his duties [13] and does not speak at all about good and evil. Yet even while presenting its majestic cosmology and locating human life as highest in the context of the whole, Genesis 1 subtly hints at the reasons why man is existentially and morally so troublesome.

In this sense, the first chapter of the Bible prepares the rest. It not only tells of the temporal beginnings, answering our questions about ultimate causes; it not only uses the temporal account to convey the intelligible order and the hierarchy of being; it also begins the moral education of the reader.

It seems, then, that Genesis 1 is guided overall by a moral intention, that it is in fact an *ethical* text at least as much as it is a cosmological one. We need a third look at the text from this point of view.

LISTENING MORALLY: AWAY FROM THE HEAVENS

The *cosmology* of the creation story is discussible entirely within the confines of the first chapter itself; but properly to discern the *moral intention* of this beginning requires reading ahead in Genesis. Nevertheless, in anticipation of such further reading, we can find the appropriate clues present already from the start. Indeed, much of the relevant evidence has already been presented and needs only to be recollected.

A main teaching—perhaps *the* main teaching—of Genesis 1 is the nondivinity of the cosmos, and in particular of the sun, the moon, the stars—in short, of everything connected with heaven. Heaven and its occupants are not eternal, they come into being; there is something temporally before, causally behind, and ontologically above the cosmos; the Hebrew word for heaven, *shamayim,* is grammatically plural (actually, dual), not singular; the account begins focused on a primordial earth, and there is no primordial heaven; the heavenly bodies are not living gods but lifeless creatures; they are not even named by God; they are presented as merely useful for the earth, and their rule extends only over day and night, not over the earth and man. The special demotion of the sun— regarded by other peoples as a god—has already been well documented: light, time, and even vegetation are presented as not requiring the sun. Not heaven but man has the closest relation to God; heaven is not said to be good. Heaven, the enduring vault of the cosmos, the stunning star-studded sphere that ceaselessly circles above and to which ancient peoples looked with awe and fear, wonder and admiration, is, according to the Bible, not deserving of such respect.

---

13. A certain imprecisely specified work is assigned to him (to rule the animals) and a certain kind of duty is placed upon him ("be fruitful and multiply").

Why such an effort to demote the dignity of the cosmos, and especially of heaven? And could there be some connection between the fact that heaven is not said to be good and the fact that man is not said to be good?

These questions may strike the modern reader as odd. Not for centuries has Western man seriously flirted with nature worship or pantheistic belief.[14] In modern times, the antipantheistic teaching of the Bible has been reinforced by the antianimistic teaching of science, which also denies special dignity to sun, moon, and stars, indeed, to the universe as a whole. Moreover, we no longer live in ways that inspire interest in or concern for the heavens. Thanks to urbanization and artificial lighting, fewer and fewer people are even aware of the wonders of the night sky, and thanks to modern science, almost no one is moved to ponder the movements of the fixed and wandering stars; astronomy is no longer regarded as an indispensable part of liberal education. And thanks to our nature-mastering technologies, fewer and fewer people live in awe of the power of the heavens: we don't pray for rain, we practice irrigation; we don't dread the full moon, we travel to it. Thus, we must exert a major effort of imagination to reacquire the natural human attitude and to adopt the posture of human beings standing before the open world and the big sky, filled, on the one hand, with curiosity and wonder, on the other hand, with anxiety and dread. By contrast, this attitude, these passions, and the beliefs about nature and the heavens that go with them are well known to the biblical author. We must consider why he regards them as primary.

Human beings, left to their own devices, naturally incline to the worship of nature. Based on their experience of the world, and the knowledge to which their senses lead them, they look up to the powers that be, and preeminently to the heavens. They cannot help but notice the stars, shining steadily, fixed in constellations that circle uniformly and endlessly. They cannot help but wonder at other "stars"—our sun and its planets—that circle endlessly but *non*uniformly, each wandering independently through the constellations—the very word "planet" is cognate with the Greek for "wanderer"—but each in a recurrent pattern whose sequences can be counted and measured. They cannot help being perplexed by the waxing and waning of the moon. And they cannot help being overawed by the sun. Because of its permanence; its regular, ceaseless, perfect circular "motion"; its power and its beauty; and above all, its importance for human life as the source of light, warmth, and the growth of crops, the sun is always and everywhere the prime candidate for natural divinity.

---

14. Such attitudes are, however, making a comeback in the environmentalist movement. Its fundamentalist wing, believers in so-called deep ecology, speaks of nature in reverent terms and even refers to Mother Earth once again as a goddess (Gaia).

These are not just primitive or foolish notions. Whether among the ancient Babylonians or Egyptians or Persians, or among Native Americans or modern-day Buddhists, we find human beings looking up to nature as something divine—not only from reasons of theory but also for purely practical reasons. Because human life is precariously dependent on sun and rain, the effort to appease, propitiate, and control the cosmic forces through worship and sacrifice and the reading of signs is a nearly ubiquitous feature of early human life, and certainly in the ancient Near East.

Thus, according to the Bible (as we will later see), the first to offer gifts to the divine—gifts not invited by God—was Cain, fittingly a farmer, no doubt concerned with rain and the appeasement of heaven. Noah, on getting off the ark, builds an altar and roasts up some of his animal charges, again without instruction, perhaps in gratitude, but perhaps also in an effort to assure no more floods. And most clearly, Babel, the universal human city, founded on reason and the arts, centers around a tower, like the ziggurats of the historical Babylon, the place where human beings first began to count the celestial happenings; in these ziggurats the priests, watchfully yet apprehensively, conducted measurements of the heavenly motions, on the basis of which they sought knowledge useful for the life of the city—forerunners of the astrological aspiration that persists to the present day.

If these inferences do not persuade, the Bible makes the point explicit. In Deuteronomy, Moses exhorts the Israelites to remember the divine voice they heard at Mount Horeb:

> Take ye therefore good heed unto yourselves—for ye *saw* no manner of likeness [*temunah*] on the day that the Lord *spoke* unto you in Horeb out of the midst of the fire—lest ye deal corruptly, and make you a graven image, even the form of any figure, the likeness of male or female, the likeness of any beast that is on the earth, the likeness of any winged fowl that flieth in the heavens, the likeness of any thing that creepeth on the ground, the likeness of any fish that is in the water under the earth, *and lest thou lift up thine eyes unto the heavens, and when thou seest the sun and the moon and the stars, even all the host of the heavens, thou be drawn away and worship them, and serve them, which the Lord thy God hath allotted unto all the peoples under all the heavens.* (Deuteronomy 4:15–19, emphasis added)

Absent special revelation—indeed, absent the special revelation of the exodus and the giving of the law at Mount Sinai—human beings would naturally be led to the worship of heaven.[15] Their natural and astronomical turn is further linked, according to this passage, to idolatry: the creation and worship of visible images and likenesses. Absent *hearing* God's word, human beings would follow their eyes, upward. Human beings, free and hence indeterminate, would *on their own* try to find their way in the world, based on their ordinary experiences; they would ultimately be led to orient themselves by the cosmic "gods" (and their anthropomorphic and zoomorphic representations). This perfectly natural human tendency the Bible seeks to oppose, and right from the first verse, by denying that the heavens—or any other natural beings—are worthy of human reverence.[16]

And what, one may rightly ask, is wrong, ethically speaking, in looking up to cosmic gods, or more simply, in trying to orient human life on the basis of knowledge of nature? After all, philosophers as diverse as Aristotle and Lucretius seem, at first glance, to have taught the life lived according to nature.

---

15. One does not have to take this on biblical authority. In this famous passage from his *Metaphysics*, Aristotle makes a similar point, reporting on a tradition that was already ancient in his time:

> The ancients of very early times bequeathed to posterity in the form of a myth a tradition that the heavenly bodies are gods and that the divinity encompasses the whole of nature. The rest of the tradition has been added later as a means of persuading the many and as something useful for the laws and for matters of expediency; for they say that these gods are like men in form and like some of the other animals, and also other things which follow from or are similar to those stated. But if one were to separate from the later additions the first point and attend to this alone (namely, that they thought the first beings to be gods), he might realize that this was divinely spoken. (1074b1–11, translated by Hippocrates G. Apostle, with slight changes [Indiana University Press, 1966], 208–9)

Astronomy, according to Aristotle, is the foundation of mythology. He believes that the additions made later for ethical and legal purposes, however salutary and useful, represent deviations from the truth.

16. The point has been beautifully made by Harvey Flaumenhaft:

> Scholars nowadays give evidence that the ancient myths of many peoples are vestiges of records made before the time of written records; tales that recount the counting that makes up the stories in the sky, tales sometimes embodied more solidly in temples—in lines of sight those buildings furnish, or in the numbers of their bricks and modules. All over the world, special numbers strangely recur; strange details related to those countings of what happens in the sky are found in accounts that do not seem to be related to the sky, or related to each other. Before the people of the book, it seems that cosmic bookkeepers did their work, impressing in the memories of men their celestial accountancy.
>
> That is why the Bible says in the beginning that what shines forth from up above is not divinities themselves but mere creations of divinity. What the heavens recount is the glory of that unique divinity which made them, we are told, and the worship of what shines forth in the heavens is the lot of all the peoples other than the recipients of this instruction given in the

The Bible's answer—a teaching it shares with modern scientific dogma—would seem to be this: nature[17] is morally neutral. The heavens may, as the Psalmist sings, declare the glory of God (Psalm 19:1), but they say not a peep about righteousness. Not only is nature silent about right and justice; absolutely no moral rules can be deduced from even the fullest understanding of nature. Knowing even that man is the highest creature, because free, does not lead to any clear guidance about how his freedom is to be used. Worse, man's awareness of nature's cosmic indifference to his needs and aspirations will likely lead him into fatalism and despair—if, that is, he knows of no supernatural divinity.

Perhaps the philosophic life, the life of contemplation, for a few private individuals, could be a life lived according to nature. Arguably, it might even be endorsed by the biblical cosmology, which begins with light, which is ordered on strictly intellectual principles, and which concludes with man as the one godlike being who can behold and appreciate the order of the world and ponder its source. Maybe so. But this attempt to reconcile Scripture and speculation seems forced: in presenting man's difference, Genesis stresses more his freedom of motion and action, less his theoretic intellect.

Bible. In the biblical instruction, idol worship is associated with the worship of the stars. Both are forms of what is rejected by the biblical instruction with its awesome either-or. Divinity, seen by some as everlasting beauty, to others rather is benevolent power. For some, an image of divinity is a statue, a graceful, static form to look at. For others, divinity is rather found calling out from fire—ever lively in its formlesssness, but having power to transform; what calls is not something to look at but to listen to, its word recorded in a book for those to read who, lively though perishable, are made in the image of the one whose glory is recounted by the shining in the sky. ("Quest for Order," *Humanities*, Jan./Feb. 1992, 31)

We shall in the next chapter explore in detail the so-called second creation story, the Garden of Eden, which explicitly examines the structure of human life and calls most profoundly into question the goodness of the human inclination autonomously to choose for oneself how to live. In that story, the knowledge to be avoided is knowledge of good and bad rooted in nature—the tree—and always within reach (at the center of our garden) through our immediate experience, once reason—the conversation with the serpent—has emancipated us from obedience to fixed ways. Suffice it to say that the second story even more radically supports the first, showing the folly of the human animal's inborn propensity to freedom and independence, to find its own way by the lights of reason and experience. But our willingness to suspect that our powers might be inadequate to the task of righteous living has been provided at the start, in Genesis 1's challenge to our native presumptions about the dignity and divinity of our given world.

17. This is a good place to repeat that there is no biblical Hebrew word for "nature." The idea of nature, both in the sense of a unified, self-moving totality and in the sense of the essence of a being, belongs to philosophy, not to the Bible. Accordingly, we run the risk of distorting the biblical teaching by referring anachronistically to the Bible's view of "nature," or indeed by using the term at all in this volume. Nevertheless, we shall do so, albeit nervously, in order to bring our study of the biblical text into conversation with other wisdom-seeking activities. We shall, no doubt, have later occasions to visit this question of nature. For now, let the reader beware.

And regarding action, society, and politics, the point is incontestable: the cosmos can have nothing at all to say or teach about all the important questions of human beings *living with other human beings.* Not even the basic prohibitions against cannibalism, incest, murder, and adultery—constitutive for virtually all human communities everywhere and always—can be supported by or deduced from the natural world. From the point of view of *righteousness,* indeed for all *practical* purposes, cosmic gods are about as helpful as no gods at all.[18] The doctrine of creation, whatever else it accomplishes, seems crucial to the Bible's moral-political intention: to bring righteousness and holiness into the center of human life.

We must return to look at the question of creation. Because we are interested ultimately in the truth of the matter, we shall not make things easy for ourselves. As we consider the question of creation, we shall deliberately keep before us modern science's great challenge to the biblical account, the theory of evolution. When the Bible was first written and read, its readers were summoned to do intellectual and moral battle with the ancient naturalism of the Mesopotamians; today its readers find themselves embattled intellectually and morally with the modern naturalism of the Darwinians. We read with our eyes and our minds open, suspecting that the stakes are very high.

CREATION AND EVOLUTION

We pause for a moment to retrace our steps. Our attempt at a literal and philosophical reading of the first chapter of Genesis has shown how its apparently temporal account conveys what we might call an ontological or metaphysical order of the entire world, beginning with all the familiar beings that appear universally in human experience. Moving us to think beyond our experience, Genesis discloses the immanent, hierarchic *order* of our world and its *intelligible principles,* both of them accessible to human beings as human beings, on the basis of reason alone. We see how this ontological account serves an overall *moral* intention, namely to show, in small print, the incompleteness and ambiguity of

18. Nothing in our modern science, including our theory of evolution, requires us to abandon this biblical teaching. Indeed, as I pointed out at the start, modern science altogether shares the Bible's view of the nondivinity of nature, the silence of nature regarding the human good, and therefore the insufficiency of human efforts to find our way of life by thinking about cosmic nature.

Yet whereas evolutionary theory suggests no alternative to nature, the Bible begins beyond nature with its divine Creator and moves throughout to supply our defect of ethical knowledge with its own stories and instructions regarding how to live. Though most of that moral instruction comes later in the Bible, the assertion of creation by God at the very start of the story seems crucial to its moral intent and to its hope of ultimate success.

the human, and in bold print, the nondivinity and moral irrelevance of the entire visible cosmos.

None of these biblical teachings needs to be retracted because of the findings of evolution. The nature, rank, and dignity of the various beings of the world remain unaltered, independent of the process by which they all came to be. In particular, the ambiguous metaphysical and moral status of human beings—in between, in some respects godlike yet not good, and morally indeterminate—can still be affirmed, taking men as they have been and are, evolutionary origins or no evolutionary origins.

Furthermore, if the major intention of the first chapter is not historical but ontological, ethical, and theological, Genesis is not the sort of book that can be refuted—or affirmed—on the basis of scientific or historical evidence. This is, I repeat, not because it is myth or poetry, but rather because its truths are metaphysical and ethical, not scientific or historical, because it teaches mainly about the status and human meaning of what is, rather than about the mechanism by which things work or came to be.

But surely, someone might say, I have skirted the main point of the entire first chapter: creation, and creation by God. The perfectly intelligible cosmology, accessible to human reason, is overarched by an assertion regarding divine creation (with God as the ultimate cause), an assertion for which the Bible offers no direct evidence or argument. Indeed, the passage from Deuteronomy quoted above suggests that, absent hearing the *voice* of God, and by extension, absent the revealed *speech* of the Bible itself, human beings would not readily come to the conclusion of creation, would not readily understand that there is an invisible, intelligent source of the visible and intelligible world. The *intelligibility* of the created order may be known by man as man, but about the *createdness* of the intelligible order—and all the more, about its creator—we readers know only by biblical assertion, that is, only by revelation.

Perhaps we should leave it at that. Yet because today's controversy concerns precisely the matter of creation, and because science and evolutionary theory do pose some challenges to the letter of the Genesis account *as it is ordinarily read* by many people, we should carry the analysis somewhat further—not least because such important matters are at stake.

To recapitulate: Creation, according to Genesis 1, is the bringing of order out of primordial chaos, largely through a process of progressive separation, division, distinction, differentiation. If there is to be a world, it must be articulated into distinguishable beings; if there are to be *living* beings, capable of self-perpetuation, each individual must belong to a kind or species that by and large breeds true, that is, after its kind. (Of this, more soon.)

At this level of generality, the biblical account is perfectly compatible with the fact of a slowly evolving cosmos, with life arriving late, beginning in the sea and only later emerging on earth, progressively distinguished into a variety of separated kinds.

Further, since the separations, actually made or appearing in the world, were all beforehand *makable*, one might even conclude that the biblical creatures—or at least the broadly possible *kinds* of creatures—were present *potentially* in the world, even before they were called forth into being (that is, created).

With this addition, one sees how one might find in Genesis 1 elements of a doctrine of evolving or unfolding creation, or conversely, how *certain* evolutionary accounts of the emergence of living forms are compatible with the Bible's account of a graded and sequential unfolding of the cosmos, through progressive acts of separating out implicit, or at least latent, possibilities.

True, evolution through the unfolding of latent possibilities is not the same as evolution through the natural selection of accidental variations—it is more Lamarckian than Darwinian. But leaving aside such questions of mechanism, creation and evolution might be perfectly compatible, at least in principle; everything depends on what is meant by each notion.

I do not yet fully understand these notions; and I rather suspect that evolution *solely by natural selection*—orthodox Darwinism—cannot be simply squared with the biblical account. But if the question about creation and evolution is to remain open for further reflection, we need to challenge some common assumptions—especially about the biblical text—that usually lead people to see them simply as opposed.

First, *evolutionists deny the primacy and even the intelligibility of natural kinds or species.* Some of them ridicule as typological or essentialist thinking the focus on natural species, characteristic not only of Genesis 1 but also of common human experience. Evolutionary theory, like natural science in general, shares the Bible's teaching regarding the intelligibility of the cosmos, but the intelligibility it seeks comes in the form of universal laws of natural change, rather than the specific forms of the separable natural beings. Indeed, the whole point of Darwin's researches was to discover the natural processes by which new species emerge from preexisting species, through descent and modification.

Yet the transformability of species does not refute the status or importance of species as a natural category; even Darwin's own title *(Origin of Species)* presupposes the reality of species or natural kinds. Moreover, species remain a principle of intelligibility, maybe not for how the animals came to be the way they are, but certainly for *what* they are and *do*. In reproduction, like still mates with like, and the progeny are, for the most part, always like their parents in kind. Genealogy may explain lines of descent or kinship of genotypes, but existent organisms behave largely true to their type. Is not your average rabbit much more impressed by the difference between a rabbit and a fox than he is by the fact that they have the same genetic code or that they are mutually descended from a common mammalian forebear? Species, however mutable, still make sense.

Second, evolutionists, rejecting the notion of fixed species and insisting that life, like the universe, is constantly in flux, oppose this view to the Bible, which they assume *proclaims a static world, created once and for always the same.*

Yet the account in Genesis, contrary to popular belief, does *not* assert the eternity or fixity of the species. On the contrary, Genesis asserts—along with modern science—the noneternity of the species: like the entire visible universe, each species had a beginning in time. More important, there are several subtle indications in the biblical text that invite us to think that God's created order is, in fact, subject to considerable change, *on its own.*

Consider, for example, the fact that God's creatures, at the start, all had their distinct place or habitat: sea, air, land. Where, then, were the amphibious ones? Did God not make frogs and crocodiles? Could they be later creatures, evolving out of an exclusively watery niche? Since frogs and crocodiles were surely known to the ancient Israelites, is the text perhaps raising questions about the propriety of beings that cross boundaries and upset the distinctions that constitute the order of the world? Later, in Leviticus, all such ambiguous creatures will be declared unclean.

The possibility of organic change is more strongly supported by explicit evidence from Genesis 1 itself. After the creatures have all appeared, God speaks to man about food:

> And God said: "Behold I have provided you with all seed-bearing plants which are on the face of all the earth, and every tree which has seed-bearing fruit; to you I have given it as food. And to every living being of the earth and to everything that creepeth upon the earth which has a living soul in it, I have given every green herb as food"; and it was so. (1:29–30)

All the animals were to have been what we call vegetarian. Keeping to this diet would barely disturb the order of creation. Yet we must imagine that man and the animals as created *were capable* of eating meat. (The alternative is that meat eaters *evolved,* later.) That they needed to be told what to eat is perhaps a sign that, left to their own devices, their appetites would naturally lead them to incorporate one another—disturbing the terrestrial order and giving rise to what we now call powerful pressures for natural selection.

In this subtle way, the text hints that the harmonious and ordered whole contains within it a principle—life, or if you will, appetite, and eventually omnivorousness and freedom—that threatens any original order of the whole. Life is, in principle, destabilizing; man is so in spades. God's created order is not immune to change—indeed, as subsequent chapters relate, by the tenth generation all the earth (including the animals) has become corrupt and has erupted into violence and fury (Genesis 6:7, 11–12); the return through the flood to the watery chaos of the beginning completes the dissolution into chaos that life—and freedom—itself had wrought.

Life and freedom are only the most obvious principles of disordering and change. A scrupulously close look at the text suggests even more fundamental principles of change. First, there is the formless, watery chaos out of which everything came to be. How well does it accept form and order? Are all its native entropic tendencies abolished by the process of separation to which it is subjected? Or does its chaotic character persist beneath the forms of the world, making *any* order unstable? Does Genesis 1 subtly teach what was once known as the recalcitrance of matter?

The text speaks twice of each creative act, once to call forth ("Let there be"), once to report the act as performed ("And there was"). Only in the case of the creation of light is the report of the creative act letter-for-letter perfectly identical to the call for the creative act: "Let light be" and "Light be." [19] Only in this case is God's speech precisely and perfectly efficacious in its mode of creative and revealing "letting be." In all other cases, there is a clear difference between command and performance. For example, God asks the earth to "grass grass," [20] but the earth instead "put forth" [*totse'*] grass (1:11–12)—leading the rabbis long ago to remark that the earth was first in disobedience. A second example: God, perhaps now mindful of the earth's recalcitrance, later asks the earth to "put forth" [*totse'*] the terrestrial living creatures (1:24), but it turns out that God has to "make" [*'asah*] them Himself (1:25).

In fact, resistance to order may be present even earlier: at the very start, after God has fully separated the light from the dark, calling the one Day and the other Night, the text reports that there was *evening* and there was *morning:* the

---

19. In the original, the words that precede and follow the "and" are identical—*yehi 'or*. English requires a change from "Let there be" to "There was," but because of a peculiarity in the use of Hebrew tenses no change is needed.

20. Hebrew makes frequent use of the cognate accusative construction; English uses it rarely (as in "dance a dance"). The construction suggests an intimate link between activity and object, between the working and the work. In this case, God had asked the earth to grass grass, in seamless activity, the way a scalp sprouts hair. The earth did not—or could not—do so.

separated Day and Night, quite on their own, had drifted partially back together, blurring the boundaries between them.[21] The recalcitrance of matter, like the mischievous propensities of life, promise massive changes, even for God's created order.

Third, *evolutionists insist that the world and life emerged, and that change proceeds, by wholly natural processes,* and they reject, in particular, creation ex nihilo. But as I read Genesis 1, creation need not mean ex nihilo. The text says nothing to require such a notion; in particular, it is silent about the origin of the primordial watery chaos. And if, as I suggested, the watery stuff offers immanent resistance to the coming and persistence of intelligible order, there may even be said to be some biblical evidence against the kind of divine omnipotence that creation ex nihilo would require. And if there is not creation ex nihilo, then what is *called* creation could very well proceed through perfectly natural—even evolutionary—processes.

Can creation proceed through natural processes, or must creation mean something supernatural, something miraculous, that is, something that defies the ordinary workings of nature? What help, if any, does Genesis 1 provide on this question? What, when we finally come down to it, is the *how* of creation according to Genesis 1?

The Hebrew word "create," *bara',* is applied only to God; it occurs five times in the first chapter: once in the first summarizing sentence, once regarding the sea monsters, three times in connection with man. But this word is used, apparently synonymously, with another word, *'asah,* meaning "to make or do." *'Asah* occurs seven times in the first chapter and three more times in the first three verses of chapter 2 that conclude the first creation account. The last words of the story (2:3) assimilate *bara'* and *'asah:* "which God in creating had made." Curiously, two of the ten uses of *'asah* refer not to God but to trees, to the trees "making" (or bearing) fruit. Is it possible that one could learn something about creation altogether by learning about the natural process of fruit trees making fruit? Here, once more, is Leo Strauss:

> The fruit tree making fruit, what kind of making is this? The fruit is originated almost entirely by the tree and, as it were, within the tree. Secondly, the fruit does not have the looks of a tree. Thirdly, the fruit is a complete and finished product. And last, the fruit can be separated from the tree. Perhaps creation has a certain kinship with this kind of making as distinguished from the following kinds of making: first, the making of some-

21. I was first made aware of these deviations by Robert Sacks, St. John's College, Santa Fe.

thing which does not originate almost entirely in the maker, artifacts, which require clay and so on in addition to the maker; secondly, the making of something which looks like the maker, the generation of animals; third, the making of something which is not complete but needs additional making or doing, the eggs; and finally, the making of something which cannot be separated from the maker: for example, deeds, human deeds, cannot be separated from the man who does them.

If creation through separation were, in fact, more like a tree making fruit than, say, like a man making pottery, could it, just possibly, be an entirely natural process?

I have perhaps gone too far. If the analogy is strictly applied, creation becomes a process of God's fructification, out of God's own substance; and the distinction between God and world on which the text manifestly and vigorously insists would be lost.

But it has been useful to have pushed the account of creation this far in the naturalistic direction, for we can now turn the tables and put a hard question back to the evolutionists. Let us assume that creation *is* evolution, and proceeds solely by natural processes. What is *responsible* for this natural process? What is its *cause*? What is the *ultimate* source of the intelligibility of the natural order or of the actual intelligence that emerged within it with the coming of man? Can a dumb process, ruled by strict necessity and chance mutation, having no rhyme or reason, ultimately answer sufficiently for life, for man, for the whole?

Darwin himself was utterly baffled by how life first arose; in the last words of the last edition of *Origin of Species,* he repairs to "the Creator" as the ultimate source of the first breath of life. Descartes before him had understood that if the human *mind* is thoroughly determined by physical causes there can be no such thing as scientific truth; he therefore was compelled to invoke God as the source of man's rational powers. And when we finally allow ourselves to come face-to-face with the mystery that there is anything at all rather than nothing, can we evolutionists confidently reject the first claim of the Bible—"In beginning, *God* created the heavens and the earth"?

Beyond Creation, Beyond Morality

Our three readings of the text—visual-historical, intellectual-metaphysical, moral-theological—have not yet finished the job. The six-day story of creation as told in the first chapter is incomplete. It has a coda, related in the first three verses of chapter 2:

And the heaven and the earth were finished, and all the host of them. And on the seventh day God [was] finished [with] His work which He had made; and He abstained [or ceased or rested: *vayisheboth*] on the seventh day from all His work which He had made. And God blessed the seventh day, and hallowed it [*vayeqadesh*], because in it He abstained [or ceased or rested: *shabath*] from all His work which God in creating had made.

Six days of work are followed by a seventh day of abstention from work, a day of rest, which completes (or perhaps transcends) the "merely" finished work of creation. The principle of separation, crucial to the whole account of creation, is here further enshrined in the distinction between work and rest. God hallows the seventh day and, in so doing, sanctifies the principle of distinction by making *distinction* the principle of holiness: *qadesh,* the root of the verb "to hallow," means something separated, set off, apart. Curiously, the metaphysical principle of separation will become incorporated in human affairs in the transmoral principle of holiness, for which the observance of the separated and sanctified Sabbath day is crucial, even paradigmatic.

The sanctification of the seventh day continues and completes the critique of beliefs in celestial divinities. The Mesopotamians (Babylonians and Assyrians), before the coming of the Bible, already reckoned seven-day cycles, connected with the phases of the moon. They set aside the seventh, fourteenth, twenty-first, and twenty-eighth days of the lunar months; they had their own Sabbath, *sabattu* or *sapattu,* the day of the full moon.[22] Among the Babylonians, these days—especially *sabattu*—were fast days, days of ill luck, days on which one avoided pleasure and important projects. In contrast, the seventh day among the children of Israel was completely independent of all ties to the heavens, save to the Creator of heaven. It established a calendar completely dissociated from the cycles of the heavenly bodies, commemorating instead their Creator, one who stands above and beyond their ceaseless motion. In Israel, the seventh day will become a day of rest and benison, a day of joy and refreshment, a day on which man would rise above the need for toil, becoming like God, separated from the changing world He created, at rest, apart, hallowed. As Cassuto puts it:

Every seventh day, without intermission since the days of Creation, serves as a memorial to the idea of creation of the world by the word of God, and we must refrain from work thereon so that we may follow the

22. The cycle of seven was not consecutive; the seventh day of a new moon cycle comes either eight days (in a defective, twenty-nine-day month) or nine days (in a full, thirty-day month) after day twenty-eight of the previous lunar month.

Creator's example and cleave to His ways. Scripture wishes to emphasize that the sanctity of the Sabbath is older than Israel, and rests upon all mankind. . . . [T]he commandments concerning the proper *observance* of the Sabbath . . . devolve only upon Israel. Thus in the Ten Commandments is it said, *REMEMBER the seventh day to keep it holy.*

The natural order of the cosmos thus acquires a more than natural significance. God not only creates, He also blesses and hallows. Three blessings are given, two for creatures, the third for the seventh day: to the fish and the fowl for fecundity ("Be fruitful and multiply"; 1:22); to man for fecundity and rule over other living things ("Have dominion"; 1:28); and to the seventh day, not only blessed but separated, hallowed, made holy (2:3). Three blessings: for life, for rule, and for holiness, or as we scholars might say, the natural, the political, the sacred—an ascending order that is imitated in the Torah's unfolding account of human life. The blessing of the fish and fowl is directly quoted; not only are the blessings of the man and woman directly quoted, but God's speech is explicitly said to be addressed *to them* (verse 28). In contrast, we have only the text's *report* of the blessing of the seventh day, not the actual words. The seventh day and its holiness are, to begin with, beyond the human realm altogether. A major concern of the subsequent biblical teaching will be to bring the human into relation to the holy and the holy into everyday human life. But for now, the holy is altogether mysterious.

The story thus ends, as it began, with mystery capable of inspiring awe. We have seen not only the created *order* but also the order as *created,* not only the intelligible separations and forms but also the largely mysterious source of form, separation, and intelligibility. We can discern the distinctions in things, but *we* have not made them separate. Neither have we made that power of mind that registers the articulations of the world and permits us to recognize distinctions. Attentive to this majestic story, addressed not through his trusting eyes but through his respectful ears, the rational man discovers, as the text proclaims, not only that he is godlike but also that he is only an image. Brought by his mindful appreciation of formed order before the mystery of form, order, and mind, the reader must bow his head—as he alone can—to powers greater than human reason. The upright animal, his gaze uplifted and his heart filled with wonder and awe, begins to suspect that he may in fact stand tallest when he freely bows his head. Our moral and spiritual education has begun.

CHAPTER TWO

THE FOLLIES OF FREEDOM AND REASON:
THE STORY OF THE GARDEN OF EDEN (I)

*T*he story of Adam and Eve in the Garden of Eden is perhaps the most famous story in Genesis, indeed, in the whole Hebrew Bible. Read simply and superficially, it tells the tale of man's disobedience and its doleful consequences: the loss of ease, innocence, and psychic wholeness, the gain of a burdened and painful mortal existence. Read carefully and searchingly, with attention to all its details, it opens a window offering profound insights into our human nature and the human condition.

The Garden of Eden story presents a view of our humanity vastly different from the one offered in Genesis 1. This so-called *second creation story* (which begins in Genesis 2:4) departs from the first not only in content but also in tone, mood, and orientation. It addresses or answers different questions and makes a different point, but as we shall see, a point complementary to that of the first story. If read *historically*, it shows *how* and *when* human life got to be so difficult. If read *philosophically* and *anthropologically*, it reveals the basic and often conflicting psychosocial elements of our humanity, thus making clear *why* human life is *always* so difficult. And if read *morally*, it enables us to see clearly and to experience powerfully the primary sources of many of our enduring moral dilemmas and much of our unhappiness. Like every truly great story, it seeks to show us not what happened (once) but what always happens, what is always the case. Like every truly great story, its truth may lie not so much in its historical or even philosophical veracity as in its effects on the soul of the reader.

WHY A SECOND CREATION STORY?

But, you may rightly ask, are there really two distinct creation stories? And more important: if so, why? These questions can be fully addressed only after the Garden of Eden story has been carefully expounded. Still, to encourage a wisdom-seeking approach to the story, it may be useful in advance both to demonstrate concretely how the two stories are different and to suggest how they might be related. By doing so, we may be able to counteract two opposing but equally misleading biases about this story: the prejudice of some pious readers and the prejudice of many biblical scholars. The pious readers, believing that the text cannot contain contradictions, ignore the major disjunctions between the two creation stories; they tend to treat the second story as the fuller, more detailed account of the creation of man (and woman) that the first story simply reported. On the other side, the scholars, though keenly aware of the differences in the two stories, have little interest in relating their content and meaning; practitioners of source criticism, they focus on the differences to prove that the two accounts came from different sources—the so-called P (Priestly) and J (Yahwistic) documents—that were subsequently redacted or compiled. They rarely consider *why* the redactor or compiler might have deliberately selected and juxtaposed these two somewhat contradictory versions.

The first creation story focuses on heaven and earth, on the entire cosmos; the second focuses on human beings in their terrestrial situation. In the first, the cosmic beginnings are watery and amorphous (1:2); in the second, the earthly beginning is dry (2:5). The first story ends with man; the second begins with him. In the first, the animals come first and man is to be their ruler; in the second, the beasts come after, as man's possible companions. In the first, man is to be the master of life on earth (1:28); in the second, he is to be the servant of the earth (2:5, 15). In the first, male and female are created together; in the second, they are created sequentially, male first (or alternatively, the first human being is, to begin with, androgynous). In the first story, man is made directly in the image of God (1:27); in the second, he is made of earthly dust and divine breath (2:7) and becomes godlike only at the end—"now the man is become like one of us" (3:22)—and only in transgressing. In the first, things are said to be "good"; in the second, there is a tree of knowledge of good and *bad*, nothing is said to be "good," and one thing—man's aloneness—is said (by the Lord God) to be "*not* good*." In the first, the name for God is *'elohim*, in the second *YHWH 'elohim*. In the first, plants are given to living things for food (1:29–30); in the second, man is to serve and keep the plants (2:15), but the fruit trees are given for food (2:16). In the first, in need of encouragement, man is given a positive injunction, for procreation and dominion (1:28); in the second, in need of restraint, he is given a negative commandment (2:17). In the first, God names and blesses (1:22, 28; 2:3); in the second, man names but God curses (3:14, 17). In the first story, God's first blessing concerns reproduction (1:28), and only later are there remarks about food (1:29); both are positive. In the second story, food comes before sex and reproduction, and each is tinged with ambiguity and sorrow: there are, first, generous remarks about eating, but with one restriction (2:16–17), followed by the emergence of sexuality, first without shame (2:25), later with it (3:7); only later in the story (in the "punishment") do we learn (for the first time) about childbirth, that it will be painful (3:16), and the truth about food, that it will come only with toil (3:18–19). In the first story, human freedom appears to be our badge of distinction; in the second story, human freedom is the source of our troubles.

The first story addresses the reader as a spectator and offers a cosmic vision, majestically presenting man's place in a cosmic whole. Though the viewer's vantage point is terrestrial, the scene viewed is remote and all-encompassing, and what is seen is eternal. Relatively open regarding man's work, the story addresses us mainly intellectually, providing "metaphysical" scope and knowledge, and it inspires in us wonder and cosmic awe. In contrast, the second story maintains a strictly terrestrial focus and addresses the reader as a suffering moral agent, presenting him a poignant account of why misery shadows human life. The perspective is close and earthy, the view is genealogical and human. It focuses on human work, in toil and generation, showing us both our complex nature and what is responsible for our life's being the way it is. It addresses us mainly experientially, personally, and emotively, with moral scope and knowledge, and (as we shall see) it inspires in us shame, fear, and moral awe. The second story is *not* just a magnified version of the human portions of the first. It is, in fact, utterly distinct and independent, and reveals a different but equally true aspect of human existence.

Once we recognize the independence of the two creation stories, we are compelled to adopt a critical principle of reading if we mean to understand each story in its own terms. We must scrupulously avoid reading into the second story any facts or notions taken from the first, and vice versa. Thus, in reading about the origin of man in the story of the Garden of Eden, we must not say or even think that man is here created in God's image or that man is to be the ruler over the animals. Neither, when we try to understand the relationship of man and woman in the garden, are we to think about or make use of the first story's account of the coequal and coeval creation of man and woman. Only after we have read and interpreted each story entirely on its own should we try to integrate the two disparate teachings. By proceeding in this way, we will discover why these two separate and divergent accounts have been juxtaposed and how they function to convey a coherent, noncontradictory teaching about human life. In the belief that an early glimpse at this teaching will encourage readers to follow the long argument more thoughtfully and fruitfully, I state the conclusion at the beginning—and beg the pardon of anyone who would rather have been kept in suspense.

Although the two accounts differ widely, and although they even contradict each other if they are read as historical accounts, the two stories in fact complement each other and form part of a coherent whole. Indeed, there are good reasons—both theoretical and moral—for putting together the separate meta-physical-cosmological and the moral-political stories.[1] First of all, reading theoretically, this separation and juxtaposition of the two stories is a way of indicating that the two aspects of our world, the natural-cosmic-metaphysical and the moral-political, although both true, are nonetheless also utterly dis-joined. The first story, addressing us as seekers of natural-cosmic knowledge, documents an eternal, intelligible, and hierarchic order of the world, in which we human beings stand at the top of the visible beings; the cosmos itself is not divine, for it has a higher, invisible, and partly mysterious source. Man, not the sun, is godlike: sufficient proof is contained in our mental ability to grasp the cosmology offered in the text. But as the second story shows, addressing us as seekers of moral-political knowledge, human life, considered here on earth and in its own terms, is for the most part hardly godlike: it has a sorrowful content for which we sense that we are somehow responsible. A life of sinless innocence and wholeheartedness is virtually impossible for a human being, thanks to free-dom, imagination, reason-and-speech, self-consciousness, and pride, and in the face of neediness, sexuality, ignorance, self-division, dependence, and lack of self-command.

Second, reading morally-politically, we learn from these two separate sto-ries that neither cosmic nature nor human reason will suffice to help us live well. Cosmic knowledge cannot heal our self-division or teach us right-eousness, not least because—as we learn from the first story—the cosmos is neither divine nor a source of such moral-political teaching. And—as we will soon learn from the second story—our own native powers of mind and awareness, exercised on the world around us, are inadequate for discerning how to live happily or justly.

In short, the first story challenges the dignity of the natural objects of thought and the ground of natural reverence; the second story challenges the human inclination to try to guide human life solely by our own free will and our own human reason, exercised on the natural objects of thought. Ordinary human intelligence, eventually culminating in philosophy, seeks wisdom re-garding how to live—that is, knowledge of good and bad—through contem-plation of the nature of things (that is, for short, of heaven). The Bible opposes, from its beginning, this intention and this possibility, first, in chapter 1, by denying the dignity of the primary object of philosophy, the natural things, and

1. These terms—"theoretical," "metaphysical," "cosmological," "moral," and "political"—are, of course, not biblical; they come from philosophy. As many people have observed, the word "nature" does not appear in the Bible. Nonetheless, in a wisdom-seeking reading of the Bible, the distinctions here employed seem to be valuable and illuminating, and the insights afforded by their use may justify any possible distortions caused by importing these anachronistic and foreign terms.

second, in chapter 2, by rebutting the primary intention of philosophy, guidance for life found by reason and rooted in nature. God, not nature, is divine; obedience to God, not the independent and rational pursuit of wisdom, is the true and righteous human way.

SPEECHLESS INNOCENCE: THE BASIC STRATUM OF HUMAN LIFE

Alerted to what is at stake, we turn now to the text and to this story's account of the primordial human being. The text's picture of man—his powers, his activities—comes to us sequentially, in layers built up in order from the inside out; for this reason, we must not ascribe human capacities to our "hero" before they are explicitly presented in the text. We can learn most from the story by regarding it as a mythical yet realistic portrait of permanent truths about our humanity, rather than as a historical yet idealized portrait of a blissful existence we once enjoyed but lost.

> Every shrub of the field was not yet in the earth, and every herb of the field had not yet sprung up; for the Lord God had not yet caused it to rain upon the earth, and there was not a man ['adam] to till [or serve: la'avod] the ground ['adamah]; but there went up a mist from the earth, and watered the whole face of the ground ['adamah]. (2:5–6)

As our story opens, the earth is hard, dry, and lacking in vegetation. Yet every shrub and every herb are, in fact, latently present, awaiting the right conditions to spring forth.[2] The earth's fruitfulness, we learn from the start, needs both the rain of heaven and the workings of man. The text hints that the future lurks in the present, not only for the earth but also for the human being. Even before we meet him, man is defined by his work: less the ruler over life, more the servant of the earth,[3] man will till and toil, needily waiting for rain, apprehensive about the future. The story begins convincingly, conveying a nearly universal truth about human life.

2. The Hebrew original says, literally, "Every shrub of the field before it was in the earth." In this subtle way, the text suggests that what follows is an account that unfolds and reveals what is inherently always there, rather than an account that tells of a once-upon-a-time event. In the same way, we shall learn about the unfolding of man's character from its inherent and permanent roots. I am grateful to Yuval Levin for this observation.

3. The verb in the expression "to till the ground," 'avad, means "to work" but also "to serve." It is cognate with 'eved, "servant" or "slave." We shall have occasion in later chapters to examine the activity of farming and, in particular, whether it represents mastery of or subservience to the earth.

But *why* is this our life? What is responsible for its being so difficult? The sequel intends an answer.

> Then the Lord God formed [*or* fashioned: *yatsar*] man [*or* human being:
>   '*adam*] of the dust of the ground ['*adamah*],
> and breathed into his nostrils the breath of life;
> and man became a living creature. (2:7)

Human troubles are foreshadowed by man's dual origins: he is constituted by two principles, the first one low ("dust of the ground"), the second one high ("breath of life"). The human being here first comes to sight not as image of God but as formed and animated (or breathing) dust of the ground. Higher than the earth, yet still bound to it, the human being has a name, '*adam* (from '*adamah*, meaning "ground" or "earth," from '*adam*, meaning "ruddy" or "tawny"), which reminds us (and perhaps him) of his lowly terrestrial origins. A groundling or earthling, man is, from the start, up from below.

Although formed from the ground, man is not alienated from it. On the contrary, simply as a living creature, he appears at first to be right at home, in a world that seems absolutely made for him.

> And the Lord God planted a garden eastward, in Eden;
> and there he put the man whom He had formed.
> And out of the ground made the Lord God to grow every tree that is
>   pleasant to the sight and good for food;
> the tree of life also in the midst of the garden,
> and the tree of the knowledge of good and bad.
> And a river went out of Eden to water the garden;
> and from thence it was parted, and became four heads. . . .[4]
> And the Lord God took the man and put him into the garden of Eden
>   to work it [*or* to serve it: *le'avdah*] and to keep it [*or* to guard it *or* to
>   watch it: *leshamrah*].

4. At this point the text identifies four rivers, only the last two of which are clearly known to us: Pishon, Gihon, Tigris, and Euphrates. That the Garden of Eden is a purely mythic place—a mere utopia, literally "no place"—is indicated by the fact that there can be no single terrestrial place that could serve as the common source of these four widely separated rivers. True, the Tigris and Euphrates rivers do meet, but the lands the text associates with the first two rivers are clearly separated from the Tigris-Euphrates valley, the first to the north, the second to the south. (A similar device is used by Homer in the *Odyssey*, where he locates Ogygia, the home of Calypso, at "the navel of the waters.") What we learn through the use of this poetic trope is that this story of human beginnings applies universally: the elementary anthropological truths it discloses pertain to human beings who populate all the great rivers (and continents).

And the Lord God commanded the man, saying,
"From every tree of the garden thou mayest surely eat. . . ." (2:8–10, 15–16)

This prototypical human being, what is he like? The text does not explicitly tell us. Yet this very silence (as well as the contrast of this tableau with what comes later) suggests that he is a simple being, with a simple soul, living a simple life. In body he looks like one of us: upright, naked, and hairless. But in mind and heart he seems protohuman, more childlike (or maybe even animal-like) than godlike. He is ignorant, speechless, and (above all) innocent; as yet, he knows no complex or specifically human passions or desires: neither shame nor pride, anger nor guilt, malice nor vanity, wonder nor awe visit his soul. Very likely, he also lacks both fear of death and erotic desire. With his simple needs— for food, for drink, for repose—simply met (or largely so; there is as yet no tilling of the ground), he is content. Experiencing little gap between desire and its fulfillment, and feeling no opposition either from without or from within, he knows neither self-division nor self-consciousness. Solitary and independent, enjoying what Rousseau would later call "the sentiment of existence," he lives for himself, immediately and here-and-now, in a world that provides him peace, ease, and the satisfaction of his basic needs.[5]

Read as history, the text fails to persuade the skeptical reader. Man probably never lived as a solitary or in an Edenic garden. But read anthropologically and morally, the story is both revealing and moving. For one thing, it conveys truly a permanent aspect of our being. Whatever else human beings are or become, they are, always and at bottom, *also* beings with an uncomplicated, innocent attachment to their own survival and ease, beings who experience and feel, immediately and without reflection, the goodness of their own aliveness. This stratum of all *animal* being—private bodily need, privately satisfied and enjoyed—is an ineradicable part of *human* being. All human beings know hunger, thirst, and fatigue. No man, no matter how altruistic or saintly, meets his own hunger by putting food into someone else's mouth. Moreover, from the point of view of simple necessity—for food and drink—the world is a rather generous place;

---

5. Readers who know Rousseau's *Discourse on the Origins of Inequality Among Men* will recognize its influence on the terms I use here to describe the primordial human being before the creation of woman (or, to speak nonhistorically, abstracted from his sexual nature). In this *Discourse,* Rousseau mounts a critique of civilization in the name of human freedom and happiness, using as a device a mythic portrait of solitary "natural man" living in the state of nature, a portrait that is, among other things, a remarkable philosophical interpretation of the Garden of Eden story and its sequelae. My philosophical reading of the biblical account of human beginnings not only takes encouragement from Rousseau's example; it is also indebted to Rousseau's profound appreciation of our basic psychic and social proclivities. As will be seen, however, I do not follow Rousseau in the moral and political uses he makes of the biblical text.

were it not for the depredations of civilized man, it would be so still. For many of our simpler relatives, including the primates, it remains in large measure a veritable garden; and it would still be so for us, had we never risen up from animality—or for that matter, from childhood.

The basic stratum of life, with its focus on satisfying life's basic needs, is never far from the surface of human life. We continue to experience its demands, we daily enjoy their satisfaction. Though we cannot remember our own infancy, we reexperience through caring for our children the phase of human life ruled almost entirely by animal necessity. From time to time we even make great efforts to reexperience in pure form the simplest pleasures of life: we go carefree into the woods to commune with nature; we pick berries, nuts, and mushrooms and we drink from a mountain stream; we sit down under a tree to eat and drink; we lie down under a tree to enjoy (we hope) a dreamless sleep.

For all these reasons, few adult readers can be emotionally indifferent to the inviting picture of "original man" in the Garden of Eden. No matter how sophisticated and civilized we have become, most of us respond to this portrait of our mythical remotest "past" with something that feels, in fact, like nostalgia. We experience the original *'adam* as a grown-up child enjoying the pleasures of a childlike existence. With at least part of our souls, we long for a condition like his. We envy original man not only his contentment with life but also and especially his simple innocence and goodness, his psychic wholeness and spontaneity, and his lack of troublesome self-division and corrosive self-consciousness. We envy his apparent being at home in the world, at one with and in command of his surroundings. Even though we probably would not, on balance, exchange our life for his (any more than we would willingly return permanently to early childishness), we are made poignantly to experience what we have lost and to wonder why. The text's answer is right before us.

DISTURBING KNOWLEDGE, DANGEROUS FREEDOM

The simple, primordial human being, because he is primordially *human*—or perhaps, instead, *potentially* human—is not quite simple. As the story already hints, there is something disquieting in his original nature. Some innate capacities or potentialities in the human soul dangerously threaten to upset the tranquillity of man's simple and innocent life. Two possible sources of disturbance are subtly identified, metaphorically, in the form of the two special trees, trees that are distinguished from those "pleasant to the sight and good for food" (2:9), each an object of potential desire: the *tree of life* (in the midst of the garden) and the *tree of knowledge of good and bad*. Later, another source of trouble will be introduced, centering on man's aloneness and the remedies provided for it—sexuality and sociality. At this point, however, the elements under scrutiny are intrapsychic rather than interpersonal.

The tree of life, offering deathlessness, stands in the center of man's garden. As is true of any other animal, man's immediate attachment to his own life implies an instinctive fear of death, which, should it become active by becoming conscious as an *actual* fear, could—and does—greatly disturb man's tranquillity. But unless and until the fear of death is accompanied by something like self-conscious *knowledge* of death as a *badness,* the creature will have no interest in trying to overcome death by seeking immortality from the tree of life. The original human being shows no interest in the tree of life; indeed, as we shall see, he never eats of it prior to his expulsion from the garden, presumably because concern with death does not penetrate the consciousness of his simple soul.

The more important threat to the contentment of elementary human life is represented by the tree of knowledge of good and bad, about which we shall soon speak at length. The tree stands as the object or goal of an (at least) latent tendency in the prototypical human being to seek a certain kind of knowledge or a certain kind of awareness. Once attained, this knowledge will necessarily disturb the psychic peace and harmony of the living creature. In its presence the human being cannot without trouble enjoy his own existence. In its presence he cannot remain undivided within himself. To reinforce the threat that such knowledge poses to his own health and happiness, the danger is here revealed to human beings—both the one in the story and the ones reading it—by the highest authority. Not mere local custom, but the highest principle of Being attests to the trouble that comes with and from a certain kind of dangerous knowledge.

The warning the story puts in the form of a divine command.

> And the Lord God commanded the man, saying, "From every tree of the
>   garden thou mayest surely eat [*literally,* eating thou mayest eat];
> but of the tree of the knowledge of good and bad, thou shalt not eat of it;
> for in the day that thou eatest thereof thou shalt surely die [*literally,* dying
>   thou shalt die]." (2:16–17)[6]

Generally overlooked in this commanding speech is its largely good news about food: the bounty of the entire natural environment is at human disposal; the world is, at least for the purpose of nourishment and self-preservation, a hos-

---

6. In contrast to the first creation story, the first divine speech in this story is moral, not creative. Further, in speaking to the human being, the Lord God does not bless, as He does in the first story; He commands.

pitable place. But the story's focus rightly falls on the one exception to God's generosity, and on the fact of commanded interdiction and limitation of human appetite.

We take it as an axiom that God is unlikely to waste His commandments and prohibitions, issuing them where there is no need.[7] Thus, from the fact that it is here prohibited, we infer the existence of a human propensity that leads toward the tree. Man must be the kind of being that has at least a potential to seek the kind of knowledge represented by the tree. Man must be the kind of being for whom such knowledge is always in his vicinity, but an arm's reach away, so to speak. To see why a benevolent God might try to keep his creature from it, we need first to try to say what this prohibited tree *is* and why knowledge of good and bad might be deadly.

We note first that one should regard the knowledge it represents as knowledge of "good and *bad*" rather than the more familiar "good and evil." The Hebrew word translated "bad" has a much broader meaning than moral evil. Pain is bad, and so are sickness, ugliness, and disorder. It is therefore better to begin with this very broad, and not exclusively moral, understanding of "bad." Second, the tree of knowledge is obviously a metaphor; knowledge does not grow on trees. Nevertheless, the metaphor is powerful, as we can see by pondering it. Why does the Bible present knowledge as if it were embodied *in a tree*, obtainable by eating? What, for openers, is a tree?

A tree is a seemingly independent being, self-developing, self-sustaining, and apparently self-caused. But seeming is not being. God caused this tree to come out of the ground—like all trees. The tree's appearance of independence— its on-its-ownness—is deceptive. Though separate and distinct, the tree in fact belongs to the earth. Though it appears lofty to the human eye, it is in fact of lowly origins and contains no breath of life. A tree may be attractive to sight and tempting for food, but it is silent; it has nothing useful to teach about life. In short, a tree is a natural, terrestrial, low but seemingly lofty, attractive (to sight) but amoral being, seemingly—but only seemingly—autonomous and self-sufficing.

Consider next the name of our special tree. The phrase "knowledge of good and bad" is ambiguous. Some have held that it is an idiom meaning knowledge of all things, others that it means political knowledge, especially knowledge of how to rule. But on its face, the name suggests rather knowledge of how to live, of what we would call practical knowledge, including but not limited to moral knowledge. Yet it is unclear whether it signifies *(a)* knowledge

---

7. An obvious if trivial example: God does not command man or the animals to breathe. A less obvious but nontrivial example: God does not command mothers to love their children.

only *that there are* good and bad or *(b)*, in addition, also a *concern* with good and bad or *(c)*, further, *true* knowledge of what good and bad *really are*. In the light of the sequel, I am inclined to think that the tree offers the human being not *true* knowledge of good and bad, but merely a concerned awareness of their presence and difference, coupled with opinions, not necessarily reliable, about which is which.

Putting together the generic characteristics of "tree" with this particular tree's name suggests that the tree of knowledge of good and bad stands for some autonomous knowledge of how to live, derived by human beings from their own experience of the visible world and rooted in their own surroundings (nature; trees in the garden). Once the potential for human freedom and choice emerges, human beings live by their own lights, learning solely from their own experience. It is precisely this natural and uninstructed human way that the Bible warns us against by having God attempt to prevent man from attaining, or even pursuing, that freedom and its correlative, autonomous knowledge. By means of the image of a divinely prohibited tree, the story means to make clear to the reader that human freedom—or, what is the same thing, human reason—is itself deeply questionable, and the likely source of all our unhappiness.

The point is even better made if we pursue a purely formal analysis, dealing not with the substance of the tree but only with the fact that it was *prohibited*. Man in this story is defined by his need for a prohibition; he is a free being, or rather a "too free" being. Accordingly, the crux of the story is prohibition and interdiction, which is to say—by negation—freedom and autonomy. The Bible knows that the only way to show human freedom as a problem is to come at it from its opposite: constraint. Here is how the story's logic works.

The man is told to obey a command. Obedience is called for, its opposite is proscribed. The opposite of obedience is nonobedience or disobedience, or in other words, choosing for yourself. *Any* free choice is, by definition, an act of nonobedience. To make this truth absolutely clear, the story makes free choice appear as disobedience to command.[8]

Free choice is tied to knowledge; free choice implies reason. Whereas obedience means necessarily "no *independent* knowledge of good and bad," dis-

---

8. It is, of course, true that someone might freely choose to obey a command(ment). Down the road, this is precisely what God and the biblical author will recommend. But rhetorically, the choice for willing obedience becomes more attractive if the reader first learns about the folly of nonobedience. And logically and psychologically, the only way to show that conduct has indeed been freely chosen is to show it in opposition to and in defiance of constraint—whether of law and command or even only of fixed instinct. From the outside, an act done because of obedience or necessity and the same act freely chosen are indistinguishable. Proof of freedom requires negation, requires explicit *dis*obedience.

obedience necessarily means, at least implicitly, independent or autonomous knowledge of good and bad. *Any* free choice implies reaching for and acting on our own knowledge (or opinion) of good and bad, better and worse. *Every* free choice implies some (at least) tacit *judgment* that the thing being chosen is, in some sense, good.

The meaning of the tree of knowledge of good and bad should now be clear: the knowledge prohibited is in fact the knowledge implied in violating *all* prohibitions, or in other words, the knowledge implied in *any* act of *free* choice. As everybody knows, the human being indeed chose to disobey, never mind why. He (they) chose therewith the *principle of disobedience,* which is to say, the principle of freedom and independence. The *name* that Genesis gives to the principle of disobedience is "knowledge of good and bad," [9] knowledge freestanding and autonomous—that is, just like a tree.

In the story, the human being, in the act of disobedience, appropriates to himself—makes part of himself, incorporates (that is, eats)—knowledge of good and bad. But please note: *to reach for the forbidden fruit is already to have tasted it.* As we shall see, the woman, *before* she eats of it, has already made a judgment that the tree is *"good* for food and a delight to the eyes and to be desired to make one wise." The woman judges for herself, on the basis of her own autonomous knowing of good and bad, that to eat is good. Formally speaking, the eating merely ratifies, after the fact, the human way of freedom and autonomy.

Some will argue that the problem that God sought to address (or to speak strictly anthropologically, the problem at the heart of our troubles) is not freedom itself but rather only its abuse. On this account, freedom is itself a good, even a blessing, but a blessing that can be used for both good and bad. When it is badly used, the fault lies not with freedom or reason itself but with human appetite: or, alternatively, human pride distorts free will.

Supporters of this interpretation emphasize that the prohibition seeks to limit human eating, an activity born of desire. But the context shows that eating, by itself, is not the problem: God generously provides a whole gardenful of trees "good for food," and the tree of knowledge is clearly distinguished from the trees of nourishing.[10] The text seems to imply not that freedom is corrupted

9. This formulation, as well as the basic insights of this formal analysis of the prohibition, I owe to Leo Strauss's essay "On the Interpretation of Genesis," *L'Homme XXI,* no. 1 (Jan.-Mar. 1981), 5–20.

10. The metaphor that lets prohibited eating stand for prohibited knowing is, however, pregnant. Eating is the incorporation of "other" and its transformation into "same." Eating the proper food maintains oneself and one's own wholeness. But eating improper food, food that cannot be assimilated, means taking in material that remains indigestible, that remains separate and alien. Taking in wrong food thus produces a certain duality and negativity within; it invites self-attention and

by desire, but rather the reverse: natural desire and its satisfaction are threatened as a result of human freedom and reason and a certain kind of knowledge. Because we have free choice—that is, because our desires are not simply given by instinct—and because our reason, through its working on our imagination, influences and alters natural appetites, human appetite increases beyond what is necessary and good for us. Precisely because we are rational and, hence, free, we can freely desire things that are harmful to life, health, and well-being. Thus, a proscriptive limitation on human eating and human omnivorousness metaphorically (and perfectly) highlights the dangers freedom poses to healthy natural desire.

As an empirical matter, it is no doubt true that desire and pride can and do warp human choice. But our biblical text has a much more radical teaching about the problem of freedom. Every act of uninstructed free choice, the text seems to intimate, is an implicitly prideful act, presupposing as it does the possession of knowledge of what is good for a human being. Every act of choice implicitly expresses a judgment of good and bad, better and worse. Every act of choice presupposes that the human agent knows—or thinks he knows—what is good for him (or someone else), on which basis he chooses accordingly. On this interpretation of the text, the fact that God wants to keep man from the tree of knowledge of good and bad suggests that He wants man to remain an innocent, contented, and unself-divided being who follows instinctively the path to his natural good. Or better, reading morally rather than historically, through God's command about the tree the text teaches the reader that it is his own freedom—and its implicitly yet necessarily disobedient character—that is the cause of all human troubles.

To sum up this formal part of the argument: For a human being, as for any human child, the possibility of choosing for oneself lies always within reach. To be a human being *means* that judgments of good and bad are always in one's mental garden, no more than a thought away. And as every parent teaches, and as we children learn painfully by ourselves much later, a free choice is not necessarily a good choice, not even for oneself. In the story, the generous God paternalistically seeks to keep man from sacrificing his simple and innocent happiness;[11] yet the need for such a restraint shows that the autonomous source of trouble lies already deep within, at least potentially. Moreover, man's ability

---

judgmental self-consciousness, precisely the result (in our story) of the act of transgressive eating. On the nature of eating and on the problem of human omnivorousness, see my *The Hungry Soul: Eating and the Perfecting of Our Nature* (Chicago: University of Chicago Press, 1999), Chapters One and Two.

11. By this means the text also shows the reader the reason why he too no longer can enjoy a simple and innocent happiness.

presumably to understand the prohibition, however partially, proves that he needs it: because he already has mind enough to distinguish the trees by name, he will soon enough have a mind of his own—just like the reader—and with it, the ability to make himself miserable.

It will not do, as some would have it, to blame God for our troubles.[12] To have created a human being *means* to have created a being with a tree of knowledge of good and bad necessarily in the picture. God did His best: He warned us of the problem and we did not hearken. The fault lies not with the world or with God but in ourselves—and not only once upon a time. By serving as a mirror, the story enables us to discover this truth also about ourselves.

The analysis of the meaning of the tree of knowledge of good and bad has so far focused in part on the metaphor and name of the tree, in part on the formal analysis of the mere fact that it was prohibited. But there is a third way of knowing about the tree of knowledge of good and bad: from the substantive consequences of eating, that is, by the kinds of knowledge acquired through partaking of the forbidden fruit. Even if it is true, as I have suggested, that the human beings have, as it were, already partaken of the tree in reaching for it, the full meaning of that choice—and of knowing *badness*—can be seen only in the material consequences of the transgression. The problem is not just that reason and freedom lead to bad choices, owing to ignorance. They also turn us into beings who are aware of, and self-consciously caught up with, the "badnesses" already present in our existence.

Regarding the consequences of disobedience we shall speak more fully later. But for the present, consider that the knowledge of good and bad is, to begin with, knowledge of nakedness. And not just the fact of nakedness, but its quality: nakedness is bad (3:7). The first human knowledge of good and bad is in fact knowledge of a badness, is a knowledge (or is it only an opinion?) of some defect within the human being itself, rather than of some badness in the world. A certain imperfection—a badness—of our own nature is the mind's first judgmental and shame-inducing self-discovery. Shame is the painful response to a self-consciously recognized gap between our idealized self-image and the truth about ourselves. True, the discovery is a social one: shame is manifest only before the other. But the object of that shame is something within the human being itself, a defect that embarrasses our self-flattering notions of what and how

12. My students often say, "If God did not want man to eat of this tree, why did He put it there in the first place? And why did He tempt them to eat of it precisely by prohibiting it?" This is the sort of trouble readers make for themselves by reading the story as a historical event rather than a literary vehicle for conveying some permanent truths about the problem of human freedom.

good we are.[13] What it is may become clear when we consider, in the next chapter, the meaning of sexual nakedness.

To sum up the discussion of the prohibition. The formal analysis and the substantive analysis agree in this: The knowledge prohibited is autonomous knowledge of how to live, found in or procured from one's own garden (nature), based on human experience of the visible world. The opposite of obedience, it is the kind of knowledge that is implicit in the act of violating a prohibition, indeed, in *any* act of *choosing for oneself.* But this autonomous knowledge of good and bad is not *true* knowledge of good and bad; human beings on their own will not find true knowledge of how to live. This must be supplied by what is later called revelation.

Knowledge and Mortality

Completing the portrait of man in his primordial condition, is the ominous remark that accompanied the prohibition: "for in the day that thou eatest thereof thou shalt surely die." Is it a prophecy, or a threat? What does it mean, both in itself and to its addressees—to *'adam* in the story and to us, the readers? As I have pictured him, the original human being (or the primary, subrational stratum of life) lacks sufficient self-consciousness truly to understand this prophecy; a simpleminded soul could not know death. At most, "dying" to him would convey some vague kind of badness, or perhaps just the absence or loss of everything present. But beyond the puzzle of what primordial man could understand by it, there are also questions about the literal meaning of the remark and about its troubling assertion that the price of knowledge—or autonomy—is death.

On one important matter, the logical connection between the remark about death and the prohibition, the text seems clear. The comment about death gives consequences, not reasons. Death, it is said, will be a consequence or result of transgressing; but avoiding death is not the *reason* that man should obey. As we have seen, obedience was commanded for its own sake, to address the dangers of human freedom, not to prevent death. Man should hearken to God's command because God commanded it, not because he wants to avoid a bad result. Mentioning the dire consequence simply provides an added incentive for promoting the desired obedience.[14] But what precisely is the prophecy?

13. In the present instance, man might experience shame at the legacy of his animality (naked, not divine) or at the errors of his pretentious reason and inflated imagination ("I will be like God, knowing good and bad").

14. A misunderstanding of this point becomes crucial in the sequel. In her response to the serpent, the woman transforms the consequence into the reason; when the serpent then denies that the consequence will follow, the woman no longer has any reason for obeying. Transgression follows immediately. (See discussion of this matter below.)

God cannot mean that the forbidden knowledge is itself poisonous, that acquiring it will be immediately lethal; for when man and woman later eat, they immediately experience shame, they do not die. God could be threatening to kill them directly if they disobey, but if so it is a threat He later fails to carry out. More likely, "thou shalt surely die" could mean that they will become mortal, rather than potentially immortal, beings; independence and loss of innocence are incompatible with immortality.[15] As we learn later, human beings once in possession of the forbidden knowledge become subject to mortality—though the original human being, 'adam, lives for more than nine centuries (5:5). Still, from the fact that man and woman are expelled from the garden in order to prevent their tasting of the tree of life, we infer that man, formed from the dust of the earth, was mortal from creation. Thus, the dangerous result of gaining the forbidden knowledge is not mortality itself but the *recognition* of that inevitability, along with the dire consequences that flow from that recognition.

The subsequent narrative nicely fits this interpretation. Until the (transgressive) rise to self-consciousness, human beings evince no awareness of death and, hence, have no interest in finding the tree of immortal life. Once they are aware of their mortality, immortality becomes at once a conscious desire and a known impossibility. By placing a tree of life in our mythical original condition, and by showing original man's indifference to it, the Garden of Eden story speaks more to the impossible longings of its readers than of the desires of innocent man. Indeed, the Bible may even regard the human longing for (literal) deathlessness as mistaken, and limitless life as undesirable for a creature such as man.[16]

Such reflections suggest a fourth possibility: the death that follows transgression and enlightenment might best be understood metaphorically rather than literally. Eating from the tree certainly produces a death of innocence. Through judgmental self-consciousness, human beings become self-separated; the primordial childlike, unself-divided, and peaceful state of soul "dies." Thanks to reason and freedom, protoman becomes a different being—the old one dies. This death, repeated in every human life, we have all experienced for ourselves: the contented and carefree life that we knew as innocent children is in fact per-

15. This interpretation is encouraged by the text's explicit pairing of the two nonfood trees (2:9), one forbidden, the other not. That image strongly suggests that human beings necessarily face mutually exclusive and incompatible alternatives: either enduring life in childlike innocence (the tree of life without the tree of knowledge) or autonomous knowledge of good and bad coupled with mortality (the tree of knowledge without the tree of life).

16. Later, in discussing the so-called punishment, I will argue that the expulsion from the garden, denying humans the tree of life, may even be an act of benevolence on God's part, setting a finite limit to the human prospects for misery and mischief. Could mortality for humanized—that is, noninnocent—human beings be a gift rather than a curse?

manently lost to us, the inevitable result of our rise to self-conscious knowledge of good and bad.[17]

SPEECHLESS ALONENESS: WEAKNESS OR STRENGTH?

So much for the picture of "original" solitary man, the poetic incarnation of the first and deepest stratum of human nature. Beginning in the immediate sequel, with God's comment on man's aloneness, the story becomes immensely complex. As a result, we face a difficulty about how to proceed. To this point, we have followed the narrative sequence, sentence by sentence; the simple story line served well the purpose of thematic exploration, revealing the first stirrings of human nature. But from now on, this approach will prove difficult. The story that follows concentrates on the transgression and its sequelae, which it narrates dramatically, in stages, through the following episodes: God's attempt to remedy man's aloneness, through the creation, first, of the animals and, second and successfully, of woman; man's first reaction to the woman; the woman's conversation with the serpent; the act of disobedience; the discovery, interrogation, and "punishment"; and the expulsion from the garden. But embedded in the narrative are deep and subtle clues to the next layers or levels of human nature.

In the course of the story, we are introduced to the higher and complicating elements of human existence, both *psychic* and *social:* speech, reason, and self-consciousness; desire, shame, and guilt; sexuality and sociality. On the psychic side, we encounter new dimensions of the human heart and mind and the growth of human reason and desire. On the social side, we see the beginnings of human social relations, rooted in the relationship of man and woman, a relationship founded on sexual desire. In the narrative, all these elements are shown in their mutual interconnections, and properly so. In life, as in the text, human speech is as much tied up with sociality as it is with reason; sexual desire influences our perceptions of and pronouncements about the world, and conversely, our opinions about the world influence the direction of desire. In a true portrait of the human being in his full humanity, the intrapsychic and the interpersonal cannot—and need not—be disentangled. But this truth poses a terrible problem for philosophical exploration: it is difficult to see the elements clearly when they are all compounded together. Thus, for the sake of

---

17. In another metaphorical reading, "you shall surely die" could be taken to mean being separated or alienated from God and the garden. This is certainly plausible, though there is no evidence that the human being consciously experienced (read: cares about) the presence of God prior to the transgression (read: until he comes to judgmental self-consciousness).

clarity and at the risk of some distortion of the story, I shall proceed themati-
cally, separating out two crucial strands of our emerging humanity, the linguistic (or rational) and the sexual (or social). The latter will be treated in the
next chapter. In the remainder of this chapter we shall follow the tracks of human speech, reason, and self-awareness.

Speech, you will recall, played a major part in the creation story of Genesis 1—divine speech. God entered the account speaking. In His first and most
perfect (hence, paradigmatic) act of speech, God said, "Let light be," and light
was called into being, letter-for-letter perfect and exactly as summoned. God
also created everything else through speech, named a few of the creatures (the
naturally ill-delimited ones: day, night, heaven, earth, and seas), pronounced on
the goodness of the spoken-forth creatures, and spoke personalized blessings to
the human beings. Man, created in God's image, said not a word. When we
come, in the present story, to human speech we are invited to consider whether
and to what extent human speech is like God's. Is human speech central to our
being? Is it creative? Evaluative? Relational? Solicitous?[18] Though the Garden of
Eden story must itself be interpreted without reference to the previous story, the
juxtaposition of the two accounts cannot help but raise such questions in the
reader's mind.

The human being as we have met him so far in the Eden story has been silent.
He offered no comment of any kind regarding the garden, his appointed task, or
even the prohibition. Speech is no part of the fundamental human beginning, of
the basic or lowest stratum of human life. Our basic engagement with life is
speechless and subrational. In addition, the primordial human being is alone:
what need is there to speak, and with whom? We will hear him speak only after
the creation of woman; his speech on that occasion will reveal deep truths about
the character of human speaking altogether.

The original human being is not only silent. He evinces no other clear evidence of the possession or exercise of reason. True, God appears to be addressing
the man's understanding when He informs him of the plenitude of food and
when He pronounces the prohibition. By implication, one could argue, the primordial man must have sufficient reason to understand the prohibition. Fair
enough. However, it is possible also to think that man in the original condition,
being not yet fully free or fully human, lacks any active inclination toward the

18. A comparison of divine and human speech—including an exploration of these questions—is
the subject of a superb paper, "Creation and Evaluation: Human Speech and Relationality in the
Garden and at Babel," written for my 1997 class on Genesis by Kristen Dietrich Balisi, a graduate student in the Committee on Social Thought at the University of Chicago. Several of the observations
that follow I owe to Ms. Balisi.

forbidden knowledge, which is to say his reason is still merely potential and dormant.[19] To speak anthropologically, in nontemporal terms, man could be formed in such a way that he *embodies* the prohibition, in at least part of his nature. The basic self-loving stratum (or aspect) of life, being nonrational, carries an inborn indifference, or even an aversion, to thoughts about good and bad; it carries, so to speak, the instinctive equivalent of the proscription. The inner core of human aliveness knows or senses that the forbidden knowledge is bad for enjoying life and for feeling immediately its sweetness.

Only when dormant reason begins to stir (as it has, of course, for every reader of the text) will the *enunciation* of the prohibition *as a prohibition* become important: only then will the prohibition be *understood* for what it is; only then will it become *necessary*. On the basis of this analysis, one can argue that human reason is, to begin with, merely potential. Or to say the same thing in nontemporal ways, the basic stratum of human life—represented in the story by the tableau of a solitary human being, before the coming of the animals and before woman—is nonrational and suspicious of or deaf to reason, even as reason sleeps alongside, waiting to be awakened.

We readers, unlike original *'adam*, have enough reason to understand all this. Thanks to our reason and its ability to understand the speech of the text, the story can teach us about the trouble with reason and speech. We are now alerted to watch closely what happens when reason and speech finally appear.

The itch in his soul that could destroy his contentment is, as we have argued, not manifest to the simple human being. Neither is a second difficulty: his aloneness. It is not man (who as yet knows not good and bad) but the Lord God who notices: "It is not good that man should be alone; I will make him a help opposite him [*ezer kenegdo*]" (2:18). This observation sets in motion the rest of the story: it leads to and explains the creation of woman, which in turn leads to both sexuality/sociality and speech/reason, which in turn issue in the transgression, which in turn leads to and explains human life as we know it.[20] We need carefully to consider its meaning.

Why and for whom is man's aloneness not good? Is it not good for the man, or not good for the world around him, or not good for God? Is it not good because of present circumstances, or because of likely future possibilities? That is, might God be anticipating human death—which He had just mentioned as the

19. Alternatively, as Bill Rosen has suggested to me, the man may have just enough reason to understand a command, but not enough to speak or think: "Even a dog can 'understand' a fairly large vocabulary of commands, *particularly* prohibitions."

20. Understanding the full implications of aloneness, and the meaning of the remedy provided for it, thus requires also the discussions of man and woman (see Chapter Three).

inevitable consequence of gaining knowledge of good and bad—in response to which He will now provide the means of perpetuation? Or is it not good for the same reason that gaining knowledge of good and bad is not good: it invites the illusion of self-sufficiency? Much depends on how we understand the meaning of man's solitariness.

It is common and appropriate to think that "alone" means lonely or in need of assistance, that is, that aloneness is a badge of weakness. Weakness cries out for help, whether as companion, partner, or coworker; and God in fact offers to make a "help" for the human being. But "alone" could also mean self-sufficient or independent; it could be a mark of strength—real or imagined. Aloneness as strength and apparent self-sufficiency might be bad or dangerous in a variety of ways. For example, a solitary being, lacking a suitable mirror, might be inca-pable of self-knowledge. Or lacking self-knowledge and, hence, believing him-self independent, the solitary man, though he dwelt in the Lord's garden, might have no real awareness of the presence of God.[21] Or seemingly self-sufficient, he might be inclined to test the limits—like the hero Achilles or like the original circle men in Aristophanes' tale (in Plato's *Symposium*) of the birth of eros—seeking evidence for or against his own divinity. For aloneness as strength, the proper remedy is weakening, caused by division, opposition, conflict.

Fittingly, God proposes an ambiguous helper. Man's helper is to be (in He-brew) *neged*, that is, "opposite" to him, "over against" him, "boldly in front" of him, "in his face": the helper is to be (also? instead?) a contra, an opponent. Putting together "partner" and "opposition," God proposes to make man a *coun-terpart*. What is called for, whatever the reason, is not just another, but an *other* other—fitting and suitable ("meet"), to be sure, but also opposed. Company here comes with difference; and as we shall see in the next chapter, *la différence* will turn out to make a very big difference, both for good and ill.

NAMING: THE ELEMENTARY USE OF REASON

Though He promises to make man a counterpart, God does not do so straight-away. Instead, He makes the animals. For some reason, encountering the ani-mals activates or creates the mental and emotional powers that permit man

21. People who read the prelapsarian condition of solitary man in the Garden of Eden as a histor-ical or ideal state of human blessedness insist that man before the coming of woman lived in com-pany and harmony with God. But they do not take sufficiently seriously God's (Being's) own testimony that man *was alone*. Put in nontemporal terms, there is neither textual evidence nor sen-sible reason for thinking that a human being would have knowledge of or a personal relationship with the divine if he had no relations with other human beings.

to recognize and receive his fitting counterpart.[22] The result of man's first encounter with the animal others is remarkable.

> And the Lord God formed from out of the ground ['adamah] all the beasts
> of the field and all the fowl of the air, and He brought them to the man *to
> see what he would call them;* and whatsoever the man called every living
> creature, *that would be its name.* And the man gave names to all cattle and
> to the fowl of the air, and to all the beasts of the field; but for the man there
> was not found a help opposite him [a counterpart]. (2:19–20; emphasis
> added)

When God brings the animals to the man to see what he would call them, human reason is summoned to activity, to its primordial activity, naming. Indeed,
here the man acts for the first time: the prototypical or defining human act is an
act of speech, naming. Encountering the nonhuman animals actualizes the potential of human speech, thereby revealing the human difference. For the ability
to name rests on the rational capacity for recognizing otherness and sameness,
for separating and combining. It requires reason's separating power, which sees
each animal as a distinct unit, separate from all others; it requires reason's combining power, which sees also the samenesses that run through individual animals. Reason collects the same animals under their own singular idea, each idea
corresponding to a singular species, each deserving and receiving its own general name, one common noun for each kind.

Human speech differs from the divine. God's speech, in the first creation
story, had summoned the creatures of the world into being: "*Let* this named
thing *be.*"[23] In the case of the plants and animals, God had created them "after
their kind," which is to say, after their distinctive species or names. Human
speech, in contrast, does not create the creatures of the world. As the text indicates, the creatures themselves (the animals) are given; man creates only their
names. The names he gives them—say, "camel" rather than "porcupine"—may
be arbitrary, but the distinctions between the creatures that the names recognize and celebrate are not: the camel and the porcupine, by their clearly different natures, clearly deserve and invite different names. Human naming is

22. These powers could include cognitive capacities for discrimination, reflective capacities of
self-awareness (including the awareness of lack), and emotive capacities of desire.

23. As we noted in the last chapter, the first instance of divine speech, the calling into being of light
(1:3), was dramatically peculiar and unique: there was absolutely no difference between the utterance
and the thing called for. In this one perfect case, there is a complete identity of the divine speech and
the creation act that went with it: word and thing, word and deed are exactly the same. No human
speech is like that.

reason's fitting acknowledgment and appreciation of the ordered variety of an articulated world.

Yet human speech, even at its most disinterested, does not merely mirror the given world. For one thing, naming is selective and therefore partial. Names bear the same relation to things as map does to territory. A map, necessarily selective, is not a mirror image of the land; a truly complete map would *be* the territory. Like mapping, naming is always partial and incomplete. Less a passive mirroring, more an active choosing, even simple naming is a form of acting on the world. Even when it is born of appreciative wonder, it therefore represents the germ of appropriation and mastery.

Human acts of selection are shaped by interests. And interests spring from desire. The same is true of human speech, even of simple naming. Although the ability to name rests on the powers of reason, the *impulse* to name is rooted in desire or emotion. Bare reason is motiveless and impotent. Like every act of speech and thought, an act of naming is not only a cognitive response to the articulated character of the world. It is also an expression of some inner urge, need, or passion, such as fear or wonder, anxiety or appreciation, interest or curiosity. Just as every act of speech has a manifest logical content, so every act of speech reflects some (often hidden) motive that incites it. Even the most disinterested act of speech, such as naming the animals, is not an act of unmotivated reason; it is important to know one animal from the other, since some may be dangerous, others may be tasty, while still others may strike the human perceiver as amusing or awe-inspiring or potentially useful. To generalize: what A says about B *always* tells you something also about A. This does not mean that speech is necessarily arbitrary and distorted by passion. But it does mean that, as we listen to the *content* of speech, we should be attending also to the soul of the speaker.

The text tells us that the man gave names to all cattle, to the fowl of the air, and to every beast of the field, but unfortunately we are not told what those names are;[24] we do not even hear him speak. Yet this unfortunate silence invites the reader to wonder what motivates the allegedly simple human acts of naming. For we do not know whether the name giving was primarily disinterested, reflecting, say, the look or activity of the animal, or primarily interested, reflecting human hopes and fears. We do not know, that is, whether the man called the horse "swifty" or "strong-backed," the elephant "thick skin" (pachyderm) or

24. There is one exception, though we learn of this only later (3:1), when the text introduces us to the *nachash*, the serpent. Since we are told here that "whatsoever the man called every living creature, *that would be its name*," we are free to suppose that *nachash*, "serpent," was a name given by man, not by God. We shall look at this name and this creature in the section that begins on p. 80.

"ivory" (*elephas*, in Greek), the tiger "stripes" or "fang," the porcupine "thorny pig" or "don't touch," or the camel "humpy" or "burden-bearing" (*gamal* is from a Hebrew root meaning "to benefit or requite"). But as we shall soon see in the naming of the woman, human naming is hardly unmotivated.

Be all this as it may, this use of human speech is presumably neither dangerous nor objectionable to God, seeing that it was He who provoked the activity of human naming, and the names the man put forth became the names by which the animals are known.[25] Knowledge of the animals, in other words, is not part of forbidden knowledge. Yet as we shall soon see, human reason thus aroused will not stay innocently confined to the activity of naming. Indeed, there are potential difficulties in the activity of naming itself. Naming is not altogether innocent.

Human naming, while it does not create the world, creates a linguistic world, a second world, of names, that (partially and interestedly) mirrors the first world, of creatures. As the text indicates, human beings not only practice speech, they create it. Names are the first human inventions: although they point to the things named, they have a certain independence from them. Names (and other words) and the ideas they represent constitute a mental human world that is necessarily separated from the world it means to describe. The gap between the two worlds—the world of words and the world of things—raises the question of how well human speech can capture and reveal the truth about the world it attempts to bespeak: Are our words adequate to the things? To what extent is speech revelatory, to what extent obfuscating? These difficulties, which adhere even to the relatively disinterested uses of speech (like naming the animals), become magnified when reason's view of the world is colored by the presence of desires and passions. Under these circumstances, speech becomes a vehicle for projecting human wish and desire, even more than for mirroring the outside world. Down the road, the somewhat independent, somewhat interested realm of language can become the medium for human independence altogether. For human beings can productively imagine, with the help of the creative possibilities open in speech, a world different from the one they now inhabit. All that is required is the growth of the requisite self-consciousness.

The encounter with the animals, in fact, stirs the germ of human self-awareness, and with it, the germ of a new—that is, previously invisible—human desire. Man's naming of the animals reveals to him his human difference: he names the animals but they cannot name him. Man alone among the animals

---

25. According to the text, God does not *tell* the man to name the animals; rather, he seems to assume that the man, because he is human, will have an impulse to do so, even if that impulse needs outside provocation to be called forth into activity.

can name. Accordingly, man's powers of discernment turn back upon himself, and with feeling. He inwardly discovers: "I am not alone, but I am different from them. They are different from me, indeed, too different to satisfy my newly awakened desire for a mate. Now that I am not alone, I am beginning to feel lonely." To be accurate, this discovery is still latent in the man; it is only the text that notes, "But for the human being there was not found a help-opposite-him" (2:20). Why not? What was lacking among the animals? Was it speech and the possibility of conversation? Or was something else required in a counterpart that could properly remedy the problem of man's aloneness? [26]

PREDICATING AND SELF-NAMING: AWARENESS OF SELF AND OTHER

The suitable counterpart arrives in the immediate sequel:

> And the Lord God caused a deep sleep to fall upon the man [*or* human being: *'adam*], and he slept; and He took one of his ribs [*tsela'*] and closed up the place instead with flesh. And the Lord God built the rib which He had taken from the man [*'adam*] into a woman [*'ishah*], and He brought her to the man. And the man said:
> > "This one at last [*literally*, the time: *hapa'am*] is bone of my bones and flesh of my flesh;
> > this one shall be called Woman [*'ishah*], because from Man [*'ish*] this one was taken." (2:21–23)

The counterpart is created out of man himself; God builds a woman [*'ishah*] out of the man's [*'adam*'s] rib and brings her to the man. The psychosexual implications of this origin of woman, and of sexual duality in general, will be treated in the next chapter. We concentrate here only on the unfolding account of speech, reason, and self-consciousness.

The appearance of the woman prompts the first full human sentence, indeed, the first speech of any human being directly quoted in the text. We therefore expect that this speech will be especially revealing, not only about the nature and uses of language, but also about the soul that is moved to speak.

In his paradigmatic speech, the human being is not only a namer, he is also a predicator, displaying an advanced capacity to see sameness within otherness.

---

26. Insofar as that something else involves *sexual* complementarity, the rejection of the animals is tantamount to a rejection of bestiality. But as we shall see in the discussion of the serpent, this is not the whole story.

Most significantly, he not only names the woman, he states a *reason* for the name he chooses: "This one shall be called Woman [*'ishah*] *because* from Man [*'ish*] this one was taken." The articulated explanations, as well as the linguistic structure, reveal the creative, world-ordering power of human speech and man's interest in rationally ordering his otherwise confused and confusing experience.[27]

But there is more to human speech than creative dexterity. Man's counterpart stirs his soul to a new level of self-awareness. As she stands before and against him, he also sees *himself* for the first time. As a result, he now names himself: no longer (as God named him) *'adam*, earthling, generic human-being-from-the-earth, but *'ish*, individual male human being, man as male in relation to female woman. The woman's name, *'ishah*, like her origin, is derivative. Yet her place in this speech of self-discovery and self-naming is, in fact, first: only because the woman stands first before him and comes first to mind is he able to know and name himself and to recognize his maleness as a decisive aspect of his own humanity. This deep and far-reaching insight about complementarity and selfhood is beautifully conveyed by the text: in the man's speech, *'ishah*, although lexically derivative, is spoken first.

Whereas the appearance of the animals elicited names, the appearance of the woman elicits poetry. Human speech is not just neutral description; it also expresses human desire, a desire that had been stimulated by the encounter with the animals (*"This* one *at last . . ."*). In fact, the man's entire speech seems to have been incited by desire, almost certainly by sexual desire: as the names indicate— "she Woman, me Man"—the appearance of woman makes man feel his masculinity, which is to say, his desire for her. Regarded as an expression of sexual desire, the speech may accurately reveal the state of the man's soul; but at the same time, the presence of powerful desire may distort his view of woman.

27. As Kristen Balisi observes:

The reason [given for the name "woman"] reveals as much about the structural potential within language as it does about any supposed connection between word and thing. . . . Perhaps this is a singular case in which an English translation actually mirrors the resonances of the Hebrew words (*'ish*, man; *'ishah*, woman); in each language there is a palpable linguistic connection between the names of the two humans. The names are a form of wordplay, demonstrating the way in which language contains patterns and links concepts to each other. . . . As much as it refers to the realm of external reality, language establishes its own internal structure. *'Adam's* second act of naming demonstrates the human impulse to use language to create a conceptual order out of experience . . . to use speech as an organizational principle on its own. . . . [H]umans do indeed create through their speech but . . . their creation is unlike what has been seen before in the text. Human speech does not bring elements or lifeforms into being; it does not establish a physical order within the cosmos. Rather it creates linguistic "beings" and a grammatically ordered realm within which the terms relate to each other: a

Though he acknowledges the woman's otherness (she gets her own name, different from his), the man is much more impressed by her similarity; indeed, because of his desire, he exaggerates and treats similarity as sameness: "This is my flesh and bone; this is mine; this is me." [28] In naming the woman with reference to her derivation from himself, the man is not just neutrally playing with his words; he is *defining* the woman in the light of his possessive desire for her. The name, like the desire it expresses, is a form of capture, a taking-hold of her, a verbal act of (anticipatory) appropriation. As if to underscore his self-centered outlook, the text makes clear that he is speaking not to her but only about her. Human speech is dangerous not only because it can reconstruct the world through language, but because any such reconstruction will likely carry the distortions born of human passion and human pride.

The animals had been brought to the human being for the purpose of his naming them: "to see what he would call them." In naming them, the man both reflected and created a separation between himself and the animals. Indeed, his naming may be regarded as an early form of mastery. But woman, clearly his proper counterpart, was simply brought to the man—"and He brought her to the man"—and, by implication, *not* for the purpose of naming. Perhaps the sought-for remedy for man's aloneness was to have been found in sexual union rather than in speech. Or perhaps a different kind of speech—genuine conversation—offered a possibility of communion not available in naming. But the man nonetheless chose to name her—rather than speak to her—just as he had named the animals, and the woman, though capable of speech, does not speak to the man—not here, not ever.[29] Human speech does not guarantee a meeting of minds and hearts; on the contrary, insofar as it becomes an instrument of self-interest and self-regard, it may even exacerbate our aloneness. Even

---

secondary, humanly constructed vision of reality layered upon the physical and cosmological order. . . . [S]uch language use is central to human nature. ("Creation and Evaluation," 9–10. See p. 71 n. 18.)

28. In the next chapter, we shall revisit this speech as a speech of primordial sexual desire, looking precisely at its selfish character.

29. Indeed, in speaking about her, the man "lump[s] her together with the animals he has previously encountered: 'This one at last . . . ' His response is to provide her with a humanly constructed identity. . . . Sadly, no conversation takes place; the text records no speech of the woman. 'Adam's first speech thus provides a foreboding beginning which anticipates the fact that the woman and the man will never have a conversation in this text; the woman will speak to the serpent, the man will blame the woman, and at the end (in an ambiguous moment) he will *re*name her." Balisi, "Creation and Evaluation," 12. Many of the observations in this paragraph I owe to Ms. Balisi. The woman's silence as a possible clue to her sexual desire—and to sexual asymmetry in general—will be discussed in the next chapter.

before the transgression, the careful reader who attends to the nuances of the text will not simply be celebrating man's powers of speech and reason.

Questioning and Answering, False and True: The Road to Independence

After the private acts of naming, expostulation, and predication, human speech and reason rise to the level of dialogue, propelled by acts of asking and answering. These are displayed in the discourse between the woman and the serpent, presented as the Bible's first quoted conversation and begun by the Bible's first question. The voice of developed reason, sibilant and seductive, comes from the mouth of a snake.

> Now the serpent [*nachash*] was more cunning [*or* subtle *or* shrewd *or* crafty: *'arum*] than any beast of the field which the Lord God [*YHWH 'elohim*] had made. And the serpent said unto the woman, "Indeed, [*or* Could it be that] God [*'elohim*] hath said, 'Ye shall not eat of any tree of the garden'?"
>
> And the woman said unto the serpent: "Of the fruit of the trees of the garden we may eat; but of the fruit of the tree which is in the midst of the garden, God hath said: 'Ye shall not eat of it, neither shall ye touch it, lest ye die.' "
>
> And the serpent said unto the woman: "Ye shall not surely die; for God doth know that in the day ye eat thereof, then your eyes shall be opened, and ye shall be as gods [*'elohim*], knowing [*yod'ey,* plural participle] good and bad." (3:1–5)

We have here a paradigm of conversable speech, interrogative speech, and responsive speech. On display is the human willingness and ability to answer—that is, to look within oneself for a response to—a question. Also evident is reason's capacity to negate and contradict, to consider opposed alternatives, and to think that things need not be as they seem or as they are.

Needless to say, the presence of a talking serpent is something of a mystery. Nevertheless, here he is, seemingly out of nowhere, and we must not try to get much beyond this surface fact. Two other facts about the serpent may be inferred. First, the serpent in this tale shares with human beings not only speech but perhaps also upright posture (only later is he cursed to crawl on his belly), long associated with the theoretical attitude and the possibility of disinterested viewing of the natural whole. This makes it all the more plausible to regard the serpent as an externalized embodiment of certain essentially human, rational capacities.[30] Second, the serpent was presumably among the animals that were rejected as a suitable counterpart for the human being. If this is correct, three further inferences follow. First, the rejection of the serpent despite his ability to speak and think implies that suitability, for the human counterpart, means something other than rationality: a sexual counterpart, not a fellow dialectician, is what is required. Second, though he is one of God's creatures,[31] the serpent, because he is rational, acts entirely on his own, displaying that dangerous independence to which he will lead the human being. Third, the serpent's rejection (by God and man) as an appropriate partner could motivate his desire to punish the man for choosing woman instead of himself—for preferring sex to philosophy. It would explain also his clever decision to do so by corrupting the woman, and precisely through the use of subtle speech.

People wonder why the temptation comes from a serpent rather than another animal. Serpents are, of course, prominent in many myths of the ancient Near East, and they are widely regarded as both attractive and dangerous. This duality appears in the Hebrew word for serpent: *nachash*—the name, by the way, given by *'adam*—appears to come from a root meaning both "shiny" and "enchanting." But both the basis of man's fascination with serpents and their symbolic meaning are in dispute. Some treat the serpent as raw (or insidious) male power (a phallic symbol); they see here a tale of the sexual seduction of woman. Others, on the contrary, treat the serpent as fundamentally feminine, as serpents are in many ancient myths—they belong to the earth, and they possess what was regarded as a female power of rebirth and self-renewal (the recurrent shedding of their skin); these interpreters see here a tale of (female) nature's rebellion against (male) reason and law. Further, serpents are often used as images both of voracity and of hyperrationality. For the serpent is a mobile digestive tract that swallows its prey whole; in this sense the serpent stands for pure appetite. At the same time, the serpent is cold, steely-eyed, and unblinking; in this respect he is the image of pure attentiveness and icy calculation. His slithering, sinuous, and utterly silent movements also suggest cunning and wiliness. Plausible as the previous suggestions may be, our text singles out only this last characteristic. We are dealing here with some manifestation of cleverness.

The text says the serpent "was *more cunning* [*or* subtle, *etc.*] than any beast of

30. The Hebrew Bible's only other talking animal is Balaam's ass (Numbers 22:28–30), whom, we are explicitly told, God caused to speak. Not so the serpent, who speaks entirely on his own—as unaided reason naturally does.

31. The text makes clear that God made the serpent; he is not some independent demonic or divine being. There is no textual basis for identifying the serpent with Satan. Indeed, there is no mention of Satan in the Hebrew Bible before the book of Zechariah (3:1) (or if one reads the Bible in the Christian order, before 1 Chronicles).

the field which the Lord God had made" (3:1). The word "cunning," in Hebrew
'arum, echoes and puns on 'arumim, "naked," which appears in the preceding
sentence: "and they were both naked ['arumim]" (2:25). The root sense of 'erum,
"naked," is "smooth": someone who is naked is hairless, clothesless, smooth of
skin.[32] But as the pun suggests, someone who is clever is also smooth, a facile
thinker and talker whose surface speech is beguiling and flawless, hiding well
his rough ulterior purposes. As we shall see, the serpent is indeed a smooth
speaker, his true intention craftily hidden beneath his silky speech. He asks the
first question, initiates the first conversation, and challenges God's benevolence
and truthfulness. He implies that knowledge of good and bad will provide im-
munity against death; he challenges hearsay, the oral tradition, and law, implicitly counseling that one should see and experience for oneself; and he beckons
the woman to unite with natural knowledge. All these are further reasons for
an allegorical reading of the serpent: an embodiment of the separated and beguiling voice of autonomous human reason speaking up against innocence
and obedience, coming to us as if from some attractive source outside us that
whispers doubt into our ear. In making his rationalist mischief, speech is the
serpent's only weapon.

> And the serpent said unto the woman, "Indeed [or Could it be that] God
> hath said, 'Ye shall not eat [lo' to'khlu] of any tree of the garden?' " (3:1; em-
> phasis added)

What kind of question is this? Surely not a question seeking the truth. Rather
it intends to *call into question*—authority, opinion, law. It seeks to make simple
obedience impossible, in this case by challenging the goodness of the commander. The serpent's question implies that God is a being who is, or might be, not
only arbitrary but also hostile to human beings: God is the sort of being who
could have put human beings into a fruitful garden but denied them access to
all the trees. Says the serpent, "Is it really true that God has denied you all sustenance?" The serpent's question is a perfect example of mischievous speech.

The radical effect of the serpent's question does not, however, depend on his
subversive intent. The question itself is deeply disquieting. Like any question, it
intrudes upon silent and unself-conscious activity, disturbing immediate participation in life and forcing introspection and reflection. Like any question, it puts

---

32. In this very subtle way, the text may be suggesting the inadequacy of human perception
and naming. For the man who named it *nachash*, the serpent was shiny, attractive, and enchanting.
For the text, however, the crucial thing about the serpent is that he is clever, cunning, smooth,
and beguiling, a creature whose shiny surface hides and belies a nakedness that is, to say the least,
dangerous.

thoughts before the mind, thoughts that collect and stimulate feelings: just as the question as asked had meaning for the questioner apart from its logical content, so the question as received gains meaning from interacting with the addressee's desires and concerns. Questions are more than verbal interrogatives: questions stir the soul.

The particular question put by the serpent is perfect for provoking self-reflection. In order to answer it, the woman must rise to self-consciousness about food and eating, about God's commands and the world's hospitality to her needs, and about herself in relation to her needs, to God, and to her world. As long as any need is easily and simply satisfied, it goes virtually unrecognized; in the absence of obstacles, food is taken for granted and eating proceeds mindlessly. By raising the prospect of opposition to human eating, the serpent's question brings felt need into consciousness, against the imagined possibility of its denial. And by blaming (albeit falsely) this denial on a nay-saying God,[33] it stirs a sense of precarious selfhood pitted against an inhospitable world and threatened by outside imperatives. The woman is forced to discover that she has needs independent both of God's power to command them and of the world's ability to satisfy them; pondering the question, she begins to feel both her vulnerability and her independence.

Self-awareness grows largely through the encounter with error and opposition. As long as experience seems reliable and appearances go unchallenged, human life proceeds with a childlike trust in the truthfulness of things. By asking the woman about the veracity of God's alleged speech, but imputing to Him words God did not say, the serpent's question introduces the issue of truth and falsehood and, what's more, provokes the desire to correct error. The mind opens up by discovering—and caring about—the gap between the false and the true, between what merely appears to be so and what truly is. Appearances (and utterances) are scrutinized, judged, and corrected. In the space between the apparent and the real, the human imagination takes wing. As a result, the mind will soon be able to project a gap between what is and what might be; affirmation and denial will give rise to deliberate pursuit and avoidance. The free play of imagination and thought will soon direct the free exercise of choice. All that is required is a more developed sense of self, one that recognizes itself as thoughtful and free. This, too, the serpent's question generates.

Questions about oneself necessarily summon one to reflect—to look back—upon oneself and to discover oneself as a being that thinks. By forcing thoughts

33. The serpent introduces God to the woman not as a benefactor but as a naysayer and a denier: in Hebrew, the first word that the serpent puts into God's mouth is "not" [lo'], and the first speech is "Not you-shall-eat" [lo' to'khlu]. The importance of negation in the emergence of human reason and freedom will be discussed shortly.

about her food and eating, the serpent's question creates a doubleness in the woman's soul: her awareness of her belly is separate from her belly, her thoughts about hunger are not rumblings in her stomach. By focusing on her body's need for food, the woman awakens to herself *as mind*. She discovers that she herself is not simply identical to her needy body. She experiences herself not only as a being with desires, but also as a being with thoughts, a being that can inquire into the truth about her desires (and about much else).

This momentous act of self-discovery is liberating not only for thought but also for action. For to think about appetite is to cease to be its slave. It becomes possible freely to decide whether to eat or not to eat, whether to obey the imperatives of necessity (or nature or Being or God). In time, imagination and reason can even create new objects for human desires. In short, facing the serpent's question means discovering and exercising one's autonomy.

The woman's answer clearly reveals her emerging and risk-filled freedom of mind:

> And the woman said unto the serpent: "Of the fruit of the trees of the garden we may eat; but of the fruit of the tree which is in the midst of the garden, God hath said: 'Ye shall not eat [*lo' to'khlu*] of it, neither shall ye touch [*lo' tig'u*] it, lest ye die.' " (3:2–3)

The woman's response implicitly denies the serpent's tacit accusation against God, but she does not in fact explicitly reaffirm God's generosity. In answering, "Of the fruit of the trees of the garden we may eat," she forgets to remember that this is part of God's bounty; she treats it instead as a matter merely of human freedom and choice. Now aware that the imperative behind her eating resides within her belly rather than with any outside authority, she does not say, "*God said* that we may eat." Following the lead of the serpent, she too has God speak only as a naysayer. Indeed, she goes the serpent one better, making God into a double naysayer ("Not ye-shall-eat"; "Not ye-shall-touch"), albeit confining His negations to a single tree (where the serpent had made God deny all).[34]

The woman's answer also demonstrates another danger of speech: the problem of mistake and misunderstanding. The woman says the thing which is not, albeit in innocence. Eager to correct the serpent's error, she herself commits

---

34. There is a sense in which the woman's answer does not deny, but rather affirms, the serpent's view of God as the opponent of human desire: in denying them access to *one* of the trees, God is, in fact, denying them unlimited access to *all*. Such would be the likely conclusion of independent reason or freedom, which tends to regard the denial of total freedom as the total denial of freedom. (I owe this point to Yuval Levin: "By prohibiting *something*, God has not permitted *everything*, and therefore He indeed prohibited everything.")

multiple errors of speech. She answers not the question that the serpent asked (to which the right answer was simply "No"). She says more than was called for. She *mis*identifies the forbidden tree as the one "in the midst of the garden"; that one was the tree of life (2:9). She adds "neither shall ye touch it" to the prohibition and, most important, she converts the predicted dire *consequences of disobedience*—"for in the day thou eatest thereof, dying you will die" (2:17)—into the *reason for obedience:* "ye shall not eat of it . . . *lest* you die" (3:3). She does not remember that it was to be avoided *because* it was forbidden and commanded, not in order to avoid the deadly consequence. To put the matter universally: exactly because she is expanding her newly emerging freedom of thought, she (predictably) has no use for obedience.

The addition "neither shall ye touch it" exemplifies one or another of some common yet misleading uses of speech. It might represent a protective addition, born of solicitude, provided by the man, in communicating the prohibition to the woman (who had not heard it in the first place); or it could be an addition, born of fear, advanced by the woman herself. Or it could be a simple misunderstanding that arose in the transmission, as happens so often in the children's game of telephone. In any case, such additions show both the tendency toward, and the benefits and dangers of, the practice of "building fences around the law": on the one hand, fearing even to touch, the woman will be less likely to eat; on the other hand, should touching produce no bad effect, the woman will then be encouraged to eat. Be this as it may, sloppy speech is itself a corruption of law, and it opens the door to corruption in deed.

In the serpent's rejoinder, he exploits the fact that the woman respects the prohibition solely to avoid the bad consequence of death. He appeals to her awakened pride in her own powers of understanding.

And the serpent said unto the woman: "Ye shall not surely die; for God doth know that in the day ye eat thereof, then your eyes shall be opened, and ye shall be as gods [*'elohim*], knowing [plural participle] good and bad." (3:4–5)

In one short speech, the serpent manages both to impugn God's veracity and His motives and to provide the inducement for disobeying Him. By insisting, "You won't die," the serpent implies that God is a liar. By offering reasons for what God said—implicitly claiming, as reason frequently does, to know more than what is at the surface of things—he goes behind God's explicit words to expose (so he thinks) their hidden meaning and motive. By asserting that God knows that the forbidden knowledge will make you godlike, the serpent implies that the prohibition stems from God's jealous and self-protecting wish to avoid sharing His special privileges with human beings. By suggesting the existence of many gods (through the use of the plural participle *yod'ey*), the serpent encourages a belief in the possibility of apotheosis. Most remarkable, by his implicit chain of reasoning, the serpent clearly suggests that knowledge makes one not only godlike but perhaps, therefore, also immune to death. In this sense especially, the serpent is like a protophilosopher, one who respects no authority but the truth and who promises that knowledge gives one a share in immortality. We see here, perhaps, the reason why the serpent was passed over as a possible counterpart for the human being.

Crucial to the serpent's successful seduction of the woman is the rational power of doubt, opposition, negation, and contradiction: in the Hebrew text, the first word of the serpent's final response ("Ye shall not surely die") is "not." The idea of "not" is essential to human speech and reason.[35] It also anchors the human imagination in its abilities to go beyond appearances, both its creative ability to conjure images and its ability to recognize an image as merely an image, not the true thing. These powers the serpent in fact displays in this final speech. For he shows his cunning not only as a protophilosopher but also as a poet, creating the Bible's first metaphor: "Your eyes shall be opened," meaning, "You will have insight." Finally, in combination with this power of nonliteral speech, reason's assertion of the possibility of "not so" liberates the imagination to picture new alternatives for what is or could be "so": not only may things not be what they seem—even better, things need not remain as they are. Thus, speech and reason contribute to disobedience not only negatively, by undermining authority, but also positively, by conjuring new possibilities for choice.

In an even more profound way, contradiction lives at the heart of the serpent's speech. His utterances—like almost all of ours—offer a mixture of "yes" and "no," of the true and the not true. For truth be told, the serpent does not exactly lie; but neither does he tell the truth, the whole truth, and nothing but the truth. As many readers of the sequel have noticed, man does not die on the day that he eats. Also, just as the serpent announces, his eyes are indeed opened upon eating. Most impressively, God Himself verifies the serpent's prediction, namely, that the man, as a consequence of transgressing, "has become like one of us, knowing good and bad" (3:22). Yet as Yuval Levin points out:

> All of these are only partially true, as the story demonstrates in every case.
> Man does not instantly die, but he will die, and now he knows it. Death has

---

35. The centrality of negation to rationality was noted in the first chapter, in our discussion of creation through speech: the principle of distinction is identical to the principle of contradiction, that A is fully other than—is the negation of—not-A.

entered his life. Man's eyes are opened, but they show him only his own weakness. Man has become God-like in one way, but not in countless others (not the least of which is that he will die). Reason has given man answers that—like the serpent—seem glowing and attractive, but are dangerous. These answers present themselves as verifiable, and when they are verified man tends to accept them in total, not imagining that they might be only part of the answer. Humanity, seeing that there is some truth in the words of the serpent, acts on those words and gets itself into trouble.

Human reason, generally content to let its necessarily partial truths masquerade as truth entire, leads human freedom astray.

FREEDOM AND ENLIGHTENMENT:
THE MELANCHOLY RISE OF MAN

The force of this first conversation, begun by the Bible's first question, is to call into question authority and obedience. By challenging the beneficence and the truthfulness of the author, by denying the announced consequences of disobedience, and by suggesting attractive alternative benefits of transgression (that is, goods beyond food and sex, namely, god-likeness through knowledge), speech and reason completely erode the force of the prohibition. Once the prohibition is undermined, once reason awakens, *simple* obedience—whether to God or to fixed instinct—becomes impossible. With alternatives now freely before her, the woman's desire grows on its own, partially enticed by the serpent's promise of wisdom, mostly fueled by her own newly empowered imagination. Having heard the voice of serpentine reason, the woman now sees the world through eyes imaginatively transformed by what was said:

> And the woman *saw* that the tree *was good for food,* and that it *was a delight to the eyes,* and a tree *to be desired to make one wise,* and she took of the fruit thereof, and did eat and gave also to her husband with her, and he did eat. (3:6; emphasis added)

Independent reason, having mentally eroded the force of the prohibition and suggested new possibilities, now takes control also of action. Speech issues in the momentous and transforming act of free choice. Thanks to the growth of human mental powers, the woman "sees" in a new light; mind and desire both color and reflect the new powers of a liberated imagination.[36] In ascending

---

36. Without even thinking about it, she mixes together what she heard (that is, what mind says) with what she sees. This is how we permit reason to convince us to accept as wholly true its partial and hasty opinions.

order, she looks to the tree for meeting animal necessity ("good for food"), for aesthetic pleasure ("delight to the eyes"), and for enlightenment, insight, or judgment ("desired for wisdom"). True, as the text tells us in the immediate sequel, her imagination did not get it right: when their eyes are opened, the human beings discover not that they are god-like, as the serpent had promised, but that they are naked. Nevertheless, the human beings in transgressing display the powers of rational choice, distinctive of our humanity, based upon a conscious and autonomous (even if mistaken) judgment of what is good. Their eating merely ratifies (or symbolizes) the autonomous act of *choosing* to eat, a free act of choice that was based on the self-generated belief that eating would be *good*. Only a being who already distinguishes good and bad, and who has opinions about which is which, can make such a choice.

Traditional interpretation, especially Christian, refers to this act of transgression as signaling the "fall of man"—though the expression nowhere occurs in the text. But if we read anthropologically, and in a wisdom-seeking spirit, what we have here instead is in fact the *rise* of man to his mature humanity—to be sure, in all its pathos and ambiguity. Such a reading was offered already by Kant, commenting precisely on our passage (but without any reference to God, whose commandment appears in Kant's version to be rather the voice of built-in natural instinct):

So long as inexperienced man obeyed this call of nature all was well with him. But soon reason began to stir. A sense different from that to which instinct was tied—the sense, say, of sight—presented other food than that normally consumed as similar to it; and reason, instituting a comparison, sought to enlarge its knowledge of foodstuffs beyond the bonds of instinctual knowledge (3:6). This experience might, with good luck, have ended well, even though instinct did not advise it, so long as it was at least not contrary to instinct. But reason has this peculiarity that, aided by the imagination, it can create artificial desires which are not only unsupported by natural instinct but actually contrary to it. These desires, in the beginning called concupiscence, gradually generate a whole host of unnecessary and indeed unnatural inclinations called luxuriousness. The original occasion for deserting natural instinct may have been trifling. But this was man's first attempt to be conscious of his reason as a power which can extend itself beyond the limits to which all animals are confined. As such its effect was very important and indeed decisive for his future way of life. Thus the occasion may have been merely the external appearance of a fruit which tempted because of its similarity to tasty fruits of which man had already partaken. In addition there may have been the example of an animal which consumed it because, for it, it was naturally fit for consumption, while on the contrary, being harmful for man, it was consequently resisted by man's instinct. Even so, this was a sufficient occasion for reason to do violence to the voice of nature (3:1) and, its protests notwithstanding, to make the first attempt a free choice; an attempt which, being the first, probably did not have the expected result. But however insignificant the damage done, it sufficed to open man's eyes (3:7). He discovered in himself a power of choosing for himself a way of life, of not being bound without alternative to a single way, like the animals. Perhaps the discovery of this advantage created a moment of delight. But of necessity, anxiety and alarm as to how he was to deal with this newly discovered power quickly followed; for man was a being who did not yet know either the secret properties or the remote effects of anything. He stood, as it were at the brink of an abyss. Until that moment instinct had directed him towards specific objects of desire. But from these there now opened up an infinity of such objects, and he did not yet know how to choose between them. On the other hand, it was impossible for him to return to the state of servitude (i.e., subjection to instinct) from the state of freedom, once he had tasted the latter.

The first discovery of our humanity, or better, the discovery that *constitutes* our humanity, is a discovery about our sexual being (not, as others would say, about our mortality):

> And the eyes of them both were opened, and they knew that they were naked; and they sewed fig leaves together and made themselves girdles. (3:7)

Human self-consciousness is radically sexual self-consciousness.[37] Moreover, the discovery of nakedness is made not indifferently but with passing judgment: nakedness is viewed as shameful (that is, bad, rather than good or neutral), and action is taken to cover it up and to keep it from being seen. Shame, a peculiarly human passion, expresses pain over the gap between our wished-for estimable or idealized self-image and the now discovered fact of our lowliness or baseness. Shame presupposes a concern for self-esteem and the presence of

---

37. In the experienced psychic transformations accompanying puberty, each of us has access to the truth of this important claim. Self-consciousness before puberty is but childish, ignoring as it does the mystery of our sexually divided nature and its unavoidable link to our mortality. See Chapter Three.

pride: only a being concerned with self-esteem could have his pride wounded and experience shame.

The response to the discovery of shameful nakedness represents yet another important aspect of human reason: the disposition to art. The fig leaf, or rather the needle, is the first human invention.[38] Like all human craft and technology, it manifests both enterprise and cleverness. More important, like any invention, it tacitly asserts the insufficiency of the world and expresses the human urge to do something about it—what Rousseau would call "perfectibility." By taking up the needle, the human beings, whether they know it or not, are declaring the inadequacy of the Garden of Eden. By becoming artisans, they are voting for their expulsion from the garden; they are choosing civilization. Moreover, the needle symbolizes man's path of violent opposition to nature. Unlike weaving, which gently and harmoniously binds threads together without destroying anything, sewing invades and does violence to the elements it unites. The technological mentality and disposition emerge out of this very modest beginning.

Thanks to the needle, the girdle is produced. It may be flimsy, but its meaning is profound. Like all more sophisticated clothing, it provides protection, but more important, dissimulation, beautification, and adornment. Standing as an obstacle to the immediate gratification of sexual desire (as we will see in the next chapter), it represents the beginning of the rule of reason over desire. It therefore provides the space for the imagination to grow, transforming human lust into love and allowing room for courtship and intimacy. As an instance of enhancing self-esteem, it gives rise also to a concern with the beautiful; and it also represents and at the same time augments human amour propre. And as the first human transformation of the naturally given, the fig leaf girdle stands as the first mark of society and civilization; at one stroke, it manifests human reason's propensity to *techne,* custom, and law.

Learning the Limits of Reason: Civilization and Its Discontents

Yet human art does not sufficiently provide for human needs, not even for the needs of the body: fig leaf girdles are hardly adequate for protection or concealment. But human art is especially weak in addressing the needs of the soul once it knows about good and bad and assesses itself under these judgments. A being that experiences shame needs to know more than his own cleverness—and he knows it. Right after they make themselves girdles, the human beings show their first real openness to or awareness of the divine:

---

38. If we ignore the invention of language.

And they heard the voice of the Lord God walking in the garden in the evening breeze; and the man and his woman hid from the Lord God in the midst of the trees of the garden. (3:8)

This is the first explicit mention that any human being *really* attended to or even noticed the divine presence. Only in recognizing our lowliness can we also discover what is truly high. The turn toward the divine is founded on our discovery of our own lack of divinity, indeed, of our ugliness.[39]

It is a delicate moment: having followed eyes to alluring temptations, promising wisdom, human beings came to see, again through their eyes, their own insufficiency. Still trusting appearances but seeking next to beautify them, they set about adorning themselves, in order to find favor in the sight of the beloved. Lustful eyes gave way, speechlessly, to admiring ones, by means of intervening modesty and art. Yet sight and love do not alone fully disclose the truth of our human situation. Human beings must open their ears as well as their eyes, they must hearken to a calling for which sight and the beautiful beloved do not sufficiently prepare them. The prototypical human pair, opened by shamefaced love, was in fact able to hear the transcendent voice.

The ensuing conversation with this transcendent voice is, on its face, hardly encouraging; God conducts an inquest, extracts a confession, pronounces sentence. In the course of the examination, new uses of human speech emerge: rationalization, evasion of responsibility, and shifting of blame. New passions arise in the human soul, most notably a higher kind of shame,[40] guilt, and that remarkable mixture of fear-and-reverence called awe. Shame reveals a peculiarly human concern with self-perfection, guilt the sense of personal responsibility, whereas awe recognizes powers not under human control and beyond human comprehension, before which we feel shamefully small. Clothing the body's visible nakedness cannot cover over these disturbing passions of the soul. Hearing

39. It may be objected that man may have direct knowledge of God, founded, say, in God's beneficence and bounty. And the text does have God speaking to man well before the transgression gave birth to human shame and self-disgust. But man took no notice and showed no concern about the divine presence before the birth of shame. The situation is analogous to our knowledge of health and disease. Health (like God) is ontologically and logically prior, but its *discovery* by human beings comes usually, if not always, only through the experience of disease. When healthy we do not notice health; we know it and care for it only when we experience our lack of it.

40. The shame before God seems to be different from the shame before each other. Before each other, man and woman hide only their genitalia. Before God, they seek to hide themselves completely. The first—what the Greeks call *aischyne*—is social shame, and bespeaks a concern with the beautiful or the noble *(kalon)*, with looking good. The second—what the Greeks call *aidos*—is cosmic or ontological shame and bespeaks a concern with intrinsic worth under the aspect of the eternal and the divine.

an awesome voice, we duck for cover, hoping to make ourselves completely invisible.

To no avail. Man cannot escape from his deeds. The divine voice now interrogates him in a manner that will help him learn the meaning of his actions. God asks four simple questions, less to obtain information, more to induce a searching of the soul. Unlike the serpent's questions, which called into question God's goodness and veracity, God's questions—all put personally, using the second person singular—call the human addressees to account.

> And the Lord God called to the man and said to him, "Where art thou?"
> And he said, "I heard Thy voice in the garden, and I was afraid, because I
> was naked, and I hid myself." (3:9–10)

The simple searching question—"Where are you?"—has psychic as well as physical meaning: asking not only about the man's bodily location, but also about the place of his soul, it calls for self-examination and self-assessment. Man's reply is, on the surface, largely evasive, with sort of an answer given only at the end ("I hid"). But the answer does reveal man's state of mind. Out of guilty fear, he explains where he is, beginning by blaming the sound of God's voice as the cause of his going into hiding; in so doing, man freely confesses his concern with the divine presence, even as he tries to rationalize his misconduct. Hearing God's voice made him afraid, and he was afraid (so he says) not because he disobeyed but because he was naked. Is man confessing shame at nakedness, or fear because of his use of art to cover it up?[41] Or is he tacitly acknowledging that his crude art not only fails adequately to cover shameful body parts but, worse, cannot in principle cover his own painful awareness that he is, under it all, just a naked and vulnerable creature?

Perhaps because He has learned from man's speech enough about his state of soul, God does not press further the unanswered question "Where are you?" Instead, His next questions address the confessed discovery of nakedness and its connection to possible disobedience:

> "Who told thee that thou wast naked?
> From the tree I commanded thee not to eat hast thou eaten?"
> And the man said, "The woman whom Thou gavest by me, she gave me
> from the tree, and I did eat." (3:11–12)

41. He claims he is naked and withholds the truth about sewing fig leaves. I owe this observation to Adam Davis, who argues that man fears God's wrath about his art, not his nakedness. But the sequel suggests that the issue is nakedness, or more precisely, knowledge of nakedness, which in turn means disobedience.

Once again, the man answers only at the end, prefacing his confession with his excuse. Before admitting to disobedience, he shifts blame, not only to the woman (who gave me from the tree) but also to God (who gave me the woman). We may smile at the man's attempt to avoid responsibility, but we must also acknowledge that he has a point: the woman, given as a remedy for aloneness that could keep him from pursuing forbidden knowledge, has in fact led him to it.

God, accepting the man's final confession ("I did eat"), offers no demurrer, but moves up the causal chain and puts a direct question to the woman:

> "What is this thou hast done?"
> And the woman said, "The serpent beguiled me [*literally,* lifted me: *hishi'ani*] and I did eat." (3:13)

The woman, like the man, knows how to pass the buck and evade responsibility, but she too confesses. God does not argue or attempt to refute either woman or man. Readers can see how they both use speech to try to escape censure, but God accepts their confessions and, at least in small part, their defense: in the so-called punishments that follow, God begins by cursing the serpent. (Also, He does not curse the woman or the man, though He curses the ground for man's sake; 3:14–17.) Very likely, God has good reason to be satisfied with the inquest. For the all-too-human practice of shifting blame and denying responsibility for wrong-doing proclaims, despite itself, the existence of good and bad, right and wrong. Making excuses for oneself is, in fact, a concession that something needs to be excused. Neither man nor woman says, "I did it and I'm proud of it."[42] Judgmental self-consciousness gives birth to conscience. Conscience, in turn, can face the music, to learn and live with the consequences of one's wrongful choice and deed.

> And the Lord God said unto the serpent:
> "Because thou hast done this, cursed [*'arur*][43] art thou from among
> all cattle and from among all beasts of the field; upon thy belly
> shalt thou go, and dust shalt thou eat all the days of thy life.
> Enmity will I set between thee and the woman and between thy

---

42. Yuval Levin has made the case that the woman's speech, at least, is unrepentant. If one reads the verb *hishi'ani* literally, the woman is saying not, "The serpent beguiled me," but rather, "The serpent—or reason—lifted me up." "She may still think, indeed, that God is angry simply because He wants to keep her down. God, in the sentence he delivers to reason [the serpent], will be sure to point out that serpents are in no position to lift anything up."

43. We note the pun on *'arum,* "cunning." Cleverness becomes a curse.

seed and her seed; and he shall bruise thy head and thou shalt
bruise his heel."

And unto the woman He said:

"I will greatly multiply thy pain and thy travail; in pain thou shalt
bear children; and thy desire shall be to thy man, and he shall
rule over thee."

And unto the man ['adam] He said:

"Because thou hast hearkened unto the voice of thy woman and
hast eaten of the tree of which I commanded thee saying, 'Thou
shalt not eat of it':

Cursed be the ground for thy sake; in pains shalt thou eat of it all
the days of thy life. Thorn and thistle shall it bring forth to thee;
and thou shalt eat the herb of the field. In the sweat of thy face
shalt thou eat bread, till thou return unto the ground, for out
of it wast thou taken: for dust thou art and unto dust shalt thou
return." (3:14–19)

The inquest concluded (God does not interrogate the serpent), God pronounces sentence on the serpent, the woman, and the man, in three short
speeches. We observe, in passing, the major features of the new human condition, announced and foretold in these divine remarks to the newly awakened
pair, the condition within which the story of human life will hereafter—and
irreversibly—unfold: (1) There is the (partial) estrangement of humankind
from the world (or nature), evidenced by *(a)* enmity between serpent and
woman (3:15); *(b)* partial alienation of man from the earth, upon which he
must now toil for his food (3:17–19); and *(c)* pain of childbirth, implying conflict even within the (female) human body (3:16). (2) There is division of labor, defined relative to work: the one gives birth, the other tills. (3) There is
the coming of the arts and crafts: no more just picking fruit and gathering
nuts, but agriculture—the artful cultivation of the soil, the harvesting of
grain, its transformation into flour, the making of bread, and eventually also
astronomy (to know the seasons and to plan for sowing), metallurgy (to
make the tools), the institution of property (to secure the fruits of one's labor), and religious sacrifices (to placate the powers above and to encourage
rain). (4) And there is rule and authority (3:16).

To sum it up in one word: civilization. The "punishment" for trying to rise
above childishness and animality is to be forced to live like a human being.

The so-called punishment seems to fit the so-called crime, in at least two
ways. If the crime of transgression represents the human aspiration to self-

sufficiency and godliness (free choice necessarily implying humanly grounded knowledge of good and bad), the so-called punishment thwarts that aspiration by opposition: human beings instead of self-sufficiency receive estrangement, dependence, division, and rule. Second, and more profound, the so-called punishment fits the crime simply by making clear the unanticipated meaning of the choice and desire implicit in the transgression itself. Like Midas with his wish for the golden touch, like Achilles with his desire for glory, the prototypical human being gets precisely what he reached for, only to discover that it is not exactly what he wanted. He learns, through the revealing conversation with God, that his choice for humanization, wisdom, knowledge of good and bad, or autonomy really means at the same time also estrangement from the world, self-division, division of labor, toil, fearful knowledge of death, and the institution of inequality, rule, and subservience. The highest principle of Being insists that, given who and what we humans are, we cannot have the former without the latter.

This analysis leads me to believe that the so-called punishment is not really a newly instituted condition introduced by a willful God against the human grain. It is rather a making clear of just *what it means* to have chosen enlightenment and freedom, just what it means to be a *rational* being. The punishment, if punishment it is, consists mainly in the acute *foreknowledge* of our natural destiny to live out our humanity under the human condition.

The story moves to its conclusion:

And the Lord God made for the man and his wife garments of skin, and He clothed them. And the Lord God said, "Behold, *the man is become like one of us*, knowing good and bad; and now, he may reach out and take also from the tree of life, and eat, and live forever." And so the Lord God sent him forth from the Garden of Eden to till the ground from which he had been taken. And He drove out the man, and He set up east of the Garden of Eden the cherubim and the flame of the whirling sword to guard the way to the tree of life. (3:21–24; emphasis added)

Before sending them out to their toilsome and mortal existence, God provides the human pair with clothing made from animal skins. This gift not only manifests God's solicitude for his needy creatures. As real clothing, it also represents a wry comment on the inferiority of the fig leaf girdle and, to generalize, on the insufficiency of human art altogether. At the same time, it makes clear that artfulness—and covering up—will be needed in the human world. Everything will depend on whether human artfulness—and human reason more generally—will recognize its limitations and its (our) dependence on a higher source.

But man is not just a needy creature. On the contrary, thanks to his transgression and his newly awakened mind, man has become god-like ("like one of us"): in the language of the first creation story, man is now an image of God. Indeed, we readers have it on the highest authority that we have witnessed not the fall but the rise of man, at least in terms of his mental powers.

Yet man's god-like mental powers, the text suggests, will focus on his mortality, a major preoccupation of the fully self-conscious human being. Equipped at last to make judgments of good and bad, man will now recoil from death and will seek its remedy, ultimately in bodily immortality. But, says God in so many words, it is not good for man that he should live forever. Man is not God, cannot become God, and should not imagine otherwise; the rational animal's search for deathless life on earth would prove a disaster. In truth, given his chosen life of sorrowful toil, artful striving, and judgmental self-consciousness, finitude provides man a release from his troubles. More important, awareness of mortality will eventually inspire him to seek what is true, just, and holy.

The end of the Garden of Eden story proclaims that living a human life means living with mortality. As we watch the human beings leave the world of childish innocence for the real world, we hear, as an echo behind them, the closing words: "the tree of life." With their path blocked to the tree of life, human beings—both the ones in the story and the readers—can turn their attention not to living forever but to living well.

The story of man in the Garden of Eden helps readers on their way to finding the path to a life well lived. For it enables us to reflect on our basic nature and to discover the perils inherent in our special gifts of speech, reason, self-consciousness, and freedom. In following the emergence of human reason and human speech, we have pondered their activity in naming, predicating, celebrating, self-naming, explaining names, asking, answering, conversing, questioning, calling into question, denying, mistaking, challenging, and shifting blame. We have considered the multiple manifestations of self-awareness and the emergence of passions to which self-awareness gives rise. We have examined the meaning of free choice and recognized its inherently disobedient character. We have seen the birth of craft, reason's prodigal son, as well as conscience, reason's judge, and awe, the seed of piety, reason's recognition of its own limits. And we have thought about all these matters not with neutral detachment but with judgmental engagement.

The early verdict on human reason and human freedom is, to say the least, mixed. The Bible agrees with Aristotle in holding that man alone among the animals has *logos*, thoughtful speech, but it takes a much less celebratory view of our distinctiveness.[44] Speech can be an instrument of mischief and error, deception and falsehood, pride and domination. Reason creates a divided consciousness and overstimulates the imagination. Free choice is not necessarily wise choice. Judgmental self-consciousness yields vanity, shame, and guilt. Artfulness separates man from nature and creates new needs and desires, without bringing contentment.

But human speech and reason, in the form of this remarkable story and our ability to ponder its meaning, hold out a redemptive possibility. The remedy begins with our being willing to recognize and acknowledge the follies of which we human beings are capable—indeed, precisely because of our special intellectual capacities. The ill-clad human protagonists in our story become aware of their own inadequacies from hearing and experiencing the voice of the Lord God walking in the garden. Similarly, thanks to the special kind of speech that we are reading, we psychically ill-clad human readers become aware of our own inadequacies from hearing and experiencing the voice of the text. The source of our troubles, dear reader, is not in our stars but in ourselves. Suitably humbled, we are prepared to be educated.

44. To be fair to Aristotle, he too knew the dangers of human rationality. In the very passage that famously celebrates man as the rational animal, Aristotle notes that "just as man when he is perfected is the best of animals, so too separated from law and justice he is worst of all. . . . Without virtue he is most unholy and savage, and worst in regard to sex and eating." (*Politics* 1253a31)

CHAPTER THREE

THE VEXED QUESTION OF MAN AND WOMAN:
THE STORY OF THE GARDEN OF EDEN (II)

*A*nyone interested in the anthropology of the Bible starts by studying the story of the first human beings, living in the Garden of Eden. Here, in the form of a compelling tale of human beginnings, we encounter a revealing portrait of human nature, stripped of its cultural accretions and adornments. As we saw in the last chapter, the story's presentation of the problem of human freedom proves also to be a profound meditation on human speech, reason, and self-consciousness and their role in human choice and action. But the Garden of Eden story sheds light not only on matters of mind and will but also on matters of the heart: human sexual desire and erotic love, engines of human aspiration and association. As the narrative makes clear, human reason emerges only in conjunction with human sociality; and the natural seed of human sociality, the text makes plain, is sex. Gender-neutral humanity is an abstraction or, at most, a condition of childhood; real human beings come divided by sex, male and female. The primary story of our humanity is necessarily a story also about man and woman.

Man and woman. What are they, and why—each alone and both together? How are they alike, and how different? How much is difference due to nature, how much to culture? What difference does—and should—the difference make? What do men want of women, or women of men? What should they want? Do they really need each other? If so, why? What is the meaning of sexuality, natural and human? Which beliefs, customs, and institutions governing sexuality best promote human flourishing?

These very basic questions, today the subject of much talk and controversy, are in fact very old. Every culture answers them, at least tacitly, and many do so explicitly, in ways ranging from founding tales and stories to specific rules of conduct. The Bible has much to say on the subject, both descriptive and prescriptive, and Genesis itself has numerous stories that make vivid the complexity of human sexual relations. As with other matters, the first story provides the pattern: the paradigmatic account of man and woman is the one conveyed through the Garden of Eden story. It is descriptive rather than prescriptive: it does not offer a moral teaching on human sexuality; neither does it present a picture of the ideal relation between man and woman. Rather, it illuminates the fundamental and universal features of human sexuality, the nature of man and woman, and the natural bases of their complicated relationship. All subsequent treatments of these matters will build upon this foundation; the Bible's later prescriptions regarding sexuality will speak to the moral difficulties whose roots are here exposed. As we will do throughout our reading of Genesis, we look into the mirror provided by this story to see if it enhances our self-understanding and, conversely, if our experience lends credence to the truths conveyed by the tale.

SEXUAL DIFFERENCE: THE LOVE OF ONE'S OWN

As we saw in the last chapter, the basic level of human life is displayed through the portrait of the solitary human being, at home in the garden, tending to his own elementary needs. The coming of woman embodies a new dimension of our humanity, comprising augmented powers of reason, speech, and self-awareness, and (as we will now see) genuine sociality rooted in sexual difference and attraction—all in one package. Man's difference from the animals is not just a matter of rationality; it is decisively a matter of sexual self-awareness. All higher animals are sexual beings, but only man knows it. Sexual self-consciousness separates man from the animal or childlike way of life, represented by the solitary human being who is featured at the start of this story. But sexual self-awareness is no simple matter, because human sexuality is highly complex; the complications in our sexuality, in fact, arise largely from aspects in sexual desire that depend on our becoming conscious of it.

As we shall see, human sexuality comprises at least three distinct, and sometimes competing, natural elements. We meet these elements one by one in the Garden of Eden story, as it takes us through three separate "stages" in the emergence of human sexual awareness, each stage illuminating a distinct aspect of sexuality: the (animal) sex act; its humanization through concerns for attraction and esteem; and its deeper, procreative meaning. Each sexual element has its correlative aspect of erotic desire: need love, appreciative love, and generative love.[1] Looking into the mirror provided by the story, we readers can verify the existence of the separable sexual elements and distinctive kinds of erotic desire, in part because we have experienced their independent powers in the emergence

1. Although we meet these three elements of sex and aspects of love one at a time, and although they are distinguishable for purposes of analysis, they exist in human beings not as separated layers piled one atop the other but concretely mixed and intertwined. It is partly for this reason that the meaning of human sexuality is so perplexing.

of our own sexuality, beginning with puberty. Not surprisingly, the primary sexual element is not uniquely human. Accordingly, in the story it appears in the
context of man among the animals.

To prepare him for his appropriate counterpart, man's desire for company is
stimulated by encountering the animals. In the last chapter, we saw how this
confrontation awakens his dormant powers of reason, now exercised in the activity of naming. But man's naming of the animals is not merely a disinterested
scientific exercise in taxonomy; it is part of a quest to satisfy newly awakened desires. As man's powers of perception illuminate also his apartness and aloneness,
his approach to the animals reflects his need for another and excites his latent
powers of desire.

Few readers will wish to deny that the trial run with the animals served to
stimulate the man's desire for a counterpart: why else did God start his effort to
solve the problem of man's aloneness by creating the animals? But it is less clear
what sort of partner, to satisfy which desire, the man is seeking. Innocent, high-
minded, or puritanical readers will believe that the lonely man is looking for human company, for a rational soulmate, a fellow namer-and-speaker with whom
he can share thoughts and speeches.[2] But as the sequel makes plain, the desire
here aroused is almost certainly sexual.[3] This should not surprise us: no worthy
account of primordial human nature would fail to give sexual desire a central
place; any true account of primordial human sociality would focus on the bonds
rooted in erotic attraction.

In the immediate sequel, God creates the desired counterpart out of man
himself; He makes or builds a woman *('ishah)* out of the man's *('adam's)* rib,
and brings her unto the man.

> And the Lord God caused a deep sleep to fall upon the man [*or* human be-
> ing: *'adam*], and he slept; and He took one of his ribs and closed up the
> place instead with flesh. And the Lord God built the rib which He had
> taken from the man [*'adam*] into a woman [*'ishah*], and He brought her to
> the man. (2:21–22)

2. For a long time, I confess, I was such a reader. I began to reconsider when I once asked in class,
expecting a high-minded answer, "What is the man looking for?" A lusty young man blurted out,
"Sex," and after the class's nervous laughter subsided, he then proceeded to support his position with
evidence from the text, which, as we shall see, is very much about sex. It was about this time that I began to see the Garden of Eden story as conveying a descriptive and realistic picture of human nature,
rather than a normative and idealistic one.

3. If this is correct, the text's remark "but for the human being there was not found a counterpart"
(2:20) may be read, anthropologically, as asserting that animals are not fitting sexual partners for human beings (and perhaps also morally, as rejecting the practice of bestiality).

The necessary answer to the problem of man's aloneness, the duality of man and woman, is produced from within. As a result of the surgery, the original human being is no longer what he was: he is no longer whole. His original and amorphous stirrings of restlessness (freedom? loneliness? ambition? fear?) are, as we shall see, to be replaced by focused desire.[4]

Some critics see in this account of woman's origin evidence that the text is sexist: not only is man created first and woman second, but woman's being is derivative and dependent on man. But the text even more readily supports an opposite view. For one thing, the man's origin was lower, from the dust; the woman begins from already living flesh and, moreover, from flesh taken close to the heart. Also, the man is, in the process, rendered less than whole; he suffers a permanent but invisible wound, signifying a deep and probably unfulfillable desire. Because he is incomplete and knows it, the man will always be looking for something he lacks; but as the image of a lost rib suggests, the man cannot really know what is missing or what the sought-for wholeness would really be. Male erotic desire is a conundrum: it wants and wants ardently, but it is unsure of what exactly would fully satisfy it. In contrast, the woman made from the rib is presumably not in any way deformed or incomplete.[5] Besides—and this is surely the most important response—the difference in man's and woman's origins betokens not a matter of rank or status, but a difference in the character of primordial male and female desire, a matter to which we soon come.

The charge of sexism might receive an even more radical answer. 'Adam— the prototypical human being—prior to the creation of woman was, in fact, either sexless or androgynous: the female principle was within; only after the separation is there really male and female, only then does sexuality make a difference. Never mind anatomy: the original 'adam is *functionally* gender-indifferent—in keeping with the fact that the basic stratum of embodied life and its self-preservation has nothing whatsoever to do with sex. (Conversely,

4. This account of human division and its psychic consequences is usefully compared with the famous story about the birth of erotic desire told by the comic poet Aristophanes in Plato's *Symposium*. In that account, Zeus tries to remedy a dangerous tendency of original human beings to storm heaven by halving their strength and giving them some other desire to occupy them. He has Apollo perform symmetrical hemisection on the original circle men (each of whom, to begin with, had four arms and four legs, and two faces on a single head and neck), thus producing upright, bipedal creatures of human shape and appearance. As a result of the cleavage, each human being erotically longs to find and unite sexually with its missing other half, to restore a mythical lost wholeness. (The resulting coupling offers a perfect caricature of sexual concourse.) The surgery performed in the Garden of Eden is less drastic than Apollo's, but its meaning and consequences may be more alike than different.

5. Indeed, as we shall see later, the woman is created not with a deficiency but with an excess, an overflowing capacity for generating new life.

sex has nothing to do with *self*-preservation.) The original human being—that is, the first or lowest element of human life—is, even today, sexless and nonerotic.

But one must not ignore the gender asymmetry in the presentation. Though in the absence of woman he may experience nothing of his maleness and know nothing of its meaning, the first human being seems to have been male. And be that as it may, it is certainly with a *sense* of his own masculine priority and prerogative that the man reacts to the woman's appearance, as have billions of men down to the present day:

> And the man said,
>   "This one at last is bone of my bone and flesh of my flesh;
>   this one shall be called Woman ['*ishah*] because from Man ['*ish*]
>   this one was taken." (2:23)

In our analysis, in the last chapter, of this first human sentence, we noted that it is a poetic speech of pent-up desire *("This* one *at last")*. We also observed, from the names he here gives to the woman and to himself, that the appearance of woman makes man feel his masculinity, which is to say, *his desire for her.* And we saw, in his expostulation and in the explanation he gives for her name, how he is defining her in light of his possessive desire. Let us now look more closely at this speech, regarded as an expression of first sexual desire or, if you will, the germ of love.

The first thing to notice is the corporeal character of the man's description of woman, a clue to the carnal character of his desire. To him she is fleshy and bony, not brainy or soulful. To be sure, flesh and bone could be read symbolically, as a metaphor for the person or the soul. But he does not speak *to* her, as soulmate or conversation partner—he does not say, *"You* are bone of my bone"—but *about* her, as object of appetite. Moreover, throughout the sequel, the language remains unrelievedly physical. In addition, as we noted in the last chapter, the man, his vision clouded by his desire, looks upon the woman as an extension of himself, indeed, as his possession: flesh of *my* flesh and bone of *my* bone, this one is *mine;* this one is *me.* The first expression of desire is felt as the love of one's own, more precisely, the love of one's own flesh. The first element of love is, or appears to be, literally *self*ish: the other appears lovable because it is regarded as same, because it is or seems to be oneself.[6] This love seeks merging, reunion, fusion, as the text, interrupting the narration, says: "Therefore a man ['*ish*] leaves

---

6. The self-centered character of his love is also conveyed by the fact that he is speaking about her *to himself.*

his father and his mother and cleaves unto his woman: *that they may become as one flesh*" (2:24; emphasis added).[7]

This primordial aspect of sexuality is ubiquitous and well known. In Western thought, it is most famously represented in the Aristophanic tale of love as the search for one's own missing half, as the desire to close and fuse in order to restore a missing wholeness—which, tragically, cannot be restored. This root of erotic desire stirs the soul to repair or furnish a purely bodily lack. Corporeal, possessive, yet indifferent to rank or rule, unabashed because innocent and ignorant of what it truly means or wants, elementary sexual desire drives upright human beings toward a not especially human conjunction, caricatured as "making the beast with two backs." Whatever else may supervene to moderate or transform or humanize our sexual desire, this ancestral, lustful, and possessive sexuality remains present and powerful. *All* sexuality includes such an element, one that can best be "explained" on the hypothesis that its goal (unbeknownst to the participants) is the restoration of some lost bodily wholeness: the seemingly other is beloved because he or she is really just a missing part of oneself.

Perhaps one should not say "he *or she.*" The speech of desire was the speech of the man: indeed, in announcing the "She is mine, she is me" character of his desire, he *identifies* himself as a *male* human being, possessively eyeing his female counterpart. What the woman thought of all this we are not told. What about her desire? Were her feelings mutual or symmetrical? We do not know; but there is some reason to doubt it. Indeed, the different origin of man and woman, and the origin of woman from man's flesh and bone, may be literary vehicles for suggesting and communicating basic natural differences between male and female sexual desire. If males as males want possessive cleaving and fusing, what do females want? If male desire is naturally focused on woman, what is the heart's desire of woman as female?

Anyone who does not want to be self-deceived about these important matters would certainly want to consider, without prejudice, whether male and female desire are, *to begin with* (that is, by nature, before culture takes over), symmetri-

---

7. This moving remark is widely taken to be the basis of the biblical teaching about monogamous marriage. The passage is regarded as the divine institution of marriage, and references to it abound in Christian marriage ceremonies. One hesitates to disagree with tradition, especially when one applauds the sentiment and likes the edifying teaching. But given the context of the remark, I doubt this interpretation. For one thing, God's commandments and institutions are always explicitly attributed to God as author, and are introduced by remarks such as "The Lord said"; this comment lacks any such mark of divine establishment. For another thing, we are in that part of the Bible that is given over to description, not to law, and the story we are reading is set, to speak anachronistically, in the state of nature rather than the state of civil society, outside of which there may be coupling off but there is no matrimony. Coming where it does, the remark about leaving your father and mother seems to me best understood as a moral gloss not on monogamy but on the sexual love *of your own*

cal and even identical. Stepping now outside the text, but prompted by its hint of possible asymmetry, I am inclined to think that the asymmetry may be real and deep, especially if we think of sex and sexual difference in an evolutionary context. These thoughts are based on matters having more to do with reproduction than with sexual desire per se, but the implications for desire follow necessarily. For, evolutionarily speaking, sexual desire serves and is selected for reproductive success. Thus, although man—like all the other mammals—experiences lust without realizing its connection to generation of offspring, the character of his lusting would certainly be conditioned by its relation to that outcome or goal.[8]

As sex has biological meaning in relation to reproduction, sexual differences would be, to begin with, differentiated according to germinal differences regarding perpetuation. For the female, the reproductive future rests on very few eggs; in human beings, chance for reproductive success rides on one egg a month. For the female, success would be enhanced by anything that would, first, guarantee fertilization and, second, gain support of and protection for her necessarily few progeny. The male reproductive future, less concentrated, is carried by billions of sperm. Part of the most effective male strategy is multiple, frequent, and polygamous inseminations. Compared to the egg, which travels little and stays protected close to home, the sperm must travel far in hostile territory, competing with many rivals; speed, energy, and tenacity will be rewarded and perpetuated by natural selection, and not only in the sperm. The differences regarding the female and male gametes are, no doubt, correlated with differences in female and male body structure and function, and also, more to our point, with differences of psyche, including the character of sexual desire. Evolutionarily speaking, in successful mammalian species the desire for copulation must necessarily be very strong in males; it must be even stronger in any species—like the human—in which the females do not go into heat but are sexually receptive throughout the estrous cycle. Female desire need not be mutual or mutually strong or aggressive; at least as far as animals are concerned, female receptivity

---

flesh, which, strictly speaking, means (also and especially) incest, including parent-child incest. The text, intervening to prevent a possible improper inference from the man's expression of desire seeking fusion, makes clear that love of your own flesh does not—that is, *should* not—lead to incest, as it does among our primate relations.

8. After reading the first chapter of this book, my readers, I trust, will not be disturbed by my use of biological, even evolutionary, evidence in support of a biblical view of human nature. For we are the way we are, regardless of how we came to be this way. Today, because of the prominence of cultural opinion that denies the existence of human nature and that regards gender as solely a matter of cultural construction, it becomes necessary to appeal to biology to support what was until only yesterday widely understood to be true of human nature, including, especially, basic natural differences between men and women.

would be sufficient. And even if female desire were strong—indeed, voracious—the limiting factor in reproductive success would be male desire and the ability to perform.

The situation is, speaking even only biologically, much more complicated. Other sex-related psychic elements—say, those related to courtship or pregnancy or nursing—complicate the picture. The economy and balance of desire will differ among mammals, depending, for example, on whether the male and female bond monogamously for life or whether polygamy or "casual sex" are the species' natural way. Further, as we shall soon see, other aspects of specifically human sexuality can and do alter this animal foundation—even before cultural influences have their powerful say. Yet, once again, Genesis seems to speak truly, not only by presenting as a distinct aspect this basic level of sexuality—animal appetite for union with "one's own flesh"—but also in hinting that, at *this* level, sexual desire may be asymmetrically distributed, with perhaps differing focus, direction, and intensity among males and females. If this is true, the focus of woman's desire remains, for now, a mystery.

Whatever might be the case about sex differences in sexual desire, there is—to return to our story—no difference regarding *consciousness* of desire: it is virtually absent. Desire is experienced, desire energizes, desire is satisfied—and it is, as the sexually liberated now say, no big deal. Lust comes naturally (what could be bad?): "and they were both naked, the man [*'adam*] and his woman [*'ishto*], and were not ashamed" (2:25). Such lack of shame, too, is natural, as shamelessness is with all the other animals. Sexual self-consciousness is still a thing of the future; likewise, all matters of moral judgment. For now, just fuse and be glad.

JUDGMENT, SHAME, AND ADORNMENT: FROM LUST TO LOVE OF THE BEAUTIFUL BELOVED

The next aspect of the relationship between man and woman depends on the presence of judgmental self-consciousness, which depends in turn on the possession of ideas about good and bad. We have previously considered how conversation between the serpent and the woman generated the requisite self-knowledge. But we then ignored the sexual dimensions of the exchange. Why, for example, does the serpent approach the woman rather than the man? Could her susceptibility to his wily and subversive speech be related to her feminine state of soul?

Tradition has in fact come down hard on the woman, and misogynists have frequently used her role in the transgression to anchor or justify their belief in the inferiority and weakness of women. But if we wish to let the text teach us about man and woman, we must try to ignore all latter-day commentary and its harsh negative judgment on woman's deed—a judgment, it is true, not wholly unfounded given the overall context. Considering not morality and sin but only psychology and anthropology, we are compelled to notice that it is woman's soul that carries the germ of human ascent. The woman's dialogue with the serpent shows that it is she, not the man, who is open to conversation, who imagines new possibilities, who reaches for improvement. Unlike the man, with his desires sexually fixated upon the woman, the woman is more open to the world— to beauty and to the possibility of wisdom. She, in short, has more than sex on the brain. Her aspirations, however diffuse in direction and ambiguous in result, are the first specifically *human* longings. Precisely because her eros is less focused and less carnal, it can grow wings and fly. The man, who did (as he has so often done since) what was pleasing to woman, speechlessly followed her lead into disobedience or, to say the same thing, into humanity (3:6).

The first discovery of our humanity, or better, the discovery that *constitutes* our humanity, is a discovery about our sexual being (not, as others would say, about our mortality), a discovery made not indifferently but with passing judgment:

And the eyes of them both were opened, and they knew that they were naked. (3:7)

The serpent had promised, "Your eyes shall be opened and ye shall be as gods, knowing good and bad" (3:5). But as the biblical speaker points out, with irony, their eyes were opened instead to the knowledge of their nakedness, which now becomes a source of shame and distress. Before, they were naked, but being innocent and ignorant, they were not ashamed (2:25). Now they see things as they really are: they do more than observe what had hitherto escaped notice; they now *know* the *meaning* of what had merely been seen.

Irony notwithstanding, we must ponder the suggestion that the first major discovery of the human mind is a truth about the human body. We must take seriously the notion that the beginning of moral knowledge or the beginning of human wisdom is, in truth, an awareness of the meaning of nakedness. What is nakedness? Why does awareness of it induce shame? How does this awareness and our response to it alter the relationship between man and woman?

To be naked means, of course, to be unguarded and exposed—a sign of our vulnerability before the elements and the beasts. But the text makes us attend, as did our ancient forebears, to our sexuality. In looking, as it were, for the first time upon our bodies as sexual beings, we discover how far we are from anything divine. More concretely, we discover, first, our own permanent incompleteness and lack of wholeness, both without and within. We have need for, and are dependent upon, a complementary yet different other, even to realize or satisfy our bodily nature. We learn that sex means that we are halves, not wholes, and, worse, that we do not command the missing complementary half. Worse yet, fusion is impossible: copulation gets us only apposition, not the desired unification. Moreover, we are not internally whole, but divided. We are possessed by an unruly or rebellious autonomous sexual nature within—one that does not heed our commands (any more than we heeded God's); we face also, within, an ungovernable and disobedient element, which embarrasses our claim to self-command. We are made aware of powerful impulses whose true import we don't understand, precisely because they are recognizably different from the more basic and strictly self-serving desires for food, drink, and rest, with their strictly private satisfactions. We are compelled to submit to the mastering desire within and to the wiles of its objects without; and in surrender, we lay down our pretense of upright lordliness, as we lie down with necessity. Our nascent pride, born of reflection, is embarrassed by the way we need and are needed by the sexual other. Later, on further reflection, we discover that the genitalia are a sign of our perishability and that their activity is, willy-nilly, a vote in favor of our own demise, providing as it does for those who will replace us.

Finally, all this noticing is itself problematic. For in turning our attention inward, we manifest a further difficulty, the difficulty of self-consciousness itself. For a peculiarly human doubleness is present in the soul,[9] through which we self-consciously scrutinize ourselves, seeing ourselves as others see us. We are no longer assured of the spontaneous, immediate, unself-conscious participation in life, experienced with a whole heart and a soul undivided against itself. Worse, self-consciousness is not only corrosive and obstructive; it is also judgmental. Because we are now beings with a nascent sense of pride (which can easily be wounded), we care about whether we measure up to our own idealized self-image and we look anxiously to others for their assessment of our worthiness. When we see ourselves being seen by the other, we cannot hide from ourselves the painful awareness of our own inadequacies and weaknesses. We are ashamed.

The deep connection between sexual self-consciousness and shame is uni-

9. This second "doubleness" is an addition to the more fundamental one, found in all animals that reproduce sexually, namely, the doubleness of self-love and sexual desire. In human beings as in animals, sexual desire, unlike hunger or thirst, serves an end that is partly hidden from, and is finally at odds with, the self-serving individual. The salmon swimming upstream to spawn and die tell the universal story: sex is bound up with death, to which it holds a partial answer in procreation. This bifurcation between the drive for self-preservation and the self-sacrificing drive for sexual reproduction, though present blindly in all higher animals, is known only to human beings. The Garden of Eden story shows how the peculiarly human mental doubleness that is self-consciousness begins by recognizing this silent, animal doubleness of sexual embodiment.

versal. In its primordial form, it has nothing to do with puritan morality or with believing that sex is dirty or sinful; indeed, as the story clearly indicates, shame's relation to sexuality is not cultural but entirely natural.[10] Man's and woman's eyes are opened together; neither speaks a word to the other. Yet as soon as they see themselves being seen by their counterpart, their minds immediately grasp the meaning of what is right before (and below) their eyes. Proud reason discovers the embarrassing truth of our abiding animality and all that that entails.

The emergence of shame and sexual self-consciousness—mutually and equally, it should be stressed—radically transforms relations between man and woman. Sexual attraction is now suffused with a concern for approbation and a fear of rejection. Each discovers that the other is genuinely and irreducibly other, not an alienated portion of oneself. Moreover, each discovers that his or her relation to the other is not only unfree and needy, but even demanding—all reasons why one might meet with both disapprobation and refusal.

But, strangely, the discovery of unfreedom is freely made and partly liberating. If there can be refusal, there can also be acceptance. A new dimension of freedom—with momentous consequences—alters the sexual necessity. Each seeks no longer mere submission, but *willing* submission; each seeks to win not just the body but especially the heart of the other. Each partner seeks approval, praise, respect, esteem—perhaps, at first, as a means of securing sexual satisfaction, but soon enough as an end in itself. Through courtship and flirtation, inspiration and seduction, a new dialectic is introduced into the dance: approval, admiration, and regard require keeping lovers apart at the beholding distance, yet the original sexual instinct drives toward fusion. A new and genuine intimacy is born out of the delicate need to preserve and negotiate this distance and its closure. And yet, the friendship of the lovers remains inherently problematic: on the one hand, there is difference, dependence, and demand; on the other hand, the wish for approbation earned and freely given, despite the unattractiveness of sexual neediness. This tension, sometimes recognized, often not, energizes human eros and raises it to new possibilities.

The animals, too, are naked, but they know no shame. They too experience

10. For a profound discussion of shame, including its natural involvement with sex and love, and its relation to awe and reverence, see Kurt Riezler, "Comment on the Social Psychology of Shame," *American Journal of Sociology*, 48 (January 1943), 457–65. Among Riezler's many sage observations are these: "Shame asks for the concealment of our sexual actions. It guards their privacy. All peoples exclude the observer. The observer or he who consents to being observed is shameless" (460). "Mutual love banishes shame. In a sexual intercourse that we imagine to be the mere satisfaction of a biological urge and without a tinge of love shame insists on being present; without love, the companion becomes the observer. . . . Shame protects love in sex against sex without love" (461–62).

sexual and other necessity, but they neither know it nor know it as necessary. This knowledge, though humbling, is not disabling. On the contrary, it is the spur to rise. Human beings do not take their shame lying down:

And they sewed fig leaves together and made themselves girdles. (3:7)

Sexual shame becomes the mother of invention, art, and new modes of cooperative sociality: note well, it is not the woman alone who sews. If the needle is the first tool, clothing is the first product, and hiding is the first goal of art. Clothing, a human addition to nature, at first hides the sexual from view. An obstacle is symbolically presented to immediate gratification of lust. Moreover, clothing not only covers over or dissimulates ugliness; it also adorns and beautifies. It thus allows the imagination to embellish and love to grow in the space provided by the restraint placed upon lust, a restraint opened by shame and ratified by covering it up. When, in the presence of love, clothing is eventually removed, the mutual and willing exposure of sexual nakedness will be understood by each partner as a gift to one's beloved and will be received gladly and without contempt. Thanks to modesty and shame, embodied in clothing, love of the beautiful elevates human longings and declares itself triumphantly indifferent to our frailty and our finitude.[11]

One can hardly exaggerate the importance of this moment. Kant has captured it, economically and profoundly, in his commentary on the fig leaf:

In the case of animals, sexual attraction is merely a matter of transient, mostly periodic, impulse. But man soon discovered that for him this attraction can be prolonged and even increased by means of the imagination—a power which carries on its business, to be sure, the more moderately, but at once also the more constantly and uniformly, the more its object is removed from the senses. By means of the imagination, he discovered, the surfeit was avoided which goes with the satisfaction of mere animal desire. The fig leaf (3:7), then, was a far greater manifesta-

11. It is worth noticing that, on this account, the primary truth about the human body sexually considered is not beauty but ugliness: beautification occurs and embellishes, but the underlying truth is not beautiful. It follows, therefore, that human eros, insofar as it is inspired by and seeks the beautiful, rests ultimately on an illusion: the beloved is, first and last, not a perfect, undivided, imperishable, and self-contained thing of beauty, meriting unqualified and wholehearted devotion. In this respect the Bible seems to differ from classical Greek thought and sensibility, which appears to treat eros as a response solicited by the truly and genuinely beautiful, of which the beautiful unadorned naked body is the most obvious and immediate incarnation. Socrates' speech on eros in Plato's *Symposium* offers, at least at first glance, perhaps the starkest contrast with the Bible.

tion of reason than that shown in the earlier stage of development. For the one [i.e., desiring the forbidden fruit] shows merely a power to choose the extent to which to serve impulse; but the other—rendering an inclination more inward and constant by removing its object from the senses—already reflects consciousness of a certain degree of mastery of reason over impulse. *Refusal* was the feat which brought about the passage from merely sensual to spiritual attractions, from mere animal desire gradually to love, and along with this from the feeling of the merely agreeable to a taste for beauty, at first only for beauty in man but at length for beauty in nature as well. In addition, there came a first hint at the development of man as a moral creature. This came from the sense of decency, which is an inclination to inspire others to respect by proper manners, i.e., by concealing all that which might arouse low esteem. Here, incidentally, lies the real basis of all true sociability.

This may be a small beginning. But if it gives a wholly new direction to thought, such a beginning is epoch-making. It is then more important than the whole immeasurable series of expansions of culture which subsequently spring from it.

Though the seeds of sociability and civilization are, indeed, sown here, Kant's picture is too rosy. From the Bible's point of view, the human response to sexual awareness, while perfectly intelligible and humanizing, is at best partial, at worst distorting. The human couple now moves to heal the rift by looking mainly, if not solely, to each other. They turn inward, "we two against a sea of troubles." Mutual self-help and self-reliance are the order of the day. But the love born of wounded pride still bears the marks and concerns of the proud. The concern with self-esteem becomes vanity; the desire to win approval produces servility; the possibility of rejection gives birth to jealousy and enmity. These manifestations of amour propre greatly complicate the story of man and woman, as Rousseau (more psychologically astute than his high-minded student Kant) would later observe, addressing precisely this same transformation of natural lust into human love:

[T]he passing intercourse demanded by nature soon leads to another kind no less sweet and more permanent through mutual frequentation. People grow accustomed to consider different objects and to make comparisons; imperceptibly they acquire ideas of merit and beauty which produce sentiments of preference. By dint of seeing one another, they can no longer do without seeing one another again. A tender and gentle sentiment is gradually introduced into the soul and at the least obstacle becomes an impetuous fury. Jealousy awakens with love, discord triumphs, and the gentlest of the passions receives sacrifices of human blood. . . . Each one began to look at the others and to want to be looked at himself, and public esteem had a value. The one who sang or danced the best, the handsomest, the strongest, the most adroit, or the most eloquent became the most highly considered; and that was the first step toward inequality and, at the same time, toward vice. From these first preferences were born on the one hand vanity and contempt, on the other shame and envy; and the fermentations caused by these new leavens eventually produced compounds fatal to happiness and innocence.

The biblical story, at this stage, can hardly show all these difficulties, especially because it features only one man and one woman. But all these passions and their potentially violent effects are born with pride and shame, as we learn from the stories that follow in the sequel, beginning immediately with Cain and Abel. Welcome though it may be, the lovability of self-esteem is not necessarily good for love.

Yet, again returning to our text, we discover another new possibility that is also now open to the lovers—if they are not so self-absorbed that they are unable to attend. Right after they make themselves girdles, the man and the woman show their first real openness to or awareness of the divine. *Immediately* after clothing their nakedness, reports the biblical author, "they heard the voice of the Lord God walking in the garden" (3:8). Human beings, once awakened to their neediness and insufficiency, have reason to pay attention to higher possibilities. Provided that the lovers do not repose their love and longing solely with each other, their eros can turn them toward the divine and the immortal.[12]

GENEROUS LOVE: PROCREATION

Love's connection to the divine is, according to our story, largely indirect. Shamefaced love may indeed enable human beings to hear the transcendent voice. But transcendence is more immediately accessible because of a newfound awareness of the meaning of our sexual being: sex means generativity. Beyond desire for bodily union and beyond erotic love and romance, the meaning of man and woman has much to do with children, whether we know it or not. This aspect of the story of man and woman—and especially our awareness of it— gravely complicates the picture, introducing further new prospects, on the one

---

12. This matter was briefly discussed in the last chapter (see p. 90). Here we consider how an opening to the divine enters and transforms the relationship between man and woman.

hand, for divergence and conflict, and on the other hand, for unification and harmony. Let's take the bad news first.

The capacity to bear children is, to say the least, a mixed blessing for the woman.

> Unto the woman He said, "I will greatly multiply thy sorrow and thy pregnancy; in pain thou shalt bear children; and thy desire shall be to thy husband, and he shall rule over thee." (3:16)

First, there is the burden of pregnancy and the pain of childbirth, a physiological consequence and sign of our peculiar and troublesome nature. Human childbirth is painful mainly because of the disproportion between the child's large human head and the mother's relatively small birth canal. The human capacity for reason and freedom, embraced in the transgressive rise to humanhood and embodied in the enlarged cranium, is, at its source, in conflict with mere nature; and it comes at heavy bodily cost to the woman, indeed, often with risk to her very life. Furthermore, this bodily conflict between the mother and her emergent child anticipates the often much more painful act of separation, when the child, exercising the newly awakened mental powers made possible by his large head, reaches for his own autonomous knowledge of good and bad and repeats the original rise and fall from obedience and innocence in the ever-recurring saga of human freedom and enlightenment.

But second, the fact of maternity also brings with it, *quite naturally,* new, unequal, and potentially difficult relations between woman and man. How is this to be understood? What are we to make of the vexed passage "Thy desire shall be to thy husband and he shall rule over thee"? Most readers agree that it signifies the institution of patriarchy, the rule of man over woman and her progeny. But everything else about the remark is disputed. For example, some Christian traditionalists, blaming womanly weakness for man's loss of paradise, defend patriarchy as just and necessary: they attribute it to God's will, regard it as His fitting punishment of woman's disobedience, and see it as necessary protection against future womanly waywardness. In contrast, some contemporary feminists denounce patriarchy as arbitrary and unjust: because of this passage (among others) they claim that the Bible is a sexist text, written by males to justify the domineering ways of man toward woman, which shamelessly invokes God's will to support the male prerogative.

But such readers read thoughtlessly and often tendentiously. They do not stop to consider that God's speech might be predictive rather than prescriptive, that it expresses not so much His preference for how things *should* be, but rather, as I would suggest, His prophecy about how things necessarily *will* be. They do not reflect, philosophically, on possible reasons for why the husband's rule over the wife might be necessary or desirable or just plain inevitable. And in interpreting the remark about male rule, they ignore its local context and its most important element: the new fact, just announced, that woman will give birth. How might the idea "Your desire shall be to your husband and he shall rule over you" follow from childbirth and procreation? Can her special *reproductive* nature—not her alleged willfulness or independent-mindedness—explain both woman's desire for her man and his rule over her?

Woman, burdened naturally by pregnancy and nursing, burdened longer than females of other species because of the lengthy period of gestation and the still lengthier period of dependency of human infants, has trouble going it alone. More attached both bodily and psychically to nascent and newborn life, she feels sooner, more acutely, and more powerfully than does the man an attachment to her own young. Paradoxically, her focused love for her children causes her desire also for her husband—as *their father*—to grow more focused and more intense.[13] Whereas, as lustful, man looked fixedly at woman (any woman?) as his missing bodily half, woman, as generative, turns her broader desire on her particular husband as protector of and provider for her children, and as partner in their rearing. (We recall the female reproductive strategy, operative throughout the mammalian world: enlist all the help you can in support of your very few eggs and their living outcomes.)

How to gain the male's cooperation and permanent presence? How to domesticate him? A man who rules—or *appears* to rule—gets domestic authority in exchange for serving the needs of the woman and her children.[14] Or, equally likely, once woman attaches herself to him and domesticates him, man may simply *take* power, being physically stronger. To be sure, this is not a matter of conscious scheming or explicit contract. Rather, human nature itself as generative might conspire and beguile in this direction, arranging things in this new, more

13. Is it only when the children arrive that the woman's attitude changes and her man really matters to her? Or is it once she becomes aware that children are naturally central to her sexual being that she develops a keen interest in the man who will father and (especially) provide for them? Readers familiar with *War and Peace* should consider, in this connection, Natasha's intense love for and jealousy of her husband, Pierre, once she becomes a mother (see the "First Epilogue"). Young romantic readers (especially males) who have fallen in love with the irrepressible and carefree young Natasha are often astonished and distressed to discover how her love of her children has reordered her entire soul and transformed all of her longings and desires.

14. People who are acculturated to accept as natural the two-parent family rarely consider the necessity of providing inducements for males to accept domestication and familial responsibility. What, before the emergence of strong cultural influences, would lead a man to slave away in order to put food into other people's mouths, especially when food is scarce or when danger is at hand?

permanent, and seemingly hierarchical way.[15] But regardless of how this comes about, once children are present and the human family comes into being, the equality of man and woman as unencumbered lovers yields to division of labor and the hierarchy of social relations and institutions.

But there is a further reason why the institution of stable domestic arrangements for rearing the young depends on some form of man's rule over woman. If woman as mother needs the provision and protection of man, so man as father needs the restraint of woman. Pregnant woman or nursing mother may be physically weaker than her man, but her procreative capacity in fact gives her unique power in the household. Not only does she alone have life-bearing power; she alone also determines paternity and lineage. Maternity is never in doubt, paternity is rarely without it. Only the mother can name the father and establish the paternity of her children. Woman, therefore, controls legitimacy: a man's own legitimacy depends entirely on the marital chastity of his mother; the legitimacy of his putative progeny depends entirely on the sexual fidelity of his wife. No man is likely to accept the domestic role of fatherly protector and provider for a woman's children unless he can be reasonably confident that those children are his own. And no social order interested in its long-term future can be indifferent to the need for responsible fatherhood. For these reasons especially, the institution of family life is likely to require some form of male rule, especially over the exercise of female sexuality.[16] Establishing a human household requires limiting both male independence and female sexuality.

The institution of households and ordered family life, though necessary as

15. Does nature arrange male rule in the human household by something like instinct? Or do human beings consciously arrange it, through awareness of their needs and interests? The text does not enable us to decide between the alternatives. The fact that this arrangement is announced by divine speech could support either alternative: it might indicate that the arrangement results from rational and deliberate decision (rather than from instinct), or it might indicate that the highest principle of Being attests to the unavoidable necessity of this arrangement.

16. I am aware that other arguments have been advanced—and attacked—regarding the control of female sexuality. Some thinkers—Rousseau, for example—see females as more lustful than males, and call attention to the voracity, indeterminacy, and wildness of female sexual appetite; they fear that unregulated female desire will exhaust and enervate men or will neutralize their manly strength and independence. (See, for instance, the classical story, told in Book VIII of Homer's *Odyssey*, of how the sex goddess, Aphrodite, tames Ares, the god of war; consider also the biblical story of Samson and Delilah.) But there is nothing in this text, and especially in the present biblical story, to suggest such a concern. Primordial man's manliness is not the focus, as it might be in founding tales of *heroic* cultures; indeed, his independent aloneness was divinely cured by the creation of a sexual partner. More important, the explicit local context is not female sexual passion but procreation.

There are, however, other arguments for controlling female sexuality that *do* worry about female fecundity: woman's life-giving power is celebrated in pagan fertility cults and goddess worship, in those cultures and religions that elevate blood ties above reason, order, and law. (See, for example,

the nursery of humanity, is hardly trouble free. Division of labor between man and woman, implicit in generation and therefore in sexual difference as such, would, by itself, sow seeds of conflict. Especially if their separate work reflects, expresses, and also fosters differences of body and soul, different work means at least partly different outlooks and sensibilities, leading also to differences of opinion and interest. This possibility of conflict of interest all by itself points to the need for rule and authority, especially when the unruly children start to emerge. Yet the institution of rule itself carries with it, inevitably, the likelihood of inequality and, hence, the possibility of much greater conflict: on one side insensitivity and abuse of power, on the other side abasement, envy, and resentment. True, a genuine ruler rules only in the interest of the ruled; the tyrant is not, strictly speaking, a ruler. True, rule imposes on the ruler heavy burdens, cares, and responsibilities, not borne by the ruled. And both the woman's desire for her husband and his need to prove himself worthy of her desire and of remaining her lover might protect—at least at first—burdened and weaker woman from simple tyranny and, even more, from abandonment. But rule and power very often corrupt; and in any case, distinction and inequality related to children and domesticity threaten always to mar the bliss of the happy lovers, previously indifferent to their generative telos.

Subsequent stories in Genesis will indeed show the great dangers of male domination and exploitation of women. For example, we will encounter the rapacious conduct of the sons of God toward the daughters of man (6:2), which, like the rape of Helen, heralds the chaotic battles of the heroes, leading God to

the contest between the Furies and Apollo and Athena—between the earthbound deities and the Olympians—in Aeschylus's *Oresteia*.) It is more than plausible to argue that the biblical author shares this concern. Fertility cults belong to nature worship, a cultural outlook opposed by the Bible from its very beginning, where it teaches that the world is created by a single God through speech, not generated by a god and goddess through giving birth. We will soon encounter, in the very next chapter, the boast of Eve regarding her childbearing powers; we will consider how female procreative pride constitutes an obstacle to establishing the biblical way, a problem subsequently addressed by the unnatural barrenness of three of the four matriarchs. Along these lines, Herman Jacobs, a student in the Committee on Social Thought, has argued (in an excellent paper, "From Eve to Joseph: Establishing the Rule of the Husband") that the entire book of Genesis is a story of men wresting control of generation away from women, eventually fulfilling what Jacobs takes to be God's clear preference announced in the passage (3:16) here under discussion. I grant that there may be some truth in this argument, but I am more impressed by the Bible's emphasis—which I will demonstrate in later chapters—on the natural wayward sexuality of *males*, their penchant for heroic deed and the taking of beautiful women as prizes, and their frequent indifference to progeny. Domesticating males and turning them into responsible fathers, into men who will (eventually) undertake the paternal work of cultural transmission, is a far bigger challenge, from the point of view of Genesis, than regulating female fertility. The present passage shows how that process gets started, and what is psychically and socially necessary to establish the human family.

flood the earth and start again with Noah. We will note with disgust the predatory behavior of Pharaoh, who rounds up beautiful women for his harem
(12:14–15). We will witness with revulsion Lot's sacrificing his daughters to the
Sodomites (19:8) or the Hivite prince's rape of Dinah (34:2). Indeed, as I will
later argue, the coming of God's preferred new way, begun with Abraham, seeks
a decisive shift in what I am calling the uninstructed or natural male attitude
toward woman. Judaism partakes heavily not only of domestication but also
of what could once be called (not by its friends) feminization. Yet the possibility
of such softening is, in fact, naturally grounded. Indeed, as our present text
shows, it rests on an utterly spontaneous male reaction to news of the new
dispensation.

The end of God's speech to the woman, "and he shall rule over thee," leads
God to turn next to *'adam,* the being who just learned of his future position as
ruler. The report is hardly cheering:

> "Because thou hast hearkened unto the voice of thy wife, and hast eaten of
> the tree, of which I commanded thee, saying, 'Thou shalt not eat of it':
> cursed be the ground for thy sake; in sorrow shalt thou eat of it all the days
> of thy life. Thorns also and thistles shall it bring forth to thee; and thou
> shalt eat the herb of the field. In the sweat of thy face shalt thou eat bread,
> till thou return unto the ground [*ha'adamah*]; for out of it wast thou
> taken: for dust thou art, and unto dust shalt thou return [*ki-'afar 'atah
> ve'el-'afar tashuv*]. (3:17–19)

God addresses the man not as ruler but as ruled: man, ruled internally by his desire for woman, had submitted externally to her voice. Lustful man willingly ex-
changed a life of innocent simplicity, in obedience to God's command, for a life
burdened by shame-filled self-division, in obedience to the siren song of free
choice and worldly pleasure. Even if he subsequently gains rule in the household, man now knows that he is hardly a ruler; on the contrary, his choice for independence makes him like a slave who must work and serve the earth, in order
to eke out a living for himself and his family. Woman periodically will suffer
painful labor, but man will labor painfully all the days of his life. His portion is
sorrow, sweat, toil, and death: the dusty earth opposes his needs, resists his plow,
and finally devours him whole. Despite all his efforts, his labors are unavailing;
in the end, he returns to his beginning, the ground from which he was taken.[17]

---

17. This comment serves as an ironic gloss on man's earlier naming the woman [*'ishah*] in terms
of her origin from him (2:23): looking backward to the source only gets man back to his earthly and
dusty beginnings. (I owe this observation to Father Paul Mankowski.) In the immediate sequel, the
man will adopt a more forward-looking and more adequate view of woman.

The new ruler has no reason to revel in his new trappings of office—not least because he soon will have many mouths to feed. The procreative meaning of sex has heavy consequences also for the man.

Man's immediate response is reported in one of the most beautiful and moving sentences of the entire Torah:

And the man called his wife's name Eve [*Chavah*], because she was the mother of all living [*chai*]. (3:20)

The man hears the prophecy of hardship and trouble and death, the evils that he unwittingly purchased with his enlightenment, but he does not despair. Despite having his nose rubbed in the truth that he can achieve no more than a return to his earthy and dusty beginnings, the man looks instead to a promising future. Guided by one glimmer in God's speech to the woman, the soul-saving passion of *hope* fixes his mind on the singular piece of good news: "My God! She is going to bear children!" Woman alone carries the antidote to disaster—the prospect of life, ever renewable. With revelational clarity, the man sees the woman in yet another new light, this time truly: not just as flesh to be joined, not just as another to impress and admire, but as a generous, generating, and creative being, with powers he can only look up to in awe, gratitude, and very likely a good dose of envy (a point to which I shall return). Despite the forecast of doom, man's soul is lifted by the redemptive and overflowing powers of woman. He names her anew, this time with no reference to himself: only now, at last, is she known as Eve, source of life and hope.[18] This, far more than the burdensome promise of rule, can attach the man devotedly to the woman. Children, a good now common to each, can hold together and harmonize what sexual differentiation sometimes threatens to drive apart.

Despite the hardships connected with their rearing, no one who understands would see children mainly as a burden. A child is good because being is good, because life is good, because the renewal of human possibility is good. One's child is a good that is one's own, though it is good not *because* it is one's own. Rather, one's own children become one's own share of that-good-which-is-children. Through children, male and female finally achieve some genuine unification (beyond the mere sexual "union," which fails to do so): the two become

18. The woman at this point keeps silence; thus, we do not know her reaction either to God's prophetic speech or to the man's effusive reaction and her renaming. Cynics will argue that it is just like a man to glory in his wife's fecundity, while she, again, must grin—or grit her teeth—and bear the children. But as we will see in the next chapter, the woman revels in her exalted status as creator: upon the birth of Cain, the firstborn, it is Eve who boasts of her creative power while Adam is speechless, and Cain bears the name of his mother's pride.

one through sharing generous, not needy, love for this third being as good. Flesh of their flesh, the child is the parents' own commingled being externalized, and given a separate and persisting existence; unification is enhanced also by their commingled work of rearing. Providing an opening to the future beyond the grave, carrying not only our seed but also our names, our ways, and our hope that they will surpass us in goodness and happiness, children are a testament to the possibility of transcendence. Sexual duality, which first draws man's love upward and outside himself (away from his preoccupation with self-preservation), finally provides for the partial overcoming of the confinement and limitation of perishable embodiment altogether.

Needless to say, man and woman in the garden, anticipating children, would not speak of them in this way. If the desire to bear children depended on such philosophizing, the race would have long since become extinct. Rather, nature has conspired to make children attractive, lively, responsive, and lovable—directly and immediately. Nature has conspired to make parents take joy in children and to love them from the start, and even when they don't deserve it. Yet these simple passions embody and do the heavy work that the being of man and woman itself intends.

The primordial story of man and woman thus points (descriptively and prophetically) forward to the household, to that first institution of humanity, devoted finally to rearing the next generation. As Rousseau would put it centuries later, describing this aspect of nascent humanity:

> The first developments of the heart were the effect of a new situation, which united husbands and wives, fathers and children, in a common habitation. The habit of living together gave rise to the *sweetest sentiments known to man: conjugal love and paternal love.* Each family became a little society all the better united because *reciprocal affection* and *freedom* were its only bonds. . . .[19]

The relationship between man and woman, now united around their common children, takes on new coloring. Conjugal love, the love of man and woman as husband and wife and especially as father and mother, goes well beyond both animal lust and erotic passion. Its joys, claims Rousseau, are sweeter than any other.

Yet the innocence of this picture, though genuine, is partial and misleading.

---

19. Note that Rousseau describes the situation from the man's point of view: he refers to *paternal* love, not parental love. His point is that only domestication produces in men the love for children that women feel immediately and altogether naturally. The mother-child bond is fully natural; the father-child bond must be cultivated.

There are seeds of future trouble in the division of labor, difficulties that Rousseau, in fact, highlights in the immediate sequel:

> ... and it was then that the first difference was established in the way of life of the two sexes, which until this time had had but one. Women became more sedentary and grew accustomed to tend the hut and the children, while the men went to seek their common subsistence.

Even more worrisome, many men will not take easily to domestication and family life. Not only will they treasure their independence and shun responsibility; they will not see in fatherhood the vehicle for realizing their highest aspirations. Woman as life giver has a direct route to a partial triumph over mortality; man does not. Her life-giving power gains her her proper name; in contrast, lacking such an answer to mortality, he still carries the general (species) name of "earthling," a reminder of his impending death. He will thus be inclined to look elsewhere for his share in immortality. Envy of woman's fertility may compound his discontent and can spur his ambition for achievements that have nothing to do with procreation and family life: the pursuit of power, dominion, and (especially) glory in battle. Fertile woman, as mother of all living, carries within herself life's answer to mortality; but martial man, as heroic dispenser of death to those who intend his own, gains for himself his own deathless name. The naming of Eve with no reference to himself signals not only unselfish appreciation but also self-concerned estrangement and fear of anonymity: if he is to obtain a proper name, the man will have to earn it by his deeds.

The implications of these difficulties become thematic in the subsequent tales in Genesis; controversies springing from them trouble us to the present day, and most likely will continue to do so indefinitely. Still, these troubles notwithstanding, one sees in generative love and its attendant institution, family life, the basis for the deepest union of man and woman, and the one toward which sexuality as such surely points.

The tale of the Garden of Eden can hardly be called a success story, nor is the new, familial dispensation a simple or sufficient remedy. Parental interest in children is not always wholesome, and neither are the children. Indeed, when we finish the story of prototypical man and woman—which does not end with their expulsion from Eden but continues through the story of their children in the next chapter—we will discover immediately the dangers of woman's pride in her childbearing powers and of jealous sibling rivalry to the point of fratricide. Throughout the book of Genesis, we will see troubled families and the trouble families cause, even as the family principle is endorsed and even sanctified. There is parental favoritism (Isaac for Esau, Rebekah for

Jacob), more sibling rivalry (Rachel and Leah, Joseph and his brothers), and filial rebellion (Ham toward Noah). And even in the best case, Abraham's pride in his firstborn must be circumcised in the covenant, and his love for the long-awaited Isaac must be subordinated to his reverence for the Lord—precisely to prove that he is fit to be the father of his people. Yet it will be the miraculously delivered promise of a son to Abraham and Sarah—and God's refusal to allow his sacrifice—that completes Abraham's initiation into the way of God. Rightly understood, the love of one's own children and the love of the divine go hand in hand.

THE MEANINGS OF SEXUAL COMPLEMENTARITY

Before leaving this complicated story about man and woman, we should look back at what we have learned. Reading anthropologically and descriptively, in the way we have attempted, we see more sharply the various inherent elements—somatic, psychic, and social—of our own gendered and engendering existence; and we see how the tensions among them are almost guaranteed to cause trouble, both for thought and for action. There is our sexually neutral, needy, private, and self-loving interest in our own personal survival and well-being. There is complementary sexual duality without, experienced as needy incompleteness within, issuing in animal-like lust for bodily union—perhaps more powerfully felt in the male. There is, as in all sexual beings, a built-in nonconscious bifurcation in our nature, in both males and females, because sexual impulses directed outwardly toward another are in principle in conflict with self-interested impulses directed toward self-preservation. There is the differentiation into two sexes, with nonidentical desires and interests, whose differences both incite union and also threaten divorce. There is human sexual self-consciousness, and rational consciousness more generally, that add yet an additional, reflective kind of bifurcation to the human soul, part of whose meaning is expressed imaginatively in shame, modesty, refusal, adornment, flirtation, courtship, display, approbation, acceptance, rejection, beautification, illusion, vanity, coquetry, aspiration, flattery, wiliness, seduction, jealousy, the desire to please, and the search for self-esteem—all intrinsic aspects of the humanization of sex, the sublimation of lust, and the possibility of love and sociability. There is the strange problem of distance and desire that results from the inexplicable connection between sexuality and the love of the beautiful, as beauty beheld at the viewing distance drives us toward merging, unbeautifully and sightlessly, at no distance whatsoever. There is generativity and childbirth, followed by domestication and rearing, and all that that implies, including, on the one hand, rivalry and risk of inequality, on the other hand, concern for lineage and hope for transcendence—the overcoming of privacy, duality, and perishability. Finally there is, through sexual self-consciousness, an opening to the truly transcendent and eternal, whatever it may be, best evidenced in the experience of *(a)* wonder at the beautiful beloved, *(b)* respect before the mystery of sexual complementarity and its peculiarly human self-conscious and imaginative embodiment, *(c)* awe in the face of life and sex and love and other great powers not of our making and not under our command, and *(d)* gratitude for the unmerited gift of creative powers exercisable through procreative handing down of our living humanity to the next generation.

All these elements can, of course, be clothed by culture, and altered by customs, rituals, beliefs, and diverse institutional arrangements. But the elements themselves are none of them cultural constructions, nor is there likely to be any conceivable cultural arrangement that can harmonize to anyone's satisfaction all their discordant tendencies. On the contrary, political and cultural efforts to rationally solve the problem of man and woman—and we are, to be frank, in the midst of such utopian spasms—will almost certainly be harmful, even dehumanizing, to man, to woman, and especially to children, not least because the matters are so delicate and private, and their deeper meanings inexpressible.

To this point we have been proceeding anthropologically, reading descriptively rather than prescriptively, looking into the mirror of the text to discover permanent aspects of our humanity as gendered, erotic, and engendering beings. Thanks to seeing the moral ambiguity of our sexual proclivities, we are better prepared to understand our permanent dilemmas in being man and woman. But is there no positive moral teaching about man and woman in this story? Does not our human nature, here disclosed, point toward some answers regarding better and worse? Given my principles of reading—namely, that what we have here is realistic description rather than idealistic prescription—I hesitate to suggest any normative conclusions. Nevertheless, remembering that pointings are not prescriptions, I think the story may very well point to the following encouraging suggestions.

The primordial story of man and woman hints that, despite all the dangers that accompany the humanization of sexuality, it is complementarity—the heterosexual difference—and not just doubleness that may point the way to human flourishing altogether. Conscious love of the complementary other draws the soul outward and upward; in procreation, love, mindful of mortality, overflows generously into creativity, the child unifying the parents as sex or romance alone never can; and the desire to give not only life but a *good way of life* to their children opens both man and woman toward a concern for the true, the good, and the holy. Parental love of children may be the beginning of the sanctification of life. Perhaps that is what God was thinking when He said that it is not good for the human being—neither for man nor for woman—to be alone. Perhaps this is why "male and female created He them" (1:27).

Chapter Four

Fratricide and Founding:
The Twisted Roots of Civilization

*T*he so-called second creation story, told in Genesis 2–3 and discussed in our last two chapters, does not end with man's expulsion from the Garden of Eden. On the contrary, the tale of primordial man and woman continues and concludes in the next chapter of Genesis, which narrates their earthly doings and those of their children. The story of Cain and Abel, the main subject of Genesis 4, not only completes the story of Adam and Eve, of whom we shall not hear again; by presenting an account of primordial life outside the garden—the life of human beings born of woman, living under their own internal, natural knowledge of good and bad—it also shows the reader what unregulated human life is really like. Eager for such understanding, we willingly join with Adam and Eve in turning our backs on the Garden of Eden. We gladly follow them as they enter upon earthly life, in expectation of learning more about the nature of our humanity.

As part of its convincing portrait of real life, this final episode of the primordial story introduces and weaves together many fundamental elements of human existence, psychic and social. Discovering the character of these elements is, as before, our primary goal, more important than the story itself. Present for examination are the following:

1. the household and family—the first human *institution*, hence the first element of society—featuring the equally elementary yet very different relationships between parents and children and between brother and brother
2. distinctive human passions related to sociality, preeminently wounded pride, anger, jealousy, fear, and dread
3. violent death, crime and punishment, and the rudiments of natural justice
4. the emergence of agriculture and settlements, the arts and the city

5. the first attempts, through sacrifices, at a relationship between man and God

As a result, this tale manages to introduce, in a mere twenty-six verses, many of the essential elements of human nature, showing us ourselves in a mirror and making vivid how humankind would live on its own without moral instruction or law. Precisely because its significance is more anthropological than historical—to repeat, these are *paradigmatic* more than they are real people—the story helps us see clearly some of the reasons why the natural or uninstructed way does not work, and therefore why the subsequent giving of God's law might be both necessary and welcome.

To read the text in this wisdom-seeking spirit, we need to set aside certain moral prejudices that will distort our understanding of the text. This is, I admit, difficult to do, especially since some of these thoroughly decent moral opinions are derived ultimately from biblical religion itself. But the characters in the story before us do not themselves live under the biblical teachings; they have received no moral instruction, they know no imposed law, human or divine. Unlike us, they have not read the story of Cain and Abel or anything else in the Bible. Indeed, it is precisely the moral poverty of their untutored wants and ways that constitutes the value of the Bible's early stories for our moral education. Thus, if we come at the Cain and Abel story with high-minded notions about the goodness of justice or offering sacrifice or founding cities, we will read only to have our moral prejudices confirmed, without any deeper understanding—of brotherhood, for example.

The story of Cain and Abel is, quite obviously, a story about brothers and brotherhood. As the first such story, it promises—on our hypothesis that first stories are paradigmatic—to reveal the basic pattern of, and the unvarnished truth about, the natural relationship between brothers. Yet because the picture of brotherliness it paints is so dark, and the fratricidal deed of Cain so horrible, readers recoil from considering the possibility that enmity—yes, enmity to the point of fratricide—might be the *natural* condition of brothers. Rather than read philosophically, readers condemn moralistically. Rather than see Cain as the human pattern, they treat him as an anomaly and denounce him as evil. To be sure, Cain's deed *is* evil, as even he comes to see. But in order really to learn from the text, we must postpone this judgment until we see what it might be about the human soul that makes fratricide an ever-present possibility.

Everyone knows that Cain committed fratricide. But few people remember that he is also the first farmer, the initiator of sacrifices, and the founder of the first city, as well as the progenitor of a line of men that invented the arts—including music and metallurgy. Why does the first family issue in fratricide? And what has fratricide to do with the city or with all these other—and usually celebrated—features of civilized life? Is there, perhaps, something questionable, even destructive, at the heart of civilization? Could there be something wrong with offering sacrifices to the divine? The text that prompts these questions does not simply answer them. To pursue them we must submit to the careful work of exegesis and interpretation.[1]

THE BIRTH OF THE BROTHERS

The first word about life outside the garden is directly responsive to the last word heard as the human beings were leaving it. Blocked from the tree of life and the possibility of bodily immortality, man and woman answer their mortal condition through procreation.

> And the man [*ha'adam*] knew Eve, his wife [*or* his woman: *'ishto*], and she conceived and bore Cain [*qayin*], saying "I have gotten [*or* created: *qanithi*] a man [*'ish*] with the Lord." And she again bore his brother, Abel [*hevel*]. (4:1–2)

The picture of life east of Eden is not as harsh as we had been led to believe. On the contrary, it celebrates the birth of a son, without report of pain or trouble to the woman, received joyously by his mother. The man, having known his wife, quite naturally recedes into the background; as it is she who will not only

---

1. Some critics contend that the available text of the Cain and Abel story is but a fragment of a more complete version, and that therefore the analysis proposed here cannot yield the desired instruction on these matters. But Umberto Cassuto, the distinguished Italian biblical scholar, has meticulously analyzed the structure of the story and conclusively demonstrated its literary and thematic integrity (*A Commentary on the Book of Genesis, Part One: From Adam to Noah* [Jerusalem: Magnes Press, 1964], 178–248). Cassuto distinguishes five themes, treated in six paragraphs: *(a)* the birth of Cain and Abel and their occupations (vv. 1–2); *(b)* the murder of Abel by Cain (vv. 3–8) and *(c)* the sentencing of Cain (vv. 9–16); *(d)* the genealogy of Cain (vv. 17–22); *(e)* the song of Lamech (vv. 23–24); and *(f)* the birth of Seth and Enosh (vv. 25–26). Cassuto observes the evenly spaced and repetitive use of the verb "to know"—three times in the sexual sense—to set off (and to link) major parts of the story, and to highlight Cain's denial of knowledge and responsibility: "And Adam knew Eve his wife" (v. 1); "and Cain knew his wife" (v. 17); "and Adam again knew his wife" (v. 25). And in contrast: "I know not. Am I my brother's keeper?" (v. 9). This tight structure (for which Cassuto provides even more convincing evidence) encourages us to think about the story as a whole, though our emphases here will differ somewhat from Cassuto's.

bear but also name her children, there is nothing left for him to do.[2] Equally naturally—exactly as the man, in renaming her, had foreseen—Eve, in her generational fullness, occupies center stage, to her great delight. Boasting of her own creative powers, Eve, though "merely" a woman (*'ishah*), can create a man (*'ish*). Indeed, she compares herself as creator to God: though the conventional translation of *qanithi 'ish 'eth 'Adonai*, "I have gotten a man *with the help of* the Lord," makes Eve seem grateful and even pious, "with the help of" is an interpretive interpolation. In my view, the context clearly favors "I have gotten [*or* created] a man [*equally*] with God"—or in plain speech, "God created a man, and now so have I."[3]

Who could blame Eve for such an attitude? Absent some divine revelation about God's role in generation, all the evidence naturally supports Eve's view: she conceived, she labored, and she bore; and the child grew and emerged out of her own substance. Having been named Eve (*Chavah*) by her husband because she was to be the mother of all living (*chai*), she now exults in her special creative powers. She takes special delight in her firstborn, the "womb opener," whom, in keeping with her procreative preeminence, she alone names.

Cain, the pride of his mother's bearing, bears the name of his mother's pride: Cain (*qayin*), related to *qanithi*, from a root *qanah*, meaning "to possess," also perhaps related to *qoneh*, meaning "to form or shape or make or create." Cain, a formed being,[4] a being created and possessed by his mother, will become a proud farmer, the sort of man who lays possessive claim to the earth and who is proud of his ability to bring forth—to create—fruit from the ground. Cain, the firstborn, is sitting pretty.

It bears emphasis that Cain is firstborn not only in his family. He is the first human being to be born of woman—that is, to be *born* at all. His father was made from the dust, his mother from the father's rib. Thus Cain, rather than his parents, is truly the human prototype, his pride included.

In contrast to the birth of Cain, the birth of Abel, the younger, is uncelebrated by his mother. Abel, introduced only as "his brother, Abel," seems to be an afterthought. There is no described relation to his mother; instead he is important

2. Knowing his wife is the man's only deed reported in this story. With respect to the possibility of overcoming mortality through procreation, he is the minor character, and what's more, he knows it. Learning to accept his inherent limitations, symbolized in the act of sexual knowing, might be man's most important beginning knowledge. Could this be what lies behind and unites the two different senses of "knowing"?

3. Even Rashi, who does not go this far, interprets Eve's remark as asserting that she is here a co-partner with God.

4. Form created by an action of *qoneh* is not produced by separation, as is the formation of the world in Genesis 1, but rather by *imposition* of form by the craftsman, as in the creation of man in Genesis 2:7, though the verb used there (*yatsar*) is different.

only or mainly as Cain's brother. No explanation is given for his name (unlike for Cain's); scholars think that it is probably not of Hebrew origin. But his name, *hevel*, is homonymous with a biblical word that means "breath that vanishes"; readers who know Hebrew will hear the pun and think that Abel is, alas, prophetically named. As Robert Sacks puts it, "Cain is a firmly established being; Abel barely exists."

Were we to know nothing more of the two brothers, we would still have enough with which to think about their relationship. Even apart from differences in inborn nature or divisions resulting from parental favoritism or neglect, birth order alone sets the stage. Younger siblings face difficulties because they come on the scene with their older brothers or sisters already firmly established—in size, in ability, and in their parents' affections. The younger, regarded as underdog, generally elicits our sympathy. But the eldest, too, faces serious and subtler difficulties. The first carrier of parental hopes and the primary object of parental pride, he feels that more is expected of him—and more often than not, it is. More than his younger siblings, he bears the burden of a need to please; his failures he knows will disappoint.

Moreover, the birth of his sibling radically changes the world as he had known it. Previously the sole apple of each parent's eye, he now has competition—especially for his mother's attention. Why, he must silently ask himself, did they (she) have another one, unless there was something wrong with me, something they are keeping hidden? Because anger at the parents for his displacement is too dangerous and counterproductive, the firstborn lodges all his resentment with the innocent newcomer. The more beloved and favored and happy the firstborn, the more difficult it may be for him to accept the second, and the more important it will be for him to continue to prove himself superior. For all these reasons, the firstborn may be expected to cherish and jealously defend his pride of place.

Yet the cause of competition between brothers lies deeper than the psychic effects of birth order. Brothers, by the very fact of being brothers, are natural rivals. Between man and woman, two is the coupling number, each naturally seeking unification; but between brother and brother, two is the fighting number, each naturally seeking supremacy. The natural, uninstructed way between brothers is not brotherhood and brotherly love but rivalry and enmity.

Comparing the dyad of brothers with the dyad of man and woman sheds light on why this should be so. The relation between man and woman, as we saw in the last chapter, is based on natural complementarity and natural appetite. Man (*'ish*) and woman (*'ishah*) are defined relative to each other, and their relationship is incited by desire seeking fusion, which in turn points forward toward offspring. But brothers are not complementary beings, and there are no *natural* impulses or passions that seek to unite brother with brother. True, the relation of brotherliness rests on a natural fact, expressible in terms of common blood or birth from the same womb.[5] But the commonness of brotherliness is mediated and derivative: one is a brother not because of any necessity in one's nature, but only because of the contingent fact that someone else has the same parents. The primary and only necessary relation of each son is backward-looking, to the parents; and this makes the relation of the sons to one another rather like parallel lines, not intersecting ones. Moreover, unlike sexual complementarity, the natural fact of common blood is not directly experienced. What is experienced instead is, immediately, rivalry for parental attention and regard and, in the long run, competition for the place of one's father and the inheritance of family name, home, and fortune.[6] The existence of one's brother is painful proof that one is not the sole meaning of one's origins; the patrimony, the link to one's source, is contested. True, when their father's house is under attack, brothers may band together to prevent harm to their common source; for the same reason, a brother may even rise to avenge his injured brother. But in times of peace, brothers are not natural allies, not only at first but also later. When a man finally "leaves his father and mother and cleaves to his wife," he takes his lineage in his own direction, tacitly rejecting the parallel (or divergent) way taken by his brother. Precisely because each son's primary relationship is to his parents—first to his mother, and later to his father—the primary relationship of each brother to the other is unlikely to be based on brotherly love.[7]

Our text underscores the absence of natural brotherly bonds between this

---

5. The ancient Greek word for "brother" is *adelphos*, "out of the same womb."

6. Sisters, too, are like nonintersecting parallel lines, having no natural relation to one another. As we will learn much later from the story of Rachel and Leah (the only story in Genesis about sisters), sisters also are rivals. In their case, however, the rivalry is over the special womanly power of procreation and, secondarily, over the love of a husband. In the case of brothers, the primary rivalry is about pride of place in the world and, secondarily, the love of the parents (more the mother or the father?). This prototypical story of sibling rivalry to the point of fratricide is not sex-neutral. It is not by chance a story about *brothers*. (Very likely for the same reason, there is no special word for sister killing; "sororicide" is not an English word.)

7. The intrinsically tragic character, at least in a heroic culture, of the relationship between brothers (and also between father and son and between husband and wife) receives its most powerful expression in the classical Greek story of the House of Atreus, the subject of Aeschylus's *Oresteia*. The trouble begins when Atreus, inheritor of his father's throne, is cuckolded by his brother Thyestes; in revenge, Atreus slaughters two of Thyestes' children and serves them to him in a stew. In the next generation, Atreus's son Agamemnon is willing to go to war along with his brother Menelaus to avenge the rape of Menelaus's wife, Helen, but on returning home, he claims singular glory for the sack of Troy. For an excellent discussion of these matters, and of the tragic nature of all the domestic relations in the world of heroes, see Reeghan Raffals, "A House Divided: The Tragedy of Agamemnon" (doctoral dissertation, University of Chicago, 1997).

prototypical pair of brothers. In every detail, the story insistently emphasizes the things that *separate* them—birth order, namings, attitude of mother to their birth, and, as we shall next see, occupation. There is nothing to suggest natural similarity or real kinship.

OCCUPATIONAL DIFFERENCE AND MORE

The natural rivalry of brothers may be further accentuated by differences in habits and ways of life, as, indeed, they are in our present story.

> Now Abel was a keeper of sheep and Cain was a tiller of the ground [*literally,* worker of the ground *or* servant of the ground: *'oved 'adamah*]. (4:2)

The two occupations of the brothers echo two earlier remarks about the human work. Herding sheep reminds us of having dominion—ruling—over the animals, the work announced in Genesis 1 (verses 26, 28), the majestic story in which man is god-like, the world harmonious, and all is seen to be very good. Tilling or serving the earth is the way anticipated and forecast in the so-called second creation story (2:5; 3:23), the story that shows why badness and hardship enter and complicate human existence. Some readers do not choose to make much of this occupational difference, seeing farming and herding simply as the two primary and complementary ways human beings obtain a livelihood. Others treat the occupational difference as a mere narrative device, necessary for introducing the differences in what each brother will, in the sequel, bring for his offering to the divine. But given what we know (from reading ahead) of God's persistent preference for nomads and shepherds over citydwellers and farmers, it is reasonable from the start to see farming and herding as contending alternatives, with deep differences in their inner meaning and in the attitude that their practitioners have to the world.

But even if one suspects that farming and herding differ profoundly in their orientations to the world, it is not obvious how to describe their difference. In particular, it is hard to know how to characterize farming and the reason why the Bible regards it with suspicion. Is farming a manifestation of worrisome human innovation, independence, and mastery over the earth that eventually gives rise to civilization and politics? Or conversely, is farming a manifestation of human complacency, conformity, and subservience to the earth that eventually gives rise to servitude and tyranny? The text may be said to offer evidence to support both points of view.[8] Let us consider each in turn.

---

8. Curiously, as we shall see, on either account of what's wrong with the farmer, the shepherd will appear better suited to answer a call from the divine.

Cain, the new man and heir of the second account, appears to be following the life God foretold for man outside the garden. Perhaps, like many a firstborn, he takes over the family business, whether out of duty, ambition, or the desire to please—or displace—his father; alternatively, as the human prototype, he may be the first farmer, the first to take up the announced or prescribed human work. In either case, one might think farmer Cain obedient. But as Robert Sacks observes, "The only disturbing thing is his name. It implies that, for Cain, to be a farmer means to put up fences and to establish a private tract of land which one can call one's own, rather than fulfilling one's duty to the fruitfulness of the earth. Abel's way of life leaves the world open. Shepherds need no fences and roam through the whole." Yet the difference is greater still.

Farming requires intellectual sophistication and psychic discipline: wit is necessary to foresee the possibility of bread from grain,[9] to develop tools, to protect crops; self-control—indeed, a massive change in the psychodynamics of need and satisfaction—is needed before anyone will work today so that he might eat months later. In addition, agriculture comes with a new relation to the earth (and also toward the heavens): farming means possession of land and settled habitation; it represents a giant step toward human self-sufficiency, yet it is also precarious and very dependent on rain (2:5). Because he mixes his labor with the earth, the farmer claims possession not only to the crops but also to the land itself. For the same reason, he is even inclined to regard himself as responsible—creatively as maker—for the produce itself. On this view, the farmer is an audacious and self-assertive character.[10]

9. So impressive is this discovery that many other traditions ascribe it to a god. In contrast, the Bible treats all such discoveries—including the invention of languages, the initiation of sacrifices, the discovery of fire and its power to transform, the creation of music, and the fermentation of grapes—as of purely human origin. In this book, the divine gifts are moral and legal, not intellectual and technological.

10. No modern thinker has seen this as clearly as Rousseau, who, it is evident, was a careful reader of Genesis:

The first man who, having enclosed a piece of ground, to whom it occurred to say *this is mine* and found people sufficiently simple to believe him, was the true founder of civil society. How many crimes, wars, murders, how many miseries and horrors Mankind would have been spared by him who, pulling up the stakes or filling in the ditch, had cried out to his kind: Beware of listening to this imposter; you are lost if you forget that the fruits are everyone's and the Earth's no one's. (*Discourse on the Origin and Foundations of Inequality Among Men,* in *The First and Second Discourses and the Essay on the Origin of Languages,* trans. and ed. Victor Gourevitch [New York: Harper & Row, 1986], 170)

See also Rousseau's discussions of the mental prerequisites for agriculture, the connection of farming and metallurgy, and the link between landed property and the first rules of justice, as well as the contributions of property to vanity, inequality, domination, and war (*Discourse on Inequality,* Part I, par. 22; Part II, par. 19–29).

The shepherd, in contrast, lives a simple and by and large artless life. His work is mild and gentle; his rule requires no violence. The sheep graze as they roam and produce wool and milk out of their own substance, the shepherd contributing nothing but also harming nothing. Though he wanders the earth as he pleases, the shepherd has no illusions of self-sufficiency; indeed, he is likely to feel acutely the dependence of his entire life on powers not under his control and processes not of his own creation. The settled farmer seeks to design his life, the wandering shepherd allows his life to be designed by the world.

In sum, on this understanding of the two occupations, Cain's way of life, like the man, is more complex: possessive, artful, potentially harmful, and dangerous, but with the prospect of the higher achievements (and risks) of civilization. Abel's way, like the man, is simple: open and permissive, harmless, and certainly vulnerable (especially before craft, cunning, and technique) and, besides, incapable of accomplishing much of anything. Abel's way is fragile, not to say impossible; Cain's way is problematic, not to say indecent—unless it can be educated and restrained. Everything depends upon whether the possession and the use of the land are just and whether Cain's pride can be tamed by learning or remembering that not he but God—a power beyond—is the source of his farmerly success. The immediate sequel—the episode of the sacrifices—faces this question frontally.

But as we shall see, the practice of sacrifices provides evidence for the other interpretation, namely, that the trouble with the farmer is not that he is too much of a master but that he is too much of a slave. Which divine power is it that commands the farmer's attention? In part, he looks to heaven, home of the sun and the source of rain. But he also pays mighty attention to the womblike earth, source of fertility. The phrase used to describe Cain's work as farmer, usually translated as "tiller of the soil," literally means "laborer (or servant) of the ground." The verb 'avad means "to work, to labor, to serve," including "to serve" in a religious sense. Those who work the earth turn out to serve the earth, even if they think they are mastering it. Rather than serving God, farmers are in danger of serving the earth as if it were a divinity; they are at risk of becoming slaves to the earth. It is not just that they are at the mercy of the elements, of the heavenly rain from the skies above and the maternal fruitfulness of the soil below. The farmer is bound to his plot, rooted in place just like his crops, not free to leave, not free to escape the grip of necessity by which the cursed ground holds him fast, as it were, by the throat.

In contrast, on this interpretation the shepherd is the true innovator. Having the example of the farmer before him (his older brother), he refuses to live in thrall to the cursed earth, tilling it, serving it, and looking to it for his salvation.

Rather than submit to dumb nature in the form of Mother Earth, the shepherd breaks away from the bondage of farming and rises up to exercise rule over the animals.[11] He somehow intuits that it is in this way that he acts as a human being made in the image of the true God (and in the way anticipated in the harmonious created order of the first creation story). Rather than seeing the world in terms of master and slaves, he sees the importance of reasoned order and authority, all in the interest of the ruled. A leader and a ruler himself, yet feeling his dependence on powers aloft, he may be more open to the need for leadership in his own life. But precisely because he is free and independent, he is unlikely to conform to conventional opinion or submit to tyrannical authority. When it finally comes, the shepherd may be more open to the edifying and elevating call of the Lord.[12]

Having in mind these competing thoughts about man's various relations to the divine, we are exactly ready for the sequel, the gifts the brothers bring before the divine.

SACRIFICE: PRIDE OR SUBMISSION?

In the course of time [*literally,* at end of days: *miqets yamim*] it came to pass that Cain brought of the fruit of the ground an offering [*minchah*] unto the Lord, and Abel, he also brought of the firstlings of his flock and of the fat thereof. (4:3–4)

11. Historically, of course, herding probably preceded farming, agriculture requiring the massive technical, psychic, and social developments cited above. On this usual view, the farmer is the innovator, the man who takes the ambiguous step forward (or is it backward?). But our text invites us to consider the shepherd as the innovator by making him the second born, one who did not follow in his brother's vocational footsteps.

12. This second way of thinking about the farmer and the shepherd is new to me, for I have long been partial to the first view—and on balance, I remain so. It was suggested to me—nay, forced upon me—in powerful arguments made by Josh Weinstein, Dan Polisar, and Asaph Sagiv of the Shalem Center in Jerusalem, during my visit there in May 2000. We all agreed that the farmer is under suspicion, but we differed as to why. We all agreed that biblical Israel is defined in opposition to biblical Egypt, the fertile place. But we disagreed whether Egypt is rejected because it is a place of technology, administration, and other manifestations of human self-glorification leading to the tyranny of Pharaoh, or because it is a civilization that worships the earth and the river. Asaph Sagiv believes that the question of Egypt may in fact be present already in this story of Cain and Abel. He offered the interesting suggestion that the Cain and Abel story represents a biblical countermyth to the Egyptian story of Osiris and his brother Seth. In that story, Seth, an evil god of the nomads, kills Osiris, the Egyptian god of the earth's fertility. In Genesis, Cain (an Osiris figure) offers a cult sacrifice (Abel) to the earth; the Lord curses the ground for accepting the victim's blood and banishes Cain from His divine presence; and Seth appears as a substitute for the nomadic victim whose sacrifice the biblical God preferred.

Sacrifice is of human origins. God neither commands nor requests it; we have no reason to believe that He even welcomes it. On the contrary, we have reason to suspect—and will soon give ample evidence to defend this suspicion—that the human impulse to sacrifice is, to say the least, highly problematic, and especially from God's point of view. To be sure, God will eventually command sacrifices, though then only under the strictest rules. As in so many other matters, the problematic is permitted but only if regulated. Because He will not, or cannot, extirpate the dangerous impulses in men, God makes concessions to them, while at the same time containing them under explicit and precise commandments. The present story, which begins the reader's education regarding the questionable nature of sacrifices, should arouse our suspicion because it is Cain who is their inventor and founder.

Unlike the word "sacrifice," whose Latin roots mean "to make holy," the Hebrew word here translated as "offering," *minchah,* does not by itself connote anything sacred. It comes from an unused root meaning "to apportion, to bestow a share," and later, euphemistically, "tribute." An offering, in the first instance, is a share of what is *one's own,* doled out or apportioned *by the owner* as *he* sees fit. Only those who possess are free to bestow. Such echoes of self-possession may still be heard surrounding the more religious sense of *minchah,* "a sacrificial offering, usually bloodless and voluntary"—a gift, an oblation, a present to the divine.

Competing yet deep-seated passions lie beneath the human impulse to give a share or to pay tribute to the divine, to offer gifts and oblations to God or the gods. To begin with, there are fear and gratitude—fear that unless appeased with presents, the powers that be will thwart or ignore our hopes and wreck our plans; gratitude for experienced good results and good fortune, interpreted as divine favor directed at us. Less rational are the ecstatic passions, associated with bloody and orgiastic sacrifice (in ancient Greece, the province of Dionysus); these appear to play no part in the present offering, but they will figure in Noah's sacrifice after the flood and in many later and equally questionable biblical sacrifices.[13]

The impulse to sacrifice need not be at all impulsive. It is frequently a matter of rational calculation, not to say cunning manipulation. Man may seek to put the gods in his debt, or more nakedly, to bribe them into delivering benefits and withholding harms. Any human being conscious of being at the mercy of powers not under his command will attempt to do something to improve, or avoid,

---

13. One might even argue that it is these ubiquitous wild impulses that are being excited only to be repulsed in the story of the binding of Isaac, which shows, once and for all, that the God of Abraham—unlike the deities worshiped by others—does not want child sacrifice.

his fate. For primitive man—and especially for farmers, eager for rain—the powers of concern were especially the powers aloft, including the sun and moon, the wind, and the rain, but also the powers below, the teeming earth.[14] It is perfectly fitting that the primordial farmer be the first to think of sacrifice—even before he knows anything at all about who the gods really are.

Indeed, ignorance of the divine—and the wish to dispel that ignorance—is itself another powerful motive for bringing sacrifice. Men intuit the presence of higher powers, perhaps first through the experience of awe and wonder before the spectacles and phenomena of nature: sunrise and sunset, new and full moons, thunder and lightning, the fall of water out of the sky, the seasonal changes in the earth. Natural piety gives rise to the desire to close the gap between the human and the divine, to mediate the distance, to establish ties, to gain a close and firm connection to the whole and its ruling forces. This, too, is a natural and understandable desire for the first truly human earthlings.

But it is no simple matter to act on this desire. For how can and ought one communicate with what is so remote, unknown, or inscrutable? Unless man knows *who* God is and *what* (if anything) He wants, communicating will be strictly a shot in the dark. Curiously, however, human beings do not behave as if the divine is mysterious and inscrutable. On the contrary, both the fact of offering sacrifice and the particular gift offered bespeak certain clear—and clearly presumptuous—assumptions about the divine:

1. God is (gods are) the kind of being(s) that does (do) or could care for me.
2. He (or they) would be more likely to care for me—do me good and not evil—if I could please Him (them).
3. I could please Him (them) with gifts. Why? Because *I* am pleased by gifts. (Unspoken premise: the gods are just like me.)
4. He (they) must like what I like.

The deep ambiguity at the heart of the human impulse to sacrifice now stands revealed: all of the underlying assumptions—even in the best case, a sac-

---

14. Both sky and earth gods and goddesses were prominent in the religious cults of the ancient Near East. Among the Canaanites, Baal, the most important god in the pantheon, was apparently a fertility god, known variously as Lord of the Earth, Lord of the Rain and Dew, He Who Rides the Clouds, and Lord of the Heavens. Astarte, a fertility goddess worshiped among the Babylonians and the Western Semitic peoples, became associated also with the fertility of the earth, being later identified with the Egyptian deity Isis, goddess of (among other things) grain.

rifice from pure gratitude—are in fact expressions of human pride and presumption, masquerading as true submission. Any deity worthy of the name must, no doubt, see this for what it is.[15]

To his credit, Cain, the initiator, somehow divines the presence of the divine. Perhaps because he is a farmer, he is both more concerned with the powers aloft (and below) and more sophisticated about his earthly dependence on them. Perhaps, as the firstborn, he experienced natural reverence before his father and now looks to the highest power for reassurance and support in the presence of his younger rival. But the God Cain encounters is not the god he expected. This one does not just make rain or grow crops; He cares for life, for individuals (including one's rivals), and for right.

Cain addresses the divine as eater. He brings before the (to him unknown) god or gods,[16] "of the fruit of the ground," his produce—but produce (he must be aware) that depends on the gods' sending rain. In what spirit Cain brings his gift we cannot be sure. Perhaps he was worried about the lack of rain. Perhaps, conversely, he was simply grateful for a good crop. Perhaps he was showing off: "Life was supposed to be hard, but behold, I can create enough so that there is even some for you." But from the sequel one can infer that Cain offered his gift from lower and more calculating motives. And even here, the text hints at possible halfheartedness: he waited until the "end of days" to offer; more important, unlike his brother Abel's gift, which (though he was merely a follower: "he

15. God will, later, *reluctantly* command and institutionalize sacrifice, once it becomes clear that the children of Israel need sensuous experience in coming closer to God. The crucial text is Exodus 24, describing the wild sacrifice and then the sensualist experience of the elders on Mount Sinai, following which God immediately lays down the law for the building of the Tabernacle, the place of sacrifice. Finding a mean between absolute remoteness and absolute nearness, and between absolute inscrutability and complete knowledge, God permits man "to approach" by practices *already familiar to human beings*. The human and the humanly ambiguous are brought under law and sanctified by God's commandments. But one must first see—as we begin to see in the present story—why the unregulated and unsanctified human impulse is so troubling.

16. Readers, especially those who read the text purely temporally or historically, may object to my suggestion that Cain, to begin with, has no true knowledge of God. Some will assume—without any textual evidence—that his parents must have informed Cain about God. But parents do not always (often?) reveal to their children their earlier misdeeds, especially momentous ones. Also, there is nothing in the story, until the very end, to suggest that the first parents lived with anything resembling awareness of God. For all they knew, His domain was confined to Eden. A more serious objection would point out that the text clearly says that Cain brought an offering "unto the Lord" *(Yahweh)*, using the tetragrammaton name for God by which the children of Israel will later know Him. But the careful reader will notice that this represents a change from "Lord God" *(Yahweh 'elohim)*, the name used for God in the story of the Garden of Eden. This change is in keeping with the view that Cain is sacrificing to the name of he-knows-not-what, and not to the God who had dealt

also") came from the *best* portions (the fat) of the *firstlings* of the flock, Cain's gift was indifferent or worse.[17] But as we have shown, the sacrifice itself is ambiguous enough—especially when not commanded, especially when coming from a farmer like Cain. Apparently, God also had doubts—perhaps these, perhaps others—about Cain's offering.

> And the Lord had respect unto Abel and to his offering; but unto Cain and to his offering He had not respect. And Cain was very wroth and his countenance fell. (4:4–5)

The economy of the text leaves big questions unanswered. How, for example, do the brothers learn of the divine response to their gifts? Did a fire descend and consume one but not the other? Or was a sign given in the sacrifices themselves? Or—my preference—did they learn only in due course, through divergent consequences in their occupations, Abel's flock waxing great and fertile, Cain's field going barren? The text is silent. Equally hidden are God's *reasons* for respecting Abel's offer and not Cain's. Does God prefer the second-born to the firstborn? Does God prefer Abel's shepherd way of life to that of farmer Cain, a difference that (as we have suggested) might be reflected in different attitudes toward the world and the divine? Did He discern a difference in intent and disposition, along the lines hinted at above? Or, as others have suggested, is this a case of mysterious divine election, having nothing whatsoever to do with the merit or character of the human agents?[18] Again, we do not know. We are, it seems, meant to focus on the outer fact alone.

---

with his parents in Eden. Father Paul Mankowski suggested to me that we should not here translate the Tetragrammaton as "Lord" but rather as *Hashem* ("The Name"): Cain brings an offering to The Name, but he has no idea yet who or what The Name is or what it might want or demand of us.

Reading anthropologically rather than historically, I see no reason to assume that the first human being to think up the idea of sacrificing to the divine would have any clear idea of who or what the divine really was. Cain, the human prototype, divines the existence of the divine and seeks on his own to make contact, but as the story amply shows, he has no good idea of who God is or, more important, what would truly please Him.

17. In a famous Greek tale, Prometheus, who first taught men to sacrifice, showed them how to save the best portions for themselves.

18. This last view does not sit well with a philosophical reader, for it looks rather like arbitrariness: God is simply and utterly inscrutable, bestowing His gifts without any relation to what we do. But as we shall see as we go along, this view of God's doings does not accord well with God's interventions in Genesis, as God Himself will say of them. God's doings may be mysterious to some extent, but not utterly so. The skeptical reader's willingness to follow and learn from the text requires that there be reason in the deeds the text attributes to God. Beginning with the rational order of creation offered in Genesis 1, the text encourages us to regard the highest principle of being not as arbitrary and capricious but as benevolent (albeit awe-ful) and reasonable.

Looking only at what we do know, we must avoid a common misperception. As Robert Sacks has pointed out, "Cain's sacrifice was not rejected but merely not yet accepted. . . . From Cain's reaction it appears as though he understood God's disregarding his sacrifice as a simple rejection, but this is not necessarily the case."[19] The sequel will bear this out: God will address Cain in solicitous and encouraging speech. Indeed, on hearing this speech, we may find it plausible that God intends Cain's disappointment as a necessary vehicle for educating him regarding what He truly cares about. But we must first face Cain's anger ("very wroth")—the first human display of this crucially human and ever-dangerous passion—and also his shame ("his countenance fell").

ANGER, SHAME, AND JUSTICE

Both the shame and the anger have their roots in pride, wounded pride. The firstborn and elder brother, the proud farmer who produces crops by his own ingenuity and labor, first also (or so he thinks) in his relation to the divine as the inventor of sacrifices, Cain desires to be first and best, and to be so recognized. His younger brother, a lazy shepherd, a mere follower in gift giving, has surpassed him in God's respect. Even were Cain to regard himself merely as his brother's equal, his failure in the presence of Abel's success wounds his pride. Cain feels the sting of shame, as the world does not affirm his lofty self-image. But, still proud, he takes the disappointment as a slight or an insult; he not only hangs his head in disgrace, he fills his heart with rage, for he believes that he has been not only shamed but also injured. Cain's anger, though it is not pretty, expresses the world's first sense of justice—or rather, injustice: "I did not get what I deserved; I was wronged."

Through Cain's anger, the text conveys its first instruction regarding man's interest in justice. Justice is, to begin with, not an altruistic matter of doing right by others, but a selfish matter of not letting others do wrong to oneself. A concern for justice begins in the passion to get what one deserves and to get even when one feels cheated or slighted.

Suffering a loss or a harm arouses only sadness or pain; but experiencing slight, insult, and injury—from the Latin, *iniuria,* meaning "injustice"—gives rise to anger, to a demand not only for getting back what we have lost but especially for getting even with the one who has slighted us, who has knowingly treated us less well than we deserve. This deep connection between anger and

19. I would add that although God had respect for Abel's sacrifice, it does not follow that He endorsed it entirely. As we shall see at the end of this story, there will be a third brother, a replacement for Abel, who does not bring material offerings but instead "calls upon the name of the Lord."

justice has been noted since antiquity. Aristotle calls anger "an impulse . . . to revenge . . . caused by an obvious *unjustified* slight," and slight, "an active display of opinion about something one takes to be worthless." A man feels especially slighted—unjustly—by "those to whom he looks for good treatment—persons, that is, who are indebted to him for benefits, past or present, which they have received from him." Such contempt for our person, experienced as a slight, is often more unbearable than the harm itself.

Cain's display of anger reveals retroactively his state of soul in making the sacrifice. Because he had sought to place God in his debt by means of his gift, Cain feels slighted by what he takes to be God's unjustified rejection of his offering. If indeed part of Cain's anger is directed at the divine, it shows how presumptuous and hubristic were his expectations.

More likely, however, Cain's anger is directed mainly at his brother. God, after all, is invisible and (up to this point) silent; for all Cain truly knows of divinity, it may not even be a being capable of bestowing slights and favors. And be this as it may, it is surely safer to displace (not necessarily by a conscious process) his anger at God onto his human rival, in whose absence God—or anyone else—would not have found him to be merely second best. The bitterness of not having his own gift respected is nothing compared with seeing the greater success of his (lesser) brother. Cain treats Abel's success in sacrifice as if Abel had been trying to outdo him.

Cain's anger, shame, and jealousy are—sad to say—entirely intelligible and, speaking anthropologically, perfectly normal. Every human being, once he comes to self-consciousness, acquires notions of self-esteem and self-worth; absent some corrective, this sense of self-worth becomes the standard by which each of us naturally measures what he thinks he deserves from another and from the world. Rousseau has captured this essentially human (all too human) phenomenon, showing the evils that lurk in the seemingly reasonable concern for self-esteem and the ugly consequences of demanding the consideration to which we feel we are entitled:

> As soon as men had begun to appreciate one another, and the idea of regard [*considération*] had taken shape in their mind, *everyone claimed a right to it*, and one could no longer with impunity fail to show it toward anyone. From this arose the first duties of civility even among Savages, and from it any intentional wrong became an affront [*or* outrage] because, together with the harms resulting from the injury, the offended party saw in it contempt for his own person, often more unbearable than the harm itself. Thus everyone punishing the contempt shown him *in a manner pro-*

portionate to the stock he set by himself, vengeance became terrible, and *men bloodthirsty and cruel.*[20]

Once there is self-regard, there will be perceived insult experienced as injustice. Once there is perceived injustice, there will be anger and the desire for revenge. And the larger the self-regard, the greater the exacted vengeance.

When looked at in this light, Cain appears not as some monstrous deviant but as humanly prototypical. Cain, treated worse than he thought he deserved, smoldered with resentment at Abel, who in Cain's eyes was treated better than he deserved, who had in fact usurped—de facto—Cain's pride of place. No wonder he was angry.

God enters the picture in an attempt to assuage Cain's fury; indeed, He expresses surprise that Cain should be angry at all:

And the Lord said unto Cain: "Why art thou wroth? and why is thy countenance fallen? If thou doest well, shall there not be a lifting? But if thou doest not well, sin coucheth [*rovets*] at the door; its desire shall be for thee, but thou shalt rule over it." (4:6–7)

Trying to comfort and encourage Cain, God makes clear that his sacrifice has not been rejected. Rather, acceptance will come provided Cain "does well." We must now try to put ourselves in Cain's place.

No doubt Cain ought to be pleased by God's attention and interest in him. Though He respected Abel's offering, God speaks only to Cain; Cain seems to hold more interest, being both more promising and more problematic. The promise of a lifting—of his sacrifice, of his countenance, and of his fallen dignity and standing—ought to be encouraging. Yet like many an angry person, Cain may find this belated solicitude offensive, adding insult to injury: first he kicks me, then he asks, "Why are you crying?" Especially galling to the angry Cain is God's placing the onus on him: "If *you* do well . . ." But whether Cain is pleased or irritated by God's speaking to him, the substance of God's counsel is surely puzzling, not to say delphic. Indeed, this part of God's speech (verse 7) is regarded as one of the most difficult passages in the entire Bible.[21] One must not assume that Cain found it less obscure than we.

20. As Rousseau makes clear, there is a deep connection between wounded self-esteem and the demand for revenge. This is the seed of justice, and, Rousseau suggests, its later and larger growth can never completely outgrow this initial self-regarding spirit and vindictive intention.

21. The problem is not helped by the grammar. For in the Hebrew text, it is unclear whether the subject of the verb "to do well" is "you" (that is, Cain) or "lifting" (that is, the offering). The verb

God's counsel, whatever it finally means, seems to assume that notions of doing well and not doing well (and of sin and ruling over it) are present and clear
to human beings, without further instruction; for human beings do indeed have
some kind of knowledge of good and bad. True, there has been no given law;
there are as yet no well-defined crimes or punishments. Still, human beings act,
moved by their own perceptions of better and worse. "Do well," exhorted the
Lord; and even if you don't do well, and thus even if sin is in your way, ready to
pounce like a wild animal, you will be able to rule over it. If God intended to
warn Cain of the dangers lurking in his own heart, He might have found a
clearer way to do so; and, clear or not, the overall message—"Do well; you can
master the obstacles"—was not, on balance, a teaching of self-restraint. Cain,
still angry, now put his mind to doing well.

Those who wonder why God might not have produced a more powerful and
successful antidote to Cain's anger might wish to consider God's speech as if it
were, rather, the voice of reason and goodness—such as these might exist in natural man—manifesting itself (as if coming "from the outside") against a soul
filled with rage (like the appearance of Athena, who suddenly appears and prevents Achilles from drawing his sword on Agamemnon in Book I of the *Iliad*).[22]
"Be reasonable," says the voice, "bide your time, you'll get your position back. Do
well." The voice of reason is, first of all, concerned with our own good; otherwise, we will not listen. Absent very *specific* instructions and delineations, rationality is experienced not as counseling the other fellow's good but as promising
my own—not now, but later, that is, if I do well and overcome sin,[23] which
threatens to get in my way and drag me down. The sequel shows how little avail-
ing are such vague instructions in the face of vengeful passions. They might even

---

form is both second person masculine (in which case the subject is Cain) and third person feminine
(in which case the subject is "lifting"). Here, then, is an equally accurate alternate translation of the
second sentence and first part of the third sentence of God's speech: "Whether the lifting does well or
does not well, sin coucheth at the door." In this translation, with "lifting" as the subject, God would
seem to be saying, "Never mind the sacrifices, whether they go well or badly; the important thing is
sin, which is ready to pounce on you."

The ambiguity of this passage turns out to be perfect for what the story has to show us: God may
have meant one thing, while Cain understood the other—hearing what he wanted to hear about his
own "doing well." For the interpretation I offer in this and the next few paragraphs, I have worked
mainly with the other translation ("If thou doest well"), largely because I think that is the meaning
that best fits with what Cain seems to hear and with what he subsequently does.

22. The text tells us that "the Lord said *to Cain*"; it does not say that the Lord spoke loudly and
from on high so that all could hear Him. It seems rather that the communication was private, like a
voice in the ear. Would it be obvious to Cain who or what was speaking to him? *We readers* are told
that it was the Lord speaking, but the voice does not so identify Himself to Cain.

23. The word for "sin," *chatath*, comes from a root, *chata*, that means "to miss the mark." To the
morally uninstructed, like Cain, it might mean simply "failure."

be understood to *counsel* revenge—only not impulsively, but with due calculation and premeditation. Primordial human knowledge of good and bad may be
used self-righteously, but it is a far cry from righteousness. This we readers
quickly learn from the ensuing events.

FRATRICIDE: CRIME AND PUNISHMENT

And Cain appointed a place where to meet Abel, his brother [*literally,* and
said *(vayo'mer)* Cain to *('el)* Abel, his brother],[24] and it happened when
they were in the field [*sadeh*] that Cain rose up against [*'el*] Abel, his
brother, and killed him. (4:8)

Cain uses his reason to help take his revenge. He plans the event, employs speech
to arrange Abel's presence, and picks a place out in the fields,[25] where no one will
see and where no one can come to Abel's rescue. But if reason is the instrument,
jealousy remains the likely motive: the hated rival is removed. Gain also might
have been on Cain's mind; with Abel out of the way, his flocks would belong to
Cain, who might then be able to offer a respectable sacrifice. And to stretch the
point perhaps beyond what is reasonable, Cain may even have thought this was
precisely what was meant by "doing well." For how was he to know that murder
is bad, it not having been forbidden? Worse, if, as it might appear to Cain, the divine prefers animals to vegetables, might not a human sacrifice be best? Because
Cain's deed was committed not in heat but with premeditation, we must assume
Cain believed that he was doing good—at least for himself.

Whatever he may have thought beforehand, he soon learns, painfully, the
wrongness of his deed—and so do we.

And the Lord said unto Cain: "Where is Abel, thy brother?"

And he said: "I know not [*lo' yada'ti*]; am I my brother's keeper
[*hashomer 'achi 'anokhi*]?"

And He said: "What hast thou done? Listen, thy brother's blood cries
unto me from the ground." (4:9–10)

24. In this expansive rendering of *vayo'mer,* I follow Cassuto's reading, for which he argues cogently (*Commentary,* 213–15). However, little is lost to the argument by leaving the text in its original
opacity. It is important that Cain *said something* to Abel, indicating premeditation; it is not important to know exactly what he said.

25. The word for "field," *sadeh,* denotes uncultivated and uninhabited land, away from human
habitation. It is the home of the wild animals (the "beasts of the field"; 2:19) and the scene of human
crime. That Cain slew Abel *in the wild,* rather than in the cultivated fields, may be taken as small evidence against the view that Cain was offering Abel as a blood sacrifice to the earth goddess, in the
cause of his farming.

God does not begin with an accusation or an assertion, but like both a good teacher and a good investigator, with a question, and with a question that requires Cain to confront himself in his brotherliness: Your brother, Abel, your young playmate, out of the same womb—why is he not at your side? Where is he?

Cain denies knowledge of Abel's whereabouts. Though an analytic philosopher or White House lawyer might try to argue that Cain's speech was true—for where indeed is the soul of Abel now?—Cain, to protect himself, lies to God (or if you prefer, to his newly aroused conscience), but not to himself. Indeed, to keep the inquisitive voice from forcing him to fully confront the meaning of his deed, he answers the question with a question, no doubt tinged with indignation and even mocking: Why are you asking *me*? Am I supposed to be his guardian?[26] *You*, you who liked his sacrifice, you who made him prosper—aren't *you* his keeper? Why don't you know where he is? And (implicitly) what kind of a guardian are *you*?

God (or conscience) is not deceived. On the contrary, He treats Cain's question, with its blatant disregard for brother Abel's whereabouts, as tantamount to a confession. Fully understood, "Am I my brother's keeper?" turns out, in fact, to be the maxim of a would-be murderer, an expression of fratricidal intent. For to deny responsibility for your brother is, tacitly, to profess indifference to his fate. To care not at all about his existence and welfare is to be tacitly guilty of all harm that befalls him: in short, to say yes even to his death and disappearance. Thus, taking Cain's counteroffensive to be a tacit admission of guilt, God puts the well-timed question to Cain: "What have you done?" Of course I know where Abel is. I have heard *your* brother's spilled blood crying out unto Me from the earth. How could you have done such a thing to your *brother*?

Thanks to the awesome intervention of the transcendent voice, the enormity of his deed is now borne in on Cain (and on the reader). The manifest fragility of human life and, especially, the image of the screaming blood of his brother awakens Cain's horror, and ours; a protoreligious dread accompanies this picture of violent death. Very likely, guilt wells up in response to the accusation implied by the screams, as does pity for his fallen brother. Here, at last, the meaning of brotherhood is disclosed, but only through confronting the murdered brother's blood: "thy brother's blood" is the same as yours. Even the murderer cannot but be moved. Not just the will of Abel, but the cosmos itself has been violated; the crime is a crime against "blood"—against both life and kin; the

---

26. In the domain of shepherding, the *shomer* is the keeper of the feedlot, the one who tends the sheep when they are not out grazing. Using this sense of the term, Cain is asking contemptuously, "Am I the shepherd's shepherd?" (I owe this observation to Father Paul Mankowski.)

whole earth, polluted and stained with bloodshed, cries in anguish and for retribution. We anticipate precisely God's next remarks.

"And now cursed art thou from the ground,[27] which hath opened her mouth to receive thy brother's blood from thy hand. When thou tillest the ground, it shall not henceforth yield unto thee her strength; a fugitive and a wanderer shalt thou be in the earth." (4:11–12)

The earth that supports life, now defiled by life's wanton destruction—watered not by rain but by blood, shed by the farmer's hand—becomes an alien place for the murderer. The world is arranged so that murder will not go unnoticed; it will also not go unanswered. The earth shall resist the murderer's plow; nowhere on earth shall he find a comfortable place to settle, both because no one else will welcome him and because his conscience and his fears will give him no rest. A man who has once shed blood knows—as he could not know before— the deep truth of the human condition: he knows in his marrow that his own life hangs by a thread, that he lives, as it were, by the grace of God. Despite the fact that God does not exact the fitting specific (capital) punishment for his murder—as there is yet no law against it, there can be no exact punishment (see Genesis 9:6 and Exodus 21:12)—Cain is nonetheless thrown into despair.

And Cain said unto the Lord, "My punishment [*or* my sin: *'avoni*] is greater than I can bear. Behold, Thou hast driven me out this day from the face of the earth; *and from Thy face shall I be hid;* and I shall be a fugitive and a wanderer in the earth; and it shall come to pass that *everyone that findeth me shall slay me.*" (4:13–14; emphasis added)

Cain's fears lead him to exaggerate the punishment. He understands— mistakenly—that he is banished from the whole earth and that, in wandering, he will be out of sight of the divine protection, exposed to predators not unlike himself, men who will kill him for gain or for sport. Cain, the farmer, the man who sought security in settlement and possession of a portion of the earth, feels utterly bereft at the prospect of wandering—of living

---

27. The preposition here translated "from" could also be translated "by" or "of" or even "more than"; Rashi reads that Cain is now cursed *more than* the ground, the ground having been cursed for man's sake at the end of the Eden story (3:17). This translation, "cursed more than the ground," could also fit with the interpretation (discussed earlier in this chapter) that sees farmer Cain as serving and sacrificing to the earth. On this reading, the earth is here cursed for opening its "mouth" to drink in the blood of brother Abel—the blood that now cries out from the ground. The complicit blood-drinking earth is cursed, but the guilty blood-shedding Cain is cursed more.

an open life such as that of his brother, Abel. Believing that God defends only those who are settled and established—after all, God was apparently not able to protect Abel out in the fields—Cain fears for his life once he is forced to roam about among uncivilized men.

God directly addresses Cain's fear of violent death:

> And the Lord said unto him, "Therefore, whosoever slayeth Cain, vengeance shall be taken on him sevenfold." And the Lord set a mark upon Cain, lest any finding him should slay him. (4:15)

The mark of Cain—wrongly regarded as the sign of murderous guilt—is, in fact, meant to protect Cain's life in the wilderness, and to obviate the need for settled defense. As a result of this solicitous speech, Cain may at this moment glimpse the difference between a god to whom one sacrifices vegetables and the God who takes notice of, and who is outraged by, bloodshed (and who, at least for now, provides even for murderers). But moved more by dread than by reverence, Cain does not draw the most pious conclusion. Reassured but only temporarily, Cain sets out on his travels.

CAIN'S SECOND SAILING: A CITY OF ONE'S OWN

> And Cain went out from the presence of the Lord, and dwelt in the land of Nod, on the east of Eden. (4:16)

Heading backward toward the garden, longing perhaps for its safety and comfort, Cain comes to the land of Nod—literally, the land of "wandering"—and he *settles* there! Though he is in the place of wanderers, Cain refuses to wander. He lacks trust—in nature, in God, and in his fellow human beings. He would rather rely on his wits and his own flesh and blood to sustain and defend him. These he trusts because these he knows.

> And Cain knew his wife,[28] and she conceived, and bore Enoch; and he builded a city, and called the name of the city after the name of his son, Enoch. (4:17)

28. On a literalist-historical reading of the text, there is no woman mentioned (other than Eve) who might be eligible to be the wife of Cain. This silence leads to unpleasant inferences, the most palatable of which is brother-sister incest with (unmentioned) daughters of Eve. Silently, the text may be hinting that, at the human beginning, incest may be unavoidable. (My wife was kicked out of Sunday school at an early age for asking about the wife of Cain.) But read anthropologically, rather than historically, Cain is the human prototype: farmer, fratricide, and founder of the first city, in defense of his own. *That* he had a wife (and descendants), not where she came from or who she was, is what we here need to know.

Having broken his ties to his origins, now alone, vulnerable, and without refuge, Cain deals with his predicament by looking to the future. Aware of the prospect of violent death, he takes out insurance. Knowing his wife, Cain fathers a son, a son named Enoch, meaning "to initiate or discipline; to dedicate or train up." Cain initiates a family to which he will dedicate himself, a family that he will discipline and train up in the ways of dedication. Unlike the later (and precociously modern) city of Babel, whose builders seek a name for themselves here and now, the city Cain builds is dedicated to the name of his son. The city is almost certainly founded on the fear of death and with a view to safety.

The Hebrew word for "city," 'iyr, comes from a root meaning "to watch" and "to wake." In the first instance, a city is a place guarded by a wakeful watch; it is not the market or the shrine but the watchtower or outpost that first makes a city a city. Though Cain retains his pride (in his son), his confidence has been tempered by fear. But civilization as it comes into being, starting from his founding act, is tainted: the city is founded in fear of violent death, but first, in fratricide. This taint, one must believe, is, from the Bible's point of view, inherent in civilization as such. We follow its emergence in the hope of learning why and how it may be defective.

> And unto Enoch was born Irad [meaning "fugitive"];
> and Irad begot Mehujael [meaning "smitten of God" or "seer of God"];
> and Mehujael begot Methushael [meaning "man who is of God"];
> and Methushael begot Lamech [meaning is obscure].
> And Lamech took unto him two wives:
> the name of one was Adah [meaning "ornament"];
> and the name of the other Zillah [meaning "shadow" or "defense"].
> And Adah bore Jabal [from a root meaning "to flow, to lead, to bring
>   forth"]:
> he was the father of such as dwell in tents and of such as have cattle.
> And his brother's name was Jubal [same root as for Jabal]:
> he was the father of all such as handle the harp and pipe.
> And Zillah, she also bore Tubal-Cain [meaning unclear; perhaps "Tubal
>   the smith"], the instructor of every artificer in brass and iron;
> and the sister of Tubal-Cain was Naamah [meaning "pleasantness"].
>   (4:18–22)

Our attention is focused on Lamech, the seventh—the completed or fulfilled—generation of the line (through Cain) begun by Adam. It is in this generation that civilization flowers. With one wife an ornament, the other a shadowy protector, Lamech has children who teach men how to protect and adorn themselves: tents, fixed habitations against the elements and for protection of privacy; cattle, a new form of wealth;[29] music, the arts of memory and song; and metallurgy, the transformative art of forging tools and also weapons. Human beings, now externally well equipped, undergo coincident changes in their souls. In particular, vanity—the desire to be well regarded by those around—grows to dangerous proportions. Mankind now truly displays the passions and the conduct so well described by Rousseau in the passage quoted earlier: "[E]veryone punishing the contempt shown him in a manner proportionate to the stock he set by himself, vengeance became terrible, and men bloodthirsty and cruel."

> And Lamech said unto his wives, Adah and Zillah, "Hear my voice; ye wives of Lamech, hearken unto my speech; for I have slain a man to my wounding, and a young man to my bruising. If Cain shall be avenged sevenfold, truly Lamech seventy and sevenfold." (4:23–24)

Lamech combines poetry and prowess in his own person; he sings (the Hebrew is in high poetic style) his own exploits in fighting, and boasts of his great superiority, ten times greater than Cain's, greater even than God in vengeance.[30] Lamech's mention of Cain shows the presence of a historical sense, which the muse puts into a mythic past presumably already familiar to his wives and others. Yet Lamech irreverently looks down on the past and prefers his own time and his own great deeds.[31] Lamech, a combination Achilles and Homer, belongs to the peak of the Heroic Age, made possible by the arts, especially music and metallurgy;[32] he seeks nothing less than immortal fame, not to say apotheosis, by being master of life and death.

29. The word translated "cattle," *miqneh*, means "something bought," "something acquired and possessed," especially livestock.

30. Lamech's claims are not quite clear. Most translators have him taking fatal revenge on men who merely wounded or bruised him. But Cassuto, in his usual careful analysis of the precise wording, argues that it is Lamech who is doing the wounding and bruising. So great is his strength, his mere taps proved fatal: "A man I slew, as soon as I bruised [him]." In either case, Lamech boasts in song of his prowess in killing his enemies.

31. One might see here the germ of the idea of progress, the view that the present is always better than the past. (I owe this observation and the one about Lamech's contempt for the past to Yuval Levin.)

32. Sacks argues that Lamech's deeds are not dependent on these arts, which presuppose an earlier heroic past, necessary if civilization is to follow. "Hence, [civilization] cannot begin until the most impressive acts of the past have been raised to the level of the heroic. Consequently, the poet must praise arts which, were it not for his poetry, would appear as merely violent." ("The Lion and the Ass," Chapters 1–10, 75) Sacks may well be right about the order—Lamech is older than the inventors, his sons; still poetry presupposes song (the Muses) and the Heroic Age usually involved the sword and shield, made with metals.

FRATRICIDE AND FOUNDING:
THE TWISTED ROOTS OF CIVILIZATION

We are now in a position to pull together some threads, connecting the deeds of Cain and the civilization that rests upon them. Concerned with his position as number one, eager to establish himself as lord and master of his domain, Cain (like Romulus, the mythic founder of Rome) commits the paradigmatic crime of the political founder: fratricide. For the aspiration to supremacy and rule entails necessarily the denial and destruction of radical human equality, epitomized in the relationship of brotherhood. To wish to rule, to dominate, to be in command, means—by its very nature—the wish not only to remove all rivals but also to destroy the brotherly relation with those under one's dominion. The ruler, as ruler, has no brothers.

The more that rude and ambitious men have to do with one another, the more they both need to fear and seek to outdo one another. For both reasons— safety and pride—they cultivate prowess in fighting. They build city walls to protect them from their enemies; but the existence of walls creates new enmities and invites attack. The city begun in fear proudly begets one of heroic ambition. There is a direct line from the plowshare to the sword.

As we will see even more clearly later on, when we come to the city and tower of Babel, the Bible in its beginning takes sides in an ancient quarrel about the origin and goodness of the city and civilization. According to the more optimistic view, the city is rooted in need and comes to be by a process of natural growth, beginning with the household, then the tribe, then the village, then the merging of several villages to form the city. According to Aristotle, the city is the first truly self-sufficient community; it comes into being for the sake of life, but it exists for the sake of living well. According to the more pessimistic view, shared by the Bible, the city is rooted in fear, greed, pride, violence, and the desire for domination. These questionable beginnings continue to infect civilization as such. In addition, the city's aspiration to self-sufficiency is highly problematic. This, too, our story makes plain.

But the context of the story of Cain is not simply political. Cain was jealous over a matter of *divine* favor. He was the first to be interested in bridging the gap—in his case, by gifts—between the human and the divine, an impulse we have shown to be largely presumptuous or hubristic. This prototypical human being begets a line leading to civilization, the arts, and the heroes—all manifestations of an impulse toward self-sufficiency, an impulse that culminates in a desire to jump the gap entirely, in a wish to *become* a god. Lamech, the hero, acts as if he has succeeded; but we, readers prepared by what has come before, know that he is self-deceived.

For Eve, bearing a child may satisfy the human desire for immortality; "creating" life may satisfy the human wish to be as God.[33] But her man-child Cain and his male descendants have to seek such satisfactions by other means, not by giving life but by threatening it, especially in heroic encounters. Cain and Lamech are neither the last nor the greatest of those who pursue the heroic option.[34] But as Robert Sacks notes, the Bible wastes no time in calling attention to the problem their conduct represents:

> The *prima facie* opposition to the arts on the part of the Bible is fundamentally connected with its opposition to the heroic, and hence to polytheism. The heroic cannot be praised as such if there is no possibility for jumping the gap between the human and the divine. The quest for apotheosis and its ultimate failure is the most fundamental root of Greek tragedy, but without the figure of Hercules looming somewhere in the remote past, a man who had actually achieved the status of a god, the attempt itself could never be viewed as tragic. It would be no more than foolish, not sinful in the deepest sense.
>
> The same is true of those pagan myths with which our author might have been familiar. Gilgamesh's attempt to achieve the status of a god was deeply rooted in his knowledge that the god, Utnapishtim, had once been a man like himself—that apotheosis was possible.
>
> The Biblical rejection of polytheism, in part, means the Biblical rejection of apotheosis. . . . Unfortunately, too many commentators fail to understand the Bible because they assume that the objections to polytheism are clear and simple. . . . By operating within the prejudice of the absolute superiority of monotheism, many authors tend to overlook the reasons offered by the Bible for that superiority.

The present story—of Cain and Abel, and the line of Cain to Lamech—does not explicitly give the reasons for rejecting paganism; but it surely paints a vivid picture of the bloody indecency connected with the way of Cain and the pursuit of self-sufficiency and heroism. The elements of the human soul that lead in this direction are shown to be, to say the least, problematic. So too our much vaunted knowledge of good and bad. Seeing something of himself in the mirror of this story, the reader is stimulated to hope that there is an alternative to the all-too-human way of Cain.

33. This natural pride of woman is easily treated, as we will see in subsequent stories. Three of the four Israelite matriarchs, Sarah, Rebekah, and Rachel, are for a long time barren. When their children finally arrive, they do not boast of their own creative prowess.

34. Heroism is the explicit theme of the next chapter.

A New Beginning

The menacing outcome of the line of Cain—the line of pride, presumption, violence, the arts of death, and the desire for apotheosis—begs for another way. We are not disappointed. The story ends as it began, with a new birth.

And Adam knew his wife again; and she bore a son, and called his name Seth [*sheth*]: "for God hath appointed [*shath*] me another seed instead of Abel; for Cain slew him." And to Seth, to him also there was born a son; and he called his name Enosh; *then began men to call upon the name of the Lord.* (4:25–26, emphasis added)

Though the description echoes closely the birth of Cain, there are crucial differences. No longer boastful, Eve is, instead, subdued. The death of Abel hangs heavily upon her, as does the fact that it was Cain, her pride and joy (but now also lost to her), who slew him. Chastened regarding also her own pride in Cain's birth, she feels only gratitude in the birth of Seth. She feels the beneficence of powers beyond her, here manifested in the birth of a much wanted replacement—explicitly a replacement for Abel, but in fact a replacement for both her sons. Seth, unlike Cain, is received as a gift—from beyond, precious, unmerited. Seth, unlike Cain, will be less likely to suffer from excessive parental expectations. Tragedy has humbled parental pride; woman and man no longer stand as creators and claimants upon the world, but as grateful recipients of the blessings of new life.

To Seth also is born a son, whom he names Enosh, a name that means "man" understood as *mortal*—a meaning less dignified than *'adam* ("man" understood as from the earth, *'adamah*). Enosh, mortal man, in the line of Seth, corresponds to Enoch, disciplined dedication, in the line of Cain: the greater modesty of the new beginning is evident in the names. No longer disciplined in trying to jump the gap between man and god, the line of Seth is marked near its start by the memory of death—Abel's—and by the recognition of the difference between mortal man and immortal God.

In keeping with this new recognition, "men"—or at least *some* men—"began to call upon the name of the Lord." How they called or what they said the text keeps inaudible—in sharp contrast to the loud vauntings of Lamech, or even to the explicit report of the goods brought in sacrifice by Cain and Abel. True, there remains a more than residual presumption in calling upon God—as if He should care for me—and, more so, in the familiarity of calling Him *by name.*[35]

---

35. "Calling upon the Lord" is different from "calling upon the *name* of the Lord." Yet it is hard to know how one could call on the Lord if not by calling Him by name.

But at the same time, we have what seems like a spontaneous calling out—springing from the heart without calculation—probably out of need and fear, perhaps also out of longing or respect or awe. Recognizing the distinction between man and God and mindful of the gap between them, Seth, Enosh, and their kin call out across it empty-handed, hoping someone will listen. Thanks to this effort, mankind is now meaningfully divided into those who do and those who do not seek communication with the Lord. Of God's response, we know nothing. But we cannot help but think that some progress has been made: the new approach to the divine proceeds through speech and hearing, not through gifts of food that we hope God might fancy. Someone seems to have divined that it is not through material means—nor through pride of place or acquisition—that man can hope to stand in fitting relation to God. Someone seems to have divined that—more than the arts and sciences, power, and prosperity—decent human life and human relations require such a reverent and attentive orientation to the divine.

Even a civilized and sophisticated reader, living in the twenty-first century, cannot dismiss such reflections. Chastened by this profound tale that mirrors the dark recesses of our own souls and that exposes the dark and violent origins of the human city, we are ready to read on and to receive further instruction.

CHAPTER FIVE

DEATH, BEAUTIFUL WOMEN, AND THE HEROIC TEMPTATION: THE RETURN OF CHAOS AND THE FLOOD

*T*he Bible's picture of human nature, conveyed through its first stories of human life, is, to say the least, sobering. The tales of the primordial family underline the dangers of freedom and reason, speech and desire, pride and shame, jealousy and anger. They force us to acknowledge the explosive tensions lurking in any human family, both between husband and wife and (especially) between siblings. They alert us to the morally questionable origin and meaning of the human city and make us suspicious not only about politics and the arts, but even about man's interest in the divine. Although the last chapter ended on a hopeful note, with the birth of Seth and a seemingly improved attitude toward God, the sequel shows that we have not yet exposed fully the roots of our human troubles. What follows Cain and Abel is the story of the Flood.

Almost everyone has heard of Noah's ark. Indeed, the story of the Flood is among the most famous tales in Genesis, second only to the story of the Garden of Eden. But comparatively little attention is paid to the events that led up to the Flood or to the reasons why God might have caused it. This is, in a way, not surprising, for the text is rather stingy with explanatory material. Having dropped the curtain on the violent tragedy of Cain and Abel, and advertised a new beginning in the promising birth of Seth, Genesis turns cheerfully to report the gentle increase in humankind, through the many "begat's" from Adam to Noah. Then, with virtually no warning, we learn that "the wickedness of man was great in the earth" and that "the Lord repented that He had made man" and all the other terrestrial animals (6:5–7). What happened? How and why did things turn out so badly?

The only intervening material between the gentle genealogy (of Genesis 5) and God's decision to send the Flood are a few highly enigmatic verses (6:1–4) about the sons of God, the daughters of men, the Nephilim (or so-called giants), and the mighty men of renown. If these verses are to provide the answer, we need to read them fully in context. We must start farther back, taking the story from its beginning.

The relevant beginning is, in fact, the "book of the generations of man ['*adam*]," [1] that superficially boring chapter (Genesis 5) filled with nothing but ten generations of "begat's." This is, indeed, a third and wholly new creation story, distinct in content and form both from the cosmological account of Genesis 1 and from the paradigmatic story of the prototypical human beings, Adam and Eve and sons (Genesis 2:4–4:26). This third version, a purely human creation story in which God plays almost no role, tells how the human race descended and grew from its first ancestor. On its face, it is a story of success and flourishing, with mankind finally reaping the blessing of increase that was pronounced in the first chapter: "Be fruitful and multiply." But as we shall see, there is a worm in the family tree, and it makes a catastrophic world of difference.

The beginning of this new account of human origins, in fact, repeats and unites the most promising notes from each of the two preceding stories. From the first, it echoes the God-created and god-like status of man, from the second, it retains the birth of Seth as an alternative to the dangerous line of Cain.

> This is the book of the generations of Man ['*adam*].
> In the day that God ['*elohim*] created man ['*adam*], in the likeness of God
>   made He him;
> male and female created He them, and blessed them
> and called their [!] name man ['*adam*] in the day they were created.
> And Man ['*adam*] lived a hundred and thirty years,
> and begot a son in his own likeness, after his image;
> and called his name Seth.
> And the days of Man ['*adam*] after he begot Seth were eight hundred
>   years
> and he begot sons and daughters.
> And all the days of Man ['*adam*] were nine hundred and thirty years and
>   he died. (5:1–5)

---

1. I follow Robert Sacks in translating the Hebrew '*adam* as "man," human being. Adam is *not*, in the biblical text, a *proper* name (unlike "Eve," a proper name given to woman by the man). God does not name him Adam; on the contrary, He names *both* the male and the female '*adam* (5:2). Neither does man name himself Adam the way he names the woman Eve. Throughout this chapter, I will for convenience sometimes speak of Adam as if this were his name (see, for instance, the next sentence). But readers should be aware of the lack of justification for doing so.

This is as good a place as any to express my debt to Robert Sacks for my understanding of Genesis 5. It was he who first told me the anthropological secret buried in what looked like mere genealogy.

The story begins with echoes of Genesis 1. We are reminded that God created man, both male and female, in His own likeness, that He blessed them (both for fecundity and for rule over the animals), and that He named *them* "man," that is, *human* beings. Man *('adam)*, who was blessed with many sons and daughters, became a father of record (in *this* story) at age 130, when he begot—guess who?—*Seth*, not Cain, his firstborn in the previous story, who is entirely forgotten in this new account.[2] Seth, it seems, and not Cain, was the son begot in Man's likeness and image, and hence, derivatively, in the likeness (once removed) of God. The story thus begins by ratifying the hopes raised in the immediate antecedent (4:25–26), which had announced the birth of Seth, humbly and gratefully received, and the first human attempts to call on the name of the Lord. In addition, in this third creation story, the harsh life forecast for Man (in the second story) is not mentioned, nor is his death untimely. Father Adam, though he does eventually die, lives to a mighty old age, forty-six score and ten, a span of years virtually equal to that which runs from the Norman Conquest (1066) to the present day.

The line of ten generations from Adam to Noah begs to be compared to the seven generations from Cain to the sons of Lamech—Jabal, Jubal, and Tubal-Cain (4:17–22). Many of the names are strikingly similar, and two are even identical: Cain-Cainan, Enoch-Enoch, Irad-Iared, Mehujael-Mahalalel, Methushael-Methushalah, Lamech-Lamech. Yet the similarity ends with the names. The line of Cain is self-reliant; it boasts the first city, inventors of the arts, and a man (Lamech) who proudly sings his triumphs in dispensing violent death. The line of Adam and Seth, simpler and gentler, contains no inventors or warriors; and its most distinguished members are somehow closer to God: Seth's Enoch[3] walked with God (5:22); and Seth's Lamech, in naming his son Noah, remembers the Lord, accepts the mortal lot He has cast for men, and takes comfort in birth and renewal (5:29).[4] It may be too much to claim that the line of Seth is pious and God-fearing, especially when its

2. Like his mother, Eve, who is also not mentioned here, Cain will not appear again in the Hebrew Bible. Cain, the pride of his proud mother, and the proud mother herself are both remembered as belonging to a human beginning that deserves to be forgotten. Observing the absence of Eve, we notice also that this new lineage lists the names only of the male begetters. Though all the progeny are, no doubt, still born of woman, no woman's name is mentioned. As we shall see, the point of this chapter provides a reason for the male-centered character of this account, and especially regarding the commemoration of names.

3. Cain's Enoch carries the name of Cain's city, built in defiance of God's decree (or prophecy) that Cain be a wanderer.

4. In this last respect, Seth's Lamech resembles Adam when he names his wife Eve, celebrating her generative powers in the face of the dreary prospect of future toil and death that God had just announced (3:17–20). See Chapter Three, p. 117.

members are compared, say, to Abraham or Moses. But compared to the line
of Cain, the greater modesty and lack of impious pride are clearly evident.
And the men in Seth's line flourish: except for Enoch, whom God takes at
age 365, all the firstborn before Lamech live between 895 and 969 years
(Methushalah); Lamech lives a triply perfect 777 years.

To discover the worm in the family tree, we must read with a magnifying
glass—and with a timeline and calculator. Because the text reports the lives of
these antediluvians in sequence—chronicling each man's birth, the number of
years he lived before and after begetting his first son, his life span, and his
death—the complacent reader does not notice that there is more than a half
century (between the year 874, in which Lamech is born, and the year 930, in
which Adam dies) during which *all nine generations of human beings,* from
Adam to Lamech, *are alive at the same time,* with all their myriad descendants.
Then, suddenly, in the year 930, Adam drops dead. Next, in 987 (readers can do
the calculations for themselves), Enoch "was not, for God took him." And in
1042, Seth also dies. Readers of the Garden of Eden story need no longer remain
in suspense: the prophecy of human mortality ("you shall surely die"; 2:17) is, at
long last, fatally—and fatefully—fulfilled. Indeed, this may well be the purpose
of reciting the entire genealogy in all its numerological detail: to prepare the
wisdom-seeking reader to learn, in the sequel, how human beings—especially
the men—react to the discovery of their unavoidable finitude. For with the
death of Adam, and after nearly a millennium of "immortal" human existence,
natural death has entered the human world.

Cain's act of murder had shown that death might occur by violence, but not
that death was necessary by nature. And even this knowledge of the possibility of
violent death was confined to the line of Cain, with whom the line of Seth (according to the present chapter) does not yet have contact.[5] The deaths of Adam
and Seth must have shattered men's expectations and sent them reeling.

How exactly men took this discovery of their own impending deaths we
shall consider in a moment. But we note first the special place of Noah. Noah,
born in 1056, is the first man born into the world after Adam dies. Noah is
therefore the first man who could have no direct contact with the first man
and, therefore, with a living memory of the Garden of Eden and its prospect
of immortal life. More important, Noah is the first man who enters a world in

5. We should remember that both the prophecy of mortality and the murder belong to the second
creation story. Therefore, though the reader is meant to remember them, it is not proper, strictly
speaking, to use these facts in interpreting the present story. Be that as it may, the presence of natural
death as a constitutive feature of human life is made manifest for the first time only in this (purely)
genealogical narrative. In contrast, the life spans—and the *deaths*—of the descendants of Cain
(4:17–22) were not mentioned.

which death is already present, the first man who grows up knowing about death, knowing that he must die. For Noah unlike for his predecessors, mortality is a received part of the human condition: thus, Noah (not Adam or Cain) is the prototype of self-consciously mortal man. Fittingly, the name that Noah carries, received from his father, Lamech, means both "comfort" and "lament," a perfect name for new life seen in the light of inevitable death. These facts may explain, in part, why Noah would, uniquely, later find grace in the eyes of the Lord.

In the meantime, the rest of mankind goes boldly and heroically wild. Who can blame them? It is no stretch to imagine that having lived within a deathless horizon, living as if they were immortals, these oldest of men, explicitly god-like ("image of God") in their origin and nature, not only are shocked by the belated discovery of their own unavoidable mortality; they are offended and angry. They closely resemble the Homeric heroes, descendants of gods, obsessed with the affront to their god-like dignity that was their mortality. Rather than wait for death to find them hiding away in a corner, they go forth, beautifully clad, to meet it face-to-face, in the person of another death-defying warrior, who also defends himself against death by his own prowess alone. The desire for immortality is transmuted into the desire for glory—immortal fame—earned on the field of battle, in combat against equal or superior opponents. Each victory is a triumph—partial and temporary, to be sure, but nonetheless a triumph—over death, a victory not only self-consciously enjoyed but also acknowledged in defeat by the equally heroic opponent whom one kills, a victory afterward sung by the poet in beautiful verses for generations to come. Of such stuff are heroes made, and especially among those closest to the immortals. Says Sarpedon, the mortal son of Zeus, to Glaukos, on the threshold of combat:

> "Man, supposing you and I, escaping this battle,
> would be able to live on forever, ageless, immortal,
> so neither would I myself go on fighting in the foremost
> nor would I urge you into the fighting where men win glory.
> But now, seeing that the spirits of death stand close about us
> in their thousands, no man can turn aside nor escape them,
> let us go on and win glory for ourselves, or yield it to others."

Death is the mother of the love of glory, of a beautiful name for splendid deeds.

Death is also—and similarly—the mother of beauty, of a concern with the beautification of an ugly world, fated to decay, rife with death. In the face of death, artful men create beautiful objects—statues and paintings, poems and songs, vases and temples—objects that they hope will last, immune to decay as

their makers are not. In the face of death, manly men also notice and admire—
often acquisitively—the natural beauty of beautiful women. As we learn from
Homer, just as Ares, the god of war, lusts for Aphrodite, the goddess of beauty,
so the warrior heroes pursue and prize their beautiful women. The love of
Helen and the love of glory are twin faces of heroic ambition. Given the resonance of this heroic archetype among cultures on every branch of the human
family tree, from Japanese samurai to the characters of the Bhagavadgita, there
is no reason to believe that this conjunction is peculiarly Greek rather than peculiarly human.

Armed with these thoughts about death, heroes, and the love of beauty, we
are now equipped to investigate the cryptic biblical verses, looking for the reasons behind the Flood.

> And it came to pass, when men [*literally* the man: *ha'adam*]
> began to multiply on the face of the earth,
> and daughters were born unto them,
> that the sons of God [*beney ha'elohim*]
> saw
> the daughters of men [*literally,* the man: *benoth ha'adam*]
> that they were fair [*literally,* good: *tovoth*];
> and they took [*vayiqchu*] them wives
> whomsoever they chose. (6:1–2)

The troubles start as a consequence of population growth. When men begin to
multiply all over the face of the earth, people necessarily begin to live near one
another. Separate families and tribes now regularly meet. As the text emphasizes
("and daughters were born unto them"), the most important consequences of
these new contacts has to do with daughters. Men begin to notice women from
other tribes, and to notice them for their beauty ("that they were fair"). We, the
readers, are asked to notice not only the daughters but also the men who are
struck with their beauty and who take to themselves as wives whichever ones
they please. Reading with hindsight, in the light of the ensuing wickedness, we
must consider that the root of the trouble is the male attitude toward other
people's daughters, and in particular, its connection to the love of beauty. Appreciation of beauty is one thing, desire to possess it is another. Appreciation
may be shared without diminishing anyone's portion, whereas possession is exclusive. When the object of desire is not a beautiful necklace or a beautiful vase
but a beautiful woman, and when winning and losing her are also a matter of
pride and self-esteem (especially in men of the heroic temper), erotic interest in

the beautiful is hardly conducive to tranquillity.[6] Indeed, jealousy and competition over beautiful women are surely sufficient causes of bloodshed (remember Helen and the Trojan War), especially among proud men who are newly obsessed with the insult that is their own unavoidable mortality.

But our text points to additional complexities that surely bear on the outcome. The pursuit of beautiful daughters occurs across—and hence intermixes—distinct tribal lines: it is "the sons of God" who come to notice "the daughters of men," and who take them as wives. Identifying these two groupings is no easy task. Some learned commentators argue that the sons of God are superhuman beings, for example, demigods or angels or mythic heroes of the sort known in other traditions (and whom, some add, the Bible introduces here only to let them be drowned in the Flood). But the biblical text does not speak of any such creatures. Furthermore, given the local context, a simpler and more reasonable assumption (also favored by many traditional commentators) is that the two lines that meet and merge are the line of Seth (Genesis 5) and the line of Cain (Genesis 4). But which is which?

Some evidence can be adduced that it is the line of Cain that are the sons of God and the line of Seth that carries the daughters of men. For example, Robert Sacks mounts an ingenious argument based on the parallel names in the genealogies of Seth and Cain and on the fact that the line from Adam and Seth to Noah is introduced by the chapter heading "This is the book of the generations of Man ['adam]." The line of Cain includes some mighty men—beney ha'elohim, translated "sons of God," could also mean "sons of the mighty"— and it would be characteristic of heroes (like Cain's Lamech) to find and seize the beautiful daughters, almost as trophies. In contrast, the line of Seth contains Enosh (whose name means "mortal"), and it alone mentions the deaths of men, suggesting that this is the line of mortals, not gods or sons of gods. And apropos the identity of the daughters of men, it is only in the generations of Seth that we hear constantly of the birth of daughters; daughters, reminders of birth and hence of man's dependence on woman, were not mentioned in the line of Cain, the line that sought god-like self-sufficiency.

---

6. Rousseau (in a passage already cited in Chapter Three) has elegantly illuminated this "new" anthropological element, in all its moral ambiguity:

Young people of the opposite sex . . . grow accustomed to attend to different objects and to make comparisons; imperceptibly they acquire *ideas of merit and of beauty* which produce sentiments of preference. The more they *see* one another, the less they can do without *seeing* one another still more. A tender and sweet sentiment steals into the soul, and *at the least obstacle becomes an impetuous frenzy; jealousy awakens with love; Discord triumphs,* and the gentlest of all passions receives *sacrifices of human blood.*

But there is equal if not greater evidence on the other side.[7] Though it is true that the line of Seth is given in "the book of the generations of Man ['*adam*]," this text (as already noted) twice makes clear the connection of Man with God: Man is made in the likeness of '*elohim* and is created by '*elohim* (5:1). Further, Man begets Seth in *his* image and likeness: Seth is thus a likeness of a likeness of God. (Earlier, in the previous story, Seth had been named with explicit reference to God: '*elohim* "appointed" the seed for Seth, as a replacement for Abel; 4:25.) In contrast, the line of Cain, reviewed in the previous chapter, makes not even the slightest reference to God; humanist through and through, it is characterized by pride, the city, and the arts, in pursuit of full self-sufficiency. The men of the line of Seth, as already noted, are certainly not high, mighty, and proud—at least until the death of Adam.[8] Moreover, while daughters are mentioned in the line of Seth, the arts of adornment—artificial beautification—belong to the line of Cain. In sum, this reading suggests that the more god-like sons of the line of Adam and Seth, their world now shattered due to the death of Adam and Seth, are drawn to and seduced by the (perhaps merely artificial) beauty of the daughters of the line of Cain.

Yet in the end, it may make little difference whether we conclude (with Sacks) that the mighty descendants of Cain began mixing with the naturally beautiful daughters of the line of Seth or (with Abravanel) that the less impious sons of Seth began mixing with the adorned daughters of the line of Cain. Either way, the result is mixed marriage, with an illicit mixing of the god-like and the human, leading to the corruption of one by the other. The sons of God are led by their eyes toward visible feminine beauty. Who can blame them? Throughout the animal world, nature uses superficial looks (along with every other appeal that the senses can distinguish, from mating calls to aromas to pheromones) to bring the sexes together, in order to accomplish the great work of procreation. The love of the beautiful takes on still greater importance for human beings, especially as we become mindful of death and necessary decay. The beautiful lures us into regarding it as a bulwark against death, a haven from the ugliness of dis-

7. I am much indebted to the researches and arguments of Daniel Meron, whose superb paper for my Genesis course in 1987 ("The Sons of God and the Daughters of Man: A Commentary on Genesis 6:1–4") has persuaded me to favor this point of view. Meron himself begins from a similar suggestion by Isaac Abravanel, the great Jewish sage of the fifteenth century.

8. The most prominent points of comparison include Cain and Seth—the meaning of their names and the naming of their children—and the differences between the two Lamechs, Cain's Lamech boasting of his superiority to God in vengeance, Seth's Lamech accepting the human condition laid down by God. Also consider the two Enochs: Cain's is connected with the city, Seth's walked with and was taken by God. (Enoch means "disciplined" or "educated"; "walked" means walked around, zigzagging. Thus Abravanel: "God took him before he got too educated." Isaac Abravanel, *Perush 'Al Hatorah* [Jerusalem: Benei Arbael, 1964], commentary on Genesis 5.)

integration. The beautiful beckons, promising permanence and happiness: the beautiful seems to us to be the skin of the good. Yet appearances are often deceiving on the side of both viewer and viewed. Imagination, colored by human hopes, often distorts what we see. Beauty may exist only in the eye of the beholder, while artful beautification hides underlying plainness or worse: beauty may be even less than skin deep.

Even apart from such distortions, the pursuit of the beautiful may be altogether a dead end. Appreciation of the beautiful may inspire the soul, but efforts to capture it leave one unfulfilled—even when seemingly successful. For what do we really have if and when we "possess" the beautiful? Can a beautiful wife really satisfy our soul's longings for the eternal or the good? Does union with a beautiful woman make us any less ugly or any less perishable?

The visibly beautiful, through its harmonious and well-proportioned appearance, always seems to promise some underlying goodness. Were it able to deliver on its promise, the love of the beautiful might bring us to the good, and hence to our felicity. But as experience teaches, the promise is only infrequently fulfilled; what strikes us as beautiful is rarely yoked to the good. Nonetheless we persist, seduced by the next beauty into believing that this time we shall gain our heart's desire. We willingly allow ourselves to be betrayed by the testimony of our eyes; we naturally and repeatedly mis-take the beautiful for the good.

The Bible has already demonstrated, in the Garden of Eden story, how what seems good in the eyes of men can be very far from what is truly good— or good *for them*.[9] Now again, in the present story, the text subtly hints at the same difficulty: "The sons of God *saw* the daughters of men that they were good [*tovoth*]—very likely, a mistaken seeing that mis-takes the fair for the good. Choosing their wives—perhaps even taking them off by force—on the basis of their looks alone, the sons of God were oblivious to matters of character and moral goodness, much more important to the work of marriage and perpetuation. This will not be the last story in the Bible in which the human love of beauty—especially the desire of men for beautiful women, and their wish to be esteemed by them—is shown to have unfortunate consequences.[10]

An unsuspecting reader, perhaps himself subject to the attractions of beautiful women, will be unmoved by these philosophical musings and may not by himself become suspicious of the new aestheticism of the god-like men. He should therefore be jolted from his complacency by God's reaction to all this.

---

9. See Genesis 3:6: "The woman *saw* the tree *that it was* good [*tov*] for food." Does she *see* truly?

10. See, for example, Jacob's infatuation with Rachel and the troubles it causes him; or Joseph's coat of many colors; or his attractiveness for Potiphar's wife. Generally speaking, the love of the beautiful will be shown to be a form of idolatry, unless properly subordinated and directed.

And the Lord said, "My spirit shall not judge [*yadon*] from within man[11] forever, for he also is flesh; therefore shall his days be a hundred and twenty years." (6:3)

God's speech is difficult to translate, much less to understand. Yet it is clearly a negative comment and, in context, a response to and a criticism of the deeds of the sons of God—who are, by the way, here clearly identified as human. In interpreting God's remarks, Robert Sacks glosses as follows:

> The antediluvian period was marked by its pre-legal character. God had made suggestions from time to time, but they were never enforced. Cain was neither punished for killing his brother nor was the suggestion that he become a wanderer ever carried out. The time before the Flood was a time in which there was no external law. God's statement to Cain, *If thou doest well . . .* (Gen. 4:7), presupposed that there was a faculty within man capable of judging. But when God says *My spirit shall not always judge from within man* He recognizes that the ability of man to judge *from within* is not sufficient for human needs. Only two ways are open: the total destruction of the world or the imposition of external law. The present verse [6:3] does not make clear which of these two paths God will choose.

Later, after the Flood and Noah's ambiguous sacrifice, God will elect the path of external law. But for the time being, He contemplates a different tactic: to shorten the human life span to 120 years. Presumably very great longevity invited only very great mischief and danger. The ultra-long-lived descendants of Seth, all begotten in the image of God, may have been overly impressed with their own god-likeness and their ancestral tie to the divine Creator. They may have forgotten that they were at most merely god-*like*, that they were—as God's remark "He also is flesh," here reminds us—also flesh and blood, like the other animals. Because death was for so long so far out of sight, these men were able to forget their mortality and pretend to immortal godliness. Yet when the inevitable happened, they behaved worse than all the animals. Perhaps a shorter life span could limit the damage any beastly man might cause. Perhaps a shorter life span, more obviously finite, would produce, by itself, the requisite moderation, without the need for external law: *Memento mori.* Perhaps if men learned from observing the deaths of others that they too had limited time, they would

11. I follow Robert Sacks's very literal translation of *yadon be'adam* as "judge from within man," rather than the more conventional "strive with man."

use it better. Perhaps if they could not pretend to immortality, they would be more open to the truly eternal.[12]

But the strategy of a shortened life span is to no avail, at least in the short run, as the sequel makes plain.

> The Nephilim [the fallen ones *or* the fellers] were on the earth in those days and also afterward, when the sons of God were coming in to the daughters of man and they were bearing [children] to them; they are the heroes [*hagiborim*] that from yore [*that is,* always: *me'olam*] are the men of name [*or* renown: *'anshei hashem*]. (6:4)

For the time being, at least, the Age of Heroes—mighty men, warriors, men of strength—prevails. These are the children of the mixed marriages, borne by the daughters of men (in our preferred reading, the proud line of Cain) to the sons of God (the line of Seth). In place of simplicity and (relative) righteousness, these fallen men—sons of corrupt mothers—make their names great by felling men. Their name, Nephilim, usually (but perhaps wrongly) translated "giants," comes from the root *naphal,* meaning both "to fall" and "to cause to fall." Descendants of the sons of God but now fallen due to improper marriages, the Nephilim—like Cain's Lamech—celebrate their status by hewing down men like timber.[13]

The age of heroes produces a result not to God's liking, and for good reason:

> And the Lord saw that the wickedness of man was great on the earth, and that every inclination of the thoughts of his heart was only bad all the day. And it repented the Lord that He had made man on the earth, and it grieved Him at His heart. And the Lord said, "I will blot out man whom I have created from the face of the earth; both man and beast and creeping thing and fowl of the air; for it repenteth Me that I have made them." (6:5–7)

Curbing man's life span might help in the future. But now, every inclination of the human heart was bent on badness, so much so that God regretted His entire

12. There is, of course, a danger that a shortened life span would only make death more hateful and insulting, especially to men of heroic temper. God's remark about the reason for a shorter life span, made to Himself, may therefore be aimed more at the reader than at the men of the Heroic Age. We who might wish for added longevity need to understand that longer would not necessarily be better.

13. See, for comparison, *Gilgamesh:* "My hand I will poise and will fell the Cedars, / A name that endures I will make for me" (quoted in Sacks, "The Lion and the Ass," Chapters 1–10, 82).

creation of man, and indeed, of all terrestrial (animal) life. Self-conscious men, recoiling from their mortality and lacking women's procreative power to answer it, betake themselves to war and to beautiful (but not good) women, seeking recognition for their superhuman prowess. Whether from rage over mortality, from jealousy and resentment, or from a desire to gain favor from beautiful women, or to avenge the stealing of their wives and daughters, proud men are moved to the love of glory, won in bloody battle with one another. The world erupts into violence, the war of each against all. What ensues is what Hobbes would later call "the state of nature," that is, the state characterized by absence of clear juridical power and authority, in which the life of man is nasty, brutish, and—through violence—short. Bloody destruction covers the earth.

With their would-be ruler turned to rioting, even the animals depart from the desired peaceful way and descend into beastliness: "The earth was corrupt . . . and . . . filled with violence; . . . *all flesh* had corrupted their way upon the earth" (6:11–12; emphasis added). For the animals, this can only mean that they have taken to eating one another, in clear violation of the original life-and-order-preserving dispensation that would have had them eat only herbs, grass, fruit, and seeds (see Genesis 1:29–30).[14] This state of wickedness could be repaired, if at all, only by the imposition of law—reasoned rules of conduct, backed by sufficient force to compel obedience. But things have deteriorated so much that there is not enough sanity on earth with which to legislate. The experiment in anarchy—in living law-less-ly—has failed miserably, so much so that God Himself despairs of His creation. In an extraordinary remark—one that should give pause to those who think that the biblical God is either omniscient or omnipotent—God says that He *repents* His creation of man and the other animals. More in sadness than in anger, and lacking any remedy, God decides entirely to erase his creation, perhaps to start again.

But Noah found grace in the eyes of the Lord. (6:8)

Because of Noah, God must modify His decision and plan for *total* destruction. More important, because of Noah, God can indeed start a human (and living) world over again without needing to re-create another Adam from the

---

14. The reasons for the corruption of the animals are not given. Was it due to population increase and resultant scarcity of food? Was it the emergence of an always latent ferocity, perhaps related to the birth of an unself-conscious animal equivalent of the rudiment of pride? Or as the textual context might suggest, was it caused by the corruption of their ruler, man? And on the subject of corrupted eating, the human animal too might have taken to eating not only animal flesh but also flesh of his own kind. Cannibalism surely would be the ultimate meaning of life's corrupting its way upon the earth.

dust . . . which is apparently not God's preferred course. Starting with Noah insures against the unexpected loss of innocence about mortality, a crisis that a human race stemming from a second Adam would someday necessarily face, and which is the cause of the current catastrophe. What was it about Noah that gained him election?

> These are the generations [*toledoth*] of Noah. Noah was a man righteous and simple [*'ish tsadiq tamim*] in his generations [*bedorothav*]; Noah walked with God. And Noah begot three sons, Shem, Ham and Japheth. (6:9–10)

Noah is a saving remnant because of his saving virtue. He is distinguished, in these wicked times, for his righteousness and his simplicity and for "walking with God." What it means, in this context, to be righteous *(tsadiq)* or simple *(tamim)* or to walk with God we are not told; but we are put on notice that it is these qualities, not heroic manliness (prized everywhere else), that are divinely favored.[15] The text is also wonderfully ambiguous about whether Noah's virtues are absolute, and therefore all the more remarkable in *these wicked* generations (despite near universal evil, Noah was righteous), or merely relative (compared to the wicked others, Noah was righteous). In either case, we suspect that Noah's righteousness may be related to his simplicity: simple (-minded) Noah did not rage against mortality, but accepted it as part of his human condition.[16] Nor was he seduced by the lure of the surface attractions of womanly beauty. He is both simple *and* pure—*tamim* also means "pure" or "perfect" or "wholehearted" and includes sexual simplicity or innocence as well. In combination, these are good reasons for choosing Noah. A viable alternative to the chaos caused by the heroic temptation must include both the acceptance of mortality and the domestication of sexuality; procreation, not the search for beauty or glory, offers a more moderate and peaceful way to pursue immortality. Noah is a likely candidate for a new beginning.

Noah must yet prove himself worthy of election by accepting his commis-

15. These are indeed the decisive biblical virtues. Righteousness is the supreme virtue in actions dealing with others, while wholeheartedness is the supreme virtue of the well-ordered soul; both, it turns out, will depend on being and acting in proper relation to God. Noah is the first person who is described as righteous and simple (or wholehearted), and the second said to walk with God (Seth's Enoch was the first). Later, in the covenant with Abraham (Genesis 17), Abraham will be charged to be *tamim* and to walk before God. And prior to the conversation with Abraham about the fate of Sodom and Gomorrah (Genesis 18), God will indicate that His principal interest in Abraham is tied to Abraham's becoming a teacher of righteousness.

16. "By always having known death Noah was never forced to learn about it. His simplicity was both his wisdom and his naivete" (Sacks, "The Lion and the Ass," Chapters 1–10, 84).

sion. Accordingly, God informs Noah of his plan to destroy the earth by flooding, commands him to build an ark according to precisely prescribed instructions, promises to establish His covenant with Noah, and commands him to take aboard the ark his family and two of every kind of living creature (6:13–21). Noah asks no questions and raises no objections. Speechlessly, he obeys: "Thus did Noah; according to all that God commanded him, so did he" (6:22). Noah takes instruction in the service of preserving not only his own life but also the life of the whole world. Though he will not be its helmsman—the ark, being but a box, will merely float upon the waters, unguided by human art—Noah willingly accepts responsibility to manage affairs aboard the ark, exercising dominion over the animals *for their own good* (see 1:28). In complying with God's command, Noah vindicates his election and raises hope for the future.

For the rest, God sends the Flood, a fitting response to the self-destructive conduct of the heroes. For the Flood, in restoring the watery chaos of the ultimate beginnings (1:2), merely completes the descent into chaos that anarchic and heroic men—and animals—were bringing upon themselves entirely on their own. The text even makes the point linguistically: the word God uses for "destroy"—"I will destroy them with the earth" (6:13)—is the same word translated "corrupt," used to describe what man and the animals were doing on their own—"all flesh had corrupted His way upon the earth" (6:12). The sympathetic and thoughtful reader understands that the Flood is necessary and fitting. Identifying with Noah, he allows his aspirations to climb aboard onto Noah's ark, dreaming of a new world order.

∾

Because of our interest in the new world order—the subject of our next chapter—we shall not comment on the details of the story of the Flood itself, interesting though they are.[17] But to understand more completely the meaning of the biblical Flood, and its place in the emerging anthropology of Genesis, it is useful to place this story in cultural context. As we did with the first story of creation (see Chapter One), we need to consider what alternative teachings the Bible is here rejecting (albeit silently). For the tale of the Flood proper is much more than a charming story; it carries important and radical teachings about nature,

---

17. I cite only one example. Everyone knows that it rained for forty days and forty nights. This marks the first of many episodes in the Bible associated with the number forty (or four hundred), including the four hundred years of Israel's bondage in Egypt, the forty days Moses spent on Mount Sinai, and the forty years the Children of Israel wandered in the desert. Sacks comments: "Each of these periods implies a time of waiting in which nothing happens and yet a time without which nothing could happen. . . . It would be difficult to know why the number 40 was chosen to imply a period in which nothing appears on the surface and yet quietly a seed is growing. However, it is worthy of note that nine months make approximately 40 weeks."

God, and man. As is the case for the other early stories in Genesis, its most important truths are not historical but anthropological, theological, and moral.

Scholars have long associated the biblical deluge with floods known in other ancient Near Eastern traditions, in particular with the Sumerian and Akkadian cultures of Mesopotamia. The Mesopotamian stories, already circulating by 2000 B.C.E., were almost certainly known to the biblical writers. Indeed, some scholars believe—I think rightly—that the biblical account is written as a quiet but insistent polemic against them. A brief comparison of Genesis's story of the Flood with the most famous of these Babylonian tales, the *Gilgamesh* epic, reveals some startling conclusions that strengthen the interpretations we are advancing both in this chapter and in this book as a whole.

The hero Gilgamesh, terrified of death and eager for eternal life, seeks advice from Utnapishtim, who had been saved from the flood and then transformed into a god. Utnapishtim, in order to teach Gilgamesh that his deification was due to special and nonrepeatable circumstances, tells him the story of the flood. A council of the gods (led by Enlil) decides to send a flood upon the earth, destroying the cities of men. (No reason is given for this decision, though in another version of the legend, one of the gods complains that the noisy human beings are interfering with his sleep.) One god, Ea, secretly sends a warning dream to his favorite, Utnapishtim, urging him to pull down his house, build a ship, abandon his possessions, and save life by going aboard the ship. Utnapishtim then describes, in great detail, the design and construction of his ship and tells Gilgamesh how he took aboard not only his household, his relations, and all his animals, but also his gold and silver and all his craftsmen. A six-day storm ensues, so frightening that even the gods are panic-stricken; on the seventh day the storm abates, the flood ceases, and the ship rests atop a mountain. Utnapishtim sends out a dove, then a swallow, then a raven in search of dry land; the first two returned to the ship, the last did not. Utnapishtim tells how he then offered sacrifice and burned incense, in "seven and seven bowls," and how "the gods smelled the sweet odor and . . . gathered like flies over the sacrificer." Disputes break out among the gods around the offerings, some complaining that Enlil, chief instigator of the flood, should not now enjoy the sacrifice, and Ea complaining that the destruction was excessive. As a result, a softened Enlil boards Utnapishtim's ship, lifts him and his wife, and makes them into divinities, to dwell far off with the other gods.

Readers familiar with Genesis's story of the Flood will immediately recognize numerous similarities. Like the Gilgamesh legend, the Bible reports a divine decision to destroy earthly life by flooding; the salvation of one man, his family, and representative animals by a divine injunction to build a vessel that could survive the flood while housing all who would be saved; the grounding of the vessel on a mountaintop; the sending forth of birds (dove and raven) to see if dry land had reappeared; the offering of sacrifices after the deliverance; and a divine blessing for the saved. But it is not the similarities but rather the differences that are crucial for understanding what the Bible is doing with this story. Noah differs decisively from Utnapishtim, and God differs decisively from the gods of the *Gilgamesh* epic. These differences, taken together, comprise the point of the biblical tale.

1. God's decision to destroy the earth, unlike Enlil's, is not arbitrary; it is a response to the near-universal wickedness and corruption of life on earth. Not so much by punishment as by purgation or purification, God seeks to erase the evil that has polluted His creation.

2. Unlike Ea, God decides to spare Noah not out of caprice or favoritism, but on account of Noah's virtue.

3. Unlike the gods and goddesses of the *Gilgamesh* legend, who are terrorized by the wild natural forces they themselves have loosed and who later quarrel among themselves, God is in full command of chaotic waters and, needless to say, is at one with Himself.

4. Unlike the Mesopotamian deities, who, starved for human offerings, swarm over the sacrifices eager to eat, God merely smells the odor of—He does not eat—Noah's burnt offering (which is completely consumed in the flames).

5. Unlike Utnapishtim, Noah does not himself design the ark, but merely executes, to the letter, God's very detailed instructions. Moreover, there is no gold and silver, and there are no craftsmen or helmsmen, on Noah's ark.

These important differences convey the Bible's dim view of the goodness and adequacy of human artfulness:

- Whereas Utnapishtim builds himself a ship, fitted with a helm and directed by a helmsman, Noah builds but an ark with no clear fore and aft, incapable of being steered in any direction.
- Whereas Utnapishtim reports how he closed himself inside the ship, the Bible reports that "the Lord shut him [Noah] in" (7:16): man, on his own, cannot guarantee his survival.
- Utnapishtim is a crafty commander; Noah is an obedient servant.
- The point of Noah's ark is not to save a vestige of civilization, but to preserve and perpetuate life, in all its profusion and variety—"of all flesh . . . two of each . . . to keep alive . . . male and female" (6:19); "of

every kind" (6:20; 7:14); "after its family" (8:19)—and to restore the peaceful harmony of the original creation.

Perhaps most important, unlike Utnapishtim, Noah is not elevated to divine status at the end of his ordeal. On the contrary, he remains as mortal as before, yet with a difference. Instead of apotheosis, the goal of both Gilgamesh and the Bible's antediluvian men of renown, Noah will get a blessing that both reinforces his mortal condition and shows him how human beings are to deal with it. Noah (as we shall see in the next chapter) will be blessed with fecundity and with a new mission that binds him—and, through him, all humanity—as God's earthly partner in executing justice in defense of human life.

We hazard to put the matter in a nutshell. Just as the Flood drowns the heroes and washes away the violent world they produced,[18] so the story of the Flood seeks to wash away the heroic temptation in the reader. It seeks permanently to drown the natural human aspiration to apotheosis through heroic deed and to replace it with an acquired human commitment to righteousness and the perpetuation of life on earth. Sobered by the tale of the Flood, we are ready for the new dispensation.

18. The last of the long-lived descendants of Seth and the oldest living human being ever, Methushalah, dies in 1656, the year of the Flood, we presume by drowning.

CHAPTER SIX

ELEMENTARY JUSTICE: MAN, ANIMALS,
AND THE COMING OF LAW AND COVENANT

*O*bedience to law and the doing of justice are crucial biblical concerns. So too is the idea of covenant. All three notions are introduced into human life—and into the thought of the reader—in the form of the Noahide law and covenant, the subject of the present chapter. It is impossible to exaggerate their importance. For the coming of the way of law and covenant marks a permanent shift in the psychic and social conditions of humankind. Human beings accept the need for self-restraint and the responsibility for curtailing dangerous natural impulses. Human society becomes governed by general rules that oblige proper conduct toward others, and not just toward your own flesh and blood. Moral man and civil society are both the product of the institution of law. But these developments the Bible regards ambiguously. The emergence of law, though absolutely necessary, is not simply celebrated as a story of unqualified success. It is, first of all, a response to the evils that lurk in the hearts of men. To control these evils, law must not only accept their unavoidable existence; it must also offer them concessions and, moreover, even enlist their aid in support of civil peace.

At the end of the last chapter, we left Noah and his ark silently adrift between the old world and the new, yet pregnant with new life and new possibility. As we again look down on the scene, we remind ourselves of how and why things have come to this pass.

The first beginnings of human life ended in violent chaos. Left to their own devices, human beings followed the inclinations of their hearts, informed only by their ill-formed judgments of good and bad, advantage and harm. Prompted by fear of death and love of glory, driven by greed and anger, lust and vanity, they made endless war upon one another and managed to destroy all hopes of peace, prosperity, and happiness. Anarchy bred lawlessness and death. The excesses of life threatened to wipe out the articulated and harmonious order of the earth, created against the primordial chaos only by divine effort.

Noah appears to promise a viable alternative to the violent chaos of the world of the heroes. God contemplates a new earth, begun afresh after a cleansing, this time under the leadership not of an innocent (like Adam) but of the naturally righteous (like Noah). Noah is to be a new, yet different, Adam. Through him, and through the vehicle of the ark, God tries to renew the first creation. He tries again for a peaceful and harmonious terrestrial order, in keeping with the intelligible cosmological order of the whole.

The ark is a microcosm of the projected new earthly order. Afloat amidst the watery chaos, it bears male and female of every species of terrestrial and avian life, in order to begin again. The complete variety of living forms is represented: the new order preserves not only the phenomenon of life but also the many-splendored kinds that make an articulated world. In charge of preservation and order is the human animal, guardian of all animal life. Will he be willing and able to maintain order and to preserve life? We should not underestimate the obstacles to his doing so. For life as such always poses a danger to life, and the human animal threatens it most of all.

Preservation of living beings, always vulnerable and needy, requires food; and food for animals is, necessarily, other living things. Whether the violent carnivorousness of the past can be reversed in the new world we shall soon discover. But in a passage often overlooked among the details of the Noah story, the text has clearly pointed to the problem. In presenting His plan for Noah's ark, God's last instruction to Noah was, as with Adam in chapter 1, about food:

"And take thou unto thee of all food that is eaten, and thou shalt gather it to thee: and it shall be for food *for thee and for them.*" (6:21; emphasis added)

God in fact tries to circumvent life's threat to life by again providing nonviolent nutrition: all the animals on the ark—including the human beings—are again to be vegetarians, sharing exactly the same food.[1]

Noah, as we noted in the last chapter, does exactly as he is commanded: "Thus did Noah; according to all that God commanded him, so did he" (6:22). The ark is built, according to instructions followed to the letter; the animals are brought aboard two by two, male and female; and the food is gathered. As the waters drown corrupt and violent life, the harmonious voyage to the peaceful new world begins.

1. Compare the original dispensation regarding food in the first creation story: "And God said: 'Behold I have provided you with all seed-bearing plants which are on the face of all the earth, and every tree which has seed-bearing fruit; to you I have given it as food. And to every living being of the earth and to everything that creepeth upon the earth which has a living soul in it, I have given every green herb as food'; and it was so" (1:29–30). Though all creatures are to be vegetarian, human food (seed-bearing plants and fruit) and animal food (green herbs) are different.

Most of us rarely stop to ponder life aboard ship, and the text seems completely uninterested in the subject. Nothing is said about how Noah managed to keep order, not to speak about keeping clean. Yet for more than a year (compare 7:11 and 8:14),[2] Noah, his family, and their animal roommates apparently lived together in peace. As far as we know, while on the ark the lion and the lamb broke straw together, and no species practiced war anymore. Rehabilitation of the entire living world seemed possible—or almost possible. Only one small clue gives the reader pause: Noah's first scout for dry land was the raven. Remembering the raven's carnivorousness, Noah must have hoped the bird would return with rotting flesh, but the ravenous scout "went to and fro until the waters were dried up from the earth" (8:7). The herbivorous dove, sent second, returned, because she "found no rest for the sole of her foot"; sent seven days later, she brought back an olive leaf freshly plucked (8:8–11). Yet while redemption was celebrated aboard ship, the spirit of the hungry raven, no doubt fed up with seeds and looking for meat, still hovered over the face of the deep. As the sequel shows, Noah himself, for all his virtue, turns out to harbor some of the wildness of antediluvian man.

The Ambiguous Sacrifice: Man's Evil Inclination

When the earth is again dry, the time arrives to renew its vitality and living splendor. God tells Noah to leave the ark and to bring forth with him "every living thing that is with thee of all flesh," in order that they might all "be fruitful and multiply upon the earth" (8:17). As in the first creation, described in Genesis 1, the present plan calls for life, growth, and fruitfulness, not just for man but for every living thing. Yet a strange and unforeseen event occurs immediately after the ark is emptied. Noah, without any divine instruction, builds an altar unto the Lord and roasts up large numbers of his animal former roommates as burnt offerings to God—a strange answer indeed to the exhortation to arrange for the animals to be fruitful and multiply.

> And Noah builded an altar unto the Lord; and he took of *every* clean beast and of *every* clean fowl and offered burnt offerings on the altar. (8:20; emphasis added)

What is going on?

---

2. Though it rained for only forty days and nights, it took almost ten times as long for the waters to subside. To restore order is much harder than to destroy it.

Noah, presumably in an act of thanksgiving and perhaps also hoping to stave off further rain, sacrifices some of the animals he rescued from the antediluvian world of violence and bloodshed.[3] It is not difficult to imagine what moves him to do so. Overwhelmed by the destructive power of nature but perhaps even more impressed by his own salvation, man is moved by strong feelings of dread, awe, and gratitude to acknowledge the superiority and importance of the divine. Noah's protracted and close encounters with the other animals would, by themselves, have convinced him that he is more than just the chief among the animals. But his new awareness of divine power and divine providence—awareness not shared by the animals—confirms him in the belief that his species is special and, thus, separates him from his animal relations. Noah's self-defining first act in the new world is an act of violence against the living world.[4] A simply harmonious world order, led by a human being, seems to be impossible.

Noah's impulse to express gratitude is, under the circumstances, thoroughly intelligible, but his belief that God would like to gorge Himself on roast meat—or, more modestly, enjoy its aroma—is utterly unfounded. Noah, like most gift givers (as we saw with Cain's offering), assumes that the Lord would like a gift, and a gift from me. Not knowing *what* He would like, Noah further assumes that He would like what I like, because He is more or less like me, only more so.

3. Although Noah sacrificed many animals, he chose only from the *clean (tahora)* ones, both beasts and fowl. This difficult matter deserves some comment. *Tahor,* from a root meaning "bright," means clean or pure, in both physical and moral senses. Later, in Leviticus, the distinction between clean and not clean plays a crucial role in the Hebrew laws of sacrifice and purity, including the dietary laws that permit the eating only of clean animals. (See my *The Hungry Soul: Eating and the Perfecting of Our Nature* [Chicago: University of Chicago Press, 1999], chap. 6, "Sanctified Eating: A Memorial of Creation.") But the meaning of "clean" and "not clean" at this stage of things can only be unclear. Noah had in fact been instructed earlier to take with him onto the ark seven males and seven females of the clean animals, in contrast to the single pair of the not clean animals (7:2–3). From this command, commentators have inferred that God intended Noah to use them in sacrifice, but God in fact says nothing at all about why they are singled out, or even about which animals are which. For good reason, Noah at first seems perplexed about which animals are clean. When the report is made of the embarkation (7:15), all the animals go into the ark "two and two of all flesh." There is no distinction made between clean and unclean animals, and there is no mention of the required seven and seven. Noah, who seems to be as unsure as we are about the meaning of clean and unclean, may just be guessing in his selections at the time of the sacrifice, just as he is guessing about the propriety of sacrificing altogether.

4. This is, indeed, Noah's first major free act altogether (if we treat as minor acts his sending forth the raven and the dove). His offering, unlike his building of the ark, is made without command. Noah builds and enters the ark in obedience; he leaves the ark in freedom. (In this connection, it is revealing to contrast the order in which Noah and his family actually leave the ark [8:18] with the order prescribed in God's command to do so [8:16], a topic that we shall discuss in Chapter Seven.)

The ambiguity of Noah's deed is confirmed by the ambiguity of God's re-action:

> And the Lord smelled a sweet savor; and the Lord said in His heart, "I will not again curse the ground anymore for man's sake; *for the imagination of man's heart is evil from his youth;* neither will I again smite anymore every living thing as I have done. While the earth remaineth, seedtime and har-vest, and cold and heat, and summer and winter, and day and night shall not cease." (8:21–22; emphasis added)

The text's opening remark, "And the Lord smelled a sweet savor," is generally taken to be evidence that God was pleased with the sacrifice itself, and not only with Noah's impulse to offer it.[5] Perhaps so. But when we hear what God Him-self says immediately thereafter, in directly quoted speech, we have strong reason for doubt. In His response to Noah's sacrifice, God does not praise man's gener-ous impulses. On the contrary, He complains that "the imagination of man's heart is evil from his youth" (compare 6:5). From this explicit negative judg-ment, we might reinterpret the beginning remark to mean that God discerned that the smell of roast meat was sweet *to Noah.* Not having been told how to ex-press thanksgiving, Noah gave God a gift on the assumption that God would like what he, Noah, liked. Animal sacrifice, in fact, reveals nothing about God. But like his selection of the raven, it reveals a good deal about *Noah:* a preference for meat—or at the very least, a willingness to shed blood. To give of what one trea-sures most is praiseworthy; to kill animals and to relish their flesh is not. Even Noah, righteous and simple Noah, the new and better Adam, is not pure at heart and has a taste for blood.

Explicitly for this reason, God now decides against blotting out and starting over: "I will not again curse the ground anymore for man's sake." Why? Because it is now clear to God, and He here makes it clear also to the reader, that it would be no use to start over—not then, not now, not ever. To put it in simple terms, no human being, following uninstructed only the native inclinations of his heart, will ever be content to be a pacific, nonviolent, fruit-and-seed-eating steward of living flesh. The way of nature must be replaced by the way of law.

Our expectations are not disappointed: the covenant with Noah and the Noahide law follow in the immediate sequel (indeed, in the very next verse). The

5. This account is usefully compared with the gods' reaction to a parallel sacrifice made by Utnapishtim after his deliverance from the flood in the *Gilgamesh* epic (see Chapter Five, p. 165). In contrast to the latter, the biblical account denies that the Lord eats or is interested in eating the of-fering, in keeping with the Bible's resolute refusal to endorse any belief in God's corporeality. The rest of God's comment suggests that He has no interest in sacrifices altogether.

institution of law is the direct answer to Noah's animal sacrifice and to the Dionysian impulses of the human soul that lie behind it.

In fairness to Noah, and therefore to nascent civil man, one should observe that the sacrifice—seen even at its worst—is not a manifestation simply of animal blood lust. An altar is built, fire is used, whole animals are offered, and no blood is orgiastically strewn. Noah's reaching for divinity—even in all its ambiguity—partly constrains, by the form of ritual, the otherwise unrestrained human use of animals, even in the act of violence done to them. There is method in his madness, order in his destructiveness.

As we shall soon see, the law that follows will both make explicit and also regulate what is implicit in Noah's sacrifice. Noah displays self-conscious separation from the animals; the law will respond by establishing man's nearly complete alienation from the animals, embodied in a near absolute permission to eat meat. Noah displays a taste for shedding blood; the law will respond by absolutely prohibiting the eating of animal blood and by demanding in-kind retribution for the shedding of human blood. Noah seeks a new relationship with the divine, through sacrifice; the law will establish a new relationship with God, through a demand for justice. A divinely backed law humanly enforced and a divinely pledged covenant humanly recognized together form a precise response to the inner meaning of Noah's sacrifice, seen as a search for contact with the divine.

Right after Noah's sacrifice, a new world order is established, marked by the first law for all mankind. To use nonbiblical language, man here emerges from what later writers will call the state of nature and becomes civilized or political; it is, as Rousseau will later put it, "the moment when, right taking the place of violence, nature was subjected to law." In the state of nature, might (which is to say violence) alone makes right; only under the rule of law is might forced to submit to an independent notion of what is just. True, for the philosophers of the social contract, like Hobbes, Locke, and Rousseau, human beings, *on their own*—that is, without God's help—reason out the necessity of instituting laws and punishment; human beings, on their own, contract to form societies on the basis of these laws. But even nonbelieving readers of Genesis might learn something unavailable to them in Hobbes, Locke, or Rousseau, precisely if the Bible's version of the arrival of law rests on ontological ground, a ground more solid than mere human agreement. Readers might learn something universal and true about law and its foundation if the new law makes explicit the relations between man, animals, and the whole, relations that Noah—read: self-consciously mortal man—*could divine on his own.*

In this connection, it is worth emphasizing that the Noahide law is not especially or uniquely Jewish; it is not parochial but universal. Announced as a law for all humankind, it is instituted ten generations before the election of Abraham, the first of the Israelites. Indeed, many commentators over the centuries have treated it as part of the so-called natural law: a law discernible by human reason and constitutive for all human societies, a law valid for all human beings everywhere exactly on account of their humanity.

We too shall look at the Noahide law in this spirit. Continuing our philosophical reading, we shall regard it as the primordial and, hence, prototypical law. We shall first consider the law's inner meaning and logic, its rational basis and ontological ground, and its significance for human life, ignoring any part that God (or any other god or gods) might play in instituting such a new dispensation. But there is no getting around the fact that, according to Genesis, the primordial law was not discovered by Noah, thinking for himself; it was directly commanded by God. Thus, even though we read philosophically—or better, precisely *because* we read seeking wisdom—we will also try (toward the end of this chapter) to understand just how and why man's new life under law requires and reflects a relationship to the divine.

THE FORM OF LAW AND ITS FORMATIVE POWER

The new world order takes human beings as they are, not as they might be. It does not try to obliterate their tendencies to wildness and violence; it tries, rather, to accommodate and restrain them by means of law. But this seemingly small innovation is of monumental importance. For the institution of law transforms the human world, and thereby the world altogether. It creates new relationships between man and animals, man and man, man and the cosmic order, and between each man and himself. It requires and promotes new powers of mind and heart, largely unexercised before (or unless) man becomes law-abiding. It makes possible a new form of sociality, civil society, founded on shared explicit expectations and agreed-upon notions of justice and punishment. Precisely as it restrains human impulses, it liberates human possibility.

As presented in Genesis 9, the founding document of the new world order comprises two parts: the law (verses 1–7) and the covenant (verses 8–17). Together they provide the necessary and sufficient conditions—both the fear-inducing legal sanctions and the hope-inspiring belief in a durable human future—for founding civil society. Here, in full, are the seven verses that propound the primordial law:

> And God blessed Noah and his sons, and said unto them: "Be fruitful and
> multiply, and fill the earth. And the fear of you and the dread of you shall

be upon every beast of the earth, and upon every fowl of the air, and upon all wherewith the ground teemeth, and upon all the fishes of the sea: into your hand are they delivered. Every moving thing that liveth shall be for food for you; as the green herb, I give you all. Only flesh with the life thereof, which is the blood thereof, shall ye not eat. And surely your blood of your lives will I require [a reckoning]; at the hand of every beast will I require it; and at the hand of man, even at the hand of every man's brother, will I require the life of man. Whoever sheddeth man's blood, by man shall his blood be shed [*shofekh dam ha'adam ba'adam damo yishafekh*]; for in the image of God was man made. And you, be ye fruitful and multiply; swarm in the earth and multiply therein." (9:1–7)

The law is presented wrapped in a blessing; indeed, it seems to be an integral part of the blessing. Two similar injunctions "to be fruitful and multiply" frame the entire legislation. They make absolutely clear the law's paramount interest in promoting human life. Under the circumstances, no concern is more appropriate or more urgent than the growth and protection of life. After the recent devastation, human and natural, a blessing for fecundity is especially welcome. And for what is to be a postheroic age, a command to procreate, rather than to obliterate, is especially fitting.

The blessing "Be fruitful and multiply" reminds us of the identical blessing given in the first creation story (1:28). Indeed, the entire passage revisits but significantly reworks the original blessings and dispositions of Genesis 1. The differences are revealing and profound. In the creation story, the blessing for fecundity had been given also to fish and fowl (1:22); here it is explicitly given only to human beings (9:1, 7). Originally, the uniquely human blessing was for rule over—but not exploitation of—the animals (1:28); here the animals will dread and fear man, into whose hand they are now delivered as food (9:2). As in the first story (1:29-30; see also 2:16), there is an abundance of food (9:3); but whereas in the first creation there was only encouragement of eating and no explicit limitation of human appetite, here the bounty comes with definite restriction ("not the blood," 9:4; compare also 2:17). Utterly novel in the present story, without precedent in the first, are the demand for retribution for bloodshed and the human obligation to exact it (9:5-6); the *new* world order, though it seeks to deter homicide, assumes that it cannot be avoided. Yet while expecting less of man's nature, it demands more of his choice, requiring him to live by law and to enforce it. Indeed, the first story's celebrated "image of God" description of man (1:26-27) here becomes the basis for a legal responsibility to execute justice (9:6). Whereas order had been originally created out of chaos through separation and distinction, here order is prevented from dissolving back into chaos through law and punishment. When, at the end of the blessing of Noah and his sons, the command to be fruitful and multiply is repeated (9:7), it will be newly heard, and it must be newly understood, in the awesome light of the intervening requirements of law and justice. The natural good of life is now bound up with the legal good of right and the legal obligation to defend it.

Before looking closely at the specific provisions of the Noahide law, we observe that it stands as a perfect embodiment of the foundations of law in general. Like law in general, this cardinal law combines speech and force: a *logos* with teeth, it is an articulate formulation of what to do or not do, backed by threat of punishment for failure to comply.[6] True, the teeth and the fear they inspire are at first glance more prominent than the *logos:* the threat of capital punishment seeks to deter murder by inspiring fear for one's own life. But because even this threat of punishment is made in speech, law addresses us as rational beings, free to obey or not, free to choose risking the threatened punishment. Law is rational also in its form and generality: no respecter of persons, law speaks in identical words to and about each person it addresses. But it speaks never in terms of personal names, always in terms of the fundamentally rational general nouns and pronouns (*"Whoever* sheds blood"; "by *man* shall . . ."). The very language of law, like reason itself, is always universal, never ad hominem.

Regardless of its particular content, the institution of law *as such* also means for each human being a new—and uniquely human—relationship to himself. Both in its articulation *as a law* and in its demand for obedience, the establishment of any law expresses a heightened moral self-consciousness not available to animals or very young children, or even to immaturely human beings like Adam and the antediluvian race. Obedience to law both presupposes and promotes the possibilities of self-command and self-restraint.

Law is, in the first instance, generally a matter of nay-saying: Do not eat the blood; do not shed human blood. Effective nay-saying depends on the self-consciousness of freedom and power; it requires an awareness that we can either do or not do, that we are, at least in part, not in the iron grip of necessity. It also requires awareness of our own impulses or inclinations to act, which we also wish, or are told, to oppose. And it requires conscious *moral* judgment, positive as well as negative; it presupposes an at least tacit awareness of some notion of good or right, and a recognition that the good is not necessarily the same as the pleasant. For all nay-saying is, at the same time, implicitly a yea-saying. Just as

---

6. Force (or might or violence) does not disappear in civil society; it persists as the strong arm of the law. The rule of law does not mean the rule of unarmed reason. As a mixture of the rational and the forceful, law reflects perfectly man's composite nature as rational animal.

negation wakens the soul to the possibility of truth as the opposite of error, so prohibition wakens the soul to the possibility of right as the opposite of wrong.[7] In all these ways, by becoming law-making and law-abiding animals, human beings display their decisive difference. Both the form and the content of the Noahide code underscore this insight. Thus, whenever man deliberately institutes, as he does here, what he regards as proper attitudes and practices toward the animals, he by that very act separates himself from all else that lives. For man is the only animal that *decides* how other animals *should* be treated.[8] And because living under law is an essential mark of our distinctive humanity, the *substance* of the primordial law is, quite fittingly, about the difference of man and the difference it makes. With poetic justice, the foundational law enunciates rules of conduct—*different* rules of conduct—concerning our relations both to the animals and to our own fellow men: a (nearly) absolute permission to eat meat (minus only the blood), an absolute prohibition against human bloodshed (plus a duty to avenge it). The Noahide laws about eating meat and about shedding human blood are necessary and complementary parts of this founding legal package.

The importance of this observation cannot be exaggerated. The permission to violate the other animals is somehow necessary to the prohibition against violating human beings. At the same time, the demand to respect the dignity of animals both marks our own higher dignity and manifests a respectful attitude toward our own abiding animality. Let us see how this works.

LAW REGARDING THE ANIMALS: BLOODLESS MEAT

The new world order, under the rule of law, begins by redefining the relationship between man and beast. All living things now will live in fear and dread of man, as they are delivered into his hand. Man is now permitted to use all living things as food; but there is to be no eating of living flesh or blood. As in the fruit-filled Garden of Eden, the big picture in the new world order is liberal,

7. This present discussion of law as prohibition reminds us of the "original" prohibition in the Garden of Eden story, the command not to eat of the tree of knowledge of good and bad. As we interpreted that story, under interdiction was human free choice altogether. Had the first prohibition been obeyed—had human beings never risen to practice free and autonomous choice—there would have been no need for the Noahide law or any other law. Human beings would have been innocent and ignorant, beneath both the need and the capacity for law.

8. This insight should put to rest, once and for all, the claims of both those animal rightists and those philosophical materialists who assimilate man without remainder to the rest of nature, either because all life suffers and dies or because, at bottom, all is just matter and motion.

only more so: all living things are fit to eat (compare 2:16). Also as in Eden, there is one minor restriction: no living flesh or blood (compare 2:17). But the original or hoped-for harmonious relation of man and animals—re-created aboard Noah's ark—in which man, like a true ruler, rules in the interest of the ruled, is gone forever; the shepherd will now tend his flock with at least part of his mind on lamb chops.[9] Yet the shepherd is not—and must not become—a wolf. He can and must abide by the restriction on eating "flesh with the life thereof."

It might seem, at first glance, that this restriction is based simply on compassion for animal suffering and repugnance for cruelty to animals. If men in eating meat are confined to eating flesh from which the life has departed, there will be no cutting off limbs from live animals or other similar barbarous practices. But there is more at stake in the prohibition against the eating of blood. Some have speculated that the reason is utilitarian: blood is to be avoided because it is unhealthy or, worse, because it embodies the vital force of another being, the incorporation of which would illicitly mix the spirit of another species with that of man. Others believe that the text is polemicizing against wild pagan practices (possibly including cannibalism) that involved drinking of blood, human as well as animal. Perhaps. But the entire biblical context in which the law is propounded suggests something neither merely humane nor self-interested, but something ontological: blood is to be avoided because of what it *is*; blood is not to be eaten because *it is the life*. The operative principle is neither calculation nor compassion, but awe and respect. Life is to be *respected*, even in the taking of it—whether we like it or not, and whether the animal suffers or not.

Modern readers should not miss the point just because we are too sophisti-

---

9. In keeping with our effort, begun in the last chapter, to see the biblical account of the Flood against the Mesopotamian alternatives, we take note of Robert Sacks's observation of the rift between man and the animals:

> Prior to the Flood, man had a natural kinship with the animals; but with the rise of the political bond, that kinship was broken. A similar account is given in the *Gilgamesh* but from a very different point of view. Gilgamesh was once told of a man named Enkidu, a man who spoke no language and who lived with the animals as one of them. He [Gilgamesh] sent a prostitute to tempt him and to bring him back into the city. After his encounter with Gilgamesh, Enkidu returned to his home, but the animals all ran away. There was no longer any place for him among them. In the Biblical account things go the other way around. It is man who rejects the animals by accepting them as food. The particular care of man for man which political life requires precludes the unity of all living things characteristic of earlier times.

Actually, the rupture with the animals was anticipated in Noah's sacrifice, which prefigured the coming of civil society. Here, the animals do not flee man but live in fear and awe of him. (Parenthetically, it is the death of Enkidu that launches Gilgamesh on his heroic quest for immortality and that leads him to seek out the deified survivor of the Flood, Utnapishtim. See Chapter Five, p. 165.)

cated to believe any longer that the blood is the life. Truth to tell, we have no rea-son to feel smug; exactly because of our sophistication, which has led us to aban-don the idea of *psyche* or *anima,* we no longer have *any* idea about *what* the life *is,* or what is responsible for it. Yet even now, if we think about living organisms rather than about either lifeless DNA or disembodied consciousness and per-sonhood, the singling out of blood is surely not unreasonable. Blood is warm and mobile and courses continuously through the whole body; everywhere it goes it supports vital activity, and no power of life is possible without it; and when blood spills or drains from the body, the life goes with it, as vital powers weaken and eventually cease entirely. But be this as it may, we must rise above the details and grasp the principle: all life, whatever it is and wherever we find it, has a claim upon us for respect—*even when we do it violence.* Unlike the other animals, we human beings are able to recognize and make good that claim.

Animals destroy other animals without restraint, and as a matter of strict ne-cessity. They know not what they do; moreover, they cannot help themselves. In the decisive respect, this excuses their conduct even as it does not cleanse the deed, which remains a violation, one that we, at least, can recognize. Even when we remember the hungry cute little lion cubs waiting for their dinner, we are still rightly repulsed by the sight of the lion sinking her teeth into the zebra (by con-trast, we are not repulsed by seeing the cow tearing up grass). We, who cannot plead ignorance and who can usually freely stay our hand, never have the lion's "excuse" of strict instinctual compulsion. Yet *some* mitigation of our violent ex-ploitation of other animals is provided if we acknowledge what is lost, through feelings of *awe* and *respect* and through appropriate voluntary self-restraint: Do not eat the blood, which is the life.[10]

Even as it departs morally from the "original" vegetarianism, the Noahide law regarding animals reflects and ratifies the order of being—the ontology—dis-closed in Genesis 1. The law reaffirms both the continuity and kinship of all life as living, while simultaneously also insisting on the decisive difference of human life as self-conscious and free. The animals, for their part, experience passion-ately the superiority of the human, in dread and fear. There is even a hint that their fear of man is not just naked fright, but terror tinged with something re-sembling awe; the word for fear, *mora',* is from the root *yare',* meaning at once

---

10. Eventually, appropriate self-restraint will entail not only respecting life, regarded homoge-neously and without distinctions of rank, but also recognizing hierarchy within the ranks of the liv-ing. Later in the Bible, the specifically Israelite laws will in fact extend and enlarge the Noahide self-restraint, especially in the dietary laws of Leviticus that, among other things, rule out eating all carnivorous animals and move human beings further in the direction of the "original" vegetarian-ism. But the positive principle of respect for life is first legitimated in the small negative restriction that, paradoxically, accompanies the legalization of eating meat.

"fear and revere." (This is the same passion that Abraham will feel toward God, and for which he will be supremely praised, in the story of the binding of Isaac, 22:12). The animals do not choose to fear man, nor does man choose to be feared. Rather the response is simply fitting to the hierarchic facts of life and to man's having consciously separated himself in a move toward god-likeness. Moreover, by showing some respect for all life's shared vitality, beyond what any animal can show, human beings manifest a superiority that is deserving of awe and reverent fear.

The reaffirmation of the ontology of Genesis 1 comes, however, with a different moral order. The order of being remains relevant, but it does not—or cannot—simply dictate conduct. The natural superiority of man now translates in practice into extensive use of animals, rather than stewardship. But use is restricted only for certain ends, that is, to meet necessity, in other words, for food; only up to a certain point; only without cruelty; and only without disdaining the animals used. Bloodshed is tolerated, blood lust is not.

In short, the dignity of animals still counts, in setting limits to the ends and means of human use and, especially—this is the main point—*in the attitude and disposition required of the human user.* The desired human attitude is ontologically grounded, and its point of view should inform all human practices regarding animals.[11] The concession to the human propensity to violate the animals is not absolute; and it is recognized always for the ontologically and morally dubious matter that it is. However, the real virtue of the law regarding the treatment of animals turns out to be its connection to the law regarding the treatment of other human beings. Animal blood may not be eaten, but human blood must not even be shed.

LAW REGARDING HUMAN BEINGS: THE IMAGE OF GOD AND THE SHEDDING OF HIS BLOOD

We remind ourselves that the law regarding animals is part of a package intended to make possible peaceful, civilized human life, a life of law and order,

11. This passage, if I correctly interpret it, refutes—or at least challenges—both those who blame and those who credit the Bible for allegedly giving man the unqualified authority to use animals in any way he likes, for his own benefit or pleasure. True, precisely *how* the Noahide attitude of respect for life might function in specific situations—say, regarding the use of animals in scientific research—will remain an open question. So, too, the legitimate *ends* for which animals may be properly used as means; much will depend on the meaning of "what is *necessary,*" always a vexed question for a being such as man, whose desires are both notoriously elastic and psychically come to be experienced as needs. But man's right to exploit and destroy is not unlimited, and the attitude that holds animal life in contempt is clearly proscribed. For an excellent treatment of this subject, see Ernest Fortin, "The Bible Made Me Do It," *Review of Politics* 57, no. 2 (spring 1995).

in the absence of which the Hobbesian state of nature would persist until primordial chaos returned. It is, in fact, this important human goal that alone justifies the exploitation of animals just discussed. God—or to speak philosophically, the wise legislator—is willing (at least at this primitive stage of civilization) to tolerate meat eating (under law) in the hope that man's ferocity would thereby be sated. If human spiritedness can be satisfied by meat, murder might become less likely.

Civil society is instituted, first of all, to protect and preserve human life; civil society stands or falls on the basis of whether or not it can do so successfully. For this reason, the foundation of civilized life demands (in practice) an unqualified respect for human life. This fundamental requirement is here powerfully expressed in the unprecedented announcement of the punishment for homicide:

"And surely your blood of your lives will I require [*that is,* I will require retribution for it]; at the hand of every beast will I require it; and at the hand of man, even at the hand of every man's brother, will I require the life of man. Whoever sheddeth man's blood, by man shall his blood be shed [*shofekh dam ha'adam ba'adam damo yishafekh*]; for in the image of God was man made." (9:5–6)

In the service of both safeguarding life and securing elementary justice, the Noahide law for the first time prohibits murder and compels its punishment.

The institution of the Noahide law regarding homicide represents an advance in righteousness over the spiraling anarchic cycles of revenge that characterized the antediluvian state of nature. Yet we are struck first by the rather ugly character of primary legal justice. The injunction is stated not as a moral rule, nor even as a negative commandment—"Thou shalt not murder" [12]—but rather as a demand for fitting, blood-shedding punishment once the implicit rule is violated. God, it seems, expects human bloodshed to continue, but it must no longer be tolerated; homicide must no longer go unpunished. Indeed, human bloodshed even by an animal must be avenged, and a fortiori, blood shed by a man's own brother—a clear reference to Cain and Abel.

Strictly speaking, the deed that is to be avenged is not solely murder but any sort of homicide or manslaughter. This primordial law makes no distinction among the differentiable crimes in which human blood is shed. The presence or absence of premeditation or intent to kill does not matter, and neither does the excuse of provocation or even self-defense; the deadly deed is all that counts. Human bloodshed is human bloodshed, no matter why it occurs and no matter

---

12. This commandment is first enunciated in Exodus 20, as part of the Ten Commandments.

who does it. Strangely to modern ears, shedding human blood must be avenged even if it is committed by an animal: "at the hand of every beast will I require it" (9:5); a man-slaughtering beast must pay with his life. What is at issue here is less what we today call crime, more what we used to call defilement. The foul deed is foul all by itself, without regard to its cause; the pollution of human bloodshed must be cleansed and "undone" through retribution.[13]

Retribution, unlike the original deed, requires intention; for retribution to be retribution, its agent must understand, at least tacitly, that he is deliberately defending something important against violation and defilement. Thus, although other animals may be guilty of polluting, only the human animal can exact the requirement of reciprocal cleansing. In the Noahide law, this "can" is transformed into a "must." The required capital punishment is to be administered not directly by God but by human beings (*"by man* shall his blood be shed"); human beings now become responsible agents of the divinely ordained, just, yet bloody retribution. (From this passage, the rabbis would later deduce the establishment of human courts of justice to "execute justice," including, quite literally, to execute those who commit murder.) Human beings, in order to live as human beings, must freely accept the harsh responsibility for defending the inviolability of human life.

Seen in context, the Noahide injunction regarding retribution is, in fact, a device for restraining much greater harshness. In contrast to the prelegal kind of revenge, men will now take no more than a life for a life, and the life only of the murderer, not also that of his wife and children. The temptation of righteous indignation to excessive vengeance, with spiraling violence begetting more violence, is strongly curtailed. Anger and force are brought under rational rule and measured proportion, which is to say, are brought into line with an idea of justice.

The murderer's life for the life he murdered in fact exemplifies the first principle of strict and equal justice: the violator gets exactly what he deserves. The

---

13. Later Israelite law will, of course, acknowledge the difference between premeditated murder and accidental homicide, and provide lesser punishments for the latter. (See, for example, Exodus 21:12–14.) The strict act-oriented justice of strict liability is a crude beginning. We are inclined to regard it as primitive. But there is something to be said for the position that this primordial justice is justice indeed, albeit more rational than reasonable. On this question, see the *Oresteia* of Aeschylus. This trilogy powerfully enacts the conflict between the clear if ugly blood-for-blood justice of the old theological order, represented by the Furies, and the clouded but peaceful justice of a fair trial by jury, one that admits arguments about intent, represented by the new, rational Olympian gods Apollo and Athena. Aeschylus shows that progress, though welcome, is accompanied by increased uncertainty about guilt and responsibility: the trial of Orestes, who is clearly guilty of matricide, ends with a hung jury; the six-six tie vote among the human jurors is broken only when Athena, mounting a sophistic defense, casts her vote for acquittal.

language of the Hebrew text—*shofekh* (sheds) *dam* (blood) *ha'adam* (of man), *ba'adam* (by man) *damo* (his blood) *yishafekh* (will be shed)—makes the point beautifully, through word repetition and inverted word order. In the mirrored (chiastic) structure—abccba—the second three-word injunction, for retribution, precisely and equally reverses the first three-word shedding of human blood.[14] As you go in, so you come out; as you do to another, so by another it will be done to you. The first deed is mirror-reversed by the second; the second deed constitutes an *un*doing of the first.[15] In addition, the retributive deed is deliberately (reflectively) an answer to the first, which had no such justifying antecedent and which need not have involved any reflection. The retributive undoing is done, as the text indicates, for a good reason. There are vital principles that need defending.

Although it speaks mainly about punishment, the Noahide law at the same time implicitly conveys a lofty moral message: radical human equality regarding the value of human life. Even before we are explicitly told that all human beings are equally god-like because they are all equally made in God's image (9:6), the retributive rule of a life for a life is itself a teacher of equality. Against our ever-present natural temptation to care only for ourselves and for our own and to depreciate or ignore the value of the stranger, and against our prideful propensity to make our own puffed-up sense of self-worth the sole standard of justice, the Noahide law teaches that, at least with respect to life itself, every human being has a claim and a standing *equal* to our own. As the text soon makes clear, such equality can be grounded only in the (recognized) equal *humanity* of each human being.

True, this (or any other) lofty moral principle is by itself too weak to withstand our violent passions—our angers, hatreds, envies, lusts, spites, and greed. It needs to be defended by armed yet just retribution. The threat of retribution deters future violations; the practice of measured retribution purges past violations and enables the community to reconstitute itself around its founding principles. For reasons not only of security but also of moral integrity, the community must insist that whosoever denies, by shedding human blood, the inviolate equal humanity of human life denies and thus forfeits his own share in it.

14. The sequence of words in this six-word chiastic phrase also provides a visual image of man's condition in the new human order. In the center, we have a picture of society (*cc: ha'adam ba'adam,* "man by man") set within bounds. Beyond these bounds, there is bloodshed on all sides. (I owe this lovely observation to Yuval Levin.)

15. This means that the executioner is not a murderer. Because it is an *undoing* of the original crime, the act of capital retribution does not itself require a response of further retribution. This is yet another indication that the law intends to put an end to the cycle of never-ending demands for revenge that characterizes the state of nature. I owe this observation to Bill Rosen.

The guaranteed strict reciprocity of life for life provides the teeth needed to defend the underlying lofty principle of human equality.

Nevertheless, murder is to be eschewed not only to avoid the punishment. That may be a motive, which speaks to our fears; but there is also a reason, which speaks to our minds. The fundamental reason that makes murder wrong—and that even justifies punishing it homicidally!—is man's divinelike status: "for in the image of God was man made." [16] Not the other fellow's unwillingness to be killed, not even (or only) our desire to avoid sharing his fate through retribution, but *his*—any human being's—*very being* requires that we respect his life. Human life is to be respected more than animal life because man is more than an animal; man is said to be god-like.

Three questions are raised by this assertion: What does it mean? How does it function as a reason, and for what? What do Noah and his sons—and what do we—understand by it?

What "image of God" or man's god-likeness means is, as we saw in Chapter One, not easy to say. (It is presumably even harder for Noah, who does not have the benefit of reading Genesis 1.) Biblical expressions generally gain their meaning both from their local contexts and from the echoes recalled from their previous occurrences, and also by the transformations that the local usage imposes on previous meanings. As we will see shortly, the notion "image of God" seems to be undergoing such an evolution in meaning for the reader. But it is also, for the first time, acquiring meaning for the human actors in the biblical narrative.

Readers will surely remember that, in Genesis 1, man was created as the cosmos's one god-like being. But those original remarks about man's god-likeness were not addressed to human hearers (except for us readers). Here, in an echo of that passage, God tells man directly (rational translation: man clearly learns [17]) and for the first time that human beings are "in the image of God." Man becomes conscious of his own god-likeness. As a result, man's special cosmic status as a god-like being—known to the reader from the creation story—acquires moral and legal meaning; for it enters human consciousness

16. The second part of verse 6 seems to make two points: man is in the image of God (that is, man is god-*like*), and man was *made* thus by God. The decisive point is the first. Man's creatureliness cannot be the reason for avoiding bloodshed: the animals too were made by God, yet permission to kill them for food has just been given. The full weight rests on man's *being* in the image of God.

17. Let us generalize the interpretive strategy. "God tells man X" conveys two distinct points: (1) man hears or learns the truth about X (if you will, authoritatively and convincingly) and (2) the source of his learning this is God. A philosophical reading will concentrate first on the first point, man's insight or understanding, leaving aside the question (and the mystery) of how that insight might have arrived. We too will bracket the matter of the source, at least for now. God's role in this story we shall consider in the last section of this chapter.

precisely at the point at which man becomes a moral and legal being. Absolutely fittingly, this teaching *about* man is here gained *by man* only when human beings, by deliberate decision, undertake to rise above their animal condition. Human beings learn about their god-likeness only when they quit the state of nature, take up the state of right, and seek a relation with the divine—in short, when they *in fact* become *more* god-like than they were before. Man discovers, right here, his in-between status: we are higher than the animals, we are like—albeit lower than—a god.

Once again, please note that the *truth* of the Bible's assertion does *not* rest on biblical authority. Man's more-than-animal status is in fact performatively demonstrated whenever human beings quit the state of nature and set up life under such a law, a law that exacts just punishment for shedding human (that is, more-than-animal) blood. The law that establishes that men are to be law-abiding and law-enforcing both insists on, and thereby demonstrates the truth of, the ontological and god-like superiority of man: "We human beings, alone among the creatures, will live by and care about what is said to be right and just."

Taking as the divine standard the activities that God displays in the first creation story, we argued in Chapter One that man's god-likeness comprises his capacities for speech and reason, his freedom in doing and making, and his powers of contemplation, judgment, and care. To these one may add, from the second creation story, man's involvement with questions of good and bad, said explicitly by God Himself to be a distinguishing mark of the divine ("Now the man is become *like one of us, to know good and bad*"; 3:22, emphasis added).[18] Human beings, like God but unlike the other animals, distinguish good and bad, have opinions and care about their difference, and constitute their whole life in the light of this distinction. Animals may suffer what is, for them, good and bad, or pursue the one and avoid the other instinctively; but they have no notion of either.

The Noahide code adds a third layer of meaning to man's likeness to the divine. The exalted position he obtains in relation to the other animals—he may use them almost at will, while they live in awesome dread of him—attests to his more-than-animal status. But it is especially in taking up the way of law, justice, and punishment that man becomes god-like in new and unprecedented ways. Only human beings—like God or gods—articulate generalized and intelligible rules of conduct. Only human beings—like God or gods—take measures to punish or redress violations of those rules. Only human beings—like God or

18. We recall that in the first creation story, man is created straightaway in God's likeness; in the second account, man is, to begin with, made of dust, and he *acquires* god-like qualities only at the end, and then only in transgressing.

gods—exercise death-dealing avenging power. Only human beings—like God or gods—undertake to rationally define and execute justice, and only they establish communal means to secure it. Indeed, as the passage establishing the law regarding homicide indicates, the very pronouncements "Murder is bad" and "Retribution will be required" constitute proof of *these* god-like qualities of human beings (as does the establishment of society founded on these beliefs and practices).

In sum, man has special standing not only because he shares in reason, freedom, judgment, and moral concern and, as a result, lives a life freighted with moral self-consciousness. He has special standing also because he uses his freedom and reason to promulgate moral and legal rules and to pass moral and legal judgments, first among which is the judgment that manslaughter is to be punished in kind because it violates the dignity of such a moral being.[19]

In the local context, man's being in the image of God serves to explain both why human bloodshed is so heinous, demanding in-kind retribution, and why human agents are both obliged to execute it and justified in doing so. Manslaughter, by violating the image, violates also the divine original. Retribution, by vindicating the image, pays homage to the divine.

Yet man is, at most, only god*ly;* he is not God or a god. To be an image (or a likeness) is also to be *different* from that of which one is an image. Man is, at most, a *mere* likeness of God. With us, the seemingly godly powers and concerns described above occur conjoined with our animality. We are also vulnerable flesh and blood—no less than the other animals. God's image is tied to blood, which is the life.

The point is crucial, and stands apart from the text that teaches it: everything high about human life—thinking, speaking, willing, loving, legislating, judging, acting—depends absolutely on everything low: ingestion, digestion, absorption, circulation, respiration, perspiration, excretion. In the case of human beings, "divinity" needs blood—or "mere" life—to sustain itself. Yet because of what it holds up, human blood—that is, human life—deserves special respect, beyond what is owed to life as such: the low ceases to be merely the low.[20] The biblical text elegantly mirrors this truth about its subject, subtly merging both high and

19. We note a crucial implication: what will come later to be known as the *sanctity* of human life rests absolutely on the *dignity*—the god-like-ness—of human beings. Contemporary discussions, such as those surrounding assisted suicide and euthanasia, that pit arguments for human dignity *against* arguments for the sanctity of life are regrettably ignorant of the interdependence of these two notions. This point will be strengthened in the next few paragraphs.

20. Modern physiological evidence could be adduced in support of this thesis: in human beings, posture, gestalt, respiration, diet, and the "premature" birth of infants into the social womb of the first year of life, among other things, all show the marks of the copresence of rationality.

low: though the *reason* given for punishing murder concerns man's *godliness*, the *injunction* itself concerns man's *blood.* Respect the god-like; do not shed its blood! Respect for anything *human* requires—*pace* philosophers of personhood and autonomy—respecting *everything* human, requires respecting human being as such. Paradoxically, human elevation is achieved only through a law that reminds the god-like man to honor and defend his precarious, animal-like mortal existence—his blood.

Taking human life is wrong—as is disrespect for animal life—for reasons *immanent* in the nature of things, above and beyond the needs of society and apart from the will of the murderer or the suffering of the victim. Indeed, human society is instituted to defend human life, and its self-understanding as *human* society rests precisely upon this insight of common humanity implicit in the law proscribing murder—a law asserted into the teeth of the equally human (all too human) propensity to kill others of our kind, out of greed, lust, jealousy, anger, or pride. The universal language of law is, to be sure, abstract and cold, and hardly commensurate with the horror and revulsion we feel at the sight (or news) of a murder—or even at the sight of a corpse. Yet that horror, like the Noahide law, bespeaks an awareness that the wanton spilling of human blood is a violation and a desecration, not only of our laws but also of being itself (compare 4:10).

The Noahide law against homicide and the responsibility for enforcing it turn out to be great gifts to the community, for at least three reasons. First, only when men accept the responsibility for executing strict retributive justice can their own lives as human beings be secure. Second, only when men join together around shared obligations and responsibilities do individuals become a genuine community: because enforcement of law is something that the human beings must do together, it unites them around a common principle or ideal. Third, only in this way can they be said to affirm in deed that they appreciate what it means to be equally in God's image, demonstrating their god-likeness by exercising moral responsibility in the name of the equal sanctity and dignity of human life.

These deeper benefits of the Noahide law may not, however, be evident at first glance. And we have no idea what Noah himself made of what he had just been told, either regarding his new obligations or the justifying explanation, "in God's image." Noah's response was silence, perhaps from incomprehension or puzzlement, perhaps from understanding all too well, perhaps from fear or reluctance to comply, perhaps from despair over the human prospect. God's speech about bloodshed and retribution could hardly have been what Noah expected to hear in response to his sacrificial offering. To address the human silence, God has to say more. God makes Noah a crucial promise.

THE IMPORTANCE OF THE COVENANT

The new world order rests not only on law but also on a covenant, God's promise never again to destroy all flesh.

> And God said to Noah and to his sons with him, saying,
> "And I, behold, I establish my covenant [*berith*] with you and with your seed after you, and with every living creature that is with you, the fowl and the cattle and every beast of the earth with you, all that have come out of the ark, even every beast of the earth. And I will establish my covenant with you, that never again shall all flesh be cut off by the waters of a flood, and never again shall there be a flood to destroy the earth." (9:8–11)

The Hebrew word *berith*, translated "covenant," comes from a root meaning "to bind together." A covenant is an agreement or promise that binds together that which is naturally—that is, in the absence of covenant—separate and apart. The covenant here announced corrects a dangerous cleavage in the antediluvian world. As Robert Sacks remarks: "After the unspoken bonds which should have unified the world in the antediluvian period were broken, they had to be replaced by external and explicit bonds." God here explicitly binds Himself to all of life—both human and animal—forevermore. God promises never again to destroy all life (at least through flooding and the return to the natural chaotic beginnings). Or to look at it somewhat differently, God's covenant, which promises to bind up nature's destructive fury, overcomes by agreement nature's indifference, not to say hostility, to human aspiration.

God's promise is unilateral, one-sided, and unconditional. It does not require human agreement; it does not ask anything of either man or the animals; it does not even depend on man's obedience to the newly given law. It expresses, from God's side alone, His voluntary and permanent self-restraint from the destruction of all life. Thus it provides for man the prospect of a terrestrial future secure against global natural catastrophe.

Belief in the covenant is crucial to the new world order; it is equal in importance to the law. Just as human nature, in the absence of law, always threatens human life through violence, so external nature, in the absence of covenant, always threatens human life through cataclysm. Thus, a belief that the outside world ("dumb nature") will not ultimately crush us is absolutely indispensable to all higher human possibilities. Civilized life, in which human beings live partly for posterity, depends upon hope for the future. Absent such hope, human beings, always seeing doom before their eyes, would be little inclined to do much of anything.[21] Most likely living only for the moment, they would hardly be inclined to accept the restraints of law or the obligations to do justice. This is why God's promise, though it comes after the law is pronounced, does not depend on man's restraint. On the contrary, man's self-restraint rests on something like trust in the substance of God's promise: no more floods.

Yet Noah and his sons, hearing God's promise, make no response. They are either dumbfounded or disbelieving. God must speak again.

And God said,[22]
"This is the sign of the covenant that I make between Me and you and
    every living creature that is with you, for everlasting generations:
I do set my bow in the cloud, and it shall be a sign of the covenant be-
    tween Me and the earth.
And it shall come to pass, when I bring a cloud over the earth that the
    bow shall be seen in the cloud.
And I will remember My covenant which is between Me and you and
    every living creature of all flesh; and the waters shall no more become
    a flood to destroy all flesh.
And the bow shall be in the cloud; and I will look upon it, that I may re-
    member the everlasting covenant between God and every living crea-
    ture of all flesh that is upon the earth."
And God said to Noah,
"This is the sign of the covenant which I have established between Me
    and all flesh that is upon the earth." (9:12–17)

The spoken promise of a secure future is insufficient. Man requires a sign, not only now but forever, especially when despair threatens to overtake him. All covenants, remarks Sacks, "require a sign since all covenants must be remem-

---

21. A comparable point is made in Greek tragedy. Before he gave to human beings the transforming gift of fire (and the arts), Prometheus gave them the gift of "blind hopes," which kept them from being preoccupied with death and freed them from gloom about the future (Aeschylus, *Prometheus Bound*, ll. 250–53). God's covenant with Noah, in contrast, appears to offer something truer and much more reliable than Prometheus's *blind* hopes.

22. "This is the first instance of a common convention of biblical narrative: when a speaker addresses someone and the formula for introducing speech is repeated with no intervening response from the interlocutor, it generally indicates some sort of significant silence—a failure to comprehend, a resistance to the speaker's words, and so forth. . . . The flood-battered Noah evidently needs further assurance, so God goes on, with a second formula for introducing speech ['And God said'], to offer the rainbow as outward token of His covenant." Robert Alter, *Genesis: Translation and Commentary* (New York: W. W. Norton, 1996), 39.

bered. Their being is in their being remembered because they lack sufficient natural foundation. Memory is such an integral part of a covenant that even God must have a sign, because without a sign there is no covenant."

According to the text, God does indeed say that the rainbow will remind *Him* of His everlasting promise; this memory will keep God from sending another Flood, even though it might be warranted. But it is far more important that Noah and other human beings both remember what God said and continue to believe it. It is we who need to be reminded of this story, of this covenant, and in particular, of God's speech about the rainbow. For it is *man's* memory of the meaning of the rainbow that sustains the human attitudes necessary for civilization.

The rainbow, a natural phenomenon visible to all, is here, through speech, given a more than natural meaning, understandable only by human beings.[23] Like the covenant itself, the rainbow *regarded as a sign* betokens a world more gracious than that of nature on her own. True, without its explicit connection to God's covenant, the rainbow might appear a perfect token of nature's grace. Coming with the reappearance of the sun after a storm, it can be, by itself, a beautiful sign of hope. But rainbows are ephemeral and natural hope fades. However, when and if the rainbow is interpreted through the prism of this story, it reminds human beings that the cosmic order is finally not inhospitable to human dreams and aspirations, and not because we are deserving. It reminds us of the great Flood, brought about by our own natural wickedness. It reminds us of nature's awesome destructive power, which God has promised not to unleash on us again, whatever we may do. It reminds us that though the evils we do might justify total destruction, the world graciously permits us to persevere and try again.

Thanks to this story and the meaning it ascribes to the rainbow, Noah and his sons—and all human beings descended from them—may come to believe that fate, the gods, and the cosmos are not arrayed against us. Remembering the covenant, we may hope and plan for the future. We may establish communities founded on right rather than might. We may be fruitful and multiply and we may legislate for ourselves and our posterity, reassured that our efforts will not be washed away.

THE EVILS OF DOING JUSTICE

Our rosy picture of the new world order is not altogether true to the text. We have deliberately avoided—until now—a troubling fact: the institution of capi-

---

23. This transformation of the natural is fully in keeping with the institution of reason-based law to replace the natural reign of violence.

tal punishment. The avengers of human bloodshed are ordered to shed human blood. Does this not make them guilty of the same violation they are avenging? How can this be just or right? And even if it can be shown to be just, how can it be good for a world order devoted to safeguarding and promoting life? [24]

Any answer must remember the context, and the context is lawlessness. As we have said before, whatever its ambiguities, the Noahide law clearly represents a big advance over the prelegal condition, in which vengeance is excessive, unlimited, and measured solely by *personal* standards of desert and injury. In contrast, we have here impersonal retribution, precisely limited in extent, universal in scope, with no exceptions for the mighty, and based on a recognizable ontological standard ("image of God"). In addition, the retribution of "a life for a life" is proportionate, reciprocal, and fitting. The killer, and *only* the killer, gets what killers deserve. This absolute violation cannot be "fixed" by ransom (money) but must be paid for in kind. Moreover, by willfully denying the god-like nature of human life, the killer denies his own share of god-likeness, becoming worse than an animal—or, perhaps, more than a man. He thus forfeits his claim to remain as a member of the human community. For all these reasons, the punishment is just. Even the killer himself, in moments of rational and fair-minded detachment, would readily agree with this verdict.

But this account focuses solely on the perpetrator, not on the avengers. How can one assert the inviolability of human life and, in the same breath, insist that human beings deliberately take human life—especially to uphold the god-like sanctity of human life? Even if we agree that the killer gets what he deserves, there seems to be a problem. True, the burden of punishment falls on the human community as a whole ("*by man* shall his blood be shed"), not on the relatives of the slain. But this just shifts the problem to the collective: the community and its representatives, in executing justice, become guilty of bloodshed.

One may seek to defend the Noahide law as providing primitive justice for primitive times, later to be improved upon. The deed and its punishment are crudely set forth. Homicide as such is to be punished homicidally, whatever the motive or intent, and regardless of possible mitigating circumstances. There is no provision that protects the wrongly accused; there is no exception even for self-defense. Later Israelite law will in fact qualify and refine the law and greatly moderate the punishment, in part out of concern for the effects of capital pun-

24. Every time I have taught Genesis, I have defended the justice of the entire Noahide law, only to be surprised again and again by strong objections from students who, for reasons having nothing to do with the text, believe that capital punishment is always immoral or unjust. But in my 1997 class, tenacious arguments by Adam Davis, Kristen Dietrich Balisi, and Margaret Litvin—arguments rooted in the text—finally convinced me that the situation is more ambiguous than I had before realized. The discussion in this section owes everything to my conversations with these students.

ishment on the avenging community. The need for these later modifications testifies to the defects of the Noahide law.

Another (and, I think, better) line of argument concedes the ugliness, and even badness, of capital punishment for the punishers, but insists on its necessity. Law insists that its just demands be backed by just punishment. If the punishment is just, and if *we* must, for our own humanity's sake, uphold justice, we have no choice. For one cannot defend human life without getting one's hands dirty. Executing justice is *necessarily* harsh and ugly.

Yet all these arguments, however reasonable, do not remove our disquiet. Suspicion persists that capital punishment, for all its justice and justification, is also a concession to human bloody-mindedness. That, after all, is the problem being addressed and accommodated.

Human beings have shown themselves to be blood shedders: recall the antediluvian violence of the Heroic Age, recall Noah's sacrifice and God's comment in response. Because there is no possibility of a simply pure and nonviolent humanity, the only hope is to contain human violence under law. The Noahide code offers two means of containment, both concessive. First, it tries to sate human wildness through the eating of meat (and hunting). Second, *it employs human wildness in the service of avenging human bloodshed; it tries to satisfy blood lust by giving it limited but honorable cover.*

Read very carefully, the text offers some support for this dark suggestion. The heart of the Noahide law is, as we have already noted, about retribution. It does not say, "Thou shalt not kill"; it says—to exaggerate—"Thou *shalt* kill." Whom shall—may—we kill? Only those who have killed. Man's bloody-mindedness, impossible to expunge, is licensed in the service of opposing bloody-mindedness.

But the foregoing arguments, however worthy, do not provide the final or decisive word. According to the text, what justifies the practice of capital punishment is that God demands it. Though He abandons the punishment of wholesale destruction, God Himself clearly indicates that individual guilty men must pay for their transgressions. God quite clearly indicates His own ongoing demand for retribution: "The blood of your lives I *will require*." But the avenging, from now on, will be the responsibility of man, not God. Man will now become God's scourge and minister, God's avenging angel: being in God's image now includes engaging in retributive justice, as God's partner and on God's behalf.[25] Taking another human being's life, especially under the banner of justice,

25. The crucial phrase, "for in the image of God was man made," comes right after "by man shall his blood be shed." It thus can be read as providing not only the reason why human bloodshed is wrong, but also the reason why human beings must avenge it capitally. Man the god-like must imitate God the avenger.

is perhaps the most god-like act we human beings can perform. But strangely, doing the deed may also remind us that we are very far from being divine.

To be sure, giving man responsibility as an avenger is an uncertain business. If it is mainly a concession to his violent side, it risks inflaming the very passions it seeks to control. But paradoxically, it may also lead him to prefer a less violent way of life. By having his nose rubbed in his own bloody-mindedness, avenging man may come to long for a more gentle way. The primary blood shedders will be deterred by the fear of death; but the avenging blood shedders, their hands stained by the blood of retribution, may themselves learn awe and reverence for human life. They may learn from their own experience as executioners to know what human life really is. God's withdrawal from direct retribution, in favor of human avengers, enables human beings to learn the limits of our vaunted god-likeness and the ungodliness of human justice—notwithstanding the fact that human justice and capital punishment have both been divinely ordained!

In the end, there appears to be no easy textual way fully to resolve the controversy about capital punishment. Perhaps that is the point. As we read about this crucial moment in the emergence of our humanity, the text invites us to consider the weaknesses as well as the strengths of nascent human society. It prods us to see how difficult it is for imperfect creatures to affirm and defend the dignity of human life. It provokes us to ask about the goodness of justice and punishment. Even as we welcome the Noahide law and covenant, we are alert to the evils that still remain in the hearts and minds of men, evils that cannot help but find a place in any human social arrangement.

THE DIVINE LAWGIVER

Up to this point, we have largely ignored the role of God in this account of the beginning of civil society. We have done so in order to show how the content of the Noahide law and covenant make perfect sense on grounds of reason, common sense, and political philosophy. In our wisdom-seeking spirit, we have continued to use the text to help us discover the truth, on the assumption that at least some of the wisdom the Bible contains does not depend on biblical authority. But fidelity to both the pursuit of wisdom and the text before us requires that we turn now to the most obvious and massive fact about what we have misleadingly been calling the Noahide law and covenant: God institutes them both, and Noah—man—says not a word. The new world order, like the created world itself, is entirely God's handiwork. What does this mean?

God plays the crucial role in both parts of the new world order. Through His unilateral covenant, He stands as the guarantor of the sustainability of the world, in opposition to the manifest inhospitality of unruly nature. In His blessing-cum-law, He stands as the more than human source for law, thus placing the law on the highest possible ground and making it deserving of the requisite awe and respect.

Political philosophers are quite familiar with stories of and arguments for the participation of the divine in the founding of law and civil society. In ancient Greece, many a city traced its mythic origins to a god; and Plato's *Laws,* his major work on legislation, opens with the question "Is it a god or some human being, strangers, who is given the credit for laying down your laws?"[26] Many political philosophers have regarded a belief in superintending gods as indispensable to any decent human society; as an old maxim had it, "No gods, no city." To this point, our own analysis has shown that decent human life requires a belief in a secure future and in the justice of law and the sureness of punishment. But such beliefs are considerably more stable in the presence of a belief in divine backing. A benevolent divine legislator serves to guarantee both requirements: the divinely supported cosmos, offering encouragement through hope; the divinely sanctioned law, offering moderation through fearful reverence.

Thus far political philosophy alone can take us. It can show us the utility, indeed, even the necessity, for politics and morals, of human belief in providential gods who care for human beings and who legislate and exact justice. To create such salutary beliefs, say those who ascribe the Bible to Moses (or to some other legislating sage), a wise legislator will put into the divine mouth those teachings he himself wants to impart, giving them the requisite supernatural authority. More generally, God or gods speak the lines their philanthropic human creators write for them. But we should not, in our latter-day sophistication about these matters, overlook the plain sense of the text. We must ponder the role of God as the text reveals it. The critical fact is this: God does not initiate the Noahide law without provocation. Noah (that is, self-consciously mortal man) has first addressed God *on his own.* Man, all by himself, divines the presence of the divine.

Noah's sacrifice had expressed a specifically human desire for a special human relation to the divine, there pursued through animal sacrifice. As we saw earlier, many things might have conspired to prompt Noah's (that is, man's) turn to the divine: his initial righteousness and simplicity, tied perhaps to his acceptance of mortality; horror at the chaos wrought by the Heroic Age; awe and dread before the mighty destructive power of the Flood; recognition of his humanity, of his difference from his animal roommates; gratitude for his own sur-

---

26. *The Laws of Plato,* trans. Thomas L. Pangle (New York: Basic Books, 1980), 3. The question is put by the Athenian stranger to Kleinias, a Cretan lawgiver charged with founding a new Cretan colony. Kleinias answers: "A god, stranger, a god—to say what is at any rate the most just thing. Among us Zeus, and among the Lacedaimonians, from whence this man here comes, I think they declare that it's Apollo. Isn't that so?" The Spartan Megillus answers, simply, "Yes."

vival, experienced as deliverance; and a generalized human desire for contact with the powers that be. The animal sacrifice itself, questionable though it was, manifested not only Noah's eagerness to communicate with the divine but also, perhaps, one or more of the states of soul that are, as we know from other cultural accounts, associated with the practices of burning incense and offering animals: an oceanic feeling, a longing for ecstasy, a wish for transcendence, a wild revolt against order, a primordial dread, a will to power.

To be sure, all these impulses may originate, without external cause, entirely from within the human soul, as expressions of need, and the god to whom sacrifice may be offered may represent merely a projection of human hope and fear. Indeed, God Himself, as we have argued, appears to attribute Noah's sacrifice—his choice to sacrifice animals—to man's evil inclinations. Nevertheless, it is likely that Noah's sacrifice was a response not only or mainly to his own inner needs and passions but also and especially to intimations of divinity offered him by and gleaned from the world. Noah, like Cain before him and with far better reason, seems to have divined the presence of some higher yet mysterious cosmic power to which human beings can and should be open.[27]

Seen in this light, Noah's sacrifice changes color (at least in part). Noah sends up questions in the form of the odor of burnt flesh: Do the powers that be like incense or roast meat, just as I do? Do they care enough for me to enter into contact with me? Noah receives an unexpected answer, one that calls attention to the meaning of his being the one kind of creature that is moved to ask such questions. The answer comes as a blessing, a law, and a covenant. Noah, the new human prototype, is told, "Yes, you have a special relationship to the divine; you are in God's image." But this means something other than possessing raw power, something other than devouring (or drowning) the animals and strewing (or drinking) their blood. It means accepting our god-like power to live justly and gratefully in a world not of our making. It means recognizing the unmerited and gracious hospitality of the world to human hopes and possibilities. A new relation between man and God is indeed established, not through bloody sacrifice but through speech and hearing—through a blessing, through commands, through a divine promise—and also through a visible sign (the rainbow), whose *meaning* is, however, known only through speech, hearing, and memory.

Noah's appeal to a corporeal God is answered by the arrival of an intellectual,

27. Noah had, of course, better access to the divine than do most men, who will, on their own, at best intuit the existence of some (unspecified) higher powers. The biblical God had given Noah precise instructions for building the ark. Noah thus experienced not only awesome and destructive divine power but also divine solicitude and care. Nonetheless, we should not therefore assume that Noah has a clear understanding of God's "character" or what He wants from human beings. Noah, unlike the reader, did not read the Bible.

moral, cosmological, and theological insight, delivered through speech to the human heart and mind (the reader's perhaps more than Noah's). This insight, packaged by the text into a directly spoken divine blessing, turns out really to *be* a blessing. Who among us can say with confidence from whence this insight came?

⁓

The new world order is really rather modest, humanly speaking: we have here only the rudiments of law and justice, tied only to the protection of life. Still the Noahide order is the prototype for all civil society. It rests, to repeat, on the belief in divinely sanctioned law to induce fearful reverence, which in turn leads to moderation; it rests also on the belief in a divinely supported cosmos (the covenant) to induce hope for the future, which in turn leads to encouragement. The divination of this perfect package of restraint and stimulation, inspired and supported by the ruling principle of the whole, is indeed the necessary basis of civil society. Knowing whether this foundation is sufficient requires reading further.

CHAPTER SEVEN

PATERNITY AND PIETY:

NOAH AND HIS SONS

*T*he Noahide code and covenant mark the founding of civil society, based on rudimentary but explicit notions of law and justice, rooted in the idea that all human beings are created equally in God's image. Humankind now faces a new prospect, founded on the hope for an enduring human future protected against natural cataclysm, thanks to God's covenant; and the hope for a peaceful social order protected against the violence of other men, thanks to the Noahide code. Human beings, rising above their animality, come to live under the first rudimentary rule of law.

With the law now established, thought naturally turns to the question of perpetuation, which is quite another matter. Founding requires the genius of new insights and the invention of new social arrangements to give them institutionalized expression. Perpetuation requires the will and the dedication to transmit those insights and arrangements from one generation to the next. The work of perpetuating law and civil society is carried on by tradition (*tradere*, "to hand over"), passed down from parents to children, from fathers to sons. Tradition requires fathers who are able to hand down and sons who are willing to receive. Perpetuation and tradition depend decisively on paternal authority and filial piety.

Paternal authority and filial piety are, not surprisingly, central themes of the Genesis narrative and crucial to its pedagogical purpose. How could it be otherwise in a book self-consciously engaged in perpetuating a tradition? As I have argued from the beginning of this book, Genesis is a work largely devoted to the education of the Hebrew patriarchs—and through them, of generations upon generations of fathers and sons—to the great work of fatherhood: the task of transmitting not just life but a way of life, a most particular way of life, devoted to righteousness and holiness and looking up to the divine. Most men, left to their own devices, do not readily leap to this paternal task. Though they may sire children, their energies are concentrated outside the home. They pursue other ways of life, devoted to wealth and pleasure, power and domination, or even to heroic quests for personal honor and glory (see Chapter Five). The greater their ambition, the more ambivalently they tend to regard their own sons. On the one hand, they welcome their sons as perpetuators of their name and preservers of their fame; and they take pride in their sons' achievements, which they see as extensions of their own. On the other hand, they see their sons as rivals to their supremacy; indeed, because the very existence and growing prowess of their sons constitute evidence of their own finitude and limitations, they may even come to resent them.[1] This ambivalence has its exact parallels on the side of the sons, for whom father is both an inspiration and an obstacle, a source of both pride and envy, someone to imitate and someone to supplant.

In order to encourage the ambivalent male reader to participate vicariously in the fatherly education of the Hebrew patriarchs, Genesis must show him first precisely why such an education is needed. Equally important, it must move him to care about whether in fact it can be obtained. These goals require demonstrating the natural or uninstructed ways of fathers and sons so as to reveal their psychic and moral ambiguity. Such a showing seems to be part of the purpose of the Bible's first tale about fatherhood, the story of Noah and his sons (Genesis 9:18–27), which, not surprisingly, is also the Bible's first tale of intergenerational conflict. As we have already seen, first tales in Genesis may be taken as paradigmatic: the story of Adam and Eve revealed fundamental and ineradicable tensions in the relationship of man and woman; the story of Cain and Abel exposed the fundamental rivalry that naturally accompanies the relationship of brothers. Similarly, we expect to discover, in this first story of Noah and sons, fundamental and troublesome aspects of the natural relationship between father and sons. We expect to learn not how things ought to be but rather how they are, absent some additional, corrective teaching.

Unlike the stories of Adam and Eve, Cain and Abel, or Noah's ark, the impor-

---

1. These complex feelings of heroic fathers for their sons are presented nowhere better than in Homer's *Iliad*. In an especially poignant example, the poet shows us the hero Hektor at home, where his wife, Andromache, pleads with him to stay within the walls of Troy and protect his family and his city instead of going out to fight Achilles. In this scene, Hektor fondly tosses about his infant son and makes prayer to the gods on his behalf: "Zeus, and you other immortals, grant that this boy, who is my son, may be as I am, pre-eminent among the Trojans, great in strength, as am I, and rule strongly over Ilion; and some day let them say of him: 'He is better by far than his father,' as he comes in from the fighting; and let him kill his enemy and bring home the blooded spoils, and delight the heart of his mother." (*The Iliad of Homer* VI.476–481; trans. Richmond Lattimore [Chicago: University of Chicago Press, 1951].) But Hektor rejects his wife's pleas and promptly goes forth to battle Achilles. Seeking his own glory, he gains only his death and the destruction of his city. His wife is taken captive and his son is slaughtered just as soon as Troy falls. Homer makes the reader see that Hektor's own ambition is, in fact, at odds with his prayer for his son. Heroic ambition does not enable men to care wholeheartedly for their offspring—or conversely, for offspring to easily accept their forebears.

tance of the story of Noah and his sons is largely neglected. Even where it is considered, its profundity is commonly overlooked, and virtually no one has seen why it happens to be one of the most significant stories in Genesis. Part of the reason for the story's neglect lies with the text itself: the tale is brief and its subject is ugly. Indeed, suspecting that it is brief because it is ugly, some scholars believe that it offers but a fragment of a larger tale known to the oral tradition, a tale that, according to one commentator, "must have seemed to the monotheistic writer dangerous to spell out." But the story is underappreciated also because of the altered sensibilities of modern readers. Many of us will have a hard time grasping what this story is about and why it matters, both for what it shows about the problem of fathers and sons and for the crucial role it plays in demonstrating the need for the biblical new way begun with Abraham. Not the least of our difficulties is our diminished attention to the meaning—and problem—of fatherhood and paternal authority. A few general remarks on the subject may set the table.

Until only yesterday, Father was a figure of authority to every young boy. To be sure, authority may have been shared with Mother, but Father was the imposing figure. His superior size and strength promised safety; his voice of authority laid down the rules and established reliable order; his patient instruction encouraged growth. At the same time—and on the other hand—Father's power often inspired fear and awe; his moral authority, shame and guilt; and his superior competence, a sense of inadequacy that could sometimes lead to envy. And then there was his pride of place with Mother, and all that that entailed—the so-called Oedipal problem, made notorious by Freud.

This highly complex aggregate of mixed feelings and attitudes made son-to-father relationships very unusual. They certainly made difficult, if not impossible, any easygoing friendship, which usually requires and fosters equality; one cannot simply be friends with someone one holds in awe. Yet these sentiments—even the uncomfortable ones like awe, fear, and shame—were (and are) perfectly suited, on the one side, to the parental task of rearing and, on the other side, to the possibility of inheriting not just life but a decent way of life from those responsible for our proper cultivation and moral development. Precisely because he is capable of inspiring awe as well as security, shame as well as orderliness, distance as well as nearness, emulation as well as confidence, and fear as well as hope, the father is able to do the fatherly work of preparing boys for moral manhood, including, eventually, their own fatherhood.

To be sure, the power can be abused: fathers can be bullies and tyrants, they can abuse both their authority and their sons. And even where paternal intentions are purely benevolent, it is often difficult to achieve a finely tuned mixture of encouragement and restraint. More important, errant paternal conduct can

easily betray the very teachings paternal authority aims to impart; a philander-
ing father, once exposed, has trouble teaching fidelity. Trust betrayed is hard
to recover, and hypocrisy is often unforgiven, *especially* by one's children. Still,
that—and how—Father exercises paternal authority, and equally, how boys
come to terms with Father, may make all the difference for the future life of the
sons—and the grandsons, great-grandsons, and so on and on.

The scope of the story of Noah and his sons is, therefore, not simply domestic. On the contrary, its purpose in exploring fatherhood and sonship is also and
especially social and political. Appearing as the immediate sequel to the new
covenant following the flood, it addresses questions related to perpetuating the
new world order: Will the new world order succeed? Will the fathers be able to
transmit a law-abiding and righteous way of life to their sons? To insure perpetuation, are the Noahide law and covenant protecting bodily life and emphasizing human equality sufficient? If not, what else is needed? Of fathers? Of sons?
Will fathers accept the paternal task of transmission? Will all sons take equally to
the ways of the father? Are all fathers equal *as transmitters;* are all sons equal *as
receivers?* If not, why not, and what can be done about it, socially, culturally, politically? All these questions are prompted by this story.

The story of Noah and his different sons also begins an account of the differentiation and divergence of humankind into multiple nations, each with a different way of life, each with a different view of the divine.[2] What accounts for
these national differences, and how do they emerge from the original unity of
the human race? Could differences in national character reflect differences in
character between their earliest progenitors? What are the fundamental alternatives in personal and national character? About these questions, too, our little
story speaks.

FAMILY ORDER, NATURAL AND CONVENTIONAL

Here is how the story begins.

> And the sons of Noah, that went forth from the ark, were Shem and Ham
> and Japheth; and Ham is the father of Canaan. These three were the sons
> of Noah, and of these was the whole earth overspread. (9:18–19)

2. The tripartite account of the origin of national diversity will continue, in Genesis 10, with a
lengthy genealogical tale of Noah's descendants, showing how the peoples of the earth evolved by descent from the three sons of Noah. Part three, Genesis 11:1–9, presents the competing yet (as we shall
see in Chapter Eight) complementary story of Babel, showing how the various peoples came to be
different as a result of acquiring different languages (and with them, I will argue, different world-
views).

The story's introduction leads back to the solitary ark of life afloat on the earth-covering, life-destroying waters and forward to a future time in which the whole earth will be overspread not with water but with people, all derived from three sons of one man. The narrative immediately focuses on the sons of Noah, and especially on Ham, the only son who is mentioned a second time, this time as *father* (of Canaan and the Canaanites; of this, more later).

We pause over the names of Noah's sons, names he presumably gave them. Shem means "name"—not only an appellation, but also "renown" or "respect"; the word "name" has already occurred many times in Genesis, referring not only to the identity of rivers (2:11, 13, 14), animals (2:19, 20), and persons (4:25), but also to fame and renown (*'anshei hashem,* "the men of renown"; 6:4). *Shem* has also been used, on at least one occasion, in connection with God: "then began men to call upon the *name* of the Lord [*beshem YHWH*]" (4:26); later, *Hashem,* "The Name," will be a pious way of referring to the Lord. Though we cannot know which meaning Noah had in mind when he named his son Shem, we suspect that because he was born in the Heroic Age, before the Flood, Shem was named by Noah in the hope of fame and renown.[3] The name of Ham, this story's central character, means "hot" or (?) "warm," from a verb meaning "to make warm, to become hot, to inflame oneself." The name of Japheth means "expansion," from a root meaning "open," though it may also be related to *yafeh,* meaning "beautiful." Three sons: "name or renown," "hot or inflammable," "open or expanded or beautiful." We wonder what Noah had in mind with these namings. We wonder also whether the namings proved prophetic, whether there is destiny in the names of Noah's sons.

But there is something strange about the order of names, Shem, Ham, and Japheth. Ham, the central character, is the youngest son; Shem, who turns out to be the model son and who is therefore always mentioned first, is the middle son; Japheth, although he is always named last, is, in fact, the eldest.[4] Natural priority—the order of birth—is not the same as virtue. If, as we suspect, the differences in their given names reflect or portend differences in character of Noah's sons, the out-of-order listing hints that the order of nature (birth) may

3. If so, Noah will have named Shem better than he knew. For as we shall see, Noah will later link Shem with the divine Name. It is through that linkage that Shem earns his reputation and renown. In this shift in the meaning of the name "Name," we may be seeing evidence of the Bible's sought-for shift from the heroic to the pious disposition.

4. The evidence about Shem and Japheth comes from three passages: Noah was five hundred years old when he first became a father (5:32); the Flood happened when Noah was six hundred (7:11), at which time his eldest son would have been one hundred years old; but Shem did not turn one hundred until two years after the Flood (11:10). Thus, Shem cannot be the firstborn. Regarding Ham, verse 9:24 tells us that he is the youngest.

need to be replaced by an order of goodness or merit—a necessity that informs much of the early part of Genesis. (In none of the patriarchal generations is the *firstborn* the right son for the work of perpetuation.)

We are moved to think about order, natural and conventional, not only by the puzzlements about the sequence of the sons but also by the reference back to the departure from the ark after the Flood: "the sons of Noah *that went forth from the ark.*" The story takes us back not to the Noahide code but to the time just before the law was established, to the end of the state of nature and the beginning of family life after the Flood, and more precisely, to the going forth from the ark. When the earth was fully dry, God had commanded Noah to leave the ark in a particular order: "thou, and thy wife, and thy sons, and thy son's wives with thee"(8:16). This prescribed order for leaving the ark differed from the order prescribed for entering it—in keeping with the fact that life prior to the Flood had entered the ark male and female but was to emerge into the new world "after their families."[5] But Noah reverses the prescribed order for disembarking. He emerges first with his sons, and only then with his wife and his sons' wives: "And Noah went forth, and his sons, and his wife, and his sons' wives with him" (8:18). Noah, a new man rescued from the Heroic Age, nevertheless apparently still holds to a heroic model of family structure: it is only the men who count. Failing to give proper place to his wife,[6] Noah has (perhaps inadvertently) failed to appreciate the right order of the household. He has failed to see that leading a family means more than sowing your seed; he has failed to recognize that it requires honoring *both* father and mother if transmission is to take place. Measure for measure, as we shall see, Noah will have his own paternal authority challenged by one of his sons.

UNFATHERING ONESELF: NOAH'S DRUNKEN EXPOSURE

Noah, it must be admitted straightaway, contributes to his own undoing:

> And Noah the master of the earth [*or* husbandman: *'ish ha'adamah*] began and planted a vineyard [*or* was the first to plant a vineyard]; and he drank of the wine and was drunken; and he was uncovered in his tent. (9:20–21)

5. Compare 6:19 with 8:19. When giving instructions to Noah about *entering* the ark, God had listed Noah's sons before his wife: "and thou shalt come into the ark, thou, and thy sons, and thy wife, and thy sons' wives with thee" (6:18).
6. We never learn the name of Noah's wife. Her anonymity may betoken her low standing in Noah's eyes and, more generally, the low standing of wives in the pre-Abrahamic (heroic) way of the world. After Eve, women are barely mentioned, and except for the two wives of Cain's descendant Lamech, none are known by name until we get to Sarah. In contrast, named and powerful wives are crucial to the stories of the three patriarchs Abraham, Isaac, and Jacob.

Noah, the saving remnant before the Flood, is now the man or master of the new earth. Like the prototypical Cain, the new big man on the earth takes to planting; unlike Cain, Noah takes to viticulture, quite on his own and without hesitation. Wine making is not a divine gift, but a human invention.[7]

Noah's interest in the vineyard—like that of any human being—is understandable. The wondrous discovery of fermentation enables the fruit of the vine to yield more than mere sustenance: wine "to gladden the heart of man" elevates the spirit and enables man to obtain (also from the ground) a partial relief from the curse upon the earth that makes him sweat for his bread. Yet at the same time, wine is the cause of drunkenness, of the erosion of the ability to make distinctions, of chaos. The Hebrew word translated "began" also has the meaning of "being profane": says the great eleventh-century Hebrew commentator Rashi, "He profaned [degraded] himself, for he should have occupied himself first with planting something different."[8]

Given his ordeal upon the waters, one can perhaps understand Noah's turn to drink. Despite God's promise of no more floods, Noah may even have sunk into despair, especially insofar as the receding waters left behind a desolate landscape littered with the skeletons and rotting corpses of animals and men drowned in the Flood. Noah may well have sought solace in the grape, or even forgetfulness. Like the Flood, which covered over the earliest beginnings, so drink covers over all painful memories of destruction and desolation.[9] Alternatively, Noah may have been overwhelmed by his new responsibilities as master of the earth, especially as defined under the Noahide code. He may have recoiled and sought escape from the harsh burdens imposed by the new law with its demands for capital punishment. Or yet again, being simple (*tamim;* 6:9) or perhaps exuber-

7. In the Greek tradition, the hero of the Flood, Deucalion, is connected to Dionysus, the god who brings wine to humankind.

8. As we discussed in Chapter Six, Noah's susceptibility to Dionysian chaos was already revealed in his sacrifice after leaving the ark. In response to this ritualized act of wildness, God immediately establishes the Noahide law and covenant—which is then challenged in the present tale.

9. Robert Sacks suggests that such forgetfulness of the Flood and the antediluvian world are necessary for the biblical way:

As we read the Book of Genesis we are forced to participate in Noah's drunken stupor. The wine of oblivion will affect our relationship to the book from this point on. The names Man [=*Adam*], Eve, Cain, Abel, Methuselah, Seth, Enoch, the Flood, the Serpent, Eden—none of these names will ever appear again within the Torah or the books of the earlier Prophets, although on rare occasions the later Prophets do allow themselves to break with this understanding of the past.

The origins of the whole must be stated in some form, but they must also be forgotten. From the Biblical point of view they may not be hearkened back to either as a paradigm or as a way of understanding. The temporal beginnings must be superseded by the Covenant.

ant without knowledge (see his sacrifice), Noah may just not have foreseen the power or consequences of wine; many an innocent is unwittingly laid low by drink.

Yet regardless of his motives, and despite his possible desire to forget the past, the important fact remains: Noah was drunk and uncovered in his tent. His drunkenness robs Noah of his dignity, his paternal authority, and his very humanity. Prostrate rather than upright, this newly established master of the earth has, in the space of one verse, utterly lost his standing. Worse, instead of escaping from his origins, Noah in fact returns to the shameful naked condition of the aboriginal state: "he was uncovered in his tent."[10] Stripped of his clothing, naked, exposed, and vulnerable to disgrace, he appears merely as a *male*, not as a father—not even as a humanized, rational animal. Noah will not be the last man who degrades and unfathers himself as a result of drink. Paternal authority and respectability are precarious indeed.

UNFATHERING YOUR FATHER: SHAMELESS LOOKING

But the real damage requires that his degradation—his dead-drunkenness and especially his exposed nakedness—be observed, and observed by his sons.

> And Ham, the father of Canaan, saw the nakedness of his father, and told his two brothers outside. (9:22)

Ham is identified again as "the father of Canaan": as we think about Ham's present conduct toward his father, Noah, we are invited to see that it entails consequences also for his son Canaan. Ham here does two things: he sees and he tells. The first might have been accidental, though one wonders what he was doing in

---

10. My friend and colleague Hillel Fradkin has suggested to me an attractive alternative reading, in which Noah is trying to escape not from his origins but only from his more recent, traumatic past and his new responsibilities. Noah may in fact be seeking the true origins, that earliest Edenic (pre-transgression) condition of innocence and wholeness; and at first glance, it appears as if he gains something like a return to this original state, a state in which human beings were naked but were *not* ashamed. Yet as Fradkin adds, Noah's condition is nothing like the originally innocent one because it has been achieved through drunkenness, which depends, in turn, on the way of Cain, the cultivated way of agriculture. I would add that Noah's reaction upon waking makes clear that he is neither innocent nor free of the sense of shame, that he cannot shed the sense of shame that attaches to exposed nakedness. Regarding the important matter of paternal authority, the moral import of Fradkin's suggested reading does not differ from the one I am elaborating. Noah's attempt to reach the shame-free beginning is tantamount to a desire to shed paternal authority, law, self-consciousness, and all awareness of good and bad—in short, a desire to give up the responsibilities of fatherhood and leadership.

his father's tent; indeed, the juxtaposition of Noah "in his tent" with "Ham . . . saw . . . and told . . . outside" suggests that Ham's first misdeed—a misdeed that tells the whole story—was his disrespectful invading of his father's private space. Be this as it may, his second act (telling his brothers) clearly shows that—for this son, at least—the seeing could just as well have been intentional. Ham looks upon his father's shame and *traffics* in it.

Two questions occur to us: What does it mean to "look upon the nakedness" of one's father? And what sort of a human being would gladly do so and boast— or at least blab—about it? In the story of man and woman in the garden, the discovery of nakedness is an epochal event, the immediate consequence of gaining knowledge of good and bad. As we discussed in an earlier chapter, nakedness in that context means preeminently sexuality itself. Sexual neediness, its dependence on another person not under one's control, its resistance to self-command, and its link with our perishability are all reasons why sexual self-consciousness is colored with shame, and why we move immediately and almost instinctively to cover up. But here, in the Noah story, we are considering the further meaning of seeing nakedness *uncovered*, of removing clothing, and not between man and woman but between father and son.

It is true that later in the Bible, the expression "uncover the nakedness of" is a euphemism for "have sexual relations with." For example, the law of forbidden unions (Leviticus 18) is expressed entirely in the form "Thou shalt not uncover the nakedness of." For this reason, some commentators have suggested that Ham performed some abominable deed upon his drunken father.[11] But there is no textual warrant for such a suggestion.[12] Besides, what Ham did is more than sufficiently odious, even though he did not lay a hand on Noah.

Noah, without his clothes, and prostrate in his tent in a drunken stupor, lies dehumanized and unfathered, stripped of all human ways (though as a result of a peculiarly human way, the way of Bacchus). Ham's viewing confirms

11. Castration and homosexual rape have both been suggested. These commentators, rabbinic scholars among them, take support from the existence of Canaanite and other legends that tell of an ancestral god who castrated his father. And some people argue that a similar tale, much cruder and uglier than what remains, was part of an oral Israelite tradition before the Torah was written. Perhaps delicacy censored the original tale, so that the one we now have speaks only euphemistically about the abominable deed. But I am inclined to the view, defended in the sequel, that even the minimal misdeeds of looking and telling are sufficiently shocking and reprehensible and, moreover, that they are perfectly suited to the story's purpose and meaning. We have already seen that the Torah deliberately retells, but only with major changes, stories from other traditions, presumably in order to convey a very different teaching. The standard for practicing proper reverence for one's father is set much higher if one may not even *look upon* his nakedness and shame.

12. A full analysis and decisive refutation of this position is given by U. Cassuto, *A Commentary on the Book of Genesis, Part Two: From Noah to Abraham* (Jerusalem: Magnes Press, 1964), 150–53.

and ratifies his father's unfathering. To put it sharply, Ham's viewing—and telling—is metaphorically an act of patricide and incest, of overturning the father *as a father*. Without disturbing a hair on Noah's head, Ham engages in father killing.

This overturning of the father is not the overturning of his biological paternity or the taking of his life: on the contrary, he is overturned precisely by being reduced to mere male-source-of-seed. Eliminated is the father as authority, as guide, as teacher of law, custom, and a way of life. Ham sees and celebrates only the natural and barest fact of sex; he is blind to everything that makes transmission and rearing possible.

Thus, as Robert Sacks has pointed out, by overturning his father as a source of authority, Ham implicitly rejects the new covenant and life under law, designed to replace the antediluvian world. Anticipating the various paganisms that will soon be founded by his descendants (and against which the Bible, from its opening chapter, is quietly polemicizing), Ham, "the father of Canaan," gives primacy to the merely temporal and amoral beginnings. He looks back to precovenantal (or natural) origins.

But the nature to which Ham looks is utterly demystified. His shamelessness not only violates paternal honor and authority; it also violates sexuality itself. To see this better we need a brief excursion into the (very complex) subject of shame.

Our English word "shame" is, I believe, too broad for the phenomenon. Help comes from the ancient Greeks, who distinguished two kinds of shame—*aischyne* and *aidos*. The origin of *aischyne* is dishonor; we experience it in violating man-made codes and mores. The origin of *aidos* is awe; we feel it especially when we stand before things that *naturally* inspire reverence, things that are mysterious, things that have a power or a secret that we should respect. We feel *aidos* when we enter the darkness of a cave or a forest, when we enter a temple or a courtroom, when we stand before mighty human figures—a Churchill, Einstein, Tolstoy, or Kant. And we feel it—or should feel it—with regard to sex: here too there is mysterious creative power to which we

---

The pivotal piece of evidence is this: "[O]f Shem and Japheth it is said, in contradistinction to Ham's action: *their faces were turned away,* AND THEY DID NOT SEE THEIR FATHER'S NAKEDNESS (*v. 23*), from which we may infer, conversely, that Ham's sin consisted of seeing only. Furthermore, the statement (*ibid.*), *and covered the nakedness of their father,* supports this interpretation: if the covering was an adequate remedy, it follows that the misdemeanour was confined to seeing" (151, emphasis in original). If Shem and Japheth did not see Noah's nakedness *because their faces were turned away,* their not seeing must be understood literally: they did not see because they refused to look.

must pay respect; here too there are invisible and secret meanings we ought to acknowledge. Not by accident did the Greeks call the sexual organs *aidoia*, the "awesome things."

Ham looks without *aidos*—without awe—upon his father's sexuality. For him, there is nothing here to respect, not even as the mysterious source and ground of his own existence. His father's genitalia are a mere anatomical appendage, perhaps potent, perhaps not; either way, in shameless looking, their meaning is excised. Ham is thus guilty also of metaphorical castration. In his simple act of shameless viewing of uncovered nakedness, he symbolically overturns his father both as source of life and as moral authority. Moreover, that he speaks irreverently about what he has seen proves that he understands and celebrates what he has done.

At first glance, it might seem that there is a possible tension between the two aspects of the crime of Ham: Is the problem a deficiency of *natural* piety—that is, of awe-shame-reverence before the naturally awesome truth of sexuality? Or is the problem a deficiency of *conventional or moral* piety—that is, of respect-shame-reverence for legal and moral authority? But further consideration makes it clear that the two aspects are intertwined, precisely because the father is the embodiment of *both* naturally rooted strength and creative power and rationally grounded moral and prescriptive authority. The father as lawgiver is, like law itself, a combination of reason backed by natural force. Later, we will see how the father is, in the same way, a stand-in for God—creator and commander, both source of life and source of law.

Ham, lacking awe and reverence, transgresses a most sacred, if unpromulgated, law and becomes the father of peoples—including the Canaanites (singled out here) and the Egyptians—whose lawless and abominable sexual practices will later be the antipodes to the Hebrew laws of purity. These pagan practices we will meet later in Genesis, for example, in the Egyptian pharaoh's predatory behavior toward women (chapter 12), in the Sodomite (Canaanite) attempts at homosexual violence against the strangers (19), in the Canaanite prince's rape of Dinah (34), and especially in the incest of Lot's daughters (born to a Sodomite mother) upon their drunken father (19)—a tale that parallels our present story. Here, in the first generation after the first institution of law, nature tosses up its first antinomian rebel, the first rebel against law and authority. Perpetuation and tradition are in trouble right from the start.

FILIAL REBELLION, FILIAL PIETY

What sort of human being is Ham? What kind of person delights in rebelling against or exposing preexisting law and authority? What kind of person is *utterly without aidos*, without awe-filled shame?[13] Most often, he is the would-be tyrant, a man who seeks self-sufficiency, who would (if possible) become his own father and author, whose creatureliness and dependence are an affront to his autonomous self-conception. Patricide (and incest)—both literal and metaphorical—are crimes of the tyrant, as we know from Sophocles' *Oedipus Tyrannos*. Like Oedipus, Ham commits patricide (metaphorically), and his descendants practice incest (literally). One of his descendants, Nimrod (whose name connotes "rebelliousness"), will conquer an empire and will seek to make himself the all-powerful and self-sufficing lord of the earth (10:8–12).

But tyrants are not the only antinomians. The philosopher, too, sees through the arbitrary character of law and custom, and looks to nature, all in an effort to learn the unvarnished truth. Even that greatest philosophical friend of moral virtue, Aristotle, insists that *aidos* is not a virtue. Put in its best light, Ham's deed might be construed as an act of shameless curiosity, of an unbridled willingness to look at or into anything, of a desire to know the origins and an unwillingness to have them obscured by either forgetfulness or custom, of a desire to see nature clearly, by and for oneself, utterly uncovered, demystified, and unhidden. After all, the Greek word for truth, *aletheia,* means "unhiddenness," that which has been brought out of hiding, that which now lies uncovered and exposed to the mind's eye.

Ham's delight in *telling* what he has seen inclines us to think him more tyrannical than philosophical; not before Nietzsche did the true philosopher shout from the rooftops his privately uncovered subversive knowledge. Seeing for oneself was, in the greatest philosophers of antiquity, generally combined with reticence and with a partiality to adhering to the law.[14] But from the Bible's point of view, it seems to make little difference. With respect to the law and, hence, with respect to the crucial matter of fathers and sons, the philosopher and the would-be tyrant are equally suspect. The disinterested gazing-upon of the philosopher and the rebellious seeing-through of the tyrant are both "against the law," are both impious. For the sake of law-abidingness, and this means for the sake of

13. We leave aside a possible explanation in terms of birth order. Ham, the youngest, has two older brothers much more pious and reverend than he. He will not be the last younger son who rebels against authority because his place in the line of reverence is occupied by his rivals.

14. See, for example, Plato's *Crito,* where Socrates, speaking to his lifelong but unphilosophical friend Crito, defends the law under which he was condemned to death.

righteousness, the attitude most needful will reverently let sleeping fathers lie, and will act to cover them up. Filial piety is the indispensable partner of law-abidingness and righteousness.

Noah's other two sons are more properly disposed. One does not envy them their situation. They were no doubt shocked by their brother Ham's disclosure (if not by the fact of *his* retailing it). Quite likely, they had never before seen or known their father to be humbled or even at a loss. Upon the sea of troubles, Noah had commanded an entire microcosm and presided over it with full authority. And Noah had been granted a special relationship to God. Could Ham's tale really be true? What should a son do on hearing report of Father's disgrace? Should he go and see for himself? Should he ignore the knowledge, preferring disbelief? Or should he act benevolently, while remaining in the dark about the truth?

Shem and Japheth rise to the occasion. They choose the latter course:

> And Shem and Japheth took a cloak, and laid it upon both their shoulders, and went backward, and covered the nakedness of their father; and their faces were backward, and the nakedness of their father they saw not. (9:23)

No sooner told, Shem and Japheth move to act in their father's defense and to come to his rescue. Rather than join in Ham's shameful boast, they reverently cover their father's nakedness. Walking backward, together, they gently deposit a draping cloak from off their shoulders; deliberately, they see nothing. They refuse to share in their father's shame; indeed, they cover it up.

We readers are touched by this display of loyalty and filial piety. Even more than their decency and respect, we admire the perfect way they found delicately to correct the problem without participating in it: they did not first look and only then cover. They intuitively understand that, were they to *see with their own eyes* their father's nakedness, their family order would be permanently altered. Moreover, by protecting Noah's dignity and authority, they safeguard their own capacity to exercise paternal authority in the future.[15]

But in our own admiration we should not overlook the stark implication: their piety *is* a kind of willing blindness. They knowingly choose to live leaving some things in the dark, without pressing back to the naked truth about temporal beginnings or ultimate origins. They knowingly choose not to know

15. Shem and Japheth *do,* in a sense, participate, albeit unwillingly, in Noah's shame. True, they do not look. True, they participate as little as possible. But they have been drawn in to cover and rescue their father, and they cannot erase the memory of their deed or of what (allegedly) made it necessary for them to perform it.

their father's shame and weakness.[16] They embrace authority and, implicitly, life under law.

THE SINS OF THE FATHER: CURSING THE SONS

When he discovers his disgrace, Noah does not take his shame lying down. Angrily, he retaliates. And for the first time in the biblical narrative, we hear Noah speak. Noah opens his mouth only to curse (and to bless):

> And Noah awoke from his wine, and knew what his youngest son had done unto him. And he said: "Cursed be Canaan: a servant of servants [*or* slave of slaves] shall he be to his brothers." (9:24–25)

Noah's anger is surely expected, as rage is the usual response to being shamed. A man who is put to shame harbors a hatred keener than any other, largely because the observer compels him to confront himself in his own meanness and ugliness. Witnesses establish our own disgrace beyond our power of forgetting and remembering. And the horror of it all is magnified many times over when disgrace is witnessed by those we love, and perhaps worst of all, by our children.

But certain features of Noah's discovery and reaction are surprising. How did Noah know who had done what, especially if we are right and nothing in fact was *done* by Ham, other than looking? Awakening, Noah must have found himself covered with the cloak and inferred the rest: those who covered him were not those who first saw him; and knowing his sons, Noah knew which was which. Ham, the hot one (in this respect, too, he is like the tyrannical Oedipus, whose ruling passion was anger), had no doubt given earlier indications of disrespect and anger. But in his own anger, Noah retaliated not by cursing Ham but by cursing Canaan. This requires explanation.

A little reflection shows the fittingness of Noah's response. Measure for measure, Noah unfathers Ham by driving a wedge between Ham and Ham's youngest son, Canaan. Should the curse be realized or effective, Canaan (whose name is from a root meaning "to be low") will blame his own misfortunes on his

---

16. One might therefore say that they knowingly choose not to know the full truth about their father. A man should know his wife, not his father. This view of what piety requires fits with the implicit teaching of Sophocles' *Oedipus Tyrannos*. Against the advice of the seer Tieresias, Oedipus insists on coming to know his father; he insists on looking shamelessly into his origins; he insists on bringing the dark and private things into full public light. Such insistence is the work of the tyrant, of the man who would kill his father and lie with his mother, becoming his own source—the very opposite of being a willing perpetuator of a way gratefully received from those who have gone before.

father's misdeed, precisely in the matter of filial piety. Ham, who seeks to free himself from parental authority and law, will be held responsible *by his son*—as a parental authority—for the evils that befall that son. Moreover, the precise evil to be suffered by Ham's descendants is also fitting: those who would live without law are destined to live under slavery; those who "see through" authority become incapable of exercising authority and must live under the rule of others; those who deny covenant are bound to accept the rule of the stronger—that is, slavery and tyranny—precisely what the rule of law was first instituted to prevent (see Chapter Six).

But however fitting, is it *just* to visit the sins of the fathers upon the sons? How could this be fair to Canaan, who himself did and saw nothing?[17] This is a vexed question; yet it takes us to the heart of the matter regarding fathers and sons.

If we regard human life as the story of solitary and independent individuals, each fully responsible for himself and each deserving to receive only what he has earned through his own effort and merit (or fault), then we will likely regard suffering for the sins of our fathers as unfair. But the premise is false. Human beings live everywhere and always enmeshed in a world made largely by the many others who came before. We almost always accept as completely fair and just the blessings bestowed on us, gratis, by generations past. Is it then just to reject as unfair the sufferings we owe to our father's errors and misdeeds?

Whatever the justice of the matter, it is almost inevitable that children suffer from the deeds of their fathers, and not because some willful or punitive God intervenes to guarantee it. On the contrary, the deeds and beliefs of the fathers directly shape the sons—whether by conformity or by rebellion—just as they shape also the world that the sons will inherit. What kind of sons would a father like Ham be likely to rear? If they follow his example, they will not heed his or any other authority; thus, like him, they become antinomian. They will lack awe, reverence, and sexual self-restraint. They will create and inhabit a world in which no one's nakedness is off limits to their impious lusts. If, on the other hand, a son rebels against the impious paternal example, he might come to wish for some orderly and traditional alternative, but he will not be able himself to supply what has been destroyed.

Such a curse upon future generations need not imply some additional and

17. There is a line of interpretation that, in order to make sense of the curse on Canaan, attributes the deed to him, instead of or in addition to his father, Ham. Accordingly, they read *beno haqatan,* "his youngest son," as "grandson," like the French *petit fils.* But this has no other warrant from the text. Rather than assume Noah's response to be simply righteous, the reader is better off pondering the rights and wrongs of cursing Canaan *as the son* of the sole guilty party, Ham.

contrary event or occurrence. It may simply be the unavoidable consequence of some unsavory or reprehensible experience, the lingering effects of an initial pollution. Having seen what he should not have seen, Ham cannot escape into blindness.[18] He is cursed to have that experience permanently with him, and the memory of it will color everything he does and feels—including how he is with his own sons (especially given his "hot," impulsive nature). Thus, one might wish to consider Noah's remark less as causing or wishing than as prophesying—to be sure, with righteously indignant satisfaction—"Canaan [will] be cursed."

Yet it is more likely that Noah is calling down, and not merely predicting and endorsing, the curse he pronounces on Canaan. Exercising what he takes to be the magical potency of imprecatory speech, he summons the powers that be to exact vengeance upon Ham by punishing his son (and descendants). But however understandable and however fitting as a form of retribution, Noah's act is not altogether kosher. It partakes of the terrible problem of administering punishment to your own. One cannot cleanse pollution of the nest caused by one of the nestlings without further befouling it. (This truth is the core of the classic tragedy of the House of Atreus.) And when the innocent are made to suffer with the guilty, there is ground for later hatred and revenge. Will not some descendants of Canaan later punish the line of Shem? Will not Noah's angry misdeed on the innocent Canaan come back to haunt the equally innocent sons of Shem? And leaving later consequences aside, is there not something wrong with calling down a curse on young Canaan, even if it is—as I have argued—an absolutely perfect response to his father's misconduct?

A later biblical echo of the present story supports our criticism of Noah's response. In Leviticus 18, at the heart of the Israelite instruction on holiness, the law proscribing forbidden sexual unions and unchastity is promulgated. It begins, comparatively, with the injunction "After the doings of the land of Egypt, wherein ye dwelt, shall ye not do; and after the doings of the land of Canaan, whither I shall bring you, shall ye not do; neither shall ye walk in their statutes. Mine ordinances shall ye do, and My statutes shall ye

---

18. In this respect (among others) the present story may be regarded as part of the Bible's ongoing reflection on the different human senses, their relative strengths and weakness. Though man is prone to favor his seeing to his hearing, man is in fact powerless before his sense of sight, especially when he comes upon shattering revelations. Once we see, we cannot unsee. What we hear we can dismiss as hearsay, but we cannot ignore what we have once seen for ourselves. The pollution of seeing what should not be seen cannot be removed, not even by putting out one's eyes. Oedipus's self-blinding, however fitting to his misdeed of uncovering the truth about his origins, was equally inefficacious. Putting out one's eyes cannot put out one's mind or one's memory.

keep, to walk therein: I am the Lord your God" (18:3–4). There soon follow fourteen verses (6–19) detailing those forbidden sexual unions—each verse proscribing "uncovering of nakedness"—which, we assume, were common practices among the Egyptians and the Canaanites, people descended from Ham, the first uncoverer of nakedness. The list of sexual misconduct is interrupted by a stark prohibition regarding child sacrifice: "And thou shalt not give any of thy seed to set them apart to Molech, neither shalt thou profane the name [shem] of thy God: I am the Lord" (18:21). Could this be a belated gloss on Noah's willingness to "sacrifice" his grandson Canaan to pagan gods and ways simply to avenge his own son's misconduct—and worse, to avoid accepting responsibility for his having disgraced himself in the first place? Did not Noah, by his fierce act of revenge, profane the name of God and join in the Canaanite ethos that he was cursing? May we fathers ever be forgiven for wishing that our grandsons pay back our sons with in-kind rebellion and disrespect—especially when we have not comported ourselves respectfully and reverently?

Difficult children are often difficult especially with regard to our shortcomings: holding themselves as partial outsiders, they see more and are not ashamed to speak up. They criticize our ways, try our patience, challenge our wisdom, and test our virtue. The more able or spirited they are, the more trouble they can cause. Moreover, contrary sons are born even to thoroughly decent and righteous fathers, who—if they are to remain righteous—do not therefore excuse themselves from the paternal task. On the contrary, it is the difficult sons who often teach us—painfully—just why and how the paternal work must be done, even against the odds, and not least because they are frequently more interesting and promising than their more dutiful brothers.

FILIAL PIETY AND THE IMAGE OF GOD: BLESSING THE SONS

Noah follows his curse with a blessing. Together with the curse on Canaan, this speech is the first directly quoted human speech after the Flood, and it means to divide the human race into cursed and blessed portions.[19] It is also Noah's last reported deed; his death at age 950 years—350 of which were after the

19. It is important to emphasize this division is Noah's, not God's. God's division begins with the call of Abraham; it seeks, through the call of one people who are enjoined to seek holiness, to spread righteousness and holiness among all the nations. There is nothing in the biblical text itself, here or later, that supports the later uses that have been made of this passage, for example, to justify American chattel enslavement of the descendants of Ham, or to justify Israelite conquest of Canaanite peoples.

flood—will be reported in the very next verses (9:28–29). The blessing itself is remarkable:

> And he said:
>   "Blessed be the Lord [*YHWH*],
>   the God of Shem;
>   and let Canaan be their servant.
>   God enlarge Japheth,
>   and he shall dwell in the tents of Shem;
>   and let Canaan be their servant." (9:26–27)

Rather than bless Shem, Noah blesses *YHWH*, the God of Shem (just as, rather than curse Ham, Noah curses Canaan). According to Cassuto, the formula "blessed be *YHWH*" "connotes thanksgiving and praise to the Lord who performed a beneficent act." He interprets the present verse to mean: "Thanksgiving and praise be to YHWH who guided Shem in the good way and taught him to conduct himself with decency and all other virtues."

But how exactly did the Lord guide Shem? Overt intervention did not take place, as far as we know; and Noah, aroused from his drunken stupor, could only be guessing. Yet it turns out that Noah speaks truly, and better than he knows. Noah divined that Shem's conduct was inspired by pious reverence, not only for him, *but also and especially for the divine.* Shem, though better in conduct than his father, had accepted and respected his father for the sake of what his father, *as father,* stood for. Shem had managed to see—however dimly—in the authoritative relation of father and son an image of the relation of God and man, and therewith a pathway to the holy. In the experience of awe and reverence before paternal authority is the germ of awe and reverence for the divine. As the stance of Ham points downward to Canaanite paganism and depravity, so the stance of Shem points upward to the sacred and the holy.

Shem, who seems to have initiated the move to cover his father's nakedness, and his older brother, Japheth, turn out to be more pious than their father, though they probably learned their lesson largely from him. The formative experience in their lives would certainly have been the Flood and the building of the ark. They could not help but be impressed by their father, who, without raising a question or uttering a sound, obeyed God's shipbuilding instructions to the letter. Aboard the ark, they saw their father, the man who "walked with God" (6:9), standing in God's stead as protector and preserver of an entire living world. And when God spoke directly to them in making His covenant (9:8), they experienced personally the God who cares for man and to whom the fatherly human being points—as generous source and sustainer of life, as awesome source of order and law.

Common experiences are not, however, necessarily experienced in common. Different sons, different dispositions. Some sons are reverent and pious, others are not. Some take easily to the ways of their fathers, others do not. But the varieties are not unlimited; indeed, there may be but a few basic natural types. The three sons of Noah may represent the Bible's view of the three fundamental human types: the tyrannical man or, alternatively, the man who is focused on sex and bodily pleasure; the decent or noble man, the generous man of refined taste and sensibility; and the pious man, the man who takes his bearings from looking up to the divine.[20] Shem, the man of the name and the progenitor of Abraham, is most closely connected with holiness. And Abraham, with the help of massive tutoring from *YHWH*, the God of Shem, will perform supremely well the paternal work of transmitting the new way. Japheth, the enlarged or beautiful or noble one (he is the progenitor of the Greeks and the other Europeans), is basically decent, but he and his kind of decency and nobility can not go it alone; Japheth must dwell under the protection of holiness ("in the tents of Shem"). But Ham—for reasons unknown—marches to a different drummer, deaf to the voice of authority and the divine call. The case of Ham clearly demonstrates the insufficiency of relying on nature or family alone to insure decency and to guarantee the transmission of righteous ways. Filial piety and paternal excellence—both indispensable for moral education—are precarious virtues, always in short supply.[21]

∼

The little story of Noah and his sons has exposed large obstacles in the path toward a decent and holy community. Perpetuation of a sound social order cannot be counted on; tradition cannot depend only on what is naturally given to fathers and sons. The ground of human authority is altogether precarious,

20. These three types should be compared to the three paradigmatic lives mentioned by Aristotle in the *Nicomachean Ethics* (1095b14–1096a5): the life of pleasure, the life of honor, and the life of contemplation, lived, respectively, by the hedonistic many, the gentlemanly few, and the philosopher. The major difference is that, in the biblical triad, the pious man stands in place of the philosopher.

21. Today, the supply may be shorter than ever. For modern times have produced a new human type—neither tyrant nor philosopher—who seems also to be deaf to authority and who knows neither awe nor reverence: democratic man. For the lover of equality, all hierarchy is suspect, all distinctions odious, all claims on his modesty or respect confining. Last names, and even familial titles like Uncle or Aunt, are much too formal. Honor and respect, fear and awe, and filial piety seem increasingly vestiges of an archaic world. Democratic fathers find it easier not to exercise authority; democratic sons find it easier not to recognize it. Sex, utterly demystified, is now sport and chatter; nakedness is no big deal. (Most of my students do not recoil from Ham's deed, and cannot under-

both because those in authority expose their weaknesses and because even small weaknesses, once uncovered, can totally undermine respect for authority, especially among those who are inclined to rebellion. Righteous Noah, excellent as preserver of life, is not natively good enough as teacher of a way of life. Not all of his sons are natively willing to walk in the ways of decency and righteousness. Preservation of family order is saved only by a pious act of willful ignorance, committed by extraordinary sons who understand intuitively the need for preserving Father's dignity and authority. The new human order seems very fragile indeed, especially as it rests on natural family relations. Even if a father did everything right, there is no guarantee that all of his sons will follow in his footsteps. We read ahead, wondering whether and how these obstacles can be overcome.

---

stand what the fuss is all about.) Many fathers and mothers traffic shamelessly in their own uncovered nakedness; sons and daughters, inured to shameless exposure, see no reason to cover it up. Severed now from their source in what is truly venerable, the customs of respect for elders and sexual modesty become anemic; increasingly petrified, they crumble beneath the avalanche of equality, explicitness, and the "right to be myself." No need for reverence or judgment: we're all pals now.

Perhaps this represents progress: liberation from archaic, demanding, and stultifying mores and attitudes. Or on the contrary, perhaps this represents decline: the disappearance of moral standards, decency, reverence, and respect. On such important matters, we must not allow ourselves to be self-deceived. Do we not see evidence that the sins of unfatherly fathers are still being visited on the sons and the grandsons? Is it not possible that Canaan is still—and again—cursed to live slavishly like a pagan?

CHAPTER EIGHT

BABEL: THE FAILURES OF CIVILIZATION

*T*he story of the city and the tower of Babel, told economically in the first nine verses of Genesis 11, is the last episode in the biblical narrative prior to God's call to Abraham. As everybody knows, God disrupts the building of the city, confounding the speech of the builders and scattering them into many nations spread abroad upon the face of all the earth. After this event, God will abandon efforts to educate all of humankind all at once; instead, He will choose to advance His plan for human beings by working first with only one nation. After Babel, the Bible will turn directly to its main subject, the formation of the nation of Israel.

In keeping with its pivotal place within the text of Genesis, as the end of the beginning, the story of Babel represents something of a completion. Read historically, as part of an ongoing temporal narrative, this tale of the universal city completes the account of the universal human story, with human beings living largely on their own and without divine instruction. Read philosophically, as part of an unfolding anthropology, this reflection on language, technology, and the first (prototypical) city exposes fully the core of civilization and man as a rational and political animal. Read morally, as part of a search for wisdom regarding how to live, this report of human failure prepares and encourages us to pay attention when, in the immediate sequel, God undertakes to educate Abraham in the new way of righteousness and holiness.

As the capstone of the universal human story, the tale of Babel also revisits and extends the consideration of several important themes treated earlier in Genesis: the status of heaven; the ambiguous power of speech, reason, and the arts; the hazards of unity and aloneness; the meaning of the human city and its quest for self-sufficiency; and man's desire for fame and immortality. The Tower of Babel that reaches toward heaven recalls the Bible's sustained opening polemic against orienting human life toward the heavens (see Chapter One); the beginning of the beginning demoted the standing of the heavenly bodies; the end of the beginning rejects the way of life that is centered upon them. The

Babel builders' uses of language and technology confirm the hazards of human speech and human artfulness, first exposed in Genesis 2–3 (see Chapter Two). The singular and undivided human city revisits, on the social-political plane, the problem of Adam's aloneness (see Chapters Two and Three) and extends our thinking about the moral ambiguity of cities and civilization, with their proud pursuit of self-sufficiency (see Chapter Four). The Babel builders' desire to make a name for themselves echoes the concern with fame and glory that characterizes the dangerous Heroic Age (see Chapter Five). Finally, the anti-Mesopotamian spirit of this entire section of Genesis—see, for example, the account of the Flood (Chapter Five)—is made explicit in this mythic story of the rise and fall of Babylon, the greatest Mesopotamian city. It is astonishing how much is packed into this little tale. Here it is, in its entirety.

> And all the earth [*kal-ha'arets*] was of one language [*safah 'echath*] and one speech [*devariym 'achadiym*].
> And as they journeyed about from the east, they found a plain in the land of Shinar, and they settled there.
> And they said, [each] man to his neighbor, "Come [*havah*], let us bake bricks [*literally,* brick bricks: *nilbenah leveniym*] and burn them thoroughly [*literally,* burn them to a burning; *venisrfah lisrefah*]"; and they had brick for stone and slime they had for mortar.
> And they said, "Come [*havah*], let us build [*nivneh*] for ourselves a city with a tower, with its top [*or* head] in the heavens;
> and let us make [*na'aseh*] for ourselves a name [*shem*], lest we be scattered abroad upon the face of all the earth."
> But the Lord came down to see the city and the tower, which the children of man [*or* children of Adam: *beney ha'adam*] were building.
> And the Lord said, "Behold, it is one people ['*am 'echad*], and they have all one language [*safah 'achath*]; and this they begin to do: and now nothing will be restrained from them which they have imagined [*or* plotted: *zamam*] to do.
> Come [*havah*], let us go down and there confound their language, that they may not understand [each] man the language of his neighbor."
> So the Lord scattered them from thence upon the face of all the earth; and they ceased to build the city.
> Therefore is the name [*shem*] of it called Babel [*bavel*], because the Lord did there confound [*balal*] the language of all the earth [*sefath kal-ha'arets*]; and from thence did the Lord scatter them upon the face of all the earth. (11:1–9)

On first encountering the story, prior to careful reflection, any reader who is not already committed to defending everything God does is likely to find the tale troubling. For the building of the city and tower appears at first glance to be an innocent project, even a worthy one. It expresses powerful human impulses, to establish security, permanence, independence, even self-sufficiency. And it is accomplished entirely by rational and peaceful means: forethought and planning, arts that transform the given world, and cooperative social arrangements made possible by common speech and uniform thoughts. Babel, the universal city, is the fulfillment of a recurrent human dream, a dream of humankind united, living together in peace and freedom, no longer at the mercy of an inhospitable or hostile nature, and enjoying a life no longer solitary, poor, nasty, brutish, and short. According to the story, however, God finds this humanist dream a nightmare. Taking strong objection to the city of man, He thwarts its completion by measures designed to make it permanently impossible. Why?

Given that the human beings want the city but God does not, our first impulse is to think that the answer depends on knowing God's reasons or seeing things from His point of view. Of this, all that we know for now is contained in God's remark, no doubt uttered with a negative judgment, "Now nothing will be restrained from them which they have imagined to do" (11:6). God, it seems, sees the likely success of the project but does not approve it. He apparently does not approve of the prospect of unrestrained human powers, exercised in support of unlimited imaginings and desires. He seems to be worried both about man's boundless capacity to dream up grand projects and, even more, about man's ability, sustained by unity of speech and purpose, to realize them. More generally, He may not like the absence of reverence, the vaunt of pride, the trust in technique, the quest for material power, the aspiration for self-sufficiency, the desire to reach into heaven—in short, the implied wish to be as gods, with comparable creative power. From God's point of view, the city of man is, in its deepest meaning, at best a form of idolatry and self-worship, and at worst a great threat to the earth.

But why should readers—especially, modern enlightened or wisdom-seeking (that is, philosophical) readers—take God's view of the matter? Should we not cherish the hopes of our fellows, those first dreamers of the humanist dream? After all, we are told, all mankind without exception thought the project right and good. Absent a meddlesome God, would there be any reason to disagree? And if, as many of our contemporaries believe, a meddlesome God is truly absent, would there not be every reason to revive the dream? If there is no city of God, the city of man is not only not idolatry—it becomes our last best hope.

A careful study of the biblical story suggests that this view is mistaken, that

God's judgments and actions regarding Babel are entirely fitting, and on grounds accessible to human reason. Pondering the building of Babel, in the context of what precedes and follows, wisdom-seeking readers may well come to see it from God's point of view.

THE CITY IN CONTEXT

We must first locate the story of Babel in the larger context of human beginnings. As we have already seen, the early chapters of Genesis take the reader vicariously through four alternative conditions of human life: first, simple innocence (in the absence of human self-consciousness); second, life without law—anarchy—based on internalized knowledge of good and bad; third, life under the primordial law, when man emerges from what later writers will call the state of nature; and fourth, the dispersion of peoples, each living under its own law or customs. Let us briefly revisit these human alternatives.

First is the condition of simple innocence, pictured in the Garden of Eden. Innocence is destroyed when human beings, their desires enlarged by newly used powers of mind, exercise their autonomy and take to themselves independent knowledge of good and bad; judgmentally self-conscious, they immediately discover their nakedness, and thus their shame and wounded pride, which they artfully attempt to clothe over. This end of innocence is, literally, the expulsion into the real world, where human beings live according to their own lights and judgments of good and bad, without imposed law (see Chapter Two). In this second state, we encounter Eve's proud birth of Cain; Cain's sacrifice, wounded pride, jealousy, and murder of his brother; the line of Cain and the line of Seth, and their ill-fated interbreeding after Adam died in the tenth generation; and the world degenerating into riotous and lewd behavior. The Flood completes the dissolution of this anarchic world (see Chapters Four and Five).

The third state appears after the Flood with Noah—righteous and simple Noah, the first man born into the world after Adam dies—when God institutes a new order based on law and covenant. An externally imposed law—to begin with, *No murder*—is now administered and enforced by human beings but with divine sanction, against the background of a world order guaranteed to be not hostile to human aspiration by God's covenant never again to destroy the earth (see Chapter Six). This new state of primitively lawful society was to have been transmitted universally, from fathers to sons, but it was not successfully perpetuated even for one generation: Noah's drunkenness and the irreverent conduct of one of his sons made universal transmission impossible (see Chapter Seven). Dispersion of peoples and election of one, under the direct leadership of God, thus becomes the next plan, featuring the nation that begins with Abraham, a people that will be called to carry God's way as a light to all the nations.

One way to speak about this series of states is to say that God keeps trying new plans after the old ones fail, in many cases making concessions to unavoidable and undesirable human weaknesses (for example, in the permission to eat meat granted with Noah). But a better way is to say that, by this means, *we* the readers learn that those other imaginable human possibilities—innocence, anarchy, universal perpetuation of law and covenant through natural lineage— have been tried and have failed, which is to say, *they are terrestrially impossible.* We are educated to believe that the human spirit of righteousness is not strong enough to rule from within but needs outside instruction, legislation, and help. The story of the city and tower of Babel is the culmination of this sequence: it shows the impossibility of transmitting the right way through the universal, technological, secular city.

The more immediate background for the builders of Babel is the Flood. Through this universal cataclysm, human beings encountered the full destructive force of brute nature. After the Flood, God promised, "Never again"; but it is reasonable to surmise that the memory of the deluge weighed at least as heavily as the hearsay report of God's promise not to repeat it. God's first postdiluvian command to Noah, to spread out and fill the earth with people, might have been a terrifying prospect under the circumstances. The connection of Babel to the antecedent Flood is in fact hinted at by the very last words of Genesis 10, the words immediately preceding the story of Babel:

> These are the families of the sons of Noah, after their generations, in their nations; and of these were the nations divided in the earth *after the flood.*
> (10:32; emphasis added)

Genesis 10 is, altogether, another and gentler account of the division of mankind, answering in its way the questions How came there to be many nations? And How came there to be many tongues? The answer of Genesis 10 is genealogical, beginning with the three sons of Noah, their descendants reflecting to some degree their own very different characters. As people multiplied and spread abroad, different families grew into diverse national populations, each speaking its own tongue, each in its own land.[1] Among the descendants of Ham, the

---

1. This naturalistic or gently genealogical account fits with a widely held, if unsophisticated, view of the world's diversity: people speak different languages because they live in different lands. Their native tongue is tied to their native land. Their *native* land is *their* native land because that is where they and their ancestors were born (that is, had their nativity). The rightness of this natural, gentle, and seemingly innocent claim to land, tongue, and nationhood—the root of national pride and

irreverent son, we find one man who is, in this version, connected with Babel. Nimrod, whose name means "rebelliousness," was "the one who began to be a mighty man upon the earth." He was "a powerful hunter in the face of God," and for this he became famous; he was also the founder, presumably by conquest, of an empire of cities in the plain of Shinar, and the beginning of his kingdom was Babel (10:8–10). By means of a large kingdom, Nimrod attempts to overcome by force the division of mankind. We should not be too quick to blame him: if what lies behind the human world is only chaos and instability, man must make his own order. Human ordering is the theme of the story of Babel.

RATIONAL ANIMAL, POLITICAL ANIMAL: SPEECH AND THE CITY

The project of creating order, the meaning and goal of Babel, is rooted in *logos*. Speech and language, reason and the arts are at the heart of the story. In keeping with its subject matter, the story of Babel is itself a wonderfully artful narrative and the words it uses are most carefully chosen. Poetic craft and linguistic subtlety are enlisted to sound an alarm about language and craft. To take full advantage of the text, we must proceed very slowly, looking at every word with care.[2]

And *all the earth* was of one language and one speech.

The story of Babel begins with all mankind united as a single, harmonious group, or as God says later, as "one people." Unlike the previous chapter's account of the differentiation of peoples, descending from the very different sons of Noah (who, though of one family, were not of one mind), this story begins with the entire human race, united and whole. Indeed, the text accentuates the unity by exaggeration, identifying all mankind as "all the earth." The project that

---

territoriality—will later be challenged by the text, as are many things regarded as good because natural. When God sets out to start His own nation, He will begin by uprooting His founder (Abram) and bringing him as a foreigner to the Promised Land, his title to which will not be natural or genealogical but rather providential. (See p. 271 n. 7 and p. 306 n. 11.)

2. Robert Alter, in a succinct but most helpful comment, observes:

As many commentators have noted, the story exhibits an intricate antithetical symmetry that embodies the idea of "man proposes, God disposes." The builders say, "Come, let us bake bricks," God says, "Come, let us go down"; they are concerned "lest we be scattered," and God responds by scattering them. The story is an extreme example of the stylistic predisposition of the biblical narrative to exploit interechoing words and to work with a deliberately restricted vocabulary. The word "language" occurs five times in this brief text as does the phrase "all the earth" . . . The prose turns language itself into a game of mirrors.

human beings are about to undertake is not the work only of Nimrod and the line of Ham; it is a universal human project. This is the first clue that Babel is not just any city but is *the* city, the paradigmatic or universal city, representing a certain universal human aspiration.

Of *one language.*

The unity of the human race was linguistic or logical, not merely genealogical. This means more than sharing uniform sounds and symbols—speaking, say, Aramaic rather than Greek; it means sharing the view of the world embedded in a language. It means sharing a common understanding of the world that any pure language implicitly contains. And because language also bespeaks the inner world of the speakers, sharing one language means also a common inner life, with simple words accurately conveying the selfsame imaginings, passions, and desires of every human being. To be "of one language" is to be of one mind and heart about the most fundamental things.

But where does this one language come from? It is strictly a human creation. It appears to come unaided, directly from the human mind. As we learn from the Garden of Eden story, man's first creative and distinctly human activity is naming the animals. Whatever name man selected became each animal's name. Beginning with this seemingly innocuous activity, human reason gradually creates in speech a complete linguistic world, layered over but distinct from the given, natural world. This second, shadow world, though it was invited by the articulated natural world, gains independence from it. The word is not the thing; the map is not the territory. True, language may point to and reflect the given world. But because speech is colored always by human perceptions, passions, interests, and desires, the world as captured in language is necessarily *partial*—both incomplete and biased—and ever-pregnant with the human impulse to do something to it. Language therefore conveys less the world as it is than it does the self-interested and humanly constructed vision of that world.

The merely constructed character of language does not, however, imply weakness. On the contrary, language, *because* it is a human creation and because it reflects human concerns, comes to hold greater sway with human beings than does the given world (that is, God's original creation)—especially when, as here, human beings come to take language for granted. The one-language unity of humankind means that the humanly constructed reality of speech has become pervasive and, as it were, second nature: "The language of *'adam* has become entrenched, institutionalized, universal; all humans are fluent in it and no other. Its words are a currency of universal acceptance. They can be depended upon at all

times and in all situations. . . . The humanly constructed vision of reality provided in language is unchallenged and essentially unchallengeable." In unity of
outlook there is strength—or so it does seem.

Of *one speech.*

The unity of the human race and its humanist dream are predicated on the
trustworthiness of language. Yet in the narrative, the immediate sequel to "of
one language" subtly hints that language—and thus the human construal of the
world—might be less reliable than we are inclined to believe. The human beings
were not only of one language, they were also "of one speech." Almost as if the
text were deliberately trying to deny the possibility of linguistic unity and clarity
just asserted, the meaning of this phrase is notoriously difficult to grasp. The
Hebrew words are hard to translate because there is a grammatical paradox
regarding number: the plural noun *devariym*, "words," is modified by the generally singular adjective "one" (*'achad*), but "one" is *here written as a plural:
'achadiym*. A variety of interpretations have been offered: "few words," implying
simple thoughts and communication; "many words but one speech," implying a
single plan; or "single words" or "one set of words," read as a synonym for a single language. But we wonder whether the strange construction, with the impossible plural of "one," might be a literary hint that the human beings' confidence
in their language was somewhat misplaced.[3] It might suggest, in addition, that
these people were confused about the being of the one and the many, and in particular about the existence and unity of the highest One. Such confusion might,
in the end, jeopardize the apparent simplicity, singleness of purpose, common
understanding, and intelligibility of their thought.

They found a *plain* in the land of *Shinar,* and they *settled* there.

Though mankind was told (after the Flood) to disperse and fill the earth, the human race chose rather to settle in one place, a fertile plain in the land of Shinar
(that is, in the Euphrates valley), that could accommodate and sustain them all.
A fertile plain very likely suggests agriculture, not hunting and gathering; agriculture suggests settlement, rather than wandering, and also forethought,
fences, and the arts. It also requires a keen dependence on heaven—on sun and
rain—a matter to which we shall return.

3. There are, truth to tell, two other places in Genesis where this paradoxical plural of "one,"
'achadiym, is used, in both cases to modify *yamim*, "days," and where the obvious meaning is "a few"
days (27:44 and 29:20). Yet it is also true that in both cases there is confusion: what is said to be "a few
days" is in fact a much longer period of time (indeed, years).

And they *said*, [each] man to his neighbor, *"Come, let us make* bricks [*literally*, 'brick bricks']."

As the story more than hinted from the start, the project for building the city depends on human speech: "And they *said*." But whereas human speech has previously been used for a variety of other purposes—naming, self-naming, questioning authority, shifting blame, denying guilt, expressing fear, boasting in song, spreading shame and ridicule, and blessing and cursing—speech is here used by human beings to exhort to action and to enunciate a project of *making*, for the first time in Genesis. "Come" (or "go to": *havah*) means "prepare yourself," "get ready to join in our mutual plan." Each man thus roused his neighbor to the joint venture: "Let us *make*." Hortatory speech is the herald of craft. And craft enables man to play creator: God, too, had said, "Let us make."[4]

God's creation of the world, we recall, also began with speech, divine speech that summoned the world into being. In the paradigmatic—but wholly unique—case of the creation of light (on Day One), there was absolutely no difference between the divine utterance and the thing called forth: *yehi 'or*, "Let light be"; *veyehi-'or*, "And [*ve*] light was" (1:3). This divine speech and the creature that it summoned were perfectly and completely identical; word and thing, deed and product were exactly the same. But in all subsequent acts of creation, God had to struggle to make the deed equal to the speech, just as He struggles continually by means of His commandments to make human deeds correspond to what He deems fitting and good. If God Himself has difficulty, right from the start, in making His will and His word effective, we have every reason to believe that no human speech will ever be perfectly embodied in the resulting human action. Yet we also have reason to believe that this fact will not keep human beings from trying to play God.[5]

Make *bricks* [*literally*, brick bricks] and *burn* them thoroughly [*literally*, burn (them) to a burning]; and they had brick for stone and slime they had for mortar.

4. See, for example, Genesis 1:26: "Let us make man in our image." The verb used there is *'asah*, "to do or make," while the verb used here by the men of Babel is *banah*, "to build or make," the same verb used in the second creation story when the Lord God builds woman from the rib of man. The Babel builders will use the verb *'asah* in the sequel, "Let us make for ourselves a name."

5. It becomes increasingly clear as we proceed that the Babel builders are making such an attempt. In the present verse, their use of the cognate accusative construction—"Let us brick bricks"—reminds us of God's command "Let the earth grass grass," a command that the earth did not precisely fulfill (see Chapter One, p. 49).

Far from the mountains where stones could be had, the men found no ready-made blocks for building, so they started by making their own materials, from scratch. This is the Bible's first mention of bricks. Were bricks, or permanent houses, known previously? It is unclear: even after the flood, Noah dwelt in a tent. The very *idea* of bricks is itself an invention, a creative act of the resourceful human mind.[6] And how and from what does one make bricks? From the ground, from the moistened dust of the ground, by means of fire. Fire is universally the symbol of the arts and crafts, of technology. Through the controlled use of fire's transforming power, human beings set about to alter the world, presumably because, as it is, it is insufficient for human need. Imitating God's creation of man out of the dust of the ground, the human race begins its own project of creation by firing and transforming portions of the earth.[7]

But there is a difference between the two "creations." In creating man, God had breathed life into the ruddy earth (*'adamah*) to create *'adam*, the ruddy earthling. In contrast, the earthlings here burn the ruddy earth into ghostly and lifeless (white) brick: the word for brick, *levenah*, comes from a root, *lavan*, meaning "white." In this subtle way, the text already hints that man's creative project is in fact a reversal of God's creation of man, and that its result may well be deadly.

> And they said, "Come, let us build [*nivneh*] for us a *city* with a *tower* with its top [*or* head] in the *heavens*."

Like so much of modern technology, the means precede and generate their own ends: "Now we have bricks. What can we make with them?" Bricks now in hand, the proudly creative imagination proceeds to a new plane: it projects a city with a tower. The meaning of the city is inextricably linked with the meaning and presence of the tower; conversely, the meaning of the tower is inextricably linked with the nature and meaning of the city.

Some insight is available through tales of other cities in Genesis. Before Babel,

---

6. The Bible here again takes issue with Mesopotamian teachings, which are replete with accounts of the divine origin of brick making. In one account of the founding of Babylon, told in the Akkadian creation myth *Enuma Elish*, the gods themselves mold bricks for a whole year, providing the materials for the building of the city. Such innovations, according to Scripture, are of purely human provenance, and their goodness is therefore, to say the least, open to question. Indeed, one should read the entire story of Babel as, among other things, a parody of the Babylonian tales that glorify cities, temples, and towers and in which the gods take the lead in all these artful constructions.

7. Regarding the importance of the controlled use of fire (or heat or energy) for the modern scientific project to master nature, and especially for its interest in reversing mortality, see Descartes, *Discourse on Method*, Part V, par. 2 and 4, and Part VI, par. 2.

there are only two references to cities. Cain, after killing his brother, Abel, is told by God that he would be a fugitive and a wanderer. But as we noted in Chapter Four, Cain settles in the land of Nod and, presumably out of fear, builds there a city, a refuge, once he has a family; and he names that city for his firstborn, Enoch. (The line of Cain includes the founders of the arts and crafts, implicit in civilization.) After the flood there is also a brief mention of the great city of the Assyrians, Nineveh, with its cluster of satellite cities (Genesis 10:11–12), whose wickedness Jonah will much later be sent to reprove. Later we will learn about the supremely wicked Canaanite city of Sodom, destroyed by God. Whatever the city means, it seems to be linked, at least in these other cases, with violence, lewdness, and corruption. But none of those features appear tied to the city of Babel—at least not yet—which proceeds through peaceful cooperation under the rule of reason.

The city—every city—is a thoroughly human institution, with settled place and defined boundaries, whose internal plan and visible structures all manifest the presence of human reason and artfulness. The city affirms man's effort to provide for his own safety and needs, strictly on his own. Standing up against the given world, it affirms man's ability to control and master the given world, at least to some extent. Although the city stands as a memorial to the ingenuity and success of those who have gone before, at any given moment the city is an expression of the human effort at self-sufficiency, at satisfying by human means alone all of the needs and wants of human life. Born in need, the human city, by meeting and more than meeting the needs of its builders, proudly celebrates the powers of human reason.

Perhaps the most celebrated passage on the origins and nature of the city is provided by Aristotle near the beginning of the *Politics:*

> The association constituted in accordance with nature for everyday needs is the household. . . . The first association made out of many households for the sake of needs which are not only daily is the village. . . . And the association made out of several villages and complete is the *polis* [the city], having already, so to speak, reached the limit of full self-sufficiency; that is, it comes into being for the sake of living, but it is for the sake of living well. (1252b28–31)

This argument that roots the city in human need and defines it by self-sufficiency is supported by a second argument, which roots the city in human speech: the city, the ground of self-sufficiency, is the natural home of human beings also because it is the embodiment of, and stage for, human speech and reason. Because men have speech, they live in cities, not just in herds or swarms:

Man is by nature a *polis*-animal[8] . . . more than any bee or any herding animal. . . . For man alone among the animals has *logos* [thoughtful speech/
reason]. . . . But *logos* is for making clear the advantageous and the harmful, and so also the just and the unjust. For this is special to men alone in
relation to the other animals; having alone the awareness of good and bad,
just and unjust, and the rest. And the community of these things makes a
household and a *polis*. (1253a3–19)

Speaking animal, rational animal, artful animal, political animal, animal distinguishing good and bad, and opining about the just and the unjust—it is all one
package: man becomes truly human only when he lives in a *polis*, providing for
himself and ruling himself by his own light of reason, through speech and
shared opinions about good and bad, just and unjust. Though the biblical author almost certainly did not read Aristotle's *Politics*, he seems to share a similar
view of the meaning of the city—though not of its *goodness*. Precisely what Aristotle celebrates, Genesis views with suspicion.

More directly and pointedly under biblical suspicion would be the Mesopotamian teachings about the city, almost certainly the intended target of the
present story about Babel, a clear stand-in for Babylon, the most famous city
in Mesopotamia.[9] Unfortunately, we have no Babylonian equivalent of Aristotle's *Politics*, nor any thematic treatment of the meaning of civic life. But in the
Gilgamesh epic there is mention of a city to which the present story almost certainly refers, albeit silently. Of special interest is the connection of the city to the
heroic aspiration:

In the first tablet of the *Gilgamesh*, the hero begins as the king of a great
city whose foundation is also made of *burnt bricks*. At the end of his voyage, when he has lost his last chance for the immortality of the gods, Gilgamesh returns, only to realize that his true immortality had already been
ensured by *the name he had made for himself* founding the city of Uruk, the
city of *burnt bricks*.

The biblical story of Babel, in contrast, has neither king nor hero; all humanity
joins equally in founding the city. Yet as we shall soon see, in the biblical under-

---

8. This phrase is usually (and somewhat misleadingly) translated as "political animal." Aristotle
means that man is by nature fitted to, and perfected by, living in a *polis*, a city, a community that can
do more than provide for the needs of mere subsistence.

9. The Mesopotamian world view is, as we have suggested, the target of the entire pre-Abrahamic
account in Genesis and the alternative against which the text is silently but insistently polemicizing.

standing a concern with "making a name" remains central to the purpose and meaning of the humanist city.

And what of the tower? How is this connected with the meaning of the city? The context of the Flood suggests a connection with safety: the tower is an artificial high ground providing refuge against future floods and a watchtower for the plain; it is even imaginable that it might be intended as a pillar to hold up heaven, lest it crack open another time. These suggestions, however plausible, do not go far enough. To this we must add what we know of the historical city of Babylon and its tower, the famous ziggurat Etemenanki, in the temple of Marduk. Marduk was the chief god of Babylon. Originally he seems to have been a god of thunderstorms, but according to the epic poem *Enuma Elish*, he rose to preeminence after conquering the monster of primeval chaos to become "lord of the gods of heaven and earth," the supreme ruler of all nature, responsible, among other things, for the motion of the stars and for fertility and vegetation. Translated from the Sumerian, the name of the tower, Etemenanki, means, "House of the Foundation of Heaven and Earth." The tower, part of the city's temple, is a human effort to link up heaven and earth. According to some accounts, the Babylonian tower was intended to pave a way for a divine entrance to the city; yet even granting such an aspiration, the project is not unambiguously pious. For unless the god or gods explicitly command such a gesture, the tower—any such conduit—must be seen as a presumptuous attempt to control or appropriate the divine, to bring the cosmic origins down into one's own midst, to encompass the divine within one's own constructions. What appears at first glance as submission is in fact, at least partly, an expression of pride.

But there is probably more to the Babylonian tower than its name and its connection with Marduk. The ziggurats of Babylon had more straightforward, even rational interests in heaven—heaven understood, quite literally, as the place of the sun, moon, and stars, and as the source of rain. Babylon was the place where human beings first began to study the stars and to plot and measure their courses. The towers would, almost certainly, have been the favored sites for astronomical observation. In Babylonia, astronomical observation was not undertaken for the restful and disinterested contemplation celebrated by the Greek philosophers, but for an apprehensive yet patient scrutiny and measurement of the motions of the heavenly bodies, in the service of calculation, prediction, and control—and not least regarding the coming of rain. The Babylonian priests ruled the city on the basis of their knowledge—and divination—regarding heaven. The House of the Foundation of Heaven and Earth thus sought to link the city with the cosmos, and to bring the city into line with the heavenly powers that be, or—perhaps, conversely—to bring the powers that be into line with the goals of the city. In more ways than one, the towered city is, in principle, "cosmopolis."

Not every human city has a ziggurat. But every human city orients itself on the basis of some intuition about the cosmic whole. Without some instruction to the contrary, human beings will eventually be inclined to look up to nature and, especially, to the heavens, for heaven is the home of those visible powers that matter so much to the life of the city, especially as the city rests on agriculture. In this respect, too, the city of Babel is a natural city, a city oriented toward cosmic nature even as it seeks to predict and, to a degree, control nature here on earth.

> And let us *make* for us a *name, lest we be scattered* abroad upon the face of all the earth.

The city is a mixture of pride and fear. Its origins, quite likely, are in fear. This immediately postdiluvian population has better reason than most to know and fear nature's wildness and inhospitality and to shrink from standing unarmed and dispersed before the powers that be. Having (at best) hearsay knowledge of God's promise to Noah (no more floods, no total destruction), these men are inclined rather to trust to self-help for protection against the state of nature and the wide open spaces. They find strength in numbers and unification, and in their ability cooperatively to craft a home in the midst of an indifferent—not to say hostile—world.

But what began in fear grew in pride. Human imagination and especially human craft are its nourishment. Whereas animals pursue their aims thoughtlessly using their own inborn powers, human beings take pride in exercising those powers that come to them as a result of their own devisings. Working from the ground up, men make bricks from the dust of the earth by the transforming power of fire. Lowly materials in hand, their ambition soars as they conceive next to build a city and a tower, with its top in heaven. The city and tower express the human conquest of necessity, human self-sufficiency, and independence. Above all, the sky-scraping tower—whatever its explicit purpose—stands proudly as a monumental achievement of proud builders, to serve their everlasting glory. The anticipatory vaunt of the builders—"Let us *make* us a *name*"—shows the towering pride, though the fear of dispersion ("lest we be scattered abroad") has not been altogether extinguished.

What is this wish "to *make* us a *name*"? The verb "to make," *'asah*, has previously been used only by God, either to announce His own makings or to command Noah's building of the ark, or, once, by the narrator to report God's making of coats of skins. The word "name," hitherto used in relation to particular names, acquires here a new sense for the first time in Genesis. Adam had named the animals, named himself and the woman as woman and man ('*ishah* and '*ish*), and later renamed the woman Eve, honoring her powers as the mother of all life. People give and receive names that are significant (Noah, for example, the first person born after the death of Adam, gets a name meaning both "comfort" and "lament"). Fame and renown are sought, and some men even boast of their deeds (for example, Lamech, who is the poet of his own heroism). But the aspiration to *make* a name goes beyond the desires to *give* oneself a name or to *gain* a name—that is, beyond the longings for fame and glory earned by great success.

To *make* a name for oneself is, most radically, to "make that which requires a name." To make a new name for oneself is to remake the meaning of one's life so that it deserves a new name. To change the meaning of human being is to remake the content and character of human life. The city, fully understood, achieves precisely that. Through technology, through division of labor, through new modes of interdependence and rule, and through laws, customs, and mores, the city radically transforms its inhabitants. At once makers and made, the founders of Babel aspire to nothing less than self-*re*-creation—through the arts and crafts, customs and mores of their city. The mental construction of a second world through language and the practical reconstruction of the first world through technology together accomplish man's reconstruction of his own being. The children of man (*'adam*) remake themselves and, thus, their name, in every respect taking the place of God.[10]

But the Lord came down to see the city and the tower, which the children of man [*or* children of Adam: *beney ha'adam*] were building.

At its midpoint, the story of Babel shifts from the human point of view to God's; but in making the shift, the narrator identifies the builders of the city as "the children of Adam." This could be a simple euphemism for human beings: sons of man, playing at being God. But it also connects the protagonists of this last pre-Abrahamic story with their oldest and paradigmatic ancestor, whose name is, in fact, not a proper name at all but rather the generic name for the entire species. The term "children of Adam" assimilates the meaning of the project of

10. Kristen Dietrich Balisi comments: "The entire project is designed to construct not simply a fortress but a *name*, or rather, a fortress through a name: renown, fame, reputation. The builders, in constructing their city, are crafting a verbal and social identity for themselves that, spread literally by word of mouth to all, will become part of the general order of things. This identity, wrought of human words, is their strength and protection. They attribute to it the power to prevent them from being scattered all over the earth."

Babel to the first activities of the first man: not only his naming of the animals but his project of appropriating autonomous knowledge of good and bad. Here, as in the Garden of Eden, men act in disobedience to definite commands, Adam to the specific prohibition about the tree of knowledge, the builders of the tower to the postdiluvian command to be fruitful and multiply and to fill the earth. The comparison of the two acts is apt, for in both cases the very deed means disobedience: in Adam's individual case, autonomy—choosing for yourself—is the opposite of obedience; in the builders' case, independent self-re-creation—making yourself—is the opposite of obedient dependence, in relation to God or anything else. The road from Adam to the builders of the city is straight and true.[11]

Civilization suffers, perhaps, when compared with the innocence and contentment of Eden; but when men come face-to-face with hostile nature or hostile men in a state of nature, the city appears as a remedy and the universal city a dream of deliverance, peace, and prosperity. In Babel, the universal city, with its own uniform language, beliefs, truths, customs, and laws, the dream of the city holds full sway in the hearts and minds of its inhabitants. Protected by its walls, warmed and comforted in its habitats, and ruled by its teachings, the children of Adam, now men of the city, neither know nor seek to know anything beyond. Contentment reigns, or so it does seem.

UNITY AS ESTRANGEMENT: THE FAILINGS OF SUCCESS

Can such a project succeed? Can such a city, if successfully founded, long endure? Even leaving God's judgment and intervention out of consideration (for the time being), can the humanist city succeed? There is some reason to be doubtful. For one thing, the goal of reaching heaven with the tower is impossible; that the Lord had to "come down" to see what the men had done is, in part, a wry comment on the gap between their aspiration and their deed. For another, the materials used by the men were poor substitutes—bricks for stones, slime for mortar—and were unlikely to secure the desired permanence. More funda-

---

11. As the end of the Garden of Eden story itself makes clear (and as we argued in Chapter Two), the so-called fall of man is in fact a bittersweet rise into civilization. God's announced future for our race—the so-called sentence pronounced in Genesis 3:14–24—embraces separation from the animals, self-consciousness, division of labor, rule and obedience, agriculture and bread, clothing and the arts, concern with good and bad, and the longing for immortality and lost innocence—in a word, civilization. There, disobedience (that is, the choice for independent knowledge of good and bad), fully spelled out, is shown to be a choice for civilization. Here, nonobedience directly and explicitly takes the form of civilization.

mentally, the unity of mind that inspired the project of the city could hardly be expected to survive the division of labor that brought the city into being. The oneness of human life would very likely be replaced by the many ways of life, as masons and carpenters and farmers and metalworkers acquired different and competing interests. Yet God's single comment would seem to imply that the project would, or at least could, succeed as conceived: "Behold, it is one people, and they have all one language; and this they begin to do: and now nothing will be restrained from them which they have imagined to do" (11:6). God strongly suggests that the city is feasible. Its failings, if any, are intellectual or moral or spiritual, not practical. They are the failings of success.

The first and most obvious failing is the matter of piety. What do the men revere? To what do they look up? At first they may look up, quite literally, to heaven, to the powers that be—the sun, moon, and stars. But implicit in the attempt to know, exploit, and control these powers—through calculation, divination, and perhaps sacrifices—is their belief in their own superiority. The aspiration to reach heaven is in fact a desire to bring heaven into town, either to control it or, more radically, to efface altogether the distinction between the human and the natural or divine. In the end, the men will revere nothing and will look up to nothing not of their own making, to nothing beyond or outside themselves, in part because they will see no eternal horizon. Content with and confined within the cave, they will forget about the truly enduring realm beyond.

This charge against the city is not peculiarly biblical, as the allusion to the Platonic allegory of the cave reminds us. In comparing our lives to those of men enchained in caves, Socrates implies that it is the Promethean gift of fire and the enchantment of the arts that hold men unwittingly enslaved. Warmed by the comforts of civilization and charmed by the familiar opinions projected by poets and politicians, the citizens are blind to the world beyond the city. Mistaking their crafted world for the whole, men live as cave dwellers, ignorant of their true standing in the world and their absolute dependence on powers not of their making and beyond their control. The city that does not look beyond itself to the truly transcendent realm cannot be a home for what is best in the human soul.

Second among their failings, the men refuse to look not only up but down. They seem willfully to forget and deny their own mortality. Unlike Cain, who named his city for his son, the men of Babel want a name for themselves here and now ("Let us make a name for ourselves"), and give no thought for their offspring. Rational, but proudly unreasonable, these self-made makers forget their animality and the need for procreation. Though called to be fruitful and multiply, they fly from procreation and pour all their energies into a constructed civic heroism. Mind and craft, they implicitly believe, can thoroughly triumph over necessity and mortality.[12]

Third are several failings regarding the crucial matter of standards. In their act of total self-creation, there could be no separate and independent (non-man-made) standard to guide the self-making or by means of which to judge it good. The men, unlike God in His creation, will be unable to see that all that they had done is good. (Indeed, in the story, the Babel builders do not even pause, as God had done, to evaluate their handiwork.) They could, of course, see if the building as built conformed to their own linguistic blueprint, but they could not judge its goodness in any other sense.

Even more important, there could be no moral and political standards sufficient for governing civic life and of guiding the proper use of power and technique. Power and technique are ethically neutral: they can be used both justly and unjustly. Worse, technical prowess, precisely because of its transformative power, creates the illusion that one can do without justice and morality.[13] The omnicompetent city lacking in justice is a menace, both to itself and to the world. Even assuming that the inhabitants wish to be just, where will the builders of Babel find any knowledge of justice, or, indeed, of any moral or political principle or standard?

Perhaps they will look up to the heavens. But looking to the heavens for moral guidance cannot succeed; the heavens may, as the Psalmist says, reveal the glory of God, but they are absolutely mute on the subjects of righteousness and judgment. One can deduce absolutely nothing moral even from the fullest understanding of astronomy and cosmology. Not even the basic prohibitions against cannibalism, incest, murder, and adultery—constitutive for all decent human communities—can be supported by or deduced from the natural world. (As we argued in Chapter One, this is a major reason why the Bible, devoted to instruction in righteousness, begins by denying the divinity of everything we see around us, and especially of the heavens.) To repeat, from the point of view of righteousness—indeed, for all ethical and political purposes—cosmic gods are about as useful as no gods at all.

The intelligentsia and the astrologer-priests of Babel know perfectly well the moral silence of the cosmic gods, but they are not without resources. The builders can build whatever is wanted. They will, accordingly, construct their

12. The contrast with the genealogical account of the origins of multiple nations, presented in Genesis 10, makes clear how the rational project seeking self-sufficiency and self-re-creation *means* a rejection of procreation, the need for which implies mortality and *in*sufficiency.

13. According to Aeschylus, the gifts of Prometheus, who, according to Greek myth, gave fire to human beings and taught them the arts, did not include justice or morality. His philanthropy was incomplete. See *Prometheus Bound* ll. 437–506.

own standards of right and good; but by this device they ultimately degrade the people they mean to serve. For if right and good are themselves human creations, if they have no independent meaning, justice eventually loses all claim upon the soul. The natural longings for the right, the noble, or the good that might arise in human beings could only be treated with contempt: the soul would be fed instead with artificial and arbitrary substitutes, cast forth by the human "makers of values." And unlike the shadows or images cast by the poets in Plato's cave, these artifacts of the just or the noble could bear no image relation to some genuine original toward which they point.

Fourth among the failings is that all speech loses its power to reveal the world. Carrying only its humanly constructed meanings, language, which was to begin with a self-consciously imperfect attempt to mirror and capture being, becomes, when taken for granted, a hermetically sealed shadow world cut off from what is real. To be sure, speech can still express human intention and serve practical purposes, as stipulated meanings, commonly agreed to, are communicated from one person to the next. One can still say, "Come, let us build," and, "Pass the hammer." But speech can no longer be used for inquiry, for genuine thought, for seeking after what is.[14] When the units of intelligibility conveyed in speech have no independent being, when words have no power to reveal the things that truly are, then speech becomes only self-referential, and finally unintelligible. Even the name one makes for oneself means nothing.

Finally, and perhaps the worst failing of all, there is no possibility in such a city of discovering all of the other failings. The much-prized fact of unity, embodied especially in a unique but created "truth" believed by all, precludes the possibility of discovering that one might be in error. The one uncontested way does not even admit of the distinction between truth and error. Self-examination, no less than self-criticism, would be impossible; there could be no Socrates who knew that he did not know. With everyone given over to the one common way, there would be mass identity and mass consciousness but no private identity or true self-consciousness; there would be shoulder-to-shoulder but no real face-to-face. Unity and homogeneity in self-creation are compatible with material prosperity, but they are a prescription for mindless alienation from the world, from one's fellows, and from one's own soul. The project for mastery and unity begins by presupposing a partial estrangement of human beings from the world, which it hopes to overcome. Yet in the end, the project for mastery—if successful—means the complete and permanent estrangement

14. In addition, the natural human desire to know the truth will atrophy and disappear in a world in which all that matters is the constructed reality born of language possessing only stipulated meanings.

from what is real. Ironically, the proposed remedy makes the disease total and totally incurable. The self-sufficient and independent city of man means full estrangement and spiritual death for all its inhabitants. One must thus reconsider the earlier judgment that the project of the builders could in fact succeed as planned. Over the long haul, could mutual understanding survive or cooperation flourish in the presence of spiritual, moral, and intellectual decay? Would not the meaninglessness of speech eventually foster, all by itself, the confusion that is Babel? Does God intervene only to push matters quickly to their logical conclusion, to make manifest, all at once, what was implicitly fatal and fated in the project from the start?

THE BLESSINGS OF MULTIPLICITY: FAILURE AS REMEDY

People are often best chastened and instructed by showing them vividly the previously hidden meaning of what they thought they wanted (for example, Midas's wish for the golden touch, or Achilles' wish for glory). In the Babel story, God's intervention would serve vividly to indicate the chaos, confusion, and alienation that are the inevitable consequences—or better, the intrinsic meaning—of any all-too-human, prideful attempt at self-creation. This is, admittedly, an unconventional way of reading the Bible, and the suggestion that God is just a workman who hastens what is necessary does not square neatly with the text. For if failure were both inevitable and desirable, why did not God just bide His time and allow the moral lesson to teach itself? And why does He speak as if the venture will succeed?

In fact, however, it is only God's intervention that could *prove* that failure was *inevitable,* and permanently so. Spontaneous failure, happening later in the ordinary course of things, might be perceived as an accident, avoidable by another and better attempt. When we remember that the story is told mainly for the edification of its readers, we who are ever tempted by the humanist dream of the universal city feel the power of hearing God's judgment and seeing His will behind its actual demise. We are moved to see that the highest principle of being cannot support—that is, brings down—any human project that knows it not. As a result of God's intervention, we discover that the inner meaning of the project for human self-re-creation is necessarily misunderstanding, separation, and alienation from one another.

God's "punishment" fits the "crime" also in the (more usual) sense of "fitting *counter*action." It opposes precisely each of the failings of the city by thwarting the plan to build it. Yet the punishment not only fits the crime; it is also a gift to treat and rehabilitate the criminal. Failure is offered as remedy.

Though He may be troubled by man's impending technological power,

God's remarks focus on the problem of human unity and human language: it is because "it is *one* people" and because "they have all *one language*" that "nothing will be restrained from them which they have imagined /plotted to do." Human unity depends on linguistic unity. The trouble lies not in the mere fact that all human beings speak a particular human language—say, Sumerian—but in the fact that the unified human language stands for and bespeaks merely a humanly constructed vision of the world and carries a purely factitious truth. It lies also in the pride human beings take in the plots and projects for "perfecting" the world that are made possible by an imagination furnished by the shared representations of a uniform language. The trouble with Babel is, at bottom, the trouble with language and the complacency and pride it tends to produce.

Accordingly, confusion of speech is the instrument of God's remedial intervention. He does not tear down the tower or the city walls; He chooses instead to "go down and confound their language, that they may not understand [each] man the language of his neighbor" (11:7). Misunderstanding and nonunderstanding make further cooperation on the project impossible, and the men leave off building the city. Dispersion, following upon the confounding of speech, leads to the emergence of separate nations, with separate tongues and separate ways, with the near certain prospect of difference, opposition, and the danger of war.

It is easy to see how linguistic and cultural multiplicity, contention, and the threat of destruction through war fit, as remedies of opposition, the aspirations to unity, harmony, and prideful self-sufficiency on which the city is built.[15] But they also serve to remedy the failings of idolatry, the denial of mortality, the lack of standards, the divorce of speech from being, the lack of self-examination, and, in sum, the full estrangement of man. In every case, it is *negativity* that fits the punishment to the crime: failure or opposition is the heart of the remedy, or at least provides its beginnings.

The emergence of multiple nations, with their divergent customs and competing interests, challenges the view of human self-sufficiency. Each nation, by its very existence, testifies against the god-like status of every other; the rivalries that spring up are, in part, both the result and the cause of the affronts to national self-esteem that such otherness necessarily implies. The prospect of war and, even more, its actual horrors prevent forgetfulness of mortality, vulnerability, and insufficiency. Such times of crisis are often times that open men most to think about the eternal and the divine.

15. It is also possible to see the punishment as revealing the inner meaning of the constructivist project. For the inability to understand one another *is* the deeper meaning of denying to the object of one's language and one's aspirations any independent, non-man-made meaning or being.

Awareness of the multiplicity of human ways is also the necessary precondition for the active search for the better or best way. Discovering the partiality of one's own truths and standards invites the active search for truths and standards beyond one's making.[16] Opposition is the key to the discovery of the distinction between error and truth, appearance and reality, convention and nature—between that which is appears to be and that which truly is. Contesting a "human truth" invites the quest for a truth *beyond* human making; the discovery of multiple human ways invites an interest in the *best* possible way.[17] The self-content have no aspirations and longings, the self-content are closed to the high.

This is not the first time that the Bible has pointed out a difficulty with unity and single-mindedness. After man was created and set into the Garden of Eden, we recall, God observes that it is not good for the man to be alone. Though it is common and appropriate to think that "alone" means lonely or in need of assistance—that it is a badge of weakness—"alone" can also mean self-sufficient or independent, a sign of apparent strength. Why might a philanthropic God find fault with such apparent human strength? Perhaps (as we suggested earlier) because the perfect man, because he was alone, could not know himself to be perfect, indeed, could not know himself at all. Or more likely, perhaps the original independent man, though he dwelt in the Lord's garden, had no real awareness of the presence of God. The coming of the woman first awakens man's self-awareness, and the result of their transgression not only heightens their moral self-consciousness but brings them to their first awareness of God. Only after they discover their own insufficiency and dependence, implicit in their nakedness, do they for the first time "hear the voice of the Lord God walking in the garden." Only in discovering the distance between ourselves and the Eternal, between ourselves and the truly self-

16. Jacques Ellul speaks powerfully of the benefit of knowing the partiality of human truth: "A humanity capable of communication has in its possession the most terrible weapon of its own death: it is capable of creating a unique truth, believed by all, independent of God. By the confusion of tongues, by noncommunication, God keeps men from forming a truth valid for all men. Henceforth, man's truth will only be partial and contested." (*The Meaning of the City*, trans. Dennis Pardee [Grand Rapids: William B. Eerdmans, 1970], 19.) For Ellul, it seems that modesty and humility are the major benefits of knowing the partial and contested character of truth. He does not emphasize how the contesting of "human truths" invites the quest for *the* truth, beyond human making.

17. Even in relations between nations, the awareness of misunderstanding is the possible beginning of the search for genuine understanding based upon recognizing the similar aspirations of the other. Such an understanding is admittedly hard to attain (in the face of mistrust and genuine conflicts of interest), but it would be an understanding much deeper than the factitious homogeneity and agreement created out of nothing. In all of these cases, failure and want—and their recognition as failure and want—are the seeds of the human aspiration to be and do better.

sufficient, can human beings orient themselves toward that which is genuinely highest. God's multiplication of languages and His dispersion of the nations is the political analogue to the creation of woman: instituting otherness and opposition, it is the necessary condition for national self-awareness and the possibility of a politics that will hear and hearken to the voice of what is eternal, true, and good.

It has not escaped our notice that the story that teaches us all these things and that shows us how human language can give rise to complacency, pride, and presumption is, necessarily, conveyed to us in language. Moreover, it is written in a *particular* language, biblical Hebrew, which—if we are to believe the story we are reading—is in fact one of the many languages that resulted from God's confounding of human speech and His multiplication of tongues. This invites troubling questions: Does this text, or more precisely, our *understanding of its meaning,* escape the imperfections of human linguistic partiality? Do we readers not risk the presumption of the Babel builders in thinking that we fully comprehend this story (and this book as a whole)? Let me suggest that the text has anticipated this difficulty and addressed it head-on. Lest we readers smugly believe that we thoroughly understand this story (or the Bible as a whole), the text—by its artful wordplay and multiple ambiguities—undermines our complacency, makes us feel our limitations, and demands that we pay close attention to the voice that is calling to us out of the text. Far from undermining the conclusion of the story of Babel, the linguistic manner of the text enables—even *obliges*—us readers to experience its teaching regarding the limits of language and to open ourselves to seek always for a truth deeper than our immediate comprehension.

AWAY FROM BABYLON: A PREVIEW OF THE NEW WAY

The story of Babel, the last episode in the universal human story, ends abruptly with the scattering of peoples across the face of the earth. The next story, the call of Abraham, which begins even more abruptly, is the first episode in a new human story, in which God's universal human way is taught first to a particular people. Standing on the threshold of the new way, we look both backward at Babel and forward across the divide, looking to see how coming away from Babel might be connected to where humankind must go next.

And the Lord said unto Abram: "Get thee out of thy country, and from thy kindred, and from thy father's house, unto the land that I will show thee. And I will make of thee a great nation, and I will bless thee, and make thy name great; and be thou a blessing. And I will bless them that bless thee, and him that curseth thee will I curse; and in thee shall all the families of the earth be blessed." So Abram went." (12:1–4) [18]

Why does God choose Abram? Why does Abram go? The text is utterly silent on these matters, perhaps in order not to distract us from the overwhelming facts that God did choose him and that Abram, without a word, got up and went. But we wonder nonetheless: could the election of Abram, and his openness to the call, have something to do with the story of Babel?

Between Babel and the call of Abram, Genesis gives the single line of descent of the ten generations leading from Shem to Abram, tying the tale of dispersion to the tale of election. With the lesson of Babel behind him, the reader is ready to hear the call of Abram. Is it also possible that, with Babel *literally* behind him, someone in the line from Shem to Abram was ready to hear the call of God? Does the text, by juxtaposing the two stories, suggest that an understanding of the beginning of Abram is linked to an understanding of Babel? Is there a *logical* and *moral* connection, not necessarily a historical or empirical one? We are encouraged to consider this possibility because of the literary structure of the text itself.

The name of the head of the line, Shem, means "name," the same as the word used in the Babel story, "to make us a name." Shem has gained a name for himself, not by pursuing it proudly but rather for his leadership in the pious covering of his father Noah's nakedness. The arch-ancestor of Abram is pious, refusing to look directly upon his natural origins; he looked away from nature in the direction of the as-yet-unpromulgated law to honor father and mother. Such a one is fit for the familial task of transmission. The inviolability, not to say sanctity, of family life will be crucial to the new way. Shem fathers Arphachshad two years after the Flood, and is followed by a succession of sons—Shelah, Eber, Peleg, Reu, Serug, and Nahor—each of whom, because of life spans measured in centuries, is still alive when, 222 years after the Flood, Terah is born.

It is with Terah, Abram's father, in fact, that the lineage of Abram becomes truly interesting. Terah, mysteriously and on his own, leaves his family home in Ur of the Chaldees and sets forth, with Abram, Lot, and Sarai, to go to the land of Canaan. "Chaldees" is a biblical synonym for "Babylonians"; Ur, though not Babylon itself, was a Babylonian city, historically a center of moon-god worship, as was Haran, the city on the way to Canaan where Terah stopped. Abram will

18. A more thorough treatment of this material will be presented in the next chapter. Here we are mainly interested in seeing the connection of Abram to his Mesopotamian origins, and in considering whether he might have learned from living among the Babylonians what the reader can learn only with the help of this text (and from its careful construction).

continue and complete the migration of his father, from Babylonia to Canaan, but in obedience to God's command. Like his father, Abram too is a refugee from Babylonia, from the land of the worship of the heavens and the heavenly bodies. He also, therefore, becomes a man without a home, without a city, without roots, and without the gods of his place of origins. Abram is the rootless, homeless, godless son of a wanderer (or radical), one who has grown out of, but who has outgrown and rejected, the Babylonian ways and gods. Two more things we know about Abram: he is married to a beautiful woman, Sarai, and he is still childless at age seventy-five when God calls, for Sarai is barren.

In his circumstances, Abram is as far as possible from the self-satisfied and secure condition of the builders of Babel: he has no gods; he has no city; he has no children; he has no settled ways; he is discontent, yet he is not despairing; he is capable of loving a beautiful woman even though she is barren. Everything else we know about Abram is speculative. He was almost certainly a man longing for roots, land, home, settled ways, children, for something great, and for the divine. About the divine, perhaps he has learned something important—albeit negatively—as a result of his experience of the Babylonian way: he has seen through the worship of heaven.

How this might have happened is, of course, pure speculation. But is it not conceivable that, on the basis of his *own* study of the stars, Abram intuited that the visible stars could not themselves be gods, precisely because, though they are many, they move in such an ordered whole? Could Abram have intuited that there must be an invisible, single intelligent source behind the visible, many, but silent heavenly bodies, moving dumbly yet in intelligible ways? Is this perhaps what is behind the rabbinic legends that Abram smashed his father's idols, having become persuaded of monotheism on *philosophical* grounds, even before God spoke to him directly? Could Abram have figured out that the truth cannot be one humanist city with many (or no) gods, but many nations in search of the one God?

God calls Abram with a command and a promise. The promise answers Abram's longing for land, seed, and a great name. (God does not condemn ambition for fame but will grant it only for pious service.) Abram goes not because he knows exactly who it is that is calling him—only later does God identify himself to Abram. Abram goes not only because he wants the promise but also because he has at least two reasons to believe that the speaker just might be a god indeed, and one able to deliver. First of all, this speaker in fact speaks—that is, this invisible being is itself clearly intelligent. Second, the voice addresses him not only personally but knowingly and with concern: marvelously, from Abram's point of view, the speaker has seen directly into Abram's heart, for the promises that are made respond to Abram's deepest longings. Nothing revered in Babylon could speak or know what men want. Abram completes the rejection of Babel and heads off to found God's new way.[19]

CODA: A COMMENT ON BABEL, BIBLE, AND MODERN LIFE

Before embarking on the journey with Abram, we pause to catch our breath and to take stock. We lift our noses out of the text and take a brief look around. Though in practicing our exegesis we aspire to be faithful readers, we do not permanently suspend our critical judgment. For we are seeking wisdom, after all, and not merely familiarity with the meaning of the text. We wonder about the meaning of the story and its relevance for us.

Did the failure of Babel produce the cure? Has the new way succeeded? The walk that Abram took led ultimately to biblical religion, which, by anyone's account, is a major source and strength of Western civilization. Yet, standing where we stand, at the start of the twenty-first century (more than thirty-seven hundred years later), it is far from clear that the proliferation of opposing nations is a boon to the race. Mankind as a whole is not obviously more reverent, just, and thoughtful. And internally, the West often seems tired; we appear to have lost our striving for what is highest. God has not spoken to us in a long time.

The causes of our malaise are numerous and complicated, but one of them is too frequently overlooked: the project of Babel has been making a comeback. Ever since the beginning of the seventeenth century, when men like Bacon and Descartes called mankind to the conquest of nature for the relief of man's estate, the cosmopolitan dream of the city of man has guided many of the best minds and hearts throughout the world. Science and technology are again in the ascendancy, defying political boundaries en route to a projected human imperium over nature. God, it seems, forgot about the possibility that a new universal

---

19. The pre-Abrahamic chapters of Genesis (1–11) are, as we have seen from the beginning, aimed against the Babylonian or Mesopotamian world view, a view the Bible presents as if it were the primordial outlook of humankind uninstructed and, therefore, incompatible with a righteous and holy social order. The man who will found the new nation devoted to righteousness and holiness comes out of and turns his back on Mesopotamia. Hereafter the new nation will define itself first against Canaan and then against Egypt. What is wrong, from the Bible's point of view, with these two alternatives is likely to be different from what is wrong with Mesopotamia. Crudely put, among the Canaanites the basic problem seems to be sexual wildness and impurity ("family values"). Among the Egyptians the basic problem is harder to specify, but it seems to be a combination involving despotism, technocratic bureaucracy, magic and mastery of nature, and a societal preoccupation with death ("political-cultural values"). As the founding of the nation is "out of Babylon," so its growth to tribal status is "against Canaan" and its emergence as a people with law and self-governance is "out of Egypt."

language could emerge, the language of symbolic mathematics, and its off-spring, mathematical physics. It is algebra that all men understand without disagreement. It is Cartesian analytic geometry that enables the mind mentally to homogenize the entire world, to turn it into stuff for our manipulations. It is the language of Cartesian mathematics and method that has brought Babel back from oblivion. Whether we think of the heavenly city of the philosophes or the posthistorical age toward which Marxism points, or, more concretely, the imposing building of the United Nations that stands today in America's first city; whether we look at the World Wide Web and its WordPerfect, or the globalized economy, or the biomedical project to re-create human nature without its imperfections; whether we confront the spread of the postmodern claim that all truth is of human creation—we see everywhere evidence of the revived Babylonian vision.

Can our new Babel succeed? And can it escape—has it escaped?—the failings of success of its ancient prototype? What, for example, will it revere? Will its makers and its beneficiaries be hospitable to procreation and child rearing? Can it find genuine principles of justice and other nonartificial standards for human conduct? Will it be self-critical? Can it really overcome our estrangement, alienation, and despair? Anyone who reads the newspapers has grave reasons for doubt. The city is back, and so, too, is Sodom, babbling and dissipating away. Perhaps we ought to see the dream of Babel today, once again, from God's point of view. Perhaps we should pay attention to the plan He adopted as the alternative to Babel. We are ready to take a walk with Abram.

PART TWO

EDUCATING THE FATHERS

(GENESIS 12–50)

Chapter Nine

Educating the Fathers:

Father Abraham

*T*he failure of the city and tower of Babel brings to a close Genesis's saga of universal human beginnings. Multiple nations arise as the necessary remedy for the proud and perilous political project of humankind united. After and because of Babel, God abandons His plans to work simultaneously with the entire human race. But He in no way abandons His universal aspirations for human beings. On the contrary, He pursues the same ends but by different means. Having dispersed mankind into many nations, He now chooses one nation to carry His way as a light unto all the others, and He takes up a prominent role as that nation's educator and guide. Accordingly, after the story of Babel, the Bible turns immediately to the effort to establish God's way through the founding of His chosen nation of Israel.

The true political establishment of Israel as a distinctive people must await the liberation from bondage in Egypt and the giving of the Law at Sinai, the major events narrated in Exodus, the second book of the Bible. But Israel has crucial prepolitical beginnings that reveal already the core of what the new way will demand: man's free choice for obedience, a concern for justice, and a disposition toward holiness, a way of life guided by awe and reverence before the divine. The remainder of the book of Genesis shows how this orientation is established in the lives and generations of the Israelite patriarchs: Abraham the founder, Isaac the transmitter, and Jacob—later renamed Israel—the progenitor of the twelve tribes that become the incipient nation of Israel.

It is easy to overlook the political and cultural dimensions of the Genesis narrative because the text concentrates on the lives of a few larger-than-life individuals and vividly displays their personal and familial struggles. Indeed, we are drawn to the text in no small measure because of the gigantic personages we meet there. Yet in several ways and for several reasons, the patriarchal tales are pointedly political and cultural, no less than personal and familial. For in telling the stories of the patriarchal generations, the Bible shows them interacting with other nations and other peoples, followers of different gods and

practitioners of different ways: the Babylonians, the Arameans, the Canaanites (including the Sodomites, Hittites, Gerarites-Philistines, and Shechemites-
Hivites), and (especially) the Egyptians. We must therefore understand that
Genesis is here pursuing national or political questions, not just personal
ones: Looking outward, how can this new nation both defend itself against
hostile peoples and avoid imitating their unjust or unholy ways? And how can
it avoid the opposing evils of defeat and assimilation, of conquest by and rule
over other nations, of proud indifference to the outside world and envious
imitation of its alien ways? Looking inward, how can it avoid the disasters to
which human relations are prone? And how can it consciously perpetuate into
subsequent generations both a spirited concern for righteousness and a humble reverence before God, while avoiding the extremes of stiff-necked pride,
on the one hand, and abject abasement, on the other? Finally, how can a
whole nation be instructed in God's way? How can such a nation, chosen to be
a light unto all the others, survive and flourish? All these matters must be in
our minds as we read ahead, watching how the patriarchs struggle with themselves and with the surrounding nations in order to begin and keep alive a
new alternative for humankind.

The patriarchal narratives reveal a still deeper connection between the per-
sonal-and-familial and the cultural-and-political. Central to the national and
political beginnings of the Israelite people is the right ordering of family relations; God's new nation must rest on firm familial ground. This is, to be sure,
partly a matter of practical necessity, because the new way needs to be transmitted from one generation to the next. But solid marriages and strong family ties
are not merely efficient means for the perpetuation of tradition. They are also
substantively at the heart of the new way. Decent, honorable, and reverent family life is itself a central goal of the new national-political teaching.

The point will be even clearer once I correct a false impression that may have
resulted from my loose usage of the term "political": the new way, here begun
with the patriarchs, is not, *strictly speaking,* political. That which is truly political concerns the doings and affairs of the city—in Greek, the polis—a settled
place, usually having walls that separate insiders from outsiders, dependent
upon agriculture and the other arts, and aiming (as we have seen) at self-
sufficiency. The beginning tales of Genesis—especially the stories of Cain and
of Babel—have already warned us about the dangers of cities and civilization,
dangers that are magnified in the case of the universal city but that are present
always in any city, large or small, and no matter how many or few of them there
might be.

In keeping with its original judgment on cities and civilization, the Bible's new national solution pursued with the Children of Israel will not be, at least for a long time, civic or political in nature.[1] On the contrary, the patriarchs will all be wandering shepherds rather than settled farmers or city dwellers, and this distinction will prove crucial for the difference between the new way and the ways of other peoples—especially in matters sexual and familial. Man's proper orientation in the world will be gained—to begin with—not within the proud and strong walls of the city but within the humble and precarious tents of the family. Abraham, Isaac, and Jacob—all tent dwellers, all finally family men—will have encounters with cities and their kings, but they will not live or rule after these more prevalent fashions. Once suitably instructed, they will live and govern "familially," not politically. It is not much of an exaggeration to suggest that the *primary*—not the last but the first—innovation of the Israelite new way is nothing other than patriarchy itself.

This point can be easily misunderstood, as indeed it often has been, especially in modern times. "Patriarchy" has become a dirty word, and the thing to which it is thought to refer—the hegemonic and arbitrary rule of men over women and children, justified simply because they are men—is roundly condemned. Moreover, biblical religion gets much of the blame for this allegedly unjust institution—not without some cause. As we will soon see, the biblical way does indeed begin with patriarchy, and the founding fathers of Israel are indeed patriarchs. But whether blame or credit is more appropriate depends on whether or not the institution of patriarchy is in fact unjust and unwise, a question too important to be decided on the basis of mere prejudice. Before we can judge soundly in this matter, we must first try to understand the biblical meaning of patriarchy, and to recognize the more dangerous sociopolitical alternatives to which Israelite patriarchy appears as a fitting answer. The rest of this book, which, like the rest of Genesis, is concerned with the Hebrew patriarchs, will attempt to shed light on these questions.

"Patriarch" and "patriarchy" are neither Hebrew biblical nor biblical Hebrew terms—though the Hebrew Bible speaks often about "our fathers, Abraham,

---

1. True enough, God will eventually have His own city, Jerusalem, and Israel will have its own king. But these are latter-day additions to what is essential, and even then, they are in part concessions to human weakness. Though ancient Israel was intended to be, and indeed became, a nation with its own land, laws, and self-government, forced to engage in war and other international affairs, the suspicion of cities and politics never disappears; and the character of Israelite communal life is decisively informed by the more-than-political purposes to which the less-than-political institutions of marriage and family point—that is, when they are rightly understood and suitably constituted. The threat that politics poses to righteousness and holiness becomes a key theme of the prophetic books of the Bible: the failure of political Israel to follow the ways of the Lord.

Isaac, and Jacob," through whom Israel has its special relationship to God.[2] "Patriarch" is Greek in origin: *patriarches*, "progenitor" or "father or chief of a race," is compounded out of two basic roots, *patria*, "family" or "clan" (derived from *pater*, "father"), and *arches*, "ruler" (derived from *archein*, "to be first").[3] Using this (or any other) foreign term when approaching our text does expose us to the risk of possible distortion, of not understanding the Bible as it wants to be understood. Nevertheless, its usage will prove illuminating, especially because the idea of patriarchy, by combining matters of both family and rule, is singularly well suited to describe the family-based solution to the problem of politics that is the foundation of the new Israelite way. Crucial for our understanding will be the effort to learn what the Bible means by "father," "fathering," and "fatherhood" and what it means by fatherly "rule," "ruling," and "rulership." As we shall see, it is one thing to beget a child (or to be preeminent in the household), quite another to do so understanding what it means and entails. To state the conclusion in advance: patriarchy *properly understood* turns out to be the cure for patriarchy properly condemned. The biblical sort of patriarchy is meant to provide the remedy for arbitrary and unjust male dominance and self-aggrandizement, for the mistreatment of women, and for the neglect of children.

The rule of the fathers is, by itself, only part of the remedy. A special understanding of marriage is also required. Indeed, the special kind of patriarchy instituted in Genesis is distinguished by the special regard it comes to have for marriage and for women as wives and (especially) mothers. Though they are, on balance, less prominent in the stories than their husbands, the matriarchs—Sarah, Rebekah, Leah, and Rachel, strong women all—come to play critical roles in the establishment of the new way, shaping crucial events and even directing their patriarchal "rulers" to pursue courses of action without which the new way would not survive. Patriarchy rightly understood thus depends on marriage rightly understood. Proper marriage no less than proper patriarchy is an essential element in promoting justice and holiness.

Proper marriage and proper patriarchy are hardly the natural ways of humankind. They have to be learned—to begin with, somewhat against the grain. Both require fidelity, not only to spouses and children, but also to the higher

---

2. When God first calls Moses out of the burning bush, He identifies Himself as "the God of thy father, the God of Abraham, the God of Isaac, and the God of Jacob" (Exodus 3:6). See also Exodus 3:15–16.

3. The word *patriarches* occurs four times in the New Testament, which was written in Greek: once in Acts 2:29, referring to David; once in Hebrews 7:4, referring to Abraham; and twice more (in the plural) in Acts 7:8–9, referring to the twelve sons of Jacob. In Jewish tradition, neither the sons of Jacob nor King David are spoken of as, or counted among, "the fathers."

moral and spiritual possibilities to which human beings are called. Neither marriage nor fatherhood, neither family nor nation can become truly what they are and should be unless they are steadily oriented toward and faithfully dedicated to something higher than themselves. As we shall see, the patriarchal narratives are all about how the founders of the new way acquire and transmit this elevated orientation and dedication.

Educating Father Abraham: A Sensible Approach

The new way begins with Father Abraham. His story occupies more than a quarter of the book of Genesis, from the report of his birth (chapter 11) to the report of his death, at age 175 (chapter 25). Nearly all of the account concentrates on the portion of his life between the call to leave his father's house, at age seventy-five, and the task of obtaining a wife for his son Isaac, sixty-five years later. During these years, Abraham undergoes numerous adventures, at home and abroad, with man and with God. By means of these adventures, Abraham gradually comes to know what is required of him as father and founder of the new way.

It is not exactly traditional to speak about the education of Abraham. Pious tales of the patriarch regard him as a precocious monotheist even before God calls him, a man who smashed his father's idols, a man who sprang forth fully obedient and knowledgeable about the ways of the Lord. But a careful reading of the biblical text shows otherwise: Abraham indeed goes to school, God Himself is his major teacher, and Abraham's adventures constitute his education, right up to his final exam, the binding of Isaac.

To appreciate God's education of Abraham, it is necessary to keep in mind the pre-Abrahamic, which is to say the natural and uninstructed, human condition and to see just what needs educating and why. The necessary background is in fact presented in the opening eleven chapters of Genesis, These primordial stories have shown us why it will be extremely difficult to establish a better way of life for human beings. For they have exposed the perennial problems in human relations and laid bare their deep psychic roots. From these stories we have learned especially about the dangers of human freedom and rationality, about the injustices that follow from excessive self-love and vanity, and about the evils born of human pride and the aspiration to full self-sufficiency. Those first eleven chapters have demonstrated the troubles within the household—between man and woman, between brothers, between parents and children—and the ever-present risks of patricide, fratricide, and misogyny. They have demonstrated the troubles with outsiders, including both animals and other, unrelated human beings, and the risks of violent conflict and injustice. And they have demonstrated the troubles in the relation between man and God.

By the time the careful reader has finished the first eleven chapters of Genesis, he is well-nigh convinced that mankind, left to its own devices, is doomed to failure, destruction, and misery. He hopes that there might be an alternative, a way of life different from the natural or uninstructed ways of men, a successful way in which mankind might flourish. According to the text, God more than shares the reader's dismay as well as the reader's hopes, and He decides to take a more direct role in the matter, beginning with Abraham. God Himself, as it were, will take Abraham by the hand, will serve as his tutor, and will educate him to be a new human being, one who will stand in right relation to his household, to other peoples, and to God—one who will set an example for countless generations, who, inspired by his story, will cleave to these righteous ways. Because of the moral education available to us through the first eleven chapters, when God calls Abraham we readers are also eager to listen.

But how should we listen? In particular, in what order and manner can we most profitably consider the account? Abraham's experiences are varied and complex, and what he learns through them is progressive, multifaceted, and not easily articulated. It is therefore difficult to know how best to present them. No doubt the order in which they occur is crucial; what a man can learn second or fourth usually depends on what he has learned first or third. Besides, as we shall see, the text recounts only certain selected episodes in Abraham's life and strings them together in a tight and carefully crafted order that best serves the Bible's overall moral-political and pedagogical purposes. The best way to proceed, therefore, would seem to be chronological, commenting chapter by chapter on Abraham's unfolding life story and paying careful attention to what prepares what and to what follows what, and why—to the inner logic of the account.

But such an approach, though truest both to life as lived and to the text as written, taxes the understanding. The mind looks for coherent threads and themes that can make experience intelligible and that can render articulate what experience teaches. A thematic approach, grouping together episodes on similar subjects (for example, on the promised land, or fatherhood, or relations with other nations or with God), might be more illuminating, despite its risk of taking episodes out of their narrative contexts or of distorting multidimensional stories by focusing only on one selected aspect. In this way it will be easier to see, for example, how the education of Abraham explicitly addresses the perennial troubles of human life.

What follows is therefore something of a compromise, reasonably faithful to the chronological narrative, but also grouping together some widely separated stories in order to show just how Abraham gains education in one crucial matter or another—in the next chapter, regarding the meaning of marriage; in Chapter

Eleven, regarding the meaning of patriarchy. But before detailing the patriarch's adventures, a question must be asked.

WHO IS ABRAHAM?

To know Abraham and his aspirations and ambitions, we must begin with his father, Terah, a member of the ninth generation after Noah, a descendant of Shem, Noah's most pious son.

> And Terah lived seventy years and begot Abram, Nahor, and Haran. Now these are the generations of Terah: Terah begot Abram, Nahor, and Haran; and Haran begot Lot. And Haran died in the presence of his father, Terah, in the land of his nativity, in Ur of the Chaldees. (11:26–28)

Terah is himself quite late to fatherhood; whereas his progenitors in the preceding seven generations begot their firstborn son when they were no older than thirty-five (35, 30, 34, 30, 32, 30, 29), Terah is a grandfatherly seventy years old when Abram, the first of his three sons, is born.[4] He witnesses the death of his youngest son, Haran, father of Lot, and sometime afterwards leaves his city and his homeland, Ur of the Chaldees (otherwise known as Babylonia), and heads for Canaan. When he goes he takes with him "Abram his son, and Lot the son of Haran, his son's son, and Sarai his daughter-in-law, the wife of Abram his son" (11:31).[5]

4. A comparison of the account of Terah with that of his eight ancestors in the line of Shem (see 11:10–25) reveals several subtle differences in addition to his late age of first paternity. First, in all previous generations, only the name of the firstborn son is given; here, where we have come to expect the formula "X lived Y years and he begot Z," we get "T lived Y years and he begot A, N, and H." All three sons are mentioned together. Although the text will focus almost exclusively on Abraham, this genealogical peculiarity alerts us to the possible importance of Terah's other two sons and their descendants to the future generations of Abraham. It will turn out that the wives of Abraham's son Isaac and of his grandson Jacob will come from the line descended from a union between Nahor and the daughter of his brother Haran. Second, regarding all previous generations the text reports that the named ancestor, after begetting his named firstborn son, "lived Q years and he begot sons *and daughters*" (none of them named). In contrast, no mention is made of Terah's fathering any daughters, an omission whose significance we will discover only much later (see Chapter Ten). I owe these observations to a superb paper, "Terah's Seed: Between Incest and Exogamy," written for my 2000–2001 Genesis seminar by Rachel Airmet, a graduate student in the Committee on Social Thought.

5. Terah apparently does not take with him his wife or wives. In contrast to what we are told about Abram and Nahor, we do not learn the name(s) of Terah's spouse(s). Presumably they were Chaldean women from the city of Ur who belong to and remain with their Mesopotamian society. (My thanks again to Rachel Airmet.)

Why Terah leaves we are not told, but even before Abram is called to Canaan, his father is, quite on his own, drawn toward what would become the Promised Land. Terah is drawn away from the Tigris-Euphrates valley, away from the land famous for the worship of heaven, the land where man first learned to measure the motions of the heavenly bodies (astronomy) in the hope of learning how to predict and control terrestrial events (through astrology). But though he was something of a radical—perhaps even sensing that there was something wrong with heaven worship—Terah did not complete his journey, but settled instead in Haran, a city, we learn from nonbiblical sources, that was, like Ur, a center of moon worship.

Abram belongs to the tenth generation after Noah, the last generation that could have known this "second Adam": according to biblical chronology, readily calculable from the genealogies given in the text, Abram is born in 1948, Noah dies in 2006. Noah, in contrast, was the first man who could *not* have known Adam. These biographical facts have symbolic moral-political meaning. Whereas Noah, the new man, represents a clean break with the man from the Garden of Eden, Abram will build on the foundation begun with Noah.

As Terah's firstborn, Abram is given a proud name that perhaps means "lofty or exalted [*ram*] father [*abh*]" or "the father is exalted." [6] Abram seems not to be bothered by the advanced age or restlessness of his father. On the contrary, he goes with Terah on his wanderings toward Canaan, whereas his brother Nahor stays behind: [7] Abram shows filial duty and/or shares his father's reason to leave. When he goes, he goes a married man:

> And took Abram and Nahor to themselves wives, and the name of Abram's wife was Sarai [princess] [8] and the name of Nahor's wife was Milcah

6. Some nineteenth-century biblical scholars, reading the text symbolically, regarded the patri- archs as symbols of natural powers, and they saw Abram in particular as the representative of the lofty heavens, the sky father, especially the sky at night. This view is surely far-fetched as an interpre- tation of the biblical character. But it may shed light on the meaning of the name he received from his father—"Lofty Father"—a name that would fit with the heaven- (moon-) worshiping ways of ancient Babylonia. It would also make more radical and significant the difference between his origi- nal name, Abram, and the name God gives him when the covenant between them is established, Abraham, "father of multitudes." The shift is from looking up to unchanging nature to looking ahead to procreation and perpetuation.

7. At least for now. Later we will meet Nahor's descendants—Rebekah and Laban, and then Laban's daughters, Leah and Rachel—living in Haran (Paddan-aram), the city to which Terah now moves.

8. Though in Hebrew Sarai means "princess," in Akkadian it means "queen," and appears to be re- lated to Sharratu, the name of the female consort to the moon god, the principal god of Ur.

[queen], the daughter of Haran, the father of Milcah and the father of Iscah. And Sarai was barren; she had no child. (11:29–30)

The wives were "taken" by the brothers, yet the fact that they are named indicates their likely importance for the sequel.[9] But whereas we are told (with emphasis) that Nahor took his orphaned niece, Milcah, we are given not a word as to the parentage of Sarai (a silence worth remembering for the discussion of marriage in Chapter Ten). Instead of hearing of her origins, we learn here only that she is childless; soon, we shall learn that she is also very beautiful.

So who is Abram? He is (before we meet him) a childless, rootless, homeland-less, perhaps godless, devoted firstborn son of an old wanderer and radical, a man who has grown out of, but who may have outgrown, the Babylonian ways and gods. He is very far from the self-satisfied and secure condition of the builders of Babel whose story immediately precedes his own. We surmise that Abram may long for roots, land, home, settled ways, children, and something great, perhaps even for the divine. About the divine, we wonder whether he might even have intuited a thing or two as a result of his experience in Ur: on his own or perhaps following his father, he may have seen through the worship of heaven. As we suggested in the last chapter, he may have figured out that there must be a single, invisible, and intelligent source behind the many silent and dumb heavenly bodies, that the truth is not one city with many gods, but many cities in search of the one God.

Closer to home, Abram stays long married to a childless but beautiful woman of lineage unknown to the reader; he is still with her at age seventy-five, when God first calls him. Hillel Fradkin argues from this fact that Abram's childless-ness is not altogether involuntary: he abstains from sowing seed with another wife because of his faithful love of Sarai, a love perhaps connected with her great beauty. Like many men, Abram's love of a beautiful woman exceeds his desire for children, at least at the start. In this erotic love Fradkin perceptively sees a basis for Abram's educability, for eros generally directs the soul to something higher than oneself. Abraham's longings are surely part of what makes him educable,

9. Sarai and Milcah are the first women whose names we know since Adah, Zilhah, and Naamah, the wives and daughter of the long since forgotten Lamech, heroic descendant of Cain (4:19–24). Sarai will give birth to Isaac, fathered by Abraham; Milcah will give birth to Bethuel, fathered by Na-hor, who in turn will be the father of Rebekah. The marriage of Isaac and Rebekah will reunite these two lines. Jacob, the son of Isaac and Rebekah, will marry two daughters of Rebekah's brother Laban. These two women and all three sons of Terah are direct progenitors of the line of the patriarchs. When, eventually, we learn of Sarai's parentage, we will see how "the patriarchal family line is a self-contained unit, originating solely in Terah, with no pathways to or from the outer world" (Rachel Airmet, "Terah's Seed").

but it remains to be seen whether the beautiful Sarai is the chief object of his aspiration or whether Sarai's beauty is the womanly asset of greatest importance
from God's point of view.

Of Abram's initial character we know little, beyond these frankly speculative
suggestions. The first real clue to what might truly move his soul comes only
when he receives the call from God. The Lord addresses Abram in a two-part
speech, first with a demanding command, then with a sevenfold promise:

> Now the Lord said unto Abram:
> "Go thee forth [*lekh lekha: literally,* go for thyself] from thy land, and
>   from thy kindred [*or* birthplace: *moledeth*], and from thy father's
>   house, unto the land that I will show thee.
> And I will make of thee a great nation,
> and I will bless thee,
> and I will make thy name great [*va'agadlah shemekha*],
> and be thou a blessing.
> And I will bless those [*plural*] that bless thee,
> and harm him [*singular*] that curses thee,
> and in thee all the families of the earth shall be blessed." (12:1–3)

Abram is commanded to abandon all that is familiar—his land, his kinsmen,
and his father's house—and to go to a strange land that God will show him. In
addition, as if to make up for what he shall lose, Abram is promised that he
will become the founder of a great (that is, numerous and/or mighty and/or
important) nation and that he will be prosperous, famous, and a standard by
which a blessing is invoked. Beyond these personal benefits, others too will
gain: those who wish him well will prosper (whereas he who mistreats him
will suffer) and—most impressive—all the world's peoples shall flourish on
his account. Addressing him out of the blue, without precedent or prior warning, God does not merely command Abram. He also appeals directly to
Abram's situation and to Abram's likely longings and ambitions—the love
of fame and glory, the love of gain, the aspiration to be a founder of a great
nation.

God knew His customer: Abram, obeying the command, goes immediately,
without hesitating and without so much as a tiny question: "So Abram went, as
the Lord had spoken unto him" (12:4). In apparent obedience,[10] he continues the

---

10. I say apparent obedience for this reason: verse 12:4 continues, "and Lot went with him." Abram
does not leave behind everything from his father's house. The consequences of Lot's presence we
shall consider in the next two chapters.

journey his father had begun on his own. But why he goes is not made clear. Does he go because he is a god-hungry man who is moved by the awe-inspiring, commanding voice? Or does he go because he is a greatly ambitious man who is enticed by the promises of founding a great nation, prosperity, and great fame among all humankind? One cannot be sure.

For a number of reasons, the second, more worldly explanation makes a great deal of sense. To establish a great and godly nation in the midst of a hostile world, God will need to tap a bold and ambitious man with political aspirations and ambitions. The meek might someday inherit the earth, but in a world dominated by the anything-but-meek, they will have great trouble establishing a secure community based on this teaching. Also, because God can neither extirpate pride from the human soul nor eliminate man's desire for greatness and fame—recall the Babel builders' unanimous wish to "make us a name"—it makes excellent sense that He should enlist man's ambition and pride in His project to subdue them.[11] Man's pride can be exploited in the effort to subordinate it in service to righteousness and holiness.

I therefore incline to the view that Abram goes not (as the strictly pious interpretation would have it) because he is already a God-fearing and obedient man of faith who knows that the voice is the voice of God Almighty. He goes because, in his heart, he is an ambitious man with a desire for greatness who wants the promise, and he goes because, in his mind, he has some reason to believe that the voice that called him just might belong to a power great enough to deliver. For what kind of being is it that speaks but is not seen and—more wondrous and more to the point—can see into my invisible soul, to know precisely what it is that I, Abram, most crave? Let's take a walk with this awesome voice and see what it can do.

Though I am partial to this interpretation, on both political and psychological grounds, we must remember that the text is absolutely (and happily) silent regarding Abram's motives for answering God's call. For now, the most important fact is that he indeed answers it—immediately, unhesitatingly, and (almost) to the letter. But the question about what is uppermost in Abram's soul is not trivial. On the contrary, it is the question of questions for the character of the new way: what will be the ultimate object of human aspiration and devotion? In his final test—that is, in the story of the binding of Isaac—Abraham will be compelled to declare whether he reveres the Commander more than he loves

11. Abram, already bearing a name betokening loftiness, may well desire fame and glory. But as God's promise implies, Abram will not be able to make his name great all by himself. Rather, *God* will enlarge—He does not use the verb *'asah*, "to make"—Abram's name (as He does, quite literally, when He renames him in chapter 17). As we shall see, Abraham gains his great name for being the (admittedly virtuous) bearer of God's covenant and founder of His new way.

His promised gifts. But here at the beginning, we are in the dark about what answer Abram would give, if pressed to choose.

The text's (indirectly conveyed but I think deliberate) ambiguity regarding Abram's initial motive—obedience or ambition, awe-reverence or pride—serves a useful pedagogical purpose for the readers. It provokes our curiosity and encourages us to consider as we read ahead just what sort of experiences or evidence might lead Abram—or for that matter, anyone else—to finally put God first. Were absolute submission required of him (or us) at the outset, few of us could even imagine taking a walk with Abram. But insofar as we too are ambitious for greatness and prosperity or desirous of fame, we can vicariously participate in his journey, and although none of us is Abraham's equal, we can learn from his inspiring example. Indeed, even if, though lacking great ambition ourselves, we have only a taste for greatness in others, cheering for Abram on his bold journey can bring us, as it brought him, to undreamed-of understanding.

These suggestions about Abram's ambitions are, therefore, not meant to disparage his achievement in answering the call. Far from it. You and I would probably ignore a voice that spoke to us in these terms. But not Abram. It is less that he has nothing to lose; in fact, he loses a great deal: his remaining attachments to land and family. And it is not only that he has much to gain; not everyone who lacks and wants land, seed, and substance would answer such a call. It is rather that, as a greathearted man, Abram has large, even political, aspirations and, more important, the courage to sacrifice present security and to risk everything to realize his dreams—to be sure, also opening himself to the possibility of receiving God's providence. True, next to the statesmanly Moses, Abram will appear to be rather mild and contemplative; Moses the liberator and lawgiver is from the start more obviously political. But seen in his own terms, Abram is no less a political man; we have it, albeit indirectly, on God's own authority: just look at how God chooses to catch this fellow. (Later, we will learn too of Abram's remarkable military prowess, as he drives back the invading forces in the war of the kings.) Abram has the right stuff for founding.

Many a man has a desire to found and to rule, many a man longs for a great name, especially one that could outlast his own extinction in death. These problematic aspirations, whose dangers have been displayed in earlier stories in Genesis, God will exploit and then educate in the founding of His new way. As we shall see, central to this education is an education about proper fatherhood and, therefore, about the indispensable role of women in the success of any great nation—even more in a nation whose greatness is to be grounded in justice and whose institutions are to aspire to holiness.

The Shape of Abraham's Journey

Abraham's education is obtained by undergoing eleven trials, from his original call through the binding of Isaac (see schematic summary in the table, p. 263). During this time he also has ten encounters with the divine, all of them initiated by God; after God calls Abraham, His subsequent interactions with him may be understood as responses either to Abraham's successes in his trials or to their consequences.[12]

In Abraham's first trial, already discussed, the Lord—out of the blue—calls him with a command sweetened by a sevenfold promise of great blessing: Abraham is commanded to go forth from his home in Haran and to go to Canaan, and he is promised fame, prosperity, and the founding of a great nation. Abraham immediately obliges. When he arrives in Canaan to find the land occupied by the Canaanites, and is therefore very likely perplexed about his prospects to become a great nation, the Lord appears to him (encounter 2) and promises to give this now-occupied land to Abraham's seed.

Second, when famine strikes, Abraham (on his own) goes down to Egypt, where his wife, Sarah, is imperiled in Pharaoh's palace. The Lord, without notifying Abraham, intervenes to rescue Sarah by sending plagues on Pharaoh's household. As a result, Abraham emerges from Egypt a wealthy man; he returns to Beth-El, the place of an altar he had built before going to Egypt, and calls on the name of the Lord. But his newly acquired wealth soon produces dangerous tension with his nephew, Lot, who had accompanied Abraham first to Canaan and then to Egypt and back, and who also has become a prosperous herdsman. This third trial is resolved when, on Abraham's initiative, the two men amicably agree to separate; when Abraham gives him first choice of territory, Lot heads for the prosperous cities of the plain, Sodom and Gomorrah. In response to Abraham's magnanimous act and his voluntary separation from his only possible heir, the Lord (encounter 3) now augments the previous promise. He tells Abraham that he will eventually have all the land visible in the region, including what he had just ceded to Lot, and He promises him seed as numerous as the grains of dust on the earth.

But Lot is soon captured in a war that pits the invading Babylonian kings against the local Canaanite kings and their minions. Facing his fourth trial,

---

12. The summary that follows is influenced by the structural analysis provided by U. Cassuto, *A Commentary on the Book of Genesis, Part Two: From Noah to Abraham* (Jerusalem: Magnes Press, 1964), 294–97. However, I depart from Cassuto's analysis in some important respects, and the generalizations I offer about the inner logic of the sequence are my own. In this overview of his adventures, for simplicity's sake, I will call the patriarch Abraham throughout, even though, as I will note, he acquires this new name only in the middle.

Abraham, who had prudently wanted to remain neutral in the war, enters the fighting to rescue his kinsman and wins a great victory, thus establishing himself as a political-military force to be reckoned with. Yet Abraham, swearing an oath by the Lord, refuses the victor's usual spoils of war. When this foray into international strife and his brush with death make Abraham anxious, the word of the Lord comes to him in a vision (encounter 4) to calm his fears, promising him His protection as well as great rewards. But with Lot returned to Sodom, Abraham remains doubtful of God's promise because he lacks an heir. When, in his first expression of a desire for children, he presses God on the matter of progeny, the Lord tells him for the first time that his heir will be a son from his own loins, and using a loftier image than before, He promises him that his seed will be as numerous as the stars of the heavens. When Abraham, impatient, demands a sign, God commands Abraham to divide some animals and enacts the "covenant between the sacrificial pieces," informing Abraham that not he but only his remote descendants will inherit the land, long after his death and only after they will have been slaves for four hundred years in a strange land. Thanks to these exchanges, which focus Abraham's mind more than ever before on his wish for his own progeny, Abraham accepts Sarah's offer to father a child by her handmaid, Hagar the Egyptian. But before Ishmael, his firstborn, can be born, Abraham nearly loses his heir due to family strife—his fifth trial—as the pregnant Hagar flees from Sarah's harshness (a response to Hagar's contempt for her barren mistress). Again not notifying Abraham (as in the episode of Sarah with Pharaoh), the Lord intervenes (through a messenger) to avert the danger: He gets Hagar to return to Sarah, Ishmael is born, and Abraham comes to regard Ishmael as his heir.

Here, precisely at the midpoint of the story, with Ishmael now on the cusp of manhood, God appears to Abraham (encounter 5) and reveals what He wants of him. In this decisive episode, God charges Abraham to "walk before Me and be wholehearted," and He then offers to enter into a binding and eternal covenant with Abraham and his seed. The previous divine promise is greatly augmented: Abraham will become the father of many nations and the progenitor of kings; the land will be given to his seed as an everlasting possession; and the Lord will be his and their God, always. Abraham has his name changed from Abram, "lofty father," to Abraham, "father of many." And he is told, for the first time, that his beloved but barren Sarah, age eighty-nine, will bear him a son, Isaac, his true heir, through whom God will perpetuate the (just announced) everlasting covenant. All that the new covenant requires of Abraham is that he execute the command to circumcise himself and all the members of his household—his sixth and central trial. Abraham complies without delay.

After he performs the crucial act of circumcision, thus accepting the covenant as founder of God's chosen people, the Lord again appears to him (encounter 6), this time through the medium of three traveling strangers. These men test Abraham's capacity for hospitality (his seventh trial); they seek to discover whether his entrance into a preferred relationship with God has corrupted his willingness to behave justly toward outsiders. When Abraham performs splendidly (in sharp contrast to Lot, to whom the same strangers next come), the visitors—now revealed to be divine messengers—confirm the promise of a son by Sarah. Next, explicitly in order to show Abraham what he must teach his son and his descendants, and taking advantage of Abraham's concern for Lot, now again in trouble (this time in Sodom), God Himself provokes a remarkable and unique conversation about justice and punishment for the wicked cities of Sodom and Gomorrah (encounter 7). Through this (often misinterpreted) conversation (trial 8), Abraham, after arguing against the destruction of the guiltless, comes to discover and accept some harsh truths about political justice and gives up the dispute. Having gained Abraham's tacit agreement to His plan, God proceeds to destroy Sodom and Gomorrah, but He rescues Lot for Abraham's sake.

Chastened by the display of God's wrathful power, Abraham wanders off into the land of the Philistines and allows Sarah to be taken by Abimelech, king of Gerar (trial 9). Once again, God intervenes (unbeknownst to Abraham) to rescue Sarah, this time through a dream sent to Abimelech, who in turn compels Abraham to acknowledge his wrongdoing regarding his wife. Only now is Isaac born in peace, when Abraham is one hundred years old. In his tenth trial, Abraham, under pressure from Sarah (who wants to defend Isaac from Ishmael's misconduct), and with God's instruction to heed Sarah's wishes (encounter 8), is compelled to banish Ishmael, his firstborn son. And when Abraham obeys, God intervenes to rescue Ishmael and promises to make also of him a great nation. His household now well ordered, Abraham enters into a covenant with his friend Abimelech and builds a sanctuary to proclaim God's name.

But just when everything looks set—in his family, with his neighbors, and with God—the Lord asks Abraham (encounter 9) to sacrifice his beloved Isaac, the son who—according to God's own promise—is to be the bearer of the lasting covenant. After Abraham, so to speak, passes this final test, binding Isaac on the altar, the Lord, through His messenger (the tenth and final encounter), halts the sacrifice and delivers the fullest version of the divine promise. Echoing and enlarging upon the promise the Lord made when He first called Abraham, the messenger blesses him with promises of seed as numerous as both the stars of heaven and the sand upon the seashore: seed that shall have victory over their enemies, and seed that shall be a blessing to all the nations of the earth. Abraham, who was willing to renounce the promise out of reverence for the

Promiser, regains—now on account of his demonstrated merit—both his son and the blessings of great-nationhood that he was so willing to surrender.

Abraham's education now complete, God does not speak with him again. Hereafter, the text recounts Abraham's final deeds, preparing the way for the next generation: buying a burial place for Sarah; finding a wife for Isaac; and entering a (puzzling) second marriage, having much issue.

The adventures of Abraham are schematized for easy review in the following table. The eleven trials are listed chronologically in the first column (the specific actions of Abraham are italicized). His ten encounters with the divine—all but one of them involving God's commands and/or promises—are listed in the second column (set chronologically in responsive relation to the trials of column one). The third column lists (in their appropriate places in relation to the trials of Abraham) five deeds performed by the Lord without Abraham's knowledge. From even a cursory examination of the schema of Abraham's adventures, a number of interesting observations emerge.

First, we note the thoroughgoing *chiastic structure* of the adventures, concentrically arranged in pairs around the central trial of circumcision. In the central (sixth) episode of his life, Abraham accepts both God's charge to "walk before Me and be wholehearted" and His covenant with Abraham and his seed, the covenant with what will become God's chosen people. Both the first and the last adventures are deeds complying with commands to "go" to places (Canaan, Moriah) that the Lord will designate; but the first is a response to both a command and a promise, whereas the last is a response only to a command that makes clear which it is—obedience to command, or love of promised reward—that is first in Abraham's soul. Trials 2 and 3 are paralleled by trials 9 and 10: Sarah, posing as Abraham's sister, is twice in trouble in the hands of foreign potentates (trials 2 and 9); and trouble brewing with Abraham's potential but improper heirs, Lot and Ishmael, is twice resolved by their departure (trials 3 and 10). In trials 4 and 8, Lot and Sodom are in danger, and Abraham intervenes to help; in the first case, he succeeds in rescuing them through warfare; in the second, because the threat comes not from man but from God, he fails to save the city (though God elects to save Lot for Abraham's sake). Whereas in the first case, Abraham enters political life as his brother's keeper, to save one of his own, in the second he acquiesces in a decision to destroy Sodom that could destroy his kinsman and accepts the necessity of harsh political justice and its claims over against the love of one's own. Finally, the trials immediately surrounding the covenant of circumcision concern questions of kin and stranger: in the fifth, Hagar, the stranger host-mother bearing Abraham's child, is harshly treated by Sarah but is solicitously cared for by God; in the seventh, the stranger guests receive outstanding hospitality from host Abraham (and Sarah).

Abraham's Trials	Divine Encounters with Abraham	Other Divine Deeds (Not Known to Abraham)
	1. COMMAND ("Go") and PROMISE	
1. Called with a COMMAND and a PROMISE, *Abraham answers the call*		
	2. PROMISE of land	
2. Sarah in trouble in Egypt		
		1. Sends plagues to Pharaoh; rescues Sarah
3. Trouble with Lot; *Abraham parts with Lot*		
	3. Increased PROMISE of land/seed	
4. Lot in trouble; *Abraham (his brother's keeper) wins victory for the king of Sodom and rescues Lot,* who returns to Sodom		
	4. Increased PROMISE of seed; COMMAND and covenant	
5. Hagar, the stranger woman, as host mother; trouble with Sarah		
		2. Appeals to Hagar; returns her to Sarah (Ishmael born)
	5. Charge and covenant: increased PROMISE and COMMAND ("Circumcise")	
6. *Enacts the covenant of circumcision*		
	6. God appears as strangers at tent	
7. *Serves as hospitable host to strangers*		
	7. PROMISE (son to Sarah); instruction re political justice	
8. Lot (and all of Sodom) in trouble; *Abraham argues the justice of destroying Sodom but eventually accepts it*		
		3. Destroys Sodom; rescues Lot
9. Sarah in trouble in Gerar		
		4. Sends dream to Abimelech; rescues Sarah; remembers Sarah (Isaac born)
	8. COMMAND ("Banish Ishmael")	
10. Trouble with Ishmael; *Abraham parts with Ishmael*		
		5. Calls to Hagar; rescues Ishmael
	9. COMMAND ("Sacrifice Isaac")	
11. *Abraham binds Isaac:* puts obedience to God's COMMAND above PROMISED rewards		
	10. Increased PROMISE	

Second, we notice (in the second column) that God directly both *commands* Abraham (five times) and offers him *promises* (seven times). The promises are more prominent near the beginning, the commands are more prominent toward the end; the carrots come before the stick. Moreover, the commands increase in their difficulty: from leaving home, to bringing animals for a sacrifice, to circumcision, to banishing the firstborn, to killing your covenant-bearing and favored son as a sacrifice—an act that means the willing destruction of everything God had promised. We suspect that what Abraham learns from his earlier trials prepares him to meet the ever more difficult demands of God's subsequent commands.

Third, nearly all the trials (after the call) directly or indirectly concern *marriage and fatherhood,* and especially the matter of the *suitable heir,* to be born of the *proper mother.* Trials 3, 4, and 8 concern Lot, Abraham's nephew and, to begin with, his most plausible heir (in the face of his wife's barrenness); trials 2, 5, and 9 concern the women, Sarah and Hagar, in their sexual and childbearing capacity; and trials 3, 5, 10, and 11 involve the actual or potential loss of possible heirs (Lot, Ishmael [twice], and Isaac). The central sixth episode involves circumcision of father and son, establishing as a pattern for all future generations this sign of the covenant, marked in the flesh of the organ of generation. The only trial that is not at all about generation and progeny—number 7, offering hospitality to the strangers—reveals that Abraham has a well-ordered house, and the properly welcomed visitors reciprocate their host's hospitality by announcing the birth of Isaac, his true heir.

Fourth, these plainly familial episodes are, at the same time, also highly *political,* most obviously the war of the kings (trial 4) and the conversation about the justice of destroying Sodom and Gomorrah (trial 8). In trials 2 and 9, Abraham learns the ways of Egypt and Gerar (especially in the matter of women). Trials 3, 4, and especially 8 involve him in dealings with and about the licentious Sodomites and other Canaanite peoples. The Egyptian origin of Hagar figures prominently in the familial troubles of episodes 5 and 10. The importance of national distinctiveness and the correlative danger of xenophobia are the themes, respectively, of the neighboring trials of circumcision and hospitality (6 and 7). All these encounters with other nations probe the dangers of destruction and assimilation, while at the same time providing Abraham with experience in negative cultural alternatives against which the new way must come to stand.

Fifth, the trials of Abraham are, of course, also and ultimately about man's *relation to God.* Issues of obedience, trust, and faith run through the entire set of adventures. Not only through God's explicit commands, but also through seeing the fittingness of His responses to Abraham's deeds does Abraham come increasingly to know who it was that called him and what it is that He wants from him.

Sixth, the overlapping and interweaving of the familial, the political, and the religious aspects of the adventures of Abraham are central to the meaning of the education he is meant to receive. A full understanding of what Abraham learns about his mission as founder of the new way will therefore require integrating the implicit teachings about marriage and family, justice and politics, and standing rightly and humbly before God.

Finally, we notice (column three) that God undertakes a number of interventions about which Abraham apparently knows nothing. Most of these are rescue operations involving foreign nations or individuals, and *all of them are connected to sexuality and generation:* God (twice) rescues Sarah from princely harems; God rescues Lot when He destroys the sexually corrupt city of Sodom; and God compassionately (twice) addresses Hagar, the Egyptian concubine, and rescues her son, Ishmael. In the latter cases, we are told that God acts for Abraham's sake: it is for Abraham's merit that God saves Lot, it is because Ishmael is Abraham's son that God guarantees his safety and his future. But no such reasons are given for God's interventions to save Sarah. Indeed, in both these cases it is at least partly Abraham's fault that Sarah is in danger. It is Abraham who passes her off as his sister, first in Egypt with Pharaoh, then in Gerar with Abimelech. Abraham does nothing to solve the problem he thus creates; God must on both occasions intervene, in Egypt with plagues, in Gerar with threatening dreams. Abraham also does nothing to solve the conflict between Sarah and Hagar, a difficulty caused by Abraham's agreeing to sire a child through Hagar (once again denying Sarah's wifeliness). Indeed, the schema shows at a glance that there are exactly three trials confronting Abraham that God alone solves, and solves without Abraham's participation or knowledge: *the three trials involving woman or wife* (2, 5, and 9, corrected by the divine deeds 1, 2, and 4 in column three). From this evidence we come to suspect that Abraham was not only incapable of *solving* the difficulties involving his wife; he was probably—to begin with—unaware that he had done something wrong in bringing them about. Whatever his beginning virtues, Abraham seems, to say the least, clearly inept in the matter of women, wives, and marriage.[13] This crucial failing receives much divine atten-

13. Four of the five episodes in which God intervenes without telling Abraham concern the women: the first and fourth with Sarah, the second and fifth with Hagar. The central episode concerns the rescue of Lot, without his wife; the sequel involves father-daughter incest. There is thus good reason to believe that the beginning of the education for the new way will be an education regarding sex, marriage, and procreation.

tion in Abraham's education. That he should need instruction in these matters should not surprise us.

~

Abraham is eager to be the founder of a great nation. But he has an incomplete understanding of how a nation becomes truly great. It must, of course, be able to preserve itself, to survive in a world threatened by its enemies and by those who would profit from its downfall. Accordingly, it requires leadership and manly prowess, to rule the unruly and to inspire the timid, at the very least in order to safeguard what is their own, perhaps even to expand and extend their influence and dominion. These matters Abraham likely can see for himself.

But virtuous leaders, indispensable especially for founding, cannot secure a nation's greatness alone; nor can they alone preserve their own great name. Their own mortality—which is in large part a spur to their ambition—necessitates a concern for perpetuation, for progeny, for the next generation. However manly the man, founding a great nation is absolutely dependent on woman, on her generative power. She holds the key to the future, not only by her natural capacity to give birth but also by her moral and educative influence over her children, an influence itself rooted in the powerful mother-child bond imposed by natural necessity. This educative influence is all the more important because natural excellence cannot be counted on in each generation: the sons of the founder rarely have the father's virtue (and the greater the virtues of the founder, the less the likelihood that they will be replicated), yet they must be reared well enough to replace him and perpetuate his successes and his ways. Rearing becomes still more important—indeed, supremely important—if the ways of the fathers are to be not the typical ways of mankind uninstructed, but the ways of a people devoted to righteousness and holiness. For all these reasons, founding and sustaining a great and godly nation is absolutely dependent on women, and not just any women, but the right women: women who are able to attach their husbands to the high-minded and reverent rearing of the next generation.

It is no wonder that Abraham, to begin with, does not understand this truth. Rarely do great men, with great dreams, like to acknowledge their dependence, least of all on the seemingly weaker sex. Strong men are not easily domesticated. Ambitious men do not readily accept the need for those who will replace them. Proud men are not given to yielding to their wives. Before he can become a founder, and even a proper father, he must become a proper husband and appreciate Sarah as a wife.

In the course of educating him for the work of founding, God will exploit Abraham's childlessness to move him forward, holding the prospect of his own offspring before him as a carrot. In part to teach Sarah and Abraham that children are a gift, not a human achievement, God delays the birth of Isaac. But the delay is also indispensable for educating father-to-be Abraham regarding the importance of woman and, in particular, the meaning of wife and the meaning of marriage—the subjects of the next chapter.

CHAPTER TEN

EDUCATING FATHER ABRAHAM:
THE MEANING OF MARRIAGE

*T*he primordial relations of human life are the relations of the household, first among which is the relation of man and woman as husband and wife. But man and woman are not by nature husband and wife. Marriage is a conventional institution, not merely a natural one. Nature may, to some extent, point the way, but it is clearly insufficient: natural sexual desire does not require, and natural human eros does not necessarily respect, the instituted bonds and boundaries of matrimony. Law, custom, and instruction are everywhere needed to shape and transform the natural attractions between man and woman into the social and moral relations of husband and wife.[1]

Up to this point in Genesis, we have had no positive instruction about marriage and no teaching about the meaning of "husband" or "wife." The only explicit moral-legal teaching to date, the Noahide code, is silent on this subject. To be sure, the different emerging nations will all have their differing sexual and marital customs, but virtually nothing has been said about them in the text, and certainly not by God. Abraham will be the first human being to receive any instruction in family matters, yet even here the manner of education will be somewhat indirect. Thus, if we wish to follow closely God's education of Abraham regarding marriage, we should remind ourselves of the uninstructed or "natural" ways of human sexuality.

The natural elements of the relationship between the sexes were revealed in the account of the primordial couple, living in the absence of law and custom in the Garden of Eden, previously discussed in Chapter Three. There, with the text's help, three aspects of human sexual love were distinguished, each with different implications for the relationship between man and woman: (1) *lustful sexual desire,* seeking bodily union; (2) the *love of the beautiful and ad-*

---

1. The first and most obvious example of such cultural delimitation of natural sexual activity is the near-universal taboo on incest, a subject, as we shall see, of central importance for the present chapter and for God's new way.

mirable, seeking not merely sexual gratification but approval and admiration from the one worthy beloved; and (3) *generative love,* the complex attachment of man and woman, tied to their care for and involvement with their common children.

The most basic aspect of sexual love is sexual desire itself, experienced as needy incompleteness and issuing in lust for bodily union with one's "missing half." This primordial and possessive erotic desire is experienced as the love of one's own, more precisely, the love of one's own flesh.[2] The first element of sexual love is literally selfish: the other appears lovable because she is (regarded as) same, because she is (or seems to be) oneself.

The second element of sexual love is tied to human awareness of the shame-filled meaning of sexual nakedness.[3] Proudly self-conscious human beings recognize with chagrin that sexuality means needy dependence on another, one who is *not* our own and not under our command; that sexuality means enslavement to a disobedient appetite that embarrasses our claim to self-command and that wants of us more than we understand; and that sexuality means perishability, providing as it does for those who will replace us. Eager now for approbation and afraid of rejection, man and woman seek not just sexual gratification, but also approval, praise, respect, and esteem in the eyes of the other. The ugly is covered over (the fig leaf), the body is adorned and beautified, and elemental lust is transformed into lofty eros, as lovers seek to transcend their shameful apartness through mutual pursuit of beauty and nobility.

The third element of sexual love concerns generativity, the bearing and rearing of children. This entails painful childbirth for the woman, domestication of the man, division of labor and its attendant dangers of conflict, inequality, and rule, and yet also the creative, regenerative, and redemptive possibility of renewal through children. In the face of the harsh reality of human life, generativity—especially the woman's power to bear—holds out hope for transcendence of separation, duality, and mortality.[4] Woman is a generating and creative force, with powers man can regard either with awe and gratitude or, rather, with envy

2. This aspect found expression in the narcissistic and possessive speech of the man aroused by the first sight of the woman: "This at last is bone of my bone and flesh of my flesh; and this shall be called Woman [*'ishah*] because from Man [*'ish*] this was taken" (2:23). (For the most radical meaning of "love of one's own flesh," see our discussion in Chapter Three, especially p. 103 n. 7.)

3. This, the reader will recall, was the first discovery gained from the dangerous knowledge of good and bad: "And the eyes of them both were opened, and they knew that they were naked. And they sewed fig leaves together and made themselves girdles" (3:6–7).

4. This simultaneously divisive and unifying aspect of sexuality appeared in the text with God's grim forecast of the human future, vexingly different for woman and man, a future whose only glimmer of hope is immediately seized upon by the man when he renames the woman "Eve," "because she was the mother of all living" (3:16–20).

and resentment, both because he has no share in them and because he is absolutely dependent on woman for his existence and perpetuation.

In uninstructed relations between man and woman, these three elements of human erotic love coexist warily side by side and often come into conflict. Self-love and the selfish love of one's own are at odds with love of the other and the self-forgetting love of the beautiful. Both are at odds with the self-sacrificing love of a child, seen as one's replacement: a man's love of his beautiful beloved may be at odds with her desire or love for children. Besides, each partner (as male or female) has nonidentical interests and desires, whose differences not only incite union but also threaten divorce.[5]

Furthermore, none of the elements of human sexuality is unambiguously good: possessive male lust for union can be degrading to woman, making her but an object of man's satisfaction (as we shall soon see in the story of Pharaoh and Sarah); excessive "love of one's own flesh" means incest (as we shall see in the story of Lot and his daughters); pride-filled love of beauty and concern for self-esteem can give rise to jealousy, discord, and bloodshed (as we saw in the rapacious conduct of the sons of God toward the beautiful daughters of man [6:2], which heralded the chaotic battles of the heroes [see Chapter Five]); and womanly pride in her generative capacity can give rise to domestic strife, injustice, and impiety (as we saw in Eve's boastful celebration of the birth of Cain, who, bearing his mother's pride, kills his brother out of wounded pride and jealousy [see Chapter Four], and as we shall soon see in the rivalry between Sarah and Hagar and, later, between sisters Leah and Rachel). Man and woman, left to their own devices, are bound for trouble.

Taming the dangerous female pride in her generative powers, which led Eve to boast that "I have gotten a man [equally] with God," is relatively easy: institute a prolonged period of barrenness before allowing childbirth, so that the woman (and her husband) will understand that a child is not the woman's creation and possession, but an unmerited gift. In keeping with this strategy, three of the four Israelite matriarchs—Sarah, Rebekah, and Rachel—will become mothers only after long periods of infertility.[6] But taming male possessive lust or correcting man's pride-filled love of womanly beauty or combating his indifference to—or even resentment of and flight from—the need for procreation is vastly more dif-

---

5. Division of labor, inequality, and rule and authority enter the sexual picture with the coming of children: the woman's desire, God predicted, would be to her man, and he would rule over her; he, in turn, would toil and trouble to provide for her and her children (3:16–19).

6. Countering the danger of excessive and smothering maternal love of children is another matter, not so easily dealt with. We shall touch briefly on this matter in our discussions of the covenant of circumcision in Chapter Eleven and again when we take up the relation of Jacob and his mother in Chapter Fourteen.

ficult, as is inducing him to stand rightly with respect to his wife as the prospective mother of his children. Educating a man to esteem woman as mother and to respect the task of moral and spiritual transmission is all the more difficult if he is, like Abraham, personally ambitious for fame and glory. All the more reason, then, why we should expect instruction regarding the meaning of marriage to be a central part of God's education of Abraham. That he badly needs such education we learn in the episode that follows almost immediately after he responds to God's call.

ABRAM IN EGYPT: WIFE, OR SISTER?

When the Lord calls and commands him to go, Abram answers the call and goes as commanded. But he does not go alone, for "Lot went with him, and Abram was seventy-five years old when he departed out of Haran" (12:4). Perhaps out of responsibility for his dead brother's son, perhaps because he still clings to his family of origin, but perhaps because he regards Lot as tacit heir apparent, Abram (entirely on his own initiative) takes Lot along on his divinely appointed mission. Whether Abram intends this or not, Lot, an as-it-were adopted son, represents perpetuation insurance for a man who wants to found a great nation and whose sixty-five-year-old wife is barren. When Abram arrives in Canaan with his little band, he makes his way to the oracular tree at Mamre (near Shechem), perhaps to consult the oracle, for "the Canaanite was then in the land" (12:6).[7] In response both to Abram's obedience in hearkening to His command and to his likely perplexity in finding the land occupied, God appears to Abram, promising that He will, in the future, assign this land to Abram's

---

7. Yuval Levin, in a marvelous essay, "The Promised Land: Canaan and the Covenant in the Book of Genesis," written for my 2000–2001 Genesis class, comments on this verse:

That "the Canaanite was then in the land" seems obvious—who but the Canaanite would be in the land of Canaan? But the next line tells us who: Abram. Before this, land and people defined each other in a simple natural way. The Canaanite lived in Canaan, the Urite in Ur, the Egyptian in Egypt. The name of the land reminded the people only of themselves, and the name of the people reminded others only of their land. There is something about God's action regarding Abram that runs against the grain of this way in which things naturally fall. God must put a non-Canaanite into the land of Canaan, to get away from the simple natural way of things. To be a Canaanite in Canaan requires no effort, no action, no thought. To be a Hebrew in Canaan will require attention and exertion. The uneasy and less than obvious juxtaposition of people and land will be a constant reminder that someone has made this happen; it did not happen on its own. This, in turn, might hopefully turn the Hebrews' attention to that someone: to God. . . . By giving Canaan to non-Canaanites, God is acting against the simple order of things, and ensuring that things will never settle down in the promised land. There will always be a question about the validity of the new people's claim on the land, and the question

seed—by silent implication, not to him. Abram, presumably in gratitude and awe, builds an altar.[8]

But the promised land proves even more unpromising, owing to famine. Abram goes, uninstructed, to Egypt, the fertile place, to gain food, that is, to secure his own preservation. In this place, as the descendant of Shem meets the descendants of Ham, Abram has his first instructive encounter with another nation. In Egypt, the place of sustenance for the body but of mortal danger for the soul, Abram's education begins.[9] Prefiguring the experience of his descendants who will later be enslaved in Egypt, Abram endures being a stranger in a strange land. He encounters the decadent and unjust ways of the greatest civilized nation, *the* alternative to what will become God's new way. He learns what it is like to be treated unjustly because one is a stranger: he suffers firsthand what happens when people prefer the love of their own (self-love) to the requirements of justice. But truth to tell, Abram acquiesces in this common error by repeating it, in his dealings with his own wife.

And it came to pass, when he was come near to enter into Egypt, that he said unto Sarai, his wife: "Behold please [*hineh-na'*], I know thou art a woman beautiful to look upon [*yefath-mar'eh*]. And it will come to pass, when the Egyptians shall see thee, that they will say: 'This is his wife'; and they will kill me, but let thee live. Say, I pray thee, that thou art my sister, that it may go well with me for thy sake and that my soul may live because of thee." (12:11–13)

---

will always point to the answer, the God of Abraham. God's new way would not succeed among a people who simply let things be as they are; it demands a people willing to become what they have not always been.

This profound reflection shows how starting with a foreigner is God's response to the natural emergence of nations descended from the sons of Noah, described in Genesis 10 (and briefly considered in Chapter Eight, especially in the first footnote). Because our interests lie elsewhere, we shall ourselves not be following up this very important subject of the "promised land," what Levin astutely calls "a central silent character in the narrative of Genesis."

8. In the immediate sequel, Abram moves to the mountain on the east of Beth-El, builds another altar, and calls on the name of the Lord. (Our interpretive suggestion: "Are you *here* also, Lord?") The Lord does not respond. Especially in a world in which people understand the gods to be gods of specific places, Abram, who could have no independent way of knowing that the Lord is indeed God *everywhere*, might have been dismayed at this result. If so, we can more readily understand his choice to continue wandering and his independent decision to go down to Egypt, the place of his next adventure and trial.

9. Why does Abraham's education begin in Egypt? Why, generations later, will the Israelite nation emerge only out of a contest with Egypt? If we could know the "essence" of Egypt, at least as the Bible understands it, we might be able to understand how Israel emerges in opposition to what is Egyptian. We shall consider this matter later in the book, when we come to the story of Joseph.

In this, his very first biblical utterance, Abram speaks to his wife about her beauty and the danger it now poses. Fearing for his life, he asks Sarai to deny their marriage and to pose as his sister, fully expecting that the Egyptians will be attracted by her beauty and interested in having her. Events will show that his fears are well founded—if anything, even underestimated. He does not reckon that it will be Pharaoh himself who will take her, sight unseen, on the recommendation of his henchmen, who are apparently always on the prowl for their master, rounding up beautiful women for his harem:

> And it came to pass, that, when Abram was come into Egypt, the Egyptians beheld the woman that she was very beautiful. And the princes [*sarey*] of Pharaoh saw her, and praised her to Pharaoh, and the woman was taken into Pharaoh's house. (12:14–15)

Abram has a genuine dilemma, with which one must sympathize: either he can try to save his own life at the expense of his wife's honor, or he can risk his likely death, after which his wife will also be taken (only this time as a widow). Thinking about God's promise of his becoming a great nation, Abram may well reason that it depends on his own survival even more than it depends on Sarai's fidelity and marital chastity; and should he have considered the matter, he probably concluded that there was no risk of confounding his lineage through adulterous union, for Sarai was barren. Indeed, there is no evidence that Abram *at first* believed that his becoming a great nation depended on his having his own progeny: had not Nimrod, in his own lifetime, created a great empire, presumably by conquest? But whatever his motive or reasons, in his choice his priorities are clear: he places self-preservation above marriage. Abram in his heart willingly commits Sarai to adultery.

Some might say that Abram should have trusted in God to protect him, but they read with hindsight; Abram would have had no reason to rely on God. God had not sent him to Egypt, God did not promise to protect him. And for all Abram knew, God might have no power in Egypt, which had its own gods, among them apparently Pharaoh himself. Under these circumstances, Abram's conduct could be justified, and not only as a matter of prudence in the face of necessity: if Abram is to realize the divine promise, he might even have an (inferred) duty to keep himself alive, at all costs. This is not only his opinion: Sarai, his wife, accedes to his request, willingly dishonoring herself for his sake, honoring instead his request "that it may go well with me . . . and that my soul may live because of thee."

The deception succeeds. Not only is Abram's life spared; Pharaoh does well by

Abram for her sake. In exchange for his "sister," he acquires sheep, oxen, he-asses, menservants, maidservants,[10] she-asses, and camels.

But Abram's choice is at best unsavory, at worst criminal and unholy; and his own conduct aside, the fate of Sarai is offensive to the Lord, who "plagued Pharaoh and his house with great plagues *because of Sarai, Abram's wife*" (12:17; emphasis added). For Pharaoh she was a nameless beauty fit for the harem, for Abram she could be passed off as his sister (his "own flesh"), but for God she was *Sarai,* Abram's wife. God intervenes to end this adulterous (and cross-cultural) liaison because He cares for Sarai, but for Sarai especially as Abram's *wife.* Unlike Abram, God, it seems, is concerned to defend the dignity of woman as wife. What this means, we—along with Abram—must gradually learn, for we—and he—are not here given any reasons, at least by God.

After putting plague and plague together and coming up with adultery,[11] Pharaoh—not God—rebukes Abram for his deception:

> "What is this that thou hast done unto me? Why didst thou not tell me that she was thy wife? Why saidst thou, 'She is my sister,' so that I took her to be my wife? Now therefore behold thy wife, take her and go!" (12:18–19)

Pharaoh blames Abram, with justification, for Abram had lied, though he might also have faulted his own predatory behavior; and though Pharaoh tacitly offers the principle—no adultery—he does so only out of his own current afflictions.[12] Absent the plagues, there is no evidence that he would have regretted the adultery, or that he would not have killed for the woman as Abram had feared.

Abram makes no response to Pharaoh's complaint, but one should not conclude that he has learned his lesson. The reader has been told, but Abram was not, that God is behind Pharaoh's change of heart and Sarai's deliverance. True, Abram might harbor suspicions along these lines; he sees that there are limits to Pharaoh's power, that this demigod and ruler of *the* supreme human society

---

10. Including, presumably, Hagar the Egyptian, later Sarai's slavegirl (see p. 278).

11. The nature of the plagues is not indicated, but it is likely that they were somehow connected to sexuality—for example, genital boils or impotence—so that Pharaoh could infer from them their probable cause. (The Hebrew root for plague, *n-g-ʿ*, can mean both "to afflict or plague" and "to molest or harass sexually.") Confronting Sarai as the likely cause of the problem—she alone would not be afflicted with the plagues—Pharaoh would have almost certainly been able to extract a confession from her.

12. Pharaoh, complaining about what Abram "hast done unto *me*," makes no mention of the plagues suffered by his household. His attitude and concerns should be contrasted with the more public-spirited response of Abimelech, king of Gerar, when he finds himself in a similar position (see pp. 282–88).

must yield. But it is doubtful that Abram now knows that he himself must honor his wife.[13] On the contrary, he leaves Egypt a wealthy man (12:16; 13:2); it has indeed gone "well with him on account of Sarai." Not only has he profited from his deception and "wife sacrifice"; it may even seem to him that his newly acquired wealth constitutes the beginning of the fulfillment of God's promised prosperity. (A truly nasty reader may even suspect that Abram has discovered the profit available in running the oldest profession.)

The attentive reader may learn from this story that though one may choose a wife, one cannot choose what "wife" means, that a wife is not transmutable into a sister or a concubine when it serves one's purposes. But Abram does not yet understand this. God's plagues made Pharaoh the instrument of instructing Abram about his misdeeds, but Abram doesn't get the point, partly because of who brings the message and how he delivers it, partly because Abram comes to no harm and indeed grows rich from his bad behavior. He is very likely quite impressed by his success in Egypt, and much more than he is by any suspicion that the founder of a great nation must not be indifferent to who becomes the mother of his children (or who fathers the children born to his wife). Abram is not yet ready to become a father or a founder of God's new way.

Sarai, too, may not be ready, though we are given no help from the text about her thoughts and feelings. She had freely complied with Abram's request without a reported word—just as Abram had freely complied with God's command. Whether from slavish obedience to the rule of her husband or (more likely) from noble generosity to save her husband's life and to serve his great calling, Sarai allows herself to be abandoned as wife and used for a monarch's pleasure. This is said not to judge or cast blame; no doubt Sarai's position was very weak, and she could hardly have done otherwise even had she wished to. But she participated willingly—unlike, say, Isabella in Shakespeare's *Measure for Measure*—in her own degradation. In deed if not in wish, she allowed her husband—and Pharaoh—to rule over her with utterly no regard to her personal well-being or, more important to the story of the new way, to her position *as Abram's wife*. As we shall see, it will be Sarah's later assertion of her place as wife that will finally teach Abraham about the meaning of marriage and how it is related to his founding mission.[14]

The adventure in Egypt does result, perhaps, in one small sign of movement on Abram's part. When Abram had left Haran, he "took Sarai, his wife, Lot, his brother's son, and all their substance that they had gathered, and the souls that they had gotten in Haran" (12:5). But when he goes up out of Egypt, he goes first

13. He will later again pass Sarah off as his sister, with Abimelech (see p. 282).
14. I happily confess that I owe the insights and instruction in this paragraph to my wife.

"with his wife, and all that he had," and (last) "together with Lot" (13:1).[15] There seems to be, indirectly, a greater closeness to his wife, manifested in a new distancing from Lot as possible heir, a distancing that is completed in the next adventure or trial. There, thanks in part to the great wealth first accumulated in Egypt, Abram parts with Lot to avoid fratricidal conflict. (Lot, choosing first, takes the well-watered plain of the Jordan, which looked to him "like the garden of the Lord, like the land of Egypt" [13:10]; whatever might be the case with Abram, Lot has not had enough of things Egyptlike.) When this happens, Abram is left without even an adopted son.

HAGAR THE EGYPTIAN: THE WIFE SURROGATE

In the first episode that threatened their marriage, Abram acted toward his wife entirely without regard to the question of procreation and children. Self-preservation, colored by the desire for God's promised greatness and prosperity, was his animating principle. But a new interest in progeny leads Abram, this time at Sarai's behest, to threaten his marriage a second time, and in a manner that reveals how the shadow of the Egyptian adventure continues to hover over husband and wife. This episode should be approached by briefly noting its preparatory antecedents.

Sometime after he and Lot separate, Abram enters the war of the kings in order to rescue Lot, who had been captured by the invading Babylonians when they conquered Sodom.[16] His encounter with death in battle produces a change in Abram. After the war, he for the first time expresses an interest in having children. When God appears to him in a vision after his victory and promises him a great reward—"Fear not, Abram, I am thy shield, thy reward shall be exceeding great" (15:1)—Abram, fearfully contemplating his mortality, complains for the first time of his childlessness. Abram, who had said nothing when God first called him, speaks out—in this, his first reported and directly quoted speech to God—to bemoan his lack of seed, his lack of a proper heir:

> "O Lord God, what wilt Thou give me, seeing I shall die [*literally,* I shall go] childless, and the one in charge of my house is Eliezer of Damascus. . . . Behold, to me Thou hast given no seed, and, lo, my steward will be my heir." (15:2–3)

---

15. Compare this voluntarily undertaken small shift toward the wife with the failure of Noah to effect a comparable shift—in his case, commanded—when he and his family were leaving the ark. (See Chapter Seven, p. 202.)

16. This trial will be discussed in the next chapter.

God responds by saying that not the steward but "he that shall spring from your own loins shall be your heir" (15:4). In the awe-inspiring covenant between the sacrificial pieces that follows, God gives Abram some bad news: not he but only his seed will inherit the land, and then only after they have suffered four hundred years of slavery as strangers in a strange land. God concludes with remarks about Abram's own fate:

> "But thou shalt go to thy fathers in peace; thou shalt be buried in a good old age. And in the fourth generation they shall come back hither." (15:15–16)

Forced by God directly to contemplate his own death, Abram now more than ever longs for a son. It is in this frame of mind that, in the immediate sequel, he receives and eagerly accepts Sarai's offer to try to have a child of his own by Hagar the Egyptian.

Abram no doubt recalls God's prophecy of an heir sprung "from your own loins" when opportunity knocks, in a novel proposal tendered by Sarai, who is still, now ten years later (at age seventy-five), unable to conceive.

> Now Sarai, *Abram's wife* [*'ishah*] bore him no children; and she had a slave girl, *an Egyptian,* whose name was Hagar. And Sarai said unto Abram: "Behold please [*hineh-na'*], the Lord hath restrained me from bearing: go in, I pray thee, unto my slavegirl; perhaps I shall be builded up [*or* I shall have a son] through her." And Abram hearkened to the voice of Sarai. And Sarai, *Abram's wife*, took *Hagar the Egyptian,* her slavegirl, after Abram had dwelt ten years in the land of Canaan, and gave her to Abram, *her husband,* to be his wife [*or* concubine: *'ishah*]. And he went in unto Hagar and she conceived. (16:2–4; emphasis added).

Sarai is desperate for children. In this, her very first quoted utterance (and her first words to her husband), she announces herself in terms of her barrenness.[17] But although she is frustrated by her inability to bear Abram an heir, she is not without resource or power. And although she attributes her infertility to the Lord, she does not recommend or resort to prayer. Instead, she offers Abram a concubine surrogate, following a custom well documented in the ancient Near

---

17. In Abram's first speech to Sarai—which also began, "Behold, please" (12:11)—Abram had spoken of her beauty; Sarai, by contrast, is focused on her lack of maternity. This difference between the way the man looks at his woman and the way the woman looks at herself is unlikely to be accidental or peculiar to Abram and Sarai.

East. In a gesture seemingly self-effacing, she hopes instead to be "builded up" in his esteem and in her power. And Abram, not the last man to believe that God helps those who help themselves, readily accepts the offer: here is a chance for the promised son out of his own loins.

God neither interferes with nor approves the surrogate arrangement. But the text, in telling of this exchange, hints loudly at the difficulties. Sarai is twice said to be Abram's wife and he her husband: how then can Hagar be his wife? And how can any resulting child be truly Sarai's? How will the slavegirl view her mistress—and her husband—should she bear the master's child? We are forewarned: should Hagar become pregnant, the lineage will be confounded and marital harmony challenged. And there is more: Abram's child will have an Egyptian mother—just as Sarai in Pharaoh's house might have born a son to an Egyptian father.

As these final observations suggest, the present episode is in several respects the mirror image of the episode in Egypt. In Egypt, Abram asked Sarai to disown the marriage and accept another partner, for his sake ("that it may be well with me"), and she obliged. Here, Sarai asks Abram to take another partner and in a sense disown the marriage, for her sake ("perhaps I shall be builded up"), and he obliges. In Egypt, Abram (and Pharaoh) seemed to exercise rule and power; here, Sarai seems to be in charge and Abram obeys: "And Abram hearkened to the voice of Sarai."[18] The mirroring of the two stories also invites thought about justice and retribution. For whether she knows it or not, Sarai's proposal amounts to measure-for-measure payback for the near-adulterous liaison in Egypt. Just as Abram had pushed Sarai into adultery with Pharaoh, so Sarai pushes Abram into quasi-adultery (actually, polygamy) with Hagar, this time casting herself, as it were, in the role of "sister." Just as Abram had been moved by fear for his life and perhaps also the desire for gain, so Sarai is moved by shame and the desire for advancement: neither Abram nor Sarai shows any regard for their *joint* future as husband and wife. Lest there be any doubt about the connection of the two episodes, Hagar is clearly identified as "Hagar the Egyptian," a legacy and part of the wealth gained in the wife-sister misrepresentation with Pharaoh. Abram is induced to imitate Pharaoh in beginning a harem; he accepts a quasi-adulterous threat to his marriage for the sake of progeny—whereas, in

18. This remark ominously recalls the beginning of God's complaint against Adam after the transgression (3:17). In the Garden of Eden, hearkening to his wife meant, of course, not hearkening to (obeying) God. Here, no such disobedience can be implied, as no commandments about marriage have yet been given. Indeed, later in this chapter we shall see how God weighs in on the side of hearkening to one's wife, telling Abraham to do whatever Sarah says. What all this implies for the meaning of marriage and for the prophecy "Your desire shall be for your husband and he shall rule over you" we shall take up at the end of the chapter.

Egypt, he had proposed it for the sake of his own survival.[19] (It is worth noting that the Bible's first two episodes of adultery or near adultery arise not from lust but from calculation. That they are nonetheless problematic shows that the trouble with adultery—in the Bible's view—may be more its threat to lineage, social identity, and transmission than its cost in alienating marital affections.)

The result is as we feared: the surrogacy stratagem backfires.

> And he went in unto Hagar and she conceived, and when she saw that she had conceived, her mistress was despised in her eyes. And Sarai said unto Abram, "The outrage against me is upon thee [*that is,* is because of you, is your fault]: I myself put my slavegirl in thy lap and when she saw she had conceived, I was despised in her eyes. May the Lord judge between me and thee!" And Abram said to Sarai, "Behold, thy slavegirl is in thy hand; do to her whatever seems good in thine eyes." (16:4–6)

Hagar—fertile like Egypt, from whence she came—conceives and, as a result, shows contempt for Sarai. Sarai, who had hoped to be builded up, is in fact lowered down. In the Bible's first reported two-way dialogue between wife and husband, she petulantly blames Abram for this state of affairs and quarrels with him. To keep peace in the household, he defers to her, telling her to do with the maid as she pleases (proving, by the way, that he cares not for Hagar herself; she was to him but a seedbed). At least at this point, Abram chooses to support his wife over against the mother of his child-to-be.[20]

But Abram cannot solve the problem created by his sowing his seed in, so to speak, foreign soil. Sarai, in an inversion of the later Egyptian oppression of the Israelites, deals harshly with Hagar, who flees from her mistress. God intervenes

19. This episode is but one of numerous instances in biblical narrative in which unsavory actions, even those undertaken as a matter of strict necessity, later receive their retributive answer. Harm and wrong, even if necessary, do not cease to be harm and wrong, and the one who is responsible—or, more often, his descendants—will be paid back. The biblical author is not a Machiavellian: necessity may justify, but it does not simply excuse, and the world remembers misconduct. As Robert Sacks has beautifully put it, "Deeds get hidden away in rocks; they do not disappear."

20. The psychological genius of the biblical text is wonderfully illustrated in this marital exchange. People—especially those who are close—often blame others (especially their partners) for their own foolishness, yet not without some justification. For example: "You didn't correct my error; you even acted on it; therefore, you must have wished for it yourself." Or: "You agreed that I might be built up by having a child; you too must think that my childlessness is a disgrace; therefore, you must share in Hagar's contempt for me." Likewise, people are often willing to escape all responsibility for their complicity in folly by washing their hands of the matter. Although they may be moved by a desire to avoid conflict and to restore peace, they are thereby complicitly responsible for what happens as a result of their withdrawal—as much as they were by originally acquiescing in the foolish deed.

(through a messenger)[21] to comfort Hagar but also to urge her to return to Sarai and to submit to her hand. As a compensation, He informs Hagar that she will bear a son whose name shall be Ishmael ("God heareth"), who "shall be a wild ass of a man; his hand shall be against every man, and every man's hand against him; and he shall dwell in the face of all his brethren" (16:12).[22] Ishmael is described in terms suitable for the utterly natural child that he is, sprung from his father's loins but conceived without regard to the permanence of marriage or to the difference between the ways of Egypt and the ways of God.[23] Three times in the last two verses of the story (16:15–16) does the text rub our nose in the fact that it was Hagar, not Sarai, who bore a son, Ishmael, to Abram (when the latter was eighty-six years old).

To readers familiar with the subsequent turn of events, God's intervention may seem puzzling. If there is something wrong with surrogate motherhood and the tensions it causes for the marriage, and if Isaac (later to be born to Sarah) is to be the proper heir, why not just let Hagar flee with her unborn child? Perhaps it is necessary for their education regarding marriage that Sarai and (especially) Abram live with the consequences of their mistake. Though He comforts Hagar, God weighs in on Sarai's side of the dispute, urging Hagar to accept her mistress's harsh punishment for her vaunting over her fertility. Yet the presence of Hagar in the house can only continue to aggravate Sarai, especially once Ishmael is born. More important, God's action here guarantees that Abram will have the merely natural—and hence unsuitable— heir he wants in Ishmael. Yet because of the presence of Ishmael and his rivalry with Isaac, Abram will later have to face the fact that concubinage and

21. As Robert Alter points out, "This is the first occurrence of an 'angel' (Hebrew *mal'akh*, Greek, *angelos*) in Genesis. . . . 'Messenger,' or one who carries out a designated task, is the primary meaning of the Hebrew term, and there are abundant biblical instances of *mal'akhim* who are strictly human emissaries. One assumes that the divine messenger in these stories is supposed to look like a human being, and all postbiblical associations with wings, halos, and glorious raiment must be firmly excluded. . . . [I]t is anyone's guess how the Hebrew imagination conceived agents of the Lord three thousand years ago, and it is certainly possible that the original traditions had a blurry notion of the difference between God's own interventions in human life and those of His emissaries."

22. The expression "in the face" is the literal translation of *'al-peney*, often translated "before" or "in the presence of" or even "in the company of." But the confrontational and oppositional connotation is ever present, as it is in our current idiom "in your face."

23. The text offers what may be a small hint regarding this difference. The messenger of the Lord, in offering Hagar the name of Ishmael ("God heareth") for her son, explains the name by saying, "The Lord hath *heard* thy affliction" (16:11). But Hagar called the name of the Lord who spoke unto her "God Who *Sees* Me" (*'el ra'i*; 16:13). The difference between the Lord who speaks and hears and who expects His followers to hearken and a divine being who sees and/or is seen may well reflect the difference between the beliefs and ways of Israel and the beliefs and ways of Egypt. This theme of hearing and seeing will return in the story of the binding of Isaac, discussed in Chapter Eleven.

surrogacy are incompatible with marriage rightly understood, at least within the new way.

The attempt to pinch-hit for the wife, possibly innocent in intent, is thus, in result, anything but. Not only is there still potential trouble in the household; worse, Abram will later be compelled to banish his firstborn son, and the descendants of Ishmael will later make trouble for the descendants of Isaac—as they do until the present day. But for the time being, thanks to their error, both Abram and Sarai—and the reader—may perhaps stand a bit closer to discovering the meaning of wife and the meaning of marriage: Abram, that a wife is more than a seedbed; Sarai, conversely, that bearing the child oneself is important; both of them, that joint rearing even more than bearing may be the true work of husband and wife. But before they can really be ready for the work of rearing, they will need even more to discover that the fulfillment of their relation as husband and wife depends finally on providence. They must remain open to procreation *within the marriage,* against all odds, trusting in higher than human powers—rather than human resourcefulness—to deliver the wished-for gift of life.

ABRAHAM IN GERAR: WIFE AND SISTER?

Abram will soon have one more chance to demonstrate his understanding of the meaning of marriage and his trust in divine providence regarding procreation within the marriage. But before he can be tested in this matter, he needs some explicit and authoritative instruction. This he receives when God introduces the subject in the very next episode, the central story of the covenant of circumcision (to be discussed at length in the next chapter). In the course of His speech to Abram announcing the new covenant, God renames Abram as Abraham ("father of multitudes") and tells him that Sarai "thy wife" will henceforth be renamed Sarah (still "princess"). More important, God tells a disbelieving Abraham (age ninety-nine)[24] that He will give him a son by Sarah (age eighty-nine), that He will bless her and that she will be a mother of nations, with kings of peoples springing from her (17:16). Abraham, incredulous, laughs *(yitshaq)* in disbelief and perhaps even in bitterness and derision, and he says "in his heart: 'Shall a child be born to a hundred-year-old, and shall Sarah that is ninety years old give birth?' " (17:17). Abraham clearly prefers the son in the flesh to the one in the mind. He says to God, "O that Ishmael might live before thee" (17:18). But God, rebuking him, insists on the importance of the right son, by the right

---

24. That is, twenty-four years after the promise of great nationhood and thirteen years after the birth of Ishmael.

mother, which is to say by his wife: "Nay, but Sarah, *thy wife*, shall bear thee a son . . . and I will establish My covenant with him for an everlasting covenant for his seed after him" (17:19; emphasis added). Ishmael, God says, He will bless on Abraham's account, with fruitfulness and twelve princely descendants, and He will make of him also a great nation (17:20). But, pointedly again addressing Abraham's disbelief, God concludes by reemphasizing that the covenant here being established will be transmitted only through his wife's son, Isaac: "But My covenant will I establish with Isaac, whom *Sarah shall bear* unto thee at this set time in the next year" (17:21; emphasis added).

Sarah, for her part, also will get a birth announcement and, with it, an opportunity to demonstrate trust in God's promise. It is delivered shortly after the circumcision, by the three strangers (men-messengers) who visit Abraham in his tent. Abraham immediately offers them superb hospitality, the excellence of which partly depends on the fact that Sarah is present to help out. (This well-ordered household is sharply contrasted with that of Lot, living in Sodom, to whom the same strangers next come. There, Mrs. Lot, a native Sodomite, is out of the picture, and in a parody of hospitality, the poorly wived Lot is compelled to offer his own daughters to a rapacious mob in order to try to save his guests from homosexual rape. The same daughters will later commit incest with their father.) Sarah overhears one of the stranger-messengers tell Abraham that within the year, "Sarah, thy wife, shall have a son" (18:10). Sarah, like Abraham in the last episode, laughs in disbelief within herself: "After *I am waxed old* shall I have pleasure, my *lord being so old?*" (18:12; emphasis added). In a delicate touch, God, in repeating Sarah's response to Abraham, tactfully alters it to omit any reference to Abraham's advanced age ("Why did Sarah laugh, saying, 'Shall I surely bear a child, *I who am old?*' " [18:13; emphasis added]), and He reiterates His promise that Sarah will next year have a son, rebuking them both with the rhetorical question "Is anything beyond the Lord?" (18:14). Sarah, in response, is now chastened and denies that she laughed, "for she was afraid" (18:15). But the Lord, leaving her, insists, "No, but thou didst laugh."[25] Retaining hope in the promise of a child, we are given to understand, is no laughing matter. Neither is trusting—or *not* trusting—in the word of the Lord and in His promise of intramarital procreation.

Despite God's repeated and reassuring promises of a child of their own, promises made to both husband and wife, Abraham fails to honor his wife and their marital bond. He again abandons his wife to a prince's harem at the first

---

25. This, as Bill Rosen pointed out to me, is God's first speech to a woman since He chastised Eve in the Garden of Eden. Fittingly, it also concerns childbirth and the woman's lack of trust in God's word.

available opportunity. Traveling in the land of Gerar, after witnessing the destruction of Sodom and Gomorrah (19:27–29), Abraham (although the text here again insists that she is his wife) announces to the nations that Sarah is his sister (20:2); and Abimelech ("father of the king"), king of Gerar, sends for Sarah and takes her for his harem. (Those who refuse to believe that an eighty-nine-year-old woman could attract a king's desire have not properly imagined how extraordinarily beautiful Sarah really was, perhaps all the more so now that she is rejuvenated as a result of the news of her imminent motherhood. The less erotic may prefer, as an alternative, that the king may have sought through this union an alliance with Abraham for reasons of political or economic gain.)

Given the announcement of Sarah's impending pregnancy, Abraham's conduct here is especially hard to fathom: perhaps, as he will later say when his lie is exposed, he still fears for his life; perhaps he is simply continuing a practice that proved so profitable to him in Egypt. But whatever his motive, in passing Sarah off as his sister Abraham displays a certain recklessness with the promise of Sarah's restored fertility. Could it be that he is still banking on the ascendancy of Ishmael, his firstborn? Does Abraham doubt God's word about Sarah? Could Abraham, fresh from experiencing the dreadful destruction of Sodom and Gomorrah, be doubting God altogether? [26]

Abimelech is a man much superior in virtue to Pharaoh, so God treats him not with plagues but directly, speaking to him in a prophetic dream. In fact, God will use Abimelech, a noble man but one whose virtue lacks the fear of God, to instruct Abraham in the meaning of marriage. In the dream, He informs Abimelech that the woman he has taken is another man's wife, and He threatens to kill him on her account (20:3). Abimelech, who had not come near Sarah, protests his innocence and (in contrast to Pharaoh) his concern for his people:

"Lord ['adonai], wilt Thou slay even a righteous [tsadiq] nation? [27] Said he not himself unto me: 'She is my sister'? and she, even she herself said: 'He is my brother.' In the simplicity [tam] of my heart and the innocency of my hands have I done this." (20:4–5)

26. If he is indeed filled with dread and doubt after Sodom, Abraham would be in a position similar to Noah's after the destructive flood, or perhaps also to his own situation when famine struck the promised land—in response to which Abraham went on his own to Egypt and survived by passing his wife off as his sister.

27. Abimelech's question echoes Abraham's questioning of God in their conversation about the punishment of Sodom: "Wilt thou indeed consume the righteous with the wicked? . . . Shall not the Judge of the whole earth do justly?" (18:23–25). See Chapter Eleven for the discussion of this episode.

God, continuing to speak to him in the dream, does not dispute the allegation of deception by Abraham and Sarah, and He accepts Abimelech's defense, at least in part:

> "Yea, I know that in the simplicity of thy heart thou hast done this, and I also withheld thee from sinning against Me. Therefore suffered I thee not to touch her. Now therefore restore the man's wife; for he is a prophet, and he shall pray for thee, and thou shalt live; and if thou restorest her not, know thou that thou shalt surely die [*literally,* dying you will die: *moth tamuth*],[28] thou and all that art thine." (20:6–7)

God acknowledges that Abimelech acted in the simplicity of his heart, but He does not agree that his hands were completely innocent: Abimelech, a harem keeper, *took* Sarah, after all, and he still has her; and, God adds, it was He alone who kept Abimelech's hands from touching her. Most important, He informs Abimelech, who though an honorable man seems as yet to have no fear (or awe or reverence) for the Lord, that it was to keep "thee from *sinning against Me*" that He prevented the adulterous contact. Abimelech is thus the first biblical character to learn that adultery is not only an imprudent act but may be also a sin or an offense against the divine. Promising Abimelech that the "prophet" will intercede for him if he does what is right, God insists that the man's wife be restored to Abraham, under penalty of death.

Awakening early the next morning, Abimelech relates his dream to his servants (slaves); they, like their king, fear for their lives. But Abimelech does not simply save his skin by returning Sarah; he demands an explanation from Abraham. (Pharaoh, we recall, had simply thrown Abram out.) Armed with the knowledge that a powerful god stands opposed to (this) adultery, Abimelech calls Abraham to account, as it were serving as God's own messenger and witness:

> "What hast thou done unto *us?* [compare 12:18] and wherein have I sinned against thee, that thou hast brought on me *and on my kingdom a great sin?* Thou hast done unto me *deeds that ought not be done.*" (20:9; emphasis added)

---

28. God uses the same expression that He used when warning man of the deadly consequence of eating from the forbidden tree of knowledge of good and bad (2:17). Adultery is, in God's eyes, a capital matter.

Abimelech, accusing him of committing an offense against the innocent,[29] insists to Abraham that adultery is a great sin, a sin that stains an entire people, a deed that ought not to be done; and he begs for an explanation of how Abraham could have promoted such a heinous deed. When Abraham does not answer, Abimelech continues to question him: "What sawest thou that thou hast done this thing?" (20:10).

Abraham, who on the previous occasion had said nothing to the explosive Pharaoh, now responds with a twofold defense. First, he was afraid of how he as a stranger would be treated:

"Because I thought: Surely the fear [or awe] of God is not in this place; and they will slay me for my wife's sake." (20:11)

Abraham's concern is surely not far-fetched. The love of your own and the mistrust (even hatred) of the stranger are the natural human way. Only when human beings come to realize that the stranger shares in a common humanity, each one equally in the image of God—and in this sense at least, that the stranger may in fact be a god in disguise—will strangers be treated justly (that is, with the "fear-awe of God").[30]

But it is Abraham's second reason that comes as a complete surprise, at least to the reader:

"And moreover she is indeed my sister, the daughter of my father, but not the daughter of my mother; and she became my wife." (20:12)

Sarah was first of all Abraham's (half) sister, the daughter of Terah; only later did she become his wife. (We understand now the text's silence, back in Genesis 11, regarding Sarai's ancestry when it reported on her becoming Abram's wife. We also see now that *all* the important progenitors of the line of the Israelite patri-

29. Abraham is thus accused of being just like the Sodomites, whose wickedness causes the righteous to suffer. Robert Licht, observing that Abraham might have concluded from God's destruction of Sodom that there were *no* righteous people in cities, suggests that Abraham himself (at least when he comes into the city) proves to be no exception: he lies and he causes a near adultery, inflicting harm on innocent people. On another interpretation of this passage, Abraham is accused of being guilty of the same misdeed—*punishing* the innocent—that he sought to prevent God from committing against Sodom.

30. That Abraham is himself welcoming of strangers is no reason for him to expect that most people are like him. His general suspicion would be supported by his experience in Egypt; and the reader who recalls the story of the strangers who come to Lot in Sodom should share his wariness (Genesis 19; see our Chapter Eleven).

archs are children of Terah, descending through two initial *endogamous* marriages: Abram and his half sister Sarah, Nahor and his niece Milcah, daughter of Terah's third son, Haran.)[31]

As a defense, Abraham's speech is obviously defective. Even if Sarah is his half sister, Abraham's announcement of that truth in fact amounts to a lie: the only relevant fact, namely, that she is also his wife, he fails to reveal. Readers of the text who know that marrying your sister or half-sister is later forbidden (see, for example, Leviticus 18:9 and 20:17) may assume, wrongly, that sister and wife are here mutually exclusive categories, and that Abraham had explicitly denied that Sarah was his wife when he announced that she was his sister. But as we shall soon see, that is not the case, for Abimelech finds perfectly acceptable the fact that Sarah is both sister and wife. Abraham's lie consists not in what he said but in what he did not say: he stated only half the truth and concealed the crucial other half.

Abraham concludes his apologia before Abimelech:

> "And it came to pass when the gods [*or* God: *'elohim*] caused [the verb is plural!] me to wander from my father's house, that I said unto her: 'This is the kindness which thou shalt show unto me; at every place[32] whither we shall come, say of me: He is my brother.' " (20:13)

Abimelech, unimpressed with this defense, does not answer Abraham's speech with words but with deeds, deeds that demonstrate his (perhaps now godfearing) superior understanding of marriage and the respect owed to a wife. He compensates Abraham with gifts (sheep, oxen, menservants, and maidservants), "restores him *Sarah, his wife*" (20:14), and graciously allows him to dwell in the land where he pleases. But his choice speech he reserves for Sarah:

> "Behold, I have given *thy brother* a thousand pieces of silver; behold, it is for thee *a covering of the eyes* to all that are with thee; and before all men thou art righted." (20:16; emphasis added)

---

31. I owe this last observation to Rachel Airmet. See the discussion of Terah in Chapter Nine.

32. As far as the reader knows, this request Abraham made only once before, and it was specific for the danger that lurked in Egypt (12:11–13); Abraham did not say "at every place." Yuval Levin (in a personal communication) remarks: "Abraham seems to suggest, even if he does not himself recognize it, that once such an arrangement is established it has a permanent effect on the relationship of husband and wife. If he was able to think of her as sister once, then he is not easily able to think of her as wife, at least until he comes to realize his error. There is no doing such a thing just once; it has a permanent impact."

Abimelech, a virtuous and magnanimous man, understands that Sarah has been shamed and compromised, even if with her consent. The gift of a thousand pieces of silver is intended to clear her name of all wrongdoing and impurity and to restore her reputation as a chaste and faithful wife. As "a covering of her eyes," it restores to Sarah a veil of modesty and a sign of wifely chastity; it also prevents others from looking at what had taken place, sparing her any humiliation or disgrace; in short, it vindicates her completely. Just as Shem and Japheth, covering Noah's nakedness, restored his social status as their father, so Abimelech, covering Sarah's eyes, restores Sarah's reputation and status as Abraham's *wife*—not just for his fellow Gerarites, but also for Abraham himself. Her eyes now metaphorically veiled to *all* that are with her, Abraham too must see her solely *as his wife* and recognize his own guilt in having "unwived" her. In the noblest touch of all, in speaking with Sarah, Abimelech—though he has restored her to Abraham as *"his wife"*—still plays along with the designation of Abraham as her *brother;* Abimelech spares Sarah the shame of knowing that he knows that her husband has unwived her.

Abimelech's deed in defense of marital fidelity finds its fitting response in a newly chastened Abraham. Astonished by Abimelech's delicate and noble response and by his obvious regard for Sarah *as Abraham's wife,* Abraham turns to prayer. Abraham prays to God—for the first and only time in Genesis! What he prayed for we do not know, but the act itself indicates Abraham's returning to God (for the first time since the destruction of Sodom and Gomorrah) and a tacit admission of having sinned. God responds by healing Abimelech, his wife, and his maidservants, who now all bear children, "for the *Lord had fast closed up all the wombs* of the house of Abimelech, because of *Sarah, wife of Abraham*" (20:18; emphasis added).[33]

This time around, thanks to the virtuous Abimelech, who bears moral witness against Abraham and who displays a clear appreciation of the honor due to Sarah as a wife, Abraham is forced to confront the sinfulness of his own conduct. Very likely he sees what the reader is told, in so many words: that God insists on the dignity and honor of the woman as wife; and that the blessings of fertility

---

33. God's "political strategy" in this episode deserves brief comment. He first tells Abimelech that Abraham is a prophet who will intervene for him and his people. But Abimelech serves as God's prophet to teach Abraham that adultery is a sin and that it stains an entire people. Abraham, seeing his own misdeed, prays (for his one and only time) in an act of contrition *(teshuvah).* When God then heals Abimelech's people, Abimelech must conclude that Abraham is indeed a prophet, and of a mighty God. This recognition makes possible the covenant that Abraham and Abimelech will enact in their next encounter (21:22–34). The story shows both how outsiders sometimes help the patriarchs to learn about their God and how, in turn, the patriarchs' relation to God can become a moral blessing to other peoples.

and progeny—the promised great nation of innumerable descendants—depend upon man's proper regard for the status of wife and the meaning of marriage, informed by the call to transmit a righteous and holy way.[34] Up until now, marriage (or rather women) had been regarded as important to the divine promise only instrumentally, as a source of sons. Now it becomes clear that marriage and the household must be informed by and devoted to the transmission of the covenant and the perpetuation of its ways.

SARAH AS WIFE

The time is now ripe for the long-promised birth of Abraham's true heir, to Sarah, which happens in the immediate sequel:

> The Lord *took note of* [*or* remembered *or* visited] *Sarah* as He had said, and the Lord *did for Sarah* as He had spoken. And *Sarah conceived and bore* to Abraham a son in his old age, at the set time of which God had spoken. And Abraham called the name of his son that was born unto him, *whom Sarah bore to him,* Isaac [*yitshaq:* he laughs *or* he will laugh]. And Abraham circumcised his son Isaac when he was eight days old, as God had commanded him. (21:1–4; emphasis added)

Twenty-five years after he received God's call, the first concrete evidence of the veracity of God's promise is finally provided: Abraham receives the right son and heir, whose rightfulness as heir consists entirely in the fact that he

---

34. Commenting on the phrase "for the Lord had shut fast every womb," Robert Alter insightfully observes:

> It is noteworthy that only in this version of the sister-wife story is the motif of infertility introduced. Its presence nicely aligns the Abimelech episode with what precedes and what follows. That is, first we have the implausible promise of a son to the aged Sarah; then a whole people is wiped out [LRK: Sodom and Gomorrah, most likely for sexual perversity]; then the desperate [LRK: incestuous] act of procreation by Lot's daughters in a world seemingly emptied of men; and now an entire kingdom blighted with an interruption of procreation. The very next words of the story—one must remember that there were no chapter breaks in the original Hebrew text, for both chapter and verse divisions were introduced only in the late Middle Ages—are the fulfillment of the promise of progeny to Sarah: "And the Lord singled out Sarah as He had said."

Alter sees much of the sequence that we treat as Abraham's education in sex and marriage, but he does not explicitly treat the episodes pedagogically. He therefore does not see how this final wife-sister episode with Abimelech finally prepares both Abraham and Sarah for the birth of the son of the covenant.

is born to Abraham's wife, as promised. God shows His fidelity to Abraham by showing His fidelity to Sarah: the Lord remembered Sarah; the Lord did for Sarah. From her first troubles in Egypt, the Lord has protected Sarah as Abraham's wife; now He makes clear the reason for His solicitude by making her a mother of the son of the covenant. By becoming the proper mother of his proper heir, Sarah at last becomes Abraham's wife, fully and unambiguously.

Sarah's barrenness and the couple's childlessness were, in fact, evidence that she was not yet, in the strict sense, Abraham's wife. Both her childless condition and his behavior toward her in Egypt and in Gerar attest to their "less than married" condition. Only when Abraham acknowledges that a wife is something absolutely other than a sister does Sarah become pregnant; and only then is she a wife in the full sense.

God has remembered Sarah, but Abraham remembers God and the covenant. He names his son *Yitshaq*, "He Laughs," "He Will Laugh"—a joyous yet permanently embarrassing reminder both of his and Sarah's earlier lack of trust and also of the fact that God has had the last laugh. And he circumcises Isaac as God had commanded him, committing his son to the binding covenant God had proposed with the people of the new way. Sarah, too, acknowledges her indebtedness to the divine: "Laughter [*tsehoq*] hath God made me; everyone that heareth will laugh [*yitshaq*] on account of [*or* with *or* at] me" (21:6).[35]

But Abraham's household is not yet well ordered, and Sarah still has important wifely work to do. A few years later, when Isaac was weaned, Abraham made a great feast for all to celebrate. But Sarah "saw the son of Hagar the Egyptian, whom she had borne unto Abraham, making sport [*or* mocking: *metsaheq*]" (21:9). Immediately perceiving a threat to her son,[36] she insists that Abraham take appropriate action:

35. Robert Alter comments: "The ambiguity of both the noun *tsehoq* ('laughter') and the accompanying preposition *li* ('to' or 'for' or 'with' or 'at me') is wonderfully suited to the complexity of the moment. It may be laughter, triumphant joy, that Sarah experiences and that is the name of the child Isaac ('he-who-laughs'). But in her very exultation, she could well feel the absurdity . . . of a nonagenarian becoming a mother. *Tsehoq* also means "mockery," and perhaps God is doing something to her as well as for her. . . . All who hear of it may laugh, rejoice, with Sarah but the hint that they might also laugh at her is evident in her language." The ambiguity of "laughing with" and "laughing at" precisely anticipates the sequel.

36. The precise nature of this threat is uncertain. The verb translated "making sport," *metsaheq*, from the same root as "laughing," elsewhere would be best translated as "ridiculing," "joking," or "playing": making fun of or mocking Isaac would, on this reading, be Ishmael's perceived offense. The word can also mean "engaging in sexual play"; accordingly, some interpreters, in order to ex-

"Cast out this bondwoman and her son; for the son of this bondwoman shall not be heir with my son, even with Isaac." (21:10)

When Sarah last had trouble with Hagar, Abraham had sided with her but had turned the problem over to her to solve on her own. This time she insists that he take the corrective action—partly because Abraham's other son is involved, partly to get him to choose between her son and the Egyptian's, between the son promised them by God and the son gotten by his (their) own resources. Even if she is acting simply out of jealous love for her own, Sarah intuits that the proper ordering of their household for the fulfillment of their parental task within the covenant requires the banishment of Hagar the Egyptian and her son, Ishmael.

Abraham, notwithstanding the miracle of Isaac's birth, is still attached to his firstborn, his as-it-were natural child. The deed Sarah proposes is grievously painful to Abraham "because of his son." Addressing him in his turmoil, God intervenes on Sarah's side, though with due regard also for Ishmael:

And God said unto Abraham: "Let it not be grievous in thy sight because of the lad, and because of thy bondwoman; *in all that Sarah saith unto thee, hearken unto her voice [shema beqolah]*, for in Isaac shall seed be called to thee. And also of the son of thy bondwoman will I make a nation because he is thy seed." (21:12–13; emphasis added)

God does not merely tell Abraham what action to take. Using a phrase with ominous echoes (see note 18 above), God tells Abraham to be obedient to his wife—"hearken to the voice of" is an idiom for "obey"—and what's more, in *everything* that she says to him. At least when it comes to her children's welfare, a wife has, and ought to have, authority with her husband. This Abraham learns from the highest authority of all.

Abraham, hearkening now to the joint voice of both God and Sarah, acquiesces and banishes Ishmael and Hagar. He gives up his harem; he accepts the "rule" of his wife; he establishes the right order of his household. In all these ways, he for the first time ratifies by his deeds the meaning of his marriage. Regarding his firstborn, Ishmael, he must trust that God will look after the lad; and

---

plain Sarah's strong reaction and harsh response, have suggested that Ishmael was engaging in homosexual play, perhaps even with Isaac. As a third interpretation, Robert Alter, noting that Isaac's name is inscribed in this crucial verb, suggests that Sarah sees that Ishmael is "Isaac-ing it," that is, playing the role of Isaac and presuming to be the legitimate heir. As is so often the case, the uncertainty of the precise meaning of this particular deed is a pedagogical blessing: it compels the reader to think about just what ought to outrage a mother on behalf of her child and how she should go about protecting him.

we later learn that Ishmael does indeed flourish. But he does so outside of the new way. Although he had been circumcised by his father within the covenant, Ishmael, hearkening to his own mother, becomes lost to God's new way. In the last we hear of Ishmael (until he and Isaac together come to bury Abraham) his mother takes for him a *wife out of the land of Egypt* (21:21). In this allegedly patriarchal text, the maternal influence is hardly slighted. Women matter. And good wives matter most.[37]

WIFE, OR SISTER? THE MEANING OF MARRIAGE

It is time to pull together some threads and to venture some generalizations about what Abraham—and what we—have learned on the subject of marriage. Three times we have Abraham and Sarah involved in adventures that confound the meaning of "wife"—twice with "sister," once with the Egyptian slavegirl or concubine. That Sarah is in fact Abraham's half sister as well as his wife is the clue to the deeper meaning of these adventures. So long as he is willing to treat her as a sister—which he does several times to avoid the consequences of her great beauty—Sarah remains barren. Only when he is prepared to look upon her simply as a wife does she in fact become one in the full and proper sense.

When Abraham and Sarah went to Egypt to escape the famine, Abraham asked Sarah to say that she was his sister so that "my soul may live because of you." If Sarah appears as his wife, Abraham's life will be in danger. The perceived threat is, in the first instance, quite literal: the Egyptians may indeed kill him in order to gain the beautiful Sarah. But the connection between denying marriage and avoiding death goes much deeper: admitting to having a wife is tantamount to accepting the fact of one's own mortality and one's dependence on woman's generative and nurturing powers. For as we learn along with (and perhaps even before) Abraham, woman *as wife* means not "one's own missing flesh," nor even a beloved because beautiful adornment to one's self-esteem, but one's chosen and committed equal partner in generation and transmission, providing for one's own replacement by making a home that will rear well the next generation. Abraham at the beginning acts as if the promise of becoming a great nation can be realized by himself acting alone; thus preoccupied with his own survival and indifferent to the matter of progeny, he doubly "sacrifices" his wife—first by

---

37. Judaism has always considered a child's mother to be the key determinant of the child's Jewish identity, and not simply because only the child's mother can be known with certainty. Judaism recognizes the crucial importance of the maternal influence in child rearing. Even in the Bible, whereas tribal affiliation and priestly status are determined patrilineally, membership in the nation of Israel is determined by the ethnoreligious identity of the mother. The right mother makes a world of difference.

denying her wifeliness and then by abandoning her to Pharaoh's harem—symbolically enacting his belief in his own self-sufficiency (or at least his own lack of need for woman).

Years later, now preoccupied with his wish for an heir, Abraham accepts his need for woman but not yet his need for a wife. He sheds his wife again (albeit on her suggestion), this time to use the Egyptian slavegirl as a surrogate womb. It is not enough to say that this was then a customary practice in the ancient Near East; such a practice has an inner meaning that God's new way rejects. For a woman is not merely a seedbed or even, to speak less luridly, just the creative "mother of all living" (as Adam had put it, thinking only of Eve's *natural* power of generation). For these purely natural deeds, any woman will do. But because *human* procreation means rearing as well as bearing, the naturally loose relations of male and female must be transformed and fixed by the legal or conventional *singular* relation of husband and wife—that is, by marriage.

This lesson Abraham does not begin to learn until Abimelech, acting under the enlightenment of a divinely sent dream, teaches him the sinfulness of adultery and the need to respect the honor and chastity of his wife. And the lesson is completed only with the wondrous, divinely promised birth of a son within the marriage and with Sarah's subsequent instruction of her husband, again divinely backed, regarding the long-term well-being of their son, on whom the cultural transmission of the covenant will depend. Lest anyone be in doubt about the importance of these matters for God's new way, the reader, like Sarah and Abraham, is shown that God Himself supports all three crucial elements of the marital bond: (1) respect for woman's chastity and marital sexual fidelity, which anticipates (2) the gift of children within the marriage, which makes necessary (3) the right ordering of the household, with the husband endorsing his wife's devotion to the well-being of their children.[38]

Woman as wife means primarily something very precise: a long-term partner for rearing the next generation, or in other words, for transmitting the way of life that is the spiritual lifeblood of the family and the nation. As the story makes plain, it will not do, from the point of view of rearing and transmission, to sow one's seed in culturally foreign soil, to have as the mother of one's children a woman who follows other gods or none at all. And one certainly cannot found or perpetuate God's new way by Egyptianizing one's descendants or, worse, by adopting Pharaoh's own tyrannical practices, including those with respect to women.

---

38. This conclusion, though accurate, will need to be reexamined in the light of the episode of the binding of Isaac (see Chapter Eleven).

In the Garden of Eden story, God had informed the woman that because she was to bear children, her desire would henceforth be to her husband (as father of her children) and he would rule over her. God was not—we argued in Chapter Three—prescribing but predicting; he was forecasting what would happen naturally between man and woman once the children began to appear. And be that as it may, God was surely not endorsing tyranny of husbands over wives. For the natural way of male dominance does not serve best to secure God's new way of justice and holiness. On the contrary, as we learn from God's interventions in the Abraham story, God intervenes to oppose the uninstructed tendency of men to lord it over their women. God attempts to teach Abraham that his rule in the household is, in fact, tantamount to hearkening to his wife, and to supporting her deep-rooted concern for the next generation.

But if the work of rearing the next generation is best conducted with a spouse who shares one's customs, ways, and gods, why exogamy rather than incest? Why would not sister and brother be the marital ideal?[39] For both share not only common origin and common blood, but also, more important, common rearing and common mores. We who have lived so long with the taboo against brother-sister incest—a taboo we owe, by the way, to biblical religion and the new way begun with Abraham—take for granted that wife and sister are mutually exclusive categories, so much so that we cannot remember the reasons why this should be so—except perhaps for latter-day scientific arguments about the genetic dangers of inbreeding. We also have forgotten—or are too well brought up to consider—that brother-sister unions may in fact be the more natural and uninstructed way of the human race, as it is among our primate cousins.

Rousseau, a man not shy about such matters, paints a vivid picture of human generation in the earliest times:

No, there were families, but there were no Nations; there were domestic languages, but there were no popular languages; there were marriages, but there was no love. Each family was self-sufficient and propagated itself from its own stock alone: children of the same parents grew up together and gradually found ways to make themselves intelligible to one another; the distinction between the sexes appeared with age, natural inclinations sufficed to unite them, instinct served in lieu of passion, habit in lieu of predilection, people became man and wife without having ceased to be brother and sister.

39. Brother-sister incestuous marriage was practiced by the Egyptian pharaohs. It was also the way of the Greek gods.

Rousseau's account is in fact quite compatible with the anthropology of the early chapters of Genesis, which preserves delicate silence about, say, the wife of Cain, and which finally reveals that Abraham took to wife his own half sister. Rousseau, in a note appended to the just-quoted passage, adds this powerful moral (albeit utterly secular) commentary:

> The first men had to marry their sisters. In view of the simplicity of the first morals, this practice continued without prejudice as long as families remained isolated and even after the most ancient peoples had come together; *but the law that abolished it is no less sacred for being by human institution.* Those who view it solely in terms of the bond it established between families fail to see its most important aspect. In view of the intimacy between the sexes that inevitably attends upon domestic life, the moment such a sacred law ceased to speak to the heart and to awe the senses, men would cease to be upright, and the most frightful morals would soon cause the destruction of mankind.

The biblical author, to say the least, shares Rousseau's view of the supreme importance of putting an end to incest. The promulgated law that explicitly forbids the practice, given later in Leviticus, is indeed held to be sacred, not only because it is God-given but because it is part of the so-called holiness code of the Children of Israel, who are enjoined to be holy as the Lord is holy. But the need for such a law is anticipated already in the stories of Abraham and Sarah, in which there is movement from the original *sister-become-wife* to *wife-who-is-also-sister* to simply *wife*. Abraham is led from the natural toward the marital and legal, from an outlook that says that "incest is best" or that "any woman will do" to an outlook that makes instituted exogamous marriage the sacred norm. Let me exaggerate to make the point: Abraham is so to speak "given" a wife who is also his sister in order to educate him—and the reader—in the crucial difference between wife and sister and to lead him—and us—to embrace with understanding the singular meaning of woman as wife.[40]

It remains only to attempt to specify just why this difference is so important. There are, of course, likely psychological and social difficulties with brother-

40. Careful readers, especially those who are supporters of Natural Law or who hold a more ancient and teleological understanding of nature, may well object to our suggestion that incest is *natural,* and that God's instruction consists in replacing the way of nature with the way of right (we argued similarly, in Chapter Six, regarding the institution of the Noahide code and covenant). We happily concede the point; indeed, we embrace it. One might say that a proper understanding of the inner procreative meaning of sexuality—and especially of *human* sexuality—points exactly to the institution of exogamous and monogamous marriage as the institution best suited to rearing decent

sister sexuality and marriage, especially if there are more than two children. Sex between siblings contaminates the sibling relation with the exclusive and dyadic attempt to fuse two lives in a merger that denies the meaning of siblinghood. To take a brother as a husband is as much an act of metaphorical fratricide as it is an act of metaphorical wife killing to pass a wife off as a sister. Moreover, motives for literal fratricide are also amply provided by brother-sister sex, owing to sexual jealousy.

Deeper than these adverse psychosocial consequences lies the matter of how one stands in the world, whether as a child or as an adult. First, in incestuous unions there is no need to learn the adult restraint of sexual impulse, for with an object of gratification near at hand, instinct spills over into satisfaction: "natural inclination suffice[s] to unite them." More important, in brother-sister marriage, both partners cling as children to the family of origin, in a relation that hearkens back to their common emergence out of the same womb ("flesh of my flesh"), under the protection of the same parents. There is no brave stepping forth unprotected into the full meaning of adulthood, to say permanent good-bye to father and mother and to cleave to your wife, to accept their death and, what is more difficult, to accept your own mortality, the answer to which is not narcissistic sexual gratification but a sober and deliberate saying "yes" to reproduction, transmission, and perpetuation. To consciously take a wife from outside the nest is deliberately to establish a family of perpetuation, in at least tacit recognition that human maturity entails both a willingness to die and a desire for renewal and continuity, through birth and cultural transmission—a matter of enormous importance when there is a special way of life to be perpetuated.

Finally, in an incestuous union between brother and sister there is no experience of the other as truly other. There is no distance, no sexual strangeness, no need to overcome fumbling, embarrassment, shame: the inward-looking love of one's own flesh is naked but it is not ashamed. For this reason, the other is taken for granted and approached in tacit expectation of full compliance with one's desires; the other is not easily an object of respect. Because of familiarity there is likely to be contempt. There is little possibility of awe (what the Greeks called *aidos*) before the sexual other: awe before the uncanniness of sexual difference, of the radical independence and otherness of the other; awe before the uncanniness of sexual complementarity, of the remarkable possibility of mediating the

---

and upright human children, that is, children who are truly human (or as our text might put it, worthily in God's image). Yet natural sexual impulses will not by themselves establish the proper institutional forms. Moreover, from the point of view of the Bible, many peoples in establishing their sexual mores get them wrong; setting Israel (and humankind) straight on sexual and marital matters will be a crucial part of God's later legislative efforts. For the clearest example, see the law of forbidden (that is, incestuous) unions in Leviticus 18.

sexual difference; awe before the mysterious generative power of sexuality, of the wondrous capacity to transcend sexual difference altogether in the creation of a child, who is the parents' own commingled being externalized in a separate and persisting existence. And because there is no awe before the sexual other, there is less likelihood of awe before the divine Other in whose image created He them, male and female.

It is one of the remarkable features of human existence how things wondrous and awesome become familiar and banal, how we live in the world complacently and self-satisfiedly blind to its marvels. Such sightless trust is in some respects helpful, in some respects harmful, but it is nonetheless eerie how much of our lives is lived within this unknowing familiarity. To a child, his family (if it is a healthy family) is a given, a unity, something that appears to him to be as natural as the rising sun. He does not see, unless and until he goes *out* to make his own family, how what appears to be a natural "one" is in fact a two-made-to-become-one. He does not discover, save through the practice of *exo*gamy, how the nursery of his own humanity was the product of deliberate human choice, not of blind nature, and the choice of one man and one woman to become husband and wife for precisely this purpose. Finally, only through exogamy is he likely to appreciate the deepest mysteries of being: the possibility of sameness through otherness, of life through death, of the eternal through the everyday. Man's openness and willing submission to his counterpart properly understood as wife partakes of his openness and willing subordination to the One who is truly other and who inspires us—and commands us—to live knowingly, decently, and gratefully in this astonishing world.

CHAPTER ELEVEN

EDUCATING FATHER ABRAHAM:
THE MEANING OF PATRIARCHY

*E*ducating the patriarch Abraham, father of the nation of Israel and, ultimately, father of three great monotheistic religions, entails many things, but none more important than teaching him to be a proper husband and father. The perpetuation of God's new way will depend not on a fortuitous succession of naturally virtuous men and women but on the proper rearing of the young in every generation to the task of transmitting their moral and spiritual heritage. In the last chapter, we saw how this task of transmission is at the heart of the meaning of marriage. In marriage rightly understood, man will cleave to his wife not because she is "flesh of his flesh," nor because she is beautiful or because she loves him back, but because she is his coequal partner in the work of perpetuation. In this chapter, we shall look more closely at the work itself. We shall look at Abraham's education in fatherhood.

A comparable discussion could, of course, be presented about Sarah's education in motherhood. Central to this tale would be the wondrous birth of Isaac, after a lifetime (ninety years) of infertility, which leaves no doubt that children are a gift, not a maternal product and possession.[1] Equally central would be those episodes—such as the covenant of circumcision and the binding of Isaac, both treated in this chapter with regard to Abraham—that make clear that children are in fact *given* only in order to be *returned*, that is, dedicated to what is right and holy. But an account of Sarah's education must remain for another day. Our concern here is Abraham, who, like most men, needs much more instruction in these matters than does his wife.

Abraham's education is hardly confined to the marital or familial sphere: the patriarch rules a larger domain. As his household grows, he inevitably becomes increasingly involved in external affairs. Through these encounters he comes to know the ways of other nations—including, especially, the unjust ways of

---

1. As we suggested when discussing Eve's proud boasting at the birth of Cain, this latter opinion is the perfectly natural belief of womankind. Woman, seen as the "mother of all living," has obvious cause to feel pride in her generative prowess, even to the point of being god-forgetting.

cities—and he comes to understand what just political rule requires. In the end, his political education, like his paternal education, is completed with the realization that proper founding and proper rule, like proper fatherhood, must be reverently oriented toward the divine. Patriarchy rightly understood readily acknowledges the "fatherhood" of God.

FATHERS AND SONS: THE UNINSTRUCTED WAY

In the absence of suitable instruction, fathers (and sons, the prospective fathers) do not naturally understand these matters, as we learned in the prototypical story of Noah and his sons (Chapter Seven). Noah, we recall, "unfathered" himself through drink and lay dehumanized in his tent, stripped of all authority and respectability. His disrespectful son, Ham, viewing Noah in disgrace and trafficking in his shame, metaphorically killed his father *as a father*, reducing him to mere male-source-of-seed. Destroyed was the father as authority, as guide, as teacher of law, custom, and a way of life. The danger of such a reversion to the merely natural, shameless, and amoral view of human affairs lurks in every household, both from disreputable fathers and from impious sons.

In such cases, the iniquities of the fathers are often visited upon the sons and, eventually, upon their national descendants. Noah, awakening to discover what Ham had done, cursed Canaan, the son of Ham, measure for measure driving a wedge between Ham and his own son. Ham became the father of peoples—including the Canaanites and the Egyptians—whose abominable sexual practices (and hence whose family life) become the antipodes to the Israelite laws of purity. In contrast, Shem, the son who piously covered his father's nakedness without even looking upon it, became the father of the line that leads to Abraham. Shem, we know not how, appears to have divined the sacred meaning of the authoritative relation of father and son. But as we saw from Noah's Dionysiac weakness and Ham's antinomian rebellion, one cannot rely on nature alone to ensure decency and reverence or to guarantee the transmission of righteous ways. Fathers and sons will both need instruction in how to promote patriarchal devotion and filial piety and how to secure the work of cultural perpetuation. Fathers and sons who, in reading the text, are willing to walk with Abraham through his adventures may benefit from vicariously participating in his instruction.

ABRAHAM'S PATERNAL BEGINNINGS: HIS FATHER AND HIS NEPHEW

As was noted in Chapter Nine, Abraham had an unusual father, and not merely because he came to fatherhood very late. More important, Terah was a radical, a man who left behind the land and presumably also the ways of his fathers in search of something new. A severed link in his own cultural chain, Terah set the example for Abraham's own radicalism. Cultural discontinuity was part of the cultural teaching on which Abraham was raised. Terah also lives long enough to feel the isolation that often comes with having abandoned the ancestral ways: one of his three sons (Haran) dies in his young manhood, a second (Nahor) refuses to follow his father on his journey toward Canaan, and the third, Abram, leaves him behind in Haran, where he lives alone for sixty more years and dies, perhaps without heirs to bury him.[2] Though Abram stems from Noah's pious son Shem, and though he himself was more attached to his father than was his brother Nahor, Abram's immediate paternal ancestry is not a model for the work of cultural perpetuation. Yet for that very reason, it leaves him open to receiving or founding a new cultural way not tied to the ways of an ancestral past.

Abram's condition as a homeless, rootless, godless, childless son of a radical makes him a natural candidate to respond to God's promise of land, seed, rule, and fame. But for the same reasons, he is not, to begin with, well educated in the successful art of fatherhood, in the work of transmission. Such lessons—and they will prove complicated—he must gradually learn through his adventures.

When God calls Abram out of his father's house, Abram is clearly enticed by the promise of greatness and prosperity. The content of the promise is plainly political, and its scope is global: Abram will become the blessed founder of a great nation and will acquire a great name, and all the families of the earth will be blessed because of him. Not bad work if you can get it, and Abram, age seventy-five, sets off immediately, "as the Lord had spoken unto him." But not unaccompanied: "and Lot went with him" (12:4). The promise of founding a great nation might have seemed odd to a childless man, and so Abram maximized his prospects by taking not only his barren wife, Sarai, but also his nephew, Lot, the son of his deceased brother, Haran, whom Abram had in effect adopted. When Abram arrives in Canaan, to find it occupied, God appears and informs him,

2. This is the impression given by the text, though it may not be true. There is no clear evidence either way. However, Abraham will later learn, soon after the binding of Isaac but just before the death of Sarah, of the descendants of Milcah and Nahor, his brother (22:20–24), who, it turns out, *are now living in Haran* (Paddan-aram) (24:10; 25:20; 28:2, 5, 10; 29:4 ff.). Perhaps Nahor (or his son Bethuel) moved there when they learned that Terah died. The timing is about right. Terah is 70 years old when Abraham is born, 145 when Abraham leaves (at age 75), and 170 when Isaac is born (Abraham is then 100 and Sarah is 90). Sarah dies at age 127, when Isaac is 37 and Abraham is 137. But when Sarah dies, Terah has been dead for two years (he lives to 205). The news Abraham receives of Nahor's family might have contained news of Terah's death.

"Unto thy seed will I give this land." God hints that Abram will yet have seed, but the focus is on the land, this promised land. Abram is not yet thinking in a fatherly way—and for obvious reasons.

Circumstances change. After the episode in Egypt, recounted in the last chapter, Abram and Lot come to a parting of the ways, an unexpected yet not surprising consequence of their newly gained wealth: "for their substance was great so that they could not dwell together. And there was strife between the herdsmen of Abram's cattle and the herdsmen of Lot's cattle" (13:6–7). Wishing to avoid trouble more than he wishes to preserve his family intact—"Let there be no strife, I pray thee, between me and thee, and between my herdsmen and thy herdsmen, for we are brethren" (13:8)—Abram takes preventative action before the conflict reaches its potentially life-threatening—and indeed, fratricidal—possibility. He magnanimously offers Lot the first and finest choice of the available land. Attracted by civilization, Lot, understandably but unwisely, chooses the fertile plain of the Jordan, which seemed to him "like the garden of the Lord, like the land of Egypt," and ends up—later—near Sodom.[3] The two men "separated themselves the one from the other" (13:11). Abram is left without even an adopted son.

This fateful separation, and the polar opposition between the wandering herdsman and the city dweller, will be the basis for Abraham's later crucial lesson in political justice. Anticipating that lesson, the narrator here gives us an early warning: "Now the men of Sodom were wicked (ra'iym) and sinners (chata'iym) against the Lord exceedingly" (13:13). But of Sodom and cities, more soon.

3. "And Lot lifted up his eyes, and beheld the plain of the Jordan, that it was well watered everywhere, before the Lord destroyed Sodom and Gomorrah, like the garden of the Lord, like the land of Egypt. . . . So Lot chose him all the plain of the Jordan, and Lot journeyed east . . . and Lot dwelt near the cities of the plain and moved his tent as far as Sodom" (13:10–12). The rich Jordan valley, with its cities, reminds Lot not only of fertile Egypt but also (wondrously!) of the Garden of Eden. Moving toward the rising sun, Lot—like most men—evinces a desire to return to Edenic conditions, albeit by means of civilization. If this choice tells us something about Lot, it tells us nothing about Abram, the person of greater interest. The text offers no clue as to whether Abram would have chosen as Lot did, had he taken first choice himself. If Abram, unlike Lot, had been chastened by his time in Egypt, he might not have chosen as Lot did; choosing first, Abram might have taken the same, less attractive land (and the wandering existence that goes with it) that remained to him after Lot chose first. If so, Abram's apparent magnanimity is less impressive. Continuing this train of thought, one might even consider that Abram gives Lot first choice, knowing in advance what Lot would probably choose, so that Lot cannot later blame anyone but himself for the fate that later befalls him in Sodom. By allowing him first choice, Abram enables Lot to reveal his soul. At the same time, however, Abram, by this means, allows his nephew to go to the dogs. Abram has here averted a potentially fratricidal conflict, but it is far from clear that he has acted as his brother's keeper—a point perhaps pertinent to Abraham's later arguments with God about Sodom (see below).

Lot having departed, Abram, in the immediate sequel, no doubt feels a sense of loss and is in need of consolation. The Lord is precisely responsive:

And the Lord said unto Abram *after that Lot was separated* from him: "Lift up now thine eyes, and look from the place where thou art, northward and southward and eastward and westward, for all the land which thou seest, *to thee* I will give it, and *to thy seed* forever. *And I will make thy seed as the dust of the earth: so that if a man can number the dust of the earth, then shall thy seed also be numbered.* Arise, walk through the land in the length and breadth of it; for unto thee I will give it." (13:14–17; emphasis added)

Compensating Abram for the recent loss of the more favorable land, God stresses in beginning and ending how the lost land and more will eventually be Abram's.[4] But in the center, addressing Abram's loss of his probable heir, God speaks explicitly and graphically about Abram's own unborn progeny, augmenting His earlier promise of nationhood with an image of innumerable progeny (and also inverting the symbol of man's mortality; compare 3:19). God tries to put Abram in mind of his prospective paternity. But Abram remains attuned to matters political, and he still hasn't reconciled himself to the loss of Lot. Nonetheless, he removes his tent and comes to dwell at Hebron, near the terebinth tree at Mamre, and builds there an altar unto the Lord.[5]

ABRAHAM'S POLITICAL BEGINNINGS: MILITARY VICTORY AND THE SPOILS OF WAR

Issues of politics and progeny, promised land and posterity, come together in Abram's next (fourth) adventure, the so-called war of the kings (Genesis 14).[6] In this episode Abram, not meek but warlike, has his heroic moment, succeeding against famous kings. But it is family concern, not heroic ambition, that drags Abram into battle; and it is battle that, in turn, increases his concern for family. His nephew, Lot, is (indirectly) the cause of Abram's going to war; his experience

4. God uses what is apparently ancient Near Eastern legal language for land conveyance. And He has Abram perform symbolic acts (namely, walking through the full length and breadth of the land) that give legal validation of title.

5. As Robert Sacks observes, Abram now sees the whole of the Promised Land from the same vantage point as the spies that will, much later, be sent out by Moses (Numbers 13:22). Abram continues to live through in advance the future life of his descendants. We should thus expect next a war with the local inhabitants.

6. For my understanding of the political implications of this story and its place in the Abrahamic narrative I am much indebted to an astute term paper by Bret Stephens, then a second-year undergraduate at the University of Chicago, now the editor of *The Jerusalem Post*.

of war will, in the sequel, lead Abram for the first time to care powerfully about paternity.

Four kings of Babylon invade Canaan to suppress a rebellion against their rule. After laying waste many nations along their route, they are finally met by a Canaanite war party, led by the kings of five Canaanite cities, including Sodom and Gomorrah. Abram takes no part in the battle; indeed, in the first half of the chapter, which is replete with the names of kings and places, his name does not even appear. The silence invites us to wonder how Abram stands with respect to the war.

Just before the war started, Abram had received from God the great promise of all the land now in dispute and had been told to walk around it, in a prefiguration of forthcoming ownership. Does Abram now see the war as an opportunity to acquire the land by conquest? Will entering the war on one side or the other help to realize the promise? Prudence would seem to counsel against joining either side. Self-interest might lead him to wish for the defeat of the Canaanites, but the heaven-worshiping and conquering Babylonians, from whose land he was called away, are both religiously and politically dangerous, unlikely partners for a man with his divine mission. By the same token, so too are the city-dwelling Canaanites, already notorious for their wicked and sinful ways (see 13:13). Thus Abram, having moved his tent to Hebron and away from the sites of conflict, wisely decides to sit out the war. But Abram is no pacifist. At the same time he prepares himself for possible trouble by entering into alliances with three Amorite chieftains, Mamre, Eshcol, and Aner, and also by training his own men for battle.

In the war, the Canaanite kings are routed, Sodom and the other cities are sacked, and Lot—who, since we last saw him, had moved *into* Sodom—is taken captive by the Babylonians: "they took Lot, *Abram's brother's son,* who dwelt in Sodom, and his goods, and departed" (14:12; emphasis added). A refugee (perhaps sent by Bela, the defeated Sodomite king) comes to "Abram the Hebrew"—an identification that tacitly recognizes him as a national or political entity—and informs him that "*his brother* [*that is,* his kinsman] was taken captive" (14:14; emphasis added). Without saying a word, Abram immediately and unhesitatingly enters the fighting, in order to rescue Lot—this, despite the fact that Abram's strategic interests would best be served by doing nothing and allowing the Canaanite nations to remain defeated. Abram, who had been fearful of death in Egypt and who avoided possible conflict with Lot in the name of brotherliness, now bravely goes to war in loyal defense of his own, risking his life and, with it, the divine promise: unlike Cain, Abram is very much his brother's keeper. He leads forth his band of 318 trained men into battle and, by clever strategy, wins a mighty victory against superior numbers; he smites the enemy, pursuing them past Damascus, and brings back all the goods, all the people, and his kinsman Lot (who promptly returns to Sodom). Abram returns to Canaan, the Promised Land, as a conquering hero.

Upon learning of Abram's military success, we readers naturally wonder about its aftereffects, political and psychic. Will Abram gain territory? Will his victory make him proud and demanding? As the king of Sodom comes forth to greet the returning hero, a strange event occurs, bearing on these questions:

> And Melchizedek [righteous king] king of Salem [probably Jerusalem] brought forth bread and wine, for he was priest to God-Most-High [*El Elyon*]. And he blessed him, and he said: "Blessed be Abram to God-Most-High, maker [*or* possessor] of heaven and earth, and blessed be God-Most-High, who hath delivered thine enemies into thine hand." And he [Abram] gave him a tenth [that is, a tithe] of all. (14:18–20)

Melchizedek, a Canaanite king and priest of a different god,[7] blesses Abram and attributes his victory to divine intervention. Abram, who had entered the war without divine instruction and without prayer or sacrifice, and who has given no sign that he knows that God was behind his victory, is moved by this outside witness to remember the Lord and His original promise. Have I not, through this victory, become a great (in the sense of mighty) nation? Does not Melchizedek invoke my name as a blessing, just as the Lord had promised? Abram rewards Melchizedek with a priestly tithe, fulfilling the Lord's promise that those who bless him shall prosper.

Thanks to this possibly providential appearance of Melchizedek, God is on Abram's mind when the king of Sodom offers him the spoils of war. Unlike in Egypt, where he grew rich at Pharaoh's hand, Abram refuses. In rejecting King Bela's offer, Abram swears an oath—the Bible's first—by "the Lord, God-Most-High, maker of heaven and earth":

> "I have lifted my hand in oath unto the Lord [*YHWH*], God-Most-High, maker of heaven and earth, that I will not take a thread nor a shoe latchet nor aught that is thine, lest thou shouldest say, 'I have made Abram rich';

7. In Hebrew, *El Elyon* means God-the-Most-High. But El is the name of the Canaanite sky god, and Elyon is perhaps the name of another local deity or, perhaps, an attribute like "lofty," one that befits the sky god. Perhaps the text means to suggest that Melchizedek worships the highest or loftiest of the gods and in that respect is on his way toward monotheism. But there is no suggestion that Melchizedek knows the Lord who called Abram. However, when Melchizedek invokes *El Elyon*, Abram thinks of the God-Most-High that he knows. Melchizedek, without meaning to, reminds Abram of the Lord.

save only that which the lads have eaten and the portion of the men that went with me, Aner, Eshcol, and Mamre, let them take their portion." (14:22–24)

Justly not wanting ill-gotten gain (the property of wicked cities) and prudently not wanting to provoke later angry resentments or to compromise his sovereignty through indebtedness, Abram—with a hyperbolic flourish: "not a thread or shoe latchet"[8]—declines the king of Sodom's offer for himself, though he allows his youthful warriors and his Amorite confederates their fair share. Abram is magnificent and magnanimous in victory.

Though he is not interested in extending his power or ruling his neighbors or occupying their lands, Abram acquires and exercises the political-military power that great nationhood entails. Unlike the fratricidal city father Cain and unlike the imperial city builder Nimrod, Abram does not gain political success at the expense of moral good. He vanquishes his foes, rescues his kin, negotiates his own national independence, spurns the seductive gifts of his Canaanite beneficiaries, and establishes diplomatic relations with his neighbors, acting shrewdly and bravely but also justly. He is even moved through all this—thanks perhaps to Melchizedek—to remember the Lord and His promises.

ABRAHAM'S RELIGIOUS BEGINNINGS: FINITUDE AND AWE

But all is not well. Abram attempts to return to his previous life but cannot do so. He is now mixed up in international politics, complete with alliances and enemies, but he has no land of his own to rule. And although he has, in a way, acquired a great name and become a blessing, he feels rather his own weakness and vulnerability. His brush with death in battle, his fear of reprisals, and perhaps, too, the irrevocability of Lot's separation weigh on his mind.

God is, as usual, exactly responsive. He speaks to Abram in a vision: "Fear not, Abram, I am thy shield, thy reward shall be exceeding great" (15:1).[9] But God

8. Robert Sacks, commenting on this chapter in Genesis, refers to a later biblical episode in which Israelite victors in war are forbidden (by Joshua) to take any spoils and offers the following profound suggestion: "All of the things a man owns and uses every day, and that usually vary in size and shape from city to city and from people to people, carry with them ghosts of the goals, customs, and ways of life that their maker put into them. It is hard to cook in the pot of another man without, in part, eating his food. Joshua's strict instructions to the men not to enrich themselves by the spoils of the city were based on his keen awareness of the relation of men to the things they make."

9. Adam Davis has suggested to me that, far from reassuring Abram regarding his new fears, God is in fact here telling Abram to be afraid—of God! According to Davis's reading, Abram's victory in the war and his subsequent almost grandiose display of indifference to the spoils are signs not of Abram's justice but of his growing pride (and also his already sufficient wealth). The covenant God

partly misses the mark, for Abram now for the first time is weighed down with a concern for his childlessness, a concern that his encounter with death has now made acute. Abram, who had met all of God's previous interventions with silence, now boldly addresses the Almighty *for the first time,* and with pathos and passion:

> "O my master Lord [*'adonai YHWH*], what wilt Thou give me, seeing I shall die childless, and the one in charge of my house is Eliezer of Damascus? . . . Behold, to me Thou hast given no seed, and, lo, my steward will be my heir." (15:2–3)

No other gift, says Abram, invoking the Lord by His special name, could compensate for not having a son who can inherit his household.

God, in reply, now seeks to give reassurance on the subject of inheritors:

> "This man shall not be thine heir; but he that shall spring forth from thine own loins shall be thine heir." And He brought him forth abroad, and said: "Look now towards heaven, and count the stars, if thou be able to count them"; and He said unto him: "So shall thy seed be." (15:4–5)

With a more specific promise about his own progeny, and with a loftier image (celestial stars, rather than dust of the earth) to convey their innumerability, God for the time being calms Abram's fears and increases his trust: "And he [Abram] trusted in the Lord, and he [*or* He] counted it to Him [*or* to him] as righteousness [*tsedaqah*]" (15:6).[10]

---

soon enacts between the sacrificial pieces, described later in Genesis 15, is a surefire remedy for pride, and the experience does indeed fill Abram with awe and dread. But from the nature and manner of his complaint in his next speech (about his childlessness), Abram seems to me at this point to be more frustrated and fearful than proud.

10. This is the first mention in the text of the central biblical idea of righteousness, *tsedaqah,* and we are eager to grasp its primary significance. The lexicon tells us that its adjectival root, *tsedek* (derived from an Aramaic source meaning "straight," "even," "speaking the truth"), refers to someone who is truthful, righteous, just, and clear—in government, in personal dealings, in all speech and deed. But we are hampered in our efforts to understand the term in its present context. Unfortunately, there is an unresolvable yet highly important ambiguity in the second clause of this verse: we cannot know who is its subject and who is credited with righteousness. If God ("He") is the subject, then the sentence means something like this: God regards Abram's trust in Him as a sign of Abram's righteousness, and hence of his worthiness of the promised reward. (In other words, faith in God becomes, by itself, the essence of righteousness. This is the interpretation of Saint Paul; see Romans 4.) However, if Abram ("he") is the subject (as he is of the first clause), then the sentence means something like this: Abram regards God's promise as a sign of His righteousness—that is, God keeps to

Continuing the conversation, God turns to the other vexed subject, the question of the land:

> And He said unto him, "I am the Lord [*YHWH*] that brought thee out of Ur of the Chaldees, to give thee this land to inherit." (15:7)

Identifying Himself by (His tetragrammaton) name to Abram for the first time, the Lord states His intentions toward him and renews the promise of the land.[11] But Abram's doubts and fears have not been fully assuaged; after all, the threat of Babylon is still present, and thanks to his own military efforts, the Canaanites are reestablished in the land. Accordingly, Abram, in response, impatiently demands proof that he will indeed inherit the land as promised: "O my master Lord ['*adonai YHWH*], how shall I *know* that *I* shall inherit it?" (15:8; emphasis added). Regarding offspring and paternity, Abram's doubts were quieted with a prophecy of a son of his own, supported by a beautiful image of the brilliant and countless stars. But regarding the political question of land and (especially) of *his* inheriting it, Abram's doubts insist on further evidence. Abram wants to *know* for sure.

In response to Abram's demand for proof God counters with awesome display. He immediately directs Abram to gather five animals—a heifer, a she-goat, a ram, a turtledove, and a pigeon—for what will become known as the covenant between the sacrificial pieces: "You demand a sign, Abram? I will give you one to remember!"[12] God's pact or covenant will stand as guarantor for the promise of land, but the conditions of the covenant will overawe Abram and squelch his in-

---

His word and God will do what He says for those who stand by Him. On this reading, which I tend to prefer—both because biblical Hebrew does not generally change its subjects in midsentence and because it seems to me to make better sense in context—Abram's continuing trust in God is based on his belief that God is just (that is, honest and truthful) and will keep His promise. This reading makes much clearer what is at stake for Abraham in the famous conversation about justice and the fate of Sodom (see below).

11. Indeed, the Lord indicates that it was *for the purpose* of giving him *this* land (Canaan) that He brought Abram out of Mesopotamia. Later, prior to the discussion between the Lord and Abraham about Sodom, the Lord will give an additional reason for his interest in Abraham: that he and his seed keep the way of the Lord, doing righteousness and justice (18:19). It is worth considering how receiving a providential gift of land might contribute to the mission of pursuing righteousness. (See also p. 271 n. 7.)

12. On the basis of later biblical instruction about the use of the same animals in sacrifices, offered by the different classes of the Israelite community, Robert Sacks suggests that the animals used in this covenant stand for the ruler (she-goat), the priests (heifer or ram), the average Israelite (heifer or ram), and the poor (birds). The use of these animals, Sacks argues, anticipates the sacrifices of lives from all ranks of the children of Abraham that will have to be made in order to gain the land.

sistence on concrete and rational evidence. Abram divides the animals (not the birds) for the anticipated covenant, employing an ancient Near Eastern custom in which each party to an agreement thereby symbolically invokes the fate of the cloven animals upon himself should he violate his agreement. At nightfall, as a deep sleep and a great dark dread descend upon Abram, God announces and enacts the awe-inspiring covenant between the sacrificial pieces:

> "Know knowing [= know for sure] that thy seed shall be a stranger in a land that is not theirs, and shall serve them; and they shall afflict them for four hundred years. And also that nation, whom they shall serve, I will judge; and afterward they shall come out with great substance. *But as for thee, thou shalt go to thy fathers in peace; thou shalt be buried in a good old age.* And in the fourth generation they shall come back hither; for the iniquity of the Amorite is not yet full." And it came to pass that when the sun went down, and there was thick darkness, behold, a smoking furnace and a flame that passed between these pieces. On that day the Lord cut a covenant with Abram, saying, "Unto thy seed I *have given* this land, from the river of Egypt to the great river, the river Euphrates; the Kenite and the Kenizzite and the Kadmonite; and the Hittite and the Perizzite and the Rephaim; and the Amorite and the Canaanite and the Girgashite and the Jebusite." (15:13–21; emphasis added)

God's message is mixed. The good news is that He now specifies both the time for delivery of the land as well as its boundaries. Abram also learns that God's gift of the land is tied to justice: the inhabitants can't be expelled until they deserve it. But on balance, God's news for Abram himself is hardly cheering. Seeking evidence that he will inherit, he learns instead that he won't: not he but only his seed will inherit the land, and then only after they have suffered four hundred years of slavery as strangers in a strange land. Regarding his own personal fate, he learns only of his death and his burial—albeit in peace and in "a good old age." When God, in concluding, says that he *has already given* the land to Abram's *nonexistent* seed (!), the patriarch can scarcely be simply reassured.

By forcing Abram to live through in advance the [unjust] enslavement of his people, God compels him to think in terms of the distant future and the fate of his remote descendants. In response to Abram's preoccupation with present personal rewards, God's speech directs him to care ardently for those nearby, but always in the light and for the sake of the future. The heroic expectation of future fame and glory, the typical aspiration of conquering heroes, is sharply undermined. Abraham's "great name" will be won, if at all, in a different and God-fearing way. Indeed, Abram's fame and the rest of God's promise will be not so much won as bestowed, a gift of God's providence, to which the Lord here pledges Himself unconditionally.

Hearing God's eerie speech as he slept deeply in the gloomy darkness, amidst cleaved animals between whose parts travel a mysterious smoking furnace and flaming torch, Abram keeps awestruck silence. Abram experiences here, for the first time, the fear of the Lord.[13]

FATHERHOOD FOR PATRIARCHS:
THE COVENANT OF CIRCUMCISION

Forced by God directly to contemplate his own death and to take the long view of his fame and fortune, Abram now more than ever longs for a son. It is in this frame of mind, and remembering God's promise that his heir will spring from his own loins, that—in the immediate sequel—he receives and eagerly accepts Sarai's offer to try to have a child of his own by Hagar the Egyptian. As we saw in our examination of this episode in the last chapter, God neither interferes with nor approves the surrogate arrangement, and Abram gets the son he wants in Ishmael. At age eighty-six, fatherhood at last.

But fatherhood is more than siring, just as God's new way is more than the way of nature. Now that Abram has a son, the crucial task of perpetuation begins in earnest, and Abram must be shown what is required. The natural son must become, through his parents' deeds, a child also of God. Proper paternity requires, first of all, a proper orientation toward the divine—the theme of Abram's central adventure and trial (Genesis 17).[14] As Ishmael approaches young manhood (age thirteen), God, looking to the future, appears to Abram. He comes to propose a new covenant and to give Abram a new charge:

13. Actually, the text tells us nothing of Abram's reaction, in contrast to the report that he trusted in the Lord when he was brought forth to contemplate the countless stars in the heavens (15:5–6). That experience induced trusting wonder, perfectly compatible with a bespeakable reaction; this experience, we surmise, induced fearful awe and reverence, perfectly expressed by speechlessness (both Abram's and the text's). Though the crucial phrase "fear of the Lord [*yirath YHWH*]" does not occur here, it seems reasonable to suggest that Abram felt it.

14. Genesis 16 ends with the birth of Ishmael: "And Abram was four score and six years old when Hagar bore Ishmael to Abram" (16:16). Skipping the events of the next thirteen years—what happened during those years is irrelevant to the narrative intention—the text leaps forward to "when Abram was ninety years old and nine" (17:1). The juxtaposition of the tales of Ishmael's birth (via Hagar) and the new covenant of circumcision, using this abrupt literary compression of time, signals the importance of transforming paternity from a strictly natural relationship into a "supernatural" one. It anticipates the provision in the new covenant, shortly to be announced, that circumcision must follow almost immediately after birth (at eight days).

"I am God Almighty [*El Shaddai*]; walk before Me [*hithhalekh lefanay*] and be thou wholehearted [*or* perfect *or* blameless: *tamim*]. And I will make My covenant between thee and Me, and will multiply thee exceedingly." (17:1–2)

The new covenant, shortly to be announced, is introduced with explicit reference to the theme of procreation and perpetuation. But the covenant and the promised "multiplication" are preceded by a charge, given in this preamble, concerning Abram's stance and orientation toward the Lord: "Walk *before Me* and be thou *tamim*." Letting Abram know immediately before whom he must walk and with whom he will covenant, God speaks intimately to him, as it were, person-to-person: God right away identifies Himself *(El Shaddai)*, and in the sequel will give Abram a new name. (When God first called Abram [12:1], no names were mentioned.)

Why a new covenant and a new charge, and why now? Is there perhaps an implicit rebuke in the need for these new arrangements? Did Abram err in fathering a child by an Egyptian woman? In taking the matter of progeny into his own hands, has Abram been less than wholeheartedly walking in God's ways? Or rather, has Abram merely reached the proper moment in his education—as a father whose son is entering adult manhood, soon to take his place—to teach him his mission so that it can be well transmitted? The text gives us no explanation as to why God chooses this time to approach Abram. But on the assumption that God's "moves" are often responsive to human ones—recall how the covenant with Noah was God's answer to Noah's problematic sacrifice—we might well imagine that He is led to intervene now because of Abram's (unstated) reaction to his son's impending manhood. Abram might have been thinking of initiating Ishmael into manly adulthood, perhaps through some current Mesopotamian or Canaanite rite of passage. God's covenant addresses this impulse, but as we shall see, it does so to specify its form and to transform its meaning.[15]

But whatever the reason, Abram's circumstances demand a new delineation of his relationship with both God and his descendants. Previous speeches of God to Abram only made promises or commanded going from here to there ("where I will show thee"); they said nothing about how he was to live. Here, for the first time, God calls Abram to undertake a specific way of being and doing in the world. The contrast is, in fact, clearly indicated by a difference in the commands. When God first called Abram (12:1) and commanded him, "Go," the word "go" *(holekh)* meant taking a bodily journey from one place to another.

15. I owe the suggestions of the last three sentences to Will Wilson, an undergraduate student in my most recent seminar on Genesis.

Here, "walk" (same verb, *holekh*, only in its reflexive and iterative form: "be-walking-around-for-yourself") means adopting a certain path or way of going and doing, living and being.

That desired way of living is to be "before Me," literally, "to My face." The image is at once perplexing and wonderfully suggestive: In My presence. In My sight (not hiding out, fully under My observation). Under My shadow. Under My protection (I am backing you; I am watching your back). As My messenger and prophet (like a servant processing before the king). Know where I am. Align your ways always with Me. In sum: go as my champion and emissary before My observing, protecting, guiding, and judging presence.[16]

Abram is also charged to "be *tamim*"—to be undivided, simple, complete, perfect, wholehearted, blameless.[17] God's charge does not make clear the connection between "walking before Me" and "being wholehearted." They might be independent tasks, or either one could be a prerequisite for the other. Thus, a man can walk in the desired divinely oriented direction only if he aspires and chooses to do so, wholeheartedly. Conversely, a man can become whole or perfect or undivided only if he chooses to walk before God. Either way, Abram is charged with becoming, in his heart and soul, wholly oriented with the Lord and wholly committed to His way.

We readers—never mind Abram—can hardly know precisely at this point what this task will require, but we can be confident of its immense importance. We can see how aspiring to such a disposition can address dangerous human tendencies that the text noted long ago. It promises an answer to the incompleteness (the "not-good-ness") of the human being, noted in Genesis 1: man is perfected or completed not by human knowledge of good and bad but by a command to orient himself wholeheartedly toward God. It promises an answer to the dangerously unlimited character of human freedom, noted in both Genesis 1 and 2 and again at Babel: freedom is here properly tethered and delimited, as man eagerly keeps step and direction, walking in God's way. It promises an answer to human self-division and self-conflict, noted in Genesis 3: human psychic turmoil is overcome by unifying our aspirations wholeheartedly around the simple—undivided—preference for the divine. Last but not least, it exactly an-

16. When God last addressed Abram, after the war of the kings, He said, "I am your shield." The shield image suggests that God will be in front of Abram, a defensive and protective presence between him and his enemies. Here, in a passage that addresses Abram's relation not to outside enemies but to members of his own people, God charges Abram to be "out in front" of Him. As Bill Rosen has observed, "This is, both literally and metaphorically, the point at which God stops serving Abram, and Abraham starts serving God."

17. Noah was said to already have this quality, "a man righteous and simple [*tam*] in his generations"—though perhaps only relative to others "in his generations" (see Chapter Five). For Abram, being *tamim* appears to be a lifelong task or goal.

swers human pride: the undivided soul, humbly focused on God, rises above amour propre and vainglory. This is not to say that these answers will be—or ever can be—perfectly achieved; they serve rather as a direction and a goal, informing and guiding a disposition of heart and mind. To the properly prepared soul, God's charge, to walk before Him and be *tamim*, will appear at once daunting and inspiring.

Abram's answer to God's new call and charge is speechless prostration—"And Abram fell on his face" (17:3)—a simple deed that speaks volumes. Expressing awe and reverent submission, and perhaps also gratitude, Abram both acknowledges that God is the speaker and tacitly accepts His offer. True, *falling* on his face may signal that he does not know how to *walk* before God and has doubts about whether he can do so; human beings will need further speech—and eventually laws—to uplift themselves for the work of holy "walking." But by bowing down and by hiding his face, Abram tacitly admits to his imperfections (his need to become "blameless") and gives over his pride (consider, in this regard, the meaning of his having instead remained standing). Yet he does not flee in fear and dread: Abram holds his place if not his standing. He acknowledges that it is hard to do what he has been asked to do, but at the same time he affirms his wish to do it. Revealing that he knows before whom he stands (and falls), Abram's speechless deed speaks loudly for his willingness to be the bearer of God's new way.

With Abram down on his face, God proceeds to announce the terms of the covenant, beginning from His side of the pact:

> "As for Me, behold, My covenant is with thee, and thou shalt be the father of a multitude of nations. No longer shall thy name be called Abram, but thy name shall be Abraham ['*Avraham*]; for the father of a multitude of nations have I made thee.[18] And I will make thee exceedingly fruitful, and I will make nations of thee, and kings shall come out of thee. And I will establish My covenant between Me and thee and thy seed after thee throughout their generations for an everlasting covenant, to be a God unto thee and to thy seed after thee. And I will give unto thee, and to thy seed after thee, the land of thy sojournings, all the land of Canaan, for an everlasting possession; and I will be their God." (17:4–8)

God's part of the covenant is very generous and full—not to say fecund. It is also emphatically and movingly personal.[19] He will make Abram exceedingly fruitful, the father of nations and the progenitor of kings; in anticipation of this new

18. *Raham* is the Arabic word for "multitude"; *ab* (or in Hebrew *'av*) is (again) "father."

19. The second person singular pronoun appears eighteen times in these five verses. This personal multitude prefigures the promised multiplication of Abraham. (The first person pronoun occurs ten times.)

future, He gives Abram a new identity and a patriarchal name, "father of multi-tudes."[20] Also, He will be his personal God and the God of his seed, forever; and He will give them the land of Canaan as an everlasting possession.

The change of Abram's name, offered in conjunction with God's abundant promise, is in fact deeply significant. "Abraham's very identity is now inextrica-ble from God's promise of abundant offspring. His *being* depends on God's speech. If God breaks his promise, Abraham ceases to be Abraham."

As for Abraham (and his seed), the obligation of the new covenant is remark-ably simple: keeping the covenant simply means *remembering* it, that is, marking its token or sign in the flesh of every male throughout the generations, by the act of circumcision:

> "And as for thee, thou shalt keep My covenant, thou, and thy seed after thee, throughout their generations. This is My covenant which ye shall keep, between Me and you and thy seed after thee: every male among you shall be circumcised. And ye shall be circumcised in the flesh of your fore-skin; and it shall be a token of a covenant between Me and you. And he that is eight days old shall be circumcised among you, every male throughout your generations, he that is born in the house, or bought with money of any foreigner, that is not of thy seed. He that is born in thy house, and he that is bought with thy money, must needs be circumcised; and My covenant shall be in your flesh for an everlasting covenant. And the uncir-cumcised male who is not circumcised in the flesh of his foreskin, that soul shall be cut off from his people; he hath broken My covenant." (17:9–14)[21]

Why should *this* covenant between God and Man be marked by circumcision? How might this sign be related to the new covenant and new charge? We can think of many possible reasons, all of them apt. Unlike the rainbow, the sign of God's earlier covenant with Noah and all life after the Flood—which addressed only the preservation of life rather than its moral or spiritual character and which accordingly demanded nothing from man in return—circumcision is an unnatural sign, both artificial and conventional. It is the memorial of an agree-

---

20. God is here, quite literally, enlarging Abra(ha)m's name, exactly as He enlarges on His promise of his future greatness, numerical and regal; God symbolically makes good on His original promise, "I will make thy name great" (12:2). That it is God, and not Abraham, who makes Abraham's name great is symbolized by the fact that the one new letter in Abraham's name, *h*, hay, is associated with the tetragrammaton name of the Lord.

21. The second person pronouns occur nineteen times in these six verses, and after the introduc-tory "And as for *thee*," in equal numbers of singular ("thou," "thy," and "thee") and plural ("ye" and "you") forms.

ment that deems it necessary (hence, conventional); it must be made by man (hence, artificial); yet it is marked in the organ of generation (hence, also natural). The world as given, and life even when secure ("No more floods"), are not yet completed; the best way to live remains hidden and must be revealed and instituted by additional human effort, exercised in the face of powerful human drives that lead us astray.

Male circumcision was, of course, a custom already widely practiced in the ancient world. In pagan societies, circumcision, performed at the time of puberty, was part of a male rite of passage (it may also have served symbolically as an act of human sacrifice to the gods). A mark on his maleness, circumcision was a sign not only of the youth's new sexual potency but also of his initiation into the male role and male society (putting an end to his primary attachment to his mother and the household, to the society of women and children). But in the new way of ancient Israel, the special obligation of the covenant gives the practice of circumcision a new and nearly opposite meaning. An initiation rite of passage of young males into adult masculinity is transformed into a paternal duty regarding the male newborn. Israel's covenant with God begins by transforming the meaning of male sexuality and of manliness altogether.

Covenantal circumcision emphasizes and sanctifies man's natural generative power, even as it also restricts and transcends it. To be performed on children only eight days old, it celebrates not sexual potency but procreation and (especially) perpetuation. Though it is the child who bears the mark, the obligation falls rather on the parents; it is a perfect symbol of the relation between the generations, for the deeds of parents are always inscribed, often heritably, into the lives of their children.

The obligation of circumcision calls fathers to the paternal task. Performed soon after birth, it circumcises their pride in siring male heirs, reminding them that children are a gift for which they are not themselves creatively responsible. More important, they are called from the start to assume the obligations of transmission. They are summoned to ratify the meaning of their own circumcision (and, therewith, of the community's view of manhood), each new father vindicating the promise made by his own father to keep him within the covenant. They are compelled to remember, now when it counts, that they belong to a long line of descent, beginning with Abraham, who was called and who sought to walk before God and to be wholehearted. They are reminded that bearing the child is the easy part, that *rearing him well* is the real vocation. They are summoned to continue the chain by rearing their children looking up to the sacred and the divine, by initiating them into God's chosen ways. They are required to give their children a spiritual rebirth, right from the start, in memory of God's covenant and His special charge to Abraham and his seed.[22] They must symbolically demonstrate their dedication of their present deeds to their future hopes and of their future hopes to the Eternal. And made mindful that the deeds of the fathers are always visited upon their sons, they are made aware of the consequences for their children—now and hereafter—of their failure to hearken to the call: "And the uncircumcised male . . . that soul shall be cut off from his people: he hath broken My covenant" (17:14). With circumcision, the child and all *his* potential future generations are symbolically offered to the way of God.

And why a rite applicable only to the male children? Because males especially need extra inducement to undertake the parental role. Freed by nature from the consequences of their sexuality, probably both less fitted and less interested by nature than women for the work of nurture and rearing, men need to be acculturated to the work of transmission. Virility and potency are, from the Bible's point of view, much less important than decency, righteousness, and holiness. The father is recalled to this teaching and, accordingly, symbolically remakes his son's masculinity for generations to come. True, he takes his son immediately out of the realm of women and children into the society of males, but the society of males is now domesticated and sanctified, redefined as those who remember God rather than as those who fight, rule, and make their name great.[23] When his son comes of age, he will come to see himself in a line that goes all the way back to Abraham. He will come then to understand the meaning of the bodily mark of his fathers and their covenant with God. Presumably, this self-consciousness will decisively affect how he uses his sexual powers, how he looks on the regenerative and nurturing powers of woman, and how he regards the covenant's redefinition of "manly work."

Although the charge of circumcision falls primarily on the fathers, the mothers are not in fact excluded. For them, too, celebration of fertility is not enough. In giving her newborn son up for circumcision, the mother affirms that the child is not wholly hers, is not her creature or her possession. She agrees immediately that the child belongs, and should be dedicated, to God's covenanted

22. In Jewish tradition, the child is publicly named on the occasion of his circumcision, in what amounts to a second birth. Abraham, as we have seen, was renamed—and in a sense reborn—on the day of his self-circumcision.

23. Our reading interprets circumcision—and indeed God's new way in its entirety—as a taming of maleness, putting men into the service of the (more traditionally womanly) work of child rearing. There is, of course, another (and opposed) way of reading the gender-specific character of early male circumcision. It could betoken the earliest possible removal of male children from the justice-indifferent "love of my own flesh" love of their mothers and their placement into the society of those who are defined in terms of dedication to the Lord's commands and who will care for the right and the holy even more than they love their own. There is, of course, no reason to deny that both these purposes are equally served by this covenantal practice.

way. Not the maternal ties of blood, but the divine bond of covenant gives the child his deepest identity.

God's covenant with Abraham does not forget the centrality of woman. Its terms being not yet complete, God speaks to Abraham a third time, this time, surprisingly, about Sarai, his wife:

> "As for Sarai, thy wife, thou shalt not call her name Sarai, but Sarah is her name. And I will bless her, and moreover I will give thee a son of her; yea, I will bless her, and she shall be a mother of nations; kings of peoples shall be of her." (17:15–16)

Renamed Sarah (the name still means "princess," from *sar,* "prince" or "ruler"), Abraham's wife also now stands in special relation to God, who will bless her with fruitfulness and make her the mother of nations and kings.

Abraham again falls upon his face, but this time laughing and muttering to himself, incredulous that a child could be born to a man one hundred years old and a woman of ninety. Partly out of disbelief, partly out of his attachment to and preference for his firstborn, Abraham resists God's suggestion and urges a different plan: "Oh that Ishmael might live before Thee!" (17:18). God, rebuking Abraham, emphatically reiterates His promise and His intention: Sarah will bear Abraham a son, to be named Isaac (*Yitshaq,* also spelled *Yitshak,* "He Laughs"),[24] within the year. Isaac, son of Sarah, not Ishmael, son of Hagar, is to be Abraham's true heir within the new covenant. Ishmael will prosper, "but My covenant will I

---

24. This is the first mention of the son of the covenant and the next patriarch, named in advance by God. Nahum Sarna offers this helpful comment:

> Hebrew *yitshak* is a verbal form meaning, "He laughs." It is almost certainly an abbreviation ("hypocoristicon") of an original, fuller theophoric form *yitshak-'el,* "El laughs," after the pattern of *yishma'-'el* ["God hears," the meaning of the name of Ishmael; see 16:11]. The full form is never found in the Bible, nor is any other proper name ever compounded with this stem. Nevertheless, all three biblical traditions relating to the birth of Isaac (cf. 17:19; 18:12; 21:6) emphatically connect the name with human laughter. The explanation for all this is twofold. On the one hand, there is a deliberate dissociation from the pagan, mythological origin of *yitshak-'el,* which reflects the laughter and merriment of the gods, something entirely devoid of moral and historical significance. On the other hand, the laughter of God in the Bible, by contrast, invariably expresses His reaction to the ludicrous attempts of men to act independently of His will and in defiance of it (Psalms 2:4; 37:13; 59:9). The repeated laughter of humans in connection with the birth of Isaac is, in a sense, the inverse of God's laughter, for it is a questioning of divine sovereignty (cf. 18:14). The person of Isaac, therefore, represents the triumph of the power of God over the limitations of nature. No wonder he receives his name from God Himself.

We shall have more to say about the significance of Isaac's name in the next chapter.

establish with Isaac, whom Sarah shall bear unto thee at this set time in the next year" (17:21). On this note, delivered with firm finality, "He left off speaking with him, and God went up from Abraham" (17:22).

Whatever his state of belief about Sarah's possible fertility, Abraham does not hesitate to act. He immediately moves to execute his part of the covenant. As commanded, he circumcises himself (at age ninety-nine), his son, Ishmael, and all the males attached to his house. Yet even as the text emphasizes (three times in five verses [17:23–27]) that Abraham circumcises Ishmael, *his son*, the reader is given to understand that, to overstate the point, Abraham is here with Ishmael undergoing basic training, as it were, just practicing to become the father of Isaac. Now he obediently circumcises his son; only later, on Mount Moriah, will he demonstrate that he truly knows what it really means.

HOSPITALITY FOR PATRIARCHS: STRANGERS AND THE LORD

The adventures of Abraham soon turn explicitly political, and not surprisingly. For the covenant marked by circumcision is a nation-making event, establishing a clear separation of Abraham and his people from the rest of humankind. At the same time as it imposes special obligations, this designation as chosen nation also threatens to arouse in Abraham's clan two deep-seated human passions (especially dangerous when felt in excess), self-love (or the love of one's own) and pride or vanity—passions that lead men to ignore or mistreat their neighbors. Yet precisely because God's covenant with Abraham is ultimately for the sake of bringing the blessings of righteousness and holiness to *all* human beings, his privileged relationship with the Lord must not lead Abraham (or his clan) to xenophobia, undue "homophilia," or injustice. In his next adventure (immediately following his acceptance of the covenant of circumcision), Abraham is tested in this regard, as the Lord appears to him in the guise of three stranger-travelers who station themselves outside his tent, waiting, as it were, to discover how he will treat them.

And the Lord [*YHWH*] appeared unto him by the terebinths of Mamre [Hebron], as he sat in the tent opening in the heat of the day.

And he lifted up his eyes and looked, and lo, three men stationed themselves by him; and when he saw them, he ran to meet them from the tent opening, and bowed himself toward the ground. And he said: "My lord ['*adonai*], if, please [*na'*], I have found favor in thy sight, pass not away, I pray thee [*na'*], from thy servant. Let please [*na'*] a little water be fetched, and wash your feet, and recline yourselves under a tree. And I will fetch a morsel of bread, and stay ye your heart; after that ye shall pass on; forasmuch as ye are come to your servant." And they said: "So do, as thou hast said."

And Abraham hastened into the tent unto Sarah, and said: "Hurry! Make ready three quick measures of fine meal, knead it, and make cakes." And Abraham ran unto the herd, and fetched a calf tender and good, and gave it unto the servant; and he hurried to dress it. And he took curd, and milk, and the calf which he had dressed, and set it before them; and he stood by them under the terebinth tree while they ate. (18:1–8)

The story has a wondrous and puzzling beginning. Three visitors suddenly and mysteriously appear outside Abraham's tent. Abraham quite clearly sees the strangers as "three men." Yet according to the first sentence, which functions as the title to the tale (and the entire chapter), the story tells what happened when the *Lord* appeared to Abraham. The text's deliberate ambiguity regarding the nature of the visitors brings the easygoing reader to attention. He apparently needs to be told that the appearance of what seems to be merely *human* beings is—also and at the same time—identical to the appearance of the Lord. The deliberate conflation of the divine with the human also anticipates the story's main questions: Will Abraham be able to see for himself what the reader has had to be told? Will Abraham be able to discern the presence of the Lord in the person of these strangers? Will he be able to recognize the divine within the human, and especially within those who are not his own?

Abraham, sitting in the opening of his tent, sees the three strange men and immediately *runs* to meet them, bowing before them in a greeting one offers to honored guests. In addressing the men, Abraham speaks nobly yet humbly, presenting himself as "thy servant" and employing polite forms of address (three times he uses the particle *na'*, "please" or "I pray thee"). He upholds the strangers' dignity by graciously understating or even denying their neediness (he implies that they are just passing by and that they need at most a *little* water to wash their feet and a shady place to rest). Moreover, he belittles the fare he offers to provide ("a morsel of bread"), understates the work it will take to prepare it (only "fetching" is said to be required), and makes it appear as if they would do him honor by pausing at his home and accepting his modest service.

But although formal and measured in speech, Abraham is quick and openhanded in deed. He organizes Sarah and his entire household to the task of preparing food; he provides a lavish feast of fresh cakes of fine meal (prepared by Sarah, not Hagar), a tender dish of dressed veal, curds, and milk; and he serves his guests himself—all with energy and dispatch.[25]

In the immediate sequel Abraham's guests reciprocate his generosity in divine measure: they announce the long-wished-for (and now forthcoming) birth of a son to Sarah (18:10,14). Abraham, newly circumcised into God's covenant, had graciously and humbly treated the stranger-men as god-like beings, as creatures bearing the image of God. His hospitality, a gift offered with no expectation of recompense, is matched by his blessed visitors. In fitting response, the strangers show themselves also to be agents of grace. They bless Abraham and Sarah's house and marriage with the promise of procreation, the one gift that will perpetuate the divine image in the light of the divine covenant.

Abraham, who in Egypt had experienced what it feels like to be a stranger in a strange land, passes his (first postcovenant) test with flying colors, treating the stranger-guests with extraordinary hospitality and magnanimity. Becoming a member of the chosen tribe does not require indifference to the needs and concerns of outsiders. On the contrary, as Abraham shows so graciously, the willingness to walk before God becomes the ground of treating *all* human beings with the respect and justice that the new covenant with the seed of Abraham was instituted to promote.

Hospitality toward strangers recognizes the importance of moderating, even while preserving, the distinction between the same and the other, between one's own and the alien. It may seem strange to suggest that exclusive and sectarian communities, if they are to be decent and just, depend radically on acknowledging the existence and dignity of the broader human community, most of which they exclude. Yet if a community is to carry God's new way (and especially as a light unto the nations), the otherwise arbitrary and largely conventional division of mankind into heterogeneous sects or associations must pay homage to the nonarbitrary and natural sameness of the human species and its dignified place in the created order.

JUSTICE FOR PATRIARCHS: A PAINFUL LESSON

Up to this point, Abraham's trials (with the exception of the war of the kings) have been largely domestic. He has come to understand that founding a great

---

25. The excellence of Abraham's conduct will become even clearer when we can compare it with Lot's treatment of two of the same strangers later on their journey, when they come to the city of Sodom (Genesis 19; below). These two chapters (18–19) constitute a single unit, revealing the differences between the way of the tribe (under God's tutelage) and the way of the (godless) city regarding hospitality and its unjust perversions.

nation and gaining a great name requires a concern for progeny and transmission, and in particular requires rearing one's sons in full memory of God's promised solicitude and care. Abraham is also in the midst of a protracted education about the meaning of marriage, without which he cannot fully enter into proper fatherhood. We have just seen how, in the light of the covenant, Abraham puts his entire household in the service of proper hospitality to strangers. Yet for all his personal rectitude in dealing with *individuals*, Abraham remains largely innocent of what justice finally requires. His next trial, immediately following, is the cure for his innocence—and also for ours.

Right after the strangers leave Abraham's tent to head toward Sodom (with Abraham accompanying them to see them off), God undertakes to give Abraham some instruction in political justice, indispensable for a national founder who cares for righteousness. This sobering instruction greatly alters Abraham's view of the world, including his understanding of fatherhood. He begins to see that proper fatherhood must be grounded not on the natural love of your own but on the acquired love of the right and the good. I refer to the famous conversation between God and Abraham about the fate of Sodom and Gomorrah.

This conversation is one of the dramatic high points of the narrated life of Abraham, indeed of the entire book of Genesis. In this unique exchange—there is no other conversation like it between God and man—Abraham dares to challenge not only God's proposed conduct but even His very justice. And for at least a brief moment, the two interlocutors address each other in a manner of speech that betokens equality. Commentators frequently see fit to praise Abraham's concern for justice and compassion, all the more remarkable as it is on behalf of unrelated strangers. They see it as a human triumph, a sublime display of Abraham's extraordinary nobility of character. Says Nahum Sarna in his new *JPS Torah Commentary: Genesis:*

> The next dialogue with God involves a concern for the welfare of others, total strangers. Abraham displays an awareness of suffering and an ability to respond beyond his immediate personal interests. He shows himself to be a moral man, a compassionate person. His behavior at this moment makes him the paradigm of "the just and the right," qualities that are to characterize his descendants.[26]

26. The Hertz Pentateuch commentator is even more effusive in his praise: "[O]ne of the sublimest passages in the Bible or out of the Bible. Abraham's plea for Sodom is a signal illustration of his nobility of character. . . . Abraham proves true to his new name and embraces in his sympathy all the children of men. Even the wicked inhabitants of Sodom were his brothers, and his heart overflows with sorrow over their doom."

I do not wish entirely to quarrel with this reading, though it seems to benefit from hindsight, not to say from certain modern prejudices. But be this as it may, there are certain aspects of the discussion between God and Abraham that this interpretation tends to overlook. Those aspects, perhaps exaggerated here, by way of overcompensation, constitute a particularly difficult and painful lesson for Abraham about the difference between personal and political justice, a lesson any political founder needs to learn.

The encounter is arranged by God, and precisely for such political purposes—as He makes clear in a speech (to Himself) that reveals for the first time His true interest in Abraham:

And the Lord said: "Shall I hide from Abraham that which I am doing, seeing that Abraham shall surely become a *great and mighty nation,* and *all* the nations shall be blessed in him? For I have known him *to the end* that *he may command his children and his household after him,* that they *keep the way of the Lord to do righteousness* [*tsedaqah*] *and justice* [*or* judgment: *mishpat*]: to the end that the Lord may bring upon Abraham that which He hath spoken of him." (18:17–19; emphasis added)

Abraham, the founder of a great nation, must do righteousness and justice,[27] and command his children after him to do likewise, for only in this way can Abraham bring the Lord's righteous ways to the entire world, and thus be a blessing to all the nations of the earth. Although he has shown himself to be *personally* righteous, Abraham, because he is to be a *political* founder, needs also some instruction in political justice, that is, in justice regarding whole communities—cities or nations. God, the teacher, not only wants Abraham, the student, to know about the judgment against Sodom and Gomorrah; He also wants him

---

27. These two crucial terms, closely allied, are nonetheless different. "Righteousness," *tsedaqah,* has been partially discussed above, page 305 n. 10, in connection with verse 15:6. Whatever ambiguity may have existed there—for example, whether righteousness referred to Abram's trust in God or, rather, to God's truthful speech—here it is clear that righteousness refers to the character of one's deeds ("to *do* righteousness"), and not just one's beliefs or faith. "Doing righteousness" means acting in a way that shows that one is aligned truly on a straight (not crooked) path. Deeds are even more clearly the domain of "doing justice" or "doing judgment," *mishpat.* "Doing *mishpat*" (the verbal root means "to judge" or "to govern") has a more juridical and legal tone than "doing righteousness." It entails passing and executing judgment in cases of dispute, crime, violation, and sin; and it includes pronouncing and carrying out any sentence judged to be fitting. One way to relate doing righteousness and doing justice is as follows: failures in righteousness become matters requiring judgment and rectificatory justice. Later, when the law is given (in Exodus), these judgments will be tied to specific *mishpatim* or legal norms. But a forerunner of passing judgment on unrighteousness is to be found in the present conversation between the two "judges," Abraham and God, regarding what is the fitting judgment and sentence upon Sodom and Gomorrah.

to understand its rightness. More important, God also intends that Abraham share responsibility for the punishment as a result of his participation in the judgment. Through this conversation, which is revealed to be far more than merely a master class in political science, Abraham is to become God's partner, as it were, in executing political justice.[28]

The Lord makes known, presumably within Abraham's hearing, the problem that demands His attention:

"Verily, the cry of Sodom and Gomorrah is great, and verily, their sin [chata'tham] is exceeding grievous. I will go down now, and see whether they have done altogether according to the cry of it, which is come unto Me; and if not, I will know." (18:20–21)

The cry of injustice rising from these two cities has brought God to investigate: He does not rely on hearsay, He will see for Himself. What He intends to do about it is not stated. Abraham draws near the Lord and initiates the conversation:

"Wilt Thou indeed consume [safah] the righteous [tsadiyq] with the wicked [rasha']?[29] Perhaps there are fifty righteous within the city; wilt Thou indeed consume and not forgive the place for the fifty righteous that are therein? That be far from Thee to do after this manner, to slay the righteous with the wicked, that so the righteous should be as the wicked; that be far from Thee; shall not the Judge [shofet] of the whole earth do justly [ya'aseh mishpat]?" (18:23–25)

---

28. As noted previously, our use of the term "political," here and throughout this chapter, is deliberately broad. Strictly speaking, what is political refers only to the affairs of the city (polis), which is a special sort of community. Abraham is becoming the founder of a clan or nation, not—indeed, most emphatically not—the founder of a city (like Cain or Nimrod or the Babel builders). In fact, one might say, and rightly, that Abraham is here receiving an antipolitical (that is, anticity) lesson, in that he is being taught the (perhaps unavoidable) evils of city life as such. But as we hope to show, the teaching about communal justice that he receives through this conversation is applicable also to nations that do not live in cities. The lesson will go beyond the negative conclusion "Beware the city, for it is a den of iniquity."

29. The terms here translated "righteous" and "wicked" are sometimes translated, after their later legal usage, "innocent" and "guilty": the person judged "not guilty" in a court of law will be called tsadiyq. The quasi-legal proceedings in which Abraham steps forward to argue his clients' case before the Judge of the whole earth could justify the more legal usage. But given that the case is occasioned by the cry of outrage on account of grievous sin, rather than by a violation of specific statute, I prefer the moral to the legal meaning. As we shall see when we meet them, the Sodomites are wicked beyond any mere lawbreaking.

We are immediately struck by the boldness and intensity of Abraham's speech; unlike most of his subsequent offerings in this conversation, he makes here no preface and offers no apologies for his challenge, and the repetitions of certain phrases (for example, "that be far from Thee") indicate his passion. But closer examination provides some clues about just what it is that moves Abraham so. It is not compassion for strangers, but a concern for justice centered closer to home.

Note first, by the way, that it is Abraham, not God, who introduces the punishment of destruction; God was still investigating, but Abraham, far from shrinking from punishing the wicked, is the one who suggests it. Not compassion or mercy, but justice, is on Abraham's mind, as it is on God's. But Abraham's leap to questioning the punishment of wholesale destruction may be motivated by something nearer and dearer. Here is the crucial clue: God had announced his interest in the wickedness of two cities, Sodom and Gomorrah, but Abraham in his questioning speaks only of *one* city ("within *the* city"; "forgive *the* place"), although he does not name it. God, reading Abraham's mind, will in His next response speak only about Sodom, and by name. As a result, we learn that Abraham's concern for the fate of Sodom is not disinterested; for Sodom is still the home of his nephew, Lot. The commentators who hear in Abraham's pleas only a concern for total strangers have forgotten the place and importance of Lot—the importance of Lot *to Abraham*. Abraham, who risked his very life—and with it the divine promise—to rescue Lot in the war of the kings, has not become indifferent to the fate of his kinsman just because he now has an heir in Ishmael. It is Lot's presence among the wicked in Sodom that captures Abraham's attention and engages his passions; Lot becomes the hook God exploits for catching and enlarging Abraham's concern for justice. Because it would be both ignoble and unjust to engage in special pleading, Abraham cannot make his argument in personal terms; he must make it in terms applicable both to his own and to the strangers alike.

Even leaving aside the question of Lot, Abraham's point of departure is clearly a concern for *personal* justice: is *each* person getting what he deserves? More precisely, Abraham focuses entirely on the danger of injustice for the *righteous:* he is not at all arguing that the wicked should be spared out of mercy or compassion, only that the righteous not suffer with the guilty. This concern for personal justice, and especially for the fate of the righteous and the innocent, is also not disinterested; Abraham surely wants to know whether his own righteousness will be rewarded as promised. If God is capricious or just plain careless with the righteous, Abraham could suffer unjustly despite his efforts at righteous conduct; he too could fare much less well than he deserves.[30]

---

30. In this respect, Abraham's concern is not all that different from Cain's—or ours.

Yet lurking in these personal concerns are also larger and even more important questions, crucial to Abraham's relationship to God and to his founding mission. For Abraham desperately needs to know whether divine justice bears a sufficiently close resemblance to our human intuition about justice, namely that the good shall prosper and (only) the wicked shall suffer. Is God's justice, seen from this human viewpoint, arbitrary or capricious? If so, will it be possible to follow Him wholeheartedly as God commanded? For this reason especially, Abraham insists on learning whether the righteous must suffer with the wicked.[31]

The conversation about the fate of the righteous is important not only for Abraham (and the reader), enabling him to find out whether God's justice and human justice are basically congruent. It is crucial also for God and for the main lesson that He wants to teach man through Abraham, a lesson about which Abraham already has his suspicions. For Abraham is dimly aware that there may be a tension between what is just for a city and what is just for individuals. He senses that if the city gets judged *as a whole*, the results for individual city dwellers will not be just, because some righteous will suffer with and for the guilty. At this Abraham rebels—at first. He ignores the political perspective and focuses entirely on the fate of the righteous individuals—and probably for all the reasons mentioned. No wonder he demands to know if the Judge of the whole earth is going to act justly, that is, render to each person exactly and only what is owed.

In contrast with Abraham, God is much more interested in the city and its wickedness than in individuals, even the righteous ones; after all, it was the grievous sins of the cities that brought Him to investigate. Still, He welcomes Abraham's insubordination in the name of personal justice in order to educate him. In accepting Abraham's plea about the fifty righteous, He promises to spare the city if they be found in Sodom, but He subtly tries to get Abraham to think also about the problem of the whole. Where Abraham had asked Him "to forgive the place for the fifty righteous therein" (18:24), God stresses the totality: "I will forgive *all the place* for their sake" (18:26; emphasis added).

Abraham, when he speaks next, repeats God's use of "all," but he clearly hasn't grasped the point. Looking away from "all the city," he wants God to look *only* at the group of the vulnerable fifty righteous: "Perhaps there shall lack five of the fifty righteous; wilt thou destroy all the city for the *lack* of *five?*" (18:28; emphasis added). In His response, God, although again allowing Himself to be moved by

31. Abraham is so concerned over the fate of the righteous and innocent that he is willing to let the wicked escape their fitting punishment; in effect, he is asking that the wicked prosper as the righteous. Thus, Abraham's preoccupation with securing justice for the righteous leads him to defend *injustice,* treating the wicked the same as the righteous.

Abraham's plea, nonetheless rejects its focus and the terms Abraham had used. Abraham had looked only at the fifty righteous and implied that God might destroy the whole city for a mere *lack* of *five* such. God, correcting Abraham's calculations, promises not to destroy the city if He *finds there* the positive *presence* of *forty-five* righteous men: "I will not destroy it, if I find there forty and five" (18:28).

Abraham gets the point. From now on, accepting God's correction, Abraham will do the bargaining solely in terms of the size of the saving remnant. Encouraged by God's answers, he continues to work down the number, making the case for forty, thirty, twenty, and, finally, ten. But curiously, Abraham on his own and voluntarily—"I will speak yet but this once" (18:32)—stops the bargaining at ten. This is strange. On the principle that has driven him from the start, and that has apparently been supported at every turn by God's response—namely, that the righteous ought not suffer—Abraham might have pressed the case to its logical conclusion: to spare the city for the sake of one righteous man. Why does Abraham break off at ten? Why does he not push all the way to one?

Abraham may have been afraid or ashamed to push to the limit, either out of a gradually increasing fear that God will judge him presumptuous or out of embarrassment at revealing a personal interest in his one kinsman, Lot. In addition, encouraged by God's concessions, he might have become increasingly moved by feelings of awe.[32] But fear, shame, and awe aside, Abraham may have broken off the bargaining because he had learned something. Encouraged by God's accepting of his conditions, he is gradually brought to adopt the divine perspective. Like God, Abraham has begun to think about justice for a whole city. He comes to see that to care about justice for a whole city or a whole nation means that one must be willing to overlook, at least to some extent, both the natural preferences for one's own kin and the demand for absolutely strict justice for each individual. By stopping the bargaining at ten, Abraham (at least tacitly) accepts the possible destruction of Lot, the man he once called "brother." And he (at least tacitly) accepts that politics—the life of cities and communities—*necessarily* involves the suffering of at least some innocent and righteous people. If one is to care for the justice of a nation, and especially as its founder, one must not only be willing to moderate the love of one's family and the love of personal justice; one must even be willing to sacrifice them, at least in part. Political founding and political justice are a sobering business, because political justice is not altogether just.

There is for Abraham, of course, also some very good news: God is indeed

32. As the conversation proceeds, Abraham, each time he speaks, tempers his initial boldness with prefatory remarks acknowledging God's superiority: "I who am but dust and ashes"; "Let the Lord not be angry and I will speak"; etc. (18:27, 30, 31, 32).

moved by every appeal Abraham actually makes. There is no known gap between God's notion of justice and Abraham's. God is willing to make accommodations, but apparently only if there is a truly saving remnant, only if there exists a possibility to lift up the city as a whole, that is, only if there are *enough* righteous men to effect reform. (If not, the innocent and righteous necessarily go down with the guilty—as they do in every wicked city, down to the present day.) By showing Abraham their common ground about the *principles* of justice, God enables Abraham to gain His perspective on the *practice* of justice in the communal realm. Abraham comes to see that one must come to care about the righteousness or wickedness of the world, and not only about one's own kin and one's own goodness and its rewards. Most important, Abraham learns that one virtuous man does not make, and cannot save, a nation by his own merit alone.

For Abraham, the lesson could not be more pointed: his excessive preoccupation with God's personal promise, with his own merit and its reward—that is, with personal justice—is in fact at odds with the fulfillment of the purpose of God's promise that he become a great *nation*, steeped in righteousness and doing justice, to become a blessing to all the others. The implication could not be plainer: because a community once founded will stand or fall together, and because one man's virtue is not sufficient, there is urgent need for education and transmission, beginning with a well-ordered house and with political measures to secure justice in the community. And this lesson could not be timelier. For it is administered to Abraham, via this conversation, just after he has learned that Sarah will bear him the long-awaited son of the covenant within the year. Before Isaac arrives, Abraham is compelled to think less like a natural father, more like a righteous founder—or more to the point, a righteous *father*, who, like a righteous founder, will care more for what is right and good than for his own. Thanks to this lesson, he will be able to fulfill his mission as true patriarch: to "command his children and his household after him, that they may keep the way of the Lord, to do righteousness and justice" (18:19).

THE INJUSTICES OF THE CITY: A REJECTED ALTERNATIVE

Having agreed to Abraham's final request ("I will not destroy it for the ten's sake"; 18:32), the Lord "went His way" and "Abraham returned to his place" in the hills of Hebron. Like Abraham, we readers are left in suspense regarding the fate of Sodom. Can ten righteous men be found in Sodom? Will the city be spared? While we wait, with Abraham, for the denouement, the text allows us—but not Abraham—to see what goes on in Sodom and to discover for ourselves what the fuss is all about. Having listened in on the abstract argument about what is owed to the wicked city, we now get to see civic wickedness and injustice

in the flesh. Because the truth about any city is most clearly revealed in its behavior toward outsiders, the story, not surprisingly, concerns the treatment of
strangers. It begins with a second and parallel tale of hospitality, involving the
same visitors, but this time with Lot, a relatively decent man but a city dweller, in
place of Abraham. Though Abraham plays no part in this story, it sheds much
reflective light on Abraham's conduct and education in the episodes that preceded it.

Having left the tents of Abraham, two of the strangers come to the city of
Sodom (Genesis 19). We have been hearing of Sodom for some time, ever since
the city was first mentioned in defining the boundaries of the Canaanites, descendants of Ham (10:19);[33] now, for the first time, we get to go inside. Vicariously, we shall experience city life through the encounters of the strangers. In the
very first words of the account, an important clue heralds for us the difference
between this story and the last: when they come to Sodom, the men are called
"angels," and they appear to Lot as such. Lot apparently would not be able to
penetrate their disguise; unlike Abraham, he would not have been able to see the
divine hidden (always?) "within" the human.[34]

> And the two angels came to Sodom at evening; and Lot sat in the gate of
> Sodom; and Lot rose to meet them; and he fell on his face to the earth. And
> he said, "Behold, please [na'], my lords, turn aside, I pray you [na'], into
> your servant's house, and tarry all night, and wash your feet, and ye shall
> rise up early, and go your way." And they said, "Nay, but we will abide in the
> broad place all night." And he urged them greatly, and they turned in unto
> him, and entered into his house; and he made them a feast, and did bake
> unleavened bread and they did eat. (19:1–3)

Lot is not at home but is hanging about the gate of the city, the passage through
the encircling wall built to keep out dangerous outsiders. In contrast with Abraham, Lot does not rush forth to meet the strangers. He bows excessively ("fell on
his face"), insists with unseemly urging that they enter his house, makes them a
much less gracious and generous offer, and prepares a less adequate meal ("un-

---

33. All of the cities and most of the other questionable human societies we meet in Genesis belong
to the descendants of Noah's most impious and questionable son.

34. Yet while Abraham may well have seen the divine in his guests, nothing in the text indicates
that he is aware that they are anything but human. He offered them simple hospitality with no apparent plan to curry favor with the powerful. Lot, as we will see, is completely opposite, not just in
his behavior, but in his probable motives. (I owe this observation to Bill Rosen.) A point by point
comparison with the detailed particularities of Abraham's hospitality, only some of which is prepared by the observations that follow, would reveal much more of the deep difference between the
two men and their social circumstances (city versus tribe).

leavened bread"—later, the bread of affliction of the Hebrew slaves in Egypt). All that Lot does he does all by himself; the nameless Mrs. Lot (a Sodomite native), soon to become famous as a pillar of salt, is not in evidence, and Lot's entire household is poorly organized to receive strangers. It is hard, it seems, to be gracious to strangers in the city. The walls raised against strangers are not merely those of brick.

Lot, it must be conceded, despite his limitations, at least offers the strangers shelter and hospitality. His fellow Sodomites, in contrast, see them merely as objects for their own pleasure. They come menacing Lot's guests, showing the utmost contempt for their dignity: they seek to rape them.

> But before they [the men-angels] lay down, the men of the city, even the men of Sodom, compassed the house round, both young and old, *all the people* from every quarter. And they called unto Lot, and said unto him: "Where are the men that came in to thee this night? Bring them out to us *that we may know them.*" And Lot went out unto them to the door, and shut the door after him. And he said, "I pray you, *my brethren,* do not so wickedly. Behold now, I have two daughters that have not known man; let me, I pray you, bring them out to you, and do ye to them as is good in your eyes; only unto these men do nothing, inasmuch as they have come under my roof." And they said, "Stand back." And they said: "This one fellow came in to sojourn, and *he will needs play the judge [vayishpot shafot]!* Now we will deal worse with thee, than with them." And they pressed sore upon the man, even Lot, and drew near to break the door. (19:4–9; emphasis added)

All the men of the city, from every quarter, young and old—including, presumably, also the married ones, and among them, presumably also Lot's sons-in-law! (see 19:14)—come to abuse the strangers. They seek to "know them" merely carnally, and even then, not freely but forcibly, not face-to-face like human beings, but from behind like animals.

Lot, courageously but foolishly, goes out (shutting the door) and pleads with his fellow Sodomites not to do wickedly. He flatters them by calling them "my brothers" and, in a perverse excess of hospitality, offers them his own virgin daughters (the two unmarried ones) to protect his guests from violation. (Offering his own daughters to his "brothers" is, symbolically, an invitation to commit incest, a deed that his daughters will later—in a deed of fitting payback—perform upon him.) But the Sodomites reject Lot's offer, and, their lust turned to rage, they focus instead on his imputation of their wickedness. They turn on Lot, threatening him with worse than rape, ostensibly because, although he is in truth only an outsider, he presumes to judge them (19:9). Perhaps they know deep down that they are wicked, and therefore hate the messenger who dares to tell them so. More likely, they hold themselves beyond good and evil, bound only by their own habitual selfish ways. For these city folk, outsiders are of no account, and even less so are their notions of justice and right: rejecting Lot's assertion that what they demand is wicked (in some absolute sense), the Sodomites insist on adhering only to their own Sodomite ways. The Sodomites thus endorse not only xenophobia and sodomy, but also moral relativism—all exaggerated expressions of the "love of same."

Lot and his family are saved only when the visitor-messengers pull Lot inside, shut the door, and blind the attackers "so that they wearied themselves to find the door." In this place where strangers are improperly treated, finally not even one's own kin are safe. In the city walled against strangers, even doors cannot—without providential assistance—defend a man and his family against his hot-blooded, lusting, and raging neighbors. Moreover (apropos Abraham's conversation with God about the fate of the righteous), one decent man cannot save or reform a city.

The visiting angels urge Lot to gather his family and get them out of town, before the Lord destroys the city. Lot tries to rouse his sons-in-law to leave, but they think he is joking. Early the next morning, the angels again urge Lot to flee, lest he be "swept away in the iniquity of the city" (19:15). When he lingers, they forcibly drag him, his wife, and their two unmarried daughters out of town. Told to escape to the mountains to avoid the coming onslaught against the cities of the plain, the fearful Lot begs to be allowed to go instead to "a little city"; he either has not yet grasped the essential wickedness of urban life or is too attached to or dependent upon the ways of civilization to be willing to go it alone. When Lot and his wife and daughters come unto the city of Zoar, the Lord rains brimstone and fire upon Sodom and Gomorrah: "He overthrew those cities and all the plain, and all the inhabitants of the cities, and that which grew upon the ground" (19:25). Lot's wife, disobeying an order not to look back, turned for a last glimpse of her native town and was turned into a pillar of salt (19:26).

Unlike Lot's wife, we readers have been permitted—nay, forced—to witness the destruction of Sodom and Gomorrah, but in a context that moves us to learn from what we have just seen. Through these two linked and juxtaposed stories about the treatment of strangers, proper and improper, the Bible invites us to discover the problem of communal justice and injustice and to see why the city—not just Sodom, but the city as such—is a breeding ground for injustice, without and within. Sodom is a city notorious for injustice, for that unqualified love of one's own and that unqualified hatred and mistreatment of strangers, exemplified in the attempted homosexual rape of the men-angels visiting Lot. But the Sodomites also turn sadistically against their own when their passions are aroused and their desires are opposed. These unjust practices, a little reflection will show, might not be peculiar to Sodom.

Every city defines itself with walls to protect it against hostile outsiders (access limited, through the gate), yet its houses come to need doors to protect—although, in the end, they *fail* to protect—its citizens against their predatory neighbors (compare Abraham's tent opening, freely communicating with the world). Both physically (by walls) and psychically (with attitudes), every city defines itself by magnifying the importance of the distinction between who's in and who's out, between those who are like us and those who are other. As with Babel, the city as a city strives for a certain unity and homogeneity, both in opinion and in practice. In any given city, this drive for "one-ness" creates opposition not only to outsiders but even to the smaller groupings that comprise it: the *archetypal* city *as a whole* looks with suspicion on the family and the household, inasmuch as family loyalties dilute and undermine wholehearted and unanimous devotion to the larger collective.[35] In its exploits, the city manifests a collective selfishness toward outsiders, to begin with by merely being indifferent to their interests and well-being, but eventually by taking perverse pleasure in violating them. Moreover, as the city grows and prospers its feverish activities and successes serve to inflate and inflame desires; licentiousness triumphs over self-restraint. Paradoxically, because of the city's quest for self-sufficiency, city dwellers are more likely to forget about human vulnerability and man's dependence on powers not under human control. The city thus blinds its inhabitants to the truth silently carried by all strangers and beggars (and explicitly taught by many ancient peoples): any stranger or beggar may be "a god in disguise"— which is a poetic way of saying that he, and by implication we, continue to survive only by some power of grace. For all these reasons, men in every city will commit injustice toward strangers—eventually also toward neighbors—unless the city is informed by teachings of hospitality, teachings that are in turn informed by fear-awe-reverence for God and the ability to discern the divine image equally present in all human beings.

But Sodomite injustice goes beyond mere inhospitality and violence toward strangers. It has an explicitly sexual character. This city's special brand of injustice is, in fact, epitomized in its own sexual perversions: the acts of sodomy (practiced by the citizens) and the acts of incest (later practiced by Lot's daughters on their father). Each is an excessive embodiment of the principles of love of like, aversion to unlike, principles in fact not peculiar to Sodom but, as is argued

---

35. The tension between city and family is most famously explored in Plato's *Republic*, where Socrates shows how full devotion to civic justice would require the abolition of the family, the city's most powerful rival for human loyalties and attachments.

above, to some extent native to all cities. Each is also an expression of sexual self-ishness; each is a manifestation of misogyny and contempt for marriage and procreation.

Misogyny, though prevalent in the other social arrangements of the ancient world, reaches its fullest expression in the city. In Egypt, where Pharaoh rules as a god, women are relegated to the harem; the tyrant uses beautiful women for sexual pleasure only. In the tribe (including, as we saw, the tribe of Abraham—before he was instructed), women are mistreated through concubinage; woman's procreative power is esteemed but her status as wife is demoted, as the master treats all women as seedbeds, equally good for providing him with heirs. But here, in the city, whose characteristic sexual "error" appears to be homosexuality, misogyny is taken to an extreme and women are treated with complete disdain.[36] Devoted both to political unity and immediate self-satisfaction, and indifferent to their vulnerability and the need for replacement, the city dwellers take nonprocreative sex to its logical and sterile conclusion: sodomy. In contrast with members of a tribe, no one in the city will naturally feel compelled to be fruitful and multiply; everyone can leave that obligation to his neighbor. For oneself, only the present and the passionately pleasant matter.

The end of Sodom, conveyed in the story's final images, reveals the city's life-denying truth:

> God annihilates "the entire Plain" including "the vegetation of the ground" (19:25). That fatal fertility, so like Eden, is withered in the flames and the earth that bore it scorched. In its place is left the sterility of the salt of the Dead Sea and of the pillar into which Lot's wife is turned. The punishment fits the crime, since in the midst of that fecundity, Sodom had enjoyed only her sterile attachments, generating nothing.[37]

As the salt and ash rub their painful meaning into our eyes, we city-dwelling readers look around us and tremble.

So too does Abraham. For his God-given lesson in justice did not end with the conversation. Its conclusion, which requires that he learn what happens to the city, comes the morning after the conversation, as Abraham awakens to see

36. One can argue that Lot's offering of his daughters to the Sodomite mob is an expression of Lot's own misogyny. On the other hand, one can also argue that this offer shows, in a perverse way, that Lot esteems his daughters, giving up what is absolutely most precious to him in order to keep honored guests under his roof from violation and abuse.

37. Paul Ludwig, "What's Wrong with Sodom?" (an unpublished paper written for my graduate seminar on Genesis, 1993). My discussion of Sodom over the past few pages is indebted to Mr. Ludwig's remarkably perceptive and finely argued paper. Among his many interesting suggestions, he explores how the fiery punishment of Sodom fits its crimes. The following passage comes immediately before the lines quoted here in the text:

smoke rising from the cities and all the land of the plain, "like the smoke from a furnace" (19:28). The text says not a word about Abraham's reaction, but we can try to imagine what went through his mind. For sure, God's evident and mighty power over human life inspired in him awe and dread. But what about the righteous for whom he had bargained? There could have been as many as nine who perished with the guilty—not to speak of innocent newborn babies—as the city went down together. And what of Lot? As Abraham watched, he no doubt concluded that Lot died in the conflagration. With heavy heart, he felt his own responsibility for Lot's death—not only because he agreed in speech to let any less than ten righteous die with the guilty, but perhaps also because he had earlier failed to educate Lot in justice and (in order to avoid strife) had allowed him many years ago to go off to settle in Sodom. The burdens of the father, the founder, and the judge are heavy indeed. Abraham's reflection on the deed of the destruction completes and fixes the political lessons of the conversation of the day before.

As if to tell the reader of Abraham's heavy heart about his "sacrifice" of Lot, the text speaks of smoke ascending like smoke in a furnace, using the words for smoke and ascent connected with the making of burnt offerings. (Indeed, the word used here for ascent, 'olah, is also the word for burnt offering that we shall meet again soon.) True, in the immediate sequel, we are told that "God remembered Abraham, and sent Lot out of the midst of the overthrow, when He overthrew the cities in which Lot dwelt" (19:29). God shows his mercy, saving Lot for Abraham's sake. But—and this is crucial—He does not tell Abraham that He has done so. There will be time enough later to teach Abraham and his descendants about God's mercy. For the time being, the painful lessons of the father's and the founder's justice must be allowed to sink in without a word of consolation.

Instead of water from above the firmament raining down to increase an anarchy already ongoing, God rains down sulfurous fire from Himself out of heaven onto Sodom (19:23). Two metaphorical connections between Sodom and fire are possible: the burning of desire, the concupiscible passions; and the burning of anger, whether God's anger visited upon them or the Sodomites' own irascible passions displayed when, incensed, they attack Lot and attempt to break down the door (19:9). The irascible passions can take their ignition from the concupiscible ones, as this incident bears out. Tempers flare more quickly among men inflamed by sexual desire; the thumotic or spirited response is actually the means by which the erotic desire can be fulfilled should it meet with resistance. To justify the violence toward which their desires compel them, and to spark its outbreak, they work themselves into an anger over a pretext. This is one origin of violence out of sexual sin. It is only too predictable that roving gangs of such ravishers would put the houses they had violated to the torch. The city's crime may thus be its own punishment. From fire the name of Sodom takes the second of its etymological meanings: "burning" (Anchor Bible Dictionary). If water brought back chaos for the heroes, fire brings for Sodom purification.

We wonder whether something of what he learned as he witnessed the smoke rising from Sodom and Gomorrah may have prepared Abraham for his greatest trial, enabling him to respond without so much as a peep of protest about the suffering of the innocent when God asks him to become not just an accomplice in the death of Lot but an actual killer of his own beloved son.

GOD'S COVENANTAL PROMISE FULFILLED: THE WONDROUS BIRTH OF ISAAC

After the episode with Sodom and Gomorrah, which teaches Abraham both about God's awesome power and about the need to serve righteousness, and after the second wife-sister episode, involving Abimelech, which completes Abraham's education regarding the meaning of wife, Sarah at last conceives and Isaac is wondrously born, when his mother and father are, respectively, ninety and one hundred years old (see Chapter Ten). The circumstances surrounding his birth oblige both Abraham and Sarah to see the permanent truth about parenthood: children are *not* man's or woman's products or creatures, and thus the pride that human beings naturally take in their own children as *their own* children is vanity and self-delusion. God commands not only the awesome power of executing justice and destruction; He is also the source of the renewal of life through children, who are life's true answer to mortality.

Abraham, his pride suitably humbled, "circumcise[s] his son Isaac when he [is] eight days old, as God had [earlier] commanded him" (21:4). Isaac, from his birth, is brought within the covenant that commemorates God's new way and man's commission to walk wholeheartedly before Him. His mother Sarah rejoices both in God's beneficence ("God hath made laughter for me"; 21:6) and in this fulfillment of her marriage to Abraham ("For I have borne him a son in his old age"; 21:7). Abraham too is joyous, and makes "a great feast on the day that Isaac was weaned" (21:8).

Yet there is still trouble in the house, on account of Ishmael, which must be remedied in order to insure Isaac's ascendancy. At Sarah's insistence, Abraham, with heavy heart and great reluctance but with God's approving endorsement of Sarah's plan, banishes Ishmael and Hagar, bringing the family for the first time into its proper order and harmony. We readers who are gratified by this result should not underestimate the difficulty Abraham probably had in, as it were, "sacrificing" Ishmael, his firstborn, the first bearer of his great hope for posterity. Only because of his growing sense of what it might mean to walk wholeheartedly before God and because of the wondrous existence of the long-promised heir in Isaac was Abraham able to lose Ishmael, as he had lost Lot before him. Even so, we should consider the possibility that it was Abraham's great reluctance to part with Ishmael that made necessary the more horrible test of separation from Isaac, reported in the story that we will soon discuss at length.

His household reordered, Abraham next secures good relations with his neighbors, Abimelech and the Philistines. Imitating God's practice with him, Abraham becomes a covenant maker, entering into a pact of mutual respect and recognition with Abimelech at Beer-sheba. In gratitude for his new blessed circumstances, "Abraham planted a tamarisk tree at Beer-sheba, and called there on the name of the Lord [*YHWH*], the everlasting God. And Abraham sojourned in the land of the Philistines many days" (21:33–34). Everything appears to be set, ordered, and harmonious: Abraham is ready to be both father and founder of his—and God's—great nation. Abraham's course of instruction would appear to have been completed.

Appearances are deceiving. The hardest and most difficult lesson is yet to come. The story of the binding of Isaac is Abraham's final test.[38]

ABRAHAM'S FINAL TRIAL: THE BINDING OF ISAAC

No story in Genesis is as terrible, as powerful, as mysterious, as elusive as this one. It defies easy and confident interpretations, and despite all that I shall have to say about it, it continues to baffle me. Indeed, my approach seems even to me to be too shallow, precisely because I am attempting to be reasonable about this awesome and shocking story.

This interpretation rests on some assumptions. First, about its timing. It comes precisely at this time, when all earthly arrangements are apparently set, so that it may clarify Abraham's relation to God, but—and this is crucial—therefore also his relation to his own and to others: Abraham must show that he understands that one's *spiritual* orientation is decisive also for *all human relations,* both personal and political. Second, although he has from the start shown something of how he stands in relation to God, Abraham at the beginning would have been incapable of meeting this test; thus, the test must be interpreted in the light of his education. His previous adventures have taught him more than a little about the divine and have readied his soul for this final trial

---

38. The story of the binding of Isaac follows on the heels not only of the tale of Abraham's banishment of Ishmael but also, and more immediately, of the account of Abraham's covenant with Abimelech, after which Abraham *calls on "the name of the Lord,* the everlasting God." Kristen Dietrich Balisi has suggested to me that this latter deed might also help to explain the "need" for the test of the binding. Abraham, who here shows himself perhaps too comfortable invoking God's name, will soon be hit in the face with God's awesomeness and remoteness. The story of the binding of Isaac will reveal as much about the nature and identity of the God who called Abraham and whose name Abraham called as it does about the merit of Abraham himself. Abraham—and the reader— are poised to learn most important lessons about God and His ways with human beings.

and lesson. He has repeatedly heard God's call and His abundant promises. He has experienced awe, the religious passion, during the dark vision between the sacrificial pieces; he has enacted the new covenant marked by (self-) circumcision—a symbolic act of "partial sacrifice," betokening dedication to God's ways; he has been God's partner in the judgment on Sodom and Gomorrah and, in his own heart, has accepted responsibility for (what he thought was) the "death" of Lot; he has learned of God's support of Sarah, his wife, and of the importance of marriage; he has beheld the wondrous birth of Isaac and endured the banishment of Ishmael. He has witnessed not only God's dreadful power but also His insight into men's souls, as well as His solicitude, honesty, justice, restraint, and providence. He has received (from Melchizedek, king of Salem and priest of the Most High God [14:18–20], and from Abimelech [21:22]) the testimony of foreign witnesses to (his own) God's majesty. Last but in importance first, he has known intimately God's benevolence toward him in the gift of Isaac, delivered as promised—the first clear manifestation of the great blessings vouchsafed him when God first called him. Abraham has learned all his lessons now, but one. In all his previous adventures, Abraham has performed the deeds that were required, but the question remains whether he has understood their inner meaning and intent. Now, as a result of what he has learned about God—and about himself—Abraham is now ready to make clear, to God but also to himself, how he stands in the world. He is ready now to demonstrate, fully and unambiguously, why and how he is a follower of God.

The stark story has a stark beginning:

And it came to pass after these things that God *did test* Abraham. And He said unto him, "Abraham!" and he said, "Here-am-I [*hineni*]." (22:1; emphasis added)

From the start, the reader is told—but Abraham is not—that what follows is a test: Abraham, at the end of his education, is being summoned for his final examination. But we are not told exactly what is being tested. Figuring that out and thinking it through, one might say, will be the test for us. For this is a crucial episode not only for Abraham. It is decisive also for those of us who have vicariously been taking the walk with Abraham and on whom the book has been working its deeds. In experiencing this tale, we must not only discover what is being tested. More important, we must also answer for ourselves whether, in *our own* eyes, Abraham passes. The text, by letting us in on God's secret ("This is [only] a test"), invites us to sit with Him in judgment on Abraham's conduct. We must decide, now when push comes to sacrifice, whether we can in our own hearts and minds continue to walk with Abraham in the new way.

Generally and safely speaking, we suspect that the trial will be a test of Abraham's disposition toward God. But of *which* disposition: Obedience? Faith or trust or hope? Love? Fear or reverence? Wholeheartedness? Zeal? Righteousness? Several of these together? We must wait and see.

And He said unto him, "Abraham!" and he said, "Here-am-I [*hineni*]." (22:1)

God calls Abraham, out of the blue and without warning—just as He did the first time. This time, however, He calls him most personally; for the first and only time, God calls him by his new name and *only* by name: " '*Avraham!*"— "Father of Multitudes!"[39] This call by name is more than a prelude to the announced test. It is itself part of the examination, inasmuch as the test turns out to be, in a sense, a test of Abraham's name. Will Abraham answer to his name, not merely verbally and superficially but also deeply? Will Abraham, father of Isaac, remembering the covenant through which he was given his new name and new calling, be willing and able to live up to his name as the covenant-bound father of multitudes—especially if it requires ceasing to be the father of Isaac?

Just as he did when God first called him, Abraham responds immediately and without hesitation. Then, commanded to go, he did as he was told without uttering a word. Now, called by name, Abraham answers the call in revelatory speech. He replies—as he will do two more times in this story—with the famous and pregnant one-word answer, "*hineni*"—literally, "Behold me"—"Here-am-I, just as you named me, 'Father of Multitudes,' fully present to you, inclining toward you, wholly ready for your word." One is tempted to suggest that Abraham, by responding as he does, almost passes the test even before it begins: he knows (without having to be told) who is calling and before whom he stands, and he makes himself fully available to a source beyond himself.[40] Hearkening as the one who is called "Father of Multitudes," Abraham stands wholeheartedly before the One who calls; the father of many stands ready to be the servant of One. It remains to be seen how he will stand—or whether he will even remain standing—when he hears next what the Caller asks him to do.

---

39. When God first spoke to Abram (12:1), He began with an imperative, "Go thee forth [*lekh lekha*]." When He came to him in a vision (15:1), He began with an imperative, "Fear not, Abram." When He appeared to him for the covenant (17:1), He began by identifying Himself—"I am *El Shaddai*"—and then with an imperative, "Walk before Me and be *tamim*." Here, and only here, does God begin with the pure call of the name, "Abraham!"

40. To answer such a call is to acknowledge that one is not the center of one's world and that one is dependent on powers not at one's disposal.

> And He said, "Take, *please* [*na'*], thy son, *thine only one,* whom thou *lovest,*
> Isaac, and get thee [*lekh lekha*] into the land of Moriah; and offer him there
> for a burnt offering [*'olah*] upon one of the mountains which I will tell
> thee of." (22:2; emphasis added)

God indeed asks—"Take, please"—but what He asks for is horrible: the "Father
of Multitudes" is asked to offer up his son—his only one, the one he loves,
Isaac[41]—as an offering to the Lord. Abraham is asked to surrender that which is
most his own and that which he most loves; he is asked not only to give it up but
also to turn it to ashes in a burnt offering. As we nervously await Abraham's reaction, we eagerly remind ourselves that this is a test, and, we hope, *merely* a test.
Having heard God's request, can we now say what is being tested?

    Unlike many interpretations, this one does not assume that this is intended
primarily as a test either of Abraham's *obedience* or of his *faith or trust or hope* in
or *love* of God—though one or more of these dispositions may enter in
Abraham's response. For one thing, God does not exactly *command* Abraham to
sacrifice Isaac, He requests it of him; as Robert Sacks points out, God says
"please." (Nearly all translators fail to translate the Hebrew particle *na',* which
accompanies the imperative verb, "take.") Thus Abraham is in fact free to refuse,
as he would not be were he simply commanded to obey. Also, it is not easy to
specify how faith or trust is being tested: faith or trust in what? That God will
turn this awful deed into some discernible good, say, by restoring the slaughtered Isaac from his ashes? Or, more shallowly, that God doesn't really mean it?
Abraham would have no reason for believing in the possibility of the former,
and the story makes no sense as a test and loses all its horror if he believes the
latter. To be sure, those who, following Kierkegaard, see here only irrationality
and contradiction—for how can one reconcile God's earlier promise that Isaac
would carry the covenant with God's current demand for Isaac's destruction?—
and who therefore insist that it is human *reason itself* whose sacrifice is being
called for have no recourse but to explain Abraham's conduct as a "leap of
faith"—a claim that we shall revisit. But properly understood, God's request is

---

41. Robert Alter offers a fine commentary on this seemingly redundant sequence:

The Hebrew syntactic chain is exquisitely forged to carry a dramatic burden. . . . The classical
Midrash . . . beautifully catches the resonance of the order of terms. Rashi's concise version is
as follows: "*Your son.* He said to Him, 'I have two sons.' He said to him, '*Your only one.*' He said
to Him, 'This one is an only one to his mother and this one is an only one to his mother.' He
said to him, '*Whom you love.*' He said to Him, 'I love both of them.' He said to him, '*Isaac.*' " Although the human object of God's terrible imperative does not actually speak in the biblical
text, this midrashic dialogue demonstrates a fine responsiveness to how the tense stance of the
addressee is intimated through the words of the addresser in a one-sided dialogue.

not as irrational as it seems. On the contrary, it makes perfect sense if we look at it not on its own but in the context of Abraham's overall education.

When God first addressed Abra(ha)m, we recall, He did so with a command accompanied by a promise. We wondered then whether Abram obeyed and went because he was a god-hungry man moved by the awe-inspiring command-ing voice or because he was a greatly ambitious man enticed by the promises of founding, fame, and prosperity. Again, when *El Shaddai* offered Abram an ever-lasting covenant in exchange for ritually circumcising his sons, we wondered whether Abram—exactly when he was renamed Abraham—fully understood the meaning of the requested dedication and its connection to his renaming and to the exalted promise. At no point up until now has it been possible to answer these questions. Only now that God has delivered the first installment of the promised blessings can the two "reasons" for following God be pitted against each other. Only now can Abraham prove that he knows what it means to cir-cumcise your son in memory of the covenant and to answer the call to "walk be-fore Me and be wholehearted." Only now can Abraham be tested to demonstrate in deed what he holds first in his soul: ambitious desire for the promised bless-ings or humble reverence for the One who calls and promises. If it was his ambi-tion that initially drew Abra(ha)m to answer God's call, has it been educated and subsumed in awe?

Here, then, are two ways to formulate the implicit—and utterly intelligible—question being asked of Abraham in this final test: Will you, Abraham, walk rev-erently and wholeheartedly before God even if it means sacrificing all benefits promised for such conduct? Do you, Abraham, fear-and-revere God more than you love your son—and through him, your great nation, great name, and great prosperity—and more even than you desire the covenant with God?[42]

Horrible though it is to say so, the test God devises is perfect: for only if Abra-ham is willing to do without the covenant (and, as proof, is willing to destroy it himself), out of awe-reverence for the Covenantor, can he demonstrate that he *merits* the covenant and its promised blessings; only in this way can he demon-strate that he is fit for patriarchy, for both fatherhood and founding. With fear and trembling I am suggesting that, far from being irrational, this test makes very good sense as a test both of the father and of the founder, as a test for the would-be "Father of Multitudes."

42. Robert Sacks presents the case similarly: "God and Abraham had made a Covenant. God would give Abraham a son and make his name great if Abraham were willing to devote that seed to the establishment of the New Way. He asked Abraham whether he would be willing to give up that seed and the Covenant. The question is whether Abraham would be willing to relinquish the seed while remaining perfect in the sense discussed at the beginning of Chapter Seventeen ['Walk before Me and be *tamim* (perfect)']."

But as Robert Sacks has astutely observed, the test is also risky, and not only on Abraham's side. Abraham could refuse God's request, producing a permanent cleavage between them; for in refusing, Abraham would demonstrate his lack of wholeheartedness, and hence his ultimate untrustworthiness. If God then, in reaction to such refusal, nullifies the covenant, He would in turn seem, from Abraham's point of view, to be equally untrustworthy. "In a strange way the present passage speaks more about God's faith in Abraham than Abraham's faith in God."[43]

God's trust in Abraham is vindicated: Abraham is ready and willing to meet the test.

> And Abraham rose early in the morning, and saddled his ass, and took two
> of his lads with him, and Isaac his son; and he cleaved the wood for the
> burnt offering, and rose up, and went to the place of which God had spo-
> ken to him. On the third day Abraham lifted up his eyes and saw the place
> afar off. (22:3–4)

Not hesitating, and without saying a word (not to God,[44] and probably not to Sarah), Abraham "arose early in the morning," as if he were wholeheartedly in sympathy with the request. But he is no zealot, eager to practice child sacrifice or insensitive to the horror involved; this we learn from the austere, steady, and dignified way he proceeds, as indicated by the simplicity, compactness, and austerity of the verbs used to recount his actions: *arose, saddled* (his ass), *took* (two

---

43. This thought is present also in Midrash: "[Following the feast given] upon the 'child's having grown and being weaned' (Gen. 21:8), Satan spoke up to the Holy One, 'Master of the universe, out of the entire feast that this old man, upon whom You bestowed fruit of the womb at the age of one hundred—out of the entire feast he prepared, could he not have spared, say, one turtledove, one fledgling, as an offering to You?' The Holy One replied, 'Is it not true that Abraham prepared the feast in honor of his son? Still, if I say to him, "Sacrifice your son to me," he will sacrifice him at once.' Satan said, 'Try him.' At once, 'God tried Abraham.' " God has faith that Abraham will refute Satan's claim that he too is, at bottom, self-centered and God-forgetting.

44. Many a reader has been perplexed by the fact that Abraham does not plead with God for the life of Isaac, as he had done for the (righteous) inhabitants of Sodom. But the cases are not the same, and one can give many plausible reasons for the difference (beyond the obviously wrong explanations that Abraham knew that God would in the end spare Isaac, or that he, Abraham, had [unconscious?] desires to harm his son). First, Abraham is much less likely to plead for himself or for his own; special pleading for oneself is base, whereas Abraham aspires to be noble. Would Abraham have been deemed worthy had he said, "Why my son?" Second, because it was a request not a command, Abraham was free to refuse, and his refusal did not require any argument about the justice or injustice of the matter. Indeed, third, the issue here is clearly not one of justice. True, shedding of innocent human blood had been pronounced a capital offense (9:6), and Abraham might have

youths with him and Isaac, his son),[45] *cleaved* (wood for the burnt offering), *rose up*, and *went*. Of what he thought and felt on the three-day journey is left to our imagination; from the text's point of view the important thing is what he did: Abraham went, and went steadily, to the place of which God had spoken.

The Genesis narrative, and not only here, is more concerned with deeds than with words, with actions than with beliefs—not because inner life doesn't matter, but because true character is best displayed in action. The text does not share our modern preoccupation with motives and feelings, and does not even hint at Abraham's psychic turmoil or distress. We therefore have no clear warrant for trying to enter his psyche, much less for projecting into it feelings of our own. Nevertheless, it is almost impossible to set aside one matter that surely must catch Abraham's attention as he travels on his somber three-day journey: how to square God's current request with God's earlier covenantal promise. The test may be "perfectly rational" from God's point of view, and Abraham himself

---

thought to refuse to do the deed on those (divinely pronounced) ethical grounds. But as the question was not about reward of the righteous or punishment of (only) the wicked (as with Sodom) but about a gift or an offering, the guilt or innocence of the "victim" is beside the point (indeed, the offered one is almost invariably pure, innocent, unblemished). And if, perhaps, one still insists that some question of justice is involved, Abraham might well believe, on the basis of his conversation with God about Sodom, that God would neither ask nor do anything incompatible with His justice or righteousness. Moreover, as Isaac was a wondrous gift and not a paternal possession, as God gave, so God may take back.

But even more attractive, in my view, than these plausible reasons for Abraham's silent acquiescence in the horrible request are the following: (1) Abraham had learned, in the episode over Sodom, that the pursuit of righteousness and the following of God's way may require sacrificing your own; (2) he felt and feared both the awesome power of God and also His righteousness; and especially, (3) he understood immediately the meaning of the test, namely, that he was being asked to show what was first in his soul: was it the love of his own (and of the promise and the covenant), or was it the fear-awe-reverence for God? As the whole story suggests, Abraham, newly a father of the promised-son-of-the-covenant and newly the founder of a new nation, *understood* that the true father and true founder must devote himself and, hence, also his offspring and his people to something higher than offspring and peoplehood, *even at the cost of losing them*. I shall amplify this decisive point in the text at the end.

45. It is not clear how old Isaac is. It is also not clear that it matters. Isaac was last mentioned on the occasion of his weaning (age two or three). He will next be mentioned on the occasion of his marriage to Rebekah (24:62 ff.), at age forty (25:20). In the immediate sequel to the story of Isaac's binding, we learn that Sarah dies at the age of 127 (23:1). (Born when Sarah was ninety, Isaac is thirty-seven when she dies). Readers who see a causal connection implied in this juxtaposition of Sarah's death with the story of the binding—namely, Sarah dies of shock upon learning what Abraham had done to Isaac—argue that Isaac must have been thirty-seven years old at the time of the binding. But the manner and content of Isaac's speech suggest someone much younger.

Yet this speculation about Isaac's age on Mount Moriah may well be beside the point. From the fact that we do not know Isaac's age, we are perhaps meant to see that the meaning of the story about father, son, and God is entirely independent of such contingent details. That one is the father and the other is his beloved son is the only thing that matters.

might even understand precisely the meaning of God's request. But not knowing that he is merely being tested, Abraham must be deeply perplexed, not to say distressed, by the contradiction between God's earlier promise, oft repeated, that it will be through Isaac that the covenant will be perpetuated and God's current request that Isaac be annihilated. It is regarding this contradiction that the argument that Abraham acts from trust, faith, and hope gains its greatest strength. To escape from the contradiction, so the argument goes, Abraham must have faith in God's providence and/or (at least) hope that the covenant carried through Isaac will still be (miraculously) fulfilled.[46] But logical argument is not yet textual evidence. We must watch closely for any clues that might reveal Abraham's true state of soul as he and his little group reach Moriah.

> And Abraham said unto his lads, "Abide ye here with the ass, and I and the lad we will go yonder, and we will worship, and we will return to you." And

---

46. Here is how one powerful advocate puts it:

If you say that Abraham, when he goes up Mount Moriah, neither hopes nor believes in the slightest that Isaac will somehow be saved or restored at the end of it all—if you say that Abraham has resigned himself wholly to the loss of his son Isaac—then you must also say . . . that Abraham is here offering Isaac to a God whom Abraham believes to be a liar. For did not God *promise* that "it is through Isaac that offspring shall be called for you" (21:12)? Was not God's covenant with *Isaac*—not with Ishmael or Lot, nor with some other son of Abraham—to be an "everlasting covenant for his offspring to come" (17:19)? Abraham's name itself bears the mark of this covenant. So does Abraham's flesh—and so does the flesh of Isaac. God, who required the circumcision of Isaac (21:4), now requires Isaac's death—and with it, the breaking of the promise that the mark of circumcision signified. Abraham will bear the mark of his own circumcision for the rest of his life as a mark of a cosmic joke. The mark will testify to God's lie, and to Abraham's foolishness; for Abraham had put all his hopes in the promise, which now will have been proven a mirage.

. . . Do we really believe that Abraham takes God's request as a sign that "all promises are off," that Abraham hopes not at all for the miraculous fulfillment of the covenant? . . . If so—if this present request shows that God's earlier promise was false—then Abraham should think twice before trusting in God here. To make Abraham into simply a man of resignation here . . . is to face an absurdity. For God's request, taken without faith in God's provision, is worthy of no awe and respect. What Abraham is being asked to commit is not just the act of murder but the act by which God is to be *proved* a liar. . . . If [Abraham is moved simply by fear and awe, not also by faith and hope in God's providence], then surely Abraham must be thinking, walking up Mount Moriah, that God—the "Judge of all the earth" (18:25)—is a cruel, deceitful demon.

The author is Andrew Varcoe, a former student at the University of Chicago and a recent graduate of Harvard Law School, who is—among his other virtues—a profound reader of Scripture. This excerpt comes from a lengthy paper he wrote for me, not on assignment, taking powerful issue with a published article of mine in which I argued that not Abraham's faith or trust but *only* his fear-awe-reverence were being tested in this story. Mr. Varcoe is responsible for showing me the problem with

Abraham took the wood of the burnt offering and laid it upon Isaac, his son, and he took in his hand the fire and the cleaver; and they went both of them together [*vayelkhu shneyhem yachdav*]. (22:5–6)

Once the appointed place becomes visible, Abraham leaves his youthful servants behind to attend to the ass and his other possessions; among other things, he surely wishes to spare them the horrible sight. Moreover, he understands that the affair is primarily about himself, Isaac, and God, and about their interrelationships: in speaking to his lads, Abraham turns his trial into a project for both himself *and Isaac* ("*we* will go"; "*we* will worship"; "*we* will return"). After Abraham places the wood upon Isaac's shoulders and takes in his own hands the fire and the knife, Abraham and Isaac ascend the mountain *together:* "and they went both of them together" [literally, "unitedly," *yachdav*, from a root meaning "to be one"] (22:6). Are father and son also together—one—in mind, heart, and purpose?

The answer to this question is immediately provided in the momentous conversation between Isaac and Abraham, the only one between them recorded in the Bible,[47] a conversation that may therefore reveal the core of the relationship between father and son. Though the drama of the story will unavoidably draw us forward to focus on Abraham's deed, it is rather here, in his *speech* to Isaac, that Abraham makes clear the disposition of his soul, regarding both his son and God. In this singular act of instruction is the true heart of the story, at least with respect to transmission from father to son.[48]

Isaac, summoning his father, breaks the tension of silence, but at the same time increases the tension both by how he speaks and by what he brings forth into articulate consciousness between them.

And Isaac spoke unto Abraham his father, saying, "My father [*'avi*]." And he said, "Here-am-I, my son [*hineni beni*]." (22:7)

_____

my former interpretation, which I have here modified considerably. (He is *not* responsible for the errors that doubtless remain in my current interpretation.) Every writer and teacher should be blessed by having been so ably corrected on a matter of such importance, especially by one of his students.

47. This conversation is, in fact, the first father-son exchange reported in all of Genesis. Adam never spoke with Cain or Abel (or Seth). Noah spoke about but never with his sons; in his only directly quoted remarks, Noah spoke to curse and bless them (see Chapter Seven).

48. I owe this insight to Yuval Levin, a graduate student in the Committee on Social Thought. Mr. Levin supports this claim by pointing out the elaborate chiastic (or concentric) structure of the entire story, which features the three calls of Abraham and his three identical responses, "*hineni*." Framing the story are God's two calls of *'Avraham* and Abraham's two "*hineni*" responses, followed in each case by a divine request or command (22:1–2 and 22:11–12) and then by a report of Abraham's responsive deeds (in 22:3, he "rose, saddled, took, cleaved, rose up, and went"; in 22:13–14, he "lifted up his eyes, looked, went, took, offered, and called"). Next within are (another) parallel pair of re-

The three spoken words poignantly verify the paternal-filial tie. Calling his father to attention, Isaac says, " *'Avi,*" not, " *'Avraham,*"—*"my* father,"[49] not "father of multitudes." Isaac is summoning Abraham to answer and behave like the *personal* father Abraham is supposed to be for him, to live up to his role as "father mine." Accepting Isaac's invitation to live up to this name as well, Abraham replies, "I am fully present to you, my son"—that is, *as the father you summoned.* Abraham, we recall, had previously answered *"hineni,"* "Here am I, fully present to you," when God had called him by name to the test (22:1). We readers, who unlike Isaac have heard Abraham on both occasions, wonder whether and how Abraham, given his present mission, can be "fully present" both to God and to his son. Nevertheless, we experience this "my father"/"my son" exchange as assuring the veracity and depth of the son-father conversation that follows.[50]

And he [Isaac] said, "Behold the fire and the wood; but where is the lamb for a burnt offering?" And Abraham said, "God will provide Himself [*literally,* will see-for-Himself] the lamb for the burnt offering, my son." And they went both of them together [*vayelkhu shneyhem yachdav*]. (22:7–8)

Isaac, who apparently has seen sacrifices done before, recognizes that something is wrong, that something is missing. Isaac's question bespeaks childlike wonder or mild confusion, though it may also be tinged with a faint suspicion. His failure to mention the knife among the things he sees ("the fire and the wood") may

---

ports of Abraham's deeds (in 22:6, he "took, laid, and took"; in 22:9, he "built, laid, bound, laid, stretched forth, and took"). Next within, and immediately surrounding the central father-son conversation featuring its central call of Abraham and Abraham's *"hineni"* response, is the paired identical remark about father-son unity, "and they went both of them together-as-one" (22:6 and 22:8). Mr. Levin remarks (in a personal communication):

The chiastic structure of the binding story can be seen as painting a kind of picture of a proper life, in which the relationship between the generations is the center and the key. If the structure is drawn out, and the resulting picture is considered as a depiction of the life of man, it provides an image of a life in which transmission is at the core (the conversation, pointing the next generation to God). Around it is family (father and son walking together). Around that are the simple pious actions of a man (Abraham's austere acts in accordance with a commandment), and around that is the word of God. This extraordinary picture is a kind of reward for the reader willing to get past the initial shock and horror of this story, and to examine its structure for sources of insight.

49. Alter translates *'avi* as "Father," commenting that "that noun [*'av;* "father"] with the possessive ending is the form of intimate address in biblical Hebrew, like *Abba* in postbiblical Hebrew."

50. Robert Sacks comments: "The elegant simplicity of the dialogue gives it an aspect of eternity which makes it seem to last the whole of their lives. Very few dialogues in literature bring men so close together."

be an expression of his own fear, which could put the knife beyond the margin of perception.

In response, Abraham gives authoritative, fatherly, and pious reassurance. Indeed, as an answer to a perplexed and anxious son, Abraham's speech, spoken out of paternal solicitude, is simply perfect. Abraham uses Isaac's trust in his father to encourage his son's trust in God's providence: Yes, I am your father; but (*or* and) as your father I inform you that it is God who will provide what is needed. Whatever the meaning of Abraham's words *to Abraham*, Isaac hears from the man he most trusts that God Himself will see to it that the missing lamb will be provided on the mountain. Isaac, whose thoughts began with things visible ("Behold, the fire and the wood") and who then wondered about visible absence ("Where is the lamb?"), is moved straightaway ("God will see") to reorient his mind and heart and to put his trust in the invisible but seeing-and-providing God.

Although Isaac hears that the lamb will be on the mountain, Abraham for himself must almost certainly believe that "the lamb" is already at his side. Yet it is clear that, even if he accepts the inevitability of Isaac's sacrifice and answers as he does mainly to reassure his son, Abraham does not exactly lie. For in Abraham's eyes it was God who had wondrously provided Isaac, the sacrificial lamb, presumably for the very purpose of being offered up in His service. Even when interpreted in this way, Abraham's speech still affirms a belief in God's providence. Were we readers to hear nothing more in his answer, we would marvel at Abraham's composure and steadfastness.

But Abraham's one-sentence answer is pregnant with additional meaning. Just as there are faint tinges of fear in Isaac's question, so are there faint tinges of hope in Abraham's answer: hope in the Lord to find us a way out of this. More important, Abraham, hopeful or not, surely speaks better than he knows: he may hope for Isaac's deliverance, but he surely cannot know it, and his subsequent conduct shows no hesitancy in acting against any such hope. Yet it will turn out that Isaac's simple and reassuring interpretation of his father's words was entirely correct. Abraham's faithful fatherly speech is thus all the more astonishing and awesome. What is it in Abraham's soul that enables him—or anyone else—to speak prophetically? Is there perhaps some mysterious power of insight, more perspicacious than hope, that enables a man to "speak better than he knows"?[51]

The conversation between son and father is over. It produces no change in the father-son relationship: they continue to go up the mountain as before, both of

---

51. When Abraham later names the place, he will interpret the entire event in the light of his speech to Isaac.

them, *yachdav,* united as one. Not only is their unity not ruptured; it is intensified and now articulately pointed in the direction of the God-who-will-see-for-Himself. More deeply joined as a result of their conversation, they go together now in spirit as well as in body, walking consciously and freely in the way of the Lord.

The story moves toward its climax, Abraham acting with the same simplicity, austerity, and dignity as before:

> And they came to the place that God had told him of; and Abraham built the altar there and laid the wood in order and bound Isaac his son and laid him on the altar, upon the wood. And Abraham stretched forth his hand and took the knife to slay his son. And the angel of the Lord called unto him out of heaven, and said, "Abraham! Abraham!" And he said, "Here-am-I [*hineni*]. (22:9–11)

In slow motion, the text records how Abraham deliberately *built* the altar, *laid* the wood, *bound* Isaac, his son, *laid* him on the altar, upon the wood, *stretched-forth* his hand, and *took* the knife to slaughter his son. At the last moment, the angel of the Lord calls out to him, twice,[52] by his new name, "Father of Multitudes." Abraham, for third time in the story, comes to full attention and answers the call: *"hineni,"* "Here-am-I, just as you called me, fully present and ready to hear." Abraham continues to be—or is once again—responsive to his name and inclined to the voice of God.

To everyone's great relief, the angel commands Abraham to desist and to leave the lad untouched. Of greatest interest is the reason the angel offers for Isaac's deliverance.

> And he said, "Lay not thy hand upon the lad, neither do thou anything unto him; *for now I know* that *thou art God-fearing* [*yere' 'elohim*], seeing thou hast not withheld thy son, thine only son, from Me." (22:12; emphasis added)

At long last the question about the nature of God's test is answered. "Now I know"—and so does the reader, and on the Highest Authority—what the ordeal was meant to demonstrate: *the depth of Abraham's awe-fear-reverence before God.* Later, perhaps, men can learn to *love* God, but it is the *fear* of the

---

52. Why twice? For emphasis. To make sure that Abraham heard. Because he did not answer to the first call. Because he was so committed to and involved in the deed that a single call would not have penetrated.

Lord that is the beginning of wisdom. The test is over because Abraham has passed.

The word translated "fear," *yare*, means more than simple fright. In moral terms, it connotes also awe, dread, reverence; it is the primary religious passion, experienced in recognition of a form of being beyond our comprehension, of a power beyond our control, of a force before which we feel small and toward which we look up. Curiously, awe in acknowledging the gap thereby partly overcomes it: awe or reverence establishes a relationship across the unbridgeable divide. Though a disturbing passion that holds one back from the thing feared, awe also holds one fast, attracted and transfixed before it: we flee from the simply frightening, we approach the beautiful or the lovable, but we attentively keep our place at a respectful distance before the awesome. Of special importance here, awe-reverence is evoked also by the voice of authority, in which we hear something *morally* compelling and powerful that commands our attention but that remains partly hidden and mysterious because we cannot take its full measure.[53] It is thus the primary passion experienced not only before the divine, but also, at least in reverent sons and daughters, before one's father and mother: in Leviticus, when the Children of Israel are commanded to "fear every man his mother and his father. . . . I am the Lord your God" (19:3), reverence before parents and reverence before God are brought into explicit alignment, as they are in the present story.

The wonders of the story do not end with the angel's saving speech:

And Abraham lifted up his eyes, and looked, and, behold [*hineh*], behind him a ram was caught in a thicket by its horns, and Abraham went and took the ram and offered him up as a burnt offering instead of his son.

53. Perhaps the best biblical illustration of the relation between authoritative speech and awe is the account—a parallel to our present tale—of how God catches Moses, speaking to him out of the burning bush (Exodus 3:1–6). Moses approaches a wondrous and attractive sight, a burning bush that continues to burn without being consumed, hoping to take its measure. But he is arrested by a voice that calls to him out of the midst of the bush, addressing him (twice) by name. After Moses, like Abraham, answers *"hineni,"* the voice tells Moses not to approach farther and identifies Himself as the God of Abraham, Isaac, and Jacob. In response, "Moses hid his face, for he was afraid [*yare*'] to look upon God" (Ex. 3:6). Sight gives one the impression, often mistaken, that one has full access to the meaning and being of the visible object: what you see appears to be all there is, and it beckons you to know it. But through sound and speech, one can be confident only of the *presence* of a being, without any clue regarding its totality, never mind its nature. We know through speech—at most— only so much as the speaker chooses to reveal to us, the rest being hidden from our perception. Before a speaker who addresses us personally, and with commanding power and authority, our ignorance and perplexity naturally give way to awe-fear-reverence, in this case, the awe-fear-reverence of the Lord.

And Abraham called the name of that place *YHWH-yir'eh* [*literally,* the Lord sees], as is said to this day, "On the mount of the Lord it [*or* He] shall be seen." (22:13–14)[54]

As soon as the angel finishes speaking, Abraham "lift[s] up his eyes" (compare 22:4) and sees a ram caught by his horns in the thicket. This act of sight the text shrouds in mystery: does the ram suddenly appear out of nowhere, or does Abraham suddenly see what was previously present but beyond his ken? Although God does not ask him to do so, Abraham takes the ram and offers it as a burnt offering in place of his son. Remarkably, he also reveals his understanding of what has transpired. In renaming the place *YHWH-yir'eh*, Abraham endorses the truth of his previous speech to Isaac ("God will *see-for-Himself* the lamb for the offering"): the Lord sees, the Lord sees-to, the Lord provides. The Lord has seen, through Abraham's deed, into his awe-filled heart; the Lord has seen to the sheep for the offering; the Lord has seen to it that Isaac is spared and the covenant is preserved.[55] The Lord has even seen to making true Abraham's fatherly speech to Isaac. Having spoken then better than he knew, Abraham now knows—wonder of wonders—how truly he had spoken.

After Abraham's sacrifice of the ram and renaming of the place, the angel responds by calling once again to Abraham out of heaven, this time to report verbatim the Lord's own speech: a new blessing, God's last and best blessing of the patriarch.

" '*By Myself have I sworn,*' said the Lord, '*because thou hast done this thing,* and hast not withheld thy son, thine only son, that in blessing I will bless thee, and in multiplying I will multiply thy seed as the stars of heaven, and as the sand which is upon the seashore; and *thy seed shall possess the gate of his enemies;* and in thy seed shall all the nations of the earth be blessed; *because thou has hearkened to my voice.*' " (22:16–18; emphasis added)

As a reward for Abraham's willingness to surrender the love of his own to the service of God, the Lord, swearing an oath (!), renews and expands His covenant and His promises. The image of innumerable progeny here combines the two previous ones (stars and sand), the lofty and the earthly. Also, for the first time, Abraham is told that his seed shall be victorious in wars with its enemies—

54. The expression in common use is multiply ambiguous: it could mean "He sees" and/or "He [it] will be seen." It could mean that "God sees" and/or that "God is seen." Abraham's naming of the place is, by contrast, quite clear: "*YHWH* sees."

55. As Bill Rosen has pointed out to me, Abraham promised a lamb, but a ram—the lamb's father—appeared in its stead. The "lamb," Isaac, is spared and returned to his father; in response, the "ram," ruler or father, Abraham, sacrifices himself to the Lord.

which means, of course, that there will be later need for God-fearing men to sacrifice their sons, this time in battle; in the absence of fathers who are willing to pay such a price, God's way on earth cannot survive in the world against its enemies. Finally, Abraham is told that all the *nations* (compare 12:3, "all the families") will be blessed in his seed. Why? Because he *hearkened*, in awe-fear-and-reverence, to the *voice of the Lord*. For all the talk about "lifting the eyes" and "seeing," Abraham's supreme virtue resides in his hearing and hearkening, born of awe-fear-reverence, yet not without hope.[56]

If God learns from this test about the state of Abraham's soul, Abraham—and we—learn something equally important about God. It seems that He wants dedication and reverence, not sacrifices. He is not the sort of god who wants human flesh or the sacrifice of innocent life;[57] indeed, He here puts a curb on any such human impulse. More important, God does *not finally* require that men choose between the love of their own and godliness, between the goods of terrestrial life and the path of reverence for the Lord. Though it took a horrible episode to demonstrate this fact, harmonization is possible between a reverence for God (who loves righteousness and wholeheartedness) and the love of one's family or nation, rightly understood. God, the awesome and transcendent power, wants not the transcendence of life but rather its sanctification—in all the mundane activities and relations of everyday life. Thus, God displays Him-

56. In view of God's expanded final blessing, we feel confident in setting aside a powerful and radically alternative reading of this tale, first suggested to us in conversation by a friend and colleague, Michael Fishbane, professor of Judaica. This interpretation, which regards this trial as a test of Abraham's zealousness for the divine, holds that Abraham *fails* the test, by *not* refusing God's command and by yielding instead to the all-too-human predilection for child sacrifice and slaughter of the innocent, manifested by zealots and religious fanatics, then and now. The only possible textual basis for this reading makes much of the fact that it is an angel rather than God Himself who calls a halt to the sacrifice. God, suggests Fishbane, is so embarrassed by Abraham's willingness to sacrifice his son that He refuses to speak with him directly, but sends His messenger instead. Moreover, God never speaks to Abraham again. But, as already indicated, Abraham at no time shows even a tinge of zeal or wildness; in his dealings with Isaac up to the deed itself, he shows solicitude, steadiness, and calm resolution. More important, Fishbane's sensitive account, which does justice to *our* own horror at Abraham's deed, cannot handle the manifest fact that the angel speaks for God, who swears by Himself and who increases Abraham's blessing as a response to his hearkening to the divine voice. Whether *we* like what Abraham did or not, we have it on the highest authority that Abraham passed the test, summa cum laude. Can we pass *our* test as readers if we fail to acknowledge this judgment? Are we not invited by the text not only to recognize Abraham's achievement but also to endorse it? We shall take up these questions shortly, in the concluding section.

57. There is no evidence that God wanted or even appreciated the sacrifice of the ram. The text is utterly silent on these matters. Much later, of course, God will order the Israelites to institute regular—and massive—animal sacrifice, but a good argument can be advanced that this change is concessive to human need and weakness, much like the permission to eat meat granted in the Noahide code.

self to be exactly the sort of god whom one could not only fear-and-revere but even come to love—"with all thy heart, with all thy soul, and with all thy might" (Deuteronomy 6:5).

Abraham, called by God to be the father of a new nation that will carry God's righteous ways to the rest of the world, is educated by God Himself in the proper roles of father and founder, and proves his readiness in his final test. After this, he has but a few remaining tasks to perform in order to complete his work as father-founder, after which he can quietly leave the scene. He purchases the cave at Machpelah as a burial place for Sarah, a deed simultaneously of familial and political significance, done not least for Isaac's and his descendants' sake (Abraham will also be buried here, as will Isaac and Rebekah, Jacob and Leah); the ground is consecrated as a memorial, helping to keep alive in memory the deeds of the founding mothers and fathers. Ownership of this small plot of earth will be the Children of Israel's sole legal claim in the promised land during their four hundred years of exile in Egypt. Not agriculture but burial is the first title to land. The Holy Land is holy *first* because it is the land where my fathers (and mothers) died.

The land having been sacralized in perpetuity, Abraham next completes the work of perpetuation by arranging an appropriate marriage for Isaac; no father worth his salt can be indifferent to who it is that his children marry. In Rebekah, as we shall see in the next chapter, he found more than any father of sons could ask for, a woman of worth who, even more than her husband, will be responsible for safeguarding the new way into the third generation. At age 175, his work complete, Abraham "expired, and died in a good old age, an old man, and full of years; and was gathered to his people. And Isaac and Ishmael,[58] his sons, buried him in the cave of Machpelah. . . . There was Abraham buried, and Sarah his wife. And it came to pass after the death of Abraham, that God blessed Isaac, his son" (25:8–11).

THE MEANING OF PATRIARCHY

It is time for us to take stock. In so doing, we also submit ourselves to the book's test of the reader. Abraham has been shown many things and succeeded in all his trials. But what about us? What have we learned about Abraham and about patriarchy?

Father Abraham, I submit, is the model father, both of his family and of his people—yes, even in his willingness to sacrifice his son—because he reveres

---

58. Though banished by his father, Ishmael returns (out of the blue) to perform the filial duty of burial, in the company of his "supplanter," Isaac. Modern readers, prone to believe that we should honor parents only if they treat us well, should ponder this remarkable example of filial obligation.

God, the source of life and blessing and the teacher of righteousness, more than he loves his own. He is a model not because all fathers should *literally* seek to imitate him; almost none of us could, and fortunately, thanks to him, none of us has to. He is a model, rather, because he sets an admirable example for proper paternal rule, in which the love of one's own children is put in the service of the right, the good, and the holy.

Truth be told, all of us fathers devote (that is, "sacrifice") our sons to some "god" or other—to Mammon or Molech, to honor or money, pleasure or power, or worse, to no god at all. True, we do so less visibly and less concentratedly, but we do so willy-nilly, through the things we teach and respect in our own homes; we intend that the entire life of the sons be spent in service to our own ideals or idols, and in this sense we do indeed "spend"—or try to "spend"—the life of our children. But a *true* father will devote his son to—and will self-consciously and knowingly initiate him into—only the righteous and godly ways. He will understand that, like Abraham, and unlike Noah, only a father who feels awe before the true source can deserve the filial awe-and-reverence of his sons By showing his willingness to sacrifice what is his for what is right and good and highest, he also puts his son on the proper road for his own adulthood—the true test of the good father. He will *not* finally love his son solely because he is *his own,* but will love only that in his son which is good and which is open to the good, including his son's own capacity for awe before the divine. In this sense at least, he is ever willing to part with his son as *his* son, recognizing him—as was Isaac, and as are indeed all children—as a gift and a blessing, from God.

Just as Abraham as true father learns the limits on the love of one's own, so Abraham as the true founder learns the limits of politics and of the founder's pride. All founders, like all nations, even Sodom and Babel, look up to something; a *true* founder will know from the start that there is something higher than founding and higher than politics, in the light of which one should found. Accordingly, he will strive to devote the nation or the polity to what is truly highest. Righteous politics requires not only a desire for greatness, but also a willingness to subordinate that desire to the source of righteousness, in which subordination is true greatness to be found.[59] Finally, the true founder knows and accepts the fact that his innocent sons *will suffer* for the sake of the righteous community and that their "sacrifice" is no proof that they are not properly loved as sons. On the contrary, the true founder, like the true father, shows his love for

---

59. As Sacks points out, the ram that served as a substitute for Isaac is throughout the Bible an image of the ruler, his horns an image of his pride and lofty aspiration. Symbolically, the ruler is here trapped by his pride and ambition; he must, like the one who would be a true ruler, be dedicated to God.

his followers when he teaches them, often by example, that one's life is not worth living if there is nothing worth dying and sacrificing for.

~

We are almost at the end of the story of Abraham. But one vexing question has been utterly neglected: Isaac. The story has been considered solely from Abraham's point of view. But fatherhood is not fatherhood without sonship, and we must in concluding—and in honesty—cast a short look at what Isaac may have felt, and learned, during *his* ordeal. For it would be a tragic and self-defeating result if Abraham proved himself a worthy father only at the price of his son's alienation. Is it possible that Abraham (like Noah in his tent) unfathered himself on Mount Moriah?

On the surface, there is no apparent rupture on the mountain. Isaac does not resist being bound, Isaac does not struggle, Isaac does not even cry out. Isaac, it seems, is complicitous in his own sacrifice. Yet a closer look shows that his relation to his father is indeed broken as a result: indeed, from the very moment that he is wondrously returned to Abraham, Isaac becomes estranged from him, perhaps forever. Although going up the mountain, as the narrator stressed twice, "they *went both of them together* [*vayelkhu shneyhem yachdav*]," at the end of the story, the narrator reports pointedly, "*Abraham* returned unto his youths, and *they* rose up and *went together* [*vayelkhu yachdav*] to Beer-sheba; and *Abraham* dwelt at Beer-sheba" (22:19; emphasis added). Isaac does not go down the mountain with his father; Abraham now goes alone, leaving his son to fend for himself.

This result, we discover after a little reflection, should not surprise us, for it was prepared by the text itself—and its import has general and profound significance. Abraham chose to return or dedicate the gift of his son to God, in effect sacrificing his bond to his son, even in an act that fully displays his patriarchal excellence. His supreme act of fatherhood was not the sacrifice of his son but the sacrifice of his natural paternal authority. That, after all, was the gist of Abraham's sole paternal speech to Isaac: "Not I, my son, but God will provide for our needs and your perplexities and fears." Though Isaac is spared, Abraham's fatherhood is not, as the bond of father and son remains broken. Abraham regains his son only to lose him—like most good fathers who understand fatherhood. We rear our children not for ourselves, we rear our children to do without us, we rear our children to take our place, aspiring to righteous and holy ways.

But can this transmission be successful if the bond is broken? If Isaac does not later return to Abraham, will he at least remain attached—or later return to—Abraham's God? The prospects are not rosy. Isaac and Abraham will not appear together again (in the text) until Isaac and Ishmael come to bury Abraham. Later Isaac is explicitly said to be grieved by the death of his mother, Sarah, not by the death of his father. One might go so far as to suggest that this trauma at the hands of his father explains Isaac's subsequent shortcomings as a father of his own sons, Esau and Jacob, including his preference for the strong, ruddy, earthy, present-centered hunter Esau (whom Isaac loved, we are told, because he loved to eat of his venison), and his apparent indifference to the paternal work of transmission. Everything points to the fact that Isaac—like so many of us sons—neither understood nor approved of what his father did or stood for, and, you might wish to add, in Isaac's case for good reason.

But if we are lucky to live long enough, many of us discover that our parents get smarter as we get older, especially if we are blessed with children of our own to rear. They were right, our parents, when they said to us, "Just you wait until you have children! Then you'll see." Why we cannot learn by being told and while we live under their rule is a long question; but most of us must separate ourselves from our parents in order to learn the hard way, before we can, in returning, step up to take their place. This, I believe, happens also to Isaac, albeit late in his life. Yet before we can examine this possibility, we must take up the life of Isaac in its entirety, the subject of our next two chapters.

CHAPTER TWELVE

INHERITING THE WAY:
FROM FATHER TO SON

When God sets out to institute His new way among humankind, He calls on Abraham to be its earthly father and founder; by definition, therefore, and despite Abraham's individual greatness, these are roles he cannot fully realize alone. Everything depends on what happens in future generations, and in the first instance, on what happens with Isaac, his son. Only if the son grows up to take the father's place is the father's work successful; only if his way is followed does the founder truly found.

Just as Abraham was tested as first father and founder, so Isaac is tested as son and inheritor, the first of myriad generations to follow. Whereas Abraham alone stands at the head of a tradition, Isaac, like every son that comes after him, stands *within* a tradition. In this respect, Abraham, is unique, Isaac is not. For this reason, the transition from Abraham to Isaac may have a more universal significance. As the Bible's paradigmatic instance of inheriting the new way, it illuminates the traditioning relationship between fathers and sons, with all its special difficulties. Other traditions tell comparable stories of first transmission involving first father and son. But for the biblical version, everything is shaped by one decisive fact: the inheritance to be handed down is the patriarchal covenant with the divine, and the special orientation and obligations that it entails. The biblical way of life looks back not to nature or first origins but to a particular event, the covenant between Abraham and God that accompanied the charge to "walk before Me and be wholehearted." [1]

The story of Isaac is thus the preeminent story of a son-of-the-covenant. Isaac is not the Bible's first son; that honor belongs to Cain. Nor is he the prototype of the "natural son," one who stands in relation to his father without special instruction; that honor belongs perhaps to the rebellious Ham, perhaps to the pious Shem or Japheth, the sons of Noah (see Chapter Seven). Isaac is a special

---

1. Another singular event, the giving of the Law at Sinai, will later become the event that forms the people of Israel. But Sinai can be understood as giving specificity to the obligations tacitly implied by the new way established by the covenant made with Abraham.

son of a special father, the first child to be *born into* the new way. He isn't even Abraham's first son; that honor belongs to Ishmael, who was born before the covenant, and he was therefore not circumcised until age thirteen (17:25). We thus expect that Isaac's story will illuminate and address not only the general difficulties of being a son of any father, not only the special difficulties of being a son of a *great* father and national founder, but also, and most important, the unique challenges of being the anointed son of *this* great father-founder— Father Abraham—a man who is patriarchal in the name of the Lord, charged to do justice and to pursue wholeheartedness before the Lord.

Every son, though a person in his own right, is, by virtue of being a son, defined in relation to his parents. To be a son *means* to be derivative and dependent, secondary and subordinate—not only physically and generatively, but also psychically, socially, and culturally. To be the son of a great father is to be still more subordinate, at risk of being permanently overshadowed, even when one reaches one's prime. Sons (and later descendants) of heroes and political founders are throughout their lives frequently torn between worshiping their famous fathers (and ancestors) and striving against them for independence or superiority. But to be the son of a great father whose greatest achievement was to surrender the entire promise of worldly greatness to the divine is to be junior in a most peculiar way. On the one hand, such a son is doubly, even supremely, subordinate: he depends on and looks up to his great father, who in turn looks up to and submits himself to God. On the other hand, it is precisely the father's submission to the divine that largely levels the difference between son and father. Unlike a founder king who towers over his princely son, the biblical father and his son are equal in being equally overawed by the Lord.

It follows from this analysis that the prime exemplar of the biblical son will be far from grand or heroic. On the contrary, he should appear at first rather ordinary and unprepossessing. Precisely to reveal the problem of sonship, especially within the covenant and the new way, the script calls for a man weaker and paler than Abraham who nevertheless will not in the end reject his father's example. The text does not disappoint expectations. Compared to Abraham, Isaac appears drab, passive, and gullible, more victim than hero, a man of few words and prosaic deeds whose wife must be chosen for him and who never converses with God. Yet despite—or is it because of?—the absence of large natural virtues, Isaac finally succeeds his father as a conveyer of the covenant. If such a son can inherit from his superior father and grow into his father's replacement, perhaps anyone can—especially if they remember and take to heart this prime example.

To be sure, the son's relative weaknesses do not, by themselves, make transmission easy; they do not mean that he can readily be molded into becoming his father's and the covenant's heir. On the contrary, as we shall see, there is absolutely no guarantee that the son will gladly follow in his father's ways. His own relative weakness may, if recognized, lead him through envy or resentment to rebel against what his father accomplished or stood for. And even should he instead welcome his inheritance, his limitations may simply prevent him, at crucial times, from being able to defend and protect the new way. Something in addition to the absence or presence of natural virtue is necessary.

In every respect, Isaac turns out to be the perfect candidate for the test of sonship. To grasp his situation, we must revisit parts of the text already discussed, now to consider them in relation to the questions of sonship, inheritance, and perpetuation.

BEING A SON: THE DEDICATION OF LAUGHTER

We first hear about Isaac a year before he is born, indeed, even before he is conceived. In the course of elaborating to Abraham His new covenant, the Lord renames Sarah and announces that He will give Abraham a son through Sarah, a son whom the Lord will then bless (17:16). In response, Abraham first "flung himself on his face and laughed," almost certainly in disbelief that his eighty-nine-year-old barren wife should now bear a child. Instead of expressing gratitude for the news, Abraham then pleads on behalf of his firstborn, Ishmael: "Would that Ishmael ['God Heareth'] might live before Thee" (17:18). God indeed "heareth" both Abraham's laughter and Abraham's plea. He responds by repeating the announcement, this time also giving the prophesied son his name. It is in God's reply that readers (twice) hear Isaac's name for the first time:

> And God said, "Nay, but Sarah, thy wife, shall bear thee a son and thou shalt call his name Isaac [*Yitshaq*] and I will establish My covenant with him for an everlasting covenant for his seed after him. . . . My covenant I will establish with Isaac, whom Sarah will bear you by this season next year." (17:19,21)

For the patriarch, the annunciation of Isaac's birth and name is intended to counter his disbelief and to point him toward his covenantal future. But for the son, the announcement of his birth means that he will be born into—and for the sake of—an existing covenant with God, the reason for his being having been determined for him even before he comes to be. Where Abraham had to choose to leave his family of origin in answer to God's call and later had to choose to accept the offered covenant, Isaac will enter the world with a divinely promised inheritance already laid out before him. He will get God's covenant both as a reward for his father's merit and, more important, for the sake of his own seed after him. Even before his conception, Isaac is conceived as a link in the covenantal chain, the first such link that has ties to both past and future, under the aegis of the Lord. This, at least, is what Isaac's birth is *supposed* to mean; whether he will come to accept its meaning becomes the challenge of his life.

Not only Isaac's place and purpose but also his name is known in advance of his birth. Like his half brother, Ishmael, Isaac gets his birth name from God: *Yitshaq*, "He Laughs" (or "He Will Laugh" or "He Who Laughs"; from *tsahaq*, "to laugh").[2] God names Isaac with laughter in mind, but it is not obvious what He wants the parents—and the son—to be reminded of by means of the name "He Who Laughs," partly because the (grammatically male) subject of the verb "he laughs" is unclear. (The likely "laugher" could be Abraham, Isaac, man, or God.) Isaac's name will certainly recall his father's—indeed, his parents'—skeptical laughter on hearing of his coming birth. For not only Abraham but also Sarah (in the next episode) laughs in disbelief when she overhears the confirmatory news about her childbirth from the three stranger-messengers come to Abraham's tent (18:12 ff.). But "He Who Laughs" also suggests that God laughs at man's ignorance and disbelief and does as He pleases, having as it were the last laugh. As the old Yiddish proverb puts it: *"Der mentsch tracht, un Gott lacht"*— "The human thinks [*or* schemes], and God laughs [*or* is amused]. "He Who Laughs" would also remind everyone that the bearer of the name owes his existence to an act of divine merriment and that he is a divinely inspired eruption of joy into the sad human world.

But Isaac's name does more than commemorate his parents' skepticism and the fact that his coming was not taken seriously. The name "Laugher" is also perfectly fitting for Isaac's status as son-of-the-covenant.

Laughter, whatever its cause, presupposes detachment from the thing that provokes it; a pratfall is not funny to the man who experiences it, nor to a parent

---

2. It is rare for God to name children at (or before) birth: Ishmael and Isaac are in fact the only two instances in Genesis. (Abraham né Abram, Sarah née Sarai, and Israel né Jacob are renamed by God late in their lives.) Ishmael, "God Hears," was the name God announced to Hagar when, after she became pregnant, she ran away from Sarah: "because the Lord hath heard thy affliction" (16:11). When the child was born, Abraham named him Ishmael, presumably out of gratitude for what he thought (wrongly) was the answer to his plea for an heir. In contrast, Isaac, "He Laughs," is named by God in relation to Abraham's ridiculing the announcement of the son who would in fact be his true heir. "God hears" and "man laughs" are richly suggestive names for pondering the difference between man and God, and the difficulty even the best human beings have in understanding and aligning themselves with the divine. In this connection, Abraham's only other act of naming, the naming of the binding place on Mount Moriah as "the Lord sees," may be said to be a correction of the earlier namings of his sons and the thoughts and feelings that lay behind them. God not only hears men's desires; He also "sees for Himself."

whose infant is its victim.[3] In order to provoke laughter, the incongruous or the absurd or even only the whimsical must first be *recognized* as such by an "objectifying" act of the inspecting mind. If great enough, laughter-producing detachment can give rise to alienation in the form of ridicule and mockery: for example, when Lot warns his sons-in-law of the impending destruction of Sodom, their own skepticism and separation from Lot lead them to think Lot is joking or mocking them *(metsaheq)* (19:14). And as we have seen, Sarah forces Abraham to banish Ishmael because he was mocking Isaac or making sport *(metsaheq)* at Isaac's expense (21:9).[4]

But laughter can also be a manifestation of joy and delight. When Isaac is born and named "He Laughs" by Abraham, Sarah makes her joyous laughter explicit:

"Laughter has God made me [*tsehoq 'asah li 'elohim*],
Whoever hears will laugh at [*or* with] me [*yitshaq li*]." (21:6)[5]

Delighted not only by Isaac's birth but also surprised by joy itself, Sarah credits God with the gift of laughter. She marvels at the gracious gift of a child in old age, a wondrous antidote to barrenness and decay, a miraculous seed of renewal sprung incongruously—not to say absurdly—from withering flesh. "He Who Laughs" now refers also to God, who "has made me laughter." Speaking better than she knows, Sarah pronounces comedy divine.

Yet Sarah's joyous laughter is probably not unmixed. Tacitly acknowledging that God has had the last laugh regarding her powers of childbirth, she may be atoning for her skepticism by laughing at her earlier disbelief. And despite her joy, she still feels the absurdity of her aged maternity, enough to hint that others may be laughing not with her but at her. Yet even if her laughter here is purely joyous, laughter remains far from awe or reverence, the religious passions. Abra-

---

3. By contrast, tears evoked by another are a manifestation of sympathy, closeness, and even identification.

4. While laughter implies distance from the thing laughed at, it can create closeness with fellow laughers. In the only example we have of Isaac laughing or engaged in play, Abimelech catches Isaac and Rebekah laughing or playing *(metsaheq)* together—the meaning is clearly sexual—and discerns from this fact alone that they are husband and wife (26:8–9). See Chapter Thirteen.

5. I follow Robert Alter's translation. Alter comments:

> The ambiguity of both the noun *tsehoq* ("laughter") and the accompanying preposition *li* ("to" or "for" or "with" or "at me") is wonderfully suited to the complexity of the moment. It may be laughter, triumphant joy, that Sarah experiences and that is the name of the child Isaac ("he-who-laughs"). But in her very exultation, she could feel the absurdity (as Kafka noted in one of his parables) of a nonagenarian becoming a mother. *Tsehoq* also means "mockery," and perhaps God is doing something to her as well as for her. . . . All who hear of it may laugh, rejoice, with Sarah, but the hint that they might also laugh at her is evident in her language.

ham will not laugh when he banishes the mocking Ishmael. And there will be no trace of distance or levity when, a chapter later, he willingly offers "He Laughs" as a sacrifice to the Lord.

The question for Isaac, carried always in his name, "He Laughs" or "Not Taken Seriously," is whether, like his father, he will traverse the distance from skepticism to submission, especially after his ordeal on Mount Moriah. To be sure, the capacity to laugh betokens the capacity to recover, even from the most horrific experiences. But one cannot live or live well only at a laughing distance from life's true gravity. Will there come a time when "laughter" turns to awe, when the child embraces seriously and wholeheartedly the work of his father and service to his father's God? Will the fear of the Lord enter into the one who laughs, that he not become a mocker, a debunker, a cynic?

His father has every intention that this should occur. When Isaac is newly born, Abraham, in memory of the covenant, dedicates his son to the way of the Lord: "And Abraham circumcised his son when he was eight days old, as God had commanded him" (21:4). Isaac is the first person to be entered into the covenant while still an infant. Whether the sign inscribed in his son's infant flesh will achieve the correlative orientation of that son's adult soul remains—as it does in every generation—something only time will tell.

Isaac, as a small child, is closely identified with his mother. True, Abraham names him (as God had foretold or commanded), circumcises him, and makes a great feast on the day he is weaned. But it is Sarah who fights fiercely for his preeminence, demanding of a reluctant Abraham that he drive out the mocking Ishmael in order that "the son of the bondwoman [Hagar] shall not be heir with my son, with Isaac" (21:10). Though the Lord backs Sarah, Isaac's closeness with his mother may become an obstacle to his stepping into his father's ways, a problem we shall revisit when we come to speak of Sarah's death and of Isaac's taking a wife.

These early hints of the problem of Isaac's sonship are, however, trivial when compared with the story of the binding of Isaac, in which the difficulty emerges full-blown, albeit indirectly.[6] If this story presents the paradigmatic test of being a father, it must also convey the paradigmatic difficulty of being a son. Abraham passes the patriarchal test by delivering up his son as a sacrifice to the Lord. Though Isaac survives the ordeal, at least in body, he is set adrift. He will have a long way to go before he can accept what transpired on Mount Moriah and

6. Recognition of this aspect of the binding story I owe to Kristen Dietrich Balisi, graduate student in the Committee on Social Thought, whose profound paper (written for my seminar), "The Sacrifices of Isaac," is the source and guide of much of the analysis that follows. It was Mrs. Balisi who first made me see that Isaac, as the first person to grapple with an inherited tradition, exemplifies the problem of all subsequent sons of the covenant.

before he is willing to stand toward his sons and his God as Abraham stood toward his. We look again at the story of the binding, this time not to see how it functions as the test of Abraham but to discover how it displays "a vision of Isaac's transitional identity and the corresponding challenge of tradition set before him."

When God addresses Abraham at the start of the story, His words of request/command to the father tacitly disclose the true situation of the son:

> "Take, please, thy son, thine only one, whom thou lovest, Isaac . . . and offer him there for a burnt offering." (22:2)

Isaac is first of all identified as "son," a being defined by his tie to his father: "Take your *son*." His identifying individual name appears last, only after his social identity as his father's unique son has been articulated. Before he is Isaac, Isaac is "son of Abraham." Second, God's relation to Isaac is indirect, mediated through his father: "Take *your* son." At no time in this episode will God speak directly to Isaac; at no time will Isaac have direct access to the divine. It is not even clear from the text whether Isaac hears the divine voice that, at the last moment, stays Abraham's hand from his slaughter. Isaac, as son, is not only defined socially as a son to a father, but he is also related to the divine only through his father's mediation. Third, Isaac is passive to his father's action, Isaac is someone who is to be *done to: Take* your son." Agency belongs to the father, patiency to the son. Finally, Isaac is not only to be taken, he is also to be offered: "and *offer* him."

These four features—social linkage to a past, mediated relation to the divine, passivity, and dedication—are not just idiosyncrasies of Isaac, tied, say, to his allegedly weak character. They are constitutive and essential features of the condition of sonship under the covenant. The first three, in fact, may be attributed to sonship in general. All sons, as sons, are tied to their fathers and born into a social and cultural context that they do not create but inherit. All sons, in every tradition, generally learn about the divine indirectly, through teachings and ways exemplified and transmitted by the fathers. All sons, in every tradition, are, to begin with, passive before the shaping ways of their fathers. But in the tradition that carries the new way, something new has been added. Isaac, as the paradigmatic inheritor of the covenant, is not so much taught by his father as sacrificed: "Inheritance of this legacy is as much to *be given* as to receive." Paradoxical as it may sound, Isaac inherits by being given up to his father's God.

Isaac, as we know from the story, is not destroyed; what is destroyed, rather, is Abraham's claim to paternal possession of his son. Abraham deliberately and knowingly dedicates his son's life to the Lord. But this offering and surrender implies a correlative loss on the side of the son: in the decisive respect, Isaac is no longer simply the son of his father. Whether he knows it or not, he is now also and especially the son of the covenant, a link in the chain that carries the new way. Abraham's near sacrifice of Isaac in effect becomes, for Isaac, the sacrifice of his father, or, to speak more carefully, the rite of passage in which Isaac is forced to say good-bye to his primary identity as the son of his father. Isaac passively is bound and placed upon the altar. He witnesses his father's raised hand poised to strike him a deadly wound. He sees his father halt just before striking (he may or may not hear the divine messenger to whose intervention he now owes his entire existence);[7] he sees his father place the ram on the altar in his stead. Not a word does he say; not a word is said to him. When Abraham returns to his men, Isaac is not with him. For Abraham the test is over; for Isaac it is just beginning. Isaac is on his own.

Not surprisingly, Isaac at this first crucial point in his life surely knows nothing about inheritance and transmission. He almost certainly does not understand the meaning of his near sacrifice. The text's silence about Isaac's state of mind, and even his whereabouts at the end of the tale, is thus wonderfully apt to his existential situation. Isaac knows only that his father was willing to sacrifice him to the Lord, but he knows not why. Little does he understand of what it means to dedicate your son to God; little does he understand of what it means to be so dedicated. At best confusion, at worst dread and anger at his father rule his soul. "My father took his knife to me: how could he? Why did he? What did God want of him and of me? What now should all this mean for me?" Yet Isaac also knows that his father stopped short, that something summoned him to stop, that his father offered a ram in his stead, that his own life was restored to him even as it was being given up. Even if he has not heard the voice of the divine messenger, he has reason to suspect that he owes his life less to his father, more to gracious powers invisible; that his life—like any human life—is an unmerited gift from beyond. How to put all this together is not an easy task for a youngster, and Isaac, like most sons, is not yet ready. Yet the singular experience burns its way into the young man's soul, where it will remain alive and at work on him, until such time as he is ready to learn its significance. For now Isaac is cut loose to fend for himself. Though Isaac is spared, Abraham has "lost" *his* son, Isaac has

7. Yuval Levin (in a personal communication) comments: "Whether Isaac hears the voice of the messenger of God or not seems an absolutely crucial point for determining what he may have learned from this episode. If he does not hear it, then he had seen a terrifying display of his father's power, as if his father has said, 'I can kill you if I wish, and you will live from now on only because I have spared your life.' If he does hear the voice, then he learns what his father knows—which is that Isaac's life is a gift from God. His experience, if he knows what has happened, could show him that he lives because God chose to let him live. It would certainly make a better point if he does hear the voice, but the text simply does not tell us." Levin is surely correct in this assessment. But as we shall soon suggest, Isaac still has something to go on even if he does not hear the messenger.

"lost" his father. Still, below the surface, his father's sacrificial act and his own deliverance live, constituting (along with his covenant-remembering mark of circumcision) the core of his inheritance.

As a trial of Abraham, the binding of Isaac tested which was first in his soul: the love of his own or reverence-awe for the Lord. But as "gift" to Isaac and to his descendants (and to all who read this story), the inherited message of the binding encourages and challenges them to surmount this dichotomy. It teaches that belonging to God's new way permits—nay, requires as a permanent challenge and obligation—the joining of ties to one's family and one's community with one's devoted service to the divine. In this respect the story sets the pattern and poses the perpetual challenge of perpetuation:

> The vision of Isaac the reader receives through his relation to Abraham in the sacrifice vividly portrays what it means to inherit a religious tradition and the unsettling, dangerous nature of perpetuating a tradition. Inheritance, the text is bold enough to say, is problematic and the negotiation of transmission is not easy or beautiful. Still, it provides the very possibility of a community establishing a relationship with God and with each other, for the possibility of something other than mutually exclusive alternatives [loving your own versus serving God]. If covenant is to exist, spiritual experience and commitment cannot be isolated, individual, direct phenomena; they must be rooted in practices that flow from the elder generation to the younger, from the past to the future. Readings of chapter 22 [the binding story] which interpret its events as singular because of its horror miss the truly unsettling conclusion. Without denigrating the greatness of Abraham's action (and the intimation of his understanding of that action) one can see that it is *not* enough. Isaac's position as an inheritor is not singular, but the prototype of every future generation. If this is the case, then the action of Abraham does not hang over the story of Genesis as a ghostly spectre of the past; rather, it permeates the story, setting a precedent which always calls—part request, part demand—for fulfillment. The dedication of children must be repeated with every generation if a tradition is to be maintained and to grow, if the covenant is to be remembered by the people. The child, after all, becomes the parent. Thus, the truly sobering element of the sacrifice is that it is not a completion but a beginning.

But this analysis, notwithstanding its profundity, omits a crucial piece of Isaac's inheritance. What remains with Isaac from the event on Mount Moriah is not only the memory of his father's terrifying deeds but the memory of his father's uplifting speech. The meaning of the deed alone would surely leave Isaac confused and filled with questions, especially if he did not hear the celestial voice. But Isaac has already been taught by Abraham where to look for answers to such questions.

As we argued in the last chapter, the heart of the story of the binding is the conversation between father and son as they went together up the mountain, the conversation that began with Isaac's question and that ended with Abraham's speech that proved prophetic: "God will see for Himself the lamb for the burnt offering, my son" (22:8). Even if Isaac did not hear the divine voice that soon after saved his life, and even if he subsequently feels estranged from his father and from the God to whom he was offered, he will never forget his father's interpretation of the event. Somewhere in his soul he will always remember that singular conversation of transmission in which Abraham counseled him regarding the deep perplexities of life. Somewhere in his soul he will always remember that Abraham taught him to place his trust not in his father but in the Lord.

REMEMBERING THE DEAD, SANCTIFYING THE LAND

Though Isaac must hereafter make his way on his own, choosing whether he will accept his reserved place as inheritor and perpetuator within the covenant, Abraham does not simply step aside. Instead, looking to the future, he seeks to smooth the path to his replacement. In three successive chapters (23–25) Abraham undertakes three deeds that prepare for the transition to the next generation. All three deeds are almost certainly informed by Abraham's awareness of his own mortality; all three deeds are informed by his awareness of what his son will need in order successfully to perpetuate his inheritance. First, addressing the passing generation in a way that will preserve its memory for the living, Abraham purchases a burial place for Sarah (23). Second, addressing the rising generation in a way that will secure its future, he arranges for a wife for Isaac (24). Third, addressing the anticipated needs of future generations, he remarries and produces six half brothers for Isaac, some of whom are progenitors of quasi-kindred and friendly nations (for example, the Midianites) that will prove helpful to the emerging nation of Israel (25). We consider these in order.

As soon as the test of the binding of Isaac is complete, the text signals the need to think about the next generation. Immediately after reporting that Abraham (alone) returned to his men and that he removed to dwell at Beer-sheba, the text tells us that Abraham learns of the fruitfulness of his brother, Nahor, who has sired twelve sons (eight by his wife, Milcah, four by his concubine, Reumah). Of greatest importance, he is also told about the birth of Rebekah, fathered by Bethuel, the eighth son that Milcah bore to Nahor (22:20–24). Abraham and the reader are put in mind of Abraham's ancestral home and of his young grandniece,[8] the woman who will soon play a crucial role in securing the future of the covenant by becoming the wife of Isaac.

But Isaac is not yet ready for marriage: his mother is still alive. Before Isaac can cleave to his wife, he must be completely cut loose from his family of origin and especially from his ties to his mother. It is necessary that, immediately after Isaac's world is set askew on Moriah, it must collapse completely. Already separated from his father, he now has to endure the death of his mother.

> And the life of Sarah was one hundred and twenty and seven years, the years of the life of Sarah. And Sarah died in Kiriarth-arba—this is Hebron—in the land of Canaan; and Abraham came to mourn for Sarah and to weep for her. (23:1–2)

Sarah's death, the first death reported since the call of Abraham, hits the reader—as death generally does—like a bolt of lightning, utterly without warning. Why Sarah? Why now? The placement of Sarah's death immediately after the story of the binding of Isaac invites the reader to link the two events, perhaps even as cause and effect: when she learns what her husband had just done with her son, Sarah drops dead from shock and horror.[9] Or, alternatively, Isaac now being safe and secure as Abraham's heir, Sarah's work on earth is now complete; having nothing important left to do, the matriarch can now leave the scene fulfilled.[10] Indeed, given the closeness of Isaac and his mother, his stepping forth into marriage and adulthood requires that he be separated from Sarah—just as he was separated from his father after Mount Moriah. But whatever its cause

---

8. Rebekah is the granddaughter of Nahor, Abraham's brother, and of Milcah, Abraham's niece. Rebekah is thus both grandniece and great-grandniece to Abraham. (For the discussion of the genealogy and the family of Terah, see Chapter Nine.)

9. The possible linkage is suggested by many commentators. According to a midrash, Isaac himself during the binding is most concerned for his mother:

> Then Isaac said, "Father, hurry, do the will of your Maker, burn me into a fine ash, then take the ash to my mother and leave it with her, and whenever she looks at it she will say, 'This is my son, whom his father has slaughtered.' " . . . When Abraham was about to begin the sacrifice, Isaac said, "Father, bind my hands and my feet, for the urge to live is so willful that when I see the knife coming at me, I may flinch involuntarily and thus disqualify myself as an offering. So I beg you bind me in such a way that no blemish will befall me." So Abraham "bound his son well" (Gen. 22:9). Then Isaac said to Abraham, "Father, don't tell Mother about this while she is standing over a pit or on a rooftop, for she might throw herself down and be killed."

10. Against this view, and in favor of the former, is the fact that the text does not say that Sarah died "in a good old age" or "full of years" or "full of days." Compare the remarks about the deaths of Abraham (25:8) and Isaac (35:29).

or reason, Sarah's death is a heavy blow to Abraham. Annihilated is the bride of
his youth, vanished is the woman to whom he clung notwithstanding her barrenness. Once, when God renamed Sarah and foretold her childbirth, Abraham
had laughed the Bible's first laugh; now, when Sarah dies, Abraham weeps the
Bible's first tears shed for the dead. Abraham's tears are more profound than his
laughter.

We see Abraham mourning and we hear Abraham weeping. But strangely, we
neither see nor hear Isaac. The text is altogether silent as to his whereabouts and
his reaction to his mother's death. (Genesis 23 is the only chapter between his
birth [21] and his sending out of Jacob [28] in which Isaac is not even mentioned.) Later, we will learn indirectly of the depth of his grief (see Genesis
24:67); for now, he is out of sight and out of mind, lost to his father, lost to the
reader, utterly lost.

Sarah's work may be finished, but Abraham's is not. In the first place, he must
attend to Sarah's corpse:

> And Abraham rose up from before his dead, and spoke unto the children
> of Heth, saying, "I am a stranger and a sojourner with you; give me a pos-
> session of a burying place with you, that I may bury my dead out of my
> sight." (23:3–4)

As we approach the Bible's first treatment of burial, we should pay careful attention. For although Abraham acts here without divine instruction, his conduct
may reveal something of the Bible's approach to the newly dead.

What to do with the dead body? The first thing is to get it out of sight, "out
from being before me" (*milfanay;* literally, "from before my face"). The sight of
the corpse before us is most distressing. It assaults us with what we have lost: this
is she but she is no more. It mocks our trust in bodily existence: what is most human turns out to be (at least partly) invisible, what is visible turns out to be less
than human. It impresses us with life's—our life's—fragility: how quickly vanished is the breath of life that animates the dust of the ground. Human beings
cannot live with death staring them in the face. The dead body must be removed.

But how removed? And where? Abraham chooses burial, not cremation, and
direct burial in the earth, not embalming and entombment (say, in a mau-
soleum or a pyramid).[11] The body of *'adam,* the creature formed from the dust
of the ground *('adamah),* is returned to the ground, lifeless but intact and

---

11. Later this form of treating the mortal remains will be contrasted with that of the Egyptians.
Both Jacob and Joseph are embalmed and receive an Egyptian funeral.

"whole." Both respect for the life that was and regard for the lives that remain require respectful treatment of the mortal remains (to begin with, no mutilation).

Proper burial is even more for the survivors than for the deceased. Hence, burial in the earth cannot just be anywhere. A special site, clearly identified and easily found, is set aside as a sacred ground of remembrance. Although located on the outskirts of daily life, it remains close enough to be kept in mind and regularly visited. Abraham will purchase such a place, a cave (me'arah, "dark," "cavern") at the end of a field, the cave of Machpelah, which becomes the burial place of all the patriarchs and their wives.

But there is a political obstacle blocking the way to the burial of Sarah. Though he dwells in the land and has grown prosperous there, Abraham is a stranger among the Canaanites, and strangers generally lack the right of burial. Although God has told him that his seed will later come to possess the whole of Canaan, Abraham must now plead his cause as an outsider. He does so with extraordinary skill.[12]

Abraham begins his remarks to the Hittites, collected in public, by playing the needy suppliant come to beg a favor. He pleads that he is but a "sojourning settler"—for us, a resident alien, one who dwells in the land but only temporarily and as an outsider—yet he asks that they give him with them a "burial holding," a "possession of a burying place" ('ahuzath qaver, an inheritable burial place). The Hittites answer graciously but shrewdly: "You are not just a stranger, you are a mighty prince. Choose, therefore, as you wish from among *our* sepulchres to bury your dead; no one of us shall deny you the use of *his* sepulchre" (23:6, paraphrased, with emphasis added). Though they grant Abraham burial privileges, the Hittites deny him possession; the burial places will remain theirs.

Abraham quickly acts to take advantage of the Hittite offer of burial space; he uses it, however, to press his case for ownership and possession. He bows to the people of the land, showing deference. But at the same time, he commits them to the generous part of their last speech: If you are serious about letting me bury my dead in your land, then—listen up—entreat Ephron to "give me the cave of Machpelah, which he hath, which is in the end of his field; for the full price let him give it to me in the midst of you for a possession of a burying place" (23:8–9). Abraham describes precisely, in legal terms, the specific site he wants—

12. Some commentators see the sale that follows as a revealing example of ancient Near Eastern legal transactions and land deals. Others comment on the shrewd and indirect manner of bargaining and negotiating said to characterize the ancient Near East. But few see the political problem Abraham faces or address the reason why *ownership* of the burial land is so important to Abraham. Robert Sacks, an exception, offers an astute analysis of Abraham's entire negotiating strategy, focusing on the matter of purchase and possession. Sacks's analysis informs our account of the negotiations, yet the speculations about why ownership matters so much for Abraham will be our own.

the cave at Machpelah, at the end of Ephron's field—and he repeats his desire for possession, now adding that he will pay money for it, at full worth. Ephron, flushed out by Abraham's remark from among the congregated Hittites, rises and gives answer before the assembled witnesses ("in the hearing . . . even of *all* that went in the gate of his city" [23:10]): "It's a done deal—I have already given it to you! Bury your dead." [13] Ephron quite clearly does not want to yield Abraham legal possession.

Having provoked Ephron to declare himself in public, Abraham now takes the upper hand. Bowing again to the people, as they are his witnesses, he addresses only Ephron, but in everyone's hearing. Without again using the term, he addresses the vexed question of possession: "You have already *given* me what I want? Good. Now I will *give* you *money* for the field. Take it of me" (23:13; paraphrase, with added emphasis). Abraham, imitating Ephron, will not speak of buying, selling, or ownership, but only of giving: he will give money for the land. Such a "gift" before witnesses, of course, amounts to a purchase.

Ephron, taking the bait and intent on profit, now speaks about money, seemingly to dismiss its importance: "A piece of land worth four hundred shekels,[14] what is that betwixt me and thee? Bury therefore thy dead" (23:15). In this expression of apparent unconcern with money, Ephron continues to refuse what will look like a sale: "What do I need of your gift of money? Just go ahead and bury her." Yet by naming the worth of the land, he tacitly agrees to "an exchange of gifts," not explicitly to a sale. Abraham immediately makes the exchange:

And Abraham heard [*or* hearkened] unto Ephron; and Abraham weighed to Ephron the silver that he had named in the hearing of the children of Heth, four hundred shekels of silver, current money with the merchant. So the field of Ephron, which was in Machpelah, which was before Mamre, the field and the cave that was therein, and all the trees that were in the field, that were in all the border thereof round about, were made sure unto Abraham *as a possession in the eyes of the children of Heth,* before *all* that went in at the gates of the city. And after this Abraham buried Sarah, his wife, in the cave of the field of Machpelah before Mamre—the same is Hebron—in the land of Canaan. And the field and the cave that is therein were *made sure* unto Abraham *for a possession of a burying place* by the children of Heth. (23:17–20; emphasis added)

13. This again is a paraphrase. Three times in his single sentence Ephron repeats, "I have given it thee" (23:11).

14. Comparisons with prices paid for other purchases in the Bible show that this is in fact a huge sum. Ephron is no philanthropist.

Abraham gains exactly what he wanted: not just the burial of Sarah, but an inheritable possession of a deeded burial ground, acknowledged to be his by all the local peoples.

Why all the fuss about ownership? And why about ownership of burying ground?

Ownership of burial land is crucial for both familial and political reasons. Sarah would have received a decent burial regardless of whether Abraham had purchased the cave. But Abraham has his mind also and especially on what is needed for future generations, beginning with Isaac. By purchasing a family burial site, Abraham provides as a permanent holding a special place where the ancestors may always "dwell" among the living, a place of memory and filial piety. Indeed, Abraham is arranging his own place of interment and safeguarding it in advance through purchase so that his son will have a secure place to bury him, side by side with Sarah, his wife and Isaac's mother. Isaac will not need to go begging for burial in Hittite sepulchres; Isaac will not need to bargain as Abraham had done; Isaac will know where his loss should lead him: back to his ancestral roots. Even without further instruction, Isaac at the time of his father's death will be directed to reunite his father with his mother and to recognize in their union the wondrous source of his being. He will be compelled to think of himself as standing in their lineage. He will be moved to recall their deeds. He will be encouraged to try to walk thereafter in their ways.

Abraham's interest in purchasing the burial place is thus part of his education of Isaac. Prevented by their separation from teaching him face-to-face, Abraham must from now on speak to him indirectly. The burial arrangements Abraham makes today for Sarah (and himself) will speak for him to Isaac after Abraham has died, precisely when Isaac will need to hearken.

With the purchase of the cave, the new way also gains a political foothold in the Promised Land. Neither birth in native soil[15]—a "natural rootedness"—nor military conquest, but mortality honored through burial provides the Israelites' first title to land. The nascent nation of Israel is thus tied to the land not by conquest or agriculture, and not even only by God's promise, but also by ancestral piety, by reverence for those who embarked on the new way in special relation to God's promise. The land—more precisely, a portion of it—becomes Israelite land because that is where their founding fathers and mothers are buried: the Holy Land is holy *first* because it is the land where my fathers (and mothers) died. Isaac and Rebekah will be buried in the cave at Machpelah; so too Jacob and Leah. Moreover, during the four hundred years of slavery in Egypt the pur-

---

15. Isaac alone of the patriarchs and matriarchs is born in Canaan; only he has both his beginning and his end in the land. Indeed, he never leaves it.

chased cave at Machpelah, containing the remains of the patriarchs and three of the four matriarchs, will embody the Israelite presence in the land, past and future. Ownership of this small plot of earth will be the Children of Israel's sole legal claim in the Promised Land during their lengthy exile. The way to the political future is linked in sacred memory to the venerable beginnings, beginnings themselves defined by and suffused with a relationship to the Truly Venerable.[16]

ENTER REBEKAH: "A MAN SHALL LEAVE FATHER AND MOTHER AND CLEAVE TO HIS WIFE"

The land having been sacralized in perpetuity, Abraham next addresses more directly the business of perpetuation: finding a wife for his son Isaac. When the story begins Abraham is now "old and well stricken in age, and the Lord had blessed Abraham in all things" (24:1). As he becomes more mindful of death, Abraham must be increasingly preoccupied with the future of the covenant and the dangers that lie ahead. For how can the new way be preserved and handed down without succumbing or reverting to the evils of the uninstructed ways, when it rests on the shoulders of a son who is not only not the man his father was but who is also—since the binding—apparently estranged from him? In Abraham's generation, the challenge had been to sire and keep a son (Isaac) born to the right and proper wife (Sarah). But in the next generation, the challenge will be, first, to find a proper wife for a seemingly less than right man, a wife who will, second, be able to lead him to anoint the proper son as his and the covenant's heir. No father worth his salt can ever be indifferent to who it is that his children marry; but the choice of wife in the present circumstance is especially crucial. In Rebekah, as we shall see, Abraham found more than any father of sons could ask for, a woman of worth who, even more than her husband, will be responsible for safeguarding the new way into the third generation.

Genesis 24, the longest chapter in the book, brings about the transition in the generations from Abraham to Isaac and does so by solving the problem of finding the fitting wife for Isaac. At the start of the chapter Abraham is center stage; by the end of the chapter the spotlight shines on Isaac, now in his father's place. But the central and pivotal roles belong to Abraham's servant and, of course, Rebekah. Not Abraham but only his loyal servant can both embody and effect the continuity between father and son. Sent out by Abraham but returning to Isaac, the servant in speech moves from saying "my master Abraham" to "my master

16. This beginning link to the land, though necessary, is not sufficient. The land finally becomes Israel's not because it houses the bones of the ancestors but because it was given to the Children of Israel, as promised, by God. Yet these patriarchs and matriarchs are distinguished from ancestors in general because they lived their lives in relation to the covenanting and promising God.

Isaac." (The central verse of the chapter reads: "And he said, 'I am Abraham's servant' " [24:34].) Truly to serve Abraham means caring to perpetuate the covenant that Abraham has chosen to serve. Though God does not directly intervene in the events of this story, readers are made to feel that a providential hand is guiding the whole affair. Abraham's servant himself will more than once credit the Lord with leading him to Rebekah. He, in turn, leads Rebekah to Isaac. Rebekah, in due course, will lead Isaac both to Jacob and to the God of his father, Abraham.

Abraham sets things in motion by charging his servant[17] to attend to a most urgent matter: the marriage of his son.

> "Put, please, thy hand beneath my thigh. And I will make thee swear by the Lord, God of the heavens and God of the earth, that thou shalt not take a wife for my son of the daughters of the Canaanites among whom I dwell. But thou shalt go unto my country, and to my kindred, and take a wife for my son, for Isaac." (24:2–4)

Abraham underscores the gravity of the matter by insisting on a sworn oath, using an unusual (indeed, unique) invocation for the name of the divine.[18] Abraham's charge, straightforward on its face, also quietly hints at a double difficulty: a wife has to be found for Isaac because he cannot find one on his own; and she must not come from the local peoples because such a wife would threaten the covenant, partly owing to her Canaanite ways, but partly also owing to Isaac's weakness and/or falling away from his father's path. Back in Abraham's own land and family, there might be a kinswoman whose familial ties might equip her for the task of being wife to such a man.

The servant's response (which implies that Abraham might not be alive on

---

17. The servant is, surprisingly, unnamed throughout the story, though tradition has generally assumed that he is Eliezer of Damascus, the servant named by Abraham when complaining to God about his lack of a son (15:2; see Chapter Eleven). Yet the servant's anonymity here makes sense, on several grounds. First, the crucial identity of the man is exhausted in his serving Abraham. Second and more important, his anonymity increases the reader's sense that it is a mysterious and higher power that is the true agent of this story. This will not be the last time in Genesis that an anonymous man providentially plays an absolutely crucial role in safeguarding perpetuation of the new way.

18. The oath is sworn with the servant's hand beneath Abraham's loins, the place in biblical idiom from which children are said to spring; for example, "the souls . . . that came out of his loins" (46:26). The practice of swearing with the hand on or near the genitalia—there was no Bible on which to swear an oath—was apparently practiced in other ancient societies. It manifests the enormous trust that is being placed in the person who takes the oath: he holds a man's life and posterity in his hands. He also symbolically agrees to permit the man's progeny to exact retribution from him should he swear falsely. In the present circumstance, the servant is swearing on circumcised loins that he will fulfill his oath to secure the future of the covenant of circumcision.

his return) picks up on the hints of fatherly worry and brings the problem of
Isaac's weakness into the open:

> "Perhaps the woman will not be willing to follow me unto this land; must
> I indeed bring thy son back unto the land from which thou camest?" (24:5)

Which is worse, the servant wants to know, returning empty-handed without a
wife (in which case Isaac must either remain unmarried or take a Canaanite
wife), or taking Isaac away from the Promised Land to Haran (in which case he
might get a wife from Abraham's people but will have to live in their midst)?
Abraham's answer—the last words we ever hear from the patriarch[19]—reveals
that he knows well the danger the covenant faces from the weakness of his son.

> And Abraham said unto him, "Guard thyself, *lest thou bring my son back
> thither.* The Lord, the God of the heavens, who took me from my father's
> house and from the land of my birth, and who spoke to me and who swore
> to me saying, 'Unto thy seed will I give this land,' He will send His messen-
> ger before thee, and thou shalt take a wife for my son from there. And if the
> woman be not willing to follow thee, then thou shalt be clear from this my
> oath; only my son *thou must not return him thither.*" (24:6–8; emphasis
> added)

According to Abraham, the Lord, the God who cares especially for Abraham,
will send His messenger to conduct the servant to the right place, but He cannot
guarantee the return of the woman: she must herself be willing to go. But both
at the beginning and at the end of his speech, Abraham insists that Isaac not be
taken back to Haran. Abraham senses that Isaac's return to Haran would not
only separate him from this Promised Land. It would also very likely lead to the
abandonment of God's promise, as Isaac would wander off into foreign ways.
The first and everlasting threat to God's new way comes not from outside enemies but from internal weakness and lack of dedication. Should Isaac leave the
Promised Land, the promise would leave with him, disappearing without a trace
as he gets absorbed into the comfortable and comforting ways of near relatives
who nonetheless follow alien ways. Better no wife at all than a wife that will incorporate Isaac into her family's ways. First and best of all, a wife who willingly
will reject those ways and repeat Abraham's journey from Mesopotamia to
Canaan, to join the Lord's way.

19. We do well to compare these last quoted words of Abraham, expressing his full confidence in
the Lord, with his first quoted words (15:2, 8), expressing fear of dying childless and doubt in God's
providence. Abraham has come a long way.

After swearing the oath as Abraham had commanded, the servant takes ten camels and an ample supply of gifts and heads for Mesopotamia and the city of Abraham's brother, Nahor. Rather than go directly to the home of Abraham's kin, however, the servant stops before the public well at evening and awaits the arrival of the women who come to draw water for their households. The wise servant is not content to settle only for kinship; perhaps because he too knows the truth about Isaac, he wants also a woman of character. He devises a perfect test, a test not only for the woman but also for the Lord, God of Abraham:

> And he said, "O Lord, God of my master Abraham, please make it happen before me this day and do kindness [*chesed*] unto my master Abraham. Behold, I stand near the fountain of water and the daughters of the men of the city come out to draw water. Let it happen that the maiden to whom I shall say, 'Let down, please, thy pitcher that I may drink,' and she shall say, 'Drink, and also thy camels will I give drink,' be the very one that Thou hast chosen for Thy servant, for Isaac, and thus I shall know that Thou hast done kindness [*chesed*] unto my master." (24:12–14)

The servant's test seeks a kind and generous woman, hospitable to strangers and even to dumb animals, who will eagerly and energetically attend to their needs, well beyond the minimum. But will the test of character square with the additional requirement of kinship? The servant prays to the Lord that He should guarantee the coincidence. "Make it occur," says the servant, "that my criteria accord with Your will." Should this happen, the servant (and the reader) will know that the Lord is indeed kind and gracious to his master Abraham.

Whether by chance or divine providence, the servant's prayers are immediately answered, even before he has finished speaking: "Rebekah came out, who was born to Bethuel the son of Milcah, the wife of Nahor, Abraham's brother, with her pitcher on her shoulder" (24:15). The reader is told, but the servant does not yet know, that Rebekah comes from the right family. But servant and reader see at once that she is altogether winning: she is very good looking *(to-vath mar'eh me'od)*,[20] pure (a virgin), and lively. When the servant runs up to her and, understating his need, asks for a little water, she responds graciously in speech and quickly in deed: " 'Drink, my lord' [her first words]; and she hastened, and let down her pitcher and gave him drink" (24:18). "And when she had done giving him drink"—the servant and the reader are kept a moment longer in suspense—"she said, 'I will draw for thy camels also, until they have

---

20. Rebekah is not beautiful *(yefath mar'eh)* like Sarah or Rachel. Beauty is, as we have seen and will see again in the story of Jacob, highly problematic.

done drinking' " (24:19; emphasis added). As the servant watches in amazement, but holding his tongue, Rebekah is true to her word. "Hastening" and "running to the well," in an astonishing flurry of activity, she draws enough water to satisfy fully ten dehydrated camels.[21] Producing a golden nose ring and two gold bracelets, the servant now seeks to learn of her identity:

> "Whose daughter art thou? Tell me please. Is there room in thy father's house for us to lodge?" And she said unto him, "I am the daughter of Bethuel, the son of Milcah, whom she bore unto Nahor." And she said, "We have both straw [*or* bran] and provender enough, and room to lodge in."
> (24:23–24)

Rebekah's answer does more than satisfy. She is not only from the right household; once again she offers hospitality beyond what was asked for (not just lodging, but also food; not just for the men, but also for their animals).[22] The servant, overwhelmed with gratitude, prostrates himself before the Lord: "Blessed be the Lord, the God of my master Abraham, who hath not forsaken His lovingkindness [*chesed*] and His truth toward my master; as for me, the Lord hath led me in the way [*baderekh*] to the house of my master's brethren" (24:27). On seeing and hearing the servant praying, Rebekah, duly impressed, immediately runs off to tell her mother's house all that just happened, no doubt also including the servant's praise of the Lord. The Lord, as the servant says, may have brought him to Rebekah, but it is the servant who first brings to Rebekah knowledge of the Lord.

Rebekah's brother Laban, impressed by her story but even more by the gold ring and bracelets, rushes forth to meet the stranger and invites him home.

---

21. The typical camel will drink roughly twenty-five gallons of water when rehydrating.

22. Some readers, frankly more suspicious than I am about Rebekah, question her behavior in this scene. She speaks to a stranger, hastens to serve him, and responds quickly and favorably to his request for a place to lodge. Her critics charge her with behaving forwardly and immodestly, or at least imprudently. They have a point: as we learn in the Dinah story (see Chapter Sixteen), terrible things can happen to young women who meet up with strange men away from home. Yet the text offers (admittedly subtle) clues that indicate that Rebekah's conduct is unimpeachable. Readers are told that she is a virgin and that no man has known her; perhaps this means that she looks and acts accordingly, that we can read her modesty in her dress and carriage and her innocence in her ingenuous and energetic manner. The servant, who had intended to say, "Let down, please, thy pitcher that I may drink" (24:14), on seeing Rebekah's modesty makes of her a more modest request: "Give me please *a little water* of thy pitcher" (24:17). Through small signs such as these, both Rebekah and the servant take the measure of each other. Moreover, the aura throughout is one of hospitality to strangers, not sexual coyness. Nothing unseemly is even hinted at—though one cannot rule out that Rebekah may have long dreamt of meeting a magnificent man who would take her away and make her his wife.

There the servant relates the whole story, but in a manner artfully designed to secure Rebekah as a wife for Isaac. He prudently makes several alterations that will impress or flatter; he shrewdly omits certain details that point to religious differences or that would make the match seem less attractive. He expands greatly on his master Abraham's prosperity and accumulated wealth; he emphasizes that it all goes to the master's son; and he adds to the content of the oath he was made to swear that the wife should come out of Abraham's father's house, like Abraham himself. On the other hand, he leaves out Abraham's identification of the Lord as "the God of the heavens and the earth"; he makes no mention of the covenantal promise of the land to Abraham's seed; and he fails to repeat Abraham's remark that it was God who had taken him away from his father's house. Most significantly, he omits any mention of not bringing or allowing Isaac to come to Haran. Finally, in recounting what just transpired at the well, he reverses the order of his own deeds, claiming that he put the ring in Rebekah's nose and bracelets on her wrists only after he asked after her origins. The servant concludes by reporting how he "blessed the Lord, the God of my master Abraham, who had led me in the true way [bederekh 'emeth] to take my master's brother's daughter for his son" (24:48). Everything is said to win the consent of Rebekah and her family. They are made to see and wonder at the excellence and prosperity of the father, backed by his special relationship to divine providence, both—prosperity and relationship—now bequeathed to his son.

The servant's speech is persuasive. When he finishes his tale, Laban and Bethuel do not hesitate. Indeed, they answer that they have nothing to say in response, inasmuch as "the thing proceedeth from the Lord" (24:50). They readily accede to the servant's request:

"Behold, Rebekah is before thee. Take [her] and go, and let her be the wife of thy master's son, just as the Lord has spoken." (24:51)

The grateful servant bows down to the Lord, then offers gifts (jewelry and clothing) to Rebekah and to her brother and mother. Then, together with his men and Laban's entire household, the servant feasts and celebrates all night. But Rebekah, to this point, has not been consulted. She will soon have to declare herself.

In the morning, the servant, eager to return, asks to be sent away. But Laban and his mother ask for a delay before they allow Rebekah to go. Fearing that a delay may presage or produce a change of heart or worse, the servant asks for a prompt departure. It is only at this point that Rebekah's own wishes are considered.

And they said, "We will call the maiden and inquire at her mouth." And they called Rebekah and said unto her, "Wilt thou go with this man?" And she said, "I will go ['*elekh*]." And they sent away Rebekah their sister and her nurse, and Abraham's servant and his men. (24:57–59)

Rebekah answers in one word, simply yet decisively: "I-will-go." Rebekah courageously and willingly leaves her father's house in Haran, exactly as Abraham had done a generation before, to go to Canaan. She has a mind of her own and knows her own mind, consenting without hesitation to the proposed marriage.[23]

The servant, now returning, leads the camel train bearing Rebekah back to Canaan and to Isaac. The story ends with an account of their first meeting.

And Isaac came from the way of Beer-lahai-roi; for he dwelt in the land of the South. And Isaac went out to wander [*or* languish] in the field at evening; and he lifted his eyes, and saw, and behold, there were camels coming. And Rebekah lifted up her eyes, and when she saw Isaac, she alighted from her camel. And she said unto the servant, "Who is that man walking in the field to meet us?" And the servant said, "It is my master." And she took her veil and covered herself. And the servant told Isaac all the things that he had done. And Isaac brought her into his mother Sarah's tent, and took Rebekah, and she became his wife, and he loved her. And Isaac was comforted for his mother. (24:62–67)

When Rebekah comes upon her future husband, we see him uncared for, languishing, in the place where Hagar wept; the text reports that "he lifted up his

23. Maurice Samuel offers a beautiful gloss on Rebekah's decision to go at once to meet her intended, against the wishes of her family:

Let us bethink ourselves that Rebekah and her mother—and no doubt the nurse, too—sat up half the night, talking about this fairyland turn in their lives. They saw the miracle as a whole *à laisser ou à prendre* ["to leave or to take"], and since it was *à prendre* ["to take"], Rebekah understood that one did not linger over such things, one did not draw them out with increasingly tedious banquetings and farewells. It was all thrashed out in the night. Even the preparations were begun. How else could she have left on such short notice? When Rebekah's mother joined Laban in saying: "Let the damsel abide with us a few days," she did so out of deference to her son, perhaps also her husband, who is very much in the background. And when she joined in the question, it was with foreknowledge of the answer.

Something more, and that of crucial significance. Instinct—by which I mean the totality of her character—told Rebekah that it would be good for her husband to know, and to remember for the rest of his life, that when she was called to him she turned to her family and said: "I will go—at once."

eyes, and saw, and behold, camels were coming." But Rebekah too "lifted up her eyes and she saw Isaac, and she alighted from the camel," saying, "Who is that man?" On receiving the answer, her energy and perspicacity (both still power-ful) hide behind her modesty, as she veils herself to announce in the language of visibility that she willingly "belongs" to him. The text subtly compares her en-ergy to his limited vision, her modesty to his being comforted for his mother, as he took, wived, and loved her. From now on, Rebekah will exercise her leader-ship indirectly and from behind the scenes. Just as God led Abraham's servant to the right woman, Rebekah, so Rebekah will lead Isaac to Jacob, the right son and proper heir. Thanks to his father's forethought and his servant's genius—not to mention divine providence—Isaac is now on the threshold of adulthood and re-covery, largely because he has married well. We are ready to discover whether he will transmit what he has inherited and whether he will make adequate provi-sion for his own sons to take their place in the eternal chain.

THE LAST ACT OF ABRAHAM

Isaac, now married, is comforted for the loss of his mother. But his father still lives and lives vigorously. Despite his advanced age, Abraham takes another wife, Keturah, and sires six sons by her.[24] The placement and significance of this story are puzzling, to say the least. Because of the sparseness of the account and its ap-parent lack of connection with what comes immediately before and after, we lack evidence to do more than freely speculate. Someone might suggest that, notwithstanding the arrival of Rebekah, Abraham is hedging his bet on Isaac, providing other sons who might step forward should Isaac falter. But the text plainly says that "Abraham gave *all* that he had unto Isaac," while to the sons of the concubine he gave gifts but *"he* sent them *away* from Isaac *his son, while he yet lived,* eastward, to the east country" (25:5–6; emphasis added). It is Isaac, son of Sarah, and Isaac alone whom Abraham anoints as his sole heir under the covenant; the other "natural sons" are sent eastward, toward the rising sun.

Whether he intends it or not, Abraham's marriage to Keturah and the sons he produces with her alters the constellation of nations in the region. In addition to the Mesopotamians from whom he came, the Egyptians from whom he escaped,

24. Commentators are troubled by the suggestion that a man who was described as old in chapter 24 should now be marrying and fathering again. To solve this problem, they suggest that the mar-riage to Keturah and the birth of her sons took place much earlier. But this is highly doubtful. Abra-ham would almost certainly not have taken another wife while Sarah was alive, especially given the trouble with Hagar and Ishmael. When Sarah dies at age 127, Abraham is 137 years old and Isaac is 37. Isaac, we learn in Genesis 25:20, is 40 years old when he marries Rebekah—three years after Sarah's death. But Abraham lives to age 175, thirty-eight years after Sarah's death.

and the Canaanites among whom he lives, Abraham now fathers a host of nations that are closer kin to the children of the covenant. Unlike Ishmael, whom he has also sired but sent packing, these sons—also Isaac's half brothers through a common father—are not purely vessels of enmity for Isaac and his line. The descendants of these sons become the nomadic peoples of the Arabian Peninsula and the region east of the Jordan. Many of them crop up in later stories, both for good and for ill. Perhaps most important are the Midianites, who figure prominently in the future life of Israel. It will be Midianites who rescue Joseph from the pit where his murderous brothers had placed him and sell him into Egypt (37:28); it will be a priest of Midian, Reuel, who takes in the fugitive Moses, escaped from Egypt, and gives him his daughter as a wife (Exodus 2:16 ff.); it will be the same Midianite, now called Jethro, who tells Moses to establish a law for his emancipated nation of slaves (Exodus 18:1 ff.) Much more study would be needed to track all the encounters of Israel with the other Abrahamic nations. But it looks as if Abraham, in his last act, has made the world a little more hospitable for the future of the covenant, blurring somewhat the distinctions between kin and stranger, friend and foe.

At age 175, his work now complete, Abraham "expired, and died in a good old age, an old man, and full of years; and was gathered to his people. And Isaac and Ishmael his sons buried him in the cave of Machpelah . . . there was Abraham buried, and Sarah his wife. And it came to pass after the death of Abraham, that God blessed Isaac his son" (25:8–11). The patriarch is dead and buried. Lest we start to worry about the future, we are told immediately that God Himself blessed Abraham's son.[25] Just when and how is the subject of the next chapter.

25. Abraham does not bless Isaac before his death. He leaves him in God's hands. God does not disappoint: right "after the death of Abraham," the text says, "God blessed Isaac his son."

CHAPTER THIRTEEN

THE EDUCATION OF ISAAC:
FROM SON TO PATRIARCH

*F*ather Abraham, founder of the new way, has done everything that could be asked of him and then some. He has shown his willingness to walk before the Lord and to dedicate his son and his entire future to wholehearted service of the divine. Mindful of the likely gap created between him and his son, he has looked after the succession and taken several worldly measures to increase the chances for his son's success as inheritor of the new way. But more than this no father can do. Sooner or later, every son must take the reins of his own chariot. And when his father dies, every son will necessarily stand forth on his own, revealing at last how he stands in the world and what he stands for. The early career of Isaac suggests that he will have trouble not only filling his father's shoes but also walking in his path.

ISAAC, GENERATOR

After the death and burial of Abraham, the account turns immediately to his sons. As expected, the focus will be on Isaac. Straightaway we are told that "after the death of Abraham, God blessed Isaac, his son" (25:11). But instead of hearing about how Isaac prospered we are treated to a recital (albeit in a mere four verses) of "the generations of Ishmael, Abraham's son whom Hagar the Egyptian, Sarah's handmaid, bore unto Abraham" (25:12). Ishmael, the banished son, is fruitful and multiplies. He sires twelve sons, each mentioned by name, each a prince of what will become one of twelve distinct nations that once ranged widely over the Near East. Then, with his death (at age 137) duly noted, Ishmael disappears permanently from the text with a closing enigmatic comment: "In the face of his brothers [*or* in defiance of his brothers], he fell [from the covenant? upon them?]" (25:18). The Pentateuch's last word about Ishmael, father of princes, reports his "fall."

When the account turns now to Isaac, the contrast with the account of Ishmael could not be greater. Indeed, the beginning words regarding Isaac's career as a patriarch are altogether strange:

And these are the generations of Isaac, Abraham's son: Abraham begot Isaac. (25:19)

Where we expect to find the names of Isaac's children, we are instead told (twice) only about Isaac's father. In no other case in biblical narrative does the account of "generations" begin with the "being generated" of the person whose generations are to be recounted. It seems that the most salient fact for the future generations of Isaac, Abraham's son, is that he was generated by Abraham. Could this, rather than immediate fruitfulness of the sort enjoyed by Ishmael, be the core of what makes Isaac blessed by God?

Be that as it may, this peculiar beginning immediately calls our attention to the theme of transmission. Regarding the generations of Isaac, the question will be not whether Isaac begets children but whether he transmits to them what he received from his founding father. For Isaac is not just another son who one day comes to have sons of his own. As the special son of Abraham, Isaac is born and circumcised into a special covenant that his father had made with the Lord. That covenant, as we saw, seeks to transform the merely natural relations between the generations—and especially the heroic version, in which fathers and sons are rivals for glory—into a vehicle for teaching righteousness and holiness. Abraham, as the father and founder of the new way, knowingly chose to accept such a transformation. Isaac, his son, did not. Rather, the choice was made for him, by his father, even before he was born. The question for the future is this: Will Isaac make the same choice for his own children? Will he be a link in a chain perpetuating the covenant, or will he be the last in its line? Every son of the covenant, whether he knows it or not, shares Isaac's fateful question.

A second salient fact about Isaac's "generations" is his marriage:

And Isaac was forty years old when he took Rebekah, the daughter of Bethuel the Aramean, of Paddan-aram, the sister of Laban, the Aramean, to be his wife. (25:20)

Isaac, as chosen transmitter, has been incubating silently for (the gestational number of) forty years. Now we are going to learn whether what he alone was born to carry forward can be safely delivered, brought to life, and made to flourish. For that task, Isaac's taking of Rebekah as his wife will prove a godsend. At first glance, her pedigree as repeated here is not exactly promising. Though Rebekah is Isaac's blood relative (she is his first cousin, once removed), she comes from outside ways: both her father and her brother are pointedly said to be Arameans. Yet Rebekah will prove to be more devoted than her husband to the Lord, God of his father, Abraham. Though she leaves her father's house to join the household of the God of Abraham, leaving the foreign gods of her family as Abraham had done a generation earlier, it is especially her route to motherhood that contributes to her superior piety.

Having heard that God blessed Isaac and been reminded of his distinguished paternity and his fitting marriage, we expect to learn of his generations, of his progeny. If so, we are, to begin with, disappointed. Through the first twenty years of their marriage, Rebekah is barren. It looks as if the "blessed" Isaac may not only fail to transmit; he may even fail to sire. Rebekah is not the first, nor will she be the last, barren matriarch: Sarah had and Rachel will have trouble conceiving. But where Sarah and, later, Rachel complained to their husbands and induced them to practice concubinage, Rebekah eschews this dangerous expedient. Instead, Rebekah's husband, Isaac, acting on behalf of his wife, appeals to God for help. She may have put him up to it; and he waited twenty years before taking action. But when Isaac is finally moved to act, he turns to the right place:

> And Isaac pleaded with the Lord on behalf of his wife because she was barren; and the Lord granted his plea and Rebekah his wife conceived. (25:21)

Because conception follows only upon prayer, Rebekah (and Isaac) will most likely regard her (their) children not as a human creation and possession but as a gift and a blessing.

But Rebekah's pregnancy is not exactly the one prayed for. The trouble of barrenness is replaced by trouble in the womb, a harbinger of more serious trouble to come. Rebekah, acting on her own, seeks counsel not from soothsayers or pagan deities, but from the Lord.

> And the children crushed [*ratsats*] each other within her, and she said, "If it be so, why am I this ['*im-ken lamah zeh 'anokhi*]?" And she went to inquire of the Lord. (25:22)

Rebekah's question, elliptical and confusing to the reader, may perfectly express her own multiple perplexities and doubts. In part, Rebekah may be concerned about herself: "If pregnancy is this difficult ['so'], why am I pregnant? Why am I alive? What good is my life?" But she may also be concerned about the meaning of the struggle itself: "If there is at last to be an heir ['If things are *so*, set, *just*-so'], why is there this struggle ['why am I divided']? Why is there not a smooth transition to the next generation?" Feeling the struggles within her, she anticipates troubles ahead and goes to inquire what the present struggles mean and what they might presage for the future.

To Rebekah's enigmatic question the Lord gives an oracular answer:

And the Lord said unto her,
"Two nations are in thy womb,
Two peoples from your loins shall issue.
And [one] people over [the other] people shall be stronger [or shall prevail],
And the elder shall serve the younger [or the elder, the younger shall serve]." (25:23)

Rebekah had asked about her present and personal condition. The Lord instead answers about the future and gives a "political," not a personal, interpretation: He speaks of two *nations* in the womb and of two *peoples* that will come out. Rebekah will give birth not just to twins but to two different peoples. Moreover, these peoples will struggle against each other, but the struggle will not lead to mutual destruction: one will prevail and rule, the other will submit and serve. Only one line of her descendants, at most, will belong to the way of Abraham.[1]

But God does not identify *which* line and *which* people will prevail. As indicated, the Lord's last comment can be translated with either brother—elder or

1. Rebekah's double pregnancy and its God-given dichotomous political interpretation stir up speculations, especially in a book that opened with an account of creation produced by separation (division by two) and that will later suggest that there are really only two ways of life, the right way and the wrong way. Could it be that the two nations in Rebekah's womb (later called Israel and Edom) represent perennial human national alternatives, one people bearing witness to the way of the Lord, the other people turning its back on the Lord, preferring instead to rely on human powers alone (in, for example, a revival of the project of Babel)? In this connection, we do well to remember that the line of Esau leads ultimately to Rome, the greatest of the pagan civilizations, the nation that once ruled much of the globe. It was Rome that (in the year 70) destroyed the Second Temple in Jerusalem, leading to nineteen centuries of Israelite exile from the Promised Land. Today, although the Roman Empire is no more, the opposing national outlooks once represented by Israel and Rome remain human possibilities.

Hillel Fradkin follows up this line of thought in a highly interesting recent essay, "Two Nations Were in Her Womb: Contemporary Liberal Democracy and the Political Teaching of the Bible," presented at a conference in Lisbon, Portugal, on "Liberal Democracy and Religion" in June 2000. Fradkin develops his argument from the following suggestion: "Perhaps it [that is, American liberal democracy] contains within itself a modern democratic nation and a Biblical nation, a modern Rome or Edom (the Rabbinic term for ancient Rome) and a modern Israel, separate yet joined in some complicated way. Perhaps liberal democracy became and could only become most successful by reaching an accommodation with the Biblical nation. Perhaps the political teaching of the Bible retains some of its ancient validity."

younger—as dominant or enslaved. In addition, the meaning of "stronger" is ambiguous. Does God mean natural (bodily) strength, strength of arms—or another kind of strength, lodged in wit or tenacity? The meaning of "younger" and "older" is clear; the meaning of "stronger" or "prevailing" is not. Birth order—the order given by nature—will be obvious but not decisive; what is decisive will not be obvious. In this way, God hints that other, nonnatural traits are more important. Rebekah has asked for an interpretation of natural strife within her. God's answer turns her away from nature in order to learn what the future may or should hold. Rebekah is encouraged to look for other qualities that may determine supremacy, though what they are she is not told. Rebekah came to God with a question. She leaves, not with an answer, but another question.

Also puzzling, not least for the reader, is the *status* of God's remarks, especially given their delphic character. Is this a report of predestination, prediction, or perhaps just puzzling advice? Does God look at the intrauterine situation, see the two different natures struggling there, and simply predict the outcome, short and long term? Or does He, by announcing this prophecy to Rebekah, contribute to its fulfillment by influencing the actions of Rebekah and her approach to her husband and children? Is God giving Rebekah license to act in a certain way, required by the difficult situation she now knows that she will have to face? Or is He rather encouraging her to understand that her participation will be needed to bring about the predicted future?

Subsequent events do little to resolve these ambiguities. It is never made clear how God's response to Rebekah's inquiry functions in the subsequent story. To the extent that it is efficacious, however, it seems to work through the efforts of Rebekah herself. She alone hears the prophecy, and she alone must try to discern its meaning (there is no evidence that she tells Isaac of its contents). She alone will prove responsive to the struggles in her household. She alone will be responsible for taking the measures necessary to achieve the predicted or desired result.

Rebekah is smart. She knows, from her troubled pregnancy, that something is up. She asks God, "Why have You put me into this position?" Whatever God is actually saying to her, she seems to hear, "Look, you face a difficult choice, between two alternatives: only one of your two sons will be right for the task. A choice must be made, whether you like it or not, and *you* are the one who is going to have to make it." Whatever she finally makes of the oracle, this much can be safely said: whether with more anticipation or more foreboding, Rebekah comes to childbirth with her eyes on the long-range view, with a concern for the future and not only for the here and now. In this respect she differs from her husband, whose preferences will be governed by more immediate satisfactions.

And when her days to be delivered were fulfilled, behold, there were twins in her womb. And the first came forth ruddy ['*admoni*] all over like a hairy [*se'ar*] mantle, and they called his name Esau ['*esav*]. And after that came forth his brother, and his hand had hold on Esau's heel ['*aqev*] and his name was called Jacob [*ya'aqov*]. And Isaac was threescore years old when she bore them. (25:24–26)

The existence of twins means that this first generation of perpetuation must . confront, right from the start, all the problems that bedevil the transmission of any inherited way. The new way, like the old, must face the dangers of sibling rivalry and divided parental loves. As the Bible shows us repeatedly, nature is not a reliable ally in the work of transmission. The fertile womb, source of life, is also the breeder of conflict. More than one son guarantees rivalry. The firstborn may not be the right one for the birthright; moreover, as we saw with Cain and Abel, the natural prejudice in favor of the firstborn often works, through parental pride and favoritism, to insure that the firstborn will turn out to be the wrong one. Furthermore, superior natural prowess—symbolized by coming first in the race to be born—may not be the superiority needed for handing down the way of the God of Abraham. Indeed, the natural problem of brotherly enmity, made vivid in the Cain and Abel story, is accentuated by twinning. For one thing, twins make manifest the arbitrariness of respecting birth order: even though one twin necessarily comes out first, both are the same in age,[2] and the "younger one" has even more reason than usual to feel the injustice of being relegated to a lower rank.

Twins not only embarrass the principle of primogeniture. They also show powerfully the opposition between brotherliness, ontologically a relation of equality (both from the same womb, here also at the same time), and rule or preeminence, a relation of inequality. Leadership generally requires and fosters inequality. But when leadership is contested between twins, preeminence can be had only by struggling against the person to whom one is naturally most akin. Can it be obtained without destroying one's brother, literally or figuratively?

Finally, the existence of twins is also a powerful vehicle for conveying two problems on the side of parents, parental favoritism and paternal weakness. Nearly all readers of this story will recognize the first problem, but very few will see the second one, far more important in the present context. Isaac's limitations as a perpetuator are revealed to the reader through the device of giving him *two* "firstborn" sons. As we shall see, Isaac prefers the wrong son, and for a bad rea-

2. Here especially so. With the hand of the second on the heel of the first, Esau and Jacob are delivered as a single package.

son. Indeed, Isaac makes little effort to secure the future of the way of the covenant. A beginning clue: the text does not tell us that Isaac circumcised his sons. Though one might quite properly assume that he did so, the text's silence on the subject, especially when contrasted with the clear report of Abraham's circumcision of Isaac (21:4), hints at Isaac's probable deficiency as a transmitter of the covenant. In short: thanks to seeing all the problems created by the birth of Isaac's twins, the attentive reader gets to learn vicariously about the problems the reader himself may confront in playing his part as transmitter.

But the presence of the twins not only exposes difficulties. It also makes possible personal growth and understanding. The existence of twins makes it easier to teach both the father and his true heir some important lessons—about fatherhood and brotherliness, about struggle and suffering. In the previous generation, God Himself had to intervene to reverse the birth order of Abraham's two sons by banishing Ishmael, Abraham's firstborn, against his father's wishes. Here, Isaac must tackle this problem on his own—with the special help of his wife, Rebekah—as a result of which he comes eventually to be able to take his father's place as perpetuator.

Jacob, too, benefits and learns from his dangerous rivalry and strife with Esau. Through rivalry and struggle, he perfects his powers of resourcefulness and endurance. Through struggle and suffering, he eventually discovers something about his own limitations and about his need for God. In all these ways, Rebekah's bearing of twins is pregnant with significance for the question of proper transmission.

Rebekah's twins are not identical. Even their first appearance heralds important differences. Esau looks like an animal, ruddy ('admoni) like the earth ('adamah) and covered with hair. He appears to be the physically stronger, having prevailed in the uterine contest for primacy. In contrast, Jacob, described not by his look but by his deed, comes out grasping Esau's heel, trying, as it were, to trip him up or to pull him back into the womb. Jacob appears energetic, ambitious, and grasping, physically weaker but (quite literally) manipulative.

The initial differences grow with the boys, manifesting themselves in their work and ways.

> And the lads grew; and Esau was a knowing [or cunning: yode'a] hunter, a man of the open field [sadeh]; and [or but] Jacob was a simple [or quiet: tam] man dwelling in tents. Now Isaac loved Esau for the game in his mouth, but Rebekah loved Jacob. (25:27–28)

Esau is out in the wild, an eater of meat, roaming with and hunting the animals. Jacob is a simple fellow who hangs around home (and, we soon learn, stews vegetable soup). The text pointedly contrasts Esau's knowing with Jacob's simplicity or quietude—a contrast, echoing earlier uses of the terms, that is very much to Jacob's credit. Yet as the sequel shows, the text is surely being ironic, at least in part: Esau, the *knowing* hunter, will come home empty-handed, Jacob will show himself to be anything but simple and very far from "perfect" or "wholehearted" *(tamim)* in the covenantal sense.

But the contrast between the sons and their ways of life are, in context, important mainly for the light they cast on Isaac and Rebekah in their roles as parents and perpetuators. Isaac prefers his firstborn, his earthy and manlier son, but the reason for his preference is low, a function of pure appetite. Indeed, as Robert Alter points out, the Hebrew idiom "for the game in his mouth" pictures Esau as a kind of lion bringing home prey in its mouth as well as putting game into his father's mouth. "The almost grotesque concreteness of the idiom may be associated with the absurdity of the material reason for Isaac's paternal favoritism." The perverse picture of son feeding father, where one would expect to see father rearing son, is a telling early clue to Isaac's failure as a patriarch.

Rebekah's love of Jacob is unexplained, but the text's silence implies that it is neither low nor self-serving. It may well be related to the prophecy, with its concern for the future. But Rebekah's preference almost certainly rests also on the differences in character between her sons, for she surely sees and knows her boys. The story of the sale of the birthright that follows immediately shows those differences clearly. "You ask why Rebekah loved Jacob? Listen to this tale, and you will understand the reason."

> Now Isaac loved Esau for the game in his mouth, but Rebekah loved Jacob. And Jacob stewed a stew; and Esau came in from the field and he was famished. And Esau said to Jacob, "Let me gulp down, please, some of this red red [stuff] [*ha'adom ha'adom hazeh*], for I am famished." Therefore is his name called Edom ['*edom*]. And Jacob said, "Sell now thy birthright to me." And Esau said, "Look, I am going to die, so what is to me [*lamah-zeh li*] a birthright?" And Jacob said, "Swear to me now," and he swore to him and he sold his birthright unto Jacob. And Jacob gave Esau bread and lentil stew, and he ate and he drank and he rose up and he went off; and so Esau despised [*or* spurned] the birthright. (25:28–34)

This story offers early insights into Jacob's character, about which more below. But in its local context, the story makes clear how we are to regard the just-mentioned differences in the parents' loves. It casts grave doubts on Isaac's preference for Esau; it illuminates possible grounds for Rebekah's preference for Jacob. Esau, a slave to present appetites, proves his unfitness by the contempt he shows for the birthright; Jacob (unlike that first younger brother, Abel) has the natural gifts to survive and carry on—ambition and striving, cleverness and forethought. Most important, Jacob recognizes the significance of the birthright, the preeminent place of responsibility in the household. The text's final remark, "And so Esau despised the birthright," is a unique instance of editorial comment: in no other place in Genesis does the text itself pronounce judgment on the deeds of any character. In the context of the theme of perpetuation, the meaning is unmistakable: Isaac preferred his firstborn for the sake of tasty food; his firstborn, however, had contempt for the rights and duties of the firstborn, which he spurned (also) for the sake of food. Isaac's choice of Esau over Jacob stands condemned in Esau's contempt for being the chosen one.

The problem for which the trials of Abraham were the solution was this: how to channel the ambition and energy needed for founding a great nation into the path of wholehearted devotion to the requirements of the covenant. The problems for "the generations of Isaac" are different: First, how to replace the order of birth and strength with the order of merit, without fratricide. Second, how to do this with the support and blessing of a less-than-right father, who, to begin with, foolishly prefers the wrong son. To transmit Abraham's new way, a reversal is needed, but how can it be arranged?

Clever Jacob may think he has solved the problem in purchasing the birthright. Moreover, in agreeing to the sale, Esau shows himself perfectly willing to change places, thereby confessing to the unfitness that makes such an exchange absolutely necessary. But for reasons that will appear more clearly when we discuss this story again in the next chapter, Jacob's solution is inadequate. Jacob cannot make himself the heir of his father without his father's knowledge and blessing. Finally only Isaac can solve the problem of the generations of Isaac—with some extraordinary help from his wife.

ISAAC IN THE WORLD

Having introduced the problem within Isaac's household, the text leaves it simmering and moves to Isaac's career on the world stage. His exploits, which are all described in but one chapter (Genesis 26), present echoes of the life of his father: there is a famine; there is a visit to his father's friend Abimelech, with whom Isaac repeats his father's wife-sister subterfuge and with whom he also establishes a covenant at Beer-sheba; there is a redigging of his father's wells. But there are no great adventures: no trip to Egypt, no war of the kings, no conversation with God about Sodom and Gomorrah. The world stage of Isaac's adventures is in fact geographically limited; he spends his entire life in Canaan, in the Promised Land. And even in the episodes in which he imitates the deeds of his father, Isaac shows he is no Abraham. At the same time, however, his achievements are not negligible. In worldly terms, he not only survives but flourishes—with a little help from the Lord.

From the start, the story of Isaac's worldly career invites us to compare it with that of his father: "And there was a famine in the land, *beside the first famine that was in the days of Abraham*. And Isaac went unto Abimelech, king of the Philistines, unto Gerar" (26:1; emphasis added). With the recurrence of famine, Isaac, like Abraham before him, heads for the southwest, toward Egypt, stopping on the way to visit with his father's friend Abimelech. It is here where Isaac will make his mark; it is here where he can best be compared to his father. In order to arrange for Isaac's proper venue, the Lord appears to him in Gerar and addresses him for the first time:

> "Go-not-down [*'al-tered*] into Egypt; dwell in the land I will tell thee of. Sojourn in this land and I will be with thee and I will bless thee; for unto thee and unto thy seed I will give all these lands, and I will establish the oath that I swore unto Abraham, thy father. And I will multiply thy seed as the stars of heaven and will give unto thy seed all these lands; and by thy seed shall all the nations of the earth bless themselves, because Abraham hearkened to My voice and kept My charge, My commandments, My statutes, and My laws." (26:2–5)

When God spoke first to Abraham, He bade him to go; when He speaks first to Isaac, God bids him to stay put. He commands Isaac not to go down into Egypt but to remain in Gerar, where He promises to be with him and to bless him. Isaac is not a man fit for an encounter in Egypt; he can succeed only in less hostile territory, and then only with God's promised help. Reiterating many parts of His initial promise to Abraham—the gift of land and countless seed, the source of blessing to all the nations of the earth[3]—God now transfers His promises to Isaac simply because of his father's obedience. Isaac makes no verbal reply, but simply conforms to God's request: "And Isaac remained [*or* dwelt] in Gerar" (26:6).

Isaac immediately encounters a problem with the Gerarites on account of his wife. Showing interest in Rebekah, "the men of the place asked about his woman" (26:7). Isaac, alarmed by their inquiry, passes Rebekah off as his sister, fearing to admit that she is his wife lest they should kill him in order to possess her. When this episode is compared with Abraham's use of a similar stratagem a generation earlier (see Chapter Ten), important differences between father and

---

3. Nothing is said to Isaac about his or his seed's possessing the gates of Isaac's enemies.

son appear. Equally important, we discover that a single virtuous leader—such as Abimelech—cannot by himself establish decent ways for a whole people. Abimelech, king of Gerar, is a naturally noble fellow, as he displayed in his earlier dealings with Sarah and Abraham made clear. But as we learn in this episode and also in their later struggles with Isaac over the wells, Abimelech's people do not inherit his gentlemanly virtues. Indeed, this might be the text's main purpose in showing us two Israelite generations (Abraham and Isaac) dealing with the same Abimelech and his men: a naturally inferior man (Isaac) may succeed as an inheritor and perpetuator of righteousness because he lives under God's covenant, whereas a naturally superior man (Abimelech) may fail because he and his people know not the Lord.

When Abraham went abroad, he had prudently anticipated the danger to himself; well in advance, he told Sarah in advance to say, wherever they went, that she was his sister. Isaac, less sophisticated or farsighted, responds only when the risk is right upon him. Moreover, in Isaac's hands, the deception does not succeed.

> And it came to pass, when he [Isaac] had been there a long time, that Abimelech king of the Philistines looked out at a window, and saw, and behold, Isaac was sporting [*yitshaq metsaheq*] with Rebekah, his wife. (26:8)

Whether because he is innocent or reckless, whether loving or lustful, Isaac imprudently exposes his own deception. He gets caught in broad daylight—by the king himself, looking out a window (!)—engaging in sexual play with his wife.[4] Fortunately, Abimelech remains honorable.

> And Abimelech called Isaac and said, "Surely, behold, she is thy wife; how couldst thou say that she is thy sister?" And Isaac said to him, "Because I said, 'Lest I die because of her.' " And Abimelech said, "What is this thou hast done unto us? One of the people might easily have lain with thy wife, and thou wouldst have brought guilt upon us." And Abimelech charged all the people, saying, "He that toucheth this man or his wife shall surely be put to death." (26:9–11)

---

4. Robert Alter comments: "The meaning of the verb here is clearly sexual, implying either fondling or actual sexual 'play.' It immediately follows the name 'Isaac,' in which the same verbal root is transparently inscribed. Thus Isaac-the-laugher's birth is preceded by the incredulous laughter of each of his parents; Sarah laughs after his birth; Ishmael laughs-mocks at the child Isaac; and now Isaac laughs-plays with the wife he loves. Perhaps there is some suggestion that the generally passive Isaac is a man of strong physical appetites: he loves Esau because of his own fondness for venison; here he rather recklessly disports himself in public with the woman he has proclaimed to be his sister."

In the earlier episode with Abraham and Sarah, the wife was taken by the king himself, and God had to intervene to keep Abimelech from touching her. When asked to explain his wife-sister subterfuge, Abraham answered that he believed the place lacking in the fear of God. Here, the danger comes not from the king but from his subjects. In explaining his deception, Isaac stammers out only something about his own fear of death and says nothing about the people's fear of God. But Abimelech knows his subjects. Acting swiftly, this time without any need for divine prompting, he himself takes the place of God and puts them in fear of their king, a substitute for the fear of God: he charges his people, on penalty of death, to keep away from Isaac and Rebekah. Thanks to Abimelech's nobility and firmness, the marriage of Isaac and Rebekah, crucial for the perpetuation of the new way and put at risk by Isaac, is restored and protected.[5]

Isaac, under kingly protection in Gerar, now begins to prosper, thanks both to his own efforts and to God's providence:

Isaac sowed in that land and found in the same year a hundredfold; and the Lord blessed him. And the man waxed great and grew more and more until he became great. And he had possessions of flocks and possessions of herds and a great many servants. (26:12–14)

Isaac is the first and only successful farmer in Genesis; he becomes wealthy also in livestock. But although he becomes someone to be reckoned with, he has as yet no firm possession in the land. The wells that Abraham had dug during his sojourn there the Philistines had filled in with earth, not only blocking their life-giving water but also effacing Abraham's tacit claim to the land. Now, envying Isaac's spectacular prosperity, the Philistines ask him to leave their land. Isaac departs quietly and camps in the nearby dry riverbed (*nachal*; in Arabic, *wadi*); there he digs again the stopped-up wells of his father, calling them by the names his father had called them. His servants succeed twice in digging a new well of flowing water, but the herdsmen of Gerar lay claim to them. In each case Isaac retreats, avoiding confrontation, but he and his men continue to dig for water. On a third try, a well is dug for which the men of Gerar do not contest. Grateful

5. This episode very likely takes place before the birth of the twins, reported in the previous chapter of Genesis: the presence of children would have made the wife-sister subterfuge impossible. (The alternative—namely, that the children are grown when Isaac goes to Gerar—seems highly unlikely.) In the case of famine, all would go together; and, in the sequel, the grown sons are still present to Isaac's household. Leading with the story of the twins, out of strict chronological order, permits the highlighting of the problem of perpetuation. And placing the wife-sister story in the context of Isaac's international relations exposes the difference between another nation and the incipient nation of Israel, founded on a divine covenant.

and relieved, Isaac names the place Rehoboth ("broad place," "room"), saying, "For now the Lord hath made room for us and we shall be fruitful in the
land" (26:22).

When Isaac returns to Beer-sheba, the Lord appears to him for the second
time:

> And the Lord appeared unto him the same night and said, "I am the God
> of Abraham, thy father. Fear not, for I am with thee and I will bless thee,
> and multiply thy seed for My servant Abraham's sake." (26:24)

Isaac in response builds an altar and calls on the name of the Lord. It is his first
explicit act of recognition of the divine. At this point Abimelech and his henchmen come from Gerar to pay Isaac a visit of state. Acknowledging that "the Lord
was with thee," they propose a covenant of peace with Isaac in order that "thou
wilt do us no hurt, as we have not touched thee, and as we have done thee nothing but good, and have sent thee away in peace: thou art now the blessed of the
Lord" (26:29).[6] Isaac makes a feast for his guests and the following day they
swear an oath and enact a covenant. Isaac, acknowledged by the Philistines to be
"now the blessed of the Lord," is now explicitly recognized as a national entity.
The same day water appears for the first time in the newest well—Isaac called it
Shiv'ah—recently dug at Beer-sheba. As a man living among other men, Isaac is
now established in the promised land.

Like any man living among other men, Isaac must make his own way in the
world. He must dig again the wells his father had dug, he must make again the
treaties that his father had made, he even has to name the same city Be'er-sheva,
but for a reason of his own.[7] In the world, Isaac—like each member of any new
generation—must fend for himself. But Isaac is not just an ordinary man living
only in relation to the world, to the earth and his fellow creatures. He is also a
link in the covenantal chain, living in relation to God, His promise and His
charge. In this respect, Isaac is not simply on his own. Rather he may—nay, he
must—rely on the foundations laid by his father, Abraham, and seek to transmit

6. Robert Sacks comments: "Abimelech seems to have understood the full power of Isaac's apparently foolish actions. In Verse Twenty-nine he shows that he understands what it means to be blessed
of the lord even though he himself is not so blessed. Somehow he has seen that Abraham succeeded
in the one crucial point where he himself failed. Abraham was able to establish a house and a tradition, but Abimelech's great virtues are to die with him." As we shall argue in the sequel, Isaac may already be blessed of the Lord, but he has yet to succeed in making secure the tradition of Abraham.

7. When Abraham made a covenant with Abimelech, he named the place Be'er-sheva ("the well of
seven" or "the well of swearing," in relation to the oath they swore and to the seven ewe lambs Abraham had set aside as a witness that he had dug the well (21:28–32). Isaac names the place Shiv'ah,
meaning "good fortune," and the well and the city Be'er-sheva, "well of fortune" (26:32–33).

them to his sons. It is this inherited God-revering way of life that Isaac must hand down if it is to exist in the next generation. It is this activity that should be the central focus of his patriarchal life. There is no guarantee that the wells fathers dig will be there for their sons. But if fathers maintain their relationship with God and teach their sons the ways of the covenant, these can survive intact into the next generation, serving as a wellspring of moral and spiritual guidance to elevate and dignify human life.[8]

Although he has succeeded in providing necessary food and life-giving water, although he has grown prosperous and gained recognition and a place in the land, Isaac has not succeeded as a patriarch of the new way. True, he has made it on his own as a man in the world. True, he has reopened the life-preserving channels begun by his father. But he has fallen short as a transmitter of his father's way of life. He not only prefers the wrong son and for a wrong reason; unlike his own father, he makes no provision for the marriage even of his favorite son, Esau. To call the reader's attention back to this deficiency, the last verses of the chapter that reports Isaac's worldly successes starkly point to the crucial area of Isaac's failure. Esau, at the revelatory age of forty, quite on his own takes two Canaanite wives,[9] wives who "were a bitterness of spirit unto *both Isaac and Rebekah*" (26:35; emphasis added). Isaac, though materially blessed and prospering, has averted his gaze from both the future and the past. He has lived with apparently little awareness of what he and he alone can transmit. But when Esau, his favorite, takes foreign wives, even Isaac is dismayed. The covenant with Abraham is in grave danger. Isaac seems impotent to save it.

REBEKAH TO THE RESCUE

Into the breach moves Rebekah. Thanks to her, Isaac is brought into a proper relation to his sons, his father, and the covenant; thanks to her, Jacob is compelled to recognize—and obtain—the blessings of his father; thanks to her, fratricide is (for the time being) averted; and thanks to her, Jacob is sent off to find a proper wife, on a journey that will also tame his cleverness and bring him at last into a more proper relation to his brother and, even more important, to God.

Rebekah does this in the only way possible, not by force and not by confrontation, but by guile. At the same time, she acts with tact, delicacy, and affection; though she arranges his deception, she does whatever she can to preserve

8. I owe the insights of this paragraph and a few of the formulations to Yuval Levin.

9. "When Esau was forty years old, he took to wife Judith the daughter of Beeri the Hittite, and Basemath, the daughter of Elon the Hittite" (26:34). Esau's wives are daughters of men whose naturalistic names mean, respectively, "well" and "oak tree." Esau, the earthy man, finds earthy women.

and promote the dignity of her husband, whom she serves out of love. By the end, Rebekah's Isaac rises to the work of transmission and becomes truly the son of Abraham. And Rebekah's Jacob, under the command first of his mother and then of his father, goes off to prepare himself to take his father's place as a link in the covenantal chain.

The transformation occurs in the famous story of the stolen paternal blessing, a drama in seven scenes (Genesis 27:1–28:8).[10] In each scene, there is conversation between two and only two people: Isaac appears in five scenes, Jacob in four (once disguised as Esau), Rebekah in three, Esau in two. Isaac alone speaks with all the others, Esau speaks only to his father, neither Rebekah nor Jacob speaks with Esau. By the end of the story, the household is reordered and the covenant is preserved. A careful look at each scene shows how Rebekah enables Isaac to discharge his responsibilities as transmitter of the new way.[11]

> And it came to pass that when Isaac was old and his eyes were dim so that he could not see, he called Esau, his elder son [*literally,* his large son: *beno hagadol*], and he said unto him, "My son [*beni*]," and he said unto him, "Here-am-I [*hineni*]." And he said, "Behold, please, I am old; I know not the day of my death. So now, take up please thy equipment, thy quiver and thy bow, and go out to the field and hunt me game; and make me a tasty dish [*mat'amim*] such as I love and bring it to me that I may eat, so that my soul [*nafshi*] may bless thee before I die." (27:1–4)

10. The word for "blessing," *berakhah*, occurs in the story a completed number of times (seven), and its verbal form occurs an emphatic thrice seven times (twenty-one).

11. Yuval Levin has shown me how the structure of this story reveals Rebekah's double education of her husband and her son, referred to in our text above:

Isaac calls and sends out the wrong son
  Rebekah sends the son after the father
    Jacob deceives his father
      Isaac discovers his error
    Rebekah tells Jacob to flee
  Rebekah sends the father after the son
Isaac calls and sends out the right son

Within the education of Isaac by Rebekah, there is an education of Jacob by Rebekah. Jacob goes from confident deceiver to nearly helpless and fearful wanderer, cutting his self-reliant arrogance down to size, while Isaac learns of his own error. Isaac goes from sending the wrong son for the wrong reason (Esau, to get food) to sending the right son for the right reason (Jacob, to find a proper wife); and Jacob goes from clever homebody to (more) humble wanderer. He has been given the task of carrying on the covenant, and has been made better suited for taking it on. (Yuval Levin, private communication.)

Isaac, old and dim-sighted,[12] fears his death is near. When Abraham was in a similar condition, he arranged for a wife for his son. Isaac, in contrast, merely wants a last good meal so that he can bless before he dies. His relation to his beloved Esau is, again, through appetite, hunted food. But Isaac greatly exaggerates the imminence of his death; he lives for at least another twenty—and probably closer to forty—years.[13] Like his Esau (who, in the birthright story, also exaggerated the nearness of his death), Isaac will give something permanent and irrevocable—*his* "birthright"—in return for the transient pleasure of a good meal.[14] In this first reported father-son conversation, various words and phrases—"My son [*beni*]," "Here-am-I [*hineni*]," "that I love"—offer perverse echoes of the awesome story of the binding of Isaac, none of them to Isaac's favor: Isaac, taking the part of the Lord, calls his son, in the place of Abraham, for a meat "offering" "such as I love" (compare "whom thou lovest"; 22:2). Moreover, in speaking about the blessing he is about to offer, Isaac makes no mention either of God or of Abraham: "that *I* may eat, so that *my soul* may bless thee before I die." Yet in this very self-absorbed remark, Isaac may be speaking better than he knows. He identifies himself as the eater but unwittingly refers to something else within him—his innermost self—that will give the blessing.

Rebekah, ever alert and well attuned to her surroundings, has been listening in on Isaac's conversation with Esau. The account of her first reported action since the birth of her twins begins by noticing the sharpness of her hearing (in contrast to Isaac's dimness of sight): *"And Rebekah heard* when Isaac spoke to Esau, his son"* (28:5, emphasis added). As Esau goes off to do his father's bidding, Rebekah is quick to formulate a plan of action: Jacob, disguised as Esau, must receive the father's final blessing. Rebekah's plan is more than bold. It is fraught with certain danger. Even if it succeeds, the deception will necessarily be discovered when Esau returns, and there will no doubt be hell to pay. Isaac will be distressed, Esau will be furious, Jacob may be forced to escape, she may lose her favorite son. All this the prudent Rebekah surely knows when she concocts her scheme, yet she also knows she has no other choice. She must act now and be

12. The story will touch on all of Isaac's five external senses, four of which are either defective (sight) or easily deceived (touch, smell, and taste). Isaac's only intact sense, hearing, he does not trust. Isaac, a sensualist, is misled by his senses; to begin with, he does not hearken to the word.

13. Isaac dies at age 180, sometime after Jacob returns from his twenty-year journey to Paddanaram. Other calculations, to be shown later, suggest that Jacob may have been as old as 77 when he left home (at the end of the present story). Given that the twin boys were born when Isaac was 60, we estimate his age at this time to be 137 or less, with forty-three or more years left to live.

14. Whereas Esau was ravenously hungry, Isaac is interested in delicacies: the root of the word translated "tasty dish" is *tam*, "tasty."

prepared to handle the consequences. Despite its certain costs, she does not hesitate to put her plan into effect.

Rebekah summons Jacob, informs him of the situation, and commands him to play his part:

> "Behold, I heard thy father speak unto Esau, thy brother, saying, 'Bring me game and make me a tasty dish, that *I may eat* and *I may bless* thee *before the Lord* before I die.' So now, my son [*beni*], *hearken to my voice* [*shema' beqoli*], to that which I *command* thee. Go now to the flock and fetch me from thence two good kids of the goats; and I will make them into a tasty dish for thy father such as he loveth. And thou shalt bring it to thy father that he may eat, so that he may bless thee before his death." (27:6–10; emphasis added)

The contrast between Isaac's and Rebekah's relation to their sons is striking. Isaac, feeble and blind, pleads for a fine dinner (twice in two sentences Isaac says "please"); Rebekah, energetic and sharp-eared, speaks and commands with authority yet is mindful of the divine. Whereas Isaac speaking to Esau had forgotten to mention God, Rebekah, in reporting her husband's words to Jacob, improves them, placing the Lord's name, so to speak, onto Isaac's tongue—and also into Jacob's mind. (This is the first time in the text that the name of God is mentioned in Jacob's presence.) Soon, thanks to Rebekah's successful plotting, Isaac will bespeak his own and God's blessing upon the proper son. But here, even as she embarks on deceiving him, Rebekah tries to enhance Isaac's dignity and Jacob's respect—both for his father and his father's God—by improving upon Isaac's piety and sparing him humiliation in the eyes of her son. She also impresses upon Jacob that the blessing to be given will be given "before the Lord."

Rebekah has to reckon not only with Isaac's weakness but also with Jacob's cleverness and his penchant for self-reliance. Having gotten his attention with her report, she pleads for his compliance: "Now you, my son, hearken to my voice [*shema' beqoli*], to that which I command thee" (27:8), and she outlines the plan to get Isaac's blessing bestowed on Jacob.[15] Jacob resists, not because he thinks such deception is wrong but because he fears that it will fail: his father will grope at him and discover that he is not hairy Esau but smooth Jacob; he, Ja-

---

15. Note that while Isaac has sent Esau out into the Canaanite fields to hunt the food he desires, Rebekah sends Jacob to the family's own flock for that purpose. The two sons get wives in the same fashion (Esau from among the Canaanites, Jacob from the family's own daughters). The text may be quietly hinting that Isaac is at fault for Esau's seeking of wives from among the Canaanite women. (I owe this observation to Yuval Levin.)

cob, will be an imposter in Isaac's eyes; and he will earn Isaac's curse and not his blessing (27:11–12). Jacob, shrewd and self-reliant, does not want trouble. More important, perhaps, Jacob knows that he already owns the birthright, and he seems not yet to understand why he needs his father's—and God's—blessings.

Rebekah persists: "Upon me [be] thy curse, my son, only hearken to my voice [*shemaʿ beqoli*] [*that is,* obey me] and go take [them] to me" (27:13).[16] Moved by her earnestness and her self-sacrificing attitude ("upon me be thy curse"), Jacob respectfully submits and heeds his mother's voice. Unlike Isaac, who is dim of sight and a partisan of taste and who will later rely on touch and smell when he should have trusted his hearing, Rebekah holds her son through speech and command. Jacob, like the true son of the covenant, listens, hearkens to her voice, and obeys. Tradition, passed on through command and story, depends on hearing and hearkening—not on seeing and fending for yourself (compare Ham's relation to Noah). Rebekah overcomes her son's resistance and brings him closer to the line of his fathers.

In a flurry of activity, Rebekah now prepares the food, transforming goat meat into a likeness of the delicacy her husband loves. Next she sets about transforming Jacob into a likeness of Esau, the son her husband loves. She takes Esau's clothes and clothes Jacob with them,[17] puts goatskins on his hands and the smooth of his neck, and puts the delicate dish and the bread that she had prepared "into the hand of Jacob, her son" (27:14–17). Through her command, guile, and competence, the future of the covenant now lies, as it were, in Jacob's hands.

The deception of Isaac, cruel though it may seem, will turn out to be a blessing in disguise, and not least for Isaac himself. Isaac is, to begin with, presented pathetically. When Jacob comes to his father with the meal Rebekah prepared and calls to him, "Father," Isaac answers, "Here-am-I; who art thou, my son? [*hineni mi 'atah beni*]" (27:18)—an exchange that echoes, to Isaac's disfavor, the parallel exchange one generation earlier, when Isaac, walking up Mount Moriah, calls, "Father," and Abraham answers, "Here-am-I, my son" (*hineni beni*; 22:7). In Isaac's mouth, *hineni*, "Here-am-I," turns out to be a parody; for how can he be fully present to "Who are you"? Unwittingly, Isaac confesses his weakness: he

16. Rebekah's repeated use of *shemaʿ beqoli* deserves notice. This phrase seems to be used only by God and by women in Genesis, and one of God's uses (21:12) is to tell Abraham to listen to his wife. Women, inferior in power, must rely on their power of speech. This may also imply that they are more attuned to the biblical preference for hearkening over seeing for yourself.

17. This changing of clothes symbolizes the change that proper inheritance must work upon natural birth order. It reminds of the famous story of corrective justice. Two boys, one small and one large, owned coats that did not fit; the small boy owned a large coat, the large boy a small coat. The wise man, holding that justice consists not in having what is your own but in having what is fitting, exchanges the coats of the boys. (See Xenophon, *Education of Cyrus* I.3.17.)

does not know one son from the other—and in the sense that really matters, not only now. Jacob, in response, lies to his father: "I am Esau, thy firstborn [*bekhorekha*].[18] I have done according as thou badest me. Arise, please, sit and eat of my game, that thy soul [*nafshekha*] may bless me" (27:19). (Jacob does not add, as Rebekah had done, "before the Lord.")

Isaac is or soon becomes suspicious, partly because of Jacob's voice, partly because of the speed with which "Esau" has returned, but mostly, it seems, because of the answer Jacob gives to his question about how he found food so quickly: "Because the Lord your God brought it before me" (27:20). Jacob shrewdly may be giving expression to what he takes to be Esau's piety: for Esau, Jacob's remark implies, the Lord is the god of the hunt. Alternatively, Jacob, caught off guard, may be speaking for himself in a way that Esau never would, thus arousing Isaac's suspicion: Esau never speaks of the Lord anywhere in the text, and seems unlikely to do so here. But whatever his meaning, Jacob's mention of the Lord distances Jacob from Him: he calls the Lord "your God," not "my God" or "our God." Jacob, speaking better than he knows, puts the Lord into Isaac's—and the reader's—mind, and raises the possibility that God is somehow at work behind and through this poignant episode. However his suspicions are aroused, Isaac, at this critical moment, calls Jacob near and, groping him, seeks to determine his true identity. Isaac prefers to trust his deceived sense of touch to his well-functioning sense of hearing: "The voice is the voice of Jacob but the hands are the hands of Esau" (27:22). Those who do not hearken are destined, it seems, to learn in other ways.

Isaac's other senses also deceive him. He eats and drinks but does not notice the difference between venison and goat. Any remaining suspicion is dispelled when he calls Jacob over to kiss him and smells the smell of his garments: for Isaac, smell, the lowest and most animal of the senses, turns out to be decisive. Immediately, without further ado, Isaac pronounces on Jacob the blessing he had intended for Esau, beginning with a rapturous encomium to Esau's smell: "See, the smell of my son is as the smell of a field [*sadeh*] which the Lord has blessed" (27:27). Isaac, the heir of God's covenant, delights especially in the smell of the wild field of the hunter, the place of bloodshed,[19] so much so that he imagines the wilderness to be the recipient of the Lord's blessing. Nowhere in our text does the Lord bless a field or show any delight in hunting or bloodshed.

18. A lawyer for Jacob might claim that Jacob does not altogether lie. Now the owner of the birthright *(bekhorah)*, Jacob is now de jure Isaac's firstborn *(bekhorekha)*. Isaac had summoned Esau not as the firstborn but as the greater or elder son, his "great or large son" *(beni hagadol)*.

19. The field is the place where Cain lured Abel in order to murder him. Isaac, though a gentle farmer and herder himself, prefers the wild world of the hunter to the tame world of the shepherd or farmer.

Isaac now pronounces the blessing proper:

"May God give thee of the dew of heaven and of the fat of the earth, and
plenty of corn and wine.
May peoples serve thee and nations bow down before thee;
Be lord over thy brethren and may thy mother's sons bow before thee.
Those who curse thee be cursed, and those who bless thee be blessed."
    (27:28–29)

The blessing, in three parts, is largely material and political: prosperity from the
soil; preeminence in, mastery over, and reverence from the world and the family;
proper punishments for enemies, proper rewards for friends. Only in the small-
est ways does this blessing resemble the Abrahamic blessing, and then primarily
to call attention to the differences. There is no promise of land and no mention
of progeny. Though God *('elohim)* is mentioned, the Lord *(YHWH)* is not.
There is no mention of the covenant with the Lord. There is no mention of Father Abraham. Isaac, the transmitter of God's new way who has been told by
God Himself that his seed will inherit the covenant, gives Jacob-as-Esau-his-
favorite what amounts to a purely pagan blessing.

The story now reaches its climax, in the fourth and central scene. No sooner
does Jacob depart with "his" blessing than Esau returns from the hunt, prepares
the meal, and brings it to his father. "Let my father arise and eat of his son's
game," says Esau, solicitously and politely,[20] "that thy soul may bless me." Isaac,
his father, now thoroughly perplexed, asks, "Who [art] thou [*mi-'atah*]?" Comes
the plaintive answer, "I [am] thy son, thy firstborn [*bekhorekha*], Esau"
(27:31–32).[21] It is the moment of truth for Isaac:

> *And Isaac trembled [charad] with an exceedingly great trembling [vayeche-*
> *rad Yitshaq charadah gedolah]*, and said, "Who then is he that hath taken
> game and brought it to me and I ate everything before thou camest and
> have blessed him? And yea, blessed he remains." (27:33; emphasis added)

Isaac is at long last brought to his senses. Remarkably, when he discovers that he
has been fooled, he is not angry but, rather, awestruck: "And Isaac trembled with

20. Jacob has spoken in imperatives: *"Arise,* please, *sit and eat."* Esau is quite clearly attached and
devoted to his father.

21. Jacob, in answer to Isaac's question, had begun with the lie "I am Esau" (27:19). Esau begins by
stressing his sonship, mentioning his name only last. The poignant sequence—"thy son," "thy firstborn," "Esau"—reminds of the sequence with which God asked Abraham for the sacrifice of his son:
"thy son, thy only son, whom thou lovest, Isaac" (22:2). This is another small clue that invites us to
connect the present episode with the painful story of Isaac and his father.

an exceedingly great trembling." He is overpowered by the recognition that he has given an irrevocable blessing where he had not intended, and he knows to whom; a moment later he will answer his own question: "*Thy brother* came with guile and hath taken away thy blessing" (27:35; emphasis added). Isaac trembles because he senses that the blessing has been given *through* him to the proper son, by powers beyond his control. As he had said, prophetically but unwittingly, when he sent Esau out at the start of this episode, *he* would eat but *his soul* would bless (27:4)—and so it happened. Despite himself, something that was living in him and through him gave the blessing to the son for whom it was suited. Jacob now has the birthright and his father's blessing, and Isaac now knows enough to know that it must be so. Rebekah's plan has brought father and son into (partial) alignment, with each other and with the line and way of Abraham.

But there is more to Isaac's trembling. In this moment of revelation, Isaac, long estranged from his father, Abraham, suddenly finds himself in his father's place. He has just participated in "sacrificing" *his* beloved son, not literally but more than metaphorically. In blessing Jacob with familial lordship over his brethren, he has called down upon Esau a life of servility. Very likely, he also senses that a higher power is somehow behind all this. No wonder he trembles: O my God! Is this what my father suffered and understood and felt on Mount Moriah?

Isaac's pain is made worse by Esau's reaction:

> And when Esau heard the words of his father he cried out [*vayits'aq*] [22] with an exceeding great and bitter cry [*tse'aqah*], and said unto his father, "Bless me, me also, my father." And he said, "Thy brother came with guile and hath taken away thy blessing." (27:34–35)

Though he feels Esau's anguish, Isaac is helpless: I don't have *your* blessing anymore; your brother has it. Several more times Esau pleads for a blessing; Isaac says that, having made Jacob Esau's master and having given him corn and wine for sustenance, he has nothing left to give. When Esau offers one final plea and then lifts his voice and weeps, Isaac finally blesses him:

> "Behold, from [*or* far from] the fat of the earth shall be thy dwelling, and from the dew of the heavens above. And by thy sword thou shalt live, and thou shalt serve thy brother. And it shall come to pass when thou becomest restive, thou shalt break his yoke from off thy neck." (27:39–40)

22. The Hebrew word for "cried" creates a pun on the name of Isaac, *Yitshaq,* "He Laughs." The son of "He Laughs" shrieks in anguish over his father's unwitting casting him aside.

The blessing, though somewhat like the one given to Jacob, is more ambiguous: it is not clear whether Esau will live "off" or "away from" the fat of the land. In either event, Esau will rather live by the sword, in violence and pillage; eventually, after long servitude, he will revolt and throw off his brother Israel's rule. In blessing Esau, Isaac does not mention God at all. Isaac seems to be, at the very least, resigned to the supremacy of Jacob.

But all is not yet right. The alignment between Jacob and Isaac is incomplete: through his deception, Jacob has caused and witnessed the unfathering of Isaac. And more urgently, danger still lurks due to the wrath of Esau. The birth order has been reversed but the ever-present possibility of fratricide still threatens the entire project. Esau, now a virtual outcast, burns with a desire for revenge.

> And Esau hated Jacob on account of the blessing with which his father had blessed him. And Esau said in his heart [that is, made up his mind], "Let the days of mourning for my father be at hand, then will I slay Jacob, my brother." (27:41)

But the danger is averted. Once again, Rebekah is on the scene and saves the day. Remarkably, she divines Esau's purpose, for he spoke his plan only "in his heart." Immediately, she knows what must be done. To effect the solution, she promptly goes to work on both Jacob and her husband.

As soon as she learns of Esau's murderous intent (and fearing the imminence of Isaac's death, after which the threatened revenge is to occur), Rebekah summons Jacob and warns him that Esau is consoling himself with plans for lethal revenge (scene five). Once again she commands Jacob, this time to flee to safety with Laban, her brother:

> "Now therefore, my son, hearken to my voice [*shema' beqoli*] and arise; flee for yourself to Laban, my brother, to Haran; and *tarry with him a few days* [*yamim 'achadiym*] until thy brother's fury turn away, until thy brother's anger turn away from thee, and he forget that which thou hast done to him. Then will I send for thee and fetch thee back from there. Why should I be bereaved [*shakal*] of *both of you* in one day?" (27:43–45; emphasis added)

Jacob, the homebody, has to be persuaded to go away, the quicker the better. Rebekah gives him the truth about the peril he faces, suggests to him the safe haven of her brother Laban's home, and promises to recall him home just as soon as the danger passes. But Rebekah is no fool. She surely knows that Esau's resentment will persist, that Jacob must be in exile for much longer than "a few days."[23] As it turns out, Rebekah is giving up her son's company forever: when Jacob returns home more than twenty years later, only Isaac (!) will still be alive. What's more, she *knows* she will probably never see him again. Rebekah, too, sacrifices her son.[24] The preservation of the new way requires it.

Seen in this light Rebekah's final remark to Jacob—"Why should I lose both of you in one day?"—is especially poignant. "Both of you" could mean Isaac and Jacob, the first going to his anticipated natural death, the second to be murdered by Esau—or lost in permanent exile. Much more likely,[25] "both of you" refers to Jacob and Esau, to be lost either by double fratricide or by capital punishment of the surviving sibling. Though Rebekah prefers Jacob, she cares for the life of both her boys.[26] Rebekah faces bravely the losses made inevitable by her maternal choice. At the same time she offers hope and comfort to her son. Rebekah's last words invite Jacob to leave not for his sake but *for hers!* Nothing more need be said between them. They never speak again.

Rebekah wants more than Jacob's safety. She wants him to go with his father's blessings, this time freely and knowingly given. And she wants him to marry and to marry well. Rebekah (scene six) thus turns immediately to her husband, whom she, through Jacob, has just deceived. With him she will need a different message to help get Jacob out of harm's way. She fastens on the vexed subject of the wives of Esau.

> And Rebekah said to Isaac, "I am weary of my life because of the daughters of Heth. If Jacob take a wife of the daughters of Heth, *like these,* from the *daughters of the land* [*mibenoth ha'arets*], what is to me my life [*lamah li chayim*]?" (27:46; emphasis added)

Rebekah's speech to her husband is both loving and shrewd. She spares Isaac the knowledge of Esau's murderous hatred, awareness of which might both cause him pain and evoke his anger at Jacob. Instead, she expresses to him only her

---

23. A possible clue is the word she uses for "few," *'achadiym,* the "impossible" plural of "one" (*'achad)* that we encountered in the beginning of the story of Babel. (See Chapter Eight, p. 224.)

24. In this respect Rebekah shows her resemblance to Abraham and her superiority to Sarah.

25. Robert Alter provides the evidence: "The verb *shakal* is used for a parent's bereavement of a child, so 'you both' must refer to Jacob and Esau: although a physical struggle between the two would scarcely be a battle between equals, in her maternal fear she imagines the worst-case scenario, the twins killing each other, and in the subsequent narrative, the sedentary Jacob does demonstrate a capacity of unusual physical strength."

26. This is at least a partial answer to those who condemn Rebekah for parental favoritism, her only possible defect. A fuller answer would examine whether virtuous motherhood necessarily means loving all children equally, regardless of their loveableness.

concern for another—and perhaps still greater—danger, namely that Jacob, like Esau, will take to wife a Canaanite woman. Taking advantage of Isaac's known distress with Esau over his wives, Rebekah obliquely makes Isaac look more kindly on Jacob: indirectly she encourages Isaac to feel the rightness of the blessing that he has unintentionally given his younger son. By emphasizing the problem with *these* women, of *this* land, she also hints at the desired solution: Jacob must be sent away. But Rebekah does not directly tell Isaac what to do. She states her concern and offers hints, but she leaves the remedy to him; she does not offer Isaac her plan and does not suggest to Isaac that Jacob might return to Laban in Haran. She trusts that Isaac, in his now chastened and new state of mind, will rise to the occasion. In a brilliant move, she closes her speech to her husband with a personal plea, delivered in words that echo her remarks to the Lord when her pregnancy was so difficult: if Jacob marries badly, my life will be in vain. But whereas before she was appealing to the Lord, now she appeals to Isaac and invites him to rise to the occasion.

Critics of Rebekah's conduct will say that she is once again not being honest with her husband. And it is certainly true that she is withholding part of the truth.[27] But the concern about whom Jacob will marry is not only genuine; it is also a concern that she prudently did not mention to Jacob, who, to this point, has shown no interest in women. To each of her men, Rebekah speaks fittingly: she omits the portion of the truth that would not be well received and that would thus obstruct proper conduct. Most important, by presenting to him a concern that she shares with Isaac, she allows the two of them to act in concert, as she leads Isaac to Jacob—and Jacob to Isaac—in direct and forthright speech. Her concluding remark is more than a personal plea. It is a reminder of the supreme importance of perpetuation. Rebekah invites Isaac to consider that *his* life, too, will have been a failure if Jacob marries badly and the line of the covenant is broken.

This brief speech is the Bible's only reported conversation between Rebekah and Isaac. Fittingly, it concerns the most important purpose of their marriage: the future well-being of their children and their children's children, seen in relation to the new way. The initiative belongs entirely to Rebekah. But Isaac, though he does not speak, answers her precisely and perfectly through his deeds.

27. In these respects Rebekah manifests the dilemma faced by everyone who suffers from the divorce between knowledge and power. Having knowledge but lacking power, Rebekah is necessarily forced to find indirect ways to make knowledge effective. Guile and the selective use of information are, under the circumstances, appropriate means. Would the critics of Rebekah rather that she had put her head in the sand? Bill Rosen offers an even more telling point: Rebecca (like Abraham) is displaying an awareness that there is a higher loyalty than that to family, even one's husband. Wittingly or not, she is acting in obedience to the needs of the covenant.

Thanks to the way Rebekah presents the matter, Isaac does indeed rise to the occasion—and in so doing, attains his full stature as patriarch. At long last, he now plays the true father to Jacob, absolutely voluntarily and without the need for deception. Isaac, who hitherto had taken no care for the marriages of his sons, will now command Jacob about whom to marry, a decision crucially important to the future of the covenant. Thanks to Rebekah's prompting, Isaac will send his son to the well where she was found.

ISAAC, PATRIARCH

In the final scene of the drama, Isaac and Jacob are together a second time, this time without disguises. This is Isaac's finest hour. He initiates the meeting, as he did with his beloved Esau in scene one; but this time the matter is more important than venison. Acting now with patriarchal dignity and authority, Isaac calls, blesses, and, for the first time, *commands* Jacob (who, significantly, will now look more reverently on his father):

> "Thou shalt not take a wife of the daughters of Canaan. Arise, go to Paddan-aram, to the house of Bethuel, *the father of thy mother;* and take thee a wife from thence of the daughters of Laban, *the brother of thy mother.*" (28:1–2; emphasis added)

Isaac's speech to Jacob echoes Abraham's speech to his servant, when sending him to find Isaac's wife a generation earlier (24:3–4); but whereas Abraham spoke of Paddan-aram (not by name) as the land of his kindred, Isaac speaks of it in terms of the house of Rebekah's father and brother. Isaac wishes for his son a wife like his own.

The command about marriage answers to Rebekah's concern. But Isaac is not finished. Displaying that he now knows deeply what he is doing, he immediately adds a blessing, but a blessing of a very different sort. In what are Isaac's last words in the Bible, he bestows—freely and fully—the proper blessing of the sons of the covenant:

> "And God Almighty [*El Shaddai*] bless thee, and make thee fruitful and multiply thee, that thou mayest become an assembly of peoples. And [may He] give thee the blessing of Abraham, to thee and to thy seed with thee; that thou mayest inherit the land of thy sojournings, which God [*'elohim*] gave unto Abraham." (28:3–4)

Isaac here steps fully into the paternal role. He invokes God's blessing, using the name, *El Shaddai,* that God Himself had used when He entered into the covenant with Abraham (17:1). Echoes of the Abrahamic covenant abound. Unlike the blessing he gave earlier, this blessing is not for prosperity and dominion but for fruitfulness, plenitude of progeny, the promised land, and, most significantly, the blessing of Abraham. Though Isaac does not speak of God as *his* own God, or of Jacob as "my son," he here pronounces Jacob to be *Abraham's* true heir. In this most fatherly and most pious of acts, Isaac at last enacts the linking deed of transmission: he "adopts" Jacob for his father's covenant with the Lord. For the first time since he was bound on Mount Moriah, Isaac speaks the name of Abraham—indeed, for emphasis, twice in one sentence.[28] The very last word from Isaac's lips is the name of Father Abraham.

In his last deed, "Isaac sent away Jacob; and he went to Paddan-aram unto Laban, son of Bethuel the Aramean, the brother of Rebekah, Jacob and Esau's mother" (28:5).[29] Isaac sends Jacob away to find a wife, filled with thoughts of God, thoughts of his grandfather Abraham, thoughts of his own descendants and of the divine blessing upon them, and thoughts of the land he will inherit because of the merit of Abraham, the first man who showed that he revered God more than he loved all promise of earthly rewards. Isaac at long last fulfills his mission as patriarch. Despite nature's refusal to cooperate, the chain is unbroken, the birth order is reversed without fratricide, and Jacob, with his father's uncoerced and abundant blessing, is on his way to becoming Israel.

The story of Isaac must be counted a success, against powerful odds. Isaac, lost to Abraham as *his son,* is returned to his ways as perpetuator of the covenant. Jacob, his self-reliant heir, is off on a journey that will lead to his becoming Israel. But credit must be given where credit is due. The true hero of the story is the courageous, tactful, and above all lovingly prudent Rebekah, who conducts affairs always with circumspection, often behind the scenes, but—thanks to the Torah—in full view of us, its readers. Thanks to Rebekah, the new way survives a most severe test; thanks to Rebekah and the generations of women who, inspired by her example, followed in her footsteps, it survives at least to the present day.

---

28. In this respect, Isaac's last words imitate the text's first words about his generations (25:19), where Abraham is also mentioned twice, as Isaac's source. Isaac, in his final reported speech, comes full circle, voluntarily owning up to his beginning, and thereby renewing it for his son.

29. In this, one of the last mentions of Rebekah (later we hear her name only in passing: see 29:12: 35:8; and 49:31), she appears as mother of *both* sons, but with the birth order duly reversed. This identification memorializes her accomplishment: Rebekah succeeded in reversing the birth order without fratricide.

We of the present day, what do we make of this story and this woman? Many of my students object to Rebekah's use of deception. Believers in total frankness and empowerment through assertion, they would rather she had confronted her husband and forced him to face his failure to understand his sons and his failure as a father. Others, also believers in frankness and the therapeutic, recommend the equivalent of marriage counseling or family therapy. But one must wonder whether these alternatives are really preferable, less cruel and less destructive. Is it really better for intimacy and dignity and love to, as they say, "Let it all hang out"? Or does not the judicious yet loving use of guile prove more gentle and less destructive, enabling Isaac to learn for himself, to learn from his own contribution to this deception that he has long been self-deceived—without being lectured or nagged or confronted? Do we not see that Rebekah has not only not damaged his dignity and self-esteem, but has allowed him to find it truly only as a consequence of her careful deeds and speech?

The perpetuation of the new way, then and now, depends absolutely on the right ordering of the household, devoted wholeheartedly to the noble and sacred task of rearing and perpetuation. For this task—and there is, for the Children of the Book, none higher—women appear to have special access and special gifts, especially if they hearken to the call. As the exemplar of virtuous womanhood—eager for marriage and children; prudent, tactful, and energetically farsighted; with an ear for the transcendent voice—Rebekah is a woman for all seasons.

The story has a short coda. Jacob has been sent on his way, the book on Isaac and Rebekah is now closed. But we have forgotten about Esau. The text does not. Esau, so to speak alone onstage, takes stock of what has just transpired. He sees that Isaac has blessed Jacob (a second time) and sent him off to take a wife from Paddan-aram. He sees that in blessing him Isaac commanded Jacob not to take a Canaanite wife. He sees that Jacob has "obeyed his father *and his mother* and was gone to Paddan-aram" (28:7; emphasis added). And he sees that "the daughters of Canaan pleased not Isaac, his father" (28:8; no mention of his mother). Hoping to get himself back into his father's good graces, Esau takes a bold but unpromising decision: as Jacob went to the home of his mother's brother Laban, so he should go to the home of his father's brother Ishmael. "So Esau went unto Ishmael and took unto the wives that he had Mahalath,[30] the daughter of Ishmael, Abraham's son . . . to be his wife" (28:9). But

---

30. The meaning of the name is uncertain. Some scholars say it means "sickness," from *chalah*, "to be weak or sick." Others suggest that it means "appeasement" or "mollification," from *chalah*, "to mollify or appease; to make the face of someone sweet or pleasant."

Esau goes without his father's blessing. Far from regaining his father's good graces, he moves farther and farther afield. Esau, despiser of the birthright, chooses marriages that will take him and his seed beyond the covenant. When we meet him next, twenty years later, it will be at the head of an army come to threaten Jacob and the new way.

Chapter Fourteen

The Adventures of Jacob:
The Taming of the Shrewd

With the passing of another generation, the Genesis narrative once again travels from father to son, from Isaac to Jacob. Father Isaac, almost despite himself, has kept alive the new way begun with Abraham. Yet his success will finally depend on whether his son is willing and able to live up to his inheritance and to make it his own. In the person of Jacob, however, the new way acquires a different and most difficult carrier. If Isaac is the prototype of the son who passively receives a tradition that he must actively choose to make his own, Jacob is the prototype of that more problematic son, the self-reliant type who generally acts as though he has no need for tradition.[1]

Yet it is Jacob who obtains a new name in relation to God—Israel, "God Will Rule"—the first and only person in Genesis who is so named. His name becomes the name also of the people of the new way: although the Lord will be referred to as the God of Abraham, Isaac, and Jacob, the people who follow Him will be known as the Children of Israel (that is, the descendants of the sons of Jacob). It is also in Jacob's generation that the new way begins to spread: Jacob's father and grandfather each selected a single son to carry the new way, discarding their firstborn; now the covenant becomes the inheritance of an entire clan, twelve sons in all. In Jacob, the last of the patriarchs, the new way achieves incipient nationhood—to be sure, with human troubles still unresolved, but established and pointed in the right direction. After Jacob there will be neither need

---

1. In beginning the discussion of Isaac (in Chapter Twelve), we suggested that Isaac, as the prototype of the son who is passively born into a tradition that he must then actively accept, is a universal type with whom all future sons can identify. While this is true, Isaac is also unique in two major respects. First, he—and only he—is the son of the great founder; and second, his near sacrifice on Mount Moriah, though arguably but an extreme version of paternal dedication of sons, imposes on him a special burden in trying to take his father's place. By contrast, Jacob is the son not of the founder but of the (first) perpetuator. In this respect, Jacob is the prototype: all sons who come after him have fathers who, like Jacob and like them, will have received from fathers who were born into the covenant. In addition, Jacob is representative of all sons who are not firstborn: because his inheritance is not simply given to him, he must grasp it for himself.

nor possibility of additional patriarchs. The story of Jacob, therefore, is in some sense the most significant of the patriarchal stories. If so, understanding the character and career of this remarkable man is supremely important not only for the light it sheds on the establishment of the new way but also for the help it offers in the ongoing education of the reader.

Even the most casual of readers finds Jacob and his story immediately engaging. The portrait drawn of him is richer and more complex than that of anyone else in Genesis, and his life, recounted in its entirety, occupies fully half of its fifty chapters (born in chapter 25, he dies in chapter 49). We readers witness his conception and birth, his early life, and his leaving home. We are present at his wedding, the birth of his children, the death of his beloved wife, and the disappearance of his favorite son. We accompany him to Egypt, behold his reunion with Joseph, hear his final blessings of his sons, attend his death, and participate vicariously in the long funeral procession that bears his body back from Egypt for burial in the Promised Land. We observe all of his struggles at home and abroad, with man and with God; we rejoice in his numerous triumphs and share in his abundant sorrows. We learn not only about Jacob's deeds and speeches but also—and more than with Abraham and Isaac—about his inner life: his dreams, his thoughts, his feelings. Less heroic and austere than Abraham, more robust and enterprising than Isaac, Jacob strikes us immediately as more recognizable and familiar—in many respects not all that different from ourselves.

Yet Jacob, though nearer to us, is no ordinary fellow. He is more than complicated; he is comprehensive. Jacob is, first of all, a man of uncommon cunning and cleverness, a man of many turns and many ways, the biblical counterpart of Odysseus. Like Odysseus Jacob lives after the Age of Heroes (Achilles; Abraham); like Odysseus he lives largely by his wits; like Odysseus he is made to travel far in order to learn the ways of men and God and thereby earn the day of his homecoming. Though he is from time to time in touch with the divine,[2] Jacob is mostly on his own, relying on his own powers and devices. Artfulness is his trademark, not only in speech but also, quite literally, in craft. Though to begin with a dweller in tents, he builds a house, the first in the new way. Like Cain and

---

2. Jacob has but five contacts with God, many fewer than did Abraham, and most are either indirect or limited to instructions to leave one place for another. In only one case does God appear to him directly and speak to him more fully. Jacob receives the divinely sent dream at Beth-El when he leaves home for Haran (28:12); twenty years later God speaks to him, telling him to leave Laban and return home (31:3); after the slaughter at Shechem, God tells him to return to Beth-El (35:1); when he arrives there, God appears to him and pronounces His blessing upon him (35:9); much later, God speaks to him in nocturnal visions, telling him not to be afraid to journey to Egypt to be reunited with Joseph (46:2). In addition, there is the mysterious episode in which Jacob wrestles with a man who is more than a man (32:25).

his descendants, he brings art to bear on nature, most notably in his "magical" breeding techniques. Like the builders of Babel, he—quite literally—dreams of reaching heaven, in his case with a ladder. Jacob, more than Abraham or Isaac, is the rational man at work.

But Jacob is not only the book's most rational and resourceful character; he is also the most passionate. He displays lust for gain and righteous anger, he enjoys big dreams and suffers great sorrows, and he is the first to spontaneously experience the passion of awe. Most impressive is Jacob's erotic nature: Jacob is the first biblical character who clearly falls in love. It is thanks to his erotic adventures (and misadventures) that he comes to be the father of a clan. Jacob is also tenacious and long-suffering; though very little comes easily to him, he endures and prevails. Owing to his persistent striving with God and man, he comes famously to bear the name of Israel. Jacob, both in powers of soul and in conduct of life, offers an enlarged picture of the distinctively human at work.

This means, of course, that Jacob must solve, at the highest level of complexity, the fundamental human difficulties illustrated in the pre-Abrahamic chapters of Genesis: difficulties caused by the troublesome elements of the human soul (freedom and reason; pride; greed; lust and eros; blood lust; excessive love of one's own; and the penchant for self-sufficiency) and difficulties relating to family members, neighbors and strangers, and God. In finding his place in the world, Jacob must deal with nature's indifference to human merit (the problem of birth order). In his striving with his brother, Esau, Jacob must avoid being either Cain or Abel. In relation to his father from whom he steals his brother's blessing, he must avoid being like Ham, a man who sees his father's nakedness and refuses to cover it up. He must, despite his artful nature, avoid the pride of the builders of Babel. He must, despite his erotic nature, acquire the proper attitude toward women, marriage, and procreation. He must, despite entanglements with foreign peoples, avoid the temptations of imitation, assimilation, and idolatry. And above all, precisely because of his enormous talents and self-reliance, he must avoid the all-too-human propensity to ignore or forget about God, to regard himself as his own self-sufficing source.

As was the case with Abraham, the adventures of Jacob constitute his education—though, it should be confessed at the start, it will prove harder than it was with his grandfather to say just what it is that Jacob learns and how well, precisely because he is such a complicated character. Like his grandfather, Jacob travels far and wide, and he dwells not only in Canaan but also in the two other lands—Mesopotamia and Egypt—that offer the leading alternatives to the emerging biblical way of life. In his adventures, Jacob struggles with many vexing human relationships, familial, tribal, and international. He has troubles with his twin brother, his father, and his mother's brother. He has complicated erotic and marital relationships, faces horrible difficulties as a father (including the rape of his daughter and fratricidal struggles between his sons), and he confronts peoples of different and threatening ways: Arameans, Shechemites, Egyptians. Throughout his trials, Jacob repeatedly struggles to acquire a proper relationship both with men and with God.

In following Jacob's adventures, we will proceed mainly chronologically, in most (but not all) places following the order of the narrative. This chapter concentrates on Jacob's twenty years in Paddan-aram at the home of his uncle Laban. The main focus will be Jacob in love; the main question will be the relation between the love of woman and the love of—or reverence for—God. The next chapter will concentrate on the events leading to Jacob's reunion with Esau. The main focus will be Jacob's wrestling; the main question will be the connection between brotherhood and piety. The crisis of Chapter Sixteen is the major political event of Jacob's career, the story of the rape of Dinah. The focus will be the incipient formation of the nation around an act of collective revenge; the main question will be its bearing on the character of the new way. The story of "the generations of Jacob"—that is, the tales of Joseph and his brothers—will be treated separately and thereafter. But before we can see how Jacob learns from his travels, we need to see him as he is at home. That is where one discovers why and in what way he needs to be educated if he is to fulfill his role as patriarch.

JACOB AT HOME: "IF I AM NOT FOR MYSELF"

When we first come upon the figure of Jacob, he seems a most improbable candidate for following in the ways of Abraham. For he seems hardly a pious or God-fearing man. On the contrary, he is self-absorbed and self-reliant, a man who trusts mainly in his own devices. From the moment he enters the world, hand on his brother's heel, Jacob is marked as a conniver, trying to make up for lack of natural strength or position: "and his hand was seizing the heel of Esau" (*veyado 'ochezeth ba'aqev 'esav*; 25:26). Jacob arrives trying to prevent Esau from being firstborn, trying to supplant him as first-born, tripping him up or holding him back from behind—not in face-to-face encounter but underhandedly. An even stronger reading would suggest that Jacob is trying to weaken or cripple Esau, to make him limp, to make him lame—though these readings do not suggest any conscious, scheming prenatal intention on Jacob's part. Rather, the deed is symbolic of his nature, symbolic enough to give him his name: "Heel Catcher," "Supplanter." All his life Jacob's name *(Ya'aqov)* will announce a grasping, rivalrous, devious, supplanting, and most unbrotherly inclination or nature. Jacob in many ways comes to live out that named and natural destiny.

But *Ya'aqov* means not only "Supplanter." It can also mean "Follower," one who follows in or after the tracks (*'aqevoth*) laid down by others. In this sense, also, Jacob is suitably named. He is called to follow in the path of Abraham, yet his character inclines him to be no one's follower. Jacob's name accordingly raises the crucial questions for his future: will he become a follower of Abraham, and not only as a supplanter?

However this may turn out, readers must not judge him prematurely. Because Jacob is second born, his elder brother stands in his path. Inferior in rank and seemingly in strength, he needs other weapons to flourish. His wit and drive, in truth, arm him against his more earthy and robust brother, who, we are told, had been struggling[3] with him already in the womb; Jacob stands a much better chance against Esau than did Abel against *his* elder and stronger brother. Moreover, to grasp is a mark also of aspiration and striving, of a desire to reach beyond oneself. Jacob's grasping entrance could be seen more as zeal for life and eagerness to meet the world, less as proud determination not to lag behind his brother. Can anyone know from the outside whether Jacob is moved more by erotic striving for something good or by spirited refusal to be bested by another?

The complexity and ambiguity of Jacob's soul come more clearly to light in the story of the sale of the birthright.[4] Because Jacob's life is from the start confounded with Esau's, his encounters with his twin brother—both here and later—prove especially revealing of his character. Esau, the "knowing hunter" who roams the fields with violence, returns home empty-handed to find his quiet, stay-at-home brother cooking up a meal.

> And Jacob stewed a stew; and Esau came in from the field and he was famished ['*ayef:* faint *or* weary]. And Esau said to Jacob, "Let me gulp down [*hal'iteni*], please, some of this red red [stuff] [*ha'adom ha'adom hazeh*], for I am famished." Therefore is his name called Edom ['*edom*]. (25:29–30)

Esau is weak and weary, from both exertion and hunger. The hunting has gone badly. Perhaps Esau is not such a clever hunter. More likely, hunting being less reliable than farming, today was not Esau's lucky day.[5] In Jacob's pot Esau sees some "red red" stuff to assuage his hunger: in his maiden speech, the ruddy man, who sheds animal blood for food, gives voice to his passion for "red." Esau iden-

---

3. The verb for "struggle" (25:22) is *ratsats,* "to crack in pieces," "to break or bruise or crush," "to struggle together." The very sound of the word suggests violent destruction.

4. This episode was briefly considered in the last chapter solely for its evidence regarding Isaac and Rebekah's preferences and judgments regarding their sons.

5. There is, of course, another possibility, even less favorable to Esau: he returned home with game but, feeling weary and faint, was unwilling to wait until it was cooked, insisting instead that Jacob give him some of the already prepared food.

tifies with his food; as the text remarks, he becomes what he eats, earning a new name, Edom, "Red." In addition, his request/demand for food reveals his animal-like lack of self-command: the verb here translated "let me gulp down" (and translated by others as "feed me" or "let me swallow") is generally connected with the feeding of cattle, with stuffing them with food.[6] In these subtle ways the text implies that Esau is not just hungry; Esau is rather the incarnation of animal hunger, a man of impatient and unbridled appetite.[7]

Jacob does not simply offer a needy brother food. Speaking for the first time within the reader's hearing, he shows himself to be not impulsive but calculating.

And Jacob said, "Sell now thy birthright to me." (25:31)

This is probably not the first time that Esau has come home famished; this is probably not the first time that he has implored Jacob to "let me gulp down." But first time or not, Jacob is ready with a plan. He will not simply give away his food. He will get something for himself in return.

Many readers find fault with Jacob's response. Why doesn't he feed his needy brother? Why does he take advantage of Esau's hunger to extract a bargain under duress? These objections, though appropriate, reflect too much an expectation of brotherly love—an expectation that depends on biblical instruction, available to the reader but not to Jacob. More important, they fail to take into account Esau's character, Jacob's position, and, above all, the nature of the birthright and Jacob's reasons for wanting it.

In the ancient Near East, the birthright (bekhorah)—the right of the firstborn (bekhor, literally, "the one who comes early")—is the right accorded by priority of birth to the firstborn son, though it may later be alienated or sold (as here). It includes special property rights of inheritance from the father, as well as rights and responsibilities of family leadership, including duties toward the divine (for example, the offering of sacrifices). Holding the birthright entitles the son to

---

6. The word occurs in no other place in the Bible.

7. Esau's request should be contrasted with the request for water made to Rebekah by Abraham's servant, no doubt very thirsty after he had completed his arduous journey: "Give me to drink, please, a little water of thy pitcher" (24:17). The servant says "drink" not "gulp down," asks only for a *little* water (not "*this* red red"), and unlike Esau with Jacob, acknowledges that the pitcher and water are hers ("*thy* pitcher"). The tone of Esau's remarks is also highly unusual. In speaking about the "red red stuff," he is using crude slang, highly unusual language for the Hebrew Bible and for Genesis in particular, where all the characters, however low, speak in the highest of High Hebrew. "This passage is quite jarring in the original; it is as though some Shakespearean character suddenly began to speak like a New York taxi driver, a very noticeable and attention-grabbing shift" (Yuval Levin, personal communication).

take his father's place in all respects, not least as the next transmitter of the father's ways. Yet the possession of the birthright conveys no present advantages to the *bekhor*. Thus, to care for the birthright while one is yet young implies concern and forethought for the future rather than devotion merely to the present, precisely the forward-looking attitude that proper patriarchy will require. Esau has the birthright but lacks the right concern; Jacob has the concern but lacks the right by birth. The order of birth is not the order of merit or fitness. A reversal is needed, and, especially given Isaac's preference for Esau, it is difficult to see how it can be arranged. Those who object to what Jacob does here have not sufficiently considered some of the competing alternatives, most of them involving fraud or force, not excluding fratricide.

Clever Jacob thinks he knows how to fix the birth-order problem all by himself. Whether or not one finally approves of his action, one must acknowledge that he devises what is, in a way, a perfect test. By devising the plan and by openly and directly asking for the sale of the birthright—there is no deception, force, or theft—Jacob shows both his greater desire for the birthright and his willingness to obtain it by honest means, both signs of his worthiness. Moreover, he asks for the sale under circumstances in which Esau, if he accepts the offer, will demonstrate why he does not deserve to have it. If Esau were in fact worthy of the birthright, he would probably take offense at such an offer; if, on the contrary, he is willing to give it up in exchange for a good meal, he will thereby convict himself of his unworthiness in the very act of giving it up.

> And Esau said, "Look, I am going to die, so what is to me [*lamah-zeh li*] a birthright?" And Jacob said, "Swear to me now," and he swore to him and he sold his birthright unto Jacob. And Jacob gave Esau bread and lentil stew, and he ate and he drank and he rose up and he went off; and so Esau despised [*or* spurned] the birthright. (25:32–34)

Esau does not hesitate to sell the birthright. Sealing his intention with an oath, he shows himself perfectly willing to change places, thereby confessing to the unfitness that makes such an exchange absolutely necessary. Indeed, his stated reason for disdaining the birthright—"I am going to die"—reveals the full ground of his disqualification. On the surface, Esau appears to be claiming that he is starving to death, here and now, and that he will not live to enjoy the birthright; if this is his meaning, he surely exaggerates his nearness to death. As the text points out with an elegant simplicity that can fully be seen only in the Hebrew, with the piling up of five single-word verbs, "and-he-*ate* and-he-*drank* and-he-*rose*-up and-he-*left* and-he-*despised*," Esau was in no danger of starvation. He ate, drank, got up, and went his way, as on any ordinary day, without a touch of regret.

On a deeper level, Esau's reason for accepting the sale is even more self-condemning: "I am mortal, so why should I care about the rights and responsibilities of patriarchy and transmission?" Or, exaggerating to make the point, "Eat, drink, and enjoy the present, for tomorrow we will die." Esau declares himself absolutely unconcerned with the future and with taking his father's place. A slave to appetite, he proves his unfitness by the contempt he shows for the birthright.[8]

The point of the story, however, is to take the initial measure of Jacob, not of Esau. In his favor, Jacob (unlike the prototypical first younger brother, Abel) has the natural gifts to survive and carry on—ambition and striving, cleverness and forethought. More important, Jacob recognizes the significance of the birthright, the preeminent place of responsibility in the household. But there is also something disquieting and unsavory about his doings, above and beyond the charge of taking unbrotherly advantage of Esau. Though the text comments explicitly and unfavorably only about Esau, its silence about Jacob does not imply approval. It is far from clear that Jacob is here motivated by a knowledgeable desire to set right the household order rather than by ambition, greed, jealousy, or emulation. It is entirely likely that he is interested more in the privileges that attach to the birthright (gain and honor) than in its obligations (spiritual and moral leadership). There are, in fact, reasons to be doubtful of Jacob's relation to God and his interest in perpetuating the new way.

Jacob believes, mistakenly, that he can resolve the birth-order problem without involving his father and that he can do so by his cleverness alone. In both these respects, he is at this point unfit. For how can one be suited to take one's father's place as perpetuator if one ignores the place of one's father? How can one feel awe-and-reverence for God if one lacks filial piety? And how can one be a true heir of the way of Abraham by relying solely on cleverness or strength? In order to become truly ready and fit, Jacob will have to be brought into right relation both to his father and to his father's God. And he will probably also have to mend fences with his brother. If God's new way is to be established without fratricide, he will, at the very least, have to avoid the problem of killing or being killed by Esau, who—notwithstanding his unforced willingness to swap the birthright—now has reason to feel injured and resentful.[9]

8. The common understanding of this story has it that Esau sold his birthright for a mess of pottage. But the text is much vaguer and more ambiguous about the terms of the sale. It is not clear whether the red stew was itself the payment Esau received or whether the sale was separate and prior to Jacob's providing him with food. The important point is that Esau willingly sold it.

9. It is, however, true that Esau does not reveal any resentment until Jacob later steals the blessing Isaac had intended to give to him. If it is only on his father's endorsement of the reversal that Esau gets angry, that only supports the belief that Esau does not here sufficiently appreciate what he has surrendered to Jacob. (My thanks to Bill Rosen for this observation.)

Jacob's remoteness from his father and his brother and from God is, if anything increased by his next adventure, the stealing of the blessing from Isaac (discussed in the last chapter). True, Rebekah compels a reluctant Jacob to acknowledge for the first time the importance of his father, when she forces him to seek his father's blessing. Yet even as he does so, Jacob reveals his lack of piety, toward both his father and his father's God. When asked by the bewildered Isaac how he was able so quickly to provide savory food, Jacob, lying, answers, "Because the Lord *thy* God sent me good speed" (27:20). The first time Jacob speaks of God—and the last until he leaves home—he does not acknowledge Him as his own. Worse, he is (at least tacitly) suggesting that his own cleverness can accomplish what others will believe happens only as an act of God. It is perhaps not too strong to suggest that Jacob's impious exposure of his father's gullibility is meant to encompass also his father's belief in the Lord.

Jacob's whole relation to his father also leaves much to be desired. It is true that he never was his father's favorite. It is also true that, by the end of the story, Isaac, brought to his senses, acts the patriarch with Jacob, and when he commands Jacob to leave home to find a wife, Jacob heeds his father's (and his mother's) words. He goes off with Isaac's patriarchal blessing willingly bestowed upon him and with the name of Father Abraham ringing in his ears (28:4–7). Yet even as he honors his father's wishes by obeying his orders, Jacob cannot be leaving with much filial piety. He has witnessed—indeed, he has caused—the old man's deception and humiliation. However much the deception over the blessing may at last have made a patriarch out of Isaac, it did not make a pious son out of Jacob. On the contrary, a man who so easily fools his father is liable to regard his father as a fool and his father's ways as foolish. It is quite possible that Jacob obeyed Isaac's order to leave home mainly because it happened to coincide with an identical suggestion made to him beforehand by his mother (27:43–45).

As little as he is inclined to piety, Jacob is no more inclined to love. Esau, his twin brother, at age forty takes two wives. But Jacob, self-centered and self-absorbed, shows no apparent interest in women. He is content at home, self-sufficient in his own cleverness and happy in his mother's love. Only after the episode in which he deceives his dim-eyed father into giving him the blessing intended for Esau is Jacob at long last forced to leave home. It is Rebekah who sees what Jacob does not: if Jacob is to take his father's place, another woman must take her place in his heart. Having first solidified Jacob's claim with his father, Rebekah sees to it that Jacob will be sent away to find a wife. His self-reliance will be tested by travel. His adventures will make a man out of him, perhaps even a God-fearing one.

ANXIOUS GOING FORTH, HOPEFUL LOOKING UP:
JACOB'S DREAM AT BETH-EL

Jacob, the quiet man beloved of his mother, goes out to confront the world. Two different reasons compel his departure. His mother has urged him to flee—for only a few days, she disingenuously told him—to escape his brother Esau's murderous wrath; his father has commanded him to find a wife from his mother's ancestral home, from among the daughters of Laban, his mother's brother. Jacob, who despite his advanced years[10] had shown no inclination either to marry or to leave the nest, is sent by both Isaac and Rebekah back to Haran—to the place from which God had called an already-married Abraham, the place to which Abraham would not allow Isaac to be taken to find a wife, the place to which Abraham instead had sent his servant in search of a suitable wife for Isaac. But though he is dispatched to find his own wife, Jacob goes out empty-handed—unlike Abraham's servant, who traveled with a camel train laden with riches and gifts for the prospective bride and her family. Jacob, the self-reliant and clever fellow, will have to manage by his wits alone. Almost from the start, his adventures will teach him the limits of cleverness and self-reliance. Though he owns the birthright he has purchased and the blessing he has "stolen," he has nothing to show for either. He has good reason to be perplexed about just what it could mean to be the blessed heir of his father.

Leaving his family at Beersheba, Jacob travels alone across the desert, heading north toward Haran. Already a good distance from home, he arrives at a special place (slightly north of Jerusalem), which, unbeknownst to him, was a pagan cult site as well as a place near which his grandfather Abraham had once built an altar soon after arriving in Canaan from Haran (12:8). As the sun sets, Jacob is filled with fear and apprehension, maybe even with remorse for the conniving that has driven him into exile. His past beclouded, his future uncertain, exposed and alone, he feels his own isolation and insufficiency as the eerie darkness settles upon him. Placing a stone beneath his head for a pillow (or perhaps next to his head),[11] he lies down in that place to sleep, and to dream.

---

10. Rough calculations suggest that he may be as old as 77. Jacob will die at age 147, after living his last seventeen years in Egypt (47:28). Before that was the period of Joseph's absence, roughly twenty-two years: Joseph, who was sold into Egypt at age 17 (37:2), was 30 years old when he first appeared before Pharaoh (41:46), after which it took another seven (fat) years and two (lean) years before Jacob and Joseph were reunited in Egypt. This would make Jacob 108 years old when Joseph was sold, and 91 years old when Joseph was born, in what was (roughly) the fourteenth year of his service to Laban at Paddan-aram. Recall also that his twin brother, Esau, had married at age 40 (26:34), well before the episode of the "stolen" blessing that necessitated his departure (compare 26:34 and 27:1).

11. Like so much of the story that follows, the position of the stone is ambiguous: the Hebrew *me-ra'ashothayv* could mean "under his head" or "alongside his head." The original meaning of the stone

And dream he does: a perfect dream, one precisely suited to his situation and his anxieties. In his dream, he sees a ladder (or ramp) fixed upon the earth but reaching to heaven, with messengers (or angels) of God ascending and descending upon it. The Lord Himself also appears in the picture, atop the very high ladder (28:12–13).[12] Jacob, still lying on the ground, has his gaze directed heavenward. Though the Lord is remote—more so than He was for Abraham and Isaac, to whom He appeared and spoke directly—communication is possible. Messengers go up and down, beginning from the earth. Despite His remoteness, God is accessible to men, a fact good to know especially in a time of trouble. Jacob, who lay down overcome with his neediness and lack of control, dreams of himself lying in the same position but with questions and petitions rising to the divine.

The sublime vision is enhanced by divine speech (28:13–15). God addresses Jacob personally, identifying Himself both as *YHWH* and as "the God of thy father Abraham and the God of Isaac" (28:13); Jacob is encouraged to think of himself especially as the offspring of his grandfather, founder of God's new way, and as a new link in the covenantal chain following his literal father, Isaac. This God of his dreams has a general blessing for Jacob: he and his seed will inherit the ground on which he lies; his descendants will be as numerous as the dust of the earth and will spread out in all directions; and all the families of the earth shall bless themselves by him and by his seed (28:13–14). And beyond this grand (and by now familiar) covenantal blessing for the distant future, God offers a full personal promise of protection, no doubt of greater immediate interest to the newly vulnerable Jacob:

"I am with thee; I will protect thee wherever thou goest; I will bring thee back to this land: I will not leave thee until I have done what I have promised thee." (28:15)

A personal god, promising safekeeping, safe return, and constant divine presence until the gifts of land, progeny and a blessed name will be delivered—a cheering dream indeed, and just what the doctor ordered.

---

to Jacob—later in this episode, it will be anointed as a pillar—depends in part on where he placed it. It could be a pillow; it could represent a protective barrier; it could serve, if necessary, as a weapon; it could be a memorial ("Jacob was here"); or as my wife has suggested, it could be intended as a potential grave marker, Jacob understanding full well that one cannot bury oneself. But notice: in all these possible meanings and "uses," we see the resourceful Jacob at work, even when he would seem to be utterly resourceless. Jacob refuses simply to lie down in defeat.

12. The position of the Lord is, in fact, unclear. The Hebrew prepositional phrase *'alayv* could mean "upon it [the ladder]" or "beside him [Jacob]." The ambiguity is, in a way, perfect, for it hints that the Lord can be—is—at once both near and far. For reasons that follow, I prefer the more remote positioning of God. That He would be in the picture at all, and speaking with Jacob, is nearness enough for those who wish to stress God's proximity to man.

But is it in fact *just* a dream? The text does not say that God sent the dream (as it had said regarding Abimelech's dream [20:30]) or that God spoke to him in his sleep (as it had said regarding God's speech to the sleeping and fearful Abram during the covenant between the sacrificial pieces, also as the sun was setting [15:12 ff.]). We are told only that "he [Jacob] dreamed" (*vayachalom;* 28:12). We, like Jacob, must decide both the dream's status and its truth. Much more than any direct manifestation of God, dreams require interpretation. Jacob must use his own powers of awareness to discover the meaning of the dream, both its manifest content and, more important, its significance for him.

How do people generally, and how does the shrewd and skeptical Jacob in particular, regard dreams? It will not do to assert, as many have done, that in olden times human beings simplemindedly believed that all dreams come from the gods and accurately prophesy the future. In the Bible itself, dreams are understood to have diverse origins and varying imports. Jacob himself will later rebuke Joseph for his imperial dream (about the heavenly bodies bowing to him), as if the dream were just a projection of Joseph's tyrannical wishes. But what to think about *this* dream?

It is clearly a special dream, whose vision shows the possibility of communicating with the divine: could it itself be a divine communication? It contains a speech by God, addressing Jacob personally exactly where he lies: must it not be a reliable communication? It speaks directly to his most pressing concerns (a need for protection in a strange land, a desire to return safely home) and answers them with a providential promise; ought he not to acknowledge dependence on the God who so obviously cares for him?

Jacob's dream turns out to be a perfect (not to say heaven-sent) device for confronting the rational man with the limits of his rationality. It comes to him when his power is weakest: all alone, in the wilderness, at night, when reason is idling and fears emerge. The dream occurs, to be sure, "within" his mind, and because it so clearly answers to his needs, it must be suspected of being the mind's own creation. Yet the substance of the dream shows precisely the limits of the human mind's ability to discern the truth about the world and to provide for a man's most urgent needs. The sharp-eyed man—and also the sharp-eyed reader—is invited to see the limits of his own sharp-mindedness.

Awakened by the dream, Jacob makes a remarkable response: "And he said, 'Surely the Lord is in this place, but I knew it not' " (28:16). Jacob divines God's invisible presence. By an act of mind, Jacob sees through the dream to the presence of the absent God. Also, in declaring his own prior ignorance, he intelligently attests to the limits of intelligence. True, perhaps because the dream mirrored his present physical location, he appears to connect God's presence only to *"this* place," as if the divine were not ubiquitous. But *any* recognition of God by the wily Jacob is progress.

Jacob's discovery of God's presence appropriately fills him with awe, the fundamental religious passion. But it does not render him speechless:

> And he was afraid [*or* filled with awe-dread-reverence],[13] and said, "How awe-some [*nora'*] is this place! This is nothing but the house of God and this is the gate of heaven." (28:17)

Responding to the recognized gulf between man and God, Jacob's awe is perfectly fitting, both to the fact of the dream and to its manifest content. Like the dream's messengers that appear to span that gap, awe in recognizing the gap builds an emotional bridge across it: awe, by acknowledging man's relative lowliness and dependence, paradoxically serves to connect him with the divine.

Jacob is the first biblical character who spontaneously feels and verbalizes this passion in this way.[14] True, once again, Jacob's thoughts about the divine are too localized. God is relegated to place, to a house, with its gateway to heaven. That God may indeed be not only above him but also beside him, and not only here but also everywhere, is not yet evident to Jacob. Nevertheless, even this over-localized image ("gateway to heaven") recognizes the need for *some* "gateway" if man is to have access to the divine. "This place," this special place, is distinguished at least for this: it has provided Jacob access to discovering the need for access, and it has offered—both through the fact of his dream and in its content—some promise of such connection. Such a special place might well deserve the name of House of God.[15]

Jacob's first reaction is, however, not his last. When he awakens for good, early in the morning, he takes the stone on which he slept, erects it as a pillar, and anoints it with oil ("he poured oil upon its head"; 28:18); and he names the place Beth-El, the House of God. As Robert Sacks observes, the same words for "pouring oil on its head" are used in the anointing of Aaron as priest (Exodus 29:7) and of Saul as king (1 Samuel 10:1); Sacks suggests that Jacob's deed anticipates the need for priests and kings, those who will later be "the gate of heaven" for the people.

---

13. The word is *yare*, not *pahad. Yare* implies awe and reverence, not just simply fear of bodily harm or death.

14. Lot had experienced dread to live in Zoar (19:30), Abraham had spoken of the "fear of God" that inspires decency (20:11), and the angel had praised Abraham for having the fear of God *(yere' 'elohim)* in the episode of the binding of Isaac (22:12).

15. As a result of this episode, this ancient pagan holy site is resanctified, but now on wholly different grounds.

But Jacob has a third and more considered response. With daylight comes a return of Jacob's circumspection. He vows the Bible's first vow, but its character reflects the calculating character of its maker:

"*If* God will be with me, and keep me in this way that I go, and will give me bread to eat, and raiment to put on, so that I come back to my father's house in peace, *then* shall the Lord be my God, and this stone, which I have set up for a pillar, shall be God's house; and of all that Thou shalt give me I will surely give the tenth unto Thee." (28:20–22; emphasis added)

It is hard to know what to make of the vow's conditional character, though it seems to be connected with the fact that Jacob fixes on the promise of personal providence (not the covenantal one). Interpretations that assume Jacob's whole-hearted piety see Jacob indicating only those minimal conditions needed for him to follow in Abraham's new way: if only I survive and if only I return, I will continue to serve the God of my ancestors ("The Lord shall be my God [also]"). Others see him giving voice to simple desires—for safety, food, clothing, and re-turn—whose satisfaction he now understands is wholly dependent on God's providence. But the stronger argument is that Jacob is hedging his bets. When the sun shines, Jacob, notwithstanding the dream's theophany, is still Jacob the shrewd, the calculating, the self-reliant: Will God be able to deliver His promises? How can I be certain—especially if God is but a God of *this place*? Am I right to trust dream promises? What if they are mere projections of my wishes? Let's wait and see what transpires: *if* the Lord does in fact deliver on His (dream) promises, *then* He will indeed be my God.

Although readers of the story hear Jacob's vow verbatim, his inner thoughts remain a mystery. But given his character, given his subsequent utterly self-reliant conduct, and especially given his failure to keep his promise to return to Beth-El when he comes back to Canaan, one might reasonably suspect that Jacob's opening to the divine is not yet wholehearted. He will wait and see, and so must we. Nevertheless, as Sacks points out, the oath—conditions notwith-standing—speaks well for Jacob. For himself, he indicates that he is ready now to take on the long journey in good spirits, despite hardships, and to do his best to return to the land of his fathers ("to my father's house"). And for the new way, he recognizes the need for both a political and ecclesiastical order (the of-fer of tithes and a house of God) and accepts the necessary burdens that a more sedentary and political life will impose upon his descendants. Finally, his skep-ticism is hardly total; by the end of his vow, Jacob has shifted from speaking *about* God (in the third person: "If God will do A, B, and C") to speaking *to* Him (in the second person: "Thou shalt give me . . . I shall give Thee"). The night at Beth-El marks an auspicious beginning for Jacob's odyssey and his education.

Encouraged by his dream, no longer so apprehensive, Jacob swiftly sets off on his journey—on foot!—with energy and zeal: "and Jacob lifted up his legs and came to the land of the children of the East" (29:1). Thus begins the account of what will be his twenty-year sojourn outside of Canaan, at the home of his uncle Laban. During this twenty-year period, God will not speak to him, nor will Jacob be moved to attempt to seek contact with God. Not piety, it seems, but another soul-opening passion will rule his soul: eros. Whether and how this passion and his adventures in Paddan-aram contribute to his education for leadership in God's new way remains to be seen.

JACOB AT THE WELL: LOVE AT FIRST SIGHT

The relation of love to piety is a complicated matter, to say the least, and the answer is crucial for understanding the biblical teaching. According to the dominant religious teachings of the West, love is the very heart of piety: the preeminent Christian virtue is charity, love of neighbor, in imitation of God's love for man. And Jews are commanded, later in the Torah, to "love thy neighbor as thyself" and to "love the Lord thy God with all thy heart, and with all thy soul, and with all your might" (Leviticus 19:18 and Deuteronomy 6:5).

But precisely because one is commanded to love the Lord, and with all one's heart, the ordinary, natural loves that human beings experience for one another emerge as a possible problem. By natural human love I do not mean the generalized love of neighbor, commanded as an ethical ideal. Rather, I mean what the Greeks called eros, that overpowering desire that fixes the soul of the lover steadfastly on his beloved. Falling in love, being filled with images and thoughts of the one beloved, seeking always his or her presence, longing for unification in body and in soul with the one we love—this is erotic love, something vastly more exalted than "having sex" or "being in a relationship." The question is this: is falling and being in love good for piety?

Greek thought and literature sometimes draw a close connection between the two. Aphrodite, who inspires or gives birth to eros, is herself a goddess of considerable power and influence; tragic is the lot of those who, like Hippolytos, fail to pay her homage. In the only Platonic dialogue explicitly devoted to a god, the *Symposium*, six members of the Athenian intellectual elite make speeches in praise of the god Eros.[16] In the famous image of the ladder of love, Socrates

---

16. When closely examined, none of the speeches turn out to be orthodoxly pious, to say the least. Socrates' speech even proves that eros cannot be a self-subsistent being—and hence is *not* a god, but is rather a powerful force in the soul, one that seeks the good and longs for immortality.

(and/or Diotima) presents eros as a power pointed upward, ultimately drawn by and directed toward the eternal and highest being, the beautiful itself. On this account, earthly eros, properly directed, is or becomes love of the divine.

But is the same thing true for biblical piety? Is falling in love good for being a Christian or a Jew—for being a person of the book, for following the commandments, for loving and revering and imitating God? Is eros bad for piety and observance?

There is no question that eros opens the soul to someone and something beyond oneself. When we are in love, the whole world seems brighter and better. We become more attentive to the wondrous and the extraordinary. We recognize the presence of powers beyond our control. We feel gratitude for the existence of the beloved. In all these ways, among others, eros may incline us to recognize and look toward the divine. In addition, eros itself is often experienced alternately as "divine possession," on the one hand, and "losing oneself" or ecstasy, on the other. And there are certainly Jewish and (more abundant) Christian accounts that link up the erotic and the pious.[17] Yet love of one beautiful beloved does not necessarily lead the soul upward; eros can be arrested there, with no desire to soar higher. Furthermore, the lover desires to join with his beloved, not merely to behold her; and the union of lovers effaces the distance between them necessary for the wondering appreciation of beauty that inspired eros in the first place. Finally, even if eros is divine possession or ecstasy, does either of these conditions resemble biblical piety, resting as it does on awe-fear-reverence for the Lord? Does not reverence for the Lord demand forethought and responsibility, not self-annihilation?

Relying only on our text, and not on the later religious traditions, we have relatively little to go on, beyond the Garden of Eden story. This tale did touch lightly on the relation between love and piety.[18] For it was only after the shame-inducing discovery of their nakedness that the man and woman showed their first awareness of the divine. Immediately after clothing themselves, reports the biblical author, "they heard the voice of the Lord God walking in the garden" (3:8). In recognizing our lowliness, the text implies, we human beings can also discover what is truly high. Sexual shame and awe before God were born together. But the question remains whether erotic love, which seeks to *overcome* shame and which glorifies the beautiful, reinforces or drives out this primordial fear-awe-reverence before God. Does soaring love for the beloved lead lovers

17. Consider, for example, the Song of Songs, the ecstasy of Saint Teresa (and Bernini's famous statue of same), and Dante's *Vita Nuova* and *Divine Comedy*.

18. The reader may wish to revisit Chapter Three for our analysis of the fundamental elements of human sexuality, as these emerge in the Garden of Eden story. The love of one's own, the love of the beautiful, and generative love all play a part in the present story of Jacob as lover and husband.

into side-by-side self-absorption, or does it lead them piously upward toward the holy? The story of Jacob offers the reader the Bible's first attempt at an exploration of this subject. While we follow the story of Jacob in love for its own intrinsic interest, we seek especially to grasp the connection, if any, between Jacob as lover and Jacob as Israel.

After a long journey across arid lands, Jacob arrives in the land of the children of the East, presumably tired, hungry, and thirsty. Jacob, sharp-eyed, looks out and sees a well, three flocks of sheep lying around it, and a great stone covering the well mouth. In these arid lands, the well, as sustainer of life, becomes a meeting place for the whole community, and its use is governed by unwritten rules mutually agreed upon. Local custom had it that when all the flocks were gathered, the men would collectively roll the great stone from the well's mouth, draw water for the sheep, and replace the stone. At Beth-El, Jacob himself had set up a stone in its now special place, giving it a custom-made meaning. How will he deal with this great stone and the local customs it embodies?

Understandably unsure of where he is, Jacob interrogates the shepherds and is relieved to learn that he has indeed arrived at Haran, that the men know Laban, his uncle, and that all is well with him. The otherwise laconic shepherds volunteer, "Look, Rachel, his daughter, is just now coming with the sheep" (29:6).[19] What good luck! Perhaps the blessing was not an empty promise![20]

So as to be alone with Rachel, Jacob immediately tries to send the men away: "Water your sheep and go feed them" (29:7). Though a stranger and empty-handed, Jacob bosses the local men around, tacitly even blaming them for laziness. But the men refuse to go: "We cannot, until all the flocks are gathered and they roll the stone from the well's mouth, for [only] then do we water the sheep" (29:8). Why "we cannot" is not clear. Perhaps it takes all the shepherds together to move the great stone; equally likely, *custom* dictates that all be present before the well is opened, in order that no one be left out. Indeed, to enforce this agreement and to prevent any one shepherd from taking unfair advantage, the shepherds would likely have installed a well-covering boulder too large to be moved by any one man.

In the midst of this conversation, Rachel arrives with her father's sheep, and Jacob seizes the occasion:

19. Some readers, on hearing this news, may wonder why a woman is tending the flock. Does Laban lack sons, or is Rachel her father's favorite, or is she unusually independent and outgoing? (Later we learn of another woman, Dinah, who "goes out" alone and is seen, admired, and raped.)

20. For perfectly understandable reasons, it does not occur to Jacob that Laban could have many such daughters. Isaac had commanded him to take a wife "from among Laban's daughters" (28:2); Jacob hears only that Rachel is "Laban's daughter."

And it happened, when Jacob saw
Rachel, the daughter of Laban, his mother's brother,
   and the sheep of Laban, his mother's brother,
that Jacob drew near, and rolled the stone from the well's mouth,
and watered the flock of Laban, his mother's brother.
And Jacob kissed Rachel,
and lifted up his voice, and wept. (29:10–11)

Jacob, sharp-eyed, sees Rachel and at the same time sees also the flock. No stranger to the love of gain, he may be as attracted by the one as by the other. In any case, the sheep's need for water provides him with a golden opportunity to make an impression on the lady.[21] Jacob, restoring himself to life, bursts forth into action. Inspired by the sight of Rachel, inspired also by the miraculous coincidence of her arrival in the midst of his inquiry about her family, Jacob, in a display of heroic strength, moves the great stone all by himself—"a stone that no ten men today could budge"—and hastens generously to draw water for her flock. Jacob, as it were, takes possession of the sheep and, by implication, of their shepherdess.

It is a golden moment—a moment of vigor, daring, and kindness. What woman would not be impressed? In addition, the stranger is stronger than any man in the neighborhood, able all by himself to provide life-giving access to the well. But the careful reader also notices that, in his great deed with the stone, Jacob has defied the local custom. For Jacob, the stone is but a stone, an obstacle to life-giving water, a vehicle for showing his prowess. But in Haran, the stone is the embodiment of custom, of the mores of the community that in fact protect the life of its members.[22] Jacob the deviser, the man who rejected primogeniture, has never been a man who defers much to custom. Neither is any other man in love. Jacob in love is likely to be doubly antinomian, doubly indifferent to law and custom. This, it should be added, is not simply a defect; not being bound by convention, Jacob is potentially more open to discovering a true and better way.[23]

Jacob's boldness with the boulder is matched by his boldness with the

21. The reader will certainly recall the last reported meeting at a well, where Jacob's mother made an overwhelming impression on a man whose camels were thirsty. There, however, there was preliminary speech and a modest request.

22. This is true not only in Haran. In ancient Greece, there was an explicit connection between law/custom and stones. The Greek word for "custom" (or mores, law, and convention) is *nomos*, cognate with *nemo*, to distribute by an act of designation. An early meaning of *nomos* is "pastureland," mine in contrast to thine, whose boundaries are the product of *nomos*, our conventional agreement, and indicated by a *nomos*, a heap of stones we have set up as a sign of that agreement. Before written agreements, stones suitably arranged spoke volumes to those who knew how to read them.

23. I owe this last insight to Hillel Fradkin.

woman. The flock he waters, but the woman he kisses.[24] To protect Jacob's reputation, commentators have been at pains to insist that this was a genteel kiss, a sign of respect or familial affection.[25] And Jacob truly has every reason to be overjoyed to have arrived safely and to have met up with his kin; the tears he weeps could be tears of joyous relief, his lifted voice could be an expression of thanksgiving. Indeed, Jacob could well take this fortuitous meeting—a perfect answer in the perfect place at the perfect moment—as a sign that Rachel is his destiny.[26] But his kiss is bold in any case, and, considered as a sequel to his superhuman heroics with the stone, it looks to be love-inspired. He kisses Rachel even before speaking to her. In fact, this is the only instance in biblical narrative in which a man kisses a woman who is neither his wife nor his mother. Jacob acts on strong and immediate passion, and Rachel allows it.[27] Only after the kiss and the weeping does Jacob speak, identifying himself as her father's kin and as Rebekah's son. Rachel, who has apparently remained speechless, runs home to tell her father.

Uncle Laban is, in his own right, not reticent. A generation earlier, Laban had rushed out to see Abraham's servant, come for Rebekah, and upon seeing the gifts that he bore, had offered him hospitality. Here, once again, he rushes out to meet Jacob, embraces and kisses him, and brings him home (29:13).[28] In the house, Jacob recounts to Laban "all these things," which is to say, his whole story, including his deception of his father. Hearing the tale, Laban exclaims with gusto, "Thou art surely my bone and my flesh" (29:14), affirming kinship not

24. In Hebrew, the verbs sound much alike: *yashq*, "watered"; *yishaq*, "kissed." Compare 27:25–27, where Jacob gives both drink and kisses to Isaac; on that occasion, Jacob was disguised as Esau, this time he openly reveals himself, in shining and heroic display.

25. One example: "When the Hebrew verb ["to kiss"] is, as here, not followed by the accusative case, it denotes kissing the hand as a respectful salutation" (Ibn Ezra).

26. If so, we may ask whether Jacob is a good reader of signs. The question gains force once we learn that Rachel is extremely beautiful. Of what are beautiful looks a sign? Is this sign reliable?

27. The contrasts between the meetings of Rebekah and Abraham's servant and, more relevant, of Rebekah and Isaac (24:67) are striking. Unlike Abraham's servant, Jacob offers no expression of gratitude to God for this "miraculous" meeting. Unlike Isaac, Jacob falls in love at first sight. In contrast, Isaac first took Rebekah as his wife and only later came to love her.

28. Analyzing Laban's deeds here, Rashi comments: "HE RAN TOWARDS HIM, thinking he was laden with money, for the servant of that household (Eliezer) had come there with ten camels fully laden. AND EMBRACED HIM—When he saw that he had nothing with him, he thought, 'Perhaps he has brought gold coins and they are *hidden away* in his bosom!' HE KISSED HIM—he thought, 'Perhaps he has brought pearls (or precious stones, in general) and they are in his mouth!' " There is no mention of Laban's offering Jacob food and drink; only later, at the wedding feast (29:22), will the initial kiss be matched by the gift of drink. It seems likely that Laban got Jacob very drunk on his wedding night.

only in blood but perhaps also of character.[29] This hidden warning is lost on Jacob, who moves in with his uncle.

Love has brought Jacob into a new home, a home headed not by the passive Isaac but by a man much more like himself. It is in this home of kindred blood but of foreign ways that Jacob will finally grow up to independent manhood. His ambiguous status in Laban's household—is he kinsman, or servant? insider, or outsider?—foreshadows the dilemma he faces.

After a month or so, Laban proposes that Jacob be paid for his service:

> "Because thou art my brother, shouldest thou therefore serve me for nothing? Tell me, what shall be thy wages?" (29:15)

Laban's speech is ambiguous, and his intentions hard to discern. On the surface, he is, or at least appears to be, concerned for Jacob's welfare: "Because you are my kinsman, you should not work for nothing, but should be rewarded." But his words could also be read, "What, are you my kinsman that you work for nothing?" As we shall see, Laban will treat Jacob not as kin but as servant, and Jacob too will regard himself this way. But in either case, and regardless of Laban's intention, when Jacob names a wage for himself, Jacob agrees de facto to become his uncle's hireling. Blood and business make bad bedfellows.

The ordinarily canny Jacob is blind to any potential danger in becoming his uncle's hireling. In fact, Jacob has his own reasons for welcoming Laban's offer: Jacob intends to turn service into kinship, by working to earn the hand of his beloved as wages. But things are not going to be so easy. Laban, we are now told, has two daughters, not just one. The elder, Leah (her name can mean "cow," "strong woman," or "mistress"; or, alternatively, "weary," from a root *la'ah*, meaning "to tire," "to be or make disgusted"), is described as having weak or soft or tender eyes (*'eyney rakoth); the younger, Rachel (her name means "ewe lamb"), is said to be "of beautiful form and beautiful to see" (*yefath-to'ar viyfath mar'eh; 29:16).[30] Attention is called to Leah's eyes and Rachel's looks, and therewith to the difference between the invisible soul and the visible surface.

Visible beauty is strikingly obvious; at its extreme, it can be blinding, preventing the viewer from even looking for signs of the soul. For the beautiful look

29. I owe this observation to Eric Lavoie.
30. The twice-used word for beautiful, *yafeh*, is from a root meaning "bright" or "shining." "Form" is *to'ar*, meaning "outline," "figure," "shape," "appearance." The very same words will be used to describe Rachel's son Joseph, in the episode of Potiphar's wife (39:6). Rebekah, in contrast, had been said to be (merely) very good-looking, *tovath mar'eh me'od*. In contrast with the description given of Rebekah approaching the well, no comment is made about Rachel's virginity.

conveys wholeness and self-sufficiency and advertises its bearer as self-evidently good. Indeed, so confident are we in the reliability of the beautiful that we rarely wonder whether it advertises itself truly. In contrast, we somehow know that it is less easy to read the soul, a truth mirrored for us in the biblical text by the difficulty in deciphering the description given of Leah's eyes. Do they reveal her to be weak, or tender? Is she the maternal, nurturing, or householdly sort? Could she be more discerning, a better "looker" than her better-looking sister? However suggestively the text might invite such thoughts, it surely forces *us* to look searchingly into her eyes and into what lies behind them and within. But Jacob has eyes only for Rachel.

The mention of Rachel's beauty is immediately followed by the declaration of Jacob's love—no great surprise, inasmuch as eros is born through the eyes.[31] And loving her, he sought to have her as his wife:

> And Jacob loved Rachel; and he said, "I will serve thee seven years for Rachel, thy younger daughter." (29:18)

It may seem worse than strange to modern readers that a lover would willingly demean his beloved by regarding her as wages. But we should not judge hastily. Jacob is in a very weak position: an exile and refugee, without possessions or prospects and lacking a bride price, he could have no other hope for arranging the match. To gain her father's consent, he could offer only himself and his devoted service, and Laban appears to accept the stated wage:

> "It is better that I give her to thee than that I should give her to another man. Dwell with me." (29:19)

But Laban does not exactly say yes. "Better to thee than to another" is fully compatible with "Best to no one." Laban, who seems also to have preferred his more beautiful daughter, may indeed have been reluctant to give her to anyone. Also, as we shall see, he may have other considerations that will get in the way of the straightforward agreement as Jacob proposed it. But Jacob thinks he has a bargain, and is simply delighted with it. In contrast to his demand for an oath-sworn promise when Esau agreed to sell him the birthright (25:33), Jacob here carelessly forgets to ask for assurances or swearings. Love has lowered his guard, not to say stolen his wits.

---

31. We have here another occasion to ponder the Bible's thoroughgoing examination of the reliability of the human senses, and in particular its critique of the pretensions and hazards of sight and seeing.

And Jacob served seven years for Rachel; and they were *in his eyes* like but a *few days* [*yamim 'achadiym*] *because of his love for her.* (29:20; emphasis added)

This is, for me, one of the most beautiful sentences of the entire book. No poet has spoken better of love's power to inspire devotion, to lighten hardships, and to defy the ordinary course of time.[32] Yet seven years are *not* a few days;[33] what appears to Jacob's eyes is, in this case, an illusion caused by love. Could the promise of Rachel's beauty, also delivered to his eyes, be similarly illusory? Especially in this story about deceivers and deceiving, we should be on our guard not to let our own romantic beliefs blind us to the question of where the deception really occurs. Jacob loves Rachel—and so do most of us with him. But does God share this preference?

JACOB'S WEDDING: LOVE VERSUS CUSTOM

When the seven years have expired, Jacob claims his wages: "Give me my wife, for my days are fulfilled, that I may go in unto her" (29:21). Jacob's love of the beautiful Rachel is hardly Platonic; sexual desire for her fills his soul—not surprisingly, after seven years of longing. Laban responds by gathering all the men of the place and making a wedding feast. But under cover of night, Laban takes his elder daughter, Leah, no doubt suitably veiled as a bride, and brings her to Jacob, who goes in unto her. (At this point in the story, the text keeps the reader in the dark with Jacob by postponing the denouement for one verse, as it first tells that Laban gave Zilpah, his handmaid, to Leah for a handmaid—presumably a wedding present.) But it came to pass, in the morning: "Behold! It [she] was Leah!" Jacob, the sharp-eyed, has been tricked in the dark by his uncle regarding sisters just as he had previously deceived his dim-sighted father regarding brothers.

32. Compare, for example, Ferdinand's speech commenting on the log-carrying task Prospero had set him in order to earn Miranda's hand: "This my mean task / would be as heavy to me as odious, but / the mistress which I serve quickens what's dead / and makes my labors pleasures" (Shakespeare, *The Tempest*, III.1.4–7).

33. Recall that Rebekah had told Jacob to stay with Laban for "a few days" (*yamim 'achadiym*) until his brother's anger subsides. Love (at least when unconsummated) can appear to conquer time. The question is whether time can conquer (unsatisfied) wrath. I would suggest that Rebekah had no illusions that Esau's anger would be rapidly dissolved; there is every reason to believe that she knew she would never see Jacob again, that "only for a few days" was a white lie intended to make Jacob bear more easily the pain of forced separation. Jacob, in contrast and thanks to love, is happily self-deceived about time. A sign of his error is the use (again) of *'achadiym*, the "impossible" plural of "one" (*'achad*), to indicate a *few* days. (For the two previous uses, see Chapter Eight, p. 224, and Chapter Thirteen, n. 23.)

But how did it happen? It was, of course, dark and the woman's face was covered. Moreover, Jacob was quite possibly drunk, after a full day of feasting and drinking, and in addition he may have been blinded by lust.[34] But given the local context, the story offers a powerfully ironic comment on the love of visible beauty, and shows as well the unreliability of trusting alone to sight. For where is visible beauty in the dark? Jacob, with stars in his eyes, is shown here to be blinded, not necessarily by lust or drink but by the love of the beautiful itself. He does not know one wife from the other except superficially.[35] And whereas his dim-sighted father Isaac, in *his* deception, had available to him a reliable sense, namely, hearing—"the voice is the voice of Jacob"—Jacob and Leah's lovemaking presumably took place in silence.

As it happens, there is a midrash (a rabbinic homily) to the contrary. According to it, Rachel—who had to have participated in this switching, at least by acquiescence—is present during the entire affair, speaking from beneath the bed to perpetuate the deception, and primarily to keep her sister from being exposed and humiliated: the hands are the hands of Leah, but the voice is the voice of Rachel. Indeed, for this self-sacrificing and generous behavior, the ancient rabbis greatly extolled Rachel's character, adding that she allowed Leah to take her place not only to save Leah from having to marry Esau, for whom, as eldest, she was intended, but also because she herself knew that Leah would be the better wife and mother for her beloved Jacob.[36] But all of this extratextual commentary only serves to highlight how much the text itself leaves dark, how much it begs for interpretation, thoughtful reflection, and well-considered judgment.

In any event, though we sense the justice in the trickster being tricked, we are also inclined to share Jacob's bewilderment and indignation:

"What is this thou hast done unto me? Was it not for Rachel that I served with thee? Then why hast thou beguiled [*or* betrayed] me?" (29:25)

---

34. Believing that Jacob is your typical sexist male, dominated by self-serving lust, a recent (female) commentator vulgarly suggests that the story means to teach that, in the dark, all women are for all intents and purposes interchangeably the same. According to this commentator, this view of women is encouraged, if not actively supported, by the entire biblical narrative. Such are the dangers of tendentious readings.

35. To generalize the point: although one cannot choose whom to fall in love with, one can choose whom to marry. A man who enters into marriage driven solely by erotic passion may be said not to choose at all. Waking up in bed with the wrong wife is the perfect symbol of "failure to choose," of not knowing what one has "chosen" to do.

36. All this and much more in praise of Rachel is to be found in a beautiful book, *Rachel,* by the late Samuel H. Dresner, from which I have learned much. As will become clear, however, I do not believe that the text of Genesis itself is partial to—or even approving of—Rachel as the fitting wife for Jacob.

Jacob rightly feels abused, cheated, and betrayed.[37] But Uncle Laban has an answer, which, even if he offers it only as a feigned excuse, carries moral force—with us and especially with Jacob:

"It is not done thus *in our place* to give the younger before *the firstborn* [*habekhirah*]." (29:26; emphasis added)

Laban, perhaps speaking better than he knows, implicitly rebukes Jacob as a defier of custom, as a man committed to supplanting the firstborn: pointedly Laban does not say "before the elder" but "before the *firstborn*," using a word cognate with "the birthright" *(habekhorah)*, the right of the *bekhor*, the firstborn son. Jacob must hear and feel these rebukes, at least to some extent. And so, when Laban adds immediately that, if Jacob does not repudiate this marriage to Leah, "we will give thee also the other one" (29:27), Jacob offers no protest, not even over the condition that he must afterward serve Laban another seven years to "pay" for Rachel.

To be sure, Jacob's position is weak; he is alone, without power, and under Laban's thumb. And because he still wants Rachel and can enjoy her in only one more week, he has little choice but to submit.[38] Jacob will long harbor a deep grievance against Laban for his double-dealing. Yet at this moment, clever Jacob must surely have registered the telling criticism Laban implicitly makes of him. Cleverness and self-reliance have been humbled, all thanks to love.

JACOB'S TWO WIVES: LOVE VERSUS PROCREATION

The double marriage does not change Jacob's love for Rachel. On the contrary, "he loved Rachel more than Leah" (29:30). Such preference, probably unavoidable in any bigamous marriage, promises trouble in the house.[39] In the present case, it also raises questions about the basis of the preference, and whether, from the point of view of both marriage itself and God's new way begun with Abraham, Jacob's preference is to be applauded. Jacob loved Rachel more, but was Rachel more lovable? What, besides her beauty, recommends her? However much we might be partial to love and lovers, erotic love of the sort Jacob felt for Rachel may *not* be the best foundation for marriage and family life—especially if

37. The word Jacob used for "beguiled," *ramah,* is cognate with the word Isaac used to complain of Jacob's guile, after the deception was discovered (27:35).

38. Jacob thus finds himself in a position similar to that of Esau in the birthright story: he must take the woman who has "the birthright" (to be the first to marry) if he wants to satisfy his erotic hungerings.

39. The Chinese ideogram for "trouble" pictures two women under one roof.

they are to be informed by God's covenant with Abraham and his seed, with its emphasis on righteousness and holiness. For eros for the beautiful is one thing, parenthood and perpetuation another.

As we learn in the immediate sequel, God Himself upholds this distinction, and weighs in on the side of procreation, and thus, implicitly, *against nongenerative love:*

> And the Lord saw that Leah was hated,[40] and he opened her womb; but Rachel was barren. (29:31)

Even if God does not simply favor Leah over Rachel, even if He is only compensating Leah out of pity for her being unloved, His intervention highlights for us the tension between love and generation. Jacob has one wife for love, one wife for children. It seems as if the love of the beautiful is, by itself, sterile. And Leah, who bears Jacob four sons in quick succession, seems to justify God's gracing her with offspring. For in naming her sons—Reuben, Simeon, Levi, and Judah—she makes reference to the Lord three times, a fact all the more remarkable because the Lord was not the god of her father or his household.

In becoming Jacob's wife, Leah fully and quickly accepted Jacob's God (she speaks of "the Lord," *YHWH*). Indeed, she speaks of God much more than does Jacob himself. True, in the naming of her first three sons, Leah refers also to her affliction and to her hope that her husband now will love her because she has borne him sons. But in naming Judah *(Yehudah),* she says simply, gratefully, and piously, "This time I will praise [*hodah*] the Lord" (29:35).[41] Having apparently given up on gaining love from Jacob, she delights solely in the gift of her child. Eventually, it will be Judah who, praise the Lord, rises to leadership in the house of Jacob and whose descendants exert political leadership for the people of Israel. In addition, it is the tribe of Levi—Leah's third son—that will carry out the priestly functions. Religiously (through Levi) and politically (through Judah), the leadership of Israel will belong to the sons of Leah, the unloved because unbeautiful wife.

Rachel herself is not content to be only the preferred wife and Jacob's beloved; she too wants to bear children—the desire for motherhood is powerful and its

---

40. Commentators insist that "hated" here means only "*less* loved," that Jacob did not have an aversion to Leah. That she had children by him supports this view.

41. There is a progression in the names Leah chooses: Reuben (*R'u ben,* "see, a son"), "The Lord hath *seen* my suffering"; Simeon (*Shim'on,* from *sham'a,* "hear"), "The Lord hath heard I am despised"; Levi (*Levi,* from *lavah,* "join"), "My husband will be joined unto me"; Judah (*Yehudah,* from *'odeh,* "sing praise"), "I will praise the Lord." Leah's mind goes from seeing to hearing to joining her husband to praising the Lord. (I owe this observation to Yuval Levin.)

frustration can be devastating, all the more so in a culture that esteems procreation and fecundity. Moreover, her barrenness is made the more painful by her sister's extraordinary fertility.[42] Yet the text does not mention her sadness or her frustration, but only her envy: "And when Rachel saw that she bore Jacob no children, Rachel *envied her sister*" (30:1; emphasis added). Driven by envy, Rachel petulantly confronts Jacob. Here is the Bible's only recorded conversation between them:

> And she said unto Jacob, "Give me children or else I die!" And Jacob's anger was kindled against Rachel, and he said, "Am I in God's stead, who hath withheld from thee the fruit of the womb?" And she said, "Behold my maid Bilhah, go in unto her; that she may bear upon my knees, and I may be built up, even I, through her." And she gave him Bilhah, her handmaid, to wife; and Jacob went in unto her. And Bilhah conceived and bore Jacob a son. (30:2–5)

Not only is love apparently not enough, it is not even secure as love. Rachel first implies that a life without children is not worth living, and here we may sympathize with her (though her remark "I will die" reminds us of Esau's exaggeration in the birthright story). But Rachel's desire to be built up indicates that she is moved by other than maternal impulses. Her interest in children does not look to the future and the need for perpetuation, but to the present and her own status and sense of fulfillment. Rachel, outwardly beautiful, is inwardly consumed by the ugly green monster. Ugly, too, is her demanding, not to say hysterical, speech.

But Jacob's response is much worse. His love turns to anger, as he sternly rebukes her with a rejoinder that is, at best, only superficially pious: Why are you blaming me, when it is God's fault? Jacob seems utterly uncomprehending of the depth of his wife's womanly need. One even suspects he is not interested in children, at least not from his beautiful wife.[43] Those who love the beautiful want the beautiful to remain unchangingly and forever the same ("seven years . . . like a few days"), and also to remain undividedly theirs: on both counts, pregnancy and motherhood are threatening. In addition, a woman's interest in children is proof that a man's love is not enough for her: though she is everything to him,

42. Just as Cain's disappointment that his sacrifice was not accepted was made vastly more painful because Abel's was well received.

43. In a parallel story that opens the book of Samuel, Elkanah answers his preferred but barren wife, Hannah, "Why is thy heart grieved? Am I not better to thee than ten sons?" (1 Samuel 1:8). This speech is much more beautiful and comforting than Jacob's, but Elkanah too seems unaware of, or perhaps indifferent to, the maternal impulse in his favorite wife.

he cannot be everything to her—and this recognition is enough to make him angry.

Jacob certainly does not turn to God as his father had done under similar circumstances—"And Isaac entreated the Lord for his wife, because she was barren" (25:21)—a deed to which Jacob in fact owes his very existence. Instead, to please his wife, he accepts the dubious expedient of providing Rachel an adoptable child through a surrogate (by the by, also avoiding in this way any change in Rachel's looks), a practice that had proved disastrous when the beautiful Sarah induced Abraham to get her a child through Hagar.

Sure enough, household tensions spiral as a result. Bilhah produces two sons—named by Rachel Dan, "He Judged," because "God has judged and also heard my voice and given to me a son," and Naphtali, "Wrestlings," because "in wrestlings of God have I wrestled with my sister, and have prevailed" (30:6–8).[44] Not to be outdone, Leah enters her handmaid Zilpah into the competition; and she bears Jacob two sons, Gad and Asher. But there is no rivalry so low that it cannot sink lower. With the episode of the mandrakes, we hear the sisters speaking with each other for the first and only time.

Reuben, Leah's firstborn, has found mandrakes and brought them to his mother, who presumably intended to make use of their aphrodisiac and procreative powers to win back her husband's attention and to resume bearing children. When Rachel begs for a share, Leah complains, "Is it a small matter that thou hast taken my husband? And now [thou wouldst take] also my son's mandrakes?" (30:15). Rachel makes Leah an ugly offer, but one she cannot refuse: Jacob for tonight in exchange for the mandrakes.[45] Leah accepts and, in an act at once triumphant and self-debasing, tells Jacob, "Thou must come in unto me, for I have surely hired thee with my son's mandrakes" (30:16).

Rachel may have the mandrakes, but fertility remains with the Lord: "And God hearkened unto Leah . . . and she bore Jacob a fifth son," Issachar, and also, soon, a sixth, Zebulun, both named with clear reference to the sisters' rivalry (30:17–19). Leah believes, and repeatedly says, that her husband should dwell with her, because she is the fertile source of his children. For Leah, wifeliness means mainly motherhood, not self-satisfied eros—a view that God Himself appears to support.

44. Rachel conflates wrestling her sister and the "wrestlings of God"—mighty and awesome wrestlings. Though the text uses here a different word for "wrestling" (*naftulim*, from a root "to twist"), this image reminds of Jacob and Esau grappling in the womb; more important, it anticipates the famous episode, discussed in our next chapter, of Jacob's nocturnal wrestling in which wrestling with God and wrestling with his brother are again conflated. (In this case the verb "to wrestle" is *'avaq*, "to get dusty"—from rolling around on the ground.)

45. The ugly character of this sisterly exchange recalls the brotherly exchange between Jacob and Esau over the swapping of the birthright for a mess of pottage.

After Leah completes her childbearing with Jacob's single daughter, Dinah, God at last remembers Rachel and opens her womb. At the birth of her son, Rachel joyously exults: "God hath taken away ['*asaf*] my disgrace" (30:23); yet, not content with this one blessing, and still in competition with her sister, she names him Joseph *(Yosef)*, saying, "May the Lord add [*yosef*] to me another son" (30:24). It is doubtful whether Rachel truly understands or accepts the truth she herself utters, that it is the Lord who adds and the Lord who takes away.

Though we are tracking the adventures of Jacob, it is worth noting that the tale just considered is the only story in Genesis about two sisters (except for the brief episode in which Lot's two daughters plot to have children by their father [19:30–38]). If the Cain and Abel story showed us the unvarnished truth about the relations between brothers, perhaps this one does likewise for the relations between sisters. If so, the following comparisons seem to be suggested by the text. The brothers were rivals for preeminence: to be first in paternal or divine approval, to excel in worldly standing and success, to win renown and glory. The sisters are rivals for love and "creativity": to possess exclusively the love of a man, to be supreme as "the mother of all living." (Leah is a mother who wants to be beloved; Rachel is beloved but wants to be a mother.) Brothers rage and fume, confront one another directly, and fight it out, even to the death. Sisters smolder with envy and resentment, try to enlist men to aid their cause (Jacob for Rachel, Reuben for Leah), and if they fight, they fight with speech that wounds. Both brothers and sisters fight about what a modern reader might call their "identity" in the face of our inevitable mortality, but their different roles in and attitudes toward procreation create different grounds for rivalry. In battling one another, men rebel against domesticity, the symbol of the need for those who come after; women fight for domestic supremacy and the control over the procreative future.[46]

The tale of the birth of Jacob's children is now nearly complete, and the time has come to take stock. Rivalry between the sisters has sown deep enmity in the household—though, one must add in fairness, it is also largely responsible for the abundant growth of Jacob's clan. Thanks to the competition between the wives, God's new way will be able to go from household to incipient nation in one generation. The blame for the competition lies not with Jacob but with Laban and his deception; but Jacob contributes to his own deception, just as the appetitive Esau and Isaac contributed to theirs.

What makes Jacob vulnerable to deception—and is the root cause of this situation—is eros, his love for the beautiful Rachel. Love opened the soul of this previously self-centered and self-serving man, bringing him to attention and in-

---

46. There is no English analogue for "fratricide" to name "sister killing," though the sister as rival can be "eliminated" if she is prevented from bearing children.

spiring devotion. As a result of investing his heart in someone other than himself, Jacob has become more educable. But this is not, as the Greeks might have it, because the beautiful is the skin of the good, or because eros points one to the divine. On the contrary, Jacob as lover is open to education because love has made him vulnerable to suffering, has prepared him to recognize the limits of his own powers and understanding. He wins his beloved, but he cannot fully possess her. He has what he thought was his heart's desire, yet it turns out to be less than fully satisfying. Finally, Jacob's is a love whose wisdom is called into question by the story of the sisters' rivalry and childbearing. The more life-giving, more humble, and more God-affirming spouse is shown—to the reader, not yet to Jacob—to be Leah.

STEALING AWAY: THE CUNNING OF JACOB AND THE IDOLATRY OF RACHEL

Now that his beloved Rachel has borne a son, Jacob decides it is time to leave. His second seven years of service have expired; also, now that Rachel has borne his child, Jacob has a more powerful claim to remove her from her father's house. But he is a servant, not a free agent; he must plead with Laban not only for his independence but even for his wives and children, who technically, it seems, still belong to Laban:

> "Send me away [or give me leave], that I may go to my own place and my land. *Give me my wives and my children* for whom I have served thee that I may go, for thou knowest my service with which I have served thee." (30:25–26; emphasis added)

As Nahum Sarna points out, Jacob must argue "that he is not an ordinary slave to whom a master gives a wife. In such a case, she and her offspring would belong to the master and remain in his household on the manumission of the slave." But Laban is not ready to let Jacob go. Instead, he offers him a new deal for an extended service, asking Jacob to name his wages. Jacob resists, pointing out that Laban has already benefited aplenty from his service: "for the Lord hath blessed thee wherever I turned. And now, when shall I provide also for my own household?" (30:30). Sensing, however, an opportunity to enrich himself while still in Laban's service, Jacob proposes a new contract: in exchange for tending your flocks, let me keep as wages all the speckled and spotted sheep and goats.[47]

---

47. These are uncommon types in the Near East. The sheep are white, the goats black or brown.

Laban, eager for such a profitable deal, promptly agrees—equally promptly, he removes all the white-patched goats and dark-marked sheep and gives them to his sons, leaving Jacob, to start with, with no animals at all to breed from.

But crafty Jacob is not without resources. Armed with what appears to be arcane knowledge of genetic engineering—the secret of which is lost to us!—Jacob knows how to induce the flocks to breed spotted and speckled, and he employs this "magic" only when it is the vigorous animals that are ready to conceive. As a result of Jacob's manipulations, "the feebler were Laban's and the stronger Jacob's. And the man increased greatly, and he had large flocks, and maidservants and menservants, and camels and asses" (30:42–43). Over a period of six years, Jacob becomes increasingly rich by means of his own cleverness and enterprise. His prosperity, however, lands him in a tight spot and precipitates a final conflict with his uncle Laban.

Laban's sons, envious of Jacob's prosperity, accuse him of taking away their father's wealth, and Laban's demeanor toward him also turns sour. With his situation in Laban's household now precarious, Jacob is utterly at a loss. At this crucial juncture, God speaks to him—indeed, speaks directly for the first time, now twenty years after his marvelous dream at Beth-El. God's speech is a precise answer to Jacob's deepest longings and apprehensions:

> And the Lord said unto Jacob, "Return to the land of thy fathers, and to thy kindred, and I will be with thee." (31:3)

Thanks to God's speech, with its reassuring echo of the divine promise of his dream at Beth-El—"I am with thee"—Jacob is moved to act.

His first task is to persuade his wives to leave their father's house and their kindred, and to go off with him to a land unknown. Jacob summons them out of the house into the field, among his abundant flock, and makes his case, frequently appealing to God's providence in order to convince them:

> "I see thy father's countenance, that it is not toward me as before time; but the God of my father hath been with me. Now ye know that with all my power I have served thy father, but he has cheated me and changed my wages ten times; but God did not allow him to harm me. If he said thus, 'The speckled shall be thy wages,' then all the flock bore speckled; and if he said thus, 'The streaked shall be thy wages,' then all the flock bore streaked. For God hath taken away the livestock of thy father and has given it to me." (31:5–9)

Jacob compels his wives to compare their father with his own father's God: your father's attitude toward me changes, but my father's God is always with me. I have been constant in my devotion to your father, whereas he has been devious and dishonest; and only God has kept him from harming me as he would have liked to do. Not I, but God, has taken your father's livestock.

Jacob's rhetorical appeal is powerful: whose side would you like to join, that of your dishonest and declining father or that of my steady and successful God? But for the reader, his apparent piety is suspect. The truth of the matter is that Jacob has made no appeal to God during his years in Haran. Relying on his own skill and cunning, he has lived solely by the maxim of self-help, at most perhaps believing that God helps those who help themselves. Because his prosperity is at once the source of Laban's enmity and a reason for his wives to join his party, it is terribly important that he remove all suspicion that his wealth is both ill-gotten and insecure. To nail down this point, he next tells Rachel and Leah that his great knowledge about stock breeding—the knowledge to which he owes his success at Laban's expense—came to him in a divinely sent dream, in which an angel of God told him that it would be the streaked, speckled, and mottled he-goats that would sire the flocks. But not to put too fine a point on it, Jacob's *report* of such a dream is not otherwise corroborated in the narrative. Worse, it is frankly at odds with Jacob's actual breeding practices, in which he used white-striped rods in front of mating animals to induce them to generate mottled off-spring. There is good reason to suspect that Jacob never had such a dream.

Jacob concludes the account of what God told him in this "dream":

> "I am the God of Beth-El, where thou didst anoint a pillar, and where thou didst vow to Me a vow; now, arise, go out from this land and return to the land of thy nativity." (31:13)

Jacob inserts the Lord's most recent and explicit exhortation to leave Haran into this (?made-up) dream, not surprisingly assimilating also his experience at Beth-El, and revisiting the old promises that the God in this dream reminds Jacob He made long ago. God's actual command that Jacob return to Canaan is placed, for the wives, in the further context of Jacob's sworn vows to return and serve his God. God's power, prophecy, and providence and Jacob's prosperity and pious promises all add up to one conclusion: Let us go, and follow God— and He will surely follow us.

Despite their bitter rivalry, the two sisters respond as one and just as one might have predicted, especially after such a rhetorically perfect appeal:

> And Rachel and Leah answered and said unto him: "Is there yet for us a share of an inheritance in our father's house? Are we not reckoned by him as outsiders, now that he hath sold us and also surely eaten up our pur-

chase price? For all the riches that God hath taken away from our father, that is ours and our children's; now, therefore, all which God hath said to thee, do." (31:14–16)

The shift of economic fortunes, the decline in their father's wealth, and their belief that it is God who has shifted it—not to Jacob, but to them and their children—persuades both sisters to join Jacob in his God-supported wish to flee and to return home. To say the least, the ability to offer convincing speech about God surely helps him who would help himself.

Encouraged both by God's exhortation and promise and by his wives' wholehearted endorsement, Jacob hastens to leave, "to go to Isaac, his father, to the land of Canaan" (31:18). To avoid confrontation with Laban, he escapes with them when his father-in-law is absent. In contrast with his arrival in Paddan-aram, alone and unaccommodated, he leaves as head of a large clan (two wives, two handmaid-concubines, twelve children between the ages of six and twelve, and many servants) and as a man of substance. Yet despite his prosperity, he leaves as he came, in flight from mortal danger, relying on craftiness to outwit superior force.

In use of guile, Jacob unknowingly has a partner in his wife Rachel:

Now Laban was gone to shear the sheep, so Rachel stole [*ganav*] the household idols [*terafim*] that were her father's. And Jacob outwitted [*literally, stole (ganav) the heart (lev) of*] Laban the Aramean [*ha'arami*], in that he told him not that he was fleeing. So he fled with all that he had; and he rose up and passed over the river [Euphrates], and he set his face toward the mountain of Gilead. (31:19–21)

Both Rachel and Jacob are said to engage in theft: she literally steals the *terafim* of her father, he figuratively steals the heart of Laban the Aramean,[48] by fleeing with Laban's daughters and grandchildren, as well as by not telling him of his departure. The parallel construction might imply a link between Laban's idols and matters dear to his heart. But the side-by-side reports of the two thefts also compels attention to the differences between them: stealing away means separating yourself from Laban and his ways, stealing his gods means remaining at-

---

48. With regard to the latter, Sarna calls attention to the Hebrew double wordplay: "*Lev* echoes Laban (Heb. *lavan*), while *'arami* evokes the stem *r-m-h*, 'to cheat.' Laban the heartless cheat has been beaten at his own game!" Yuval Levin suggests that in saying that both Rachel and Jacob are "stealing" something, the text may be hinting at Jacob's idol-like worship of Rachel, a worship of something visible that blinds him to higher things. Both of them are, in some sense, stealing idols from Laban. (Personal communication.)

tached to them. Laban is here identified neither as Jacob's father-in-law nor as his mother's brother or his uncle but as "the Aramean." Jacob, who for twenty years has lived abroad, under Laban's roof and following Laban's Aramean customs, now returns on God's command to his father, Isaac, seed of the covenant between God and Abraham and bearer of God's new way. Jacob's return—his stealing away—is thus described as a cultural-religious, and not only a personal, separation.

Not so for Rachel, for when she goes she takes with her the household gods "of her father." The reason for this theft has been the subject of much conjecture. The most pious interpretation, which assumes Rachel's unswerving devotion to the God of Jacob, suggests that she took them to purify her father's house, ridding it of idol worship in a final gift to her father. Others, mindful of the use of such *terafim* in divination, suggest that Rachel sought to deprive her father of the power to detect Jacob's whereabouts after he discovers the escape. But on this interpretation, Rachel would not only need to share the Aramean belief in the power of such idols; she would also implicitly be expressing doubts about the ability of Jacob's God to preserve and protect her once she leaves home. Despite Jacob's speech about his dream and God's promise, despite her exhortation (with Leah) to Jacob that he do all that God had said, Rachel here acts as if she were skeptical—even more than Jacob was on the morning after his dream of the ladder at Beth-El.

At the very least, one must consider that Rachel is hedging her bet on Jacob's God. More likely, she still subscribes to the gods "that were her father's." Whereas Jacob is *separating* himself *from the Aramean* and his ways, Rachel—the text pointedly remarks—takes *her father's gods* and ways *with her* on her journey. Those who wish to claim that Rachel is not still an idol worshiper will have a hard time explaining why she keeps the *terafim* close to her on her journey, rather than throw them away as worthless objects. Rachel's secretive theft of, and attachment to, her father's *terafim* will soon enough come back to haunt her and the entire household.

DECLARING INDEPENDENCE: JACOB STANDS UP FOR HIMSELF

Jacob's attempt to escape unnoticed does not succeed. Three days later, Laban learns of Jacob's flight and, with a large company of men, sets off in hot pursuit. After seven days, he overtakes Jacob, who, encumbered by a great party of livestock and the women and children, necessarily travels at a slower pace. Jacob, who prefers to work with subtlety and guile, will now have to confront an angry Laban face-to-face. Unbeknownst to Jacob, he gets some divine assistance. On the eve of the impending confrontation, God intervenes in an attempt to thwart Laban's plan of retribution:

> And God came to Laban the Aramean in a dream of the night, and said to him, "Take heed to thyself lest thou speak with Jacob either good or bad." (31:24)

Once before God visited someone in a dream by night—Abimelech—to prevent him from violating the line of Abraham. On that occasion, God had even threatened Abimelech with death should he not restore Sarah to Abraham. The noble Abimelech not only hearkened to the Lord but, as a result, even served as God's witness against Abraham and his willingness to pass his wife off as his sister (see Chapter Ten). But Laban is a different sort of man. It remains to be seen what he will make of the divine injunction or warning "Speak with Jacob [neither] good [n]or bad"—especially when its meaning is less than clear.[49] Is God telling Laban to hold his peace, to refrain from attempting anything at all, or is He telling him to avoid both enticing Jacob back with sweet words ("good") and intimidating him with threats ("bad")? Will Laban understand?

When the confrontation occurs the next morning, with the two camps pitched opposite each other in the mountain, Laban begins angrily, as if ignoring the dream. He accuses Jacob of wrongdoing, deception, theft, and the coercive abduction of his daughters:

> "What hast thou done?! For thou hast outwitted me [*again, literally,* thou hast stolen my heart] and thou hast carried off my daughters like captives of the sword." (31:26)

But it soon becomes clear that Laban has little intention of really making trouble. His next words are more plaintive than threatening:

> "Why didst thou flee secretly and thieve from me, and [why didst thou] not tell me, that I could send thee away with joy and songs, with timbrel and harp? Thou didst not even let me kiss my sons and daughters! Now thou hast done foolishly." (31:27–28)

---

49. Once before, Laban himself had used the expression "We cannot speak to thee either good or bad," when he had Bethuel give Rebekah to Abraham's servant as a bride for Isaac (24:50–51). The words are the same as those in the name of the famous tree, knowledge of good *(tov)* and bad *(ra')*. Because of the usage in chapters 24 and 31, where "good or bad" is regarded as an expression for "anything at all," some people argue that the tree is a tree of knowledge of *all things.*

Laban has moved from angry charges of theft to complaints that Jacob has prevented him from showing proper magnanimity and paternal affection. From what we know of Laban, we are confident that he has no such generous intentions. Yet he means for Jacob to empathize with his fatherly losses; even liars, tricksters, and bad fathers can grieve the loss of children. But Laban is not content to play only the sympathy card:

> "I have it in the power of my hand to do thee harm! But the God of thy father spoke to me last night, saying, 'Take heed to thyself lest thou speak with Jacob either good or bad.' " (31:29)

Laban asserts both his superior power and his gracious submission to the injunction of "the God of thy father." Laban does not acknowledge that he accepts this god as his own; but he does point out to Jacob that Jacob will be spared his just deserts only because of his God's concern and Laban's free choice to yield. Once again, it is an outsider who reminds a patriarch about God's providence.

Although apparently moving to put Jacob at his ease, Laban abruptly concludes by again changing course. Saving the most serious charge for the end, Laban finishes by surprising Jacob with a new outburst of angry and most serious accusation:

> "And now that thou art surely gone, because thou surely longest for thy father's house, why hast thou stolen my gods?" (31:30)

Bad as it may be to steal a man's sheep or cattle, his daughters and grandchildren, or even his "heart" and wits, far worse is it to steal his gods—even if one knows that his gods are in no way truly divine. Laban here has good reason to be angry.

Jacob defends himself vigorously. To the demand for an explanation for his secretive flight, he answers, "Because I was afraid, for I said, 'Lest thou forcibly take [that is, kidnap] thy daughters from me' " (31:31). But in answering the charge of stealing Laban's gods, Jacob rashly draws down a death sentence on the thief:

> "With whomever thou findest thy gods, he shall not live; before our brothers, discern what of thine is with me and take it to thee." (31:32)

To explain Jacob's rash confidence, the text informs us that Jacob did not know that Rachel had stolen the *terafim* (31:32). But on a deeper level, the text suggests that Jacob does not really know his beloved wife, and on the most important matter of how she stands in relation to the gods of her father. To say the least, her theft and continued possession of them place her and Jacob's entire family at grave risk.

Laban conducts a thorough search of all the tents but finds nothing. Rachel has in fact hidden them close to her person, in the camel cushion or palanquin, and sits upon them all during the search of her tent. She explains this rude and unusual behavior to her father: "Let not my lord (*'adoni*) take it badly that I am unable to rise before thee, for the way of women is upon me" (31:35). Knowing that Laban would not approach a woman in her time of menstrual impurity, Rachel prevents Laban from searching her or the camel cushion, and the *terafim* are not found.

Many commentators have seen in Rachel's conduct a display of contempt for Laban's gods. For example, Nahum Sarna says: "In light of Israelite notions of [womanly] purity and impurity, as set forth in Leviticus 15:19–24, the description of Rachel's act constitutes the culminating absurdity in the religious situation. It implies an attitude of willful defilement and contemptuous rejection of the idea that Laban's cult objects had any religious worth." But even ignoring the anachronism of reading the as yet unpromulgated Mosaic laws into this situation, Sarna and others seem not to have considered the possibility that Rachel is not telling the truth about her menstrual condition. Someone who has stolen the gods of her father would not be above lying to prevent detection, especially when the thief has just been decreed a candidate for capital punishment. Besides, there would be poetic justice in Rachel's deceiving her father by lying about "the way of women," given that *he* had deceived Jacob regarding sexual matters and denied her the sole right to her lover's bed. Only by already assuming (without—I should even say, *against*—textual warrant) Rachel's integrity and piety toward the God of Abraham can one use this episode as evidence that Rachel was herself not attached to these idols.

When Laban's search fails to uncover the *terafim* (or any other stolen goods), Jacob, now feeling completely vindicated, goes on the offensive. For the first time, he stands up to Laban face-to-face and as an equal:

"What is my trespass, what is my sin, that thou hast hotly pursued after me? Since thou hast felt about all my stuff, what hast thou found of thy household stuff? Place it here opposite my brothers and thy brothers that they may judge between us two. These twenty years I have been with thee; thy ewes and thy she-goats have not miscarried, and the rams of thy flocks I have not eaten. That which was torn by beasts I did not bring to thee; I myself made good the loss; from my hand thou didst require it whether stolen by day or by night. Thus I was: by day the drought consumed me and the frost by night; and my sleep fled from my eyes. Of the twenty years

I have been in thy house, I have served thee fourteen years for thy two daughters and six years for thy flock; and thou hast changed my wages ten times. Except that the God of my father, the God of Abraham and the Fear of Isaac [*pachad yitshaq*] were with me, surely now thou wouldst have sent me away empty-handed. God has seen my affliction and the toil of my hand, and gave judgment last night." (31:36–42)

Jacob demands an explanation for Laban's hostile acts of pursuit, false charges, and search. He taunts Laban to produce any evidence of wrongdoing, and then proceeds to insist on his perfect record of loyal service to Laban. Never has Jacob cheated him; he has even made good losses to Laban's flocks beyond what was customary. Moving from self-defense to accusation, Jacob insists that any dishonesty that has transpired is entirely on Laban's side. Despite Jacob's twenty years of impeccable and devoted service, Laban has repeatedly changed his wages. Finally, countering Laban's claims to generosity, Jacob charges that when and if Laban would have released him from service, Laban would have sent him away with nothing—just as he had come.

Having made a spirited defense of his own conduct, Jacob in the end is able to give credit where credit is due: only the protective presence of God, taking Jacob's side, prevents Laban from successfully robbing Jacob of his rightfully earned family and possessions. Jacob refers to the God of Abraham but to the "Fear of Isaac," a most unusual expression (repeated again in 31:53), referring perhaps to "He whom Isaac feared," perhaps to "the One of Isaac who caused terror," perhaps more literally to the reverent fear experienced by Isaac on Mount Moriah. Jacob, in standing up to Laban the Aramean, is moving himself closer both to his father and to the religious passion of awe-fear. He concludes by interpreting Laban's dream of the night before: God has given judgment in my favor! Though it was Laban who had put Jacob in mind of God, by relating his dream, Jacob is not slow to take the hint. For he now has even Laban's testimony as evidence for the view that the God he dreamt of at Beth-El has indeed been with him these twenty years, despite His silence. Jacob, once inclined to think himself sufficient, now acknowledges God's providence and places himself—for the first time—voluntarily and clearly within the covenant made with his ancestors by the God of Abraham and the Fear of Isaac.

Against this powerful attack, backed finally with the invocation of divine assistance, Laban is virtually powerless to respond. Feebly, he tries to assert his possessive claim as patriarch and master of Jacob, but he cannot sustain it:

"The daughters are my daughters, and the children are my children, and the flocks are my flocks, and all that thou seest is mine; yet for my daughters, what can I do for them this day, or for their children whom they have borne? Come, then, let us make a covenant, I and thou, and let it be for a witness between me and thee." (31:43–44)

Laban clings to the ancient notions—earlier, in a way, acknowledged by Jacob himself, when he *asked* to be given his wives and children (30:26)—that the entire clan and property belong to the family's chief and that when servants leave, their wives and children remain behind with the master. But Laban lacks the means and/or the will to enforce this claim, and acknowledges his impotence in midspeech. Compelled to accept Jacob's independent standing as de facto head of his daughters and grandchildren, he now offers to make the best of a bad situation and enter into an agreement with him, on behalf of the very children he is losing. It is a great concession, for this time Laban is forced to name his terms and to deal with Jacob as an equal.

Jacob readily accepts Laban's offer. He erects a pillar, sends his men to gather stones for a cairn of witness, and shares a covenantal meal beside it. Laban also calls upon the Lord to witness and watch over their agreement after they part, charging Jacob not to afflict his daughters and not to take any other wives besides them. Laban too erects a cairn and a pillar, which he designates as a boundary between them: "This heap be witness, and this pillar be witness, that I will not pass over this heap to thee, and that thou shalt not pass over this heap and this pillar to me for harm" (31:52). Laban wants to make sure that Jacob, now powerful and with God as ally, will not move aggressively against him in the future. There is to be a clean break between the clan of Laban the Aramean and the tribe of Jacob, son of the covenant.

To conclude the agreement, both men swear an oath. Laban swears by two gods, Jacob's and his own: "May the god of Abraham and the god of Nahor—the gods of their ancestors—judge between us" (31:53); Jacob, in contrast, swears by only the Fear of his father, Isaac. Jacob, now in command, offers a sacrifice (presumably of thanksgiving) on the mountain, and calls on his brethren to eat bread: "and they did eat bread and tarried all night on the mountain" (31:54). Early the next morning, Laban rose, kissed his sons (grandsons) and daughters, blessed them, and departed, returning to his place.

The ancestral ties to Haran and Mesopotamia now permanently disconnected, Jacob, too, resumes his journey homeward. But as he starts out, he is met by angels of the Lord—just as, starting out twenty years ago, he had dreamt about them. Upon seeing them, Jacob unhesitatingly declares, "This is God's camp," and names the place Mahanaim, "two camps." Unbeknownst to Jacob, he will soon again find himself in a place with two camps and will meet another mysterious messenger of the divine. Here he takes comfort and reassurance in the signs of God's continuing presence at his side or in his vicinity.

~

The twenty years of exile are ended. Jacob is returning as a patriarch of his own clan, prosperous, independent, and more confident than ever that God is with him. His trials at Uncle Laban's have not broken his spirit; on the contrary, adversity has made a man out of him. He has acquired enough children to become a tribe, enough possessions with which to provide for his family, sufficient dignity and courage to declare his independence, sufficient clout and standing to establish political agreements with other clans and nations, a newfound desire to return to the land of his father (and to Isaac himself), and perhaps most important, a growing awareness of his dependence on God, the God of Abraham, the God of Isaac, and now also the God of Jacob. None of this would have happened had he stayed home. He has struggled, he has suffered, he has endured— and he has come out much the stronger and better for it.

But a still greater challenge stands in the way of a successful return: Esau. Jacob cannot know whether his brother's murderous hatred has subsided, or whether he can cope with the intemperate Esau as well as he has succeeded with the crafty Laban. His biggest trial still lies ahead.

CODA: THE LOVE OF WOMAN AND
THE FEAR OF THE LORD

Before moving ahead with the story of Jacob's encounter with Esau, some general remarks are called for on the major theme of Jacob's story to date: the relation of love to piety. To prepare these remarks, some materials from later episodes must be incorporated so that the picture of Jacob and his wives can be completed.

Jacob's turn toward God is greatly intensified by his next trial, the necessary encounter with his brother, Esau (the subject of our next chapter). Only one point is relevant to the present topic: beset by fear, Jacob the chronically self-reliant now turns to prayer and approaches God for the first time. He concludes his supplication: "Deliver me, please, from the hand of my brother, from the hand of Esau; for I fear him, lest he come and smite *me*, the *mother* upon the *children*" (32:12; emphasis added). The jumbling of "me," "the mother," and "the children" may well be an expression of inchoate terror, but it is also Jacob's first clear identification of himself with his progeny and with his wives as mothers of his and their children. It even hints at Jacob's own mother, for he now has reason to identify with the meaning of Rebekah's life, a life given in service to perpetuation.

To this point, Jacob has demonstrated his desire for the birthright, his love of Rachel, and his interest in the wealth of livestock. Though he has become the head of a sizable clan, this was the doing of his rivalrous wives, mostly of the one he did not love or want. His twelve children were all named by the women. Perhaps he was attached already to Joseph, son of Rachel, but we have no mention of it. Indeed, there is little if any evidence that he cared very much for the children. But here, with the prospect of death looming before him, suddenly the importance of his children rises vividly in his mind, even to the point of conflating his own being with theirs. Recognition of mortality and concern for his posterity move Jacob closer to God.

After the famous nocturnal wrestling, the reunion and reconciliation with Esau, and the episode with Dinah and the men of Shechem, Jacob, on God's command, at last returns to Beth-El. God appears to him, renames him Israel, and pronounces on him the full Abrahamic blessing. This theophany and this blessing represent the peak of Jacob's relationship to God; Jacob, now as Israel, now returned to the Promised Land, is firmly established in God's grace, having earned his place as a patriarch within the covenant. The birthright and the all-important covenantal blessing are now *rightly* his; we have it on the highest authority.

And yet, just when his relationship with God is solidly established, Jacob's human love is destroyed. As the family heads south from Beth-El, toward Isaac's home in Hebron, Rachel gives birth a second time, this time tragically:

> And they journeyed from Beth-El, and there was still some way to come to Ephrath, when Rachel travailed and she had hard labor. And it happened, when she was in hard labor, that the midwife said to her, "Fear not; for this also is a son for you." And it came to pass, when her soul was departing— for she died—that she called his name Ben-Oni, but his father called him Benjamin. And Rachel died, and she was buried in the way to Ephrath (the same is Beth-lehem). And Jacob set up a pillar upon her grave; the same is the pillar upon Rachel's grave unto this day. (35:16–20)

The text preserves delicate silence about Jacob's grief; though his sorrow for the loss of Rachel will be with him forever (see 48:7), we are not allowed to hear of it.

Yet in the silence are echoes of earlier speeches, earlier episodes. We recall how, in the immediate sequel to the first (dream) theophany at Beth-El, Jacob fell deeply in love at first sight with Rachel, in a love rooted in her physical beauty. Here, after the second (waking) theophany at Beth-El, Rachel's beauty vanishes with the departure of her soul. We remember, eerily, Rachel's demand for children ("Give me children or I die" [30:1]) as well as her greedy and ungrateful speech at the birth of Joseph ("The Lord add [*yosef*] to me another son" [30:24]), a speech that endures as the meaning of Joseph's name. We remember especially the curse Jacob brought down unwittingly on Rachel, stealer of Laban's *terafim*—"With whomsoever thou findest thy gods, he shall not live" (31:32); even if Jacob never learned that Rachel was the thief, we fear that his bold words may just now have produced their effect. And we see Jacob, grief-stricken or not, reject the name Rachel on her deathbed chooses for Benjamin—not "son of my sorrow" but "son of my right hand"; this is the first of Jacob's twelve sons who will bear a name given to him *by his father.*[50]

Finally, we note that Rachel is buried on the road, alone and separated from the sacred burial site of the matriarchs and patriarchs in the cave at Machpelah, resting place of couples Sarah and Abraham, Isaac and Rebekah, the place where Jacob himself will later bury Leah and will himself also come to lie (see 49:29–31). To be sure, Rachel's tomb will later become one of the Jewish holy places; it is a famous landmark already by the time of the prophet Samuel (see 1 Samuel 10:2), and it has been a place of pilgrimage for Jews for centuries. Yet here, in the biblical text itself, Rachel in her death seems to be pushed to the side, if not from Jacob's heart, then from the people of the new way.

Rachel alone of Jacob's entourage from Paddan-aram does not return to Isaac's home; when Jacob comes back, at last, having fulfilled his father's charge to "take a wife [singular] . . . of the daughters of Laban, thy mother's brother," the wife he will be seen to have chosen will be Leah. It is an exaggeration, but in the direction of the truth, to suggest that Jacob's entering fully into God's covenant and stepping forward into the place of his forefathers is finally incompatible with the love of Rachel, the love of the beautiful. Paradoxically, we might even say that we are taught this lesson by Rachel herself, who once insisted that life without children was worse than death and who in the end sacrificed her beauty and her life in the service of perpetuation.

What, then, does this suggest about eros and piety, about the love of woman and the love of God? Love of the beautiful, this story seems to suggest, is at best a detour and a distraction, at worst a form of idolatry. Love of visible beauty is, at bottom, an attempt to make time stand still, to deny one's own mortality and insufficiency, to attach one's perishable self to some seemingly perfect and unchanging earthly form. Only if such love is transformed and domesticated by custom and marriage and turned toward its ever-present possibility, the generation of children, can it become, for the children of the book, a help to piety. For

---

50. This difference could be rationalized as follows: Jacob understands that Benjamin, like all children, replaces his mother, who, in turn, was a replacement for Jacob's mother, taken precisely for this work of perpetuation and transmission. (I owe this observation to my wife.)

it is from the recognition of our own mortality and the resulting desire to give to our children not just life, but a good and righteous way of life, that men and women can open themselves to the ways and attitudes of the Bible. In the parental love of children lies the possibility of the sanctification of life—even in today's world. Not eros as such, about which the text is at best neutral, but *procreation* is the biblical way by which the love of man and woman can lead to the love of God.

Chapter Fifteen

Brotherhood and Piety:
Facing Esau, Seeing God

*T*o find a wife. To escape his brother. These were the reasons for Jacob's leaving home. The first has been accomplished: Jacob has married, not once but twice. The second—Esau's murderous wrath—remains to be addressed. The story's focus and ours must therefore shift from marriage back to brotherhood, the keynote of the entire Jacob story.

The new brotherly encounter will be significantly different from the old, precisely because, this time, Jacob meets Esau as a married man and father—indeed, as the head of an incipient clan. As a result, facing Esau now becomes both easier and more difficult. On the one hand, taking a wife and starting a new family exacerbates brotherly rivalry. On the other hand, having a wife of one's own and becoming a father gives Jacob the incentive to ameliorate it. The twin claims of brotherhood versus marriage-and-fatherhood wrestle with each other in the soul of Jacob—indeed, of every man. As Jacob's next adventures make clear, the tragedy that lurks naturally in the bosom of every family is averted only when the human relationships are seen in the light of man's relationship with God.

There are, of course, many reasons why Jacob cannot inherit the covenant of his fathers without addressing the enmity of his brother, Esau, and the lurking danger of fratricide. The unresolved conflict cries out at least for resolution if not for reconciliation—and not only as a matter of narrative or dramatic necessity. Jacob's return to Canaan and especially to his father's house means, almost certainly, meeting up with Esau. But confronting Esau is more than a practical inevitability; it is also a moral imperative. Failure to settle accounts with Esau and to make amends for his conniving past would leave a permanent blot on Jacob's supremacy. It would also cast grave doubts on his fitness as the next patriarch under the covenant. For under God's new way—in contrast to the uninstructed human way—a man cannot properly take his father's place by denying or destroying his father's other sons, that is, his brothers.

This last reason goes to the heart of the matter. The ambiguous relationship between brothers bespeaks one of the deepest problems inherent in all family life: the tension between family of origin and family of perpetuation, and more generally, between the claims of the past and the claims of the future. Within the family of origin, brothers are, by definition, in a critical sense "created equal." Each man's brother is his equal in being equally the seed of the same father.[1] Brothers as brothers spring from their common father; fathers as fathers live (equally) in all their sons. Thus, when a man fights with his brother, he is indirectly fighting with his father. In the extreme—that is, when he commits fratricide—he also, in a sense, commits (partial) patricide.

At the same time, however, brothers are also natural rivals—even where parents do not play favorites—and not only, as Freud would have it, owing to the shared desire of all sons to replace their father in their mother's love. There is rivalry, here and now, for parental attention and affection; there is rivalry, looking to the future, for the patrimony or the blessing. Each man, especially in heroic ages, dreams of outdoing his father; and especially as he seeks to replace and outdo his father, each man also seeks to outdo his brother. As boys grow into men, they necessarily do battle with the very people and relationships that provide them their primordial identity.

Whatever rivalry brothers experience while still at home, it is marriage that exposes the depth of the difficulty. When a man, forward looking, goes out to find a wife and starts his own family, he willy-nilly stands in problematic relation to his father. On the one hand, he continues his father's line into the next generation. On the other hand, he necessarily turns his back on the other lines that lead out of his father's house, the lines peopled by his brothers. To be devoted first and most to his wife and children is to place his own seed ahead of his father's and, most obviously, ahead of his brother's.[2] An exaggeration helps to make the point: the married man, as married man, is no more than half a son and not at all a brother.

The youthful battle Jacob waged against Esau was, in fact, an expression of this deep struggle and dilemma. It was, as the text showed us, closely allied with Jacob's struggle against his father. For the desire for the birthright is, in its inner meaning, a desire both to replace the father and to supplant the brother; these

1. Actually, it is more the common mother that makes for the common tie, since, unlike paternity, maternity is known with certainty. "Brother" in Greek is *adelphos*, "out of the same womb." Still, the general point is true also regarding sons and fathers.

2. A man (or woman) who remains more loyal to the family of origin than to the family of perpetuation sacrifices the future to the past. Greek tragedy is our best teacher in these matters. For example, the married Agamemnon who went to war against Troy to avenge a violation of his brother's marriage upheld the house of his father, Atreus, at the expense of his marriage. This truth he was compelled to enact in the sacrifice of his daughter Iphigenia as a condition of being able to go to war. Sophocles' Antigone is another famous example: she defends the family of origin at the price of her own future marriage. Her name, "against generation," carries the meaning of her deed.

are twin faces of the same ubiquitous aspiration, an aspiration most boldly revealed in the heroic temptation. But for reasons just given, the full-blown opposition of Jacob and Esau depends upon Jacob's being married. It turns out that
there is a deep connection between the twin reasons for Jacob's leaving home:
finding a wife means, all by itself, fleeing brother Esau. No less than the stealing
of Esau's blessing, Jacob's marriage is a denial of brotherhood.

Such, at least, is the *natural* (that is, uninstructed) meaning of these deeds
and the *natural* character of these familial relations. It is easy to see why tragedy
appears to be the likely fate of families and why perpetuation of righteous ways
appears to be impossible. If the new way is to survive and its adherents are to
multiply, these rivalries must be overcome—or at least prevented from reaching
their naturally tragic results (fratricide or banishment). And if human life is to
be governed by justice and guided by an aspiration to wholeheartedness, a different spirit of family life must be instituted in which the path to the future is
not at war with reverence for the past and piety toward the source. The man of
the covenant violates the spirit of his inheritance from his father if he pits the
family of the future against the family of the past. And he violates the content of
the covenant if he is not at all his brother's keeper, if he is at best indifferent to
his brother's well-being, if he is at worst a robber of his livelihood, his substance,
and his life.

The new way insists on reinterpreting all natural relations of family life in the
light of man's relation to the divine. As we have seen with Fathers Abraham and
Isaac, proper patriarchy is decisively informed by the spirit of awe-and-
reverence and by the willingness to dedicate one's children to a calling higher
than one's own pride and glory. Not surprisingly, the spirit of proper patriarchy
carries correlative implications for proper sons and proper brothers. For how
one stands in relation to the other sons of one's father must have something to
do with how one stands in relation to God. My brother is my equal not only as
the son of my father. He is also my equal in humanity, a creature equally in God's
image. Given the natural rivalry between brothers, made worse by the natural
conflict between serving the family of birth and serving the family of transmission, brotherly love may be hard to come by, and it surely cannot be counted on.
But short of love, a definite acknowledgment of the claims of brotherhood appears to be crucial to the new way.

Piety under the covenant—that is, regard for the Lord and His claims upon
us—surely requires reverence for the father, especially since the new way of the
future is founded on the promises and merits of the fathers past. It also requires,
at the very least, not destroying your brother. Respect for the brother, reverence
for the father, and awe-and-reverence for the Lord are part of one package.

In the previous generation, Abraham has solved—or rather, sidestepped—

the brotherhood question for Isaac by banishing Ishmael, on Sarah's insistence but with God's backing. In this generation, banishment is not an option. To this point the alternatives seem to be buying out the brother (Jacob's first strategy) or going to war (at risk of death and fratricide). But neither alternative is in principle or in practice in keeping with the spirit of the covenant. Jacob, to become the eponymous founder of the people of Israel, must meet Esau face-to-face and recognize him as his brother.

Jacob's adventures in Paddan-aram and the events surrounding his marriage have, in fact, made it somewhat easier for him to confront Esau. The crafty man, smitten and opened by love, became vulnerable to deception. After receiving multiple tastes of his own shrewd medicine from his fellow deceiver Laban, Jacob the underhanded eventually stood up for himself against his uncle and wrested independence from his father-in-law for his entire family. Even if he does not yet fully appreciate the spiritual aspects of his covenantal inheritance, Jacob has earned the position and prosperity he once sought through the purchase of the birthright. More important, he has willingly accepted responsibility for the well-being of his wives and children. Leaving his father and mother, Jacob went out to find a wife. Returning from his uncle and father-in-law, he comes back twice a husband, many times a father, and most emphatically a man—someone who has bound himself to his posterity. In this limited sense, he has already assumed his father's place. As a result of his new condition—patriarchy and prosperity—Jacob may be more willing and able to acknowledge his brother.

Most important, Jacob has also begun—but only begun—to acknowledge his dependence on the divine. The desire for gain and status has, at least in part, given way to higher expectations. This does not mean that Jacob is filled with brotherly love or that he has laid aside his penchant for self-reliance. On the contrary, his first attempts to cope with Esau depend, as usual, on his cleverness. But thanks to his experiences with the divine, he is more prepared to try to undo the damage he earlier did to Esau by now renouncing the birthright as he had then mistakenly understood it. Even so, it will take Jacob several more trials before he comes to see that embracing Esau as his brother is the decisive step in embracing the way of the Lord.

APPEASING ESAU: HIDING BEHIND FLATTERY AND GIFTS

As Jacob prepares to reenter Canaan, having narrowly escaped a battle with his mother's brother Laban, his mind naturally turns to the danger of renewed strife with his own brother, Esau. The appearance of the two angels, however reassuring, reinforces the necessity of confronting his own "double"; and Jacob's naming of the place Mahanaim, "two camps," prophetically looks forward to the two camps of Jacob and Esau, as well as to Jacob's strategic division of his own party into two camps to prevent its complete destruction by Esau. Twenty years have elapsed since Jacob was forced to flee Esau's desire for vengeance. Although twenty years is a long time to nurse a grudge, Jacob cannot count on Esau's pacification. His own sufferings—all tied in a way to questions of birth order and deception—no doubt make him keenly aware that Esau's anger was justified, would still be justified. But is Esau, in fact, still angry? And more important, is he in a position to do something about it?

Apprehensive but keeping his wits, Jacob seeks intelligence of Esau's strength and state of mind. Just as God had just sent messengers (mal'akhim) to Jacob, so Jacob now sends messengers (mal'akhim) before him "to Esau, his brother, unto the land of Seir [se'ir], the field [sadeh] of Edom ['edom]" (32:4). The description is ominously filled with echoes of vexed past history: Esau as the hairy (se'ar) and ruddy ('admoni) man of the field (sadeh); Jacob's purchase of the birthright when Esau (also known as Edom, "Red") came from the field (sadeh) and demanded some "red red stuff" ('adom 'adom); and Jacob deceitfully gaining the blessing meant for his brother in part by faking Esau's hairiness (sa'ir). There is even an echo of Cain and Abel, who confronted each other in the field (sadeh) soon to be made red with Abel's blood.

Rhetorically and strategically Jacob faces a difficult task. He must approach Esau deferentially, flattering him and appealing to Esau's sense of superiority, yet showing his own desire and capacity for reconciliation. He must show Esau that he is prosperous, sufficiently wealthy not to need or want anything that is now Esau's, rich enough even to shower Esau with gifts and to pay him off if necessary to settle old accounts. At the same time, Jacob must also manifest strength, just in case Esau is still hostile. Also to protect what he has, he must keep Esau partly in the dark about the extent of his wealth and numbers. Jacob chooses most carefully what his messengers should say.

> And he *commanded* them, *saying:*
> "Thus shall ye *say* unto my lord to Esau:
> 'Thus *saith* thy servant Jacob:
> "With Laban I have sojourned and stayed until now;
> and I have ox, ass, flock, and servant and maidservant,
> and I have sent *to tell* my lord,
> in order to find favor in thine eyes." ' " (32:5–6; emphasis added)

Jacob wraps up his ultimate request for favor with speeches within speeches, has his messengers approach Esau as "my lord" on behalf of "your servant Jacob," speaks of his sojourn with Laban but without reference to the reason for it, circumspectly mentions his possessions but not their quantity (using the singular nouns as collectives), neglects to speak of his camels (the most valuable animals), and hints at possible gifts from these possessions, "to find favor" with "my lord," but for now offers him only this "telling." About his family Jacob says nothing. The word "brother" is loudly absent.

The gambit fails. The messengers return, reporting that they had come to *"thy brother,* to Esau"—not to "thy lord, to Esau"—and moreover, "he himself is coming to meet you; and four hundred men with him" (32:7). Esau, it seems, had somehow learned of Jacob's impending return and had independently set out "to meet him"; the company of four hundred men almost certainly bespeaks hostile intent. Accordingly, Jacob is now "greatly afraid and distressed" (32:8). A rabbinic gloss from the midrash reads that Jacob was *afraid* that he and his own would be killed, but *distressed* at the thought that he himself might have to slay his brother. The long-forestalled moment of fratricide (or double fratricide) seems now to be unavoidable. Given Laban's enmity, retreat to Paddan-aram is impossible; given the character of his company, flight for Jacob is impractical. Confrontation appears both necessary and inevitable. Jacob's first impulse is to act to minimize his losses in the impending attack, dividing the people, flocks, herds, and camels into two camps: "If Esau come to one camp and smite it, then the remaining camp may escape" (32:9).

Beholding his own defenseless position and beset by fear, Jacob the chronically self-reliant now turns to prayer. He has never prayed before; indeed, all his previous encounters with God were initiated by the Lord—the dream at Beth-El, the speech to leave Paddan-aram, the appearance of the angels at Mahanaim. In fact, rarely has anyone before now prayed to the Lord, or at least in this way, and not in the reader's hearing. Abraham had prayed unto God after the episode with Abimelech (20:17), but what he said was not reported. Isaac had entreated the Lord for Rebekah, for she was barren (25:21), but we were not given his exact words. Jacob, in his great need, pours out his heart to God, but not without using his professed humility to bolster his petition that God keep His promise to do him good. Jacob, even in prayer, is not utterly abject and resourceless.

> "O God of my father Abraham, and God of my father, Isaac, O Lord [*YHWH*], the One who was saying to me, 'Return unto thy land and unto thy kindred, and I will do thee good': I am unworthy of all the kindnesses and all the faithfulness that Thou hast shown unto Thy servant; for with my staff I passed over this Jordan, and now I am become two camps. Deliver me, please, from the hand of my brother, from the hand of Esau; for I fear him, lest he come and smite me, the mother upon the children.

"But Thou said: 'I will surely do thee good and make thy seed as the sands of the sea which cannot be counted for multitude.' " (32:10–13)

Jacob begins with an abundant, threefold invocation. He approaches God first indirectly and doubly piously, as "God of my 'father' Abraham" and "God of my father, Isaac"; then directly and by name, as "Lord"; finally, most personally, as One who spoke directly to me and urged me to come on this homeward journey and to meet up again with my kindred. Even in his invocation, Jacob seeks to remind God, first, that his current predicament is the consequence of obeying a divine injunction, second, that God had at the same time promised providential protection and beneficence. Jacob has cleverly combined God's self-identification in his dream at Beth-El (28:13–15) with God's command to return home (31:3), and, exaggerating—whether from hope, fear, or cunning—he improves upon God's speech, turning "I will be with you" (31:3) into "I will do you good." Yet Jacob does not ask for what is coming to him as a matter of justice. Rather, he confesses his unworthiness of the good that God has already shown him, as he is moved to recall how, accompanied only by his staff, he crossed the Jordan twenty years ago but now has returned large and prosperous enough to fill two camps. And lest You ask, Lord, why the division into *two* camps, I beg you, Lord, hear my supplication, and do not undo all the good You have already done: deliver me, I pray You, from the threatening hand of my brother. When speaking to God, unlike when speaking through his messengers to Esau, Jacob identifies Esau as his brother, indeed, even before he mentions his name ("from the hand of my brother, from the hand of Esau").

Noted in the last chapter was the remarkable way Jacob expresses his concern: that Esau will "smite me, the mother upon the children," Jacob's first clear identification of himself with his progeny. With the prospect of death looming before him, suddenly the importance of his children rises vividly in his mind, even to the point of conflating his own being with theirs. Jacob, who once thought himself self-sufficient, now for the first time clearly sees himself as a link in the chain that connects fathers Abraham and Isaac to his own descendants.[3]

Prompted by his mention of the children, Jacob concludes by summoning God to remember His promise concerning Jacob's posterity—to make his seed as the innumerable sands of the sea—a promise, in fact, that had been made using *this* image of countless quantity only to Abraham (22:17; compare 28:14).

3. The insight is perfectly represented in the structure of Jacob's prayer: he begins his petition with an appeal to the God of his fathers, he finishes with a plea for the children. In the light of our discussion (at the start of this chapter) of the tragic character of natural brotherhood, this self-identification also makes clear why brother Esau is in principle a threat to Jacob's progeny: though sharing the same ancestors, Esau is a link in a *different* chain.

Jacob calls on God to honor His pledge regarding his lineage. His final plea is, implicitly, Save the children!

Jacob's remarkable prayer is met with silence: there is no immediate response from God. Never one to rely on God alone, perhaps believing that God will help him who helps himself, Jacob next tries to purchase Esau's goodwill with gifts. Flattery alone has failed; perhaps propitiation—not to say bribery—will work. Jacob sends via his servants a magnificent gift of 550 animals—including thirty milch camels and their colts—in separate droves, one after another, to be delivered seriatim to Esau, with these words: "These are thy servant Jacob's; they are a gift [*minchah*]⁴ sent to my lord, to Esau; and behold, he is also behind us" (32:19). By means of this majestic and increasingly more valuable train of tribute, delivered in a manner and with a speech that suggests that he acknowledges Esau's superiority,⁵ Jacob hopes to pacify Esau's heart. By the time he himself arrives at the end of the procession, Jacob hopes that Esau will have been moved to be forgiving and magnanimous.

For he [Jacob] said, "I will appease him [*literally,* I will cover his face *(fanav)*] with the present [*minchah*] that goes before me [*lefanay*], and afterward will I see his face [*fanav*], perhaps he will accept me [*literally,* lift my face *(fanay)*]." (32:21)

Jacob, anticipating yet fearing a face-to-face encounter with Esau, seeks to cover over his brother's angry face with kindness purchased by gifts, so that Esau will then graciously elevate Jacob's own shamefaced and vulnerable status. The images of Jacob's speech remind us powerfully of the Cain and Abel story. Cain's face fell when his offering [*minchah*] was not accepted but his brother's was. In response, God told Cain that there would be "a lifting" if he "did well." Cain's killing of brother, Abel, was the outcome (4:3–8). Here, in another potentially fratricidal situation, the one with the fallen face is Jacob; the one who, according to Jacob, can do the lifting is not God but Esau, provided only that he can be propitiated—like some god—with gifts [*minchah*]. We shall soon discover whether the presents alone can do the job.

---

4. *Minchah* is the word translated "offering" in the sacrifices brought by Cain and Abel. A donation or bestowal usually made to a superior, it encompasses tribute to an earthly ruler and oblations to God. Jacob uses the term four times in this story. Its next use is in Genesis 43, when Jacob orders his sons to bring presents to the great man in Egypt, who, unbeknownst to them, happens to be Joseph.

5. Once again, Jacob, in telling his messengers what to say to Esau, avoids the word "brother." This time, however, he has them use Esau's name ("to my lord, to Esau") in speaking to Esau. (Compare 32:5–6.)

The stakes in this encounter, as the reference to Cain and Abel reminds us, include more than family harmony. At risk is the moral foundation of the new Israelite nation. As the founder of the first city, Cain not only elevated himself over his "brothers," overturning the natural equality among human beings. He also instituted distinctions among men based solely upon the conventional definition of who is and who is not a member of the political community—a definition that leads to war and that is used to legitimate killing any outsiders. Must Jacob's nation also be founded in violence? Will it be necessary for Jacob to kill or be killed, by his very brother?

As the tribute is sent off before him, Jacob himself lodges that night in the camp. This will be a night to remember, not only for Jacob, but for all his posterity, forever.

GRAPPLING WITH GOD AND MAN: BEYOND CRAFTINESS

In the middle of the night, Jacob, restless and unable to sleep, is spurred to action. He takes his two wives, two handmaidens, and his eleven children (Dinah is apparently not counted here!) and leads them across the ford of the Jabbok River along with all his possessions. Something prompts him to separate himself from kin and substance and to face his ordeal alone. Very likely, he seeks to spare them from the attack that he knows is directed properly only at himself; perhaps, also, having sought this encounter with Esau, Jacob feels called upon to stand up before his brother entirely without assistance. Whatever the reasons, Jacob, as it were, gives up everything that his love and his cleverness have gotten him, in order to stand forth "naked" before God and man: "And Jacob was left alone" (32:24).

What follows is the story famously known as "Jacob's wrestling with an angel." Scholars have suggested that it represents a transformation of pagan folktales in which the hero is confronted by river spirits who refuse him passage across their river and whom he must defeat. If so, it represents yet another instance in which the Bible, for its own pedagogical purposes, transforms tales of nature and nature gods, giving them usually an "antinatural" or "transnatural" moral and spiritual significance. Here Jacob *(Ya'aqov)* stands at the river Jabbok *(yaboq)*, a tributary of the Jordan near the frontier of the Promised Land. He expects opposition to his return to his homeland not from river spirits but from his brother, Esau, who has cause, interest, and power to obstruct him. Indeed, we know (though Jacob does not), from the oracle given to Rebekah, that Esau will become—may already have become—an "alien" nation, the inveterate enemy of the Children of Israel. Jacob must confront this obstacle on his own, and earn the right of return from the one who has every reason to deny him. No wonder "Jacob was left alone."

Jacob was once before and famously all by himself, also at night, also at the border between Canaan and Aram, the night of his wondrous dream at Beth-El. But on that occasion, he was not *said* to be *alone (levado)*. No one, in fact, has been *said* to be "alone" since the Garden of Eden, when the man, before the creation of woman, was said "to be alone [*levado*]"—it was not good, said the Lord, that the man should be alone (2:18).[6] "Alone," we recall, has two meanings, one weak and lowly, one high and mighty. Here they seem to be combined. Though Jacob is literally alone and seemingly frightened, he has voluntarily made himself alone. Moreover, his subsequent conduct will be anything but weak. He will successfully fight alone in the dark in a foreign place against a being greater than himself, relying only on his own strength, and as a result he will win a new and lasting name. No one ever again will fight such a battle. The memory of this unique battle will inform the newly named Children of Israel, who will be derivatively but permanently marked by this nocturnal struggling. The Odysseuslike schemer here has his one shining and heroic—Achillean—moment.

And Jacob was left alone; and there wrestled a man with him until the breaking of the dawn. And when he saw that he prevailed [*yakhol*] not against him, he touched the hollow of his thigh, and the hollow of Jacob's thigh was strained as he wrestled with him. And he said, "Let me go, for the dawn is breaking." And he said, "I will not let thee go unless thou bless me [*berakhtani*]." And he said unto him, "What is thy name?" And he said, "Jacob." And he said, "Not Jacob will thy name be called henceforth, but Israel [*Yisra'el*]; for thou hast striven [*saritha*] with God [*or* gods: *'elohim*] and with men and hast prevailed." And Jacob asked him, and said, "Tell me, please, thy name." And he said, "Why is it that thou dost ask after my name?" And he blessed him there. And Jacob called the name of the place Peniel, "For I have seen God [*'elohim*] face-to-face [*panim-'el-panim*], yet my soul [*or* my life: *nafshi*] has been preserved." And the sun rose upon him as he passed over Peniel, and he limped upon his thigh. Therefore the Children of Israel eat not the sinew of the thigh vein which is upon the hollow of the thigh, unto this day, because he touched the hollow of Jacob's thigh, even in the sinew of the thigh vein. (32:25–33)

---

6. When *'adam* was alone, the remedy was to create doubleness through sexual difference and complementarity. Here, when Jacob is left alone, the remedy is to create doubleness through same-sex opposition and bodily conflict.

The story of Jacob's wrestling is both superficially and profoundly mysterious, mysterious both for Jacob and for the reader. We, like the hero, Jacob, are in the dark about the identity of his opponent, the reason for the attack, the nature of the wound, the significance of the outcome, the meaning of Jacob's new name, and the importance of the story for the rest of Jacob's life—and for his people Israel. At no point in the entire Jacob saga are we more in need of careful interpretation and searching reflection.

"Jacob was left alone," begins our story, only to contradict itself. Though Jacob was alone, he was not alone: "and there wrestled a man with him until the breaking of the dawn" (32:25). Tradition has it that Jacob's antagonist is an angel, but the text itself—at least to begin with—calls him a man (*'ish,* "male human being"). True, because of his sudden and mysterious arrival and because of other peculiarities soon to be mentioned, we—and Jacob—shall have reason to suspect that the antagonist is *more* than a man, but clarity is never provided by the text. Once before, ambiguous beings visited the patriarchs: the three *men* who appeared to Abraham at his tent (Genesis 18) are called *angels* when they (two of them) appear to Lot in Sodom (Genesis 19). Abraham, it seems, was able to penetrate their disguise or, perhaps better, to see the divine through and within the human. To this point, God has communicated with Jacob mainly through angels and a dream (about angels). If this is indeed another divine encounter, it remains to be seen whether Jacob can now recognize it despite—or through—the human form. If what he is supposed to discover is that his relations to man and God are mutually implicated, the ambiguity and mystery of the antagonist's identity is perfectly appropriate.

One thing is not ambiguous: Jacob's antagonist is in fact the assailant. Not Jacob but the man initiated the wrestling. Jacob did not seek, but did not decline, the contest. The match took a long time, the whole night. The opponents were evenly matched, even perfectly so.

Insofar as the assailant is a man, who might he be? Some interpreters, choosing to read the story purely symbolically, suggest that Jacob is wrestling metaphorically, say, with his conscience or his fears. But given certain features of the outcome (especially Jacob's limp), we are compelled to see this as a genuine physical contest. A stand-in for Esau—his tutelary angel, his spiritual equivalent—is the most common and most appealing suggestion, given Jacob's present fear of the oncoming Esau, the imminence of their meeting, their equality as twins, and the already mentioned moral-political significance of their rivalry and of Esau's obstruction to Jacob's return. The struggle itself and some of its features (mentioned later) clearly remind us of the struggle in the darkness within Rebekah's womb (for example, the tenacious hold of Jacob); and Jacob's renaming here appears to be a second birth. Once again, as he received from

Esau in the birthright story, Jacob here will get something from the other under duress, this time a blessing.

Other features of the story suggest that the man could be a stand-in for another one of Jacob's other antagonists, his father. That it is a blessing Jacob demands and obtains (again in the dark) reminds us also of the "theft" of Esau's blessing, gotten from Isaac. We might even be led to recall the rivalry between the sisters Rachel and Leah, who struggled with each other with "wrestlings of God" (30:8). In this mysterious contest, the memories of all of Jacob's previous strivings appear to be conflated and embodied, ready not only for revisiting but also for reenactment.

Jacob has feared lethal combat with Esau, but instead, he is given an opportunity to wrestle, to engage in hand-to-hand combat, as close to his opponent as possible. Requiring both bodily dexterity and mental agility, wrestling will engage Jacob's entire being, psychic as well as physical, as he joins intimately with this stranger. His limbs will become so entangled with his adversary that one will not know for sure which belongs to whom. Wrestling simultaneously seeks closeness to and control over. In victory, the loser does not die or leave or fall unconscious; though he must acknowledge his defeat, he remains present, even near, in the embrace of his superior. Jacob eagerly accepts wrestling as preferable to mortal combat: in wrestling there will be no repetition of Cain and Abel, no killing or being killed, no fratricide.

The man could not overcome Jacob, at least not whilst fighting as a man. Jacob would seem to be a match for any man; he will learn his limitations only in contests with the divine:

> And when he saw that he prevailed [*yakhol*] not against him, he touched the hollow of his thigh, and the hollow of Jacob's thigh was strained as he wrestled with him (32:26).

Jacob's opponent, unable to gain victory, makes a last effort to turn the tide. He touched—laid his hand upon, struck with force—"the hollow of Jacob's thigh." Even where he touched Jacob is not unambiguous; and since it was dark, no one could see. Some think the blow landed to the acetabulum, the hollow to the outer side of the hipbone into which the head of the thighbone fits, ball in socket; surely, dislocation or even strain of the hip joint could produce the subsequent limp. But the word translated "thigh," *yarekh,* comes from a root that means "to be soft," hence "thigh" because of its fleshy softness; but it also means "loins," and is a euphemism for the genitalia. Very likely, the man grabbed Jacob in the groin.

By touching Jacob in the loins, the man, metaphorically speaking, lays hold of

Jacob's progeny.[7] In this respect, the act may even be analogized to circumcision: for all of Jacob's sons will be touched by this encounter, as they are, necessarily, touched by his struggles with his brother and with others. Jacob is compelled by this deed to think of his progeny, now in fact threatened by Esau. Jacob is made painfully aware that the iniquities of the fathers will often be visited upon the sons. By threatening his progeny, the assailant hopes at last to get the better of Jacob.

Jacob is marked but does not yield. His hip or generative parts are out of joint or strained *(yaqaʿ)*. An unblemished draw is impossible when one struggles with one's brother or one's father or even with men of other ways and other gods. One no longer goes the same way upon the earth, and one's children often suffer the consequences. Some of them may fall away from the ways of their father, others may be killed or martyred—alienated, rotted, departed, out of joint *(yaqaʿ)*.

Despite his assailant's grasp at Jacob's thigh, Jacob holds on. Jacob—the heel-grasper—again does not loosen his grip. The assailant, still in Jacob's clutches, now demands release:

> And he said, "Let me go, for the dawn is breaking." (32:27)

Perhaps fearing that he will lose his powers in daylight, perhaps concerned that Jacob in the light will discover his identity, the assailant—in the first speech between them—commands Jacob to release him. In a moment that clearly echoes the birth of the twins, his rival wants to be separated from Jacob's grip and control. Closeness goes with ignorance (or darkness), knowledge (light) requires separation.

Jacob, now in a strong position, takes advantage of the situation; he will exact a blessing for the release:

> And he said, "I will not let thee go unless thou bless me *(berakhtani)*." (32:27)

His opponent's remark about daybreak has confirmed Jacob in his suspicion that he has faced a more-than-human adversary. It is not hard to read Jacob's mind: "Such a being could bestow a blessing; and by God, this time I have earned it! Something good is surely coming to me as a result of my tenacity and prowess in the wrestling."

---

7. The same is true in an oath sworn by placing a hand under the thigh *(yarekh)*, done by Abraham's servant when he was sent to find a wife for Isaac (24:2).

Jacob's demand for a blessing as the price of yielding recalls two earlier stories: the birthright story in its tone, the Isaac-blessing story in its content. Once again, a blessing is exacted from an unwilling party who cannot see him and whom he cannot really see or understand. By the reenactment of his stealing of his brother's blessing, Jacob is reminded of his father as he is, in his strained groin, reminded of his progeny. Such intimations of mortality also bear on how we should stand toward our brothers and toward God.

Blessings given earlier in Genesis are generally given on occasions where the future is uncertain. The powers that be are called down to protect and preserve, allaying anxiety about the fearful things to come. But here the heroic Jacob—though he may fear the morrow—is in command. Why, then, does he demand a blessing? Perhaps he wants a guarantee of safe passage for himself and his family from the one most likely to contest it. Conversely, perhaps his need for a blessing is related not to his weakness but to his strength. Robert Sacks has suggested that Jacob's greater fear is that he will be forced to repeat the fratricidal act of Cain.[8] Here, Jacob spares and releases his opponent but is also blessed by him. That his adversary began the struggle means that, this time, the bestowing of the blessing is in no way tainted.

Jacob's opponent is not yet ready to bless him. Instead, he asks him to identify himself:

And he said unto him, "What is thy name?"
And he said, "Jacob." (32:28)

Unlike the episode with his father, in which Jacob lied to Isaac about his identity, Jacob this time answers truthfully: in a word, "Jacob." But this act of self-naming is also—and more profoundly—a confession: I am *Ya'aqov*, the heel catcher, the supplanter, the deceiver, the one who prevails over his opponents by means of guile and trickery. Jacob, for the first time, is compelled to confront his previous being, to describe his character in this act of self-declaration. This truthful confession of his dubious character is part of what makes Jacob eligible for renaming and for receiving the blessing legitimately, that is, earning it himself and without deceit.

Jacob's answer pleases the man:

And he said, "Not Jacob will thy name be called henceforth, but Israel [*Yisra'el*]; for thou hast striven [*saritha*] with God [*or* gods] and with men and hast prevailed." (32:29)

8. As Sacks points out, the site of the wrestling, Peniel, will later be connected with fratricidal conflicts. See Judges 8; 1 Kings 12:25–30.

Jacob has won or earned a new name; it seems to be a title of victory in the struggle, directly and not guilefully won. In this act of rebirth, Jacob becomes the first of the patriarchs to acquire a name tied to God's name.

But like so much else in this story, the precise meaning of the name *Yisra'el* is unclear, perhaps intentionally so. If Jacob is the verb's subject and God its object, the name could mean "champion or prince [*sar*] of God," one who contends with the support of, or on behalf of, God; or it could mean "striver with or against God," one who contends with or against God; or again, "ruler or prince over God," one who gains victory over, who prevails against, a divine being. Alternatively, God rather than Jacob could be the subject: the name would then mean something like "God rules" or "God prevails."[9] The explanation offered by the man for the new name does not remove the ambiguities. The verb translated "striven," *sarah*, is a primitive root whose suggested meanings are said to include "to prevail" and "to have power as a prince." Hence, Robert Sacks translates, "For as a prince hast thou power with God and with men, and hast prevailed," though the more common translation is as given above. Of the many possible ways of combining the name and the explanation, one is especially suggestive: Jacob, who prevails as a prince with God and man, carries in his new name a teaching that it is God, after all, who rules.

Apart from the ambiguities of the new name, at least two other perplexities confront the reader. Why does the man speak jointly of struggling with God and struggling with men? And why should Jacob be rewarded with a new name and a blessing for such striving?

One possibility is that the expression "gods and men" is only a merism, an idiom meaning "all and sundry." But given the now evident superhuman character of Jacob's antagonist, it is possible that the adversary is referring to himself. If so, the speaker appears to be informing Jacob that he has just been struggling directly with God or a divine being, even as he had previously striven against Esau and Laban. Alternatively, given the uncertain nature of the speaker-antagonist— is he man, angel, or God?—perhaps he means that Jacob has here been wrestling *simultaneously* with man and God and, by implication, that all his previous strivings with men have in fact also been, at the same time, strivings with God. On the eve of facing Esau, in a potentially fratricidal encounter, Jacob is ready to discover that striving with brother Esau, like himself an image of the divine, *is*, in a sense, striving with God.

---

9. Robert Alter points out that "names with the *el* ending generally make God the subject, not the object, of the verb in the name." But as Alter also observes, the etymology that is offered by Jacob's opponent has the name mean, "He strives with God."

But we must also take seriously the suggestion that Jacob has indeed been struggling literally and directly with (and against) God. Insofar as he here is wrestling with God—or with his messenger—Jacob not only accepts the confrontation. He tries by strength to hold his own with God, to hold on to God, even to make God truly *his* God. Compared with His more active role in the life of Abraham, God has been rather remote from Jacob. In the original dream at Beth-El, God appears remote atop the ladder, in heaven, far from the sleeping Jacob, and God offers no communication at all during the twenty years in Paddan-aram. Jacob's recent prayer was met first by silence, then only by this mysterious assailant. To be sure, Jacob tends to rely on his own cleverness, ingenuity, and magic (in this sense, too, his attempt at self-sufficiency could be said to be a striving against God). But Jacob also has expressed a desire for narrowing the gap between himself and God. His willingness to grapple and to close with the assailant can be said to be a sign of his desire to be close to God, even as he struggles with and against Him.

This suggestion provides a clue for answering the second question: why Jacob is rewarded for such struggling, and especially with God, to whom one might think submission or obedience would be preferable to struggle. But weak and submissive human beings can hardly be expected to defend God's new way in a hostile world of men (recall Abel's vulnerability before Cain). Given the human condition, man will necessarily struggle with man, including those closest to him. And given the human condition, men will—at best—necessarily grapple with God. But struggle or striving is vastly preferable to ignorance or indifference. In all intimate struggles—especially within the family—one does not really seek a decisive victory, but rather respect, and only from an equal or a superior is respect worth having. Jacob has never refused the struggle, not against men, not now in his wrestling with . . . is it God? He hangs on, he endures, he *holds*—and holds *on to*—his own. At no point does he despair. In short, he *prevails*.

To endure something of the contrary character of the world without losing heart, to stay close, to strive and struggle against adversity—this is the virtue most needful for the successful transmission of God's new way, a way that will be demanding of its adherents and unpopular (to say the least) with the rest of the world. Jacob, to begin with, was in his cleverness better armed than Abel for facing conflict. But through his struggles during his travels he has largely learned the limits of his own shrewdness. He has himself been victimized by cleverness, known disappointments in love, suffered the poisonous rivalry of his wives and competition with his uncle, and acquired concern for his posterity. He now feels powerfully his own mortality and vulnerability, but also his propensity to kill.

For all these reasons, he is more open to, more engaged with, God. The blessing he had gotten by guile from his father he did not think he needed; it was entirely his mother's idea. This one he knows he needs and wants. Jacob's keen sense of the limits the world places on his quest for self-sufficiency—and also his guilt for the harm done by his earlier cunning—now opens him fully to the more-than-human. Indeed, his demand for a blessing is itself (in part) a sign of deference toward God: Jacob tacitly recognizes the superiority and authority of the One who blesses. In the midst of his "prevailing," Jacob acknowledges both his own neediness (for a blessing) and the higher standing of his opponent. Jacob, in this his most heroic moment, shows that a Hebrew patriarch does not fit the true heroic mold.

Because the opponent has credited Jacob with striving with God, Jacob's curiosity is further aroused. He wants to know with whom, truly, he has been wrestling. Heroes measure the nobility of their victories by the nobility of their opponents.

> And Jacob asked him, and said, "Tell me, please, thy name." (32:30)

But to ask the name is improper—at least unduly familiar—if indeed the being is divine. All attempts to know someone's name manifests a desire to gain clarity and reduce mystery. It bespeaks an impulse to capture the other neatly in speech. For these reasons, it is one thing to be able to name the animals; it is quite another to use the name of God.[10] Jacob does not get satisfaction. The antagonist refuses the heroic and/or rational man's wishes:

> And he said, "Why is it that thou dost ask after my name?" And he blessed him there. (32:30)

Jacob is gently rebuked, either for asking for something improper (for to name is to some extent to control) or because the answer should have been obvious. Jacob is being instructed in the kinship between the One who names and the One whose name should not be uttered. In His final act, before He presumably departs as mysteriously as He arrived, Jacob's adversary blesses him then and there.

What does Jacob, by the dawn's early light, make of all this? Surely there is need to make sense of this eerie and profound encounter. Jacob is quite decisive in his interpretation:

---

10. The reader may wish to revisit our opening discussion of speech and names in Chapter Two, and in particular the implications of having a second world of names layered atop the primary world of beings.

And Jacob called the name of the place Peniel,[11] "For I have seen God ['*elo-him*] face-to-face [*panim-'el-panim*], yet my soul [*or* my life: *nafshi*] has been preserved." (32:31)

Did Jacob really see his adversary's face? Has he indeed seen God face-to-face? Can any man do so? In Exodus (33:20), when God reveals Himself to Moses, He says, "Thou canst not see My face, for man shall not see Me and live"; but later, in Deuteronomy (34:10) we are told that "there has not risen a prophet since in Israel like unto Moses, whom the Lord knew face-to-face." Jacob seems not so much to be boasting regarding what he has literally seen as he is marveling at his survival in this intimate encounter with the divine. Perhaps he has looked into his own death. Perhaps, having striven with God, he knows he does not deserve to live. Yet he has survived—prevailed—and won his deathless name.

Jacob's triumph is, however, incomplete:

And the sun rose upon him as he passed over Peniel, and he limped upon his thigh. (32:32)

Only now, as the sun finally rises (and both Jacob and the reader are no longer in the dark), do we know for sure that he had no sighting of God's face; as he passes over "God's face," Peniel, the place of that name, he is limping—the result of the adversary's straining of Jacob's thigh. Jacob, who long ago first mentioned God in a doubly impious lie to his father, "The Lord thy God has sent me good speed" (27:20), will forevermore remember that the Lord has permanently slowed him down. A little reflection reveals that the limp carries a perfect lesson for our hero—indeed, for anyone who aspires to self-sufficiency.

A man who limps is slowed down, made conscious of his gait, mindful that his plans cannot fully succeed because the perishable body does not simply execute what reason and will command. Like Oedipus ("swollen foot") who prematurely walked with a stick, a limping man is old and dependent before his time, often in need of someone or something to lean on. The limp reminds him of his lowliness, being a defect of our lowest part, the part that is both closest to the earth yet also responsible for our separation from it. The limp bends and weakens our upright posture, that mark of our more-than-animality, which permits us to see the limitless horizon and to enlarge our deeds and projects accordingly. The man who limps is now alienated from the earth. Made to feel a perpetual stranger, he knows he is always in need of gifts and forgiveness. The man who limps gets along only with the help of grace.

The Hebrew verb "to limp," *tsala'*, is from a root meaning "to curve": to limp

---

11. From *paneh*, face, and *El*, God.

is to walk as if one-sided. Curiously, the same word is the root of "rib" *(tsela')*, that curved, one-sided source of woman (2:21–22). Adam, the paradigmatic man, not good alone, was marked in the ribs by the creation of woman: "as a result," all human beings are "curved," male or female, leaning to one side or the other, but pointing always to the "other side." Here Jacob, said to be alone in a way no man has been since Adam, is marked curvedly in the thigh, and he walks one-sidedly—always with reminders of the "other side," whether brother or God.[12]

That Jacob limped *on his thigh* implies that this mark or defect will be passed on to Jacob's descendants. The sequel does not disappoint us:

> Therefore the Children of Israel eat not the sinew of the thigh vein which is upon the hollow of the thigh, unto this day, because he touched the hollow of Jacob's thigh, even in the sinew of the thigh vein. (32:33)

For Jacob, the significance of the encounter was embodied in his naming the place Peniel. But for the text, whose voice here obtrudes itself into the narrative from a time far in the future, the limping and its meaning are more important. The Children of Israel—all those who have sprung from the "thigh" of Jacob, here called Israel for the first time—are defined (for the first time in the text) in relation to Jacob's limp. But the definition of the Children of Israel is not physical but customary, a matter of diet.

The text here informs the reader of the second specifically Hebrew custom, the first since circumcision. There is now a new mark on Israelite progeny, the first of the specifically Hebrew dietary laws. The covenant with Abraham was a covenant continued biologically, albeit "remarked" in each generation, through circumcision. But with the change in birth order (Jacob over Esau), the biological principle is superseded, or rather elevated: still the loins (thigh) but now memorially sanctified in ritualized eating, because it was touched directly by God in close encounter with the eponymous patriarch, Israel. This new covenant with Jacob is binding not only on the males, but on *all* the Children of Israel. It is to be observed not only once in a lifetime, but daily in eating, the activity that both reminds us of our ultimate mortality and daily renews and pre-

12. Four famous Greek figures had leg or foot problems, in three cases clearly related to their questionable aspirations for self-sufficiency or god-likeness: Oedipus the tyrant and riddle solver; Hephaestus the god of craft, who was made lame for striving against Zeus; and Odysseus—Jacob's counterpart—who received a scar on the famous boar hunt in the company of his maternal grandfather, Autolycus. (Jacob's cleverness seems also to have been inherited down his maternal side.) The fourth example, Philoctetes, famous archer and possessor of the bow of Heracles, was bitten by a snake when he wandered heedlessly into a grove sacred to Artemis and sustained a wound in his foot that would not heal.

serves our life: "I have seen God . . . yet my life is preserved." Remembering the ambiguous trafficking of ancestor Jacob, touched by God, the Children of Israel mark themselves not only in the flesh but also in their customs regarding flesh. The law reminds them, negatively, that Father Jacob was injured in the process of grappling with God, positively, that God was close enough to be encountered and grappled with, yet without destroying him. The law has a divine origin and a reverent intent.

This new custom also promotes community—hence, the appropriate first mention of "the Children of Israel." Circumcision was a deed required of parents only at the birth of their male heirs; afterward, there is no continuing commemoration of the covenant, nor can fellow Israelites recognize one another on this basis during ordinary dealings. But with this new dietary custom, the Children of Israel—now on the threshold of becoming a people—establish visible and distinctive mores, observed daily, that define and anchor the bonds of society. As touching the thigh meant affecting all Jacob's descendants, so not eating the thigh vein is practiced by all Jacob's descendants, in order to recall *that* they are all descendants of Israel in his special relation to God. Indeed, the dietary practice is in a deeper sense a precise counterpart of Jacob's limp: separate and distinctive customs (and not just about eating) separate and alienate the Children of Israel from the rest of the human world, reminding them that they live by the grace of God. This dietary restriction, if you will, is a metaphorical limp, accompanied by grace.[13]

Jacob, "reborn" in this encounter, has acquired a new claim to the birthright and the blessing, independent of Esau's ceding it and of Isaac's forced blessing. Jacob therefore has a partly independent claim to leadership in the service of God's new way, above and beyond his being (merely) a descendant of Abraham. He has *earned*—through his own efforts at striving, suitably instructed—his place as patriarch. The people will have a second new beginning and new source of legitimacy, as does Jacob, commemorated and enshrined in the distinction between legitimate and illegitimate food. They will remember that the God of Israel is a living God who struggles with man but who allows him to live and who sanctifies his life.

But we must not let the text's remarks about the latter-day dietary practices of the Children of Israel get us too far ahead of our story. For the time being there is no nation of Israel, and its future possibility hangs very precariously upon the fateful encounter with Esau. We are eager to learn whether Jacob's confrontation with Esau in broad daylight will be as successful as his wrestling with the mysterious stranger in the dark. We don't have long to wait.

13. I owe this last insight to my wife.

FACING ESAU, SEEING GOD: TRAGEDY AVERTED

And Jacob lifted up his eyes[14] and looked, and behold, Esau was coming, and with him four hundred men. (33:1)

Though Esau's intentions toward him are still unknown, Jacob's spirit—no less than his eyes—appears to be lifted. Earlier, when his messengers had reported the movement and size of Esau's troop, "Jacob was greatly afraid and distressed"; and out of fear, he divided people and possessions into two camps in the hope that one of them might escape Esau's onslaught (32:8–9). Now, although the report of the four-hundred-man troop is verified, Jacob is no longer afraid—or at least is not said to be afraid. Once again, he makes a division, this time of his children unto their respective mothers:

> And he divided the children unto Leah and unto Rachel and unto the two handmaids. And he placed the handmaids and their children foremost, and Leah and her children after, and Rachel and Joseph aftermost. And he himself passed over before them, and he prostrated himself to the ground seven times, until he came near unto his brother. (33:1–3)

Jacob's arrangement of the mothers with children in the order of increasing dearness could be motivated by considerations of security—Rachel and Joseph are last and hence most sheltered. But given his own conduct, it is just as likely that they arranged for the purpose of formal presentation before Esau, the best saved for last. Jacob, though vastly outnumbered, does not hang back but comes forward, adopting the position of suppliant. Displaying complete submission, Jacob throughout his approach prostrates himself before his brother—in an ironic reversal of Isaac's blessing,[15] given to Jacob disguised as Esau: "Let thy mother's sons bow down to thee" (27:29).

14. In Hebrew, *vayisa' ya'aqov 'eynayv*. At Beth-El, the morning after his dream of the ladder, the newly encouraged Jacob set off for Haran: "And Jacob lifted up his legs [*vayisa' ya'aqov raglayv*]" (29:1). In both cases, there was a "lifting," then of legs, now of eyes. "Lifting up the eyes and looking (or seeing)" is often a description of elevated sightings of great moment. We have met it already in Abraham's sighting of Mount Moriah (22:4) and of the ram caught in the thicket (22:13), in Abraham's noticing of the three strangers who came to his tent (18:2), in Rebekah and Isaac's first sightings of each other (24:63, 64), in Lot's viewing of the plain of the Jordan (13:10), and in God's exhortation to Abraham to behold all the land He was now promising to him and his seed (13:14). (See also 31:10, 12.)

15. And an ironic fulfillment of Isaac's intention. We notice also that the fear of Esau intimidates Jacob into humiliating himself in front of his children, poetic justice for Jacob, who did the same thing to his blind and aged father.

We try to imagine ourselves in Esau's place. What a strange and moving sight! My hated brother, my rival, the conniving supplanter paying me supreme homage, abasing himself supremely! Is this not a confession of his guilt, an acknowledgment of my rightful superior standing? See how he places himself at my mercy, trusting me with his life? And look how he has aged and how he limps along! Does he not begin to resemble Father? Esau is overwhelmed by a sudden upsurge of brotherly affection:

> And Esau *ran* to meet him
>> and *embraced* him
>> and *fell* upon his neck
>> and *kissed* him;
> and they *wept*. (33:4; emphasis added)

One compact verse, with five active verbs,[16] suffices for this beautiful and unexpectedly affectionate reunion. In place of his originally hostile, even murderous, intention, Esau eagerly, sincerely, and wholeheartedly embraces his brother as an equal, tacitly forgiving him his wrongdoings in a marvelous display of magnanimity. Years of enmity dissolve in tears of joyous reunion and apparent reconciliation, wept equally by *both* Esau and Jacob together—though, we hasten to add, they do not necessarily weep for the same reason.[17]

Indeed, we must not lose our wits in our relief and delight in this happy denouement. As if to caution us, the Hebrew word for "and he kissed him," *vayishaqehu,* is marked in the scriptural text with dots over every letter—a unique textual occurrence. Surely the kiss is worthy of exclamation. But its unexpectedness also raises questions, if not about its sincerity at the moment, then surely about its reliability as a promise of Esau's future goodwill. The rabbis later expressed doubts about the sincerity of Esau's kiss, and attributed his astonishing behavior not to a change of heart but to a miraculous divine intervention: God—answering Jacob's prayer—turns Esau's hate into love precisely as he fell on Jacob's neck (one possible explanation for the dots over the letters of "and he kissed him").

Yet one need not question Esau's immediate sincerity to doubt its enduring significance. We know Esau to be an impulsive and easily emotional man, but not ill-natured, and the scene he has just witnessed of Jacob's supplication could

---

16. We recall the other episode in which Esau's conduct is compactly described in five active verbs: ate/drank/rose/went/despised (25:34). Here, in contrast, the last activity, weeping, Esau shares with Jacob: *they* wept.

17. When Jacob met Rachel at the well, "Jacob kissed Rachel and *lifted up his voice* and he wept" (29:11). Here, neither Esau nor Jacob lifts up his voice.

well have stolen away his anger, at least for now. When he comes to himself, Esau will perhaps remember that his brother the dissembler and deceiver could have, once again, put one over on him. Besides, much will depend on what follows, as Esau and Jacob converse together within our hearing for the first and only time since Esau sold his birthright:

> And he [Esau] lifted up his eyes and saw the women and the children, and he said, "Who are these with thee?" And he [Jacob] said, "The children whom God has graciously bestowed upon thy servant" [*hayeladiym 'asher-chanan 'elohim 'eth-'avdekha*]. Then the handmaids approached, they and their children, and they prostrated themselves. And also Leah and her children approached and prostrated themselves, and after came Joseph near and Rachel and they prostrated themselves. (33:5–7)

Esau, who last saw Jacob as a solitary, wants understandably to know about his companions—we recall that when Jacob sent messengers to Esau he withheld all information about his family. Jacob, his tears notwithstanding, has not abandoned his wits and caution. In his first sentence to Esau, six Hebrew words in toto, he manages to mention the children, God, and His grace toward Jacob, while still identifying himself humbly as *"your* servant." He preserves delicate silence about the wives and their identity, once a touchy subject for Esau and his parents. Jacob's deferential speech is followed by a parade of prostrate deference shown by the entire family.

Esau continues to be appeased, but he wonders next about those droves of livestock that had preceded Jacob and his party:

> And he said, "What dost thou mean by all this camp which I met?" And he [Jacob] said, "To find favor [*or* grace: *chen*] in the eyes of my lord." (33:8)

Even though, as he had said, God has shown grace to Jacob, it is especially grace in the eyes of "my lord Esau" that Jacob (truthfully) says he is seeking with all his presents.

Esau initially declines Jacob's gifts, in a courteous speech that is of a piece with his gracious conduct:

> And Esau said, "I have much. My brother, let what is thine be thine." (33:9)

Whereas Jacob still speaks of "my lord" and "thy servant," Esau, now softened, addresses Jacob as "my brother." He politely refuses the gifts, ostensibly because he does not need them; whether he intends it or not, Esau is even tacitly conceding any residual claim to the birthright, sold long ago under duress: "what is thine is thine." But as many commentators have noted, Esau may be just conforming to Eastern etiquette that requires a recipient first to publicly refuse a gift, taking it only after the donor, also following customs of courtesy, presses him to accept. This Jacob proceeds to do, repeatedly and most insistently, encouraged by Esau's brotherly speech and tone:

> And Jacob said, "Nay, please, if, please thee, I have found favor [*chen*] in thy eyes, then take my present [*minchathi*] from my hand; for *I have seen thy face as though I had seen the face of God* and [*or* but] thou wast pleased with me. Take, please, my gift [*literally,* my blessing: *birkhathi*] that is brought to thee; because God hath favored me [*chanani*] and because I have all." And he urged him, and he took. (33:10–11; emphasis added)

Never mind that you have much, says Jacob, "I have all." If I have found favor in your eyes even without my presents, take them anyhow and from my own hand. Why? Because seeing your face, Esau, is like seeing the face of God.

What in the world does Jacob mean in saying, "Seeing your face is like seeing the face of God"? And, more important, what does Esau hear in what he is saying?

Some interpreters, Nahum Sarna among them, treat Jacob's remark as the work of calculation:

> This rhetorical extravagance yields, perhaps intentionally, several possible meanings: encountering you, Esau, is like a pilgrimage to a shrine, which one does not make empty-handed; I have been admitted to your august presence; you have been graciously indulgent to me [that is, as only God could be]; my encounter with you is like that with a divine being. This last would be an artfully astute reference to 32:31 ["I have seen God face-to-face, but my soul has been preserved"].

But notwithstanding Jacob's likely intent to flatter, the comparison of seeing Esau's face with seeing the face of God cannot be for Jacob simply artful. Also, the "astute reference" we *readers* hear to the previous night's wrestling could not be a reference recognizable by Esau. Jacob seems rather to be offering his own profound understanding of the connection between the two encounters.

Truly face-to-face with his brother for the first time, and seeing him behave in unexpectedly gracious ways, Jacob discovers that he has not fully understood him. The mystery that is Esau, like the mystery that is God, inspires awe and reverence. Jacob sees there another divine image, the equal god-likeness of his equal brother. Further, he sees the majesty of the divine likeness, with its powers to forgive and bestow favor but also to judge and to take life. Jacob has looked into the depths, recognized his unworthiness, faced the possibility of his own deserved death, and experienced the unmerited superhuman display of grace from the one who stood ready and able to destroy him. What Cain learns only after he has murdered Abel, Jacob discovers as fratricide is wondrously avoided.[18]

In this spirit, Jacob, in his final words of urging, begs Esau to accept "my gift," using instead of the word *minchathi*, "my offering or present," the word *birkhathi*, "my blessing." Atoning for his guilt, which he here tacitly confesses (as if before God), Jacob symbolically returns Esau's blessing, whose theft from Isaac kindled Esau's hatred in the first place. Now that fratricide—both killing and being killed—has been averted, Jacob recognizes that God has truly shown favor upon him and that in God's providence he has all that he needs: "Please, take [back] my blessing that is brought to you." Jacob, who earlier sought to propitiate Esau by means of presents alone, now gives them to the (already) forgiving Esau as genuine gifts, accompanied by his blessing.

Esau, moved by Jacob's great display of humility and by this tacit admission of prior guiltiness, accepts the gift of livestock. The score of the blessing would seem to be happily and harmoniously settled.

Yet as it turns out, the "return of the blessing" presages no permanent reunion but, on the contrary, a complete break between Jacob and Esau. Esau, still amiable, invites Jacob and his party to travel with him and offers to lead the way (with his troop of armed men). But Jacob, no sentimentalist and leery about Esau's impetuous nature and the durability of Esau's current benevolence, prudently declines the offer, pleading the special needs of his tender children and his nursing flocks that preclude rapid travel (33:12–13).

> "Let my lord [note well: still not "my brother"], I pray thee, pass over before thy servant; and I will travel ahead gently at the pace of the cattle before me and at the pace of the children, until I come to my lord unto Seir." (33:14)

Though he promises to visit Esau in due time at his home in Seir, Jacob has no intention of doing so. Thus, when Esau next offers to leave him some of his men to accompany Jacob on his trip to Seir, Jacob politely but firmly declines, beg-

---

18. The importance of the wrestling episode is now even clearer. It gave Jacob access to the meaning of his encounter with Esau before it happened. The point can perhaps be generalized: man's access to the divine—and to the divine-in-the-human—(alone?) prevents fratricide. For Cain, this access came with clarity only *after* the dirty deed was done. Later, in Chapter Seventeen, we shall see how an encounter with a mysterious "man" averts the killing of Joseph by his brothers.

ging to find favor once more "in the sight of my lord" (33:15). Esau, yielding, promptly departs and returns homeward, southward to Seir. But Jacob, shifting directions, journeys instead to Succoth, and for the time being at least, settles there.

Some readers are distressed with Jacob for his failure to accept Esau's offer of company and hospitality. They blame him for his suspicions and for his failure to cultivate full brotherly love with Esau. But Jacob is a man who, wisely, does not suffer much from wishful thinking or utopian illusions. Even if Esau's extreme hatred does not return, the two ways of life represented by the two brothers are not compatible. The way of Israel needs separation from the way of Edom—and Jacob knows it, at least intuitively. His deeds show that he has absolutely no intention of living with Esau or among the Edomites. In fact, Jacob tries to arrange it so that the coming together, just concluded, will serve to effect a lasting separation. Jacob and Esau will meet again only to bury Isaac (35:29).[19]

Jacob's caution, it turns out, is not misplaced. The score between Jacob and Esau has not been permanently settled; the hatchet is but temporarily buried. Four hundred years later, Israel, returning after the exodus from Egypt, will be first attacked by the Amalekites, descendants of Esau (Exodus 17), and will be forced to face Edom (the nation of Esau), which will refuse to allow it passage (Numbers 20).[20] The iniquities of the fathers continue to be visited upon the children.

In the light of these future developments, modern readers, strongly influenced by the Bible's own teachings about brotherhood, are very likely disappointed in the resolution of the Jacob and Esau story. Their discontent, however, implies that things could have turned out differently, that there could have been another and more lasting way for establishing peace between the brothers. But they do not take sufficiently seriously the inherently tragic nature of brotherly

19. Though no other meeting is reported in the text, a somewhat different account of their permanent separation is given in chapter 36, after the report of Isaac's death. There we are told that it was Esau who left Canaan for Seir, with all his clan and possessions, to be away from Jacob, "because their substance was too great for them to dwell together, and the land of their sojournings could not bear them because of their cattle" (36:6–7)—reasons reminiscent of those that led Abraham to separate himself from Lot (Genesis 13). Esau, who apparently had previously wandered through both Seir and Canaan, now abandons the latter for economic—not cultural—reasons. In doing so, Esau tacitly accepts Jacob's title to the land promised to Abraham and his seed—that is, to both birthright and blessing.

20. Much later, in the first century B.C.E., the Roman occupation was perceived by the people of Judea as the revenge of Edom (since the ruling family placed in power by the Romans, the line of Herod, were Edomites). The notion that Esau had returned to claim the land was a fairly common way Jews described the Roman occupation early in the Christian era. (Yuval Levin pointed this out to me.)

rivalry, especially when brothers differ greatly in their dispositions and ways of life ("Two [opposite] nations are in thy womb"). They do not see how great an achievement it is to have found a viable alternative to banishment, buyout, and battle to the death. To be sure, the problem of brothers will long be with us; Jacob's own sons will threaten fratricide against their brother Joseph, provoked in part by Jacob's foolish willingness to play favorites. Yet tragedy has been averted and Jacob has been "reborn" as Israel precisely because he was finally able to see through the face of Esau to the "face" of God. Jacob repents, repairs, and repays. He achieves closure, and limping, he carries on to continue to struggle with God and men. Who would have thought it possible?

Chapter Sixteen

Politics and Piety:

Jacob Becomes Israel

With the departure of Esau to Seir and Jacob, bearer of the new way, to Succoth, it would seem to be time for the new way to take root and spread in the Promised Land. Jacob has returned from exile, safe and mostly sound (except for a slight limp). His problem with his brother has apparently been solved. His young family, an incipient clan, has been preserved intact. Life, it appears, can return to normal.

Appearances are deceiving. Political difficulties lie ahead, for the Canaanites are still in the land, just as they were when Abraham first arrived many years before (12:6). Jacob, despite his familial successes, has yet to encounter much of the world beyond the family. True, in the person of Uncle Laban he experienced the ways of the Arameans (Mesopotamians). True, in the person of brother, Esau, he had dealings with the (nascent) Edomites, soon to be a large and powerful group of nations (see Genesis 36). But in both cases, the larger political-religious issues were incidental to settling the familial matters of marriage, brotherhood, and independence from father and mother. Jacob, before his exile a homebody, has yet to meet up with the Canaanites in whose land he and his people are destined to dwell. And he has yet to show that he can survive and flourish among the other nations, avoiding the ever-present dangers of annihilation and assimilation. On the larger world stage, already filled with many highly developed peoples, the new way and its people are hardly noticeable and barely alive.

International politics is, of course, not a new subject in the book of Genesis or in its account of beginning the new way. In a sense, it has been the large if little-heralded theme since the call of Abraham. After the ill-fated project of Babel, God embarked on a new approach to the problems of human life, choosing to spread His new way by the election of one nation, chosen to be a light unto all the others. Toward that end, God first promised Abraham that He would make of him a great nation, and at several points in his adventures, God teaches Abraham about the special demands of political life. In the conversation about Sodom (Genesis 18; see Chapter Eleven), God instructs Abraham in some painful truths regarding justice and politics, so that he might teach his descendants to "keep the way of the Lord and to do righteousness and justice" (18:19).

Abraham, in fact, had a rather distinguished career in international relations. He escaped danger in Egypt, won a military victory against the invading Babylonian kings, participated in God's judgment against Sodom and Gomorrah, established a pact of friendship with Abimelech and the Philistines, and purchased burial land from the Hittites. In all these episodes, Abraham interacted with, yet remained apart from, the surrounding peoples, managing to safeguard his distinctive identity. Isaac, much more limited in scope than his father, was never severely tested in world affairs. He encountered only his father's friend Abimelech, but managed with him to preserve and extend friendly relations, through a renewed international agreement. How will Jacob conduct himself among the nations? Partly because of who he is, partly because he has received a new name that will become the name of the people of the new way, partly because his family is large enough to constitute a (proto)political entity, Jacob, more than his forebears, will face the greatest political challenges in Genesis.

Practicing politics under the covenant is no easy matter, more difficult than practicing politics under the usual, and usually Machiavellian, principles of nations. Like other nations, the nation of the covenant needs to survive in an often inhospitable world. Self-preservation requires more than providing for bodily needs; it also requires standing up to external threats and assaults, as well as to internal schism and strife. When under attack, survival depends on the presence of the martial spirit, the willingness to fight and kill and die in defense of one's own. But unlike other nations, the nation of God's covenant must preserve and conduct itself in ways that advance the cause of justice in the world. Squaring the demands of political survival and the demands of righteousness is an eternal challenge.

Sometimes survival requires harsh deeds. Sometimes the demands of political justice bring harm to the innocent. These were among the major lessons God tried to teach Abraham in the conversation about the fate of Sodom. Yet, as with the demand for capital punishment in the Noahide law, the execution of justice may stain the hands and souls of the executors. In addition, the zeal for justice aroused by injury to one's own can easily get out of hand, leading to conduct both imprudent and impious. On the one hand, reason and prudence without zeal and force of arms cannot defend themselves. On the other hand, spiritedness in defense of one's own without moderation and prudence cannot avoid injustice. The international politics of God's new way must find the proper balance. It will not be easy.

International relations for the people of God's covenant are yet more difficult and demanding, precisely because they are called by that covenant not only to practice justice but also to "walk before Me and be wholehearted [*tamim*]." Thus, in confronting other nations, they must not only avoid suffering harm and committing injustice; they must also adhere to their own distinctive ways in matters of purity, piety, and holiness. When these ways are later fully articulated in the so-called holiness code of Leviticus, the Children of Israel will be commanded to institute numerous customs and practices that regulate and sanctify everyday life, all in order to fulfill the injunction "Be ye holy, for I the Lord am holy." Here, in the earliest days of the nation, the distinctive Israelite way is explicitly embodied only in the practice of infant-male circumcision. But it is implicitly reflected also in related reverential attitudes toward women, sexuality, procreation, fatherhood, hospitality, and, of course, the transmission of the covenant itself, all looking up to the divine.[1] The nascent nation of Israel, if it is to maintain itself *as* the nation of the *covenant*, must keep itself separate from the places and ways of its neighbors, lest it let slip its covenantal character. Getting too comfortable with neighboring nations runs the risk of losing through assimilation the higher moral-spiritual purpose for which this nation was chosen.

Even if Jacob wished to avoid these problems, he cannot hope to do so. He will in fact be forced into international relations by certain inescapable difficulties in his household. Among them, two stand out: issues of unity among the brothers and issues of marriage—the perennial problems of family life, rearing their heads in the next generation. First, how will the sons of Jacob, in their generation, solve the problem of brotherly rivalry and enmity? What if anything can unify them and keep them attached to the covenant? Or will only one or two of them remain within the fold, the others being lost to other ways?[2] Second, whom will Jacob's children marry? Where will his eleven sons find wives and his daughter a husband? Despite the dangers, Israel, at least for now, must practice cultural exogamy in order to survive. Yet marrying into the neighboring Canaanite tribes risks diluting the Israelite way, even to the point of destruction through assimilation. The international problem for Jacob and his clan is greater than it was at any previous time. The next episode, the story of the rape of Dinah, brings it to the fore with a vengeance.[3]

1. These special attitudes become apparent especially when the "education of the patriarchs" is set against the prevailing ways of the Mesopotamians, the Canaanites, and the Egyptians.

2. These questions are the theme of the subsequent story of Joseph and his brothers, which brings Israel into contact with Egypt. We consider this story beginning in the next chapter.

3. The following discussion of the story of the rape of Dinah differs in several important respects from my previously published interpretation, "Regarding Daughters and Sisters: The Rape of Dinah" (*Commentary*, April, 1992, 29–38). Forceful arguments advanced by my students, especially Eric Lavoie, Kristen Dietrich Balisi, and Yuval Levin, have altered my views. I am grateful for their insights and instruction.

DANGEROUS PROXIMITY:
ISRAEL BEFORE THE CANAANITES

The rape of Dinah (Genesis 34) interrupts a series of remarkable successes for
the house of Jacob. Returning to Canaan from Paddan-aram after having made
peace with Laban, his household intact and rich in cattle, Jacob has just achieved
two great triumphs: he has successfully wrestled the man-angel, winning a blessing and gaining a new name; and he has accomplished a peaceful reunion with
his brother, Esau, who was willing to abandon a twenty-year-old grudge. Made
wiser, through his adventures, regarding the ways of man and God, and reminded by his limp of his encounter with the divine, Jacob appears ready to
settle down and to allow his now swollen tribe to cross the threshold into nationhood. As proof of his wish to settle, he builds a house in Succoth, the first
immobile dwelling of the patriarchs, and he makes booths for his cattle. After a
while, perhaps out of fear of marauders or the possible return of Esau, perhaps
out of a hankering for city life, Jacob moves to the city of Shechem. The reader is
pointedly told that Jacob comes to the city of Shechem *whole* and/or *in peace*
(shalem); he will soon be forced to flee after episodes of rape and bloody slaughter. Confident that his troubles now lie behind him, Jacob becomes a property
owner in the Promised Land. He buys the plot of his encampment outside the
city walls from the children of Hamor, the ruling prince of the city, the first purchase of land other than the cave that Abraham had purchased for the limited
purpose of burial. Jacob establishes himself self-reliantly in the Promised Land.

   Though his conduct is certainly understandable, hindsight reveals it to be unwise. Very likely, Jacob's successes have gone to his head. His conflicts with Laban
are past; his rivalrous wives are not making trouble; his beloved Rachel has at
last borne a son; he has escaped a fratricidal encounter with Esau; he has returned to Canaan a prosperous man. He thinks everything is now settled, so he
settles. Although previously careful to remain separate from the clan of Esau
(despite Esau's invitations to join him), Jacob now carelessly comes close to the
urban Canaanites.[4] He deliberately encamps "before the city"—literally, in-the-
face-of the city *(eth peney ha'iyr)*[5]—of Shechem, a move that we readers should
regard with apprehension, given what we have learned about the character of
cities. Having apparently forgotten his dream of the ladder, Jacob does not return to Beth-El (compare 28:20–22; 31:13), from whence he left promising to re-

---

4. From this act we might infer that Jacob's insistence on separation from Esau was motivated
more by a fear of future violence and a desire for peace than by a concern for cultural distinction and
a fear of absorption and assimilation.

5. Yuval Levin comments: "Rather than walking before *(lifney)* God, Jacob has settled before
(lifney) the city" (personal communication).

turn (and to which God will subsequently send him); instead, he takes up a place among—in the face of—the nations of Canaan.

Upon purchasing the land Jacob erects there an altar that he calls *'El-'Elohey-Yisra'el*, "God, the God of Israel" (33:20). Pious readers may take this to be Jacob's profession of monotheism and his faith in the one true God. But in the context, it could rather express an anxious appeal to his own *personal* deity (for "Israel" here means only Jacob), a deity whose assistance he will need now that he is settling among strangers, people with different ways and *other* gods.[6] Indeed, the name Jacob uses suggests that he may in fact be hedging his bets on which god is locally efficacious: "El" is both a generic name for a god and a specific name for the sky god worshiped by the Canaanites. In the immediate sequel, an unexpected encounter with these Canaanite neighbors straightway upsets the peace and exposes the foolishness—or at least the insufficiency—of Jacob's plans.

GOING OUT, TAKEN IN: THE VIOLATION OF DINAH

Dinah initiates the encounter: "And Dinah, the daughter of Leah, whom she had borne unto Jacob, went out to see the daughters of the land [*bivenoth ha'arets*]" (34:1). It is Dinah, not any of her eleven brothers, who is the first of Jacob's children to initiate any action. Her action, however, appears to be minimal: she goes out, she goes out alone and on her own, she goes to see, and she goes looking to and looking at outside or foreign daughters.[7] This is all that Dinah does, here or hereafter, and all we know about it.

About Dinah herself we know but little more. She is the only daughter of the household, the seventh and youngest child of Leah, Jacob's unloved wife, with whom she is here clearly identified ("the daughter *of Leah*," not "of Jacob"). Her birth was reported almost as an afterthought, and no explanation was there given for the name Leah gave her (30:21); but every Hebrew-speaking reader would know that her name—ominously—means "judgment." Finally, Dinah must be quite young, at most an early adolescent, probably no more than twelve or thirteen.[8] Everything in the story suggests a young maiden on the cusp of young womanhood.

---

6. Jacob has forgotten the pillar he had anointed in Beth-El, and his vow that "this stone, which I have set up as a pillar, shall be God's house; and of all that Thou shalt give me I will surely give the tenth unto Thee" (28:22).

7. The foreignness of the daughters of the land is conveyed more strongly by the alternate translation of *bivenoth ha'arets:* "daughters of the earth." The Canaanites were worshipers of both the sky and the earth.

8. Here are the calculations. Jacob spent twenty years with Laban, the first seven working for his bride. During the next seven years his two wives and their concubines produce twelve children. Thus Leah's seven children must come roughly a year apart. Dinah, Leah's last, is born shortly before

It is not difficult to understand Dinah's intentions and to guess at her motives for going out. One daughter among eleven sons, she may well have been lonely and eager for female company; it is the *daughters* of the land she goes out to see. Alternatively, she may have been curious, attracted not by similarity but by difference, the difference between "the daughter *of Leah*" and "the daughters *of the land*." This would not be the first time in Genesis that a woman appears who is curious and who finds "outside" matters attractive, "a delight to the eyes." (compare 3:6)

It seems that Dinah does not go merely to see, in detached beholding, but rather to visit: in Hebrew idiom, "to see, to look upon" means "to make friendship with." Perhaps she wishes to join with the daughters in matters of seeing: to see *"and be seen"* adds the Samaritan text. For how else might a single young woman, living at home in a houseful of men, ever come to the notice of prospective suitors? Her mother,[9] after all, could have taught her, from painful experience, what it meant to be passed over and unloved. And from her father's less than equal regard for her mother and his clear preference for the more beautiful Rachel, Dinah might well have concluded that it is only good looks and being seen that truly count.

The text leaves Dinah's motives unclear, as well they often are in such matters. But more likely, the text is not interested in motives, but rather in the action itself and its meaning. For Dinah's deed has a meaning quite apart from her intention, a meaning of which she was likely entirely innocent. Whatever her

---

Joseph. The next six years, Jacob works for Laban and gains his fortune in livestock. When Jacob's family leaves Paddan-aram, the children range in age from six to thirteen. Before the present episode, there is the slow journey back to Canaan, the meeting with Esau, and an unspecified length of time dwelling first in Succoth and then before Shechem. But a few chapters and a few years later, at the start of the story of Joseph and his brothers, Joseph is said then to be but seventeen years old. After the story of Dinah's rape, and before we meet Joseph at age seventeen, there are more adventures and travels: the move to Beth-El, subsequent removals to Ephrath and Migdal-Eder, where the family dwelt for a time, and the eventual return to Isaac at Hebron. On the rough estimate that the episode at Shechem occurs near the middle of the eleven-year period between the departure from Laban (when Joseph is roughly six) and the beginning of the Joseph saga (when Joseph is definitely seventeen), Joseph would be approximately twelve years old and Dinah twelve or thirteen. If this is correct, the oldest of Jacob's sons at the time of the Dinah incident is not much more than twenty, and Simeon and Levi, the ringleaders of the revenge, are in their late teens.

9. Rashi, the eleventh-century commentator, here makes much of the connection of Dinah to her mother: "THE DAUGHTER of LEAH—so Scripture calls her; why not the daughter of Jacob? But just because she 'went out' she is called Leah's daughter, since she too was fond of 'going out' [Midrash Genesis Rabbah, 80], as it is said [30:16] 'and Leah went out to meet him.' With an allusion to her they formulated the proverb: 'Like mother, like daughter.' " Rashi hints at the unsavory nature of Dinah's "going out" by delicately linking it to the time when Leah went out to demand a sexual encounter with Jacob, having purchased him for the night with her son's mandrakes.

motive, she did indeed "go out" and she did indeed go "to see." She left the home—and the customs and ways—of her mother and father, established under the aegis of *'El-'Elohey-Yisra'el*, and went *out* unprotected into alien territory. She went out *alone*, without security, perhaps even without permission. She went to *town*, to the city,[10] never—not even today—a safe place for an innocent, attractive, unprotected, and vulnerable young woman. And willy-nilly, in going *to see*, she would necessarily look upon—and be initiated into—ways that were not her own, as happens to every young person who goes abroad (or even off to college) "to see for myself." To go to town willingly to look upon other people and other ways is to accept the possibility—perhaps even the likelihood—of being *taken* (literally) and being taken *in* by them. Actions taken in innocence are often far from innocent, both in their inner meaning and in their outcome.

This is not to blame the victim: Dinah would be culpable only if these were her intentions or if she went against advice and with foreknowledge of the dangers. Yet precisely because her act is so obviously dangerous, it is culpably worse than dangerous to have ignored or neglected her. If blame for her going to town is to be meted out, it should go instead to Jacob. For Jacob knows from personal experience what can happen to a man confronted with a beautiful woman in a strange place: it was he, a stranger in a strange land, who defied men's customs (at the well) to be alone with Rachel (29:7); it was he who lost his wits and forgot to make a contract with Laban for Rachel, so infatuated was he with her beauty; it was he, lusting or perhaps just drunk on his wedding night, who did not even recognize the substitution of Leah for his beloved Rachel. Shrewd and wise to the ways of the world, Jacob certainly should have taken precautions to instruct and protect his daughter—unless, of course, he was lulled into a false sense of security by his many recent successes and by his peaceful real estate transactions with the ruling house of the town, or, worse, unless he had not yet learned *that* and *how* one must care for daughters. The text perhaps means to hint at Jacob's distance from his daughter: Dinah is introduced as *Leah's* daughter, whom Leah the unloved bore to Jacob. Just as Abraham needed help learning the importance and meaning of "wife"—one cannot innocently pass her off as one's sister and commit her to adultery—so Jacob (and, through him, we readers) must learn, painfully, the importance and meaning of "daughter."

Jacob, who had settled in the wrong place and who was now grown comfortable among the Canaanites, compounds the error by allowing his one daughter

---

10. The text says "daughters of the land," not "daughters of the city." Yet Shechem is clearly a city, with gates (34:20, 24) and therefore presumably with walls. From Dinah's innocent perspective, the city does not appear as the menacing institution it really is. The language suggests a rural or countryside encounter. This matter of city versus land or field will have important implications later. For as we learned from Sodom, there are reasons why a city stands or falls together.

to wander off waywardly toward the ways of Shechem. This mistake sets in motion the entire ugly chain of events: once Dinah "goes out," everything that follows takes on a tragic inevitability. The failure to protect the purity of innocent Dinah (whose name means "judgment") brings on her unjust defilement (the rape), in a horrible parody of the proper union of man and woman. There follow grim parodies of (1) a marriage proposal (asking for the hand of a woman already seized and violated); (2) proper fatherhood and rulership (fathers serving rather than ruling the passions of their sons; a ruler leading his city into ruin for the sake of satisfying his son's erotic wishes); and (3) the practice of just retribution by means that appear to be anything but just (the brothers' slaughter and spoiling of the entire city), involving (4) what appears to be a parody of the sacred rite of circumcision. The entire order of justice falls apart from the neglect of the purity and dignity of woman. Jacob's negligence, embodied in Dinah's going out, invites both the defilement and the destruction of the new way.

Dinah's action ends with her going out; from now on she will be acted upon. Dinah went out to see the daughters. But it was she who was seen, and not by daughters:

> "And saw her Shechem the son of Hamor the Hivite, the prince of the land, and he took her and he laid her[11] and he abased her. (34:2)

Dinah was seen by Shechem, the princely son of the Hivite ruler of Shechem, the leading young Shechemite, the first and finest young man in the town. The coincidence of the name of man and town announces that this is the paradigmatic encounter between these two "cultures" (much like the story of the sons of God and the daughters of men; 6:2). Without a word, immediately upon seeing Dinah, Shechem took, laid, and abased—or "humbled" or "defiled" ('anah, "to put down, to depress")—her.[12] He had complete power over her, and he exercised it. Shechem alone is the agent; Dinah is literally and grammatically made into an object. Her name is not mentioned; instead, she appears four times as the female pronoun, each time as the direct object of the four verbs, recounting the four deeds of Shechem (saw/took/laid/abased). About Dinah's response the text is silent. The brute fact is all we are asked to see: Dinah was raped.

---

11. Most translators say "lay with her." But the Hebrew indicates an action cruder and more violent than "lying with"; where we would expect the preposition "with," the text instead has the marker for the direct object. The crude English expression "laid her" is a perfect translation.

12. Shechem at one and the same time abased the young woman and defiled "justice": not knowing Dinah's name, Shechem was unaware that he was, by his action, also "bringing down justice" on his entire city.

Recognizing Sexual Defilement

We pause, briefly stepping back from the text, to clarify our thoughts about the crime of rape, for our current views may be inadequate for understanding our story and the biblical teaching to which it points. What exactly is the crime, and why is it so heinous?

According to Blackstone's *Commentaries,* rape is defined as "carnal knowledge of a woman forcibly and against her will." Thus, the crime against the woman has three elements: sexual intercourse; the use (or threat) of force; her unwillingness. Accordingly, there are three coincident offenses: one against her specifically female sexual nature; one against her bodily integrity; one against her will. Traditionally, our understanding of the crime focused largely on the first. Rape, though it involves the use of force and is always against the will, is not—either in common law or in common sense—just a special case of assault and battery. It is a *sexual* crime, a violation of a woman's sexual, and therefore *generative,* nature. The purity of woman's sexual being—and therewith also the purity of marriage and the clarity of lineage—was the primary concern of the law, as it was of sexual morality in general, concerned as it was to promote and protect marriage, lineage, and family.

In Roman law, according to Blackstone,

> stealing a woman from her parents or guardians, and debauching her, is equally penal by the emperor's edict, whether she consent or is forced. . . . And this, in order to take away from women every opportunity of offending in this way; whom the Roman law supposes never to go astray, without the seduction and arts of the other sex; and therefore by restraining and making so highly penal the solicitations of the men, they meant to secure effectually the honour of the women.

It was English common law that introduced an emphasis on lack of consent, yet not because it came to regard rape as a crime against the will, but for reasons of fairness and prudence:

> But our English law does not entertain quite such sublime ideas of the honour of either sex, as to lay the blame of a mutual fault on one of the transgressors only: and therefore, makes it a necessary ingredient in the crime of rape, that it must be against the women's will.

And whereas the Roman law did not recognize the rape of a prostitute or common harlot, "not allowing any punishment for violating the chastity of her, who hath indeed no chastity at all, or at least hath no regard to it," the law of England—still concerned with chastity but more willing to allow for personal reform—"holds it to be felony to force even a concubine or harlot; because the woman may have forsaken that unlawful course of life."

By contrast, today's discussions of rape, largely led by critics of this allegedly patriarchal tradition of law and sexual morality, focus almost exclusively on the absence of the woman's clear consent. Rape is regarded primarily as a violation of the will, not a violation of womanliness. To be sure, rape is still distinguished from other forms of unconsented touching. But since the entire view of relations between the sexes is increasingly seen solely through the lens of power, rape is viewed merely as a most egregious example of the generalized male tendency to dominate and violate women. If readers of Genesis think about rape only in this understanding, they will likely miss much of the importance of the present story.

Dinah's defilement will haunt us throughout; but—returning to the text—it makes no difference to Shechem, who now finds that "his soul [or inner self] did cleave to Dinah, the daughter of Jacob, and he loved the damsel, and he spoke to the heart of the damsel [na'arah: a girl from infancy to adolescence; damsel, maiden]" (34:3). We may, if we wish, take at face value Shechem's professed love for Dinah. His attitude is surely preferable to that of the man who, having taken his pleasure of the woman he has violated, cruelly abandons her out of loathing.[13] But we should not be so easily gulled. Too many men rationalize their lusts, discover that a woman they found "good in bed" suddenly seems lovable. A man who offers a woman reassuring words, his lust now being sated after he has raped her, is no less a rapist. Her abasement means nothing; new love will conquer all. True, she needs comforting; but, says he to himself, speech to the heart will overcome her regret or sorrow.[14] Once alert to these nuances, a sensitive reader will cringe at Shechem's attempt to conceal through solicitous speech the vileness of his deed, as if defilement were just a state of mind, alterable by a change of heart. While sweet-talking the damsel, Shechem—compounding the corruption—commands his father to "take me this girl [yaldah: a young girl or child] for a wife [or woman: 'ishah]" (34:4; emphasis added),[15] and his father, the

13. See Amnon's hatred for his half sister Tamar after he had forced himself upon her (2 Samuel 13). The story of the rape of Tamar contains many echoes of our present tale.

14. Rashi reads similarly: he spoke "words that would appeal to her heart: See how much money your father has lavished for a small plot of field. I will marry you and you will then possess the city and all its fields (Joma 77b)."

15. The confusion of Shechem's speech reveals the perversity: he wants the girl-child turned into a woman-wife, and he wants it done by an act of "taking" by his father, reduced to playing minister to his son's desires and commands. I owe these observations to Yuval Levin.

ruling prince Hamor, will oblige. Servant rather than ruler of the lusts of his son, Hamor will try to legalize his son's sexual possession of "this [nameless young] girl" after the fact, and to make possession permanent.

To defend Shechem's conduct, the reader can appeal only to cultural relativity. Predatory behavior—"take first, ask later"—seems to be the customary way of the Shechemites.[16] The ruling prince does not upbraid his son for rape; on the contrary, he tacitly approves it and seeks to further satisfy his son's desires. An attempt to make an honest woman of Dinah, now that Shechem loves her, seems to be all that is needed to make prior abasement and defilement null and void. Woman is for the ravishing. Shechem and Hamor mistakenly believe that their views of the matter should command widespread assent. Lust (or love) and their possessive attitude toward woman makes them blind to cultural difference regarding shame, honor, and above all, purity and justice.

The house of Jacob takes a different view of the matter:

Now Jacob heard that he had defiled [*time'*] Dinah, his daughter; and his sons were with his cattle in the field. And Jacob held his peace until they came. And Hamor, the father of Shechem, went out unto Jacob to speak with him. (34:5–6)

As Hamor goes out to gain his son's desire, Jacob hears and concentrates only on his daughter's defilement (a new word: *tame',* to be foul, contaminated, polluted, unclean).[17] But as his sons are in the field with his cattle, he bides his time, awaiting their return.

Jacob's silence has long puzzled readers, because of what we know of his previous energy, resourcefulness, and shrewdness. Very possibly, Jacob is thoroughly nonplused, astonished at what has occurred, guilty for his own failure to prevent it, overwhelmed by sadness at the pollution of his household, or unsure

16. The sequence of deeds and feelings of Shechem regarding Dinah should be compared to that of previous courtships. Rebekah, wooed for Isaac by Abraham's servant, freely consented to be married; Isaac then took her, made her his wife, and (finally) loved her. Jacob first loves Rachel, then purchases her by service to her father, then marries her, but only after he unknowingly marries and goes in unto her sister. Dinah is first taken, then loved, and then sought for marriage. The sequence here is clearly perverse, a parody of proper courtship. It bespeaks a perverse understanding of the meaning of "wife" and marriage.

17. The idea represented by the notion *tame'* is central to the Israelite way and is very far-reaching (see the book of Leviticus). Someone can be or become *sexually* unclean (or defiled or polluted), religiously unclean (for example, through worship of idols, child sacrifice, or contact with necromancers), or ceremonially unclean (for example, by contact with carcasses of animals, dead bodies of humans, unclean animals, bodily issues, creeping things, or leprosy). The categories are overlapping: sexual purity is central also to religious purity.

of what one must do under such circumstances. All of a sudden, Dinah, in her defilement, becomes *"his* daughter." No one Jacob knew had faced the question of daughters before,[18] and certainly not the question of daughterly defilement: what can one do to reverse a violation that cannot be reversed? Some interpreters, who see Jacob's silence as paralysis, locate here the beginning of the end of Jacob's power and influence over his sons.

But Jacob's silence may also reflect his usual shrewdness rather than a newly acquired timidity. Focused on the defilement, he knows that something must be done, even if the foul deed itself cannot be undone. But what can he, a lamed old man, do, especially in the absence of his sons? Jacob does not *simply* hold his peace; he says and does nothing, the text implies, (only) *because* of their absence and *"until* they came." Perhaps, as Robert Sacks suggests,

> Jacob, who dealt successfully with his brother when facing the problems of an earlier generation, decided not to intervene in the present affair. The relation between Israel and its neighbors once a house had been built became the problems of another generation. Therefore he remained silent and waited for Dinah's brothers to arrive.

In addition, Jacob may even be thinking strategically, seeing here an occasion for collective action that could unify his sons in defense of their own. Whatever the reason, Jacob waits for his sons to return.[19]

What began as a seemingly interpersonal matter between a prince and a foreign damsel now quickly and clearly becomes (as it was from the start) a political issue between peoples. But the interests, concerns, and attitudes of the two sides differ sharply. The Hivite ruler and his son are eager to obtain Dinah as Shechem's wife; Jacob and his sons are preoccupied with her defilement.

> And the sons of Jacob came in from the field when they heard it; and the men were vexed and they were very incensed, because he had done a scurrilous deed [*nevalah*] in [*or* against] Israel in lying with Jacob's daughter, such as ought not to be done [*vekhen lo' ye'aseh*]. (34:7)

18. This is not quite true. His father-in-law, Laban, had shown him a certain high-handed way with daughters, substituting the elder, Leah, for the younger, Rachel, in what Jacob thought was his marriage to Rachel. Having lain with her, Jacob was then compelled to marry Leah, who later bore him Dinah. Jacob, who—according to Laban—had tried to ignore local customs regarding marriageable daughters, was unwittingly and unwillingly trapped into a "shotgun marriage." The sins of the fathers are sometimes visited also on the daughters.

19. In doing so, Jacob will soon lose control of the situation.

As soon as they hear the news, very likely by messenger sent from their father, Jacob's sons return from the fields, grieved and incensed. They are morally outraged by the deed, and they are united in their condemnation of it. The text, through the unusual device of narrative monologue, "conveys the tenor of Jacob's sons' anger by reporting in the third person the kind of language they would have spoken silently, or to each other." Yet, true to the phenomenon of outrage, the reasons the brothers give for their anger are not absolutely lucid. What *exactly*, from their point of view, is the scurrilous deed in Israel, the thing that ought not to be done? Is it rape? Is it the deflowering of a virgin daughter or sex outside of marriage ("lying with . . . daughter"), whether by force or not? Or is it rather the fact that sex was had with an outsider ("with *Jacob's* daughter")? And who, exactly, do they hold to be the victim of the offense: Dinah herself, Dinah as Jacob's daughter, Dinah as *their* sister? Dinah as a maiden in Israel? Not so much Dinah as their familial and ethnic dignity and honor? In the face of outrage, such distinctions are not easily made.

Yet truth to tell, many of these reasons are in fact interrelated; the brothers' angry failure to distinguish between them might reflect this deeper possibility. For if rape is a crime mainly against a woman's sexual (and therefore *generative*) nature, rather than a crime against her will, it is of a piece with other violations of female chastity and, therewith, of the purity of marriage and the clarity of lineage. As the later Israelite law makes clear, respect for maidenhood and chastity is integral to a respect for marriage, and the sanctity of marriage is central to the pursuit of righteousness and holiness. The brothers in their anger, thinking crudely but perhaps better than they know, intuit some of these vital connections. They use the expression "ought not to be done" *(lo' ye'aseh)*, which was used by Abimelech when he complained that Abraham had misled him into almost committing the sin of adultery, of lying with a woman who was another man's wife. Even though laws against rape and deflowering virgins had not yet been explicitly promulgated, not even among the Israelites, Jacob's sons intuitively understood it as an immoral, even a heinous, deed. What's more, they took it as an outrage not only against Dinah but also (and especially) against the entire clan and its ways. Their first complaint, against the "scurrilous deed in— or against—Israel," objects simultaneously to an attack on the Israelite nation ("against Israel") and a deep violation of its characteristic ways ("in Israel").

Indeed, one might even say that the clan here acts to define itself: as a community that unites to defend a sister's honor. This first action of Israel's (Jacob's) sons, to avenge a vile deed committed against Israel's daughter, gives birth to the *people* of Israel, now defined morally and politically, and no longer merely genealogically and economically: for the first time, children of the covenant speak

of themselves collectively (if somewhat anachronistically) as "Israel."[20] This unification of an otherwise potentially fractious and rivalrous band of men may be
what Jacob shrewdly had in mind when he waited for his sons to return before
responding. Previously, the sons had been primarily identified as the sons of the
four different mothers. Anger in defense of their own now unites them.

Unification in the face of a common enemy is the oldest political story. There
are even famous accounts of such political self-definition in defense of women
and to avenge a rape. The glory that was ancient Greece began, legend has it, in
this way. It was the Trojan War that first united the Achaians (Greeks), who
fought to avenge the rape of Helen by Paris while he was the guest of her husband, Menelaus. But many other cultures do not take rape this seriously.

The ancient Persians, in justifying themselves for their invasion of Greece,
blame the war on the Greeks and the revenge they took for Helen. Herodotus
presents their reasons:

> "It is the work of unjust men, we think, to carry off women at all; but once
> they have been carried off, to take seriously the avenging of them is the
> part of fools, as it is the part of sensible men to pay no heed to the matter;
> clearly, the women would not have been carried off had they no mind to
> be." The Persians say that they, for their part, made no account of the
> women carried off from Asia but that the Greeks, because of a Lacedae-
> monian woman [that is, Helen], gathered a great army, came straight to
> Asia, and destroyed the power of Persia, and from that time forth the Per-
> sians regarded the Greek people as their foes.

Nascent Israel, in its first collective action, holds a view of violated womanhood closer to that of nascent Greece rather than that of Persia. Yet on closer in-
spection, the ground of Greek and Israelite collective action may turn out to be
different. In the Trojan War the crime avenged was understood to be a crime
against hosts and hospitality; it is a perversion of hospitality to take the wife of
one's host. In avenging the rape of Dinah, the sons of Israel regard it as a crime
not only against their household but also against the purity of the woman herself. This concern with the dignity of woman as such—*not* as the possession of
the husband or father—will (much later) become emblematic of Israelite collective self-understanding.

---

20. The earlier mention of the "Children of Israel," in the episode of Jacob's wrestling, was made
in the voice of the text itself, speaking from a later vantage point, and not by Jacob or any of the characters in the story.

PROPOSING UNION: PARODIES OF
MARRIAGE AND COVENANT

Speaking to Jacob and his sons assembled, Hamor begins to make his case in strictly personal terms, pleading in the name of love: "The soul of my son longeth for your daughter. I pray thee give her unto him to wife" (34:8). But he soon appeals to what he assumes is Israelite self-interest and makes a pitch for thoroughgoing intermarriage (Hamor would certainly have noticed that Jacob had eleven sons, already or soon to be in need of wives). Hamor generously invites Jacob to "*give* your daughters unto us"—if and when and to whom *you* please—and to "*take* our daughters unto you"—again, presumably, whomever *you* please (34:9). There is no allusion to compulsion or force; indeed, there is not even a whiff of Hivite *taking-as-they*-please, let alone taking without prior paternal consent. (Needless to say, for the Canaanites, the consent of the *daughter* will play no part in arranging marriages.) Appealing still further to self-interest, Hamor proposes that the Israelites may then dwell among his people, trade freely in the land, and gain possessions there (34:10). In short, if they cooperate, they may get them wives and (other) valuable goods, through free and peaceful trade.

At this point, Shechem, grown impatient with his father's emphasis on free trade and mutual intermarriage, jumps into the conversation to return it to the object of his own immediate desire and to make his own personal appeal:

> And Shechem said unto her father and unto her brethren: "Let me find grace in your eyes and that which you say unto me I will give. Ask me however much bride price and gift, and I will give whatever you say unto me; but give me the damsel to wife." (34:11–12)

Shechem, speaking to Dinah's father and brothers, shows no trace of shame or remorse. He continues not to speak her name. He makes no mention that he has already taken lustfully by force what he now proposes to buy generously with gifts ("no price is too high"). As he believed that sweet words should overcome the maiden's shame and sorrow, so he now believes that gifts of money to the men will satisfy all their concerns in the matter. The implication is clear: for a husband, woman is sexual possession; for her family, she—and even her honor—is a commodity for sale.

We readers, some of us fathers of daughters or brothers of sisters, listening to this plea and this proposal—how do we react to such a generous and useful and profitable offer? Shall we be swayed by professions of love and promises of peaceful trade and coexistence? Shall we overlook injustice for the sake of gain, overlook the violation of our daughter (sister) so that we might easily get wives for all of our sons? Or shall we side with the moral indignation of the sons of Israel, who see only the defilement of their sister and who craftily plot revenge?

Politically and morally speaking, Jacob's sons are in a tight spot. They do, however, understand their situation and see clearly their options. Shechem still has Dinah. The city has walls. The ruling power of the city, speaking for the whole, is backing the young prince and stands behind the rape. The brothers cannot simply say, "Please give her back." Their choice is either conciliation or revenge.[21] If they acquiesce in the offer and conciliate, they tacitly become complicit in Dinah's violation, especially since there has been no remorse or apology. In addition, by accepting the broader proposition of intermarriage, they will in effect be choosing assimilation, given that they are few and the Shechemites are many. If, on the other hand, they choose revenge, Jacob's sons have no alternative but to proceed with guile. Getting even with the young prince and his father, here and now, would only produce reprisals from the city and its allies. Attacking the city straightaway is out of the question. The only alternative appears to be later massive violence hidden behind prior peaceful deception. Machiavelli could not have analyzed better.

It is important to add, however, that the way of Machiavelli is not identical to the way of the Lord. True, Shechem himself has brought Dinah—"Judgment"—into and upon his city. True, God wants Israel to be agents of righteousness and justice; and He instructed Abraham that, when injustice takes over a city, the whole city must stand or fall together and the innocent must suffer with the guilty. But thus far, that is a lesson that applies to justice executed by God, not by human beings without instruction. For those who prefer a purely political reading of the present chapter it is sobering to realize that God's name does not appear even once in the present story. (It is, thus far, only the second chapter in Genesis of which this is true.)[22] Jacob and the brothers neither appeal to God and His ways nor invoke His assistance. The Lord Himself is utterly silent. These

---

21. They could, of course, simply leave the area. But such an action would not only abandon Dinah; it would also tacitly consent to her defilement.

22. The first case was Genesis 23, the account of Abraham's purchase of the burial plot from Ephron the Hittite. In retrospect, God's absence from that account raises a question about the rightness of Abraham's deed. Could there have been something questionable, from the point of view of the new way, of any ownership of the Promised Land independent of God's providence? Might there not in fact be something wrong with resting one's claim to land on either purchase or ancestral burial rather than on divine gift and the revealed law?

facts serve as a warning to those who would like to believe that the strictly political can, at the same time, also be the strictly pious.

The brothers, unified, quickly conceive a plan of action. They are not going to conciliate and let bygones be bygones. Although they are furious, they have sufficient self-control and cunning to plot a stratagem for getting back their sister and paying back the evildoers. "Because he had defiled [*time'*] Dinah, their sister," they answer Shechem and his father "with guile" (34:13). The device the brothers use is ingenious—not only strategically, but especially morally and symbolically:

"We cannot do this thing, to give our sister to one that is uncircumcised; for that were a reproach unto us. Only on this condition will we consent unto you: if ye will be as we are, that every male of you be circumcised, then will we give our daughters unto you and we will take your daughters to us, and we will dwell with you, and *we will become one people*. But if ye will not hearken unto us, to be circumcised, then we will take *our daughter* and we will be gone." (34:14–17; emphasis added)

The sons ignore the personal side of the request and treat the matter entirely politically-culturally-religiously. Just as they saw that the crime against Dinah was a crime also against Israel, so they see that the union of man and woman anticipates children and, therefore, the question of perpetuating one's ways and beliefs. Using in their reply many of the same words spoken by Hamor, they make explicit the assimilationist meaning that was merely implicit in the Shechemite proposal for intermarriage; for freely to exchange daughters means, culturally, *to become one people*. The question is, whose ways will the assimilated populace adopt? Shall they still be the people of the covenant, whose sign is marked in the flesh by circumcision? Confronted by this question, the sons of Israel assert and insist upon the difference of their ways, a difference that reminds (the reader) always of God and his promise to Abraham. Although they do not

---

Three later chapters in Genesis will also make no mention of God: chapter 36, which deals exclusively with the abundant generations of Esau, issuing in numerous Edomite peoples and kingdoms; chapter 37, which deals with the near-fratricidal struggles between Joseph and his brothers (and in which the place of Shechem is again important), winding up with Joseph being sold into Egypt; and chapter 47, which deals with Joseph's bringing of Jacob (and his sons) before Pharaoh, Joseph's institution of slavery in Egypt, during the time of famine, and the Israelites' settling in Egypt where they will later be enslaved themselves. God's absence from all these episodes—most of them about international relations—suggests a possible tension between politics as human beings will likely practice it and the politics sought by the new way.

speak directly of God or His covenant—to do so with their Canaanite interlocu- tors would be both pointless and foolish—the brothers tacitly bring the cove- nant into the picture. Without explanation, they insist on the importance of its sign, the production of which is the singular Israelite obligation under the covenant. To be sure, the use of circumcision here serves mainly as part of the strategy for revenge,[23] and we cannot be sure whether the sons understand or even care about its deeper sacred significance, since they clearly do not intend to go through with the agreement for intermarriages. Many readers blame the sons not only for their deceit but most especially because it exploits and perhaps abuses for violent purposes the sacred sign of the covenant. Still, the demand for circumcision carries moral meaning on its own, regardless of the deceitful in- tention and bloody outcome. For it reveals still more deeply the differences be- tween the two peoples and their different attitudes toward women and sexuality.

The Israelites are, of course, not the only people who practice male circumci- sion. But with them, the ritual has a high and special meaning: it is the sign of the covenant God made with Abraham, the founder. Our earlier discussion of this covenantal circumcision emphasized, among other things, its implicit sanc- tification of procreation and lineage and its implicit teaching of the spiritual pointings of the parental task and the importance of male sexual self-restraint. For people not properly disposed toward these teachings, circumcision will have an altogether different meaning.

Shechem, the rapist, was psychically as well as physically uncircumcised. First, he acted as if his *lust* entitled him to have his way with Dinah. Afterward, the ground of his claim shifted to his *desire,* to his longing for her. The generative meaning of sexuality and the attendant reverence owed to womanly shame he understood not at all; much less did he have in mind a right partner for the fu- ture work of transmission. And he will soon lead his entire city into destruction, just so that he can satisfy his heart's desire. The Shechemites, like Shechem him- self, will submit to circumcision, but with no understanding of what it means, in itself and, especially, to the Israelites. Shechemite circumcision turns out to be a parody of the covenant, just as Shechem's request to be given a bride whom he had already taken and defiled was a parody of a proper marriage proposal.

---

23. Some people believe that the brothers' deceit sought only to avoid intermarriage, not (origi- nally) to exact revenge. That is, the brothers, fully expecting that the Shechemites would refuse to comply with the condition of circumcision, made a dishonest promise of intermarriage that they had no intention of honoring. But strictly speaking, this would not be guile. The word (in 34:13) translated as "guile," *mirmah,* means "treachery," "deceit," "scam," "a putting one over," and not merely lying. Moreover, given our earlier analysis showing that the brothers felt they had no choice but to avenge the injury, only by this deception could they weaken the Shechemites sufficiently to enable them to do so successfully.

Hamor and Shechem are well pleased with the proposal of Jacob's sons, and Shechem hastens to the deed: "And the young man deferred not to do the thing, *because he had delight in Jacob's daughter.* And he was honored above all the house of his father" (34:19; emphasis added). But the proposal required that *all* the men of Shechem submit to circumcision. How could they be persuaded? To win the hearts of their fellow Shechemites, Hamor and Shechem go to the city gate (where their countrymen are assembled) and smoothly talk business:

> "These men are peaceable with us; therefore let them dwell in the land, and trade therein; for behold, the land is large enough for them; let us *take their* daughters to us for wives, and let us *give* them *our* daughters."(34:21; emphasis added)

The appeal begins quietly: the men (that is, Jacob's clan) are not warlike or troublesome, and as there is enough land, let them live here and trade. Even better, *we* can *take* their daughters (whomever *we* like) and we can *give* them—*if* and when *we* like—our daughters; in speaking to their own, Hamor and Shechem cast the liberalities differently than when they spoke to Jacob and his sons. But the cost of this bargain in spousing has yet to be mentioned, and to pay it, the people will require an even better reward:

> "Only on this condition will the men consent unto us to dwell with us, *to become one people,* if every male among us be circumcised, as they are circumcised. *Shall not their cattle and their substance and all their beasts be ours?* Only let us consent unto them, and they will dwell with us." (34:22–23; emphasis added)

The appeal succeeds: *every* able-bodied man is circumcised, presumably the married as well as the unmarried.

And unto Hamor and unto Shechem, his son, hearkened *all* that went out of the gate of his city; and every male was circumcised, *all* that went out of the gate of his city. (34:24; emphasis added) [24]

Some, perhaps, are tempted by the promise of prospective brides; others— probably the majority—more greedy than lustful, are moved by the promise of capturing through assimilation all of the Israelite wealth and cattle, so confident

---

24. The expression "all that went out of the gate of the city" means especially those who go out to wage war. This verse thus hints at the immediate sequel, made possible by the weakening, through surgery, of all the Shechemite warriors.

are they that their superior numbers and ways will prevail.[25] The Shechemites are culturally open to all customs, provided that it increases the gross national product.

DEEDS OF REVENGE: HARSH JUSTICE AND BEYOND

As it turns out, the Shechemite leaders have made false promises, or at best have exposed their own deviousness. For, at least for the time being, Jacob and Israel have no marriageable daughters but Dinah, who remains in Shechem's house, and is (in many senses) "taken." The appeal to gain and greed is perhaps a disingenuous promise to the rabble—hiding from view that only Shechem himself would profit from their acquiescence. Otherwise, if honest, the appeal to the Shechemites betrays a rather sordid view of the entire proposal to "become one people." In any case, the Shechemites circumcise themselves wholeheartedly for gain, not—as did Abraham—to gain wholeheartedness. What they gain, in fact, is their own death and the ruin of their city:

> And it came to pass on the third day, when they were in pain, that two of the sons of Jacob, Simeon and Levi, Dinah's brethren, took each man his sword and came upon the city unnoticed and slew all the males. And they slew Hamor and Shechem, his son, with the edge of the sword, and took Dinah out of Shechem's house and went forth. (34:25–26)

Calling attention to Shechemite cupidity is not an endorsement of the harshness of the penalty exacted by Dinah's (full) brothers, Simeon and Levi, who stole into the city postoperatively while the men were in pain and who slew *all* the males before taking Dinah out from Shechem's house (34:25–26). But it is a suggestion of the fitness—at least the partial fitness—of collective punishment, bearing out the earlier suggestion that Prince Shechem is somehow representative of his entire city—both as paradigm and as head. In agreeing to the circumcision, the entire male population of Shechem has tacitly endorsed the prince's actions and the principles they embody. Here is a nation indifferent to rape and

25. Yuval Levin observes that the deployment of the stratagem of circumcision is a perfect answer also to the Shechemite adherence to the principle that "might makes right," exemplified not only in the rape of Dinah but in the communal scheme to overwhelm the Children of Israel in all future dealings. Circumcision is the mark of a covenant part of whose divine purpose is to overcome the natural way of the world in which justice means merely the rule of the stronger. By making use of the symbol of that covenant, the weaker Israelites are able to overcome the stronger Shechemites in pursuit of justice. In the process, they vindicate the principle that right is not defined by might.

the defilement of women, eager for intermarriage, keen upon gain, coveting both their neighbors' wives and their neighbors' cattle—equally regarded as objects for possession. Here is a people that will accept circumcision as a price for profit, to gain a woman or to win a herd of cattle, not as a reminder of the importance of rearing your children in a spirit of reverence. No Shechemite is moved by this self-inflicted act on the genitals (the offending organ, as it were) to reflect—or to suffer pangs of conscience—on the rape or on the proper use of his sexuality. No one is moved to feel awe or reverence for the divine. Because they are insufficiently respectful of women, with corruption in their hearts, mere circumcision in the flesh can not keep the Shechemites from being cut off as a people. Indeed, the Shechemite practice—treating woman as possessions employed for sexual enjoyment only—*means,* implicitly, the ultimate disappearance of Shechem (just as sodomy does for Sodom). It is no justification of their slaughterers to say that the Shechemites are not fit to survive.

The slaughter of the entire manhood of Shechem could, in fact, also be defended as a matter of necessity and on grounds of realpolitik. Limited revenge taken upon the young prince would unquestionably have resulted in counter-vengeance: one can hardly expect the Shechemites to regard his killing as just ("once women had been carried off, to take seriously the avenging of them is the part of fools"); and justice aside, they would certainly strike back in defense of their own first family. Greatly outnumbered, Jacob's sons would have stood little chance in an all-out battle; and while the Lord's intercession might have given them the upper hand, they would have had no good reason to count on divine aid in the fighting. Besides, Dinah, their sister, was still in Shechemite hands. Guile, deception, and stealth, followed by a massive "surgical" strike of "protective reaction," would be a sound strategy under the circumstances.

Yet it is unlikely that the sons of Jacob are simply ruled by such shrewd and cool calculation. Most likely, they are driven by rage and by the desire to visit the harshest possible punishment on Shechem and his entire kind. No matter what they do, removal of the pollution cannot be accomplished, all the more reason why no amount of punishment seems to them great enough. They do not cease with killing the men. They spoil the entire city:

The sons of Jacob [presumably all of them] came upon the slain and spoiled the city, *because they had defiled* [*tim'u*] *their sister.* They took their flocks and their herds and their asses, and that which was in the city and that which was in the field; and all their wealth, and all their little ones and their wives they took captive and spoiled, even all that was in the house. (34:27–29; emphasis added)

Rationalizing their rage by holding the entire city collectively responsible—"because *they* had defiled their sister"[26]—Jacob's sons take everything, from both the city and the fields. The flocks, herds, asses, and all the Shechemite wealth they spoil; all their women and children they take captive. This last, of course, could be recommended on grounds of policy: to obliterate the possibility of future generations that will come looking for revenge. And (to be mentioned only in hushed tones) it also solves an important present problem: Jacob's sons, previously unmarried, thus acquire wives without a huge risk of assimilation to foreign ways.[27]

But the text's picture of the brothers' deeds cannot be wiped away by such rational consideration. Even if justified or necessary, the attack reeks of barbaric cruelty. Their zeal for revenge knows no limits: the innocent suffer with the guilty. Worse, the avengers profit from their revenge. It is Dinah's brothers—not Shechem and Hamor, who merely *sought* to do so—who actually grow rich from the rape of their sister. The Shechemites started it by taking one woman; the sons of Jacob finish it by taking *all* the women, having slaughtered their husbands. To avenge the honor of a woman taken by force, Jacob's sons forcibly seize and drag into slavery or marriage a townful of women whose husbands they have killed.[28] The most Machiavellian of readers cannot but experience the horror of these "necessary" acts of retribution. Doing justice—to avenge even scurrilous deeds—is not supposed to look like this.

---

26. Is this the perfectly natural but unjustified exaggeration caused by rage, or is this a genuine insight into the collective character of Shechemite guilt? Could it be both?

27. A truly nasty reader of this story might even suggest that, intentionally or not, Dinah served as the bait for the catching of wives. An episode of similar import in the mythic account of the founding of Rome is the story of the rape of the Sabine women, to which this story should be compared. See Livy, *History of Rome* 1.9–1.13.

28. I owe this point to Kristen Dietrich Balisi. In a private paper, written as a critique of my earlier published account and offering her own line-by-line commentary, she comments further:

> If the sons of Jacob, brothers of Dinah, had a true grasp of what it is to violate a woman sexually, to treat her as an object whose sexual relationships are defined by the men who have physical and/or socioeconomic power over her, they could not bring themselves to do such a thing. This would be the thing that is an outrage in Israel. Rather than making a comparison between the very young and innocent Dinah and Helen—the most beautiful, seductive woman in the world, wife of Menelaus, lover of Paris, and lover of Deiphobos—*here* would be the perfect place to bring in images of Homer. Though the revenge for Helen brings the Achaians to Troy, it is the battle of wills over possession of a captive woman—a "prize" for great deeds in battle— which initiates the feud of the *Iliad*, a book which will remind us repeatedly of the cries of women being dragged into slavery by the killers of their husbands. . . . One can hardly see the actions of Jacob's sons as demonstrative of their deep-seated respect for the proper understanding of female sexuality or of the meaning of wife. (Private communication, February 1998)

PEACE VERSUS RETRIBUTION:
JACOB VERSUS DINAH'S BROTHERS

Jacob, too, is horrified, but for different reasons. The collective action taken by his sons has backfired; it has made it impossible for him to settle peacefully in the land as he had planned. Worse, his entire tribe is now at risk; his sons, in their zeal, had failed to consider that there were other Canaanite tribes who would not ignore the slaughter of their kinsmen:

> "Ye have troubled me, to make me odious unto the inhabitants of the land, even unto the Canaanites and the Perizzites, and I being few in number, they will gather themselves together against me and smite me; and I shall be destroyed, I and my house." (34:30)

Later, at the end of his life, Jacob, in blessing his sons, will heap moral opprobrium and curses upon Simeon and Levi.[29] But here, after the deed itself, his concerns are strictly political-prudential, and mainly self-preservative. He is now a pariah and, worse, a likely victim in the land of his fathers, a land that, the reader knows, was promised to his ancestors and their seed.

Jacob, even at the end of this episode, seems not to understand that living in peace *among* one's neighbors may not be an option for people of the covenant. Jacob blames his sons for making peaceful interaction impossible, but it may never be possible if the Israelites take their divine mission and unique ways seriously. Even after all that has happened, Jacob still seems unaware of the error he made at the beginning, when he pursued peaceful and profitable interaction rather than covenant-preserving and God-fearing-and-revering separation.

Not Jacob but Jacob's sons have the last word. They reject his rebuke and his utilitarian and survivalist concerns in the name of morality, spiced with an implicit but stinging rebuke of their own:

> "As with a harlot should one deal with our sister?" (34:31)

The brothers, by emphasizing *"our* sister"—'*achothenu* is the very last word of their speech and of the whole story—tacitly chastise Jacob for his apparent in-

---

29. "Simeon and Levi are brethren; weapons of violence their kinship. Let my soul not come into their council; unto their assembly let my glory not be united; for in their anger they slew men, and in their self-will they houghed oxen. Cursed be their anger, for it was fierce, and their wrath for it was cruel; I will divide them in Jacob, and scatter them in Israel" (49:5–7). We should, of course, be cautious in assuming that Jacob is here the spokesman for the biblical author. The zeal of Levi, suitably disciplined, will turn out to be necessary for the formation of the people of Israel. Moses is a Levite, and the tribe of Levi will later become the priestly tribe of the Israelite nation.

difference to Dinah. For he had spoken only of the unhappy consequences their deed would bring upon *his own head*—in one sentence, Jacob had managed to use the first person pronoun eight times: twice in its freestanding form *('ani)*, five more times as an object suffix, and once more as a possessive suffix (*"my house"*). Dinah he had apparently forgotten, and—so the brothers seem to imply—forgotten not only now. The brothers, who like Dinah are (mainly) children of Leah the unloved, in asserting their loyalty to their own full sister, are tacitly castigating Jacob for his unfatherly neglect, perhaps not only of Dinah but of themselves as well.

Regardless of their motives, and notwithstanding their brutality, the brothers' rhetorical question about *harlotry* reverberates in our minds, especially because it is the story's last word: *"As with a harlot should one deal with our sister?"* What does this mean? And why is this the last word?

The word translated "as with a harlot" comes from the verb *zanah,* from a primitive root meaning "highly fed," and therefore "wanton." It means "to commit adultery" (especially for the female) or "to play the harlot," and in the causative form, "to cause to commit fornication" or "to cause to be (or to play) the whore." But it also easily acquires the figurative meaning, "to commit idolatry," "to whore after false gods," on the understanding that Israel is betrothed solely to God. Even if (as is likely) they are speaking better than they know, both meanings can be heard in the brothers' rejoinder to Jacob.

At first glance, the brothers' remark seems to be equating rape with harlotry, or at least suggesting that what Shechem did to Dinah might have been overlooked—or at least mitigated—were Dinah a whore, a view not foreign to the ancient world. Roman law, as noted above, did not recognize the rape of a prostitute or common harlot, "not allowing any punishment," as Blackstone put it in his *Commentaries,* "for violating the chastity of her, who hath indeed no chastity at all, or at least hath no regard to it." Indeed, similar sorts of arguments are to this day advanced in defense of accused rapists: "Look how she dresses." "She sleeps around." "What was she doing in his apartment (or that fraternity house)?" "She was asking for it." But even granting their possible relevance, such complaints of provocation never constitute an adequate defense for rape—though they might make it more difficult to determine whether what transpired was in fact rape and not, say, seduction. For this reason, the "motto" of Jacob's sons does not mean that it would be permissible to rape a harlot. On the contrary, the sons are asserting *that their failure to avenge their sister's honor* would be tantamount to regarding her as if she were a harlot. Worse, to practice turning the other cheek would mean (tacitly) to share, by acquiescence, in her defilement. In sum, the sons are insisting that *in rape—and in indifference to rape—a man (and a community) treats a woman the way a harlot treats herself.*

Regardless of their divergent motives, the deeds of rapist and harlot have a convergent inner meaning. Both deeds are without modesty, shame, or sexual self-restraint. Both are indifferent to the generative meaning of (especially female) sexuality, both regard sex purely as a matter of present and private (especially male) gratification. Both are indifferent to the fact that sex points to future generations, those to whom we give life and nurture, paying back, in the only way we can, our debts to our own forebears. Both are especially indifferent to marriage and family, those conventional institutions whose main purpose is to provide a true home for fruitful and generous love and for the proper rearing of children. And both are indifferent to the moral, cultural, and religious beliefs of the sexual partner, so crucial for the preservation of lineage and the perpetuation of one's ways.

Whether or not they understood fully what they were saying, Jacob's sons remind Jacob (who had hoped for peaceful coexistence)—as they instruct the reader—that the alternative to defending the virtue of one's sisters is to abandon them, and all future generations, to the realm of false gods. Similarly, the alternative to defending the purity of Israel's covenant with God is to abandon the nation to the same fate. Rape—like harlotry and the indiscriminate intermarriage proposed by the Shechemites—means the spiritual defilement of an entire people. The defense of chastity and the transmission of holiness are part of a single package.[30]

This is not to say that the text means for us simply to adopt the brothers' point of view, much less to approve wholeheartedly of their conduct. All fair-minded readers of the story are left with nagging questions. The brothers' motives seem unclear. Their practice of deceit and the merely cunning exploitation of the holy rite of circumcision appear problematic. The potential—in this case, actual—extremism to which proper vengeance can grow troubles us. The notion of collective guilt, especially when rendered by outraged human beings, is questionable.

We see the terrible dilemmas of settling in a land amid people who are not-God-fearing, especially if one has imprudent and zealous offspring. We see how zeal in defense of one's own or even of God's ways can lead men into war, and how, should they prove successful, the spoils of war can lead them, ironically, *away* from God's ways. We are bothered by the danger that adherence to the new way become subverted by simple loyalty to blood. We fear in the avenging deed a return of pagan heroism and the rise of organized vengeance of the sort that

30. This teaching will find concrete expression in the Mosaic Law, presented in Exodus and Leviticus. Central to the so-called holiness code is an extensive package of rules proscribing incestuous marriages, unchastity, and Molech worship (Leviticus 18). This chapter is traditionally read in the synagogue on the Jewish Day of Atonement, Judaism's holiest day.

produced the world washed out by the Flood. We find it hard to square morally the defense of one's own women with the seizure of one's enemy's women. At the same time, however, we are also moved by the suggestion that a community that will make war to defend the virtue of its women, against a community that dishonors other people's women, proves itself—by this very fact of its willingness to fight and die for its daughters and sisters—to be not only more fit to survive and flourish but also superior in justice. And even if, in such matters, the justice of retribution is not enough or even entirely just, ignoring the matter or doing nothing would seem to be much worse.

PERSISTING POLLUTION: THE FATE OF DINAH

Wherever one comes down on these political-moral questions, no one can conclude that the episode at Shechem had a happy ending. Justice is indeed not enough: Dinah, though avenged, remains defiled. The sons may have satisfaction, but she has shame. Any reading that focuses on the vengeance of the brothers and on their political transformation into Israel runs the risk of forgetting the sister, the daughter, the maiden. But one should not mistake silence—neither ours nor the story's—for indifference. True, we are told absolutely nothing about Dinah's feelings or thoughts—not about the rape itself, or the aftermath with Shechem and his sweet speeches, or the proposal of marriages, or the bloody slaughter of Shechem and the men of his entire city, not even about her rescue by her brothers. We have not one spoken word from her own lips, not before, not after. And we hear no words spoken to her by her father or brothers. In dreadful silence, we can only imagine the terrible consequences for this young maiden—psychic, social, spiritual. As far as we know, she never marries and never bears children. Her name appears only once hereafter in the entire Bible (Genesis 46:15), all alone in the list of names of the household of Jacob who accompanied him on the move to Egypt.[31]

But readers should not mistake the reticence: the silence of her shame still cries out for our sympathy and searching attention.

Unlike other women we have met in Genesis, Dinah is defined solely by her young womanliness. Unlike Sarah, who could command her husband, unlike Rebekah, a paragon of tact and prudence, unlike the rivalrous sisters Leah and Rachel, each with her own capacity for self-defense, Dinah is presented to us merely as a maid—exposed, innocent, vulnerable to male predation. Of course, she has thoughts and feelings, motives and desires; of course, she is a person in

---

31. Even her mention here in the census is oblique, as if she were only ambiguously present: "These are the sons of Leah whom she bore unto Jacob in Paddan-aram, and with Dinah, his daughter."

her own right. But for its present purposes, the text abstracts from her inner life; it wants us to concentrate entirely on the fact that Dinah is a *woman*, and more precisely, a young and *unmarried* woman, and of course, a daughter—the first daughter in Israel. Her womanly ancestors are known mainly as wives and mothers. With Dinah we are compelled to think about maidenhood—and about daughters. How should they comport themselves? And what should we, their fathers and their mothers, teach them in matters of men, sex, and marriage? How should we guide them in negotiating the transition from daughter and sister to wife? How should we help them avoid the ever-present dangers of rape, harlotry, and intermarriage?

Jacob, it seems, did not understand the need for such education and protection. His mind focused (understandably) on other matters, perhaps reassured regarding his future by his having numerous sons, he failed to see that it is reverent and virtuous daughters who safeguard a nation's heritage. No daughters, no nation. He might have known better. He himself had been sent to Paddan-aram to find a wife, so as not to marry a Canaanite woman; from the stellar example of his own mother, he should have known the importance of woman—both to insure lineage and to foster proper rearing—and taken steps to protect his daughter's purity. But though he was in when she went out, he prevented neither her going nor her going alone; he did not even warn her against the dangers. He was, to say the least, insufficiently concerned about her maidenhood—until it was too late.

Yet with the help of the story, we readers learn the need for a special education and protection of daughters. The new way's dedicatory circumcision of newborn males symbolically teaches the restraint of male promiscuity and beckons males to familial responsibility, under the aegis of the divine covenant. The present story hints at a correlative female counterpart: modesty, caution, refusal, self-reverence, and chastity, all exercised in the service of eventual marriage—fruitful, love-filled, sanctified. This is the opposite of the famous double standard, which winks at men sowing their wild oats but castigates female promiscuity. In Israel, it will be a single standard, differently applied, as befits the natural sexual differences between men and women, a standard of purity that fits the special image-of-God dignity of the human and that aspires wholeheartedly toward holiness. Jacob may have neglected these matters, but as the sequel makes clear, the text does not.

Beyond Justice to Purity: The Call to Beth-El

Although the brothers get the last word in the argument with their father, one cannot from this fact conclude that they speak for the biblical author. Unfortunately for those readers who seek authoritative answers from the text—yet happily for those who aspire to moral thoughtfulness—the Bible does not tell us what, finally, to make of the brothers' deeds of revenge. God, absent from the entire affair, does not take sides in the argument. When He finally does speak in the immediate sequel, right after the speech of the sons, He neither approves nor disapproves of what either party has said. His remarks are addressed solely to Jacob:

> And God said unto Jacob: "Arise, *go up* to *Beth-El,* and dwell *there;* and make *there* an altar unto God *who appeared unto thee* when thou didst flee from the face of Esau, thy brother." (35:1; emphasis added)

Although God has the genuinely last word, it is less than clear what it means and implies about the episode at Shechem just ended and the argument between father and sons. On one reading, God's failure to condemn looks like a divine endorsement of the brothers' deed, or at least of their final retort to Jacob. On an opposite reading, His failure to approve looks like divine rejection, and His command to go and build an altar may be read as a demand for much needed purification.

But there is a third reading, in my view a preferable one: God's silence on the acts of revenge and His indifference to the argument about justice suggests that the problem has been wrongly posed. The deeper difficulty is not one of international relations or peace versus justice, but of Israel's relation to God. God does not express displeasure with the actions of the sons, but He tacitly expresses displeasure with Jacob's original decision to settle among the Canaanites, the deed that set in motion the whole chain of events. At the same time, he offers both Jacob and his sons a more profound answer to the "problem of harlotry."

God commands Jacob to correct his plans and to change his place, physically and, by implication, spiritually. The command contains not only a reminder of God's providence but also an implicit rebuke of Jacob's previous decisions. Jacob, who had tried to settle permanently in the face of Shechem and who erected *there* an altar with an ambiguous name (*'El-'Elohey-Yisra'el;* 33:20), is told now to complete his journey. He must "rise" and "go up" from the Canaanites and from the stage of mere politics. He must give up the house he built for himself and return to Beth-El, "the House of God," to the place where Abraham had built an altar and first called upon the name of the Lord, and where Jacob himself had dreamt his famous dream of the ladder just before his departure into Paddan-aram.[32] He must return to Beth-El and "dwell *there,*" and he must "make

---

32. In fact, only now for the first time does God explicitly confirm what Jacob—and the reader—have long suspected, namely, that this dream was indeed a God-send.

there an altar" unto God, who appeared to him there when he fled from a previous life-threatening encounter. Indirectly, God reminds Jacob of his vow, made on that occasion, to serve the Lord as his God, should he come back in peace to his father's house, as well as of the pillar he erected *there*, which would, he vowed, become God's house. In short, God instructs Jacob that there are basically two places—the right place and the wrong place—and that Jacob needs to move himself from the latter to the former, to Beth-El, the House of God.[33]

Like Abraham before him, Jacob promptly answers the call: he gets up and goes, retracing Abraham's path from Shechem to Beth-El (and eventually also to Egypt). Jacob understands immediately that he has been called not just to physical relocation but to spiritual repurification. He leaves off thinking about matters of international trade, safety, and justice, and focuses on his orientation to the divine. He sees for the first time that the central question is the question of false or foreign gods. Inspired by God's call, Jacob reasserts paternal authority in his household. As his sons have just saved him from the temptation of assimilation and idolatry, so he must now save them (and all his future seed) from the same danger.[34] He commands his household and all that are with him to "put away the strange gods that are among you, and purify yourselves, and change your garments; and let us arise, and go up to Beth-El." And he gives the reason for the journey: "I will make there an altar unto God, who answered me in the day of my distress and who was with me in the way that I went" (35:2–3).[35] Jacob collects and buries all the foreign gods and the talismanic earrings (probably from the captive Shechemite women and children but also, perhaps, from Rachel), and the entire clan heads off to Beth-El. And as they journey, "a terror of God was upon the cities that were round about them, and they did not pursue after the sons of Jacob" (35:5). Whatever He may have thought of their deed, God apparently offers the departing bloody avengers His divine protection.[36]

33. I owe this observation and formulation to Yuval Levin. On three of the occasions that God speaks directly to Jacob, He speaks to tell him to go to another place: once to leave Laban and return to the land of his fathers (31:3); here, to go up to Beth-El; and later (in a dream), to go down to Egypt (46:3). Jacob, the clever man of many ways, is eminently capable of adapting himself to his surroundings, changing according to where he is. This may be why God needs to remind him so frequently about where he is and where he needs to be instead.

34. I owe this observation and formulation to Eric Lavoie.

35. Jacob delicately omits repeating the nature of "my distress," that is, his flight in fear from Esau. But he adds publicly his acknowledgment that God, who sent the dream, has indeed been with him, albeit in silence, these past twenty or more years, fulfilling the condition that Jacob had attached to his vow. (See 28:20.)

36. It is possible, alternatively, to understand "the terror of God" that afflicted the neighboring cities to be simply "the fear of Simeon and Levi, and the rest of Jacob's sons," given the invincible and destructive power they had demonstrated in Shechem.

The removal of Jacob and his clan to Beth-El marks the beginning of the end of "the Jacob cycle," the round trip of his adventures into Paddan-aram triggered by threat of fratricide and the need to find a suitable wife. Jacob returns a changed man, inside as well as out. Thus, in a compressed account (all in chapter 35), we learn of several crucial events that bring down the curtain on his earlier life: the death of Deborah, his mother Rebekah's nurse; the death of his wife Rachel; and finally, the death of his father, Isaac.

The death of Deborah occurs at Beth-El, soon after Jacob consecrates his return by building an altar as God had commanded:

> So Jacob came to Luz, which is in the land of Canaan—the same is Beth-El—he and all the people that were with him. And he built there an altar, and he called the place El-Beth-El, because there God was revealed unto him, when he fled from the face of his brother.
>
> And Deborah, Rebekah's nurse, died and was buried beneath Beth-El under the oak [*tachath ha'allon*], and so its name was called Allon-bacuth. (35:6–8)

The report of Deborah's death takes the reader by surprise: Why Deborah? And why now? Deborah has played no visible part in our story; never before mentioned by name, we know of her only from a remark made long ago, when Abraham's servant came looking for a wife for Isaac: "And they sent away Rebekah their sister, *and her nurse,* and Abraham's servant and his men" (28:59, emphasis added). How did she come now to be in Jacob's party?[37] And why are we told of her death, especially since the death of Rebekah herself will not be reported?[38] We have no confident answers to these perplexing questions. But the place of Deborah's burial, "beneath the oak" *(tachath ha'allon),* reminds of the burial of the foreign gods and earrings, also "beneath the oak" *(tachath ha'elah),* at Shechem, during the recent purification, mentioned but a few verses earlier (35:4). Deborah, the last remnant of the world of Paddan-aram, the old nurse of his mother who had been sent to watch over her as she left to join the people of God's covenant, now at last departs; with her burial "beneath the oak" are symbolically laid to rest all traces of Mesopotamian influence.

It is only at this point that "God appeared unto Jacob again,"[39] *when he came*

---

37. Jacob left for Paddan-aram alone. Rebekah had promised to send him word when it was safe to return, but it is hardly likely that she would have sent her aged nurse.

38. Of the four matriarchs, only the deaths of Sarah and Rachel, the two beautiful ones, are reported. The burials of Rebekah and Leah in the cave at Machpelah are reported in the last speech of the dying Jacob in Egypt, as he requests that his sons bury him also in that cave (49:29–32).

39. "Again": this refers no doubt to the dream at Beth-El, now known to have been a divine appearance. See 35:1.

from Paddan-aram" (35:9; emphasis added), and blessed him—for the first and only time—with a most abundant patriarchal blessing: a blessing for seed, national profusion, kingly descendants, and the Promised Land. Here it is, in full:

"Thy name is Jacob; thy name shall not be called anymore Jacob, but Israel shall be thy name"; and He called his name Israel. And God said unto him, "I am God Almighty [*El Shaddai*]. Be fruitful and multiply; a nation and a company of nations shall be of thee, and kings shall come out of thy loins; and the land which I gave unto Abraham and Isaac, to thee will I give it, and to thy seed after thee I will give the land." (35:10–12)

God's great blessing begins with a renaming: No more Jacob, but Israel shall be thy name. Here God Himself effects the change of name, in broad daylight and in the Promised Land, ratifying the renaming (or perhaps fulfilling a prophecy of such renaming) offered in early dawn and in trans-Jordan by Jacob's nocturnal adversary. Last time, successful in wrestling, Jacob was renamed by his nameless opponent for his past deeds: for having struggled with God and with men, and for having prevailed. This time there is no explanation of the new name and no mention of struggling; the meaning of "Israel" is presumably amplified instead by the blessing that follows, a blessing that looks to the future (in the light of the past promises to Abraham and Isaac).

As Nahum Sarna points out, this grand blessing fulfills the patriarchal prayer offered by Isaac (28:3–4) when he pronounces the full Abrahamic blessing on Jacob as he is leaving for Haran. It also echoes fittingly the divine promises made by God to Abraham at the time of *his* renaming and the establishment of the covenant (chapter 17), promises about progeny and about the land. Unlike Jacob's wrestling opponent, God freely identifies himself to Israel by name as *El Shaddai* (compare 17:1; 28:3), and blesses him with fertility and increase (compare 17:2, 6), the paternity of nations (compare 17:4, 5, 6), and kingly descendants (compare 17:6; Saul will come from the tribe of Benjamin, David from Judah). And with a specific reference to His earlier covenantal promises to Jacob's ancestors, God now gives to Jacob (Israel) the land He had given to Abraham and Isaac, now to him and, in the future, to his seed (compare 17:8). This theophany and this blessing represent the peak of Jacob's relationship to God; Jacob now as Israel, now returned to the Promised Land, is firmly established in God's grace, having earned his place as a patriarch within the covenant. The birthright and the all-important covenantal blessing are now rightly his; we have it on the highest authority.

As God ascends from him in the place where He had spoken with him, Jacob commemorates the event, just as he had done once before:

> And Jacob set up a pillar in the place where He had spoken with him, a pil-
> lar of stone, and he offered a libation upon it, and he poured oil upon it.
> And Jacob called the name of the place where He had spoken with him
> Beth-El. (35:14–15)

We do not know if this pillar is the same (dream) stone erected twenty years earlier, now rededicated (28:18), or if the stele is altogether new. But in either case,
the stone—like the ceremony—has new meaning; this time Jacob pours a wine
offering upon it, in addition to anointing it with oil. This time the pillar bears
witness to an explicit encounter with God; this time Jacob knows that the
promises made by the God of his dreams have been fulfilled. This "place where
God had spoken with him"—a phrase that occurs three times in verses 13–15—
Jacob again names Beth-El, this time with greater conviction and assurance.

The divine renaming of Jacob, his divine blessing, and his responsive act of
rededication are of more than personal significance. Witnessed by his entire
clan, they also serve to define the nation that will hereafter share the new name
of Israel. It is singularly appropriate that the people should be renamed—and
morally reborn—after the story of Dinah and its sequelae. Jacob's sons, near the
beginning of the Dinah story, had wittingly if angrily defined themselves as a
distinct and united people, even proleptically naming themselves as "Israel" ("a
scurrilous deed in/against Israel"; 34:7). Speaking strictly politically, the brothers' collective act of revenge may indeed have been indispensable to the emergence of the new nation. But for a nation bearing the new way as a light unto all
the nations, something more is required for collective self-definition. Only
through willing submission to God's call and the just-concluded acts of self-
purification and rededication do the sons of Jacob become truly the children of
Israel, the nation named "God will rule." The politics of God's people must acknowledge the more-than-political purpose of God's way.

COMPLETING THE CYCLE, LOOKING AHEAD

Though his relationship with God is now solidly established, Jacob's human
troubles are not finished. Soon he will be erecting another pillar, this one in sadness. As the family heads south from Beth-El, toward Isaac's home in Hebron,
Rachel dies in childbirth after giving birth to Jacob's twelfth son, Benjamin. "And
Jacob set up a pillar upon her grave; the same is the pillar of Rachel's grave unto
this day" (35:20).

With the death of Rachel, the inevitable cycle of the generations rolls hard
into the household of Israel and into the consciousness of its members. Al-

though Jacob is still in charge, family dynamics necessarily shift and the issue of succession begins to emerge. Jacob, weakened through mourning, no longer appears invulnerable. Not surprisingly, Jacob's firstborn is the first to think about asserting himself:

> And Israel journeyed and spread his tent beyond Migdal-Eder. And it came to pass, while Israel dwelt in that land, that Reuben went and lay with Bilhah, his father's concubine, and Israel heard. (35:21–22)

Reuben, son of Leah, finder of mandrakes for his mother, cohabits with Bilhah, Rachel's handmaid, whom Rachel had given to Jacob as her surrogate during her barrenness. Whatever his actual motives, Reuben's deed represents a powerful challenge to Jacob's authority. He simultaneously exacts revenge for the humiliation of his mother, prevents Rachel's concubine from again usurping his mother's place as Jacob's (primary) wife, lays premature claim to his inheritance, and most important, directly challenges his father for leadership by assertion of greater sexual prowess and preeminence over his own wives. Reuben's incestuous act is, in its inner meaning, an act of patricide, the removal of the father as a father.

The text delicately avoids giving us much more of this sordid story; in fact, the tale is interrupted in midsentence, but not before we learn that "Israel heard." What, if anything, Jacob said or did about this we are not told; but it no doubt made a big impression. Later, he will recall Reuben's wanton and vile deed in his final blessings of his sons (49:3–4). For now, whatever else he thinks, he must be acutely aware that his time as patriarch is limited and his authority precarious. The text, as it were reading Jacob's mind, turns immediately—in the very verse that reports Reuben's action—to a preview of the next generation:

> And the sons of Jacob were twelve. The sons of Leah: the firstborn [bekhor] of Jacob, Reuben, and Simeon and Levi and Judah and Issachar and Zebulun. The sons of Rachel: Joseph and Benjamin. The sons of Bilhah, Rachel's handmaid, Dan and Naphtali. And the sons of Zilpah, Leah's handmaid: Gad and Asher. These are the sons of Jacob that were born to him in Paddan-aram.[40] (35:22–26)

The family is here still intact, despite Reuben's misdeed. Yet the separation of the sons according to their mothers—Leah first—and the highlighting of Reuben's

---

40. Benjamin was, of course, born in Canaan.

place as *bekhor* (firstborn, possessor of the birthright) so soon after the story displaying his moral unfitness serve to anticipate the struggles for succession that will soon be upon us—and upon Jacob.

But first Jacob must complete his homeward journey. He returns at last to his father, and as his father's and grandfather's son:

> And Jacob came to Isaac, his father, at Mamre, at Kiriath-Arba—the same is Hebron—where Abraham and Isaac sojourned. (35:27)

No mention is made of Rebekah, Jacob's beloved mother; perhaps she has died in his absence. The earlier suspicions that Rebekah, in arranging Jacob's deception of Isaac and in sending Jacob away, knew that she would never see him again are strengthened.

Little is said about the relation of father and son or of their lives thereafter. For the main interest of our text these matters are irrelevant. Isaac's work as perpetuator of the new way was completed by Jacob's return as his true heir, fulfilling the charge he had laid upon him when he sent him off to Paddan-aram. Isaac has nothing left to do but die:

> And the days of Isaac were a hundred and four score years. And Isaac expired and died and was gathered unto his people, old and full of days; and they buried him, Esau and Jacob, his sons. (35:28–29)

In fact, the account here of Isaac's end, with its beautiful image of satiety ("old and full of days"), is well out of chronological order. Isaac lives yet quite a few years, indeed, twelve years into Joseph's captivity in Egypt.[41] But such chronological details are of no weight for the meaning of the story, whose overriding interest is the founding and perpetuation of God's new way through the patriarchal generations. From this point of view, the story of the generations of Isaac (begun in 25:19) is now over; and the story of his son Jacob now takes a radically new direction.

Genesis 35, with its many disparate stories, including multiple deaths, shows us the crumbling of Jacob's old world and his establishment in God's ordinance. Gone are his mother's nurse and his beloved wife, both of Paddan-aram; "gone" (logically, if not chronologically) is his father. Jacob, now Israel, anointed by none other than God Himself as the carrier of the promise to Abraham, has

---

41. Here are the numbers. Jacob is 91 years old when Joseph is born, 108 when he is sold into Egypt at age 17. Isaac is sixty years older than his twin sons (25:26), hence 168 when Joseph is sold. He lives to be 180. The year following Isaac's death, Joseph appears before Pharaoh and assumes his lofty station in Egypt.

stepped forward to take his father's place, knowingly accepting the supremacy of God and the place of his own father—the two chief points on which the young, conniving Jacob especially needed instruction. Everything now depends on what happens in the next generation, on how well Jacob is able to transmit what he has so arduously been prepared to receive. The challenge to his unqualified authority as father (Reuben's "patricidal" act) gives a foretaste of the difficulties that lie ahead. The vexed tale of the generations of Jacob comprises virtually the rest of the book of Genesis.

CODA: THE EDUCATION OF JACOB

Before looking ahead to the generations of Jacob, it is time to consider what Jacob may have learned in the course of his wanderings and strivings. At the start, Jacob needed to solve—or at least cope with—the enduring human problems: how to stand and act with respect to nature, family (parents, siblings, women and wives, and children), strangers, and the divine. He would have to overcome nature's indifference to merit (the birth order); he would have to avoid being Cain, Abel, or Ham; he would have to sidestep both conquest and assimilation; and he would have to resist any temptation to forget God, an especially hard task for this clever and devising man of many ways. Having taken lessons from his mother; from travel and estrangement; from the divinely sent dream of God's providence; from falling in love and, as a result, suffering the fraud of Laban; from standing up to danger with Laban, the mysterious nocturnal wrestler, and brother Esau; and from the tragic affair with Dinah and the Shechemites, Jacob completes the round-trip journey begun with the dream theophany and rounded off by the actual theophany at Beth-El. Yet is Jacob still Jacob, or has he changed significantly, either in character or in outlook?

To be sure, it seems that Jacob has learned somewhat the limits of his craftiness; he has suffered fear, loss, and disappointment; he has been outwitted and deceived; he has been slowed down and humbled with a limp. And he is no doubt more aware than he was at the start of the presence of the Lord and His care, as well as of his own neediness and dependence on God's providence. Yet it is not so easy to say how deeply these lessons have been absorbed. As the text may be subtly hinting, Jacob though twice renamed Israel will still often appear in later episodes as Jacob—unlike Abram, who, after God changed his name to Abraham, was thereafter always called Abraham. In the "education" of Jacob, unlike that of Abraham, there is no clear final test (akin to the binding of Isaac) that closes off his instruction or that clearly identifies what he has learned. This should not surprise us. For Abraham was a founder who had to walk a straight line, with God's frequent presence and assistance. In contrast, Jacob is a perpetuator who must travel partly in a circle, returning to step into his father's shoes while still in line with the covenant. Besides, Jacob is an altogether different character, more like us than was Abraham. In Jacob's life, God is more remote, as He is for us. The greater ambiguity of his education fits the greater ambiguity of the man and of his situation.

Perhaps one might sum it up this way. Jacob remains fundamentally what he was at the start, an aspiring and striving man whose mode of being is to "wrestle" with one and all. He experiences periodic illuminations about the presence of a God who cares and provides for him, and memory of these moments has taken root in his soul. Nevertheless, and especially when times are good, Jacob falls back into his natural, self-reliant mode of being and doing—just like most readers of his story. We, too, oscillate between, on the one hand, the kind of confident self-reliance that makes us forgetful of the eternal and, on the other hand, reverent gratitude for the goodness of the world coupled with awe before a transcendent power of judgment that sees our weakness, waywardness, and folly. Jacob, like the reader, sometimes closer, sometimes further from God, does return to his father as he was commanded. He returns as the head of a large clan and incipient nation to whom God has at last given the covenantal blessing. He carries a God-given name with a view to that blessing and the future prospects of his people. Jacob is at last a patriarch in Israel. Hereafter, even when he will be inclined to forget the fact, he will be unable to do so entirely. Even when he acts mainly as Jacob rather than as Israel, the discovery that "God will rule" will never be utterly absent from his soul.

CHAPTER SEVENTEEN

THE GENERATIONS OF JACOB:
THE QUESTION OF LEADERSHIP

*T*he last section of the book of Genesis, chapters 37–50, is often read as if it were a small novella, entitled *Joseph and His Brothers*. Indeed, the famous novel of that title, by the great German writer Thomas Mann, is in a sense just a massive and imaginative commentary on the riveting story described so economically yet so powerfully in less than 450 verses of Scripture. It is, to be sure, an affecting family story, a tale of malice and mastery, of near fratricide and forgiveness, featuring one of the Bible's most talented and charismatic figures, Joseph, the favorite son of Jacob. Yet if it is read only in this way, abstracted from the larger context of the emerging nation of Israel, the special significance of the story for the book of Genesis will escape the reader. For it deals with crucial questions of perpetuation and preservation at a critical juncture for the nascent people of the covenant.

In each of the first two founding generations, the covenant of God with Abraham was successfully passed to one (the younger) of the founder's two sons— first Isaac, then Jacob—while the other son—first Ishmael, then Esau—was cast to the side. Given what we know of the perennial difficulties between fathers and sons and between brothers, and given what we have seen of the obstacles the first two patriarchs had to overcome, no one should belittle the accomplishment of such successful transmission. But a household is not a nation. And it is impossible to get from the solitary founder of a new way of life to a great nation adhering to that way if only one son in each generation remains within the covenant. There needs to be not only transmission but also growth and proliferation.

Such an opportunity arises in the third founding generation, as Jacob, blessed with twelve sons, sires the seeds of a clan, the incipient nation that will bear his divinely given new name, Israel. Thus, the way of Israel now faces new challenges: the question of the unity of the clan, and the question of perpetuating the covenant on a quasi-political scale. True, a certain unification of the clan had been achieved in the vengeful attack on the Shechemites after the rape of Dinah. But what will happen when there is no external enemy against which the children of Israel must unite? What will happen when it becomes necessary for one or another of Jacob's sons to take their father's place and lead the clan into the next generation? Will they remain one, or become many? Will they adhere to the covenant, or will they be swallowed up in foreign ways, following foreign gods?

Any new political group, no matter how well founded, faces the challenge of perpetuation, which is always endangered by threats of disintegration within and of assimilation without. Internally, ways must be found to overcome division and enmity and to promote unity and peace, and the danger of fratricide must yield at least to concord, if not to full brotherhood. Externally, ways must be found to prevent absorption into neighboring polities and cultures, both willing (by assimilation) and unwilling (by conquest). Perpetuation thus requires leadership that can promote internal cohesion and preserve attachment to the ways of the fathers, in the face not only of hostile enemies bent on your destruction or subjection but also—especially also—of welcoming neighbors whose blandishments and bounties make you forget who you are.

Leadership within, and assimilation-versus-separation without, are the two big themes the text explores in the saga of Joseph and his brothers. It is these questions more than the merely intrafamilial ones that guide our reading of the text and that are the key to its most important meaning. Concretely, we shall be looking to see who—that is, what sort of man—is the fit leader of this nascent nation at this critical threshold of its growth and expansion, and what form his leadership should take. And we shall be looking to see what happens to the covenant and God's new way when circumstances drive nascent Israel into close relation with great Egypt, the peak of civilization. The story of Joseph and his brothers is simultaneously the story of leadership within Israel and the story of Egypt and Israel, of assimilation and separation. Who will lead, and how, is connected with whether and how the way begun with Abraham will survive and flourish. The story usually known as "Joseph and His Brothers" is really the story of the legacy of Jacob and the national perpetuation of the way of Israel.

INTRODUCING THE PROBLEM:
THE GENERATIONS OF ESAU AND JACOB

After the death of Isaac and his burial by "Esau and Jacob, his sons," the text turns immediately to the generations of the twin brothers. Though its concern will be almost entirely with the fate of the line of Jacob, it begins by telling us about the fate of Esau. In a lengthy account that occupies the whole of Genesis 36, we are told in great detail of "the generations of Esau—the same is Edom" (36:1). The overwhelming impression we receive is that of a man and a lineage well settled and highly successful. While he still dwells in Canaan, his three wives bear Esau five sons. Upon his voluntary removal from Canaan to the mountainous land of Seir, his tribe increases greatly. Twelve chieftains, each the source of a different Edomite tribe, emerge in Esau's line.[1] A thirteenth, Amalek, born of a concubine to Esau's first-born son, later becomes the permanent hereditary enemy of Israel.

The line of Esau is not only fertile and fruitful. It quickly becomes politically significant, in and around the land of Canaan. The text immediately locates the generations of Esau in their international context. After recording genealogies of the indigenous Canaanite peoples who dwelt in Seir before Esau's clan arrived, and after recounting a succession of nondynastic kings who ruled in the land of Edom "before there reigned any king over the Children of Israel" (36:31), the text gives us yet another list of the chiefs that come in the single line of Esau. His descendants now the dominant peoples in the land of Edom, Esau flourishes in a world of kings. Though he failed to receive from his father the Abrahamic blessing, Esau appears to be blessed both in his generations and in his possession of a land. Esau appears to be sitting pretty.

Yet if we look more closely at the account of Esau's generations, we see that something is missing. There are multiple chiefs and chiefdoms, each with its (at least transient) worldly success. But there is no unity and, more important, no unified way of life. There is political prowess, but no hint of any more-than-political aspiration, no hint of any remaining identification with the Abrahamic covenant, transmitted through Father Isaac. We wonder whether the generations of Jacob will do any better on this score.

When the text moves next to the story of Jacob, the contrast with Esau's worldly importance could not be greater:

And Jacob dwelt in the land of his father's wanderings, in the land of Canaan. These are the generations of Jacob: Joseph, being seventeen years old, was shepherding the flock with his brethren, and he was a lad with [or an assistant to] the sons of Bilhah and the sons of Zilpah, his father's wives. (37:1–2a)

Unlike Esau, who is well established in a land formerly ruled by kings, Jacob dwells—perhaps prematurely—in the land of wanderings, in the place where his father was a stranger. And when the text begins an account of his generations, instead of the expected report of Jacob's twelve sons and their progeny, we

1. Ishmael also sired twelve tribes.

hear only about Joseph, a lad of seventeen. What is most striking, the word order conveys the impression that Jacob has but a single son: "These are the generations of Jacob. Joseph . . ." (37:2).

Joseph, the youngest son but for Benjamin, appears right away at the center of the story of the next generation, the sons and heirs of Jacob. Joseph stands apart, not only in talent and charms, but also in his father's affections. In fact, it is tempting to attribute his prominence simply to his father's favoritism: Joseph is the firstborn of Jacob's preferred wife, the beautiful Rachel, now lost to him. Largely for this reason, it sometimes seems to Jacob that he has in Joseph his only *true* son. But in its immediate attention to Joseph, the text is not merely foregrounding the hero of the following saga or revealing the personal preferences of the bereaved and aging Jacob. Joseph is singled out mainly because he is the pivotal figure for the question of the "generations of Jacob" and the perpetuation of the covenant. As becomes clear almost immediately, the familial story of Joseph and his brothers is, at the same time and more importantly, an account of political rule and national survival. Is Joseph the right one to lead the clan? Can Joseph, singled out from the first as the first among equals, unify the brotherhood? Can he insure its survival and growth? Can he preserve it not only as a familial or national entity but also as a God-revering and covenant-adhering one?

JOSEPH, THE HEIR APPARENT: PORTRAIT OF THE RULER AS A YOUNG MAN

The text's introduction to Joseph immediately points, in fact, to the problem of leadership and unity. Our initial impressions of Joseph are not at all promising:

> Joseph, being seventeen years old, was shepherding the flock with his brethren [*ro'eh 'eth-'echayv batso'n*], and he was a lad with [*or* an assistant to] the sons of Bilhah and the sons of Zilpah, his father's wives; and Joseph brought evil report of them unto their father. And Israel loved Joseph more than all his sons because he was the son of his old age, and he made him an ornamented tunic [*kethoneth pasim*].[2] And his brethren saw that their father loved him more than all his brethren, and they hated him and

2. The so-called coat of many colors. As Robert Alter notes, the only textual clue about the nature of the garment comes from the only other biblical reference to *kethoneth pasim*, the story of the rape of Tamar (2 Samuel 13), where it is said to be worn by virgin princesses. "It is thus a unisex garment and a product of ancient *haute couture*." The Hertz commentator observes: "We now know from the painted Tombs of the Bene Hassein in Egypt that, in the Patriarchal age, Semitic chiefs wore coats of many colours as insignia of rulership. . . . Jacob, in giving him a coat of many colours, *marked him for the chieftainship of the tribes at his father's death.*"

could not speak to him peaceably [*or* in peace: *leshalom*]. And Joseph dreamed a dream [*vayachalom yosef chalom*] and told it to his brethren, and they hated him all the more. (37:2–5)

Joseph first comes to sight as a shepherd, a tattletale, a lad favored by his father and hated by his brothers, and a dreamer who tells his dreams to those who hate him (later we shall learn that he was beautiful, like his mother; 39:6; compare 29:17).

Let us look more closely at each description. Joseph is introduced as a shepherd, someone who guides and (metaphorically) rules. But the text leaves some doubt as to whom he is shepherding. Most people translate as we have done above. But as Robert Sacks has noted, the verse could just as well be read to mean: "Joseph, being seventeen years old, shepherded *his brothers* among [*or* with] the sheep though he was [but] a lad, that is, the sons of Bilhah and the sons of Zilpah, his father's wives."[3] But, whomever he is pasturing, Joseph is keeping his eye on his brothers, bringing "evil report of them" to their father. We can only speculate on the content of the evil report and only guess at his motives. But Joseph is, *at best*, a spy reporting on request to his father about the deeds of the brothers he was "shepherding." Giving him the benefit of the doubt, we may even imagine that he is motivated by a desire to uphold a higher morality and to bring about his brothers' reform. But it seems more likely that, acting on his own initiative, he is simply ratting on his brothers' misconduct or, even worse, is a man who libels his brothers with an evil report of his own devising— in either case, seeking to advance himself in his father's regard. We have no way of knowing whether these evil reports are true: later, Joseph will be the victim of evil reports spread by Potiphar's wife, reports we know to be false (39:14–18). We must wonder from the start about Joseph's truthfulness and justice.[4]

3. The critical question concerns the use of the particle *'eth*, which is the sign of the direct object but can also mean "with." The verb *ro'eh*, "to tend or care for/after," generally requires the use of this particle with its direct object (see, for example, 37:12, where the same verb occurs and the object is clearly "sheep": "And his brethren went to tend the flock [*lir'eoth 'eth-tso'n*]). Here, in 37:2, the particle following the verb "to tend or shepherd" is connected instead with his brothers [*'eth-'echayv*]. Whether or not he is tending (or ruling) his brothers or the sheep, Joseph accompanies only some of his (half) brothers, the children of the concubines Bilhah and Zilpah. For any number of reasons, it makes sense to keep him apart from the sons of Leah, his more significant and formidable rivals.

4. Traditional commentary casts doubt upon Joseph's veracity. Thus, Rashi: "[H]e reported to his father that they used to eat flesh cut off from a living animal, that they treated the sons of the handmaids with contempt, calling them slaves, and that they were suspected of living in an immoral manner [i.e., sexually]. With three such similar matters he was therefore punished. *In consequence of his having stated that they used to eat flesh cut off from a living animal* Scripture states (v. 31), "And they slew a he-goat" after they sold him and they did not eat *its flesh whilst the animal was still living.* And because of the slander which he related about them that they called their brothers slaves—(Ps.

Tattletale and all, there is no doubt that Joseph is his father's favorite. The reason given for this favoritism is unexpected: "because he was the son of his old age." We might have thought that Jacob loved Joseph most because he was the firstborn son of Rachel, the wife he loved most and whose great beauty Joseph inherited. Alternatively, we might have thought that Jacob favored Joseph because of his natural charisma and superiority (these the reader shall soon encounter), or perhaps because he was a dreamer and a visionary like himself. Moreover, if taken literally, the description "child of his old age," would refer not to Joseph but to Benjamin, the youngest.[5] Only if taken figuratively does the reason for preference make sense: Joseph is the son who Jacob believes will best take care of the problem that arises *because* of Jacob's old age, the problem of succession. The elegant ornamented tunic that Jacob provides Joseph is not just a decorative gift to a favorite. The garb of rule, it is the sign of Joseph's elevation. Jacob anoints Joseph as his heir apparent—and he does so relatively early in Joseph's life.

Though at this point we have only his father's opinion on the subject, we shall learn that Joseph is a man of great talent. Though he does not stand first in the order of birth, he stands out in the order of natural gifts—though we must look carefully at what it is about those gifts that persuades Jacob to make him stand out in the social order of rule and authority. We wonder whether Jacob has chosen wisely, and whether Joseph's natural superiorities are of the sort that merit the conventional superiority of leadership, especially for the people of God's new way. Does Joseph's ornamented tunic "fit" him? Does it make the man a ruler? Does it reveal, or conceal, who he really is?

Joseph, more than once, will "lose his shirt" to an angry and aggrieved opponent: first to his brothers, then to Potiphar's wife. On both occasions, he is stripped of the external marks of his apparent superiority, only to find himself at risk for his life. True, he is in these episodes the victim of injustice. But it may also be true that the "clothes" he was wearing—and the part they had him playing—did not fit him. When Joseph finally gets the clothing—and customs—that suit him perfectly, it will not be as a prince in Israel but as the lord chamberlain of Egypt.

Looking at Joseph in his ornamented tunic—bright, attractive, and visibly compelling—we are likely to be captured by his elegant display. Many people, both those in the story and those who read it, are dazzled by him. But who is it that recognizes Joseph for what he is? Are we perhaps at risk of sharing Jacob's

---

CV. 17) "Joseph was sold for a slave." And because he charged them with immorality (XXXIX. 7) "his master's [Potiphar's] wife cast her eyes upon him, etc."

5. One might try to explain Jacob's preference for Joseph over Benjamin by the fact that it was Benjamin's birth that killed Rachel. (Svetozar Minkov offered me this suggestion.)

favoritism and of anointing Joseph with our own cloak of merited preeminence? Is the one we find most attractive also the most wise and the most just? The text's report of Joseph's ambiguous conduct serves as a warning: we must read Joseph with care and interpret his every deed with caution, precisely because, like Jacob, we are given to playing favorites.

As—and because—Joseph is preferred by his father, so he is hated by his brothers. Jacob's attempt to elevate Joseph above the others produces—or perhaps only aggravates—the not surprising and perilous result: brotherly enmity, soon of fratricidal proportions. One might have thought that Jacob, well aware from his own childhood of the dangers of paternal favoritism, would have done everything in his power to keep the peace (*shalem:* wholeness) in his household. Indeed, many readers blame Jacob for injustice to his other sons or blindness to the troubles he is causing; some even see Jacob's favoritism as a sign that the old man has slipped into his dotage, no longer shrewd and savvy, reduced to sentimentality ("child of my old age"). But they have not sufficiently considered the problem of succession. Reuben, the eldest, has disqualified himself by his dalliance with Bilhah. Simeon and Levi are hotheaded zealots, perhaps useful in battle, hardly fit for persuasion, and in need of rule themselves. What alternative does Jacob have? Jacob thinks Joseph is the man for the job, and he uses his own power to get Joseph established while he (Jacob) still has authority. It is a gamble and, one suspects, Jacob knows it.

Yet even if we can understand Jacob's motives and calculations, his anointing of Joseph turns out, predictably, to be unsound. For even if Joseph possessed the political virtues needed to rule, it still would have been virtually impossible successfully to impose a leader upon the other brothers. Men resist being ruled by one of their own, and they react angrily when one of their own makes a claim to leadership. Before they can accept him, a leader of equals must first prove himself to them and gain their voluntary assent to his ascendancy. Jacob should have known that once he elevated Joseph over his brothers, they would not easily live with him "in peace": brotherliness, always at odds with leadership and rule, is always at risk of fratricide and war—and here more explicitly than ever. For Joseph's behavior only makes the matter worse, as we learn from the immediate sequel. Entirely unaware of the need for prudence and tact, secure in his father's favor, and deaf to all political tones, Joseph shows himself from the start incapable of leadership.

In the text's initial portrait of him, Joseph stands out not for his wisdom regarding human beings but for his dreams. More precisely, Joseph—as the word order hints—is enveloped by his dreaming and his dreams: "And dreamed Joseph a dream." Does his being a dreamer bode well for his becoming a leader of men? The answer depends in part on the content and, even more, on the source of his dreams. What does he dream, and where did his dreams come from? Again, the text gives us pause: by using the cognate accusative construction,[6] the text subtly suggests that Joseph may be the author or source of his dream. Regarding no previous dream has this formulation been used: Jacob's famous dream, which we later learned was indeed divinely sent, was introduced simply by the words "And he dreamed" (28:12). By contrast, the later dreams of Pharaoh's butler and baker will be described by the same locution, "dreamed a dream" (40:5, 8), and Pharaoh, in telling his dreams to Joseph, also begins the same way (41:15). Other than Joseph, the only people who "dream a dream" are Egyptians.[7]

The brothers hate Joseph not only for Jacob's favoritism and for the suggestion, implicit in his tunic, that he was going to rule over them (and perhaps also for his informing).[8] They hate Joseph also for his dreams. Does the brothers' reaction also imply that Joseph's dreams are an expression of his own nature or his own latent wishes? Or are his dreams—also or instead—heaven-sent? The text does not say. Later, Joseph's rise to high station will begin with his ability to interpret the dreams of others. Now, we find ourselves in a similar position, obliged to become dream interpreters, beginning with the dreams of Joseph himself. We are immediately given an opportunity to practice.

And he said unto them: "Listen, please, to this dream that I dreamed. And behold [or look], we were binding sheaves [literally, sheaving sheaves: me'alemiym 'alumiym] in the midst of the field, and behold, my sheaf arose and moreover stood upright; and behold, your sheaves gathered round and bowed down to my sheaf." And his brethren said to him, "Shalt thou indeed reign over us? Shalt thou indeed have dominion over us?" And they hated him all the more [literally, they increased (yosef) to hate him], for his dreams and for his words. (37:6–8)

There are two matters requiring interpretation, the dream itself and the telling of it. As to the dream's manifest content, the brothers can hardly be mis-

---

6. The object of the action is cognate with the verb that names it: dream a dream. We have met this construction many times, beginning with "Let the earth grass grass" (1:11).

7. Throughout the Hebrew Bible, this phrase seems to be reserved for foreigners—for example, the Amalekite spied on by Gideon (Judges 7:13) and King Nebuchadnezzar (Daniel 2:3). Israelites do not "dream dreams." Rather, they see or hear things "in a dream." (I am grateful to Yuval Levin for this observation.)

8. When we were told earlier that Jacob loved Rachel, we were given a reason: she was very beautiful. Here, we get no reason for Jacob's preference for Joseph. As if to cast doubt on Jacob's judgment, the text, in its first description of Joseph, shows us several reasons why Joseph is not lovable and is therefore not the one to be preferred.

taken as to its meaning. It is a dream of rule and dominion, in which Joseph, standing supreme as ruler, is paid homage by his self-abasing brothers. It is an unbrotherly dream that, even more than the ornamented tunic, denies the brothers their equal place in the house of Israel. This dream (or to be more accurate, this *report* of a dream)—which the brothers are more inclined to attribute to Joseph's wishes than to divine prophecy⁹—fills them with anger at Joseph's presumption and arrogance. They are annoyed at his cavalier attitude and his insistence on making them hear "this dream that I dreamed" (three times he exhorts them to "behold" or "look"). Yet, very likely, they also feel fear that the dream might just be prophetic. All their feelings they hide behind a tone of mocking incredulity.

But the brothers—and most readers—do not notice the oddest feature of the dream, the dominant image of sheaves. What kind of a shepherd dreams of sheaves of wheat? The imagery of the dream belongs to another place, to a more fertile place, where one man does indeed command obeisance from all around, namely, to Egypt. Joseph's dream is foreign, and not only to his brothers' tastes.

And why does Joseph tell his brothers his dream, and in what spirit and tone of voice? Is this innocent exuberance, spoiled brattiness, or arrogant and deliberate provocation? Whether naïve or knowing, Joseph's telling of the dream partakes of the theatrical: by forcing the brothers to listen to his dream-drama in which he plays the leading part, Joseph as it were enacts, here and now, the claim to superiority contained within the dream itself. And whatever else you can say about it, Joseph's telling of the dream is imprudent in the extreme: his brothers hate him even more *(vayosifu 'od)* for his dreams *and for his words* (that is, for his telling them).¹⁰

Readers who know what's coming later in the Bible will find it instructive to compare this first appearance and deed of Joseph with the first appearance and deed of Moses (recounted in Exodus 2:11–12), especially as it bears on the question of leadership. We first meet Joseph in action in relation to his brothers, blithely commanding them to listen to his strange dreams of lordship over them, utterly oblivious to the alienating effect his speech and deed will have on them. In contrast, we first meet Moses in action leaving his home in Pharaoh's house to go out "unto his brethren," indignantly taking up the cause of a Hebrew slave ("one of his brethren") and smiting the Egyptian taskmaster who was op-

9. Alter translates: "Do you mean to reign over us, do you mean to rule us?" Such a reading implies that the brothers regard Joseph's dream as a projection of his own tyrannical desires and ambitions.

10. The phrase "even more," in describing how much they hate Joseph, is from the verb *yosef*, "to increase or add," the root of Joseph's name. The brothers hated *Yosef* very much *(yosef)*. Or, alternatively, they *"yosefed"* (more) to hate him (Joseph).

pressing him. Moses, although he had had absolutely no previous dealings with them, from the start identifies with his people; Joseph, although reared in the house of Israel, from the start separates himself from them. Moses, the political man, displays spiritedness and a passion for justice; Joseph, politically deaf and dumb, displays neither. Most astonishingly, he appears to have no idea of the effect he has on those he has been anointed to lead.

Perhaps in relation to his brothers' apparent disbelief, Joseph dreams a second dream, more grandiose than the first. Again, he promptly tells it to them:

> And he dreamed yet another dream and he recounted it to his brethren, and he said, "Look, I have dreamed yet another dream, and look, the sun and the moon and eleven stars were bowing down to me." And he recounted it to his father and to his brethren, and his father rebuked him and said unto him. "What is this dream that thou hast dreamed? Shall we indeed come, I and thy mother and thy brethren, to bow down before thee to the ground?" And his brethren envied him, but his father kept the thing in mind. (37:9–11)

This time Joseph makes sure his father is present for the telling, hoping to take advantage of Jacob's presence and authority to get his brothers to accept the dream's unpalatable truth. But Jacob does not play along and acquiesce. He could not help but notice how Joseph's brothers were seething all around him. Fearing the consequences of their anger, Jacob prudently sees the necessity of taking their side against Joseph, and at the same time, of trying to teach Joseph to be more circumspect in his utterances. He publicly rebukes Joseph in front of his brothers for dreaming such an arrogant dream, and he expresses his own disbelief in its content.

The careful reader, however, notices two additional things. First, what Jacob said, he said for public consumption; privately, however, he appears to give the dream some credence: "but his father kept the thing in mind" (37:11). Second, it is Jacob, not Joseph, who gives Joseph's second dream a familial interpretation. Given the numbers (eleven stars, eleven brothers), the interpretation is surely plausible—though Rachel, Joseph's mother (the moon) is no longer alive. But Joseph's dream, taken literally rather than figuratively, is more ambitious still: it is a dream of cosmic mastery, of human rule over the heavenly bodies. In Joseph's dream, the heavens do not declare the glory of God but instead bow to the superiority of Joseph, the exemplary human being. As we shall see, this vision of cosmic mastery is part of the meaning of Egypt, the place where man, through technology, magic, and administration, tries to force nature to her knees. Joseph, from his youth, has Egyptian dreams.[11]

THE "SACRIFICE" OF JOSEPH

In the immediate sequel things turn ugly, horribly ugly if the reader keeps in mind what Jacob has just been said to keep in mind. Jacob, perhaps *because he took to heart Joseph's dream and his own interpretation of it*, forces the family conflict to its crisis:

> And his brethren went to graze their father's flock [*lir'eoth 'eth-tso'n 'aviyhem*] in Shechem. And Israel said unto Joseph, "Do not thy brethren graze at Shechem? Come, let me send thee unto them"; and he said to him, "Here-I-am" [*hineni*]. And he said to him, "Go, please, to see whether it is well [*or* safe, sound, peace: *shelom*] with thy brethren and well [*shelom*] with the flock, and bring me back word." And he sent him out from the valley of Hebron, and he came to Shechem. (37:12–14)

The brothers are off tending the flock, far away from both Jacob and Joseph, but in an ominous place, Shechem, the place of bloody slaughter, the place where Jacob's sons slaughtered their "quasi-brethren" upon their circumcision. Jacob, who could not have forgotten what happened in Shechem, nonetheless sends Joseph to meet his brothers in that place of violent death, looking to see whether they are "safe" and "at peace." Several remarks in this exchange—Jacob's "Go, please," and Joseph's "Here-am-I"—eerily echo the story of the binding of Isaac, a story of another father's willingness to sacrifice his beloved son. The alert reader will be horrified by what he understands Jacob to be saying to Joseph: "Come, let me send thee unto thy brothers who hate thee, now that they are in the murderous place."

No one can be sure whether Jacob knows what he is doing or whether there is method in his madness. It is, however, difficult to believe that he is unaware of the danger, which prompts the following, admittedly highly troubling sugges-

11. I owe this insight to Dan Sofaer. Yuval Levin carries the suggestion further: "The fact that Joseph dreams Egyptian dreams in Canaan and seems to be an Egyptian long before he ever enters Egypt can perhaps tell us something about Egypt as well as about Joseph. How can Egyptian attitudes emerge amidst the people of the covenant? What does this tell us about the attitudes themselves? Are they the offspring of beauty and cleverness, as Joseph is? And given what we are told early on about Joseph (the desire for mastery, the capacity for administration, the lack of political prudence, the dramatic flair, the charisma, the reference to but ignorance of God), what do we learn about Egypt? Is Joseph a kind of one-man Egypt? What causes this worldview to emerge in man?" (Personal communication.)

tion: Jacob knows that his family is starkly polarized, Joseph against the rest and the rest emphatically against Joseph. It seems only a matter of time before something snaps in the brothers, and then they will cast Joseph out or destroy him. But luckily, there is this encouraging dream: Joseph will overmaster his brothers. They will acknowledge his superiority and submit to his rule. Their zealousness and bloodthirsty ways (Shechem) will be brought under the rule of (his) clear-sighted reason, and the family will be "safe," "whole," and "at peace" *(shalem)*. If Joseph's dream prophesies truly, if it was indeed a godsend, Joseph will prevail against his brothers, and what's more, Jacob's own hopes for such a result will be realized. With such an auspicious portent, now is the time to have the matter resolved and Joseph's leadership instituted. With Jacob absent and hence unable to take sides, Joseph and his brothers would have to settle matters among themselves and be bound by the result. And in the terrible event that Joseph is not accepted as ruler but rather is slain, the brothers would at least have been reunited once again around a common enemy, in this case their own flesh and blood.[12] None of this need be present to Jacob's conscious mind for it to be the latent meaning of his deed. Jacob, willingly if not wittingly, sends Joseph to the fratricidal moment. And Joseph, reflecting afterward on the ensuing event, will remember only this: the last two things my father did to me were to rebuke me in the face of my brothers and to send me out to be slaughtered at their hand. My father, his heart turned against me, set me up![13]

Somehow, miraculously, fratricide is averted. The meeting at Shechem does not take place:

> And a man found him, and behold, he was wandering in the field [*basadeh*], and the man asked him, saying, "What seekest thou?" And he said, "My brethren I seek. Tell me, please, where they are grazing?" And the man said, "They are departed from here, for I heard them say, 'Let us go to Dothan.'" And Joseph went after his brethren, and he found them at Dothan. (37:15–17)

Wondrously, out of nowhere, comes an unnamed man, to find Joseph, newly arrived at Shechem but described as "wandering in the field"; the slaughtered city

---

12. If this story is read in strict parallel to the binding-of-Isaac story, we have Jacob in the place of God doing the sending out ("Go, please") and Joseph *(hineni)* in the place of Abraham. On this analogy, Joseph would be going not to be sacrificed but to do the sacrificing. Could Jacob be testing Joseph to see if he is willing, if necessary, to destroy his brothers *as his brothers,* in order to realize the dream's "promise"?

13. Only such a bitter reminiscence about the father who Joseph thought had loved him could explain why, much later, Joseph ignores (or even deliberately produces) the torment his charade with his brothers is causing his father (see Chapter Nineteen).

of Shechem has become a wild field (*sadeh;* compare 4:8, the place of Cain's fratricide). The stranger diverts Joseph to Dothan, where his brothers had gone; perhaps he had diverted them as well. The fratricidal encounter has been averted, at least at "the fratricidal place." The reader cannot help but wonder whether this is the same "man" who wrestled with Jacob on the eve of another potentially fratricidal encounter (32:24).[14]

Despite the redirection of the place of meeting, trouble waits for Joseph at Dothan. Because of his special coat, his brothers see him coming from afar and they plot his death:

> And they saw him from afar, even before he came near unto them, and they plotted against him to kill him. And they said, each to his brother, "Behold, this master of dreams, he cometh. So now, come, let us slay him and fling him into one of the pits, and we can say, 'An evil [*that is,* vicious] beast hath devoured him,' and we shall see what will become of his dreams." (37:18–20)

Still enraged by Joseph's dreams, all (or nearly all) the brothers, one to another, conspire to kill him and cast him into a pit (without burial); to explain his disappearance, they agree to say to Jacob that "a vicious beast hath devoured him."

But Reuben, the eldest, dissents from the plot and seeks to save Joseph from his brothers' murderous hands. Reuben, Jacob's firstborn, whom we have met (but not heard) twice before—once getting an aphrodisiac for his mother (30:14), once sleeping with his father's concubine (35:22)—now opens his mouth for the first time. It will be his first—and nearly last—attempt at leading the clan.

> And Reuben heard and he delivered him from their hand; and he said, "Let us not take his life." And Reuben said unto them, "Shed no blood! Fling him into this pit that is in the wilderness, but lay no hand upon him"— that he might deliver him out of their hand and restore him to his father. And it happened when Joseph came unto his brethren that they stripped him of his tunic—the ornamented tunic—that was on him. And they took him and they flung him into the pit, and the pit was empty and there was no water in it. (37:21–24)

Reuben, perhaps eager to get back into Jacob's good graces after sleeping with his father's wife, is perhaps also eager to show Jacob that he can preserve peace among the brethren. After exclaiming, "Let us not take his life," Reuben imperi-

14. We must think also of the mysterious "men" who came to Abraham's tent (18:2), later revealed to be angels.

ously commands the others to cast him into a pit. By this means, Reuben hopes later secretly to "restore him to his father." Though the brothers do as he commands, Reuben's plan, given the situation, is naïve and doubly flawed. First, restoring Joseph to his father would not resolve the fratricidal conflict, but would merely postpone it for another occasion. Indeed, sneaking Joseph back home could hardly be expected to remove the brothers' murderous impulses; on the contrary, common sense suggests that it might rather inflame them.

Second, the brothers do not truly recognize Reuben's leadership, nor do they finally agree with his plan. True, his speech does obtain for Joseph a temporary stay of execution—a recess until after lunch. But it does not really persuade the other brothers. When we compare it to Judah's speech that follows, Reuben's rhetoric, despite his attachment to the moral principle eschewing bloodshed, is defective: he issues commands, does not give reasons, and makes no argument that could move their souls (beyond the generic appeal "Shed no blood"). The brothers say nothing in response; the text does not say that they heard or agreed with him. We soon learn that they in fact still harbor notions of killing Joseph. For now, they strip Joseph of his famous coat and cast him into an empty pit, without food and water, while they themselves sit down to lunch. While they are eating, another party happens on the scene.

> And they sat down to eat bread. And they lifted up their eyes and they looked, and behold, a caravan of Ishmaelites was coming from Gilead, and their camels were bearing spices and balm and ladanum, going to carry it down to Egypt. And Judah said to his brethren, "What profit is it if we slay our brother and conceal his blood? Come and let us sell him to the Ishmaelites and our hand will not be upon him; for he is our brother, our flesh." And his brethren hearkened unto him. (37:25–27)

The appearance of the Ishmaelite traders bound for Egypt provides the brothers an alternative to bloodshed.[15] It does so by providing an opportunity for a different voice to be heard: Judah ("Praise the Lord"), fourth of Leah's sons, makes his maiden speech. Though a first reading leads many to condemn Judah for a mercenary spirit, a more careful reading, sensitive to the explosive character of the situation, would give him at least the benefit of the doubt. Judah's plan is, in fact, more prudent and even more humane than Reuben's, despite the fact that Reuben's appears at first to be more principled and moral. What's more, his

---

15. The expression "And they lifted up their eyes and they looked, and behold, a caravan of Ishmaelites was coming" echoes precisely the description of what happened in another near-fatal situation, when Abraham lifted his eyes and looked and beheld the ram caught in the thicket that became the sacrificial substitute for Isaac (22:13).

rhetoric succeeds in persuading his brothers. Unlike Reuben, who seeks to command from above, Judah speaks as if he were simply one within the group (he uses throughout the first person plural). Partly for this reason, he is able to lead. He also knows whom he is dealing with and how to move them.

Judah begins by appealing to his brothers' base love of gain. But having gained their confidence in this way, he can remind them, twice, of the higher moral point: Joseph is their *brother*, "for he is our brother, our flesh."[16] The talented Joseph, Judah very likely surmised, would land on his feet anywhere,[17] whereas no good could come from having him return home. Judah's speech, unlike Reuben's, succeeds in defusing the murderous impulse: "And his brothers hearkened unto him" (37:27). Judah's first attempt at leadership succeeds—almost.[18] Unfortunately for his plan, some Midianite merchants get to Joseph first:

> And there passed by Midianites, merchantmen, and they drew Joseph out of the pit, and they sold Joseph to the Ishmaelites for twenty pieces of silver; and they brought Joseph into Egypt. (37:28)

While the brothers are speaking over lunch, the Midianites find Joseph (he was no doubt crying out), extract him from the pit, and sell him to the Ishmaelites, who in turn deliver Joseph into Egypt.[19] This "miraculous" appearance

16. Judah's speech looks very good compared with Hamor and Shechem's speech to the Shechemites (34:20–23). They start with goodwill but finish with profit. Judah's order is the reverse. I owe this insight to Eric Schwarze.

17. If, as seems likely, it was clear to Judah (and not just to the reader) that the Ishmaelite caravan was headed for Egypt, Judah might even be credited with having somehow divined that his plan would put Joseph into a sophisticated environment perfectly suited for his special gifts and proclivities.

18. Although Judah demonstrates here his ability to lead his brothers, he is not yet fit to be a leader *in Israel*. Preparation for that role comes primarily through his experiences with Tamar, discussed later in this chapter.

19. As many commentators have noted, it is not absolutely clear from the text who exactly did what to Joseph. Verse 28 is somewhat ambiguous; and later verses (37:36; 39:1) seem to disagree on who—the Midianites or the Ishmaelites—actually sold Joseph into Egypt. Robert Sacks cogently examines the three leading interpretive alternatives: (1) The brothers took Joseph out of the pit and sold him to the Midianites, who in turn sold him to the Ishmaelites (the traditional reading). (2) There were originally two textual versions, now intermixed: in one, the Midianites sold Joseph, and in the other, the Ishmaelites did it (the modern scholarly reading). (3) The Midianites drew Joseph out of the pit and sold him into Egypt via the intermediacy of the Ishmaelites, but without the knowledge or participation of the brothers. In other words, the Midianites had the same idea that Judah had had, but beat him to it.

I favor the last reading. It makes sense of the fact that the brothers, even when they later repent, never admit to selling Joseph. It also explains Reuben's remark, made later (42:22), where he speaks as if he believes that Joseph is dead. It also explains Reuben's surprise—in the immediate sequel

of the Midianites—descendants of Abraham and his concubine Keturah—sets up the entire remainder of the story: it accomplishes Judah's plan to save Joseph's life, but it does so without his or his brothers' knowledge or participation. As a result, Joseph gets safely to Egypt, but the brothers must assume that he is dead and—most important—that they are responsible for his death. When Reuben returns to the pit, hoping still to rescue Joseph according to his own original plan, Joseph is missing. Grief-stricken, Reuben rends his clothes and returns to inform the others that "the child is not." Accepting Reuben's report that Joseph is dead,[20] the other brothers, perhaps shaken by this report, now hastily adopt the course they had previously proposed to cover their own murder of him. From their point of view, the desired result has been achieved and they are well rid of Joseph. They also get their revenge on the father:

> And they took Joseph's tunic and they killed a kid and dipped the tunic in the blood. And they sent the ornamented tunic and had it brought to their father, and they said, "This we have found. Recognize, please, is this thy son's tunic or not?" (37:31–32)

The sons cruelly send Jacob the forged evidence of Joseph's death, in the process showing him through the bloody coat what became of his plan to anoint Joseph their ruler. Just as Jacob had done with his father, the brothers deceive Jacob using a brother's garment and a goat: the cloak is the cloak of Joseph, but the blood is the blood of a kid goat. They do not exactly lie to Jacob, but neither do they tell him the truth. Rather, they command him to recognize for himself the final verdict on the coat and its owner, and therewith also on himself as giver of the coat.

Jacob has no trouble drawing the stark conclusion:

> And he recognized it, and he said, "It is my son's tunic; an evil [or vicious] beast hath devoured him; torn, torn is Joseph [*chayah ra'ah 'akhalathhu, tarof toraf yosef*]. And Jacob rent his garments and put sackcloth around his loins and mourned for his son for many days. And all his sons and all his daughters rose up to comfort him; but he refused to be comforted, and he said, "Rather I will go down to my son mourning, to Sheol," and his father wept for him. (37:33–35)

(37:29–30)—at finding the pit empty and his brothers' failure to disabuse him of the inference that Joseph has been killed. It seems to me likely that the brothers come to believe their own story that a wild animal has killed Joseph—though they know that it is entirely their fault that he came into harm's way.

20. I repeat: that the brothers do not disabuse Reuben of his view of Joseph's fate is further evidence that it was not *they* who sold him to the Ishmaelites. The brothers in fact believe that Joseph is dead.

Most readers and commentators take literally Jacob's comments about an "evil beast," seeing him as duped by the bloody cloak into thinking that Joseph met his death at the hands of a wild animal. Some also see Jacob's speech as extravagant, "perhaps something histrionic." But Jacob is neither dumb nor daft. The brothers, by the very fact of asking, "Is this *thy* son's tunic?" are in fact casting suspicion on themselves. Acting on Cain's principle—"I don't know [where Abel is]. Am I my brother's keeper?"—their cover-up is tantamount to a confession of guilt. Robert Sacks, citing other biblical passages in which the "evil beasts" are clearly *men* (Leviticus 26:6; Ezekiel 34:22–25), explicitly suggests that Jacob knows that the evil beast is, in fact, the gang of brothers:

> Jacob in this verse is also thinking of men and only hopes that the *evil beasts* will be quieted. Verse thirty-five is full of strange passions. The father will not be comforted because he knows that his comforters are also the murderers. The sons wish to comfort because they are not sure in what way they are guilty and in what way they are innocent. The story is further complicated by the fact that the brothers may now believe their own lie.

Jacob's sons, to say the least, have not been their brother's keepers. And Jacob's beloved Joseph has not been able to rule over them. Even on the most innocent view of his sending Joseph out to meet them, Jacob—like any parent who has sent a child on an errand from which he never returns—must be awash in guilt over his own part in the catastrophe. And should Jacob have knowingly foreseen and promoted the potentially fratricidal encounter, he must shoulder even more of the blame: "I, it was I who fed Joseph to the 'evil beast.' " Far from being extravagant, Jacob's poetic outburst—*chayah ra'ah 'akhalathhu, tarof toraf yosef*—surely fits a mood not only of intense grief but also of colossal guilt. No wonder he cannot be comforted.[21]

Yet if, as we suspect, Jacob knows the score about his sons, we must also marvel at his courage and resolve. Joseph is presumed dead, the brothers are (apparently) unified, and Jacob must accept the result. He will have to continue to live with his sons, knowing or at least believing that they are the murderers of his beloved Joseph. Amidst his profound grief, Jacob grasps the truth of his situation, and speaks accordingly. By acquiescing in the charade that the deadly "evil beast" was a wild animal, Jacob—without a word of inquiry or voiced suspicion—gives closure to all further speech about the matter. No one will ever have

---

21. Many readers see Jacob here as entering a period of permanent decline, awash in self-pity and losing command of himself and events. But this view is doubly flawed: Jacob's apparent senility or weakness is in fact a rather appropriate self-condemnation. And as we shall see later, the old man is still capable of sharp speech and strong deeds.

to speak of it again. Life can and must go on, even with Joseph gone, even with his killers.[22] Jacob's response also forces the brothers to bear their guilt silently and inwardly, buried away but within hailing distance of their own besmirched consciences.

Joseph, of course, is still alive. Unbeknownst to his father and (almost certainly) his brothers, Joseph at this very moment is being "sold into Egypt, unto Potiphar, as officer of Pharaoh, the captain of the guard" (37:36). Joseph's rise—and Israel's descent—into Egypt has begun.

THE OTHER CANDIDATE: THE EDUCATION OF JUDAH

At this point, the text of Genesis springs a surprise on the reader. Before continuing to narrate what happened to Joseph in Egypt, it interrupts to tell us the seemingly irrelevant story of Judah and Tamar. Few readers understand what this story is doing here at all, much less why it appears at this juncture. Modern readers, usually unfamiliar with or hostile to the practice of levirate marriage, are especially handicapped in figuring these things out. However, both the story and its position in the unfolding drama make perfect sense. Consider.

The questions facing the "generations of Jacob," we recall, are whether this brotherhood can be held together without fratricide and within the covenant; and if so, under whose leadership this can be accomplished. From Jacob's point of view, Joseph was the one and only possible choice. But the opening chapter of the saga provides strong evidence that Jacob was mistaken: Joseph, though no ordinary fellow, turns out to be neither a prudent leader of men nor a wise choice to head this family or lead this nation.[23] If we care to look, abundant clues of his unsuitability have been made visible. Even at the ripe age of seventeen, Joseph was seeking moral advantage with his father by "evil reports" about his brothers. He dreamt grandiose dreams of mastery and rulership, lording it certainly over his brothers and perhaps also over the whole universe (sun, moon, stars). And utterly oblivious of or indifferent to the effects such speech would have on them, he imprudently told his unbrotherly dreams to his brothers. Joseph is, *at best,* a talented, enthusiastic, unbridled adolescent, protected and spoiled by his father's favoritism.

When the brothers send Joseph's bloodied coat of lordship back to Jacob, they nullify Jacob's choice and permanently kill Joseph *as their ruler,* even though Joseph himself remains very much alive. Joseph lives, and will soon thrive, in the

---

22. Would God have refused to "live" with Abraham had he gone through with His demanded sacrifice of Isaac?

23. Later episodes will reveal that Joseph is clairvoyant, irrepressible, and charismatic, but his genius is for *administration,* not for statesmanship or political rule.

place that can sustain life against famine. There, he will even temporarily exercise power over his brothers and his father. But Joseph is permanently dead as a leader in Israel. Because most readers are likely to share Jacob's love for Joseph and especially because Joseph is clearly a victim—albeit not a wholly innocent one—of hate-filled and hateful men, many readers are slow to discover that Joseph was really the wrong choice. But those of us who notice that Joseph, even at the start, dreams Egyptian dreams will see that he is not right for the job, and not only because of his brothers' hatred.

But if not Joseph, who? The eldest, Reuben, impulsive if well meaning, has shown himself inept. Simeon and Levi, leaders of the assault on Shechem, are violent hotheads. The text here shows us, through a tale that is too often mistakenly regarded as a regrettable interruption in the Joseph story, that—and why— the proper choice will be Judah. Leaving Jacob in mourning for his beloved Joseph, and leaving Joseph on the threshold of his Egyptian adventures, the text shines its light on the man who has what it takes to secure the future for this family and this people. The story of Judah and Tamar, the subject of chapter 38, is the crucial event in Judah's career that prepares him for the task.

At first glance, this story does not show Judah to advantage. Though a virile man, he makes multiple mistakes having to do with procreation and perpetuation. Judah leaves his people, takes a Canaanite woman to wife, breaks a promise and violates the levirate "law," consorts with what he takes to be a harlot, and sires children incestuously. In all these ways, Judah appears much inferior to Joseph, who meanwhile, though in a subordinate position, resists an adulterous affair with the wife of his master and retains his sexual purity.[24] But closer examination will correct this first impression, not by erasing it, but by showing the deeper meaning of the entire adventure.

One might have thought that, once rid of Joseph, the brothers would now be united and content. Not so. Judah immediately leaves them.

And it came to pass *at that time* that Judah *went down from his brethren* (38:1; emphasis added).

Jacob may have had no choice but to live with his evil-beast-like sons, but Judah refuses to do so. Judah, we recall, had tried to persuade his brothers to forgo fratricide, but through no fault of his, the plan was not carried out. Now, believing that Joseph has in fact been killed, he wants nothing further to do either with the brothers who plotted and welcomed fratricide or with his inconsolable father. He heads out entirely on his own, seeking a new life. Yet his act of independence

24. This episode, the theme of the next chapter (Genesis 39), will be discussed below.

is also an act of unbrotherliness; it is an act of indifference and abandonment: Who cares what becomes of those knaves! An exaggeration will make the point: in turning his back on his brothers (and his father), Judah tacitly commits the very act of fratricide that he had tried to prevent with Joseph. Judah's going away is therefore a "going down," figuratively as well as literally, from his community at Hebron:

> And he turned in to a certain Adullamite whose name was Hirah. And Judah saw there a daughter of a certain Canaanite whose name was Shua; and he took her, and went in unto her. And she conceived, and bore a son; and he called his name Er. And she conceived again, and bore a son; and she called his name Onan. And she conceived yet again, and she called his name Shelah. . . . And Judah took a wife for Er, his firstborn [*bekhoro*], and her name was Tamar. (38:1–6)

Culturally speaking, Judah appears to be headed in the wrong direction. And his eros for a woman speeds him along. Like Esau, Judah takes a Canaanite wife; according to an account that partly echoes the doings of Shechem with Dinah, Judah *saw, took,* and *went in unto* this stranger woman (unlike Shechem, Judah did not, it seems, take her "by force" but "to wife"; compare 38:12 with 34:2, where it is said that Shechem "laid her and abased her").[25] By his Canaanite wife, Judah has three sons, Er (meaning "rouse oneself," "awake"), Onan ("vigorous"), and Shelah ("request," "thing asked for"); for his firstborn, Er, Judah finds a wife, Tamar ("date palm"), also a Canaanite woman. Yet this last decision will eventually prove to be a godsend. For it will be the ingenious and courageous deeds of his daughter-in-law, Tamar, that teach Judah about the meaning of both brotherhood and fatherhood.

Before this can happen, however, Judah has first to suffer great loss and grief. Like his father, Jacob, Judah suffers on account of his sons, two of whom fare badly as a result of their wickedness in the sight of the Lord. Leaving his people to live among the Canaanites has, for Judah, only tragic consequences:

> And Er, Judah's firstborn [*bekhor*], was wicked in the eyes of the Lord, and the Lord slew him. And Judah said to Onan, "Go in unto thy brother's wife and do-the-levirate-duty [*yabem*] unto her, and raise up seed to thy brother." And Onan knew that the seed would not be his, and so it happened that when he went in unto his brother's wife he would spill it on the

25. Apparently Judah did not get a wife from the women of Shechem as, we surmised, most of the brothers did, when they took away the women and children of the city after slaughtering the men.

ground, *lest he should give seed unto his brother.* And what he did was evil in the eyes of the Lord, and He slew him also. Then Judah said to Tamar, his daughter-in-law, "Remain a widow in thy father's house, until Shelah, my son, be grown up," for he said [to himself], "Lest he also die, like his brethren." And Tamar went and dwelt in her father's house. (38:7–11; emphasis added)

Er, Judah's firstborn, was wicked in God's sight. What he did or did not do we are not told, though the context invites suggestions that the sin was marital: according to traditional interpretations, he refused to consummate the marriage, perhaps to avoid having children, not wishing Tamar's beauty to be marred by pregnancy. Whatever it was, for his wickedness the Lord caused him to die. Judah then charged his second son, Onan, to perform the levirate duty—the obligation of the *levir*, the dead husband's brother, to marry the widow if she is childless—and to "raise up seed to thy brother." Onan, who does not overtly refuse, nonetheless fails to perform the brotherly duty: he takes his pleasure of the woman, but refuses to raise up seed to his dead brother, for which wicked failure "the Lord slew him also."[26] With his first two sons dead and for no reason known to him, Judah fears for the life of his remaining son ("lest he also die like his brethren"). He deceitfully orders Tamar to remain a widow in her father's house until Shelah is grown. But he has no intention of keeping his promise to her that the levirate duty will be fulfilled.

Understandably, Judah seeks to preserve his own son, his youngest and last. Not without cause, he very likely fears a curse on his sons through Tamar, and he attempts to escape it. But we notice that in doing so he is willing to sacrifice not only the rightful claims of his daughter-in-law, whom he further humiliates by keeping her, a twice-married woman, confined to her father's house. He is also willing to ignore the duties that are owed to another son. To save one son, Shelah, he is willing to allow Er to disappear without a trace. Earlier, Judah had proposed a plan regarding Joseph that would have caused his father, Jacob, to lose an heir; here, Judah repeats the same misdeed against his own son, Er. More generally, he is willing to neglect future generations in favor of the present one: he neglects the claims of lineage and future community needs for the sake of the love he feels for his youngest son.

26. Rightly understood, the sin of Onan is not—as is commonly thought—simply spilling one's seed (coitus interruptus) or, by extension, masturbation, but rather the sin of pretending but failing to perform the levirate duty to the deceased. His unbrotherly intention is clear from the fact that he deliberately interrupted the sex act explicitly to prevent raising seed to his brother. Whatever Onan's motive—whether he is moved by the desire to eliminate rival heirs or by plain malice—the meaning of his deed is clear: I am pleased, brother, that you have died without progeny.

Judah, in other words, ratifies the sin of Onan. Symbolically, in withholding Shelah, Judah sins—just like Onan—against Tamar, against his eldest son, and also against his entire family and the law-abiding community. He defies the commandment to be fruitful and multiply, he denies Tamar her marital and maternal fulfillment, he neglects the duty (Shelah's) to be one's brother's keeper, and he prefers the love of his own to the keeping of the law.[27]

The law of levirate marriage will surely strike the modern reader as a peculiar, even ugly and barbarous, custom.[28] Why should a man have to consort with a woman not of his choosing, to sire children that will not be his? Why should a widowed woman be prevented from remarrying as she will, and instead be compelled to accept a man she does not want or love, solely in order to preserve the lineage of a deceased husband? But if we are willing to set aside, for the moment, our current sensibilities, we may be able to discover, and even appreciate, the principles that inform this ancient custom. For, details aside, the practice of levirate marriage seeks to uphold what is centrally important in marriage altogether.

The heart of marriage, especially but not only biblically speaking, is not primarily a matter of the heart; rather, it is primarily about procreation and, even more, about transmission of a way of life. Husband and wife, whether they know it or not, are incipiently father and mother, parents of children for whose moral and spiritual education they bear a sacred obligation—to ancestors, to community, to God—an obligation symbolized first in the covenant-making commandment of *berith milah*, of circumcision.[29] The children parents may be blessed with are finally not *their* children, but rather, they profoundly hope, bearers into the future of that devoted pursuit of righteous and holy living that has been their communally inherited duty since Abraham. Precisely because of their communal commitment to care for righteousness, they must not, even in marriage that takes them from their father's house, cease to be their brothers' keepers. True, if they devote themselves *only* to their brothers, they uphold their past at the expense of their future, their ties to blood of origin at the expense of

27. Judah's deed also recalls the deeds of his father. Jacob had, long ago, been indifferent to Rachel's desire for children. More recently, he had neglected the legitimate claims of his other sons in order to indulge his love for Joseph, his (almost) youngest son—a deed he will later repeat when he risks family starvation rather than risk harm to Benjamin. But in contrast to Judah, Jacob was willing to hazard the sacrifice of Joseph for the sake of political unity, and he was even willing to live with his favorite son's murderers.

28. The levirate duty was not yet explicitly a matter of Israelite law. At this point in the unfolding account, it could only be a matter of local—and not peculiarly Israelite—custom. With the giving of the Law at Sinai, a special Israelite version of this practice becomes obligatory, but the next of kin may be released from his obligation by a self-disgracing public refusal, after which the widow is free to remarry (see Deuteronomy 25:5–10).

29. See our discussion of circumcision in Chapter Eleven.

ties to their wives and children. But if they set out, like Judah, solely on their own, indifferent to the fate of their brothers, they effectively cut ties to past and community, placing their own progeny and advantage above all else. If the home of one's progeny is to become a home also of perpetuation and transmission, reverence for one's origins is paramount; kinship and attachment to the community must triumph over sibling rivalry and moderate somewhat the drive for independence.

In levirate marriage, all these crucial principles are defended. A man serves, literally, as his brother's keeper: he refuses to allow his brother to die without a trace. Also, he refuses to nullify his sister-in-law's marriage, vindicating her claim to motherly fulfillment within her marriage. Taking seriously the commandment "Be fruitful and multiply," levirate marriage elevates the importance of progeny above personal gratification, and hence, the importance of lineage and community above the individual. In accepting the duty of the *levir*, a man simultaneously shows reverence for his ancestors, respect for the meaning and purpose of marriage, and devotion to the future of his family and his people.

Later in the history of the nation, the law of levirate marriage may serve a more explicitly political function. Robert Sacks has argued that it is crucial for the Israelite attempt, through the ingenious institution of the Jubilee,[30] to prevent the establishment of permanent classes of rich and poor. Families may be forced to sell their land when they fall on hard times, but for the Jubilee to restore the status quo ante, each family must be able to pass down what is its own into subsequent generations. Otherwise, some families would permanently be without property and forced to live as perpetual servants of others. The levirate law not only preserves the name of the man who dies without an heir; it also keeps his property from being gobbled up by larger and wealthier families.

But all this is far down the road. At present, the stakes are first of all familial and only derivatively tribal. In the present story, Tamar, though at great cost to herself, educates Judah in the true meaning of marriage, and therewith also about the meaning of brother, husband, and father.

After a good while, Judah's wife dies. Like his father, Jacob, Judah, in addition to losing two sons, grieves for a wife. After a period of mourning (literally, "When Judah was comforted"), he went up to the sheepshearing—a time of merriment and celebration—"he and his friend Hirah, the Adullamite" (38:12). As this is the first and only mention of friends and friendship in the book of Genesis, we are compelled to pause and take notice. What is it about Judah and his circumstances that lead him toward a friend, and an outside one at that? Why is friendship, a

---

30. Every fifty years, a Jubilee year would be proclaimed in which debts were forgiven, slaves were manumitted, and lands that had been sold or surrendered were returned to the families that originally owned them. See Leviticus 25.

ubiquitous human concern, so little treated in the Hebrew Bible? What does Judah's capacity for friendship imply for his suitability as a leader in Israel?

Judah's turn toward friendship is presented, twice, as an alternative to family life. Judah's original place was within the household of his father, but when he "went down from his brethren" he took up instead with "a certain Adullamite whose name was Hirah" (38:1), until he married and started a home of his own. Then, when his wife dies, Judah again joins up with the same man, now called "his friend Hirah the Adullamite" (38:12). The alternative both to dwelling in the household of Israel (the family of origin) and to married life (the family of perpetuation) is living in friendship with an Adullamite man. Friendship and marriage-and-family are mutually exclusive alternatives. Because the Hebrew Bible comes down decisively on the side of marriage and family life, it has little to say for or even about friendship. Friendship (especially male-male bonding) belongs to the ways of others.

As we learn from the example of the ancient Greeks, the celebration of friendship is linked to the celebration of manliness and the cultivation of the (aesthetic) virtues of nobility.[31] The goal appears to be a kind of independent self-sufficiency—in the heroic extreme, to become like a god, ageless and immortal (at the very least, in song and story)—in defiance of our finitude and neediness. As we have seen, this alternative view of an excellent human life has been under attack since the beginning of Genesis, and the neglect of the subject of friendship fits with the heavy emphasis on marriage and family that is central to the covenant begun with Abraham. Yet if the way of Israel is to survive and flourish among the nations, it cannot stand simply naked before the warrior alternatives. The capacity for friendship bespeaks a certain nobility of character and a certain gift for political leadership, capable of inspiring loyalty, camaraderie, and manly courage. The fact that Judah is the only Israelite character in Genesis—indeed, in the entire Torah[32]—who has a friend hints at his subsequent rise to a position of tribal leadership.

31. Aristotle's *Nicomachean Ethics* stands out among all the major moral writings in the Western philosophical tradition for its emphasis on both nobility and friendship. Aristotle insists that the end of nearly all the ethical virtues is "the noble" or "the beautiful" *(to kalon)*, the for-its-own-sake display of the beautiful and undivided soul in graceful and harmonious actions. And fully two of the ten books of the *Ethics* are devoted to the subject of friendship. The peaks of friendship are between males, the political friendship of joint action (each friend serving as a suitable mirror for the deeds of the other) and the philosophical friendship of sharing speeches and thoughts. The "friendship of husband and wife" gets but a short and cool chapter, one with no mention of "the noble." Though he regards homosexual coupling as "against nature," Aristotle—like nearly all the Greek philosophers—does not treat marriage as central to human flourishing.

32. Abimelech, the noble and gracious king of Gerar, is said to have a friend, a man named Ahuzzath (26:26). Otherwise, there are no specific friends mentioned in the Torah (the five books of

Our suspicion of the political significance of Judah's friendship with Hirah the Adullamite gains support when we remember the two major exceptions to the Bible's silence on the subject of friends: the famous friendships of Ruth and Naomi (presented in the book of Ruth) and of David and Jonathan (presented in the book of Samuel).[33] The linkages cannot be coincidental. David, Israel's most noble warrior and beautiful hero and its only real candidate for the Aristotelian virtue of magnanimity *(megalopsychia)*, is descended on one side from the union of Ruth and Boaz and on the other side from the union of Judah and Tamar, the subject of the immediate sequel. The lines leading to King David begin with people capable of same-sex friendship.[34]

While Judah goes off to carouse with his friend—returning now to the text— Tamar is still sequestered in her father's house, in widow's clothing and unfree to marry, awaiting Shelah, who had been betrothed to her as a levirate husband. She will wait no longer. Informed of Judah's doings and taking advantage of his loss of wife, Tamar takes matters into her own hands, for "she saw that Shelah was grown up and she was not given unto him to wife" (38:14). She removes her widow's garb, covers herself with a veil, and seats herself in the entrance to Enaim.[35] By deception, involving the same devices—cloak and kid—used by Judah and his brothers to deceive Jacob about Joseph (and by Jacob to deceive Isaac), she will get Judah himself to fulfill the duty of *levir*. And by clever forethought about the consequences of her deception, she arranges things in such a way that Judah will be forced to admit his breach of promise and to acknowledge his injustice to her and his firstborn, Er.[36]

When Judah saw her he thought she was a harlot, for she had covered her face. And he turned aside to her by the road and said, "Come, please, let me come in unto thee," for he knew not that she was his daughter-in-law; and

---

Moses), and the word "friend" appears only twice. In Exodus 33:11, God speaks to Moses as a man would to his friend. And in Deuteronomy 13:7, the children of Israel are warned not to allow a family member or friend entice them to follow and serve false gods.

33. The only other mention of friends is in the (arguably un-Jewish) book of Job, a very noble man.

34. In addition, Adullam turns out to be the site of two episodes in the life of David that frame his career. In the first, he escapes from Saul to Adullam, where the dissidents first rally around him. In the second, his last great military exploit, his soldiers cross through the lines to get their old king a drink of water from the well at Beth-lehem, the city of his birth.

35. The place-name, thought to mean "twin wells," offers what Alter calls a "wry allusion to the betrothal type scene: the bridegroom encountering his future spouse by a well in a foreign land." The reader will think of Rebekah at the well, as well as Jacob's meeting of Rachel.

36. In this respect, Tamar resembles Rebekah, whose deception of her husband, Isaac, brought him to his senses and enabled him to rise into his role as patriarch.

she said, "What wilt thou give me, that thou mayest come in unto me?"
And he said, "I myself will send thee a kid from the flock"; and she said,
"Only if thou givest me a pledge till thou send it." And he said, "What
pledge shall I give thee?" And she said, "Thy signet and cord and the staff
that is in thy hand." And he gave them to her and he went in unto her and
she conceived by him. And she arose and went away, and she put off the
veil from her and put on the garments of her widowhood. (38:15–19)

Tamar, dressed in the garb of a cult prostitute, is mistaken by Judah for a harlot. In crude speech, he propositions her. In equally crude speech, Tamar, continuing the charade, asks to be paid and demands a pledge now for the later
delivery of the promised payment. When asked to name the pledge, she demands Judah's signet, his cord, and his staff, the signs of his identity and authority. Tamar knows exactly what she is doing, and the choice of collateral is
ingenious: knowing that she will face mortal danger from Judah for harlotry
should her plan to become pregnant succeed, she gains irrefutable evidence of
the identity of the father of the child-to-be. Also, symbolically, in getting Judah
to part with the marks of his identity and position, she will show him that he has
willingly surrendered his birthright and standing—not only in his present purchase of sexual pleasure, but also in his refusal to uphold the rights of his son
and his son's marriage.

Judah accepts the deal and takes his pleasure, while Tamar gets the pregnancy
she wanted and deserved. Hardly a harlot, Tamar, though she bargains, acts not
for gain—she has no intention of accepting the wage of the promised kid—but
for the fulfillment of the meaning of her marriage. She wants not only what she
is owed because of a promise. She wants what she was promised because it was
owed, owed to her as a wife. Tamar wants justice.

Judah attempts to make good his pledge of the kid—he is willing to honor his
promise to the harlot to pay for his pleasure, but unwilling to honor his pledge
to his daughter-in-law to provide her a husband and child—but the woman
cannot be found. The men of Enaim, speaking better than they know, deny that
there was any cult prostitute[37] in the vicinity. Judah, now embarrassed, decides
not to pursue the matter further, lest it be discovered that he has traded the symbols of his dignity for a fleeting pleasure: "Let her take them, lest we be put to
shame" (38:23).

Three months later, when Tamar's pregnancy begins to show, Judah is informed that "Tamar, thy daughter-in-law, has played the whore, and behold, she

---

37. The term is *qedeshah,* not as elsewhere *zonah,* "whore" or "harlot." The former practiced ritual
prostitution as part of pagan fertility rites.

is with child by whoring" (38:24). Without even investigating the matter, Judah
responds hastily and high-handedly with a two-word sentence of death by burning: "Bring-her-forth [*hotsiy'uha*] that-she-be-burned [*vethisaref*]" (38:24). In
mortal jeopardy, Tamar calmly and skillfully makes her defense. She says not a
word in her own behalf. Instead, she returns a more serious charge against
Judah:

> When she was brought forth she sent to her father-in-law, saying, "By the
> man whose these are, am I with child"; and she said, "Recognize, please,
> whose are these, the signet, and the cords, and the staff." (38:25)

Tamar not only shows Judah that he is guilty of incest and the father of her child.
She forces him to confront the meaning of his sexuality and to acknowledge its
misuse. Having compelled Judah to play the role of his son Shelah so that
Shelah's brother and Judah's son not disappear without a trace, she forces Judah
to see what it means to be a father: to care for all one's sons equally and properly.
And finally, she forces him to confront his own unrighteousness.

Judah had participated in grievously wronging his brother Joseph and his father, Jacob. Though seeking to avoid the death of Joseph, Judah was perfectly
willing to sell him into Egypt, willing, that is, to allow him to disappear in Israel
without a trace. Judah had left the ways of his father and mother for foreign customs, also abandoning his wicked brothers to their fate without benefit of his
potential leadership. Now himself a father, with sons who (like Jacob's) ignore
their marital and brotherly obligations; now a widower (also like Jacob) who is
bereaved also of (two) sons; now made aware, thanks to Tamar, of the consequences of putting the love of your son above a proper regard for the community's future and for what is right, Judah is able to learn what it means properly
to care—as a father, as a brother, as a son in the house of Israel.

Tamar's words, as Robert Sacks points out, move him to consider all these
matters:

> *Recognize I pray thee:* These words jar Judah's memory and cut more
> deeply than even Tamar had expected. He had heard them once before.
> That was the time when his brothers brought Joseph's coat to his father, Ja-
> cob. They presented the coat to Jacob and said, *Recognize, I pray thee,*
> *whether it be thy son's coat or no* (Gen. 37:32). Tamar now uses these same
> words to Judah, forcing him to reflect upon his own actions toward her
> and, in consequence, upon all his feelings with regard to political unity. By
> bringing back the past and placing him in his father's position, her words
> force him to recognize the wisdom which Jacob displayed at the end of the

last chapter. At this point Judah realizes that he cannot separate himself, but must learn to teach his brothers and to lead them. Eventually it will be he and not Joseph who will be forced to accept the duties of the firstborn.

The story reaches its climax. Judah indeed recognizes his signet, cord, and staff. His spoken response bespeaks a remarkable turning of his soul:

> "She is more righteous [*tsadqah*] than I; forasmuch as I gave her not to Shelah, my son." And he knew her no more again.[38] (38:26)

The formula "She is more righteous than I" is a legal expression, which, if taken only at face value, would suggest that Judah concedes in a legal proceeding that the preponderance of evidence is more on Tamar's side than his. But no legal proceeding had been convened, and indeed, Judah, who as patriarch had the authority to convene one, had already condemned her—even without an inquest or trial—to a fiery death. But as Tamar reminds Judah through the return of his seal and staff, he had surrendered his patriarchal authority, and in a very deep way.

Even more to the point, Judah could not rightly accuse Tamar of violating her marriage, for he had violated it twice over. Though she appeared to have broken her marital obligation of chastity, she was not in fact guilty of harlotry. On the contrary, by playing the harlot, Tamar was only making clear to Judah that he (and his sons) had long been treating her as a harlot, as a woman to be used for pleasure rather than a wife celebrated for fruitfulness.[39] Judah's comment, "She is more *right* than I," thus has moral, even more than legal, meaning. Regardless of how fully she understands these matters, Tamar teaches Judah—and the reader—multiple lessons about right and duty: the justice of keeping promises; the justice of treating all sons equally (upholding the levirate duty); the duty of brothers to uphold and care for one another; and the duty of fathers to care for all their descendants and not only those they prefer and love. Bearing witness against himself, Judah is the first person in Genesis to publicly acknowledge his *own* unrighteousness, a wrong, he implicitly suggests, that is worse than harlotry.

Judah, when next we meet him, will be back with his brothers—though the text makes no explicit mention of his return. The turnabout in his outlook and

---

38. The last sentence puns on the name of Joseph. More literally translated it reads: "And he did not increase [*yosef*] to know her" (*velo'-yasaf 'od leda'tah*).

39. The entire episode may be read as a gloss on the story of the rape of Dinah, and especially on the brothers' final remark: "Shall our sister be treated as a harlot?" (34:31).

conduct can be explained only by the present story.[40] Made wiser through suffering and through the teaching of Tamar, Judah will stand as one among his brothers but now truly ready and fit to lead. He will lead not as a master to whom others bow, but as one who can live as a brother yet with the outlook of the fathers, seeing in each of his kin an equal carrier of the ancestral ways. Judah alone will be able, in the story we shall examine later, to persuade Jacob to allow Benjamin to accompany them to Egypt, pointing out that it would be wrong to let the entire clan die, "we and you *and our children*" (43:8; emphasis added), because of excessive attachment to a favorite surviving younger son. Judah will assume full legal and moral responsibility for the fate of Benjamin, offering himself and his honor as surety to his father, as the one brother responsible to and for all, and he will accept permanent guilt or innocence as his brother's keeper. And in his greatest deed, his speech to Joseph in Egypt, Judah will persuade his Egyptianized brother to think of himself again as his aged father's son and to give up the theatrical charade that has nearly cost Jacob his life in grief. The independent Joseph will get his dreamed-of worldly power and deference, but Judah will bind himself, in a forward-looking way, to his father, his brothers, and his father's ways. The way of Abraham survives another generation and becomes now the way of an entire people, thanks in small part to the brotherly leadership of Judah—"Praise the Lord"—and, of course, to the moral courage and decisive actions of Tamar.

The story ends with the full vindication of Tamar (and the repentant Judah): Tamar, doubly blessed, gives birth to twins. Having been compelled by Tamar both to rectify his misdeed against Er, by means of an incestuous union, and to acknowledge his sin, Judah raises up twin boys to Tamar and her late husband, Judah's dead son. At the same time, the twin boys also serve as "replacements" for both of Judah's dead sons; Judah will accept them as his own.[41] The birth order of the boys couldn't be more arbitrary. One twin puts out a hand and is declared the "winner" in the "race" to come first (a scarlet thread is placed upon his hand to identify him).[42] But when the first one's hand is withdrawn, the second twin bursts forth in full appearance. Tamar names this "second" son Perez, meaning "breach" or "bursts forth," and his brother, Zerah. Perez, son of Tamar

40. To be sure, other explanations can be imagined for Judah's return to the family. But on the principles of interpretation we have been following throughout, the present story—being the only account we get of Judah away from the clan—should be regarded as providing the necessary evidence, just as the story's clear connection with the previous episode ("at that time") should be looked to for the reason why he left the clan in the first place.

41. The twin boys will appear among the sons of Judah in the census of those who accompany Jacob when the Children of Israel go down to Egypt (46:12).

42. The scarlet thread links this firstborn to another, Esau, "the Red."

and simultaneously both son and grandson to Judah, will become the ancestor of King David. What better way to indicate the rightness of Tamar and the political importance of the line of Judah?

DESCENT INTO EGYPT: JOSEPH'S RISE AND SHINE

After the Judah-Tamar story ends with Judah's self-rebuke and the birth of a son who is the ancestor of Israel's future kings, the text returns to the young hero, Joseph, now come to Egypt. Joseph, like Judah, is away from the family in a foreign land, albeit, in Joseph's case, involuntarily. Genesis 39 begins a twelve-chapter saga of Joseph's fabulous rags-to-riches Egyptian career, from slave boy to prime minister and managerial genius of the world's most prosperous nation. Woven into the account of Joseph's public career is the famous story of the arrival of his brothers, who come to Egypt seeking food during a time of famine and who unknowingly find themselves at Joseph's mercy. After the brothers remorsefully confess their sins against him, Joseph reveals himself and magnanimously forgives them. Summoning his father to Egypt, he then settles his entire family in the choicest region of Egypt. At last, harmony reigns, the family buries the hatchet, and the Children of Israel all prosper. Everything turns out fine in the end.

Such, at least, is the story as it is commonly known. But the truth is much more complicated. As we have been emphasizing throughout this book, the family saga is even more a political-cultural-religious story, illuminating the difference between the way of Israel and the way of the world and exploring the permanent question facing the way of Israel: separation, or assimilation? No place exemplifies more successfully or more fully the way of the world than does Egypt. In no place is assimilation to the way of the world more tempting. With the arrival of Joseph in Egypt these considerations receive central attention, and right from the start.

The saga of Joseph in Egypt begins with the famous story of Joseph in Potiphar's house: his rapid rise from slave to chief overseer; his sexual harassment at the hands of his master's wife; and his rapid fall into prison, courtesy of the frame-up she concocted when he spurned her advances. But read in context of the larger whole, the story of Joseph in Potiphar's house assumes much greater importance. In offering us our first glimpse into life in Egypt, and our only glimpse of Egyptian domestic life, it represents a crucial chapter in Genesis's ongoing exploration of the nature of the household, man and woman, and the meaning of sexuality, and how these matters are best regulated. It also provides new material for the text's ongoing reflections on the standing of visible bodily beauty and the problem of eros, especially for the life devoted to the new way, a subject last considered in connection with Jacob's love for Joseph's mother, the beautiful Rachel. And perhaps most important, it gives us new opportunity to examine the character of Joseph, now that he is away from the sheltering presence of his doting father. How Joseph acts and fares in Potiphar's house and with Potiphar's wife sheds light on both his capacity for leadership within Israel (especially in comparison with Judah, whose dealings with a foreign woman we have just considered) and his stance toward the attractive and competing ways of Egypt. From Joseph's first Egyptian encounter we begin to see how Israel differs from Egypt. We wonder: Can Israel survive the encounter? Can and will Joseph preserve his identity? Can and will he be able to safeguard his people? With our eyes adjusted to this larger horizon, we are ready to look closely at the details of the story itself.

The five-and-a-half-verse introduction (which, along with the story's three-and-a-half-verse conclusion, forms an elegant frame) sounds forth the grand theme of Israel in Egypt and reports on Joseph's meteoric rise in his new home:

> And Joseph was brought down to Egypt, and Potiphar, an officer [*seris*] of Pharaoh's, the captain of the guard, an Egyptian man, bought him from the Ishmaelites who had brought him down there. And the Lord [*YHWH*] was with Joseph, and he was a prosperous man, and he was in the house of his master [*'adonayv:* lord]. And his master saw that the Lord was with him, and all that he did the Lord made to prosper in his hand. And Joseph found favor in his eyes and he ministered unto him, and he [Potiphar] put him [Joseph] in charge over his house, and all that he had he put into his hand. And it happened from the time that he put him in charge over his house and over all that he had that the Lord blessed the Egyptian's house for Joseph's sake; and the blessing of the Lord was upon all that he had, in the house and in the field. And he left all that he had in Joseph's hand, and he did not know anything with him there, save for the bread that he did eat. (39:1–6a)

Joseph's entrance into Egypt is described (twice) as a descent—a bringing down: all going to Egypt is described as a "going down" (see 12:10; 26:2), and we sense that the descent is not only geographical but also moral-political. Joseph, unlike Abraham, does not "go down" to Egypt voluntarily; he is *brought* down—by the Ishmaelites, who got him from the Midianites, who had lifted him up from the pit into which he had been cast down by his brothers, whose anger he had raised, largely because of his uppity dreams in which he had them bowing down before his upright and lordly self. There are good moral reasons for seeing the entrance into Egypt as a descent. When Abraham went down into Egypt, his beautiful wife, Sarah, was taken into Pharaoh's house (12:15) and made a member of his harem. Here, when Joseph is brought down to Egypt, he is taken—purchased from the hand of the Ishmaelites, descendants of Hagar the Egyptian—as a slave for his house by Pharaoh's officer Potiphar, captain of the guard, "an *Egyptian* man." The first look into Egypt reveals open slave trading; the first Egyptian man we meet serves his master, Pharaoh, but buys and masters other human beings. Lordship and bondage are the most evident Egyptian way.[43]

But Joseph, we are meant to understand, is not really all alone in Egypt. Though he has been brought low into slavery, the text hastens to tell us that "the Lord was with Joseph,"[44] and as a result he rises and prospers. First, he is made a household slave, rather than a field slave (39:2), then he becomes his master's special assistant (39:4), then he gets appointed overseer over the entire household (39:4), and finally he is entrusted with absolutely everything that belonged to his master—everything, that is, save for the bread that he would eat (39:6; we shall return to this exception). All of this, we readers are given to understand, is owed to the Lord's providence—not to Joseph's talents, not to good luck, but to the Lord's care and attention.

Yet what of this divine attention do Joseph or Potiphar understand? *We* know that the Lord was with Joseph, but Joseph himself was with his master (*'adonayv*, "lord"), the Egyptian. It is in his master's eyes that Joseph finds favor, and it is his master, for all he knows, to whom he is beholden for his advancement. Indeed, careful reading gives the reader pause: how could the master, an Egyptian man who never heard of, much less believed in, the power of *YHWH*, "see" that "*YHWH* was with him [Joseph]"? What the master does see is that everything that Joseph touches turns to his own advantage; that Joseph has a golden touch; that, as we might loosely say, "the gods are smiling on him" or "he is one of the gods' favorites." Potiphar is impressed with Joseph—his talents and his successes—not with *YHWH*. Why, then, should it be otherwise with Joseph himself? Joseph rises in his master's service, finds grace in *his* eyes, and reaps the rewards of his master's beneficence. What does Joseph know of the Lord? Joseph evinces no hint that he believes that the Lord is behind his successes. On the

43. Potiphar is described as an officer of Pharaoh's, but the primary meaning of the word translated as "officer," *seris*, is "eunuch." The emasculation of male servants, a practice deemed necessary by the holding of many women in Pharaoh's harem, writes the meaning of Egyptian bondage into the bodies of Pharaoh's highest servants.

44. The phrase occurs four times in this chapter: vv. 2, 3, 22, 23.

contrary, he has every reason to think that his own talent and competence are responsible. His successes and meteoric rise may even go to his head. Just as his father's favoritism had made Joseph overconfident and foolishly provocative in dealing with his brothers, so his master's favoritism now places him at risk for prideful overconfidence and foolish conduct in dealing with Potiphar's affairs.

Only one matter does Potiphar not leave to Joseph: "the bread [food] that he did eat" (39:6). This could be a mere idiom, signifying the withholding of nothing: Potiphar's knowledge of his household was confined to what went into his mouth; the household for Potiphar had become just a place to feed. Alternatively, the remark could be taken literally: Potiphar entrusted everything to his Hebrew slave other than the ritually crucial matter of food. (Later we shall learn that the Egyptians have strong food taboos and will not eat with outsiders; 43:32.) Yet there is also a third interpretation, supported by the sequel: "the bread that he ate" could be a euphemism for "wife."[45] This euphemistic reading offers the best logical linkage to the very next comment:

And Joseph was of beautiful form and beautiful to look at. (39:6)

The remark jogs the reader's memory. The identical words, in the identical order, were used to describe Joseph's mother, Rachel (29:17). They occur not in the account of the scene at the well, where Jacob is first smitten by her, but later, in the context of explaining Jacob's choice of Rachel as his wages from Laban. Joseph is the only *man* in the entire Bible who is described in this way. It would perhaps not be wrong to think of him as possessing a somewhat feminine beauty. Be that as it may, the text has postponed telling us of Joseph's great beauty until the present moment—even though a beautiful resemblance to the beloved Rachel could well have figured in Jacob's preference for him, in his brothers' jealousy, and even in his finding grace in the eyes of Potiphar, his Egyptian master. The text wants us rather to think of Joseph's beauty, like Rachel's beauty, in the context of issues of sex and marriage—in the previous case, the question of the more suitable wife, in the present case, the question of marital fidelity and adultery. Once again, looking on Joseph's beauty, we are on the threshold of seeing how love of the beautiful may be at odds with the nature of marriage.

Beauty, we have had occasion to see before, is a dangerous gift. It is a grace that enhances and adorns, but it is also a power that overwhelms. It can be Apollonian and inspire admiration; it can be Aphrodisiac and inspire lust. For the

---

45. See 39:8–9, quoted on p. 543. See also Proverbs 30:20: "Such is the way of an adulteress: she eats, wipes her mouth, and says, 'I have done no wrong.' "

bearer, it can be a burden[46] or it can be a weapon. In the present context, the announcement of Joseph's beautiful appearance serves two purposes at once. On the one hand, it explains in part why Potiphar's wife took an interest in him. On the other hand, it presents a problem for Joseph's character. What are the responsibilities of the beautiful ones? How should they present and carry themselves? Before whom and in what manner should they display themselves? The beautiful, we know, are easily beloved. But do they, we wonder, love back? Is beautiful Joseph a lover like his father before him? If not, does it matter for the biggest question, his place in the life of Israel?

If Joseph, like Rachel, is of beautiful form and beautiful to look at, Potiphar's wife is, like Jacob, the one to be smitten.

And it happened after these things that his master's wife lifted up her eyes to Joseph, and she said: "Lie with me [*shikhvah 'imiy*]." (39:7)

"After these things"—after his elevation to high standing in the household, and very likely also after she had long been gazing furtively but longingly upon his beauty—Joseph's master's wife at last makes eye contact and utters her two-word sexual command: "Lie with-me." This is all she says and all Joseph (or the reader) hears. Indeed, these are the only two words she ever utters to Joseph—though she will repeat them often. Their meaning is, in one sense, clear enough: we know what she wants. But as is not infrequently the case in such sexual encounters, we need to summon our interpretive powers to figure out what in fact has been going on in her soul before she speaks.

According to the most common reading, very unfriendly to Potiphar's wife, what we have here is an oversexed, lustful woman, the unsatisfied wife of Pharaoh's chief steward (who may have been a eunuch[47]), propositioning an innocent and beautiful boy, a servant in her house who cannot escape because he is owned by her husband and who must therefore do her sexual bidding. Remarks Nahum Sarna, "There are no verbal preliminaries, no expressions of love.

46. See, on this subject, W. B. Yeats, "A Prayer for My Daughter," the third stanza of which reads:

May she be granted beauty and yet not
Beauty to make a stranger's eye distraught,
Or hers before a looking-glass, for such,
Being made beautiful overmuch,
Consider beauty a sufficient end,
Lose natural kindness and maybe
The heart-revealing intimacy
That chooses right, and never find a friend.

47. See p. 540 n. 43.

Her peremptory mode of speech flows from her consciousness of Joseph's status as a slave." The Hertz commentary glossing this verse goes further: "The immorality of the ancient Egyptians, both men and women, was notorious."

But other commentators are not so quick to blame the woman. Rashi links the woman's sexual advance to his interpretation of the remark about Joseph's beauty:

> As soon as he saw that he was ruler (in the house) he began to eat and drink and curl his hair. The Holy One, blessed be He, said to him, "Your father is mourning and you curl your hair! I will let a bear loose against you." Immediately his lord's wife lifted up her eyes, etc.

Maurice Samuel, endorsing Thomas Mann's interpretation of the woman and her behavior "after these things," insists that Potiphar's wife

> was no wanton and no nymphomaniac driven helplessly to snatch at every man within reach. She was a great lady. She was a dedicated person, even as her husband, the eunuch, was. Her passion for Joseph was not a sudden and furious flare-up of lust, already sated a hundred times indiscriminately and still insatiable. It grew slowly, and it came into the open only "after these things." . . . And long before it came into the open Joseph was aware of it, and went through the gesture of discouraging it.

On this reading, Potiphar's wife, no longer capable of restraining herself, issues not so much an imperious command to a slave but a desperate plea to a man she has fallen madly in love with.

Joseph's response also is open to more than one reading. He answers her two-word proposition with a speech of (in Hebrew) thirty-five words:

> Look, my master knoweth not, with me [here], what is in the house, and all that he hath, he hath given into my hand. He is not greater in this house than I, and he hath not held back from me anything except thee, because thou art his wife. So how can I do this great evil and sin against God [or gods: le'lohim]? (39:8–9)

Joseph's speech is not exactly tight, logically or stylistically, suggesting perhaps that he could be flustered or nervous, or perhaps even scandalized. At the same time, however, he is not at a loss for words. He does not run away and he does not merely refuse. He gives reasons why the answer to her proposition must be "No." Once again, the manifest content of his remarks is clear enough: My master trusts me beyond all bounds. To take the one thing he has withheld from me would be an act of heinous ingratitude and betrayal. Such a violation of my master's trust and my master's marriage would be a great evil and a sin against the divine. How can you expect me to do such a thing?

But the *human* meaning of the speech—as opposed to the meaning of the words—depends decisively on the moral tone in which it is uttered and on the condition of soul that gave it voice. And here again, there are several possibilities. Anyone who wishes to give Joseph even a small benefit of the doubt will admire him for not yielding, especially when it might have advanced his career to acquiesce. Moreover, his reasons appear high-minded and principled: though he could get away with enjoying his master's wife without his master ever knowing about it, Joseph says that he refuses to violate the moral norms that oppose adultery and betrayal of trust and to act in a way offensive to God.

Yet Joseph says things that make us suspect that there might have been something haughty, self-righteous, and even provocative in his tone and manner. Maurice Samuel makes a good case: "He dwells on his master's helplessness and unsuspiciousness. Does he have to emphasize the fact that he could assuage her need safely if he wanted to? 'He knoweth not what is in the house.' " Does Joseph have to point out that he is the equal of her husband ("He is not greater in this house than I")? And regarding Joseph's professed piety, we also have our doubts. In speaking with the woman, Joseph's final reason concerns "sinning against God," but the word he uses is *'elohim*, not *YHWH*. Eight times in the present chapter, the text speaks about the Lord *(YHWH)*, how He was with Joseph and how He blessed him. In pointed contrast, when Joseph speaks of the divine he uses a different name: could he be thinking about a different divinity?

No doubt, for rhetorical reasons Joseph might well speak to the Egyptian lady generically about "god" or "gods" (*'elohim* is, we recall, grammatically plural; it may be translated either way). No doubt also, to imply that adultery is a sin proscribed by a generic "fear of God" makes perfect sense:[48] adultery is opposed not only in Israel, and besides, *YHWH* has yet to hand down the Ten Commandments. Yet one must not therefore attribute to Joseph a specific adherence to the God of his fathers. Moreover, appealing to divine sanction to justify his refusal would be, under the circumstances, a shrewd rhetorical maneuver. We will soon see several occasions in which Joseph talks about God, but in which we suspect he is really referring only to himself. It is therefore entirely possible that Joseph acts here not as an innocent who lives by piety and moral principle, but as a charismatic fellow who enjoys exploiting his good looks, exercising his powers, and attracting others while displaying his own aloofness.

---

48. Abraham had used such an expression in his conversation with Abimelech (20:11).

Joseph, seemingly oblivious to the danger he faces, continues in Potiphar's service. Mrs. Potiphar's importunings continue, day after day; so do Joseph's refusals: "And it happened, as she spoke to Joseph day after day, that he hearkened not unto her, to lie by her, to be with her" (39:10). Once again, the situation is murky. Do we have here a case of exemplary moral conduct, in the face of terrible temptation? Or is this rather a case of provocation, through studied indifference? Is Joseph, wittingly or not, complicit in tempting another?

Given the mounting tension caused by Joseph's steady presence, Potiphar's wife's steady insistence, and Joseph's equally steady refusal, a crisis was bound to come.

> And it came to pass on one such day that he came into the house to do his work; and there was no man from among the men of the house there in the house. And she seized him by his garment, saying, "Lie with me [*shikhvah 'imiy*]." And he left his garment in her hand and he fled outside. (39:11–13)

Those who see Joseph as an utter innocent must concede that his behavior here is imprudent in the extreme: he wanders into a house completely empty of witnesses or others in whose presence he might be seen, and he manages to wind up in her presence. Could this be a mere accident? Or was Joseph knowingly taking advantage of a golden opportunity to play once again the role of the righteous refuser of adulterous advances? Or had he, in fact, at long last, succumbed to her wiles and importunings? Much depends on the meaning of "to do his work." Was he going to do his master's accounts? Or was he going to do his "work" with the woman? Even the ancient rabbis were divided, as Rashi reports:

> Rab and Samuel differ *as to what this means.* One holds *that it means,* his actual housework; the other *that it means* to associate with her, but a vision of his father's face appeared to him *and he resisted the temptation and did not sin. . . .*

Though the matter cannot be definitively settled, we incline rather to the interpretation offered by Maurice Samuel:

> Day by day, then, he flaunted his success, his control of the situation, his mastery of himself—so easy when there was no desire to master—until the maddened woman actually assaulted him, and came as near success as it was possible for her to come; that is to say, she forced the issue, to her undoing, and Joseph's. She committed the crime, and it was Joseph who was cast into prison.

Thus on the surface. In reality it was Joseph who forced the issue, as he had done in his boyhood with his brothers, forced it steadily day by day, until the explosion came. In those days he had played with his brothers' hatred; now he toyed with a woman's love. In both instances he was the active agent, and set the pattern; and to make this clear, in both instances he had his coat torn off him—in a kind of unmasking—and was thrown into the pit.

Having pushed Potiphar's wife beyond the breaking point, Joseph the pretending but reluctant lover is caught by his own "disguise." The false charge of sexual assault she now levels against him is a fitting, even if unjust, answer to his false "assault" on her sexual desire. Joseph, who has fled her chambers naked, or nearly so, is now exposed also to her wrath.

As in so many cases of "sexual harassment," the full truth about this episode is hard to uncover, because the surface account is spare and the motives and intentions invisible. At least three different versions seem both humanly plausible and consistent with the text.

Version 1: Joseph is completely innocent and morally pure. When first propositioned by Potiphar's wife, Joseph, morally upright, tries to instruct her. Later, filled with desire, she attacks him when he passes by, but he manages to escape her clutches. Humiliated by Joseph's rejection and eager for revenge, she accuses him falsely of attempted rape. She thus causes him to lose his job and to be sent to prison. Joseph, like many an innocent victim of sexual harassment, won't defend himself, out of shame and out of a sense that it would be merely his lowly word against her high and mighty one.

Version 2: Joseph is partly complicit in his own undoing, primarily by the haughty way he refuses her advances. Insulted by having been often rejected by a Hebrew slave, Potiphar's wife seeks to entrap Joseph in order to gain her revenge. She coolly arranges for the house to be empty. He comes voluntarily, perhaps this time even for a sexual encounter, but she takes his cloak in order to frame him. He flees in fear, partly because he can't defend himself, for he has played a role in his own entrapment. Though his standing with Potiphar is high enough that his side of the story would be heard, Joseph remains silent because he knows he is not altogether innocent.

Version 3: Joseph is largely responsible for the incident, more harasser than harassed. From the beginning he toys with her feelings, all the while having no desire for the woman. Finally, he provokes her past the breaking point when he visits her when the house is empty. She is again humiliated, here doubly so, because he led her to believe that this time he was willing to satisfy her ("to do his work," "no man in the house"). Furious, she covers her humiliation with the lie that he came to take advantage of her.

A reader who finds the analysis of the scene given above persuasive will incline sometimes to the second version, sometimes to the third, but rarely to the first. The text's remarks about Joseph's beauty (with the suspicion that he is a beloved, not a lover), the proud and provocative character of his speech of refusal, his demonstrated penchant for overconfidence when he is in favor, and his (to say the least) imprudent arrival into Mrs. Potiphar's part of an otherwise empty house—all these add up to a suspicion that Joseph is *at least* complicit in and partly responsible for what happened. As with the selling into slavery, this is neither blaming the victim nor an exoneration—or even mitigation—of Potiphar's wife or Joseph's brothers, but an attempt to understand Joseph's character and the reasons for his multiple rises and falls.

Whatever the truth about how things came to this pass, the end of the story is, by contrast, relatively straightforward. Potiphar's wife, seeing that she holds Joseph's garment in hand, plots her revenge. She summons the men of her house, hoping to enlist them as witnesses to support her false charges. In doing so, she trades in part on what she presumes is their antipathy both to their master (her husband) and to the Hebrew foreigner who had risen so high in their midst:

> And she spoke unto them, saying, "See, he [Potiphar] hath brought unto us a Hebrew man to play with us [*or* to mock us: *letsaheq banu*];[49] he came in unto me to lie with me, and I cried out in a loud voice. And it happened, when he heard me lift up my voice and cry out, he left his garment by me and fled and got himself out." (39:14–15)

Appealing to the servants' solidarity with her as fellow Egyptians ("us"), over against the mocking and outrageous Hebrew outsider, Potiphar's wife implies that Joseph's very supremacy in their master's service is an insult to them all.

Holding on to the telltale garment, Mrs. Potiphar waits for her husband, Joseph's master, to return home. To him she reports the events somewhat differently.

> "He came in unto me, the Hebrew slave whom thou hast brought us, to play with me [to mock me: *letsaheq bi*]. And it happened, when I lifted up my voice and cried out, he left his garment by me and fled out." (39:17–18)

---

49. The word she uses for "to play," *tsahaq*, can mean "to engage in sexual dalliance" (compare 26:8, where Abimelech catches Isaac "playing" with Rebekah) or "ridicule," "mock," "laugh at" (compare 21:9, where Sarah catches Ishmael mocking Isaac). Here, Potiphar's wife can mean all of the following at once: her husband has enabled Joseph to make lascivious advances, to ridicule her in rejecting her advances, and to insult the men of the house by his high position over them.

Potiphar's wife refers here to Joseph as a *slave* (not, as she had to the servants, as a Hebrew *man*), reminding her husband to think again like a master and to recognize the outrage of a slave's attack on his master's wife, no matter how valuable the slave. She no longer clearly charges her husband with an intent to have her mocked, but rather attributes that intention to Joseph ("The Hebrew slave came in to me—the one you brought us—to play with [mock] me"). She also claims that she immediately cried out, which deed led to Joseph's fleeing, leaving his coat behind.

Potiphar apparently makes no response, perhaps out of shock or disbelief. More likely, he is vexed at the necessity of dealing with a problem that has, for him, only bad solutions. So his wife continues, presumably with gestures to display her claims: " 'After this manner did thy servant to me'; and his [Potiphar's] anger was kindled" (39:19). Potiphar is angry, but the text does not specify with whom. He could be angry not only at Joseph but also at his wife, perhaps suspecting her of playing false with the truth. And he surely must be annoyed at having to part with Joseph's superior service. But Potiphar has no choice but to punish Joseph: the matter has become public, his wife has "witnesses" plus the cloak, and Potiphar is compelled to uphold his wife, whatever he may think about what really happened.

But whether from doubts about Joseph's guilt or from wishes to retain his services, Potiphar does not decree the capital punishment that the offense ordinarily would warrant. Instead, "Joseph's master took him and put him into the prison house, the place where the king's prisoners were housed" (39:20a). Joseph, again cast down, again narrowly escapes being put to death. And though in a prison house, he is in good company, among prisoners of Pharaoh, through whom he will eventually rise up to great glory in Egypt. Remarkably, Potiphar has even arranged to keep Joseph nearby. As we learn from later verses, Joseph's imprisonment is "in the house of the captain of the guard" (40:3)—that is, in the house of Potiphar, the very house in which Joseph's alleged crime had taken place! Through these small clues, we are given to understand that although Joseph in the prison house is at the nadir of his fortune, he has a good chance to rise.

Sure enough, the final verses of the story—its closing frame—inform us of Joseph's successes in the prison:

> And he was there in the prison house. And the Lord was with Joseph and showed kindness unto him, and granted him favor in the eyes of the warden of the prison. And the warden of the prison house placed in Joseph's hand all the prisoners that were in the prison house, and all that was to be done there, he was the doer of it. The warden of the prison house looked

not to any thing that was in his hand, as the Lord was with him, and whatever he did the Lord made it prosper. (39:20b–23)

Just as at the start of his career in Potiphar's house, Joseph gains favor in the eyes of the ruler of the prison house. Just as before, *everything* is placed in Joseph's hand. Just as before, Joseph prospers. We readers are again told that it was the Lord who caused Joseph to prosper because "the Lord was with him" (39:21, 23). But we have absolutely no indication that Joseph is aware of God's providence. What Joseph knows for sure is that his talents are recognized and that he is once again on the rise, albeit in jail. We must wait to see whether his successes incline him more to feelings of gratitude or to feelings of self-importance. Will he again become the victim of his own prosperity? Much will depend, it seems, on what he has learned from his most recent fall from grace.[50]

Judah, at the end of his experience with Tamar, had born witness against himself and his unrighteous behavior. He had learned important lessons about fatherhood, brotherhood, and the necessity for serving the future in the light of the past. In contrast, it is not clear what, if anything, Joseph has learned from his recent experience with Potiphar's wife. We do not hear him speak and don't know what he thinks. It is not clear whether he understands how his own conduct may have contributed to his troubles. It is not clear whether, on the next occasion, he will refuse the opportunity to make himself beloved of the Egyptians or whether he will jump at the chance, only this time taking better care to succeed.

50. To this point Joseph's career has followed a familiar pattern. At home, he was the favorite of the head of the household (his father, Jacob), a first among equals (his brothers) who was thus envied and hated by his peers, stripped, thrown into a pit, and sold into slavery. In Potiphar's house he was again the favorite of the head of the household, a first among equals (the slaves) who was later hated by his master's wife, stripped, and thrown into prison. In prison, we find him again the favorite of the head of the "house," once again a first among equals (the prisoners). Can the pattern of "success breeding failure" be avoided? If so, will it require that Joseph be elevated to a position above his "equals," succeeding not as a leader of his peers but only as a minister to an all-powerful monarch?

Chapter Eighteen

Joseph the Egyptian

We do not have long to wait to see how Joseph handles his next opportunity for success in Egypt. Having shown us Joseph's descent to his lowest point, lower than a slave and bound in prison, the text now lets us witness his spectacular rise. Previously, in reporting on Joseph's elevation in Potiphar's service, the text had given us only a summary report of Joseph's success and prospering. Now it allows us to see for ourselves the details of a genius at work.

Two episodes involving dreams and dream interpretation bring Joseph from the bottom to the very top. Earlier his own grandiose (not to say Egyptian) dreams had prompted a fall into the pit, courtesy of his brothers. Now his (eminently Egyptian)[1] powers of dream interpretation, employed on the dreams of Pharaoh's servants and later of Pharaoh himself, propel his rise from the pit to the post of lord chancellor of Egypt, the prime minister to Pharaoh.

What exactly are Joseph's powers of dream interpretation? And why are they so successful in Egypt? Does Joseph possess a special gift of prophecy or clairvoyance? Or is he rather uncommonly shrewd and calculating? Or—a third possibility—does he possess a special kind of wisdom, the kind that is especially honored in Egypt? What is "Egyptian wisdom," and what the Egyptian worldview, and why is Egypt so welcoming of Joseph and his gifts? These important questions may be considered quite apart from whether God is or is not the source of Joseph's powers, and independent of whether Joseph's rise in Egypt is part of some providential plan. Properly pondered, they shed light on the crucial differences between Egypt and Israel, which is to say, between the way of the world and the way of the Lord.

---

1. Dream interpretation is an Egyptian, not an Israelite, art or science. Apart from Joseph, the only Jew who interprets dreams in the Bible is Daniel, and he too does so only in a foreign land.

INTERPRETING THE DREAMS OF FALLEN SERVANTS: UNCOVERING GUILT AND INNOCENCE

The first episode of dream interpretation takes place in the prison house. It involves Pharaoh's chief butler (or cupbearer) and chief baker,[2] both fallen from Pharaoh's favor.

> And it happened after these things, that the butler of the king of Egypt and his baker had offended their lord, the king of Egypt. And Pharaoh was wroth against two of his officers, against the chief of the butlers and against the chief of the bakers. And he put them under guard in the house of the captain of the guard, into the prison, the place where Joseph was bound. And the captain of the guard charged Joseph with them, and he ministered to them; and they were under guard for days. (40:1–4)

Despite the highly repetitive and overly precise description, the most important matters are obscure. Why the butler and the baker? What had they done to offend or sin against Pharaoh? Had they acted separately, or together? About these matters the text is silent. And how is Joseph related to them: is he in charge of them, or is he their servant? And why would the captain of the guard set them under Joseph's eye and care? Once again, not a word. The world of Pharaoh, on first meeting, is foreign and mysterious: as in a dream, surface clarity hides deeper meaning. To uncover the truth about Egypt, we are obliged to speculate.

The butler and the baker provide Pharaoh his wine and his bread, the former to gladden his heart, the latter to sustain his life. Bringers of food and drink, these servants are very close to Pharaoh.[3] Indeed, despite their seemingly lowly station, they exercise great (albeit indirect) power over his life: they can nourish

2. The word translated "butler" or "cupbearer," *mashqeh*, from the root *shaqah*, "to give to drink," means "one giving drink." It occurs in the Bible (Hebrew Bible and New Testament) only in this story; only in Egypt and in Pharaoh's service is there a cupbearer. The function of the cupbearer is not clear. At least one tradition has the cupbearer's job as that of taster, that is, one who checks to make certain that Pharaoh isn't being poisoned. But if the cup is also involved in acts of divination, the butler may have also a quasi-religious or magical function. The reference to a particular baker is also unique. Indeed, in keeping with the strangeness that is Egypt, the biblical stories discussed in this chapter contain many unusual words, some directly borrowed from Egyptian words (for example, Pharaoh, Nile, *abrekh*), others (though of Hebrew origin) referring to things that occur nowhere else but Egypt (for example, baker, butler, and—very significantly—birthday).

3. They are here not called "servants" or "slaves," *'avadim*, but "officers," *sarisim*, a term that means "eunuchs" (40:2). Proximity to Pharaoh comes at the price of emasculation, producing retainers who remain in a condition of permanent boyishness. (We have met this term before; see Chapter Seventeen, p. 540 n. 43.)

him, they can make him ill, they can poison him. This mighty man, a god to the world's highest civilization, is at the mercy of these two eunuchs—precisely because, *not* being a god, he is at the mercy of his bodily needs.[4] It is thus easy to see how these servants in particular might come to offend their king. Perhaps Pharaoh became ill or feasted on a meal that did not agree with him. Who could be responsible? Why, the butler and/or the baker. Acting on a whim, without first discerning which of them might be to blame, Pharaoh might have punished both men indiscriminately. Alternatively, he might have been in doubt as to which one was guilty, so he put them both into prison as part of a plan to discover the answer. For it is common knowledge that men while in prison often loosen their tongues, confessing or bragging about their deeds or otherwise betraying their culpability. Let's put the butler and the baker into prison, and under the careful watch of a trusted and sharp-eyed observer. Let the observer dissemble his position as an informer; let him appear instead to be their servant: "and the captain of the guard *charged* Joseph with the men, *and* he *served* them." In the guise of serving the butler and the baker, Joseph is keeping tabs on them and, no doubt, reporting what he finds to the captain of the guard, his own master, Potiphar. Once upon a time Joseph would report his brothers' wrongdoing to their father; now he will, indirectly, report the wrongdoing of Pharaoh's servants to their ruler.

After "days in the ward," opportunity presents itself in the form of a dream shared by the two men.

> And they *dreamed a dream* [*vayachalmu chalom*], both of them, each man
> his dream in one night, *according to the interpretation* [or *solution*] *of his*
> *dream*, the butler and the baker of the king of Egypt, who were bound in
> the prison. (40:5; emphasis added)

In this strange description, with its redundant and precise reidentification of the men and their location, two facts stand out. First, like Joseph earlier, the two

---

4. From the very start of our encounter with Egypt, we are impressed by the importance of the subject of food. The two servants of Pharaoh now imprisoned are charged with serving food and drink, and their dreams will be about serving food and drink to their master. Pharaoh's own dreams will be about devouring and hunger, and Joseph's high station will be devoted to gathering, storing, and selling food. Egypt, the place where people turn in times of famine, seems somewhat obsessed with food, even at the highest level of society. As we will see, this greatest of civilizations is focused on life and devoted to its preservation, perhaps above all else. Threats to life—be they poisoning, starvation, or plague—are taken with supreme seriousness. At the same time, the ruler's unwelcome recognition of his dependence on bodily necessity—and his need for butler and baker—may be taken as an insult to his god-like pretensions and may make him especially irascible in dealing with those servants who bring him food and drink.

men actively "dreamed a dream": their dream is not said to be sent by God or some outside force; rather, it seems to be the product of their own inner activity. Second, the two men in fact dreamed but one and the same dream,[5] yet each man interpreted his dream according to his own lights. What is in fact but a single dream—depicting but a single event—is experienced differently according to what each man brings to it *from within his own mind*.

Joseph arrives in the morning to find the men dejected *(za'af)*:

And he asked Pharaoh's officers that were with him under guard in his lord's house, saying, "Wherefore are your faces sad [*ra'*; the root meaning is 'bad' or 'evil'] today?" And they said unto him, "We have dreamed a dream [*chalom chalamnu*], and there is none can interpret [*or* solve] it." (40:7–8)

The text calls our attention, again redundantly, to the fact that Joseph is speaking (1) to Pharaoh's officers, (2) who were in his company (3) under guard in Joseph's master's house. The politically charged importance of the event is made clear to the reader, as no doubt it is to Joseph. In remarking to them about the sadness of their faces, Joseph uses an adjective different from the one *(za'af)* just used by the text. Joseph says *ra'*, a word whose primary meaning is "bad" or "evil," and when applied to a look on a face, is taken to mean "sad" or "unhappy." In this indirect way, Joseph may be hinting at the evil that one or both of the men may have committed, and which may be responsible for their "bad faces." In response, the men claim that their unhappiness is rather owed only to the lack of someone to interpret the dream (again, a singular dream) they have dreamed. Joseph seizes the opportunity.

And Joseph said unto them, "Do not interpretations belong to God [*or* gods: *'elohim*]? Tell it, please, to me." (40:8)

---

5. This is the first of several instances in which both the text and the characters in the story show ambiguity about "one" and "two." Two men (two) dream a dream (one), each his own dream (two) in a single night (one). Part of Joseph's power of dream interpretation, both here and with Pharaoh's dreams, lies in his ability to see that what appears to be two things is in fact one. This ability, as we shall see, is tied to a certain (Egyptian) approach to the question of the relation of "one" and "many," of "unity" and "variety," one of the deepest metaphysical questions. In his approach to Pharaoh's dreams, Joseph will collapse distinctions and assimilate variety into unity; likewise in his practice, he will assimilate into Egypt and adopt its ways. In both these ways, Joseph is turning his back on the culture that celebrates "distinction" and "separation," both in its understanding of the cosmos (see Chapter One) and in its cultural practices (see especially the so-called holiness code presented in the book of Leviticus, where making distinctions between the clean and the unclean lies at the heart of the pursuit of sanctification).

Joseph's comment is surely unusual. Many readers, taking for granted Joseph's attachment to the God of his fathers, assume that Joseph is here speaking as a pious man, giving credit to God for interpretive powers. But such an interpretation is problematic at best. It would make less than no sense to speak to high-ranking Egyptian officials about the God of Israel. And if Joseph means *'elohim* to refer to the divine in general, it is, to say the least, bold of him to claim that he can be the mouthpiece for a divinely sent interpretation. Joseph is never—not here, not anywhere—seen speaking to or even seeking out any being higher than human. Indeed, Joseph's remark, carefully considered, belies a failure to distinguish between himself and God: because only God interprets dreams, you must tell yours to *me*![6] As we shall see, Joseph has a self-interested and practical reason for wanting to hear their dreams, and a claim that he has divinelike powers of interpretation would increase the chances that they will tell him. Yet what he does with what he is told comes very close to playing God, deciding who shall live and who shall die.

With Joseph's encouraging prodding, the chief butler does not hesitate to relate his dream. His eagerness to do so we—and, no doubt, Joseph—must take as a sign of a clear conscience.

> "In my dream, behold, a vine was before me. And in the vine were three branches; and it was as though it budded, and her blossoms shot forth, and the clusters thereof brought forth ripe grapes. And Pharaoh's cup was in my hand; and I took the grapes, and pressed them into Pharaoh's cup, and I gave the cup into Pharaoh's hand." (40:9–11)

The butler dreams about himself confronted by a three-branched flowering and fruitful vine, which, in a sequence of highly compressed time, buds, blossoms, and brings forth clusters of ripe grapes. The butler, still or again in Pharaoh's service, knows immediately what to do: he presses fresh wine from the grapes into Pharaoh's cup, which he then succeeds in serving up to Pharaoh. The butler clearly remembers and revisits his active and faithful service to Pharaoh: Pharaoh's name he mentions, for emphasis, three times in one sentence (40:11).

Joseph, in responding, also mentions Pharaoh's name three times. But Joseph's most significant remark, and the key to the entire interpretation, concerns the meaning of the vine's three branches:

---

6. Such a claim, though unique among the Israelites, would not be unprecedented in the ancient Near East. In many societies, soothsayers and oracles both claim and were credited with the possession of such superhuman mantic powers. The willingness of the butler and the baker to respond to Joseph's demand presupposes that they were previously prepared to encounter men who claimed such god-like powers.

"This is the interpretation [solution] of it: the three branches are three days. Yet within three days shall Pharaoh lift up thine head, and restore thee unto thy place: and thou shalt deliver Pharaoh's cup into his hand, after the former manner when thou wast his butler. But remember me when it shall be well with thee, and shew kindness, please, unto me, and make mention of me unto Pharaoh, and bring me out of this house. For indeed I was stolen away out of the land of the Hebrews and here also have I done nothing that they should put me into the pit." (40:12–15)

The key to the entire interpretation—and this will be true of all of Joseph's successful dream interpretations—is Joseph's introduction of the idea of time and his treatment of static visible images as symbols of time: the three branches are three days.[7] The butler's vague awareness of the passage of time, reflected in the speeded-up blossoming and fructification of the grapevine and in his remembering his former successful service to Pharaoh, Joseph now brings to the surface and makes vividly explicit. Once this is clarified, the meaning of the rest of the dream is easy to grasp.

Joseph's "Wisdom": Prophecy, or Cunning?

What exactly do we think is Joseph's power of interpretation? Two possibilities suggest themselves. First, Joseph's talent for dream interpretation may represent a special kind of wisdom regarding time. Robert Sacks sees this as crucial, and not only for interpreting dreams:

The awareness of time is the crucial key, not only to this dream, but to all three dreams [the butler's, the baker's, and Pharaoh's (chapter 41)]. Apparently the difference between him who can and him who cannot interpret dreams depends to a large extent upon the interpreter's awareness of the importance of time, and hence, of remembering and forgetting.

The importance of time in interpretation is by no means limited to

---

7. The secret of interpreting or solving the code of Egyptian dreams, here and with Pharaoh, seems to be turning all numbers into units of time, a static and discrete multiplicity into a measured period of change. On the surface, the Egyptian dreams hide the passage of time and the fact of change; but Joseph puts time and change back into the picture. The significance of the Egyptian attitude toward change we shall consider shortly. It is perhaps noteworthy of a difference between Israel and Egypt that, in interpreting Joseph's dreams, his brothers and his father, Jacob, had construed numbered units to symbolize not time or change but family members and their interrelations, that is, not "physics and metaphysics" but "morals and politics." (Yuval Levin pointed me to this difference.)

Joseph's interpretation of the dreams. Time and memory have held the book [Genesis] together ever since the Flood. Only by remembering, that is by forgetting time [Sacks means defying time; forgetting its devouring ways], have we been able to understand the author's message by seeing the traditions and ways of peoples and places throughout their history. Joseph's way of interpretation has in effect served as a model for the interpretation of the book for a very long time.

Sacks sees in Joseph's way of revivifying time a model for revivifying the past, crucial for our sympathetic reading of the entire biblical narrative.

Sacks is surely correct to emphasize the importance of memory for reading the Bible and for the new way of life that it promotes. But living informed by memories of the past differs radically from living informed by divinations of the future. And in any case, the point about time goes much deeper. Attitudes toward time reflect even more fundamental ones, toward change.[8] Change, especially the change that is decay and death, is universally deeply troubling to human beings, both offensive to our attachment to life and perplexing to our understanding. Why do we have to grow old and die? How can a being or a soul be completely extinguished? Intellectually, human beings everywhere seek to explain movement and change in terms of something that does not change— whether it be indestructible ultimate particles of matter, or eternal forms, or laws of motion, or God. And in the conduct of their lives, human beings generally adopt one or another of two opposite attitudes toward change: they seek to deny or defy change, freezing time in a permanent presence; or conversely, they accept or embrace change, preserving time while partly overcoming its ravages through renewal and remembering. This difference, in fact, goes to the heart of the difference between Egypt and Israel.

The Children of Israel are, already at this point in our narrative, defined in part by remembrance of things past and in part by anticipation of things to come. They remember especially God's promise to and covenant with Abraham. They anticipate especially the fulfillment of God's promise and the obligation to perpetuate the memory of the covenant into future generations. Speaking more generally, we may say that the Children of Israel, by looking forward to perpetuate the merit and ways of the ancestors, choose to live with full awareness of time

8. In modern thought, time (along with space) is regarded as a primary category, a dimension in which change or motion occurs. But to the ancients, it is change or motion that is primary, with time being a derivative notion used to rationalize or measure the formlessness or irrationality of motion. The classical formulation of the relation between change and time was offered by Aristotle, who defined time as "the number of motion [or change] with respect to the before and the after" (*Physics* 219b).

and with full acceptance of change and unavoidable decay. The children of the new way are enjoined to embrace the temporality of human existence because of their attachment to the timelessness of God and the permanence of His promised care, which He works out in human affairs in the course of human time.

Not so in Egypt. As we will see more clearly as we proceed, Egypt, at least in its public and official teachings, is the place that seeks to abolish change and to make time stand still. To be sure, Egyptians have accurate measures of time and a precise calendar, but they use them to manage or to stay ahead of natural change—in the first instance, to predict and manage the flooding of the Nile. What the Egyptians seek is changelessness, agelessness, permanent presence, or eternal return and renewal. Whether one looks to the hieroglyph in which the mobile world is represented in static ideograms; or to the worship of the eternally circling but never-changing heavenly bodies or of the cyclically rising and ebbing river, with its life-giving overflows; or to the practices of denying aging through bodily adornment and defying death through mummification and preparation for reincarnation—everywhere one looks, one sees in Egypt the rejection of change and the denial of death.[9] Ancient Egypt is poles apart from ancient Israel.

Seen in this light, Joseph's interpretation of the static picture in the butler's dream may be taken as the importation of an alien (Hebraic) wisdom into the world of Egypt, exactly as Sacks has suggested. The butler, in typical Egyptian fashion, has represented moving time (three days) in immobile images (three branches), which Joseph, the Israelite outsider, is able to translate into the temporal truth. But there is another and opposite possibility.

As in many ancient societies, there is in Egypt a difference between exoteric and esoteric knowledge, between what is publicly taught and believed by the many and what is privately known to the few. The Egyptian elite—the priests, the intelligentsia, and the magicians—almost certainly knew the truth about the supremacy of change and motion, the truth that was publicly hidden by the official imagery of stasis and timelessness. Knowledge of change and time would then be the secret wisdom in Egypt, a wisdom in which Joseph shared. On this reading, Joseph's ability in dream interpretation shows him to be not so much a

---

9. The evidence for this proposition could be multiplied many times. To take only one more example: the Egyptians revered the scarab or dung beetle, and treated it as the symbol of immortal life. The dung beetle forms manure into a large ball (as big as an apple), with which it then buries itself in the earth. There it feeds on the dung ball and (we now know) lays its eggs. Wonder of wonders, new scarab life emerges from the dung! The Egyptians also gave this activity of "resurrection" a cosmological meaning: the dung ball represented the earth and the beetle represented the sun, ever renewing life out of the lifeless earth.

Hebrew outsider but an Egyptian sage, and moreover, a candidate for the highest and innermost circles of Egyptian elite society.[10]

But this attempt to decide whether Joseph's wisdom is Egyptian or Israelite may be off the mark, since it may not be wisdom at all. I am in fact inclined to a different and less high-flown account of Joseph's interpretive powers, in which Joseph's gift is not metaphysical and speculative wisdom, neither Hebrew nor Egyptian, but rather psychological and practical cunning. Joseph may not have been an astute reader of circumstances and their effect on the human mind when he boasted to his brothers and possibly provoked Potiphar's wife, but he certainly appears to have become so as the sharp-eyed overseer of the prison. Readers will soon learn from the text that the third day after the present episode will be Pharaoh's birthday, a day on which Pharaoh makes a feast for all his servants and bestows favors (40:20). Everyone in Egyptian officialdom would have known of the impending event, including Pharaoh's butler and baker, the captain of the guard, and of course, Joseph himself. Everyone would have felt the significance of this supremely important day in Egyptian society. For on this quintessentially Egyptian holiday (the only Egyptian holiday mentioned in the entire Bible),[11] Pharaoh celebrates both the day of his entry into life and his continuing vitality and unchanging hegemony, notwithstanding the rolling around of another year. Like pampered children in modern America who regard their own birthdays as the most important days of the year, Pharaoh rejoices in seeing himself still at the center of the world, incapable of imagining the world in his absence. All of Egypt stands ready to help him celebrate the "eternal" return of his birthday as a sign of his eternally renewable presence. All know that this is a day on which they can expect to have their merits rewarded and their petitions considered.

With the important event looming, both of Pharaoh's jailed servants would have had cause to anticipate it, and to rejoice in or fear the prospect of coming again into Pharaoh's presence. If a man were completely innocent of the alleged charges (say, of trying to poison Pharaoh), he might imagine or dream of his exoneration and his return to Pharaoh's service. If, on the other hand, he were guilty of the alleged offense, he might imagine or dream of his guilt and its possible detection and punishment. Under the pressure of such circumstances, the

10. This display of Egyptianlike capacity anticipates Joseph's ability to connect easily with Pharaoh. Pharaoh will immediately see that this Hebrew slave has the knowledge belonging only to the Egyptian elite.

11. As if to underscore the Egyptian focus on (mere) birth and (continued) life, the words for birthday, literally "the day of birth of" (*yom huledeth 'eth*), occur only once in the entire Hebrew Bible, in this present story: "the birthday of Pharaoh" (40:20). The birthday of no Israelite is mentioned, much less celebrated.

innocent and the guilty will dream different dreams or, perhaps, experience an identical dream of "three days" in utterly different ways, each according to his hope-filled or fear-driven interpretation. There is some reason to believe that precisely such psychic motions lie beneath the dreams dreamed by the butler and baker. And quite clearly, Joseph is on the spot to discover them and, moreover, *to report them to Pharaoh through his master, Potiphar.*

If we examine the situation in this light, the butler's dream appears as the dream of an innocent and loyal servant, unjustly accused of an offense against Pharaoh and eager to return to Pharaoh's service. Joseph recognizes the optimistic signs in the dream, and he predicts accordingly. What he does not tell the butler is that he, Joseph, will have something to do with the result, through the report he makes to his superior. Instead, he asks the butler to remember him when he is restored to Pharaoh's good graces, and to ask Pharaoh "to bring me out of this house." The reason he gives to justify his plea, Joseph calculates, ought to appeal to the butler: Like you, "I have done nothing that they should put me into the dungeon" (40:15). Speaking as one innocent man to another, Joseph asks the butler to reward his auspicious interpretation by arranging in turn for Joseph's elevation. Joseph's appeal to the butler's sense of gratitude we find touching, not least because of its naïveté: the butler, once freed and restored to his office, will have absolutely no incentive to do Joseph any favors. Once again, we see the human and political blindness of Joseph's vision.

THE BAKER'S DREAM: CONFESSIONS OF A GUILTY SOUL

The baker is a different case entirely. Unlike the butler, who promptly told his dream to Joseph when asked, the baker has no intention of speaking up until he hears Joseph's good news for the butler. Only for this reason does he then open up.

> When the chief baker *saw that the interpretation was good,* he said unto Joseph: "I also saw in my dream, and behold, three baskets of white bread were on my head; and in the uppermost basket there was of all manner of baked food for Pharaoh; and the birds did eat them out of the basket upon my head." (40:16–17; emphasis added)

The baker's dream, as reported, is very different from the butler's. The picture is much less sharp. There is not even a hint of time or growth. In contrast to the butler's pressing of the grapes into wine, there is here no baking of the bread; instead, in a parody of baking, the baker remembers three baskets rising in stacks on top of his head. He is frozen in his tracks, mentions Pharaoh's name but once, and never gets to serve Pharaoh. The bread in the uppermost basket, pre-pared for Pharaoh, is instead devoured by ominous birds, who, we sense, will soon be pecking at the baker's addled head. Taken as a projection of the baker's state of mind, the dream indicates both an incapacity for proper service and an unwillingness to return to Pharaoh's presence. A guilty and fearful mind has re-vealed itself to anyone who knows, as Joseph surely does, how the dreams one dreams reveal the secret thoughts and emotions of the dreamer. Joseph draws the appropriate conclusion and informs the baker:

> "This is the interpretation thereof: The three baskets are three days; within yet three days shall Pharaoh lift up thy head from off thee, and shall hang thee on a tree; and the birds shall eat thy flesh from off thee." (40:19)

Once again, the key to the dream is the interpretation of a static image as a symbol of time: three baskets stand for three days, the three days leading up to Pharaoh's birthday. Once again, there is the prophecy "Pharaoh shall lift up thy head," an idiomatic expression for personal elevation, but this time Joseph adds "from off thee," indicating that the lifting of the head in the baker's case will be literal, not metaphorical. What he does not tell the baker is that he, Joseph, has a further role to play in securing the prophesied outcome: Joseph will inform on the baker to Potiphar, who in turn will make report to Pharaoh.

Only now, as the story reaches its denouement, does the reader learn the im-portance of the "three days":

> And it happened on the third day—*which was Pharaoh's birthday*—that he made a feast unto all his servants; and he lifted up the head of the chief butler and the head of the chief baker among his servants. And he restored the chief butler back unto his butlership; and he gave the cup into Pharaoh's hand. But he hanged the chief baker, *as Joseph had interpreted to them.* (40:20–22; emphasis added)

It is traditional to read this passage as evidence of Joseph's powers of prophecy and clairvoyance; and no one can gainsay that interpretation. But our analysis suggests a less mysterious, more ordinary interpretation: the dreams of butler and baker revealed to Joseph the true culprit, and Joseph's talebearing all by it-self guaranteed the predicted results. This interpretation makes sense of one crucial fact: only now does Pharaoh mete out the punishment that the baker's crime would have deserved, because only now is it clear that the baker is truly guilty. His time in the prison house was not his punishment but rather, one might say, his trial. Only with the "confession" of his dream is the verdict rendered; only now can punishment be handed out. The only alternative to such a reading requires treating Pharaoh's differential treatment of the butler and the baker as an arbitrary expression of whim. But the Bible's opposition to things Egyptian hardly requires treating Pharaoh as a simply capricious ruler. On the contrary, it is crucial to the Bible's intent to allow Egypt and Pharaoh the highest possible dignity so that their ultimate defeat by the God of Israel will be a victory worth celebrating. Assuming, then, that Pharaoh knows what he is doing with the butler and the baker, we must conclude that Joseph is ultimately responsible for the fact that Pharaoh is properly informed.

But if Joseph was indeed counting on a suitable reward for his valuable intelligence work, he badly miscalculated. The butler, who—we know—in fact owes much to Joseph, proves forgetful. From his point of view, he owed his restoration to Pharaoh, not to Joseph. Besides, he quite naturally has no desire to remember his prison days, and once reinstated in his high position, he has nothing to gain by wasting his newly restored access to Pharaoh's ear in order to do a favor for an imprisoned Hebrew slave. Acting in his own interest, enjoying life in the present, the butler neglects to convey Joseph's request to Pharaoh: "But the chief butler did not remember Joseph, but forgot him" (40:23).[12] Joseph's good deed yielded him nothing. He would have to wait for another occasion to demonstrate his gifts, this time to Pharaoh himself. Learning from his mistaken trust in the butler's gratitude, next time Joseph will take matters into his own hands.

INTERPRETING THE ROYAL DREAM: JOSEPH PAINTS HIMSELF INTO THE PICTURE

Joseph does indeed get another chance, this time from Pharaoh himself. In a story every schoolchild once knew, Joseph successfully interprets Pharaoh's dreams and is rewarded by being made grand vizier of Egypt. In a twinkling, Joseph goes from the bottom to the top of Egyptian society, all as a result of his ability to interpret the royal dreams.

Readers who rejoice in Joseph's good fortune rarely bother to reflect on the remarkable features of the tale. How is it that Joseph succeeds where the Egyptian wise men fail? Why does Pharaoh accept Joseph's interpretation of his dreams? What does this episode tell us about the soul of Joseph—Israelite, or Egyptian?—and more important, about Egypt and nascent Israel? These questions guide our reading of the story.

---

12. One wonders whether the butler's failure to remember is meant to indicate not merely a personal but a cultural disposition toward time past, as well as toward favors bestowed.

Two years pass. Joseph remains imprisoned, with lots of time to think. No doubt he has thought long and hard about his folly in relying on the butler's gratitude. No doubt he wishes for another chance and considers carefully what he should do if he gets it. At last, fortune smiles one more time on Joseph.

One night Pharaoh has a disturbing dream. He dreamed that as he stood by the Nile, behold, seven fair to look at and fat-fleshed cows came up out of the river and grazed in the reed grass. Then came up seven foul to look at and lean-fleshed cows that stood by and then devoured the seven well-favored and fat cows. The nightmarish dream awakened Pharaoh, but he soon fell asleep only to dream a second time. This time, behold, seven ears of grain came up on a single stalk, fat and good. And behold, seven thin ears, blasted by the east wind, sprouted after them and swallowed up the fat and good ears. Once again, the dream awakened Pharaoh, and "behold, it was a dream" (41:7). Greatly agitated, Pharaoh summoned all the Egyptian magicians and wise men and "told them his dream [singular], but there was none that could interpret them [plural] unto Pharaoh" (41:8).

What is wrong with the Egyptian experts? And what is it that they cannot do? Are they incapable of offering *any* interpretation at all? That seems unlikely. Are they incapable of offering any interpretation that is acceptable or pleasing to Pharaoh? Or are they incapable of fitting the two dreams together into a coherent interpretation (Pharaoh had told his *one* dream; they could not interpret *them*)? Robert Sacks suggests that in contrast to Pharaoh, who vaguely saw the unity of the dream, the wise men and magicians, lacking the biblical notion of time, "considered them two different dreams because they were separated by time." Aaron Wildavsky, on the other hand, favors the view that the counselors feared telling Pharaoh bad news for which they could provide no remedy. Pharaoh surely must sense from his dreams a threat to himself or his kingdom, and he will not likely take kindly to an interpretation that does not show him how to avert it. Under these circumstances, a prudent courtier would very likely keep silent.

The butler, however, has a useful suggestion. He now remembers the dream interpretations offered to him and the baker by the Hebrew slave in prison, which interpretations were soon vindicated by subsequent events: "We dreamed a dream in one night, I and he; we dreamed each man according to the interpretation of his dream. . . . And he interpreted to us our dreams; to each man according to his dream did he interpret. And it came to pass, as he interpreted to us, so it was" (41:11–13). The butler suggests that the Hebrew slave is a seer or a prophet; moreover, he hints that he gives interpretations according to the dreamer's own interpretation. Joseph, the butler implies, can read dreamers as well as dreams, and clarify for them the true meaning of what is but vaguely on their minds. The butler has nothing to lose by this recollection: if it works, Pharaoh will be grateful to him; if it fails, only the Hebrew slave will lose out. Pharaoh sends immediately for Joseph.

> Then Pharaoh sent and called Joseph, and they brought him hastily out of the pit. And he shaved himself and changed his garments, and came before Pharaoh. (41:14)

The account contains echoes of previous episodes in Joseph's vexed career. The last time he was lifted out of a pit it was to be sold into slavery, and the last time he underwent a change of clothes it led to his being cast into this prison. But this time there is to be a reversal. He is to be lifted out of slavery and out of prison rags, to an audience with the mighty Pharaoh. Joseph is absolutely ready:

> While in prison, Joseph has had a long time to ponder the nature of dreams, to learn that the trick is to understand the character of the dreamer who speaks more truly of his hopes and fears while sleeping than he can bring himself to do while awake. . . . Joseph knows he needs to ingratiate himself with the Pharaoh . . . Joseph decides to give Pharaoh reason to believe there is an optimistic interpretation behind the pessimistic one, an interpretation that will enhance Pharaoh's power.

As a prelude to ingratiating himself with Pharaoh, Joseph understands he must transform his appearance, and so he does: Joseph shaves and changes his clothes. These changes are hardly trivial.

Change of clothing to improve one's appearance is, of course, entirely appropriate when one is called into the royal presence. But change of clothing also represents change of custom. Joseph not only adopts Egyptian dress. He also adopts the peculiarly Egyptian practice of shaving. The Egyptians alone among the peoples of the ancient Near East shaved their faces and also their heads, and Joseph here for the first time acquires a fully Egyptian appearance. Is he thus trying to hide his Hebrew identity, or is he rather revealing his true, "Egyptian" nature? One cannot tell.

Shaving is, in fact, a wonderful instance and image of the problem of concealing and revealing. On the one hand, the face emerges in full view from beneath the mask of hair. On the other hand, the cleanly shaven face and head hides all signs of growth, change, and senescence. No shaggy outlines or blemishes mar the perfectly smooth look. What appears to be an unveiling is actually also a disguise, a veiling of age and disorder and, to some extent, individuation. Shaving is a perfect emblem of the Egyptian penchant to deny change and to conquer decay by human effort, the bringing of self-ordering to unruly nature. By his own hand, Joseph makes himself into a youth again, manifesting both in his deed and in his appearance the core of what is Egyptian.[13]

Pharaoh now addresses the newly attired and cleanly shaven young man:

> "I have dreamed a dream [*chalom chalamti*] and there is none that can interpret it; and I have heard say of thee that when thou hearest a dream thou canst interpret it." And Joseph answered Pharaoh, saying, "Apart from me[14] [*or* it is not in me: *bil'aday*], [only] God [*or* gods: *'elohim*] shall give Pharaoh an answer of peace [*or* wholeness: *shalom*]. (41:15–16)

Joseph's answer can be heard in at least two ways. The more usual interpretation has Joseph saying, "Not I, but God (or gods) will do the interpreting." But his words can also mean, "If you don't rely on me, only God can help you." In either case, Joseph is again confidently aligning himself with divine activity, whether as vessel or as imitator. Pharaoh, encouraged by Joseph's confidence, repeats his dream, giving Joseph a slightly fuller account, emphasizing the connection of the dream of the cows to the fate of the land of Egypt ("such as I never saw in all the land of Egypt for badness" [41:19]) and remarking that the seven lean cows did not grow fatter for their eating (41:21).

Joseph, replying immediately, is quick with his interpretation. It is as if he had had it on the tip of his tongue even before Pharaoh spoke:

> And Joseph said unto Pharaoh: "The dream of Pharaoh is one; and what God is about to do He hath decreed unto Pharaoh. The seven good cows are seven years and the seven good ears are seven years: the dream is one. And the seven lean and ugly cows that came up after them are seven years, and also the seven empty ears blasted with the east wind: they shall be seven years of famine. That is the thing which I spoke unto Pharaoh: that which God is about to do, He has shown unto Pharaoh. Behold, seven

---

13. The Egyptian penchant for shaving is commented on several times by Herodotus in his *History*, beginning in the section where he points out that the Egyptians have for the most part made their habits and customs the exact opposite of other peoples'. The Egyptians shave their faces and their heads, except during periods of mourning, when they let their hair grow. The priests are said to shave all their bodies every other day, for reason of cleanliness. (They also practice male circumcision for the same reason.) The Egyptians are also scrupulously careful about hair and other "blemishes" on sacrificial animals; for example, if they find a single black hair on a bull, they regard it as impure.

14. I follow Robert Sacks's lead in opting to translate *bil'aday* as "apart from me." When the same word appears later in this episode, it is translated "*without thee* shall no man. . . ." (41:44).

years are coming of great plenty throughout all the land of Egypt. Then there shall arise after them seven years of famine; all the plenty shall be forgotten in the land of Egypt; and the famine shall consume the land. And the plenty shall not be known in the land by reason of the famine that followeth; for it shall be very grievous. And as for repeating the dream twice to Pharaoh, it is because the thing is established by God, and God will shortly bring it to pass." (41:25–32)

The key to Joseph's interpretation is, once again, his ability to recognize, first, that the two dreams are in fact but one, and, second and more important, that the seven cows and seven ears are static images of dynamic time. Going beneath the visible surface, Joseph assimilates variety into unity and sees change in stasis. Joseph not only interprets the dream for Pharaoh, but he also gives him (twice) the principles of interpretation: the two dreams are one (a statement uttered twice); the one dream is twice given because the future events it announces are divinely determined and imminent. Joseph finishes by twice invoking the divine, using the generic term *'elohim,* "god" or "gods," that would be recognizable to an Egyptian monarch. Joseph continues to offer himself as the one man around who knows what God (or gods) is (are) up to and how He (they) works (work).

We do not know how Pharaoh receives the bad news—or Joseph's claim to divine knowledge—largely *because Joseph does not pause to let him answer.* Joseph has learned from past experience that he dare not speak painful truth to power unless he offers power some advantage arising out of the predicted troubles. With the double mention of God's plan still hanging over the conversation, and barely catching his breath, Joseph rushes ahead to tell Pharaoh what to do. Joseph shifts seamlessly from the mode of interpretation to the mode of prescription:

"Now, therefore, let Pharaoh look out a man discreet and wise, and set him over the land of Egypt. Let Pharaoh do this, and let him appoint officers over the land and muster [*himesh*] [15] the land of Egypt in the seven plenteous years. And let them gather all the food of these good years that come, and lay up grain under Pharaoh's hand for food in the cities, and let them

---

15. I follow Robert Alter's translation. Alter comments: "The meaning of the verb *himesh* is disputed. It could be derived from *hamesh,* "five," and thus refer to a scheme of dividing the land into fifths or perhaps taking a levy of 20 percent from the crops of the good years. . . . But the same root is also used for the arming or deployment of troops, and the idea here may be that Joseph is putting the whole country on a quasimilitary footing in preparation for the extended famine."

guard it, and the food shall be for a store to the land against the seven years of famine, which shall be in the land of Egypt; that the land perish not through the famine." (41:33–36)

Pharaoh had sought only an interpretation, but Joseph, uninvited, goes on to give Pharaoh advice. Joseph risks being found presumptuous, but he has read the situation well. He has discerned that Pharaoh is less interested in the meaning of the dream than in its implications for his reign and power. And the plan Joseph proposes is music to Pharaoh's ears: a prime minister, loyal only to him, backed by an army of bureaucrats, will centralize control over the entire land and its food supply. A silent implication is surely not lost on Pharaoh: during the years of famine, the central administration will use the dispersal of food to further augment and consolidate Pharaoh's power, weakening all possible rivals among the Egyptian nobility and making the people entirely dependent on Pharaoh's rule and deed.

PHARAOH GETS THE MESSAGE:
JOSEPH BECOMES PRIME MINISTER

Before hearing Pharaoh's reply, let us pause to ask what we ourselves would make of Joseph's speech, were we in attendance or in Pharaoh's place. Do we, without the benefit of hindsight, accept this Hebrew slave's interpretation of Pharaoh's dream? Do we really think Joseph is truly a diviner, with, as he implies, his own pipeline to God's plans? Or is he a clever opportunist, who invents a neat and plausible interpretation—not the only reasonable one, by any means? Could it be true both that Joseph invents the interpretation and, at that same time, that God is indeed behind Pharaoh's dream and Joseph's reading of it? Or is what most impresses us not the interpretation but Joseph's plan of action and his unwillingness to let God's alleged plan be the cause of Egyptian ruin? For Joseph's plan of action contains not even a whiff of piety. On the contrary, he proposes that human beings must act so as to counter the deeds of the divine: "Here is what the gods will do, so this is what we must do in response." Joseph never considers the possibility that there might be a reason why God is sending Egypt a famine or that Egypt might need to reform its ways; Joseph simply suggests an administrative-technical remedy for the fated disaster.[16] How will Pharaoh react to Joseph's pseudo-pious boldness?

Imagine the scene. Everyone in the room is holding his breath, waiting for Pharaoh's reaction to Joseph's speech. The wise men who had failed to inter-

---

16. I owe these last observations to Yuval Levin.

pret—or refused to give bad news—are on edge, on the one hand nervous about a possible royal explosion over bad news, on the other hand worried about being bested by this Hebrew upstart. The silence is deafening. Then Pharaoh lets out a hearty laugh and the whole room relaxes: "And the thing was good in the eyes of Pharaoh and in the eyes of all his servants" (41:38). What has happened?

We should assume that Pharaoh is no fool, that he is a shrewd and able ruler, unlikely to be duped by wishful thinking. Why, then, is Pharaoh pleased? He is delighted not with the prophecy, but with the plan. Joseph, who evinces the sagacity of the elite and who speaks with a god-like assurance, has provided Pharaoh with a defensible and justifiable plan to consolidate his power and to appear as the savior of his people. A divinely sent evil requires drastic measures to avert it; with Joseph's sage advice, Pharaoh will prove himself able to reverse and overcome the fate that, allegedly, the gods had in store for him and his reign. He will succeed in the Egyptian aspiration to conquer fortune and to make time stand still. Moreover, the forecast of disaster will provide the opportunity for Pharaoh to display and acquire more god-like powers, and the plan shows him how to go about it, and most important, who can get it done for him.

Just as Joseph has read Pharaoh's dream as expressing the soul of the royal dreamer, so Pharaoh reads in Joseph's answer the soul of an administrator of genius. Pharaoh understands immediately also Joseph's ambition: his suggestion "Let Pharaoh appoint" comes with an obvious hint regarding who should be appointed. In their brief exchange, Pharaoh and Joseph have successfully communicated to each other their mutual interests and their shared cast of mind. Now Pharaoh has only to maneuver past his court to put Joseph in charge. Just as Joseph had publicly appealed to the divine as the source of his own creative interpretation, so now Pharaoh uses a public appeal to the divine to justify elevating this Hebrew slave above all his Egyptian servants and courtiers:

> And Pharaoh said unto his servants: "Can we find such a one as this, a man in whom the spirit of God [*ruach 'elohim*] [17] is?" And Pharaoh said unto Joseph, "Forasmuch as God hath shown thee all this, there is none so discreet and wise as thou. Thou shalt be over my house, and to thy mouth all

---

17. The same phrase was last used in Genesis 1, to describe the Divine Breath that was hovering over the formless watery deep, just before God began His speech and deed of creation through separation. Although Pharaoh did not have the biblical reader's experience of the creation story, the text, by using this echo, has Pharaoh treating Joseph as a stand-in for God, the one capable of bringing human order to nature's chaos. But where God produced order by introducing separations, Joseph will do so by consolidation, aggregating all distinct human holdings and assimilating them under the supreme power of Pharaoh.

my people shall yield;[18] only in the throne will I be greater than thou."
(41:38–40)

Pharaoh first informs his followers that Joseph is a singularly gifted man and,
by obvious implication, clearly their superior: he alone has the godly spirit to see
through human dreams to the divinely ordained future. Such powers ought to
qualify Joseph to be made chief of dream interpreters. But the position to which
Pharaoh elevates Joseph is more exalted and practical: it requires administrative
shrewdness and toughness, not to say ruthlessness, even more than clairvoyance,
and a willingness single-mindedly to serve his king. It requires the know-how
and the tenacity to make the secret wishes behind dreams come true. Pharaoh
will rule ("the throne"), but Joseph's word shall govern the conduct of all
Pharaoh's people. Pharaoh appears to have discerned in Joseph's self-promoting
proposal the soul of the young lad who long ago dreamed that everyone around
him would pay him homage as the supreme ruler: "You will be my equal," says
Pharaoh, "save only for the throne."

Whether because he is stunned or coolly collected, Joseph greets Pharaoh's
proposition with utter silence. Pharaoh must continue in order to prove his new
resolve, this time with deed as well as with speech:

> And Pharaoh said unto Joseph, "Look here, I have set thee over the whole
> land of Egypt!" And Pharaoh took off his signet ring from his hand and
> put it upon Joseph's hand, and arrayed him in garments of fine linen, and
> put the gold collar about his neck. And he made him to ride in the second
> chariot which he had; and they cried before him: "*Abrekh*" [meaning un-
> known: perhaps something like "Make way"]. And Pharaoh said unto
> Joseph, "I am Pharaoh, and without thee shall no man lift up his hand or
> his foot in all the land of Egypt." (41:41–44)

Pharaoh makes clear that he means for Joseph to hold sway in Egypt, second
only to himself, and he proves it by providing Joseph with all the accouterments
of command. Invested with the king's seal, bedecked in ceremonial dress and
adorned with golden mantle of office, and riding in the royal chariot, Joseph, the
new prime minister, goes as a virtual god before the adoring people, bearing
supreme power to direct every detail of their lives ("No man shall lift up his
hand or his foot"). Fulfilling at last his adolescent ("Egyptian") dream to become "the chief of sheaves," Joseph has made it to the top—or rather, to be pre-

---

18. The phrase here translated "To thy mouth all my people shall yield," taken literally, means, "To
thy mouth all my people shall *kiss*." The image is of Joseph as the perfect beloved, to whom everyone
turns in homage.

cise, *almost* to the top. Risen from rags to riches, from imprisonment to Egyptian high authority, Joseph is now prime minister, but a prime minister who ministers to and administers for Pharaoh ("I am Pharaoh").

JOSEPH THE EGYPTIAN: THE DREAMER COMES "HOME"

Joseph's Egyptianization is immediately completed by a renaming and an arranged marriage, both directly provided by Pharaoh himself.

> And Pharaoh called Joseph's name Zaphenath-paneah; and he gave him to wife Asenath, the daughter of Poti-phera, priest of On. And Joseph went out over the land of Egypt. And Joseph was thirty years old when he stood before Pharaoh, king of Egypt. (41:45–46)

Joseph's new Egyptian name may mean "God speaks, he lives" or "revealer of hidden things" or perhaps even more majestically, "the creator or sustainer of life." [19] His wife's name, Egyptian in origin, means "she who belongs to [the goddess] Neith." Her father, Poti-phera ("he whom Re has given"), is priest (the greatest of seers) of the sun god Re, worshiped in Heliopolis ("the city of the sun"; also known as On, "a column," the city marked by columns and colonnades, almost certainly laid out in relation to the changing motions of the sun through the zodiac). Joseph, the son of Israel, renamed (perhaps) as sustainer of life and tied through marriage to the sun god and its worship in the cosmos-measuring city, reaches the zenith of human possibility in the world's exemplary civilization. Whereas the wife of Potiphar got Joseph tossed into prison, the daughter of Poti-phera gets Joseph raised to full Egyptianization. Amidst all these goings on, Joseph is not heard to say a word, not about his elevation to prime minister, not even about his marriage. [20] Yet although on the outside self-contained and imperturbable, Joseph must inwardly harbor a sense of fulfillment. At long last, mastery is his.

Joseph now goes into action, for there is much work to be done. For as Aaron Wildavsky remarks,

> A dream together with its interpretation is only a prediction, a potential but not yet an actual event. Its realization depends in part . . . on the ac-

---

19. Depending upon whether the name is regarded as Hebrew or Egyptian and upon whether or not one adopts the Septuagint transcription.

20. Indeed, Joseph takes no initiative in this marriage. In this most important matter, he shows no signs of eros, unlike his father. Nor, as observed above, had he indicated any with Mrs. Potiphar. Joseph is more a beloved, less a lover—just like his beautiful mother, Rachel.

tions of the dreamer. But individuals do not operate alone; they are enmeshed in webs only very partially of their own making . . . [W]hat other people do about your dreams or in response to them is part of their efficacy.

Joseph now sets about the task of realizing Pharaoh's dream by implementing the plan he proposed to Pharaoh.

Joseph travels throughout the land of Egypt, and during the seven years of plenty, he "gathered up *all* the food of the seven years that were in the land of Egypt and laid up the food *in the cities*" (41:48; emphasis added). According to the text, Joseph does not take up merely the surplus grain; he takes it all. And by storing it in the cities, he makes the countryside dependent on the city, a crucial change that prepares the way for the administrative transformation of the land of Egypt that is to follow. We are even invited to wonder whether this excessive gathering and storage of grain—at the expense of saving enough for replanting—might itself have contributed to (not to say caused) the famine in the years that followed.

But whatever the consequences for others, Joseph, the first economist, makes a great deal out of a bad dream:

> And Joseph laid up grain *as the sand of the sea,* very much, until they left off numbering; for it was without number. (41:49; emphasis added)

Joseph's (and Pharaoh's) business is booming. But the text provides the careful reader with a small clue of impending trouble. The image for "countlessness," sand of the sea, had been used twice before in Genesis, both times to indicate the future plenitude of the children of the covenant: once in God's blessing to Abraham after the binding of Isaac (22:17), once in Jacob's prayer to God before his encounter with Esau (32:13). Here, in contrast, innumerability goes with collected grain, not offspring. The seeds of grain are being hoarded; progeny and the fruitfulness of Israel are being ignored. Joseph is on the brink of falling outside the covenant.

As if reading the reader's mind, the text immediately turns, in the next verses, to the matter of Joseph's "seed":

> And unto Joseph were born two sons before the year of famine came, whom Asenath, the daughter of Poti-phera, priest of On, bore unto him. And Joseph called the name of the firstborn Manasseh [*menasheh:* he who causes to forget]: "for God hath made me forget all my toil, and all my father's house." And the name of the second called he Ephraim [from a

root meaning "fertile land"]: "for God hath made me fruitful in the land of my affliction." (41:50–52)

At last, we hear Joseph speak. What he says betrays his predicament. Joseph's naming of his sons shows Joseph's attempt to celebrate his new beginning. As the text stresses the Egyptian character of his wife, so too Joseph is thinking like an Egyptian. He seeks to close off the past, to forget his hardships and his paternal home, and he focuses only on his new and fruitful life in Egypt.[21] Yet even as he tries to forget, he cannot do so. By naming one son "forgetting," he will always have before him a reminder of that which he sought to put out of mind. Joseph cannot, even if he wishes it, escape his Israelite past and his Hebrew roots.[22] Soon enough he will be forced to remember "all my father's house" and all his troubles there.

The seven years of plenty come to an end. The predicted famine arrives. All the surrounding lands are afflicted as well, but in Egypt there is bread. And when the famished people cried to Pharaoh for bread, he told all the Egyptians, "Go unto Joseph; what he saith to you, do" (41:55). The famine, indeed, was

> over all the face of the earth; and Joseph opened all [the storehouses] and sold unto the Egyptians; and the famine was sore in the land of Egypt. And all lands came into Egypt to buy grain, because the famine was sore in all the earth. (41:56–57)

A global catastrophe and only one source of hope: Joseph and his stuffed granaries. Joseph the Egyptian is in the position of savior of life on earth, but he will not dispense his bounty freely. Selling with prices no doubt shaped by the facts of monopoly and extreme scarcity, Joseph is saving life by making Pharaoh rich and, soon, all-powerful. While we may applaud Joseph's forethought, we are rightly made uneasy by this man who profits from exercising his god-like power over life and death.

As we see in the immediate sequel, it is a power Joseph rather enjoys exercising. He is the center of the world stage. He alone has the authority and the power to command events. All peoples from all lands come and do as he directs. Once Joseph had dreamt of precisely such mastery. Now he no longer has need for cheering dreams. Joseph no doubt agrees with Winston Churchill, who, after

---

21. Whether the fruitfulness he celebrates is his progeny or his stored grain or both we cannot tell.

22. The text underscores this point. The names Joseph gives his sons are *Hebrew* names, and Joseph's explanation of the names shows that he derived them from the meaning of Hebrew roots. Later, these two sons will be reclaimed and adopted by Jacob as full members of the household of Israel.

years in the political wilderness, finally gained the authority to direct events during a still greater world crisis: "Facts are better than dreams." But whereas
Churchill used his political authority to preserve human freedom against the
threat of foulest tyranny, Joseph uses his administrative authority to advance the
despotic power of his master. Joseph's rise to full Egyptian power is, to say the
least, highly problematic, both in itself and in its implications for the future of
the Israelite way.

CHAPTER NINETEEN

JOSEPH AND HIS BROTHERS:
ESTRANGEMENT AND RECOGNITION

*I*n the forty-second chapter of Genesis, the scene of the story shifts back from Joseph, in Egypt, to his father, Jacob, and his brothers, in Canaan. When we last looked in on the family, we saw a scene of violence, loss, and despair. The sons of Jacob, having been united in collective action to exact revenge for Dinah, have fractured the family unity by a near-fratricidal assault on the "best and the brightest," Joseph the man of dreams. Unbeknownst to the brothers, Joseph has been stolen away and sold into Egypt; Jacob, believing he is dead—killed by a "wild beast"—descends into inconsolable grief. Judah, the most prudent of the brothers, leaves the family and strikes out on his own, only to suffer the loss of a wife and two sons and to fail in his duty to his daughter-in-law, Tamar.

While Jacob and his family suffer in and on account of his absence, Joseph is doing splendidly. His plan to deal with the famine has made him the "chief of sheaves" in Egypt. Bedecked in Egyptian garb and clean-shaven, Joseph at last comes into his own, not as a ruler in Israel but as an Egyptian demigod. His original—and as it were Egyptian—dreams of mastery have been realized, through his ability to interpret and carry out the dreams of the Egyptian sovereign. But the very same famine that elevated Joseph in Egypt threatens to destroy his family in Canaan, driving them toward a new encounter with Joseph, this time on Egyptian soil.

What will be the result of their meeting? More generally, what will happen when Israel meets Egypt? Can survival and prosperity be achieved without a loss of morality or piety? Will the Children of Israel remain true to the covenant, or will they, like Joseph, be swallowed up in Egyptian ways? And what about the questions of brotherhood and family leadership: can the family survive intact and with a reconciliation of Joseph and his brothers? If so, will the reconciliation be on Egyptian, or Israelite, terms? Who will now emerge as the leader of this family? Will it be Joseph the god-like administrator, or will some statesmanlike leader emerge from among the other brothers? These questions all get explored in the saga of Joseph and his brothers, reunited this time in Egypt.

ACT I: RECOGNITION AND ESTRANGEMENT

The Egyptian story of Joseph and his brothers is a drama in three acts. By and large, Joseph is the producer and director of the drama, as well as its leading actor. But fortune—or providence—also shares the credits. Indeed, the first act is precipitated by the famine, when Jacob sends his sons to Egypt in search of food:

> "Why do ye look upon one another? . . . Behold, I have heard that there is grain in Egypt. Get you down thither and buy for us from thence; that we live, and not die." (42:1–2)

The trip Jacob's sons now take will produce the first full encounter of Israel and Egypt. Father Abraham had sojourned in Egypt during a famine, but before he entered into the covenant with God (12:10 ff.). Famine had also started Isaac in the direction of Egypt, but God intervened to arrest his journey in Gerar (26:1–2). Now Jacob unwittingly starts the process that will bring him and his people into Egypt—and as a separate people—for four hundred years. Traveling to Egypt are "Joseph's ten brethren" (42:3); in this quiet and unobtrusive way, the text informs us that Judah has returned to the family. But Benjamin, "Joseph's [full] brother," Jacob *sent not with his brethren,* for he said, 'Lest peradventure harm befall him' " (42:4; emphasis added). Jacob, believing that Joseph was probably murdered by his other sons, does not dare risk sending "Joseph's brother" with them, as he had once *sent* Joseph to them at Shechem (37:14)— this despite the fact that Benjamin is already an adult.[1] While dangers lurk on the road, Jacob regards his sons as at least equally dangerous.

The brothers arrive in Egypt amongst a great throng of people, all seeking relief from the famine, all seeking to buy grain. Necessarily, they must come before Joseph, the master of the land, the one who sold to all the people of the land:

> And Joseph's brethren came and bowed down to him with their faces to the earth. And Joseph saw his brethren and *recognized* them [*vayakirem*] but he *made himself strange* [*vayithnaker*] unto them, and spoke roughly with them, and he said unto them, "Whence come you?" And they said, "From the land of Canaan, to buy food." (42:6–7; emphasis added)

---

1. Joseph is now roughly thirty-eight or thirty-nine years old (he was thirty when Pharaoh elevated him, and since then, the seven fertile years and one or more famine years have passed); he has been in Egypt since he was seventeen, and when he left, Benjamin was already alive. In fact, Benjamin is most likely only six or seven years younger than Joseph; he was born on the road back from Paddan-aram (35:16–18); Joseph was born in the fourteenth year of Jacob's service to Laban (30:25–26); Jacob left after serving twenty years (31:41).

As Joseph looks out over the crowd of suppliants bowing before him, he picks out his brethren with no difficulty. But their arrival, in fact, presents him with a difficulty. Subtle wordplay in the Hebrew text calls attention to the problem Joseph now faces: the verbs "he *recognized*" and "he *made himself strange*" come from the same root, *nakhar* (the latter being a reflexive form). Why, in Joseph's case, does recognition—to again make familiar—give rise to estrangement? It did not do so in Judah's case: when Judah was compelled by Tamar to recognize (*haker; yoker;* 39:25–26) his staff and signet, he understood through them the deeper truth about family life and his ties to his brothers. Robert Sacks draws attention to the contrast:

> Joseph is now in somewhat the same position in which Judah had been in Chapter Thirty-eight. He has found a new life for himself and has no intention of returning to his brothers. Unlike Judah, his recognition will not cause him to return immediately. In his case, relations will become much more complicated.

Joseph's emotions on recognizing his brothers are, almost certainly, already quite complicated. He may be glad to see them, yet angry and eager for revenge ("He spoke roughly with them"). He may be sad to see them brought low, yet vindicated in seeing them bow before him (compare his adolescent dreams). He may be delighted by the opportunity to make them atone for their sin, yet also guilty for his part in provoking their anger. He may be eager to toy with them, but confused about how to do so. And he may be moved by some residuum of family feeling, yet afraid of the implications of the fact that he is their relation. This last point deserves emphasis. For in recognizing *his brethren*, Joseph also recognizes *himself* as *their* brother, as a man who once belonged—and still somehow belongs—to a different world, with different gods and different ways, from the world of Egypt into which he has so successfully been assimilated. Can he afford to have them expose him as a Hebrew,[2] now that he has become Henry Kissinger? The arrival of the brothers "from the old country" could jeopardize everything he has struggled to achieve. Joseph's question—"Whence came you?"—no doubt springs from his own turmoil about his identity; it is designed in part to prick their self-awareness and to give him room to maneuver.

---

2. Pharaoh, as well as the others with whom Joseph was early in contact in Egypt, knew him to be a Hebrew. But it was an identity Joseph had deliberately shed, in physical appearance, family life, and above all, national position. He would understandably not want to be reminded—and have others be reminded or learn for the first time—that he belongs to a foreign, uncivilized people, and he certainly would not want his loyalty to Egypt and her ways put into doubt.

> And Joseph recognized [*vayaker*] his brethren but they did not recognize him. And Joseph remembered the dreams that he had dreamed about them, and said unto them, "Ye are spies; to see the nakedness of the land ye are come." (42:8–9)

Recalling his dreams aggravates both Joseph's indignation and his fears. He recalls their hate-filled reaction to his youthful dreams of superiority and is reminded of the reason for his enduring indignation and resentment. At the same time, he recalls how in response they unmasked his pretensions and, quite literally, uncovered his nakedness by stripping him of his ornamented tunic. Both passions gain expression in his speech to his brethren. On the one hand, by accusing them of being spies, Joseph gains control of the situation, putting the brothers on the defensive and thereby compelling them to assert their innocence of the charges. In the act of doing so, they will be led to recall those deeds of which they are in fact guilty and to reenact, in memory, their crime against him. On the other hand, Joseph's remark about "seeing the nakedness of the land" surely reflects his own fear of exposure: have they perhaps come in order to reveal my origins? Will they expose the Hebrew who is hidden beneath this fancy Egyptian dress?[3] Will my whole charade as Egyptian viceroy come to an end? It would be very much in keeping with Joseph's penchant for grandiosity that he should conflate his own nakedness with Egypt's ("To see the nakedness *of the land* ye are come").

The brothers quickly deny the spying charge, insisting again that they are come to buy food: "We are *all* one man's sons: we are honest; thy servants are not spies" (42:11; emphasis added). Their rebuttal assumes that no head of a family would hazard the family's entire future by sending *all* his sons together on a spying expedition. But Joseph knows that, though they may all be sons of one man, they are not *all* of that man's sons. Having gotten them on the subject of family, he presses his case and repeats the charge: "Nay, but to see the nakedness of the land ye are come" (42:12). Their denial having been rejected, the brothers are at once zealous to prove their honesty, yet guiltily aware that they had not spoken

---

3. Although we were not told that Jacob circumcised his sons, we may assume that he did so. Joseph's nakedness might, quite literally, expose him as an outsider. As noted above, Pharaoh and probably also the palace insiders remember that Joseph was, to begin with, a Hebrew slave before he rose to power. There is even some textual evidence that some of the Egyptians have not forgotten Joseph's Hebrew ethnicity (see 43:32, a passage we shall discuss later). But Joseph has not only willingly assimilated. As far as he knows, his public influence depends absolutely on his having put his Hebrew past behind him. When a man is trying to pass, even when everyone knows the truth about his "unsavory" origins, no one wants attention called to them.

the whole truth about their family. They now feel compelled to say more than they did before and to elaborate their familial defense:

"We thy servants are twelve brethren, the sons of one man in the land of Canaan; and, behold, the youngest is this day with our father, and one is not [or no more]." (42:13)

In this second reply, the brothers add significant details: they give their number, identify their father's home, mention the existence of a missing younger brother, specify that he is alive and well and living with their still-living father, and reveal that they believe that their other absent brother—namely, Joseph—is dead. Why the brothers are now reminded of Joseph is unclear. The need to speak truthfully to Joseph may, by itself, stir their memory, especially when it is a question of guilt or innocence that they are forced to consider. Sacks suggests that it may have been his voice that, subconsciously, awakened their memory of him. Be that as it may, their answer, should he believe it to be truthful, ought to be multiply reassuring to Joseph, not only about the welfare of Benjamin but also about the brothers' intentions toward himself: they could not have come to expose him, for they believe he is dead.

But it seems that Joseph does not believe them, and their reference to "the one who is not"—namely, himself—stirs him up even more. It is precisely their previous efforts to unmask him and to make him "no more" that leads Joseph to worry that they are come again to do him in: to expose him, to depose him, perhaps even to kill him. Joseph continues his charge, now focusing on the putative "evidence" of the two missing brothers, beginning with a rejoinder that refers to their remarks about him:

And Joseph said unto them, "He [hu'] is it that I spoke unto you,[4] saying, 'Ye are spies.' Hereby ye shall be proved, *by the life of Pharaoh*: ye shall not go forward hence unless your youngest brother come hither. Send one of you, and let him fetch your brother; and ye shall be bound that your words may be proved, whether there be truth in you; or else, *by the life of Pharaoh*, surely ye are spies. And he put them in all together into ward for three days. (42:14–17; emphasis added)

4. Most translators translate the beginning of Joseph's speech as "*That* is it that I spoke unto you," using the vaguer "that" instead of "he" to translate the third person male pronoun, *hu'*. But Joseph's disbelieving reaction to the brothers' claims are mainly based on what they have just said about *him* and, even more, on what they *omitted* to say about what *they did to him*. Says Joseph, "He's the one I am talking about. It's because of him that I say you are spies." (I owe this observation to Yuval Levin.)

It is hard to tell exactly what Joseph is up to. Clearly, he intends to test his brothers, but about what? On the surface, he claims to be testing the truthfulness of their account: that they are brothers and that there is yet one more at home. Since this is their sole defense against the charges of espionage, he asks them to prove it. But Joseph may also be seeking to test whether the brothers can be trusted with the life of Benjamin and, also, whether Jacob will—despite (or because of?) what happened to him—send Benjamin out alone with these murderous fellows. The test would be risky, but Joseph, it seems, may want to have answered his own questions about his brothers and (perhaps especially) his father.

The importance Joseph attaches to his demand he underlines by twice swearing an oath, "by the life of Pharaoh": this is the only place in the entire text where Joseph swears an oath or invokes a higher power. To be sure, he may be swearing by Pharaoh in order to frighten the brothers into compliance; but he is also, in this first and disturbing encounter with his family, emphatically affirming his new Egyptianized identity. What we do not know is *why* Joseph is interested in going through with the test. Is he interested mainly in punishing them? In humiliating them? In exercising his authority and playing with them? In searching their hearts for signs of remorse and reform, perhaps in the hope of possible reconciliation? In the hope of stealing Benjamin away from his father? With a complicated and cagey fellow like Joseph, anything and everything is possible.

During their three days in ward, the brothers are filled with doubt and foreboding. Joseph, too, undergoes a change of heart: the change of plans suggests that his original reaction may have reflected emotional turmoil rather than shrewd judgment. Instead of keeping all and sending one, he decides to keep only one and send all the rest.

> And Joseph said to them on the third day, "This do and live; for I fear God ['*eth-ha'elohim 'ani yare'*]: if ye be upright men, let one of your brethren be bound in your guardhouse; but go ye, carry grain for the famine of your houses. And bring your youngest brother unto me; so shall your words be verified, and ye shall not die." And they did so. (42:18–20)

By declaring his fear of God—Joseph is almost surely not referring to the God of his ancestors; he is, as we learn in a moment, speaking to them in Egyptian and using a translator—Joseph indicates that he is moved by the demand not to abuse strangers, at least more than is absolutely necessary. He claims to be moved by a concern for the starving family members back home: perhaps only for Benjamin, perhaps also for Jacob, perhaps for the innocent women and children. Grain sent with a caravan of nine will feed more people than grain sent with only one brother. In addition, if Joseph is testing his brothers to see if they have changed since dry-gulching him, then a proper test demands that he replicate the circumstances. Testing whether one brother would sacrifice *everyone* isn't really the same as testing whether nine brothers would—as they did before—sacrifice one.[5]

Yet Joseph's seeming concern for strangers is balanced—indeed, overshadowed—by an explicit threat of death should they fail to deliver the evidence of their missing brother, Benjamin. The impression grows that possession of Benjamin may be the true goal of the entire charade. By holding one of their number prisoner, Joseph is confident that the brothers will be compelled to take, and pass, his test and deliver Benjamin to him in Egypt.

And why might Joseph be so interested in Benjamin? Many possibilities suggest themselves: As his alter ego. As his only full brother. As the sole link to his mother. To rescue him from his father and his brothers. To adopt him for himself and for Egypt. To punish his father, Jacob. We must wait to discover the source of Joseph's interest.

Joseph's speech fully stirs the brothers' guilty souls. One or more of his remarks struck home. Perhaps it was the idea of returning home to their father once again missing one brother, abandoned in this pit of a prison. Perhaps it was the need to beg Jacob for the missing Benjamin, thus raking up all the old man's horror and suspicion. Perhaps it was Joseph's mentioning of the "fear of God." Whatever it was that moved them, the floodgates of conscience burst open wide:

> And they said one to another, "We are truly guilty concerning our brother, in that we saw the distress of his soul, when he besought us, and *we would not hear* [*lo' shama'nu*]: therefore is this distress come upon us." And Reuben answered them, saying, "Spoke I not unto you, saying: 'Do not sin against the child'; and *ye would not hearken* [*shema'tem*]? Therefore also, behold, his blood is required." (42:21–22; emphasis added)

The text profoundly and beautifully displays how guilt lives in the human soul and how it can well up from deeply buried stores to regard as deserved and fitting punishment some distress that is utterly unrelated and, strictly speaking, unmerited. Imprisoned in a "pit" where there is none who can hear their distress, they recall how they failed to heed Joseph's pleading voice calling to them out of the pit—a fact previously not known to the reader. Perhaps it is the sound of his voice now that triggers a memory of their failure to hear it years ago. Reuben, in yet another feckless and ill-considered attempt at leadership, plays "I

---

5. I owe this last insight to Bill Rosen.

told you so," shifts blame, and decrees that Joseph's death must be requited by the death of another. His words, if they do not exactly fall on deaf ears, elicit no response; Judah keeps silence. So does Joseph, but he is not unmoved:

> And they knew not that Joseph understood [*literally*, heard *(shome'a)*] them; for the interpreter was between them. And he turned himself about from them, and wept. (42:23–24)

Joseph, still present, hears and, unbeknownst to the brothers, understands all their confessional talk. They had failed to hear him when he besought them from the pit, but he hears them—and his earlier self—in their distress. Just as his speech had uncorked their guilty memories, so their remarks revive his painful ones. But these familial memories and emotions are now overshadowed by cultural complications, economically but beautifully conveyed in the seemingly inconsequential remark about the interpreter.

Joseph, unbeknownst not only to his brothers but also to his Egyptian entourage, speaks and understands both Egyptian and Hebrew. His brothers' distressing conversation he thus hears twice, first in Hebrew as spoken by the brothers, then in Egyptian when translated by the interpreter. Nothing could better convey the struggles taking place in Joseph's soul: Do I belong with them, or do I belong with Egypt? No wonder he loses his composure. He weeps—probably with recalled terror and sadness for the previous episode, perhaps with genuine pleasure for their remorse, but very likely also with the, at best, bittersweet knowledge that he is still bound to them and must somehow return to them. Joseph is painfully reminded of his place in this family, a place he once coveted but lost, a place about which he is now at best ambivalent. Much as Joseph would like to turn away from them, he cannot simply do so.

Joseph will weep several more times. Understanding his tears on each occasion is no doubt important for gauging his character and state of soul. But we must be on guard against sentimentality and our tendency to sympathize with tears and to grant automatically the moral high ground to those who shed them. Often a man weeps most when he is feeling sorry for himself.

Whatever genuine softening of heart Joseph may feel on listening to his brothers, it is short-lived. His actions, coolly executed, are menacing:

> And he returned to them, and spoke to them, and took Simeon from among them, and bound him before their eyes. Then Joseph commanded to fill their vessels with grain and to restore every man's money [*literally*, silver] into his sack, and to give them provision for the way; and thus was

it done to them. And they laded their asses with grain and departed thence. (42:24–26)

Joseph personally binds Simeon[6] in front of his brothers, making them sense their duty to obtain his release. Then, with his servants enacting his carefully scripted plot, Joseph begins to play tricks on them, designed to befuddle them with wonder, awe, and terror and to make them feel that they are at the mercy of powers divine. When, at a place of lodging on the way home, one of the brothers opens his sack to feed his ass, he discovers his silver in his sack:

And he said unto his brethren, "My money is restored; and behold, it is really in my sack." And their hearts failed them [*literally*, went out] and they trembled [*vayecherdu*] each man to his brother, saying, "What is this that God hath done unto us?" (42:28)

Joseph the stage director has precipitated what the brothers regard as a miracle: the money paid to Joseph has reappeared with the grain. As is often the case, silver, like the unsavory deeds that earn it, keeps coming back into one's soiled hands, a blessing that is also frequently a curse. Having left one brother in bondage at peril of his life, and filled with guilt over another brother, whom they had intended to sell into slavery, the brothers are awestruck and terrified by the appearance of what looks like stolen profit, "earned," as was planned for Joseph, by the loss of a brother. Though they might be amazed at their good fortune, they are also and more likely terrified that they will be branded as thieves, to go along with the charge of being spies.

Like Isaac when he discovered he had given Esau's blessing to Jacob, the brothers tremble because they see here the work of powers invisible: speaking of Him for the first time ever, the brothers attribute the return of the money to God Himself. The reader, who has just been told that the miracle of the money is the work not of God but of Joseph, is invited to wonder with the brothers about divine causation. Is Joseph the instrument of a divine plan—as Joseph himself will later claim? Or do we have here an example of human gullibility, augmented by guilt, attributing to God what we cannot otherwise explain? Are the brothers in danger of confusing the workings of Joseph with the workings of God? Or is this confusion proper? Is it not true that the Lord works in wondrous ways?

6. Perhaps Simeon was the ringleader of the group that had wanted to kill Joseph. He is second oldest, after the more well intentioned Reuben. Also, Simeon, along with Levi, was the chief perpetrator of the slaughter at Shechem.

The brothers now face the unnerving prospect of reporting to their father their strange and contradictory experiences. Shifting tone slightly, they recount to him the entire tale of the Egyptian lord's confusing conduct, comprising threats and generosity, touching concern for one missing brother and arbitrary cruelty toward another. They conclude by inventing an invitational addendum for Joseph's speech to them: "and bring your youngest brother unto me; then shall I know that ye are no spies but that ye are upright men; so will I deliver you your brother, *and ye shall traffic* [or *trade*] *in the land*" (42:34; emphasis added). But opening their sacks before Jacob gets a chance to answer, they discover that each of them has his bundle of money returned in his sack, "and when they and their father saw their bundles of money they were afraid [*vayiyra'u*]" (42:35). Jacob now draws the gloomiest conclusion from the whole affair:

> "Me have ye bereaved of my children. Joseph is not, Simeon is not, and ye will take Benjamin away! Upon me are all these things." (42:36)

Jacob dwells on his great personal grief in a tone of magnified self-pity, but he does so in part because he holds himself responsible. He had sent Joseph out to his death; he had sent Simeon out with his brothers; and he must now bear responsibility should he refuse to ransom him. Like Judah in the story with Tamar, Jacob, having "lost" two sons, clings to his youngest son for fear something will happen to him. He does not trust his other sons with Benjamin; he has reason to fear the Egyptian "lord," who, because of the money, will have good reason to regard his sons, should they return to Egypt, as thieves. Seeing no way out, Jacob descends into sorrow, self-blame, and self-pity.

Reuben makes one last well-meaning but inept attempt to save a bad situation:

> And Reuben spoke unto his father, saying, "Thou shalt slay my two sons if I bring him [Benjamin] not back to thee." And he [Jacob] said, "*My son shall not go down with you* [plural]; for his brother is dead, and *he only is left*. If harm befall him by the way in which ye go, then ye will bring down my gray hairs with sorrow unto Sheol." (42:37–38; emphasis added)

Reuben, showing his firstborn's eagerness to take on the role of responsible patriarch and his willingness to match his father's losses, makes the foolish and grotesque suggestion that Jacob can kill his two sons should Reuben fail to bring Benjamin back alive. Reuben is, in effect, confessing his guilt also for Joseph: If I don't bring Benjamin back, I will deserve two sons' worth of punishment, retribution for the two sons I have caused you to lose. But as anyone with common sense can see, Jacob could hardly satisfy his anger and sorrow over losing his two sons by destroying two of his grandsons. Jacob treats Reuben's remark with contemptuous nonresponse, insisting only that Benjamin will under no circumstances be allowed to go down to Egypt. In addition, Jacob rubs salt in the wound by implying that he has now but one true son ("my son"; "He alone is left"), using remarks whose effect must be to distance Jacob still further from the sons he can neither abandon nor embrace. His attitude toward them is, to be sure, regrettable, a mixture of blind favoritism toward the sons of Rachel and a clinging to the one son who played no part in the death of Joseph (or the loss of Simeon). But like a drowning man, Jacob clings to Benjamin as his only hope and consolation.

Jacob has reached his nadir, thanks to the theatricalities of Joseph, now at his zenith. Perhaps he has what is coming to him, perhaps not. But the future looks grim, and there is no one, it seems, who will take charge. The entire household and line of Israel is in mortal danger.

JUDAH STANDS FORWARD

Time passes. The food brought from Egypt is consumed. Famine now weakens Jacob's resistance, and again leads the children of Israel down into Egypt, precipitating the second act of the drama of Joseph and his brothers. In this act, Joseph's Egyptian stage directing will reach its greatest virtuosity, while amongst the sons of Israel, a new leader will emerge, successfully displaying his political virtue. Even Jacob, albeit without much enthusiasm, will be forced to acknowledge Judah's superior wisdom and to begin to accept him as his heir apparent.

> And it happened, when they had eaten up the grain that they had brought from Egypt, that *their father* said unto them, "Go back, buy us *a little food.*" (43:2; emphasis added)

When we last heard him speak (at the end of chapter 42), Jacob, in adamantly refusing to send Benjamin to Egypt to obtain the release of Simeon, had insisted that Benjamin was his last and only son ("He only is left"). Here, gently refuting Jacob's claim by referring to him not as "Jacob" but as "*their* father," the text shows us a pathetic Jacob who must now rely on his as-it-were disinherited sons. Still in denial, he ignores entirely the Egyptian's demand for Benjamin's appearance. Instead, he speaks plaintively—as if he were, in his imagination, throwing himself on the mercy of the Egyptian grand vizier—in the naïve hope that a pitiable request for only "a *little* food" will obviate the need to comply with the Egyptian's command to produce Benjamin.

The time is now ripe for Judah to stand forward: the situation calls for leadership, and Jacob may finally be willing to listen to reason. Earlier, when Reuben
had foolishly pledged the lives of two of his sons as a surety for Benjamin's safe
return, Judah had held his tongue; Jacob was then in no mood to listen. Now Judah speaks up:

> And Judah spoke unto him saying, "*The man* solemnly warned us, saying,
> 'Ye shall not see my face, except *your brother* be with you.' If thou wilt send
> *our brother* with us, we will go down and buy thee food; but if thou wilt not
> send him, we will not go, for *the man* said unto us, 'Ye shall not see my face,
> except *your brother* be with you.' " (43:3–5; emphasis added)

Judah speaks clearly, calmly, yet forcefully. He reminds Jacob (twice) of the
Egyptian "man's" insistent demand, and he uses it to reinforce his own assertion
that Benjamin is "*our* brother," even if you, Father, regard him as your last remaining son. Most important, Judah impresses on Jacob the futility of going
back to Egypt without Benjamin, given what "the man" had said. But Joseph had
not, in fact, used the expression "Ye shall not see my face"; this appears to be an
addition of Judah's own invention, whose simple meaning would be, "Ye shall
not be admitted to my presence." But, perhaps speaking better than he knows,
Judah's remark echoes the notion—voiced by Jacob himself when he reconciled
with Esau—that seeing the face of the divine is linked to affirming the relation
of brotherhood. Judah indeed stands up to his father not only in the name of
prudence and common sense, but also in the name of the unity of the brothers.[7]
Not surprisingly, Judah's words move his old father to acknowledge that fact, but
they do not yet lead him to the proper practical conclusion:

> And Israel said, "Why dealt ye so ill with me, as to tell the man that ye had
> another brother?" And they said, "Firmly the man asked us about our-
> selves, and about our kindred, saying, 'Is your father still living? Have ye
> another brother?' And we told him, according to the tenor of these words.
> Could we know that he would say, 'Bring down your brother'?" (43:6–7)

Resisting the clear implication of Judah's direct and prudent speech, Jacob, filled
with self-pity, chastises (all) his sons for having caused the problem in the first

---

7. Bill Rosen comments: "What Judah fails to say is as important as what he says. Joseph's real
threat was not that, failing the production of Benjamin, they would fail to see his face, but that they
would die. Judah is careful not to argue that Benjamin is surety for their lives, but for the success of
their mission, a careful argument he will repeat in his big speech in Genesis 44. To the degree that he
mentions a threat, it is not to the brothers, but to the entire clan (including the 'little ones') by death
from famine, not execution by the Egyptian lord."

place by revealing to the Egyptian "man" the existence of their missing brother. Judah, his mind riveted on what must be done, does not indulge Israel's pointless complaining but allows his brothers to reply. Eager to exonerate themselves, they lie to their father: it was they—not "the man"—who, quite spontaneously, first mentioned both their father and their youngest brother, then at home with him (see 42:13).

Judah, showing his superior judgment, ignores the quarrel between father and sons and goes to work again on Jacob, bringing the discussion back to the main business:

> And Judah said unto Israel his father, "Send the youth with me, and we will arise and go, *that we may live and not die,* both we and you and *also our little ones.* I myself will be pledge for him, from my hand shalt thou require him; if I bring him not unto thee and set him before thee, I will bear the blame for all time. For except we had lingered, by now we could have returned twice." (43:8-10; emphasis added)

Judah's speech is triply masterful. First, he proposes the best course of action and gives the persuasive reason for its necessity, repeating exactly Jacob's words from the previous occasion, "that we may live and not die," but adding on his own the concern for the next generation ("our little ones"). By using Jacob's own words against him, Judah brings Jacob back to his senses. And through his own addendum, he gently instructs his father in the lesson he learned from Tamar: one must not sacrifice the future of the clan out of selfish regard for oneself and one's youngest and dearest son.

But, second, Judah does not dismiss Jacob's fears and attachments. In order to reassure his father, Judah pledges personal responsibility for Benjamin's safety and welfare ("Send the youth *with me*"). Whereas Reuben had offered the life of two sons (sacrificing the future generation for the safety of the present one), Judah stands solely on his honor ("I will bear the blame for all time"). Judah, who has already lost two sons and who has returned to care for the well-being of his family, indicates that his good name rests on whether he can fulfill his obligation to his father by protecting all members of his father's line. In this quiet but insistent way, Judah asserts his claim to leadership in the clan, and takes the place normally reserved for the firstborn, Reuben.[8]

8. Robert Sacks comments shrewdly on Judah's relation to and replacement of Reuben:

Judah and Reuben have one thing in common. They both refused to commit fratricide. But in spite of his refusal Reuben, the elder, proved to be inadequate as a leader. Judah, in his decision to return to his brothers, knew that he would have to take the responsibility of the first-born

Judah not only seeks to reassure Jacob. He must get him to overcome his stubborn resistance. This he accomplishes by his third point, a deft expression of confidence in the mission that also contains a gentle rebuke of his father: we could have gotten food (and rescued Simeon) twice by now, had "we" (that is, *you*) not tarried.

Judah's remarks succeed. Convinced that he has no other choice, but perhaps also slightly reassured by Judah's assertion of honorable and confident leadership, Jacob not only yields but—now speaking as Israel—gives orders for the journey:

> And their father, Israel, said unto them, "If it must be so now, do this: take of the best fruits of the land in your vessels and carry down to the man as tribute [*minchah*] a little balm and a little honey, spices and myrrh, nuts, and almonds.[9] And take double silver in your hand, and the silver that was returned in the mouths of your bags carry back in your hand; perhaps it was an oversight. Also your brother, take him, and arise, go again unto the man. And God Almighty [*El Shaddai*] give you mercy [*rachamim*] before the man, that he may release unto you your other brother and Benjamin. As for me, if I must be bereaved, I will be bereaved." (43:11–14)

Fearful of the Egyptian potentate who seized Simeon and who will probably seize Benjamin as well, Jacob seeks to appease him with presents (as he had done before with Esau),[10] with the repayment of the returned (and for all that Jacob knows, stolen) money, and with double payment for the new grain. Feeling once again the desperate need for divine assistance, Jacob also invokes God's help (as he had done before his meeting with Esau) in gaining mercy from the Egyptian,

---

and that this responsibility, in the mind of the author, will continue even past the days of Josiah.

Reuben and Judah had been the two brothers who refused to commit fratricide. But in this essential respect Judah, insofar as he sees the necessity of replacing his brother, was metaphorically compelled to commit fratricide in a deeper sense. Thus ultimately he was the only one of the brothers to perform the act.

Insofar as the verse [43:9] is directed to himself, his private thoughts go back to the time he spent with Tamar. When he *pledges* himself in this verse he becomes a replacement for the *bracelet, staff and signet ring* which he gave to Tamar as a *pledge* (Genesis 38:18).

9. As Robert Alter points out, the gift prepared for Joseph includes three of the items included in the list of goods carried by the Ishmaelite traders who bought Joseph from the Midianites and who sold him as a slave in Egypt (see 37:25). "As with the silver sent back and forth, the brothers are thus drawn unwittingly into a process of repetition of and restitution for their fraternal crime."

10. See 32:13–22 and 33:10. As in the episode with Esau, Jacob again uses the word *minchah*, a word the Bible mainly uses for tribute rendered to God (see, for example, 3:3).

but he lacks his former confidence and speaks with resignation of his own impending bereavement.

Readers, knowing that Joseph is behind the plot, are often quick to accuse Jacob here of histrionic self-pity. But Jacob has good reason to fear the worst, notwithstanding Judah's forceful words. He still grieves for Joseph. His beloved Benjamin, his last link to Rachel, is in the hands of the sons he suspects in Joseph's death. And most worrisome, all his sons are at the mercy of an unknown but seemingly irascible and tyrannical Egyptian potentate. As the ten brothers leave together for Egypt, Jacob is left alone with the women and children, an old man in perilous times, not knowing if and when how many, if any, of his sons will return to him alive. Who among us would trade places with him? Courageously, Jacob is now willing to risk total personal loss for the sake of a hoped-for survival of the clan and its future. Who among us could do what he does? Jacob does not yet know, but we readers must not forget, that his present suffering is entirely the gift of his favorite son, Joseph, prince of Egypt.

ACT II: KEEPING BENJAMIN, BENJAMIN'S KEEPERS

Armed with the tribute and the double money, and with Benjamin, the men arrive in Egypt and stand again in Joseph's presence. Act II of Joseph's drama with his brothers begins. When he sees Benjamin among them, Joseph orders his servant (speaking, no doubt, in Egyptian, which the brothers do not understand) to bring them into his own house for a festive noonday meal. Brought to Joseph's house not knowing why, the men are greatly frightened. Fear, coupled with time to think, provokes their guilty thoughts: "And they said, 'Because of the silver that was returned in our sacks at the first time are we brought in, in order to roll himself upon us and to fall upon us and to take us as slaves, and our asses' " (43:18). Pleading their case to Joseph's servant, they explain that they had come the first time to buy food, that they had paid for it, that their money had mysteriously reappeared in their sacks on the way home, and they were now returning both to repay the money and also to buy more grain. "We do not know who put our silver in our sacks" (43:22).

The servant, a party to Joseph's machinations, reassures the brothers with a well-crafted falsehood, attributing to God what are in fact the deeds of Joseph (a practice of which Joseph, his master, is very fond):

"Peace be unto you, fear not. Your God and the God of your father hath given you treasure in your sacks. Your silver has come to me." And he brought Simeon out to them. And the man brought the men into Joseph's

house, and gave them water, and they washed their feet; and he gave
provender to their asses. (43:23–24)

The brothers must now be thoroughly bewildered. First, they believed that they
were being held as thieves. Now, reassured on that score and reunited with the
liberated Simeon, they are treated as honored guests, yet for no apparent reason.
What could the Egyptian man want with them? Why have they been singled out
from among all the others who have come into Egypt to buy grain?

When Joseph arrives home at noon, the brothers present their tribute and
prostrate themselves before him.

> And he asked them of their welfare, and he said, "Is your father well, the
> old man of whom ye spoke? Is he still alive?" And they said, "Thy servant,
> our father, is well, he is yet alive." And they bowed down their heads and
> made obeisance. (43:28)

Eleven brothers bowing down at his feet, in a position of worship. But where is
his father? Did he really send Benjamin of his own volition, or did the brothers
wait until he died: "Is the old man still alive?" "Yes," the brothers answer, "our
aged father is alive and well. Though absent, he is your servant by proxy, a sender
of tribute to your lofty self." Joseph's boyhood dream of domination has come
true. Nothing is said about his feeling any relief at the news that his father is still
alive and well. While his brothers look down, Joseph looks up and scans the
group for the only person of real interest to him.

> And he lifted up his eyes and saw Benjamin, his brother, *his mother's son*,
> and he said, "Is this your youngest brother of whom ye spake unto me?"
> And he said, "God be gracious unto thee, *my son*." And Joseph made haste,
> for his mercy grew warm [*nikhmeru rachamayv*] *for his brother*, and he
> sought where to weep; and he entered into his chamber and wept there.
> And he washed his face, and went out, and refrained himself, and said,
> "Serve bread." (43:29–31; emphasis added)

Seeing Benjamin, Joseph sees not only a brother, but his only full brother and
alter ego, the son of his mother, Rachel, who died while giving birth to Benjamin
when Joseph was himself but a boy. Joseph recognizes him immediately—he
does not wait for a confirming answer from the brothers—and addresses him
with paternal, not to say god-like, solicitude ("God be gracious unto you, my
son"). Though he had coolly manipulated the brothers precisely to deliver up
Benjamin, the consummate master of the drama is unprepared for his own emo-

tional response to the sight of his brother, once his mother's son and now, so his heart tells him, also his own.[11] As if to underscore Joseph's distorted vision of family relations—"Is Benjamin my alter ego, my brother, or my son?"—his eyes grow misty and his sight grows dim. Joseph, for the second time, is overcome with the need for weeping and hastily removes himself to shed his tears unseen.

Joseph's tears are, the text makes clear, born of compassion or pity, based on brotherly identification: *rachamim*, usually translated "mercy" or "compassion," originally meant "brotherly feeling" (or "motherly feeling"), based on its derivation (according to many scholars) from *rechem*, "womb" (itself from a root meaning "soft"). But Joseph's brotherly feeling is not directed to all of his brothers; he is not moved by their trustworthiness with Benjamin or the indication of their remorse and reform. Joseph's compassion is rather reserved for the one brother born from the same womb, from Rachel ("His mercy grew warm *for his brother*"). But why does Benjamin's situation call for compassion? What inspires Joseph's tears? Is it merely that Benjamin is, as Joseph once was, in the hands of the ten unloved and unloving brothers? Is it also that Benjamin, "his mother's son," is, like himself, an orphan? Or does Joseph weep, in addition, to see Benjamin suffering on account of Joseph's own actions, deeds that have dragged Benjamin away from his father and brought him bowing down abjectly before him in Egypt? Could there be tears of tenderness mixed with tears of pity, as Joseph contemplates his next moves in a plan that could get Benjamin to stay with him, thus to complete the integration of the line of beautiful Rachel into the beauty-loving land of Egypt? Could Joseph, the man with little or no eros for women, be moved by erotic longings for his brother?

Whatever its cause, Joseph's impulse to tears makes clear, both to him and to the reader, that his feelings for Benjamin and his lack of self-command are incompatible with his lofty position as Egyptian viceroy and consummate manager of the present drama. Fittingly, Joseph must weep in private, shedding tears also for himself and the divisions within his soul.

His face washed to hide the evidence of tears, and struggling for self-control, Joseph returns and resumes command, giving an order to set on the food. But the meal that follows only corroborates Joseph's deep dilemma:

And they set on for him by himself, and for them by themselves, and for the Egyptians that did eat with him by themselves; because the Egyptians

---

11. The implicitly patricidal and incestuous meaning of Joseph's calling Benjamin "my son," so close to recognizing him as "his mother's son," cannot be overlooked. Only a reader who believes that Joseph is filled with feelings of pure brotherly love—and filial piety for Jacob—will read past these words without batting an eye. Joseph's blurred understanding of family relations will be corrected only by Judah's great speech; see pp. 595–604.

would not eat bread with the Hebrews, for that is an abomination [*to'evah*] in Egypt. And they sat before him, the firstborn according to his birthright and the youngest according to his youth, and the men marveled one with another. And portions were taken unto them from before him, but Benjamin's portion was five times so much as any of theirs. And they drank and they got drunk with him. (43:32–34)

Imagining the scene, we see that Joseph eats alone, separated both from his native Hebrew brethren and his adopted Egyptian compatriots. Because of his elevated Egyptian status, he may not eat with his brothers. Yet despite his power, his Egyptian underlings will not eat with him, because he is a Hebrew,[12] whose food is an abomination in Egypt.[13]

Joseph, an Egyptianized Hebrew, is simultaneously both and neither. Because his relation to these Hebrew visitors is known only to Joseph himself, only Joseph feels the poignancy of his self-isolation and emptiness at the very moment in which he enjoys his long-dreamt-of greatness vis-à-vis his brothers. Joseph has what he wished for, but it turns out to be not exactly what he wanted. Joseph learns what the reader has learned from earlier stories in Genesis: supremacy and the equality of brotherliness are incompatible.

Joseph (and the reader) may very well remember the last time his brothers ate in his vicinity, when, after they had planned to kill him and claim that a wild beast had eaten him, they cast him into a pit without food and water and sat apart eating their lunch. Now, acting either from impulse or calculation, Joseph sends portions of food from his table to his brothers, seemingly confirming some kind of link between them. The brothers are delighted by this turn of events and conviviality reigns. But as the brothers marvel over the fact that the viceroy has magically divined their birth order, this time even rejoicing over the fivefold favoritism shown to their youngest half-brother, Joseph, perhaps as

12. The text is, admittedly, not crystal clear on this point. Surely Joseph's high position would by itself be a sufficient reason why his underlings ate separately. The Egyptian refusal to eat with Hebrews could explain only why the former sat apart from Joseph's brothers. But the text describes these Egyptians as "Egyptians that did eat with him," yet it undercuts the "with him" by pointedly remarking that they ate, rather, "by themselves." From this it follows that they ate at the same time and place, but seated apart. The Egyptian taboo against eating with Hebrews, given in the next sentence, would seem to supply the reason for the separation from Joseph himself.

13. This is no trivial matter. The important biblical notion of "abomination," crucial for the Israelite laws of purity (see, for example, Leviticus 18), gains its first usage here. The Egyptian dietary taboo about eating with the Hebrews may be related to the fact that the Israelites are shepherds (not farmers) and eaters of lamb; later, we shall learn—in the only other mention of "abomination" in Genesis—that "every shepherd is an abomination unto Egypt" (46:34). What and how one eats says a great deal about who and what one thinks one is.

much in sorrow as in joy, leads the partygoers to lose themselves in drink, satisfying at once his desire both to forget and to celebrate. One can readily understand that he has much he would rather forget, not only past but also present.[14]

But the drama is not yet finished. When he sobers up, Joseph moves the plot
toward its conclusion. He commands the man in charge of his house to fill the
men's sacks with food and to (once again) put each man's silver back into the
mouth of his sack. In addition, he has his servant place "my goblet, my silver
goblet," in the sack of the youngest brother, Benjamin. His plan, most assuredly,
is to test the brothers' attitude toward Benjamin. As Robert Sacks puts it:

> Joseph has now decided to put his brothers to the fullest test. He will place
> them in a position where they will be strongly tempted to treat Benjamin
> as they had treated him. The point of Joseph's trial is that repentance is
> only complete when one knows that if he were placed in the same position
> he would not act in the same way he had acted before.

But although this stratagem works to test his brethren, it is not clear that this is
Joseph's primary purpose. He may have designs on Benjamin, for which this
same device will serve perfectly.

As day breaks, the men are sent away, their asses laden with sacks stuffed with
grain. When they have gone but a short way, Joseph sends his servant after them:

> "Rise, follow after the men. And when thou dost overtake them, say unto
> them: 'Wherefore have ye rewarded evil for good? Is not this it from which
> my lord drinketh, and whereby he indeed divineth?' "[15] (44:4)

The servant does as he is told and repeats these words. The brothers, in response,
vehemently protest their innocence, citing in evidence of their honesty their return of the money that they had found in their sacks after their first visit. In conclusion, the brothers rashly pronounce in advance a sentence of death on the
guilty one and slavery for themselves, should the divining goblet be found on
them: "With whomsoever of thy servants it be found, let him die, and we also
will be my lord's bondsmen" (44:9).

The entire occasion reminds the reader of Laban's accusing Jacob, a generation earlier, of stealing his household gods; and the brothers' speech echoes
Jacob's pronouncement of death for the thief of the *terafim*, a death, one might

14. Joseph's pursuit of this combination of forgetfulness and rejoicing (in this order) we saw
earlier in the name that he gave to his sons. See Chapter Eighteen, pp. 570–71.

15. Recall the importance of the cup and the cupbearer to Pharaoh, mentioned in Chapter
Eighteen.

say, that was later inflicted on Rachel, the guilty party. Here, without knowing it, the brothers are calling for the death of Benjamin—just as they had once knowingly plotted the death of Joseph, Rachel's other son. But in contrast with their previous and explicit wish for Joseph's death, they here also pronounce servitude for themselves, as their brother's keepers—a promising note that only slightly redeems the foolish overconfidence of their protestation of innocence. Having been lulled into a false sense of security by Joseph's unexpected and magnanimous display of hospitality the night before, the brothers are now ripe for self-destruction.

The servant is more measured regarding the proper punishment of the thief, perhaps because he is in on the plot:

> And he said, "Now also let it be according to your words: he with whom it is found shall be my slave, but ye shall be blameless." (44:10)

The servant, while agreeing that their proposal would in some sense be right, accepts a lesser (and more pointedly just) punishment: not death but only servitude, and only for the guilty one; the others, though accomplices, shall be held blameless. Whereas the brothers spoke up as a united band, the servant's speech (and Joseph's plot) is designed to separate Benjamin from the others, perhaps to test their brotherliness, perhaps to gain Benjamin for himself.

The search of sacks is conducted one by one, from eldest to youngest. When the goblet is found in Benjamin's sack, the brothers "rent their garments, and laded every man his ass, and returned to the city" (44:13). In rending their clothes, the brothers adopt in advance the garb of mourning. They mourn Benjamin as if he were as good as dead. Perhaps they also mourn in anticipation of the lethal blow that Benjamin's loss will deliver to Jacob, who had once done the same on seeing the bloodied coat of Joseph (37:34). They may even be mourning belatedly for the death of Joseph, whose demise they had also "pronounced."

But the brothers are not merely passive mourners. In addition to these displays of brotherly grief, they all ("every man") immediately load up their asses and return to the city: none of them even thinks of deserting Benjamin. At last, they clearly show themselves to be their brother's keepers. They will try to stand or fall together. They do not ask—as did Abraham of God regarding Sodom—why the righteous must suffer with the guilty. For one thing, they know that they are not righteous. For another, they are at last affirming the principle of the unity of the whole tribe. A careful reader, remembering God's conversation with Abraham about the fate of Sodom, may find in the behavior of Benjamin's ten brothers a vindication of God's principle: "I will not destroy the whole place if there be found there ten righteous men" (see 18:32, and the discussion in Chapter Eleven). The ten sons of Israel meet the moral challenge as a united group and return with Benjamin to face their judge.

ACT III: JUDAH TO THE RESCUE

Then came Judah and his brothers to the house of Joseph, and he was yet there, and they fell before him to the ground.

And Joseph said unto them, "What deed is this that ye have done? Know ye not that such a man as I will surely divine?"

And Judah said, "What shall we say unto my lord? What shall we speak? And how shall we justify ourselves? God hath found out the iniquity of thy servants; behold, we are my lord's slaves, both we and he also in whose hand the goblet is found."

And he said, "Far be it from me that I should do so. The man in whose hand the goblet is found, he shall be my slave, but as for you, get you up in peace unto your father." (44:14–17)

We have come to Act III of Joseph's drama with his brothers. In contrast with the previous two meetings, on this occasion the brothers, though all are present and united, will have a clear leader: Judah. Thus, in addition to seeing how Joseph's drama resolves itself, we readers will finally see a face-to-face contest between Jacob's two leading sons, and we will be able to compare and judge their relative virtues and their suitability for leadership within Israel. We are at a dramatic high point of the entire book. The fate of the Children of Israel hangs in the balance.

The preeminence of Judah is foreshadowed in the first sentence of the just-quoted passage: although the subject of the sentence appears to be compound—"Judah and his brothers"—the verb ("came") is in the singular. The eleven brothers are significantly divided into one and ten (not Benjamin and the others, but Judah and his brothers). But thanks to Judah's singularity (it was he who came at their head), the eleven brothers are united to the point of having their actions regarded as the deeds of one person. The clan that once stood violently together in avenging the rape of their sister Dinah and violently divided in assaulting their brother Joseph here unites in communal solidarity regarding their brother Benjamin. Judah's leadership, because it is decisively informed (as we shall soon see) by filial piety, is singularly capable of embracing all the brothers as equals. Exemplifying the special way of rule within Israel, it avoids both the patricidal (and incestuous) tendencies of tyrannical rule (Ham; Oedipus) and the fratricidal tendencies of political rule (Cain; Romulus). But we are getting ahead of the story. For now, Joseph is still in charge of the situation.

Joseph, from his commanding and morally superior position, opens the conversation with feigned indignation and an indictment of unspecified wrongdoing. Moreover, by means of a rhetorical question ("What deed is this that ye have done?"), he asserts his superiority and implies that it rests on special abilities for gaining hidden knowledge, claiming falsely that he can discover veiled truths through magical powers of divination (available to him even without the missing silver goblet).[16] Whether he actually engaged in it or not, Joseph here takes his stand on the well-known Egyptian practice—later condemned in Israel—of divination.

Joseph, without intending it, triggers the emergence of his counterpart, the true leader of the sons of Israel. Judah, speaking up for all the brothers, pleads "no contest." At the same time, through ambiguous speech, he subtly amends Joseph's claims: it was God (not Joseph, who claimed powers of divination) who found their iniquity, not the theft of the goblet, but their earlier plot against Joseph. Throughout, Judah speaks in the first person plural, stressing the brothers' collective guilt and their intention of hanging together: "What shall *we* say . . . what shall *we* speak? How shall *we* justify ourselves? . . . *We* are my lord's slaves, both *we* and also the one in whose hand the cup was found." The discovered goblet, says Judah, condemns all of *us*—we eleven, both we ten and that one, all mixed together. Judah concludes by proposing a collective and *equal* punishment of slavery for all, not, as the brothers had hastily proposed earlier (44:9), death for the guilty and servitude for the rest.

Judah's proposal accomplishes several things at once. It shows solidarity with Benjamin (without naming him or even conceding his guilt), and it tacitly confesses the other brothers' desert of such punishment (the ten brothers would have Joseph made a slave, now it is tit for tat). But in addition, understood tactically, Judah's proposal constitutes an opening gambit in a last-ditch effort to bargain for mercy and to find an escape from the dreadful alternatives now before the sons of Jacob. Thinking as a leader and loyal to his father, Judah surely knows that Jacob can hardly regard losing all his sons to slavery in Egypt as a preferable alternative to the loss only of Benjamin. Hence, Judah hopes that the winning display of solidarity and the proposal of collective punishment will move the heart of the Egyptian viceroy to let *all* his people go.

---

16. Joseph's remark—"Know ye not that such a man as I will surely divine?"—is, in fact, ambiguous. "He is saying that they should have known that a person of his standing would practice divination and so the goblet they purloined was no mere silver cup but a dedicated instrument of divination. But . . . he is also suggesting that a man of his powers would be able to divine such a theft, and its perpetrator." The practice involved is hydromancy, in which the diviner forecasts the future by reading the figures that form in moving liquid.

Joseph flatly rejects Judah's suggestion of collective punishment, insisting instead on enslaving only the guilty party:

"Far be it from me [*chalilah li*] that I should do so; the man in whose hand the goblet is found, he shall be my slave; but as for you, get you up [*'alu*] in peace [*leshalom*] to your father." (44:17)

Joseph's phrase, "Far be it from me," reminds us of Abraham's outraged insistence that God, the just judge of the whole world, not punish Sodom's righteous along with the guilty ("Far be it from thee" [*chalilah lekha*]; 18:25). We readers, therefore, may be inclined to see Joseph here enacting the role of the perfect (not to say divine) judge, giving each person only and exactly what he deserves—*until we recall that the so-called guilty party is accused on a completely trumped-up charge.* And even if one believes that Joseph is rightly getting even with his brothers, what excuses his treatment of his beloved brother Benjamin, who has harmed him not at all? Joseph's behavior makes sense only if it is part of a plan to take Benjamin away from Jacob and his sons, in order both to have him for himself and to punish (especially) his father.

Many readers, sympathetic to Joseph and thinking the best of his motives, will see here only an attempt to test the brothers, to see if they are willing to abandon Benjamin to slavery as they were willing years earlier to do the same with him. But Joseph's language suggests that he seeks to *punish* them (including Jacob) even more than to test them. "You/go-up/in peace/to your father" can also be read: "You rise-like-an-offering [*'alah*] in-wholeness-with-your-father" ("As for you, may you and your father together burn as a sacrificial offering"). Be this as it may, Joseph leaves the brothers an impossible choice: either to return home empty-handed, saving their own lives, again losing a brother, and likely killing their father; or to stay behind with Benjamin, abandoning their father and all their families to starvation and grief. It is Joseph's last remark—"Go up in peace to your father"—that triggers Judah's great speech.

THE STATESMAN'S PERSUASION

Judah's speech, the longest speech in the book of Genesis (seventeen verses, 44:18–34), is widely praised for its pathos and beauty. Judah's magnanimous offer to remain as a slave in Benjamin's place redeems Judah's reputation even in the eyes of those who have not hitherto seen his virtues. And for those readers who read Joseph's doings mainly as a well-controlled effort to test the character of his brothers, Judah, speaking in the name of all, passes the test. But few readers appreciate fully the rhetorical genius of the speech or notice that it is also a test of Joseph. Those who cannot so appreciate do not see in Judah's speech the reason why Judah, not Joseph, is fit for leadership in Israel. Joseph's trickery and powers of "divination" are more than answered by a remarkable display of brilliant speech and filial piety, which in the end bring Joseph to give over his theatrics and to recognize his human connections to his family.

The power to persuade—to move not only minds but hearts—is Judah's special gift. Judah, who had persuaded his raging brothers not to kill Joseph and his stubborn father to entrust him with Benjamin, now persuades a foreign potentate (his alienated and alienating brother Joseph) to take pity on his venerable father. Judah alone among the sons of Jacob can move the angry and stubborn hearts of men. He can cool the hot, warm the cool, and melt the icy severity of power. Does any other character in Genesis show equal powers of persuasive speech?

The only possible competition for Judah's speech—which rarely if ever receives the careful scrutiny and analysis it merits—is Abraham's much more famous conversation with God about Sodom. There, Abraham argued with God regarding the fate of the righteous in the genuinely wicked city, remonstrating with Him to do perfect justice—and he failed. Here, Judah argues with an Egyptian demigod regarding the fate of the one innocent man among a genuinely guilty band of brothers, remonstrating with him to practice mercy for the sake of an aged father—and he succeeds.

> Then Judah came near unto him and said, "I pray, my lord, let thy servant please speak a word in my lord's ears, and let not thine anger burn against thy servant, for thou art like Pharaoh." (44:18)

Judah begins with great deference and flattery, addressing Joseph as a god. Twice calling Joseph "my lord" and twice calling himself "thy servant," Judah begs Joseph not to be angry, reminding him that, because he is like the godly Pharaoh, he should be beyond anger. But this flattery is, in fact, a brilliant stroke of great boldness, and the speech of deference a device to level the difference between the two men. Judah cleverly turns the flattering bits of obsequiousness into an indictment: "If I am your servant, my lord, then you are the one responsible for what I, your agent, have done." [17] Judah courageously steps forward uninvited but unrebuffed, and stands man to man with Joseph in private conversation; the idiom for "in private"—"in my lord's ears"—conveys not only

---

17. I am indebted to Bill Rosen for this insight.

the proximity but the equality of the two interlocutors.[18] So intimate is the speech that follows that not a word is said about the presence of an interpreter. One would assume that an interpreter would be formally required, in keeping with Joseph's charade not to understand the Hebrew tongue, but as the story is presented, it is almost as if Judah's speech moves Joseph without being translated. One is even prompted to wonder whether Judah, emboldened to act in the name of the Children of Israel, may have seen through Joseph's disguise. At the very least, despite his deferential speech, Judah treats Joseph as if he were simply one of his own. And the motion of his speech—beginning from references to "my lord" but ending with references to "my father," making clear whom Judah holds in higher reverence—will in fact compel Joseph to acknowledge that he is indeed a member of Jacob's family.

The bulk of Judah's speech recapitulates the brothers' previous encounters with Joseph in Egypt. How does this retelling bring about this transformation in Joseph? Like many a great story, it holds up a mirror in which the listener—Joseph—can see and recognize the meaning of his deeds as they are seen by a seemingly neutral reporter. Because he is forced to recognize the sincerity and truthfulness of the story's narrator, Joseph is made to bear witness against himself. Joseph, a man who would forget his father's house, who has adopted foreign ways, and who even acts like a god, is summoned to acknowledge and care for his father by seeing that he himself is a guilty party, nearly guilty of (more than metaphorical) patricide. At least for the time being, Joseph, who embodies the Egyptian way of mastery and self-sufficiency, will be moved by Judah's example of and appeal to the Israelite attachment to the way of the fathers. Judah, spokesman for and leader of the Children of Israel, understands that the unity of the tribe rests on common paternity, and he demonstrates that proper regard for its future requires filial piety. By his persuasive narrative, Judah awakens in the hardened heart of Joseph the dormant spring of reverence for their father.

In retelling the story "in Joseph's ear," Judah begins with an account of their first meeting in Egypt (44:19–23):

19. My lord asked his servants, saying, "Have ye a father or a brother?"
20. And we said unto my lord, "We have a father, an aged man, and a child of his old age, a little one; and his brother is dead, and he alone is left of his mother, and his father loveth him."

18. The beginning of this passage, "And Judah came near unto him [*vayyiggash 'elayv Yehudah*]," reminds of the beginning of the conversation about Sodom, "And Abraham came near" [*vayyiggash 'Avraham*]" (18:23). There, too, a temporary relationship of equality is established by the boldness of the inferior speaker.

21. And thou saidst unto thy servants, "Bring him down unto me, that I may set mine eyes upon him."

22. And we said unto my lord, "The lad [*na'ar*] cannot leave his father; for should he leave his father, he would die."

23. And thou saidst unto thy servants, "Unless your youngest brother come down with you, ye shall see my face no more."

Comparing Judah's retelling with the original biblical account (42:7–20), we notice that Judah introduces numerous changes; he is no mere chronicler of the facts. Some of the changes he makes no doubt reflect Judah's honest interpretation of the *meaning* of what transpired and what was actually said. But everything Judah says is guided by his rhetorical intention to move the viceroy to be merciful. Let us examine the master at work.

Judah says that Joseph began the inquiry about the family (verse 19); but it was the brothers who had spontaneously volunteered their family story, in response to Joseph's repeated accusation that they were spies (42:9–13; see our discussion above). Judah's alteration of the facts prudently refrains from reminding Joseph of his initial suspicion. But it also conveys a highly plausible interpretation of Joseph's original intention in the exchange about being spies. The brothers then had taken Joseph, in accusing them of being spies, to be questioning their identity as well as their intention. And when Joseph had challenged them to prove that they indeed had a father and a youngest brother still living in Canaan, they reasonably surmised that Joseph must be interested in these familial facts. So they told Jacob, and so they now themselves believe.

Judah has Joseph asking, "Have ye a father *or* a brother?" Speaking perhaps better than he knows, Judah implies that Joseph had separated father and brother, Jacob and Benjamin; hearing this "retelling," Joseph cannot help but recognize that he has in fact separated the two, both in mind and now in fact. Judah's "recounting" of the brothers' response (verse 20) has them answering "yes" to father but speaking vaguely about "brother": *We* have a father; there is a child of *his* old age; *his brother* (not "our other brother") is dead; *he alone* is left of his mother; he is beloved of *his* father (not "our father"). The family picture that Judah paints focuses entirely on the Jacob-Rachel family, and it evokes immediate sympathy. Yes, we have a father, but our father has only this little one, the sole survivor of his mother's children, beloved of *his* father; though we are sons of our father, our father, in fact, really has only one son. Judah presents to the imagination of the Egyptian viceroy a tender and pitiable picture of a vulnerable and bereaved old man doting on the little, solitary son of his old age. And Judah does so without a grain of envy and malice, passions that such paternal favoritism, once expressed toward Joseph himself, had once aroused in the brothers. Joseph, listening to Judah, must identify with Benjamin and his special place in his father's heart. He cannot help noticing the absence of fraternal envy in Judah's narration. And, unless he has a heart of stone, he must feel, for the first time, some compassion for the plight of his father.

Into this heart-wrenching picture, Judah's next sentence (verse 21) sends an arrow of tacit yet piercing accusation: And you, once we told you this, what did you do? Hardhearted and uncaring, you bade us to bring this lad down to you, away from his father, so that you might set your eyes upon him. Lest this arrow not find its mark, Judah, in a completely invented addition (verse 22) to the original conversation, adds remarks that are intended to make perfectly clear the true meaning of the viceroy's (that is, Joseph's) earlier demand. We told you "the lad" (not "our brother"; not "the man," as Joseph had called him in verse 17) could not leave his father; we told you that, should he leave him, he would die.[19] Joseph hears from Judah that his (half) brothers were solicitous of Benjamin's and their father's welfare. They had, even then, sought to spare their father's and/or brother's life, and they had warned Joseph about the consequences of his command.

Judah continues. And you, sir, how did you react to this dire warning? Intransigently you insisted that we bring our "youngest brother"; otherwise, "ye shall not see my face again" (verse 23). Once again, a comparison with the original account (42:14–20) shows that, although the bottom line is unchanged, Judah completely alters what was said. Judah omits Joseph's renewed charges—backed by his sworn oaths (sworn by Pharaoh)—that they were spies; he omits the taking of Simeon as hostage and Joseph's angry threat of death. Again speaking perhaps better than he knows, Judah presents Joseph with a picture of himself not as someone acting out of concern with matters of state, but as someone who is trifling with family feeling and family survival. According to Judah, it was Joseph who first clearly identifies the person Judah had carefully called "the lad" and "the son of [their] father's old age" as *your youngest brother.*" In this way, Judah credits Joseph with compelling him and his brothers to face up to their *own* brotherly ties to Benjamin. At the same time, he tacitly blames Joseph with forcing them to do so in a way that would kill the common principle that makes them brothers—their common father, for whom, Judah makes powerfully clear, Joseph has shown absolutely no consideration. By inventing for Joseph the godlike remark "Ye shall not see my face again," Judah presents Joseph with a picture of himself as a remote, cold, and heartless being, indifferent to human feeling

19. As Robert Alter suggests, the ambiguity of the final "he" may be deliberate on Judah's part: "He leaves it to Joseph to decide whether the old man would die if he were separated from Benjamin, or whether Benjamin cannot survive without his father, or whether both dire possibilities might be probable."

and—contrary to his own self-understanding—hostile to the principle of brotherhood that he arrogantly believes he is defending.

Without pausing for Joseph's reaction, Judah next retells what happened when the brothers returned to their father after their first audience with Joseph (44:24–29, emphasis added; compare with the text's original account, 42:29–43:7).

24. And it happened when we came up to *thy servant my father,* that we told him the words of my lord.
25. And *our father* said, "Go back, buy us a little food" [verbatim, from 43:2].
26. And we said, "We cannot go down; if our youngest brother be with us, then we will go down; for we may not see the man's face, except our youngest brother be with us."
27. And *thy servant my father* said to us, "Ye know that two did my wife bear me.
28. And the one went out from me, and I said, 'Surely he is torn to pieces [*tarof toraf*],' and I have not seen him since.
29. Now if ye take this one also from me, and mischief befall him, ye shall bring down my gray hairs with evil to Sheol [*or the grave*]."

In this section of his speech, Judah mixes together some accurate, even verbatim, quotations and some newly invented paraphrases. And by devising for them a new order, he presents Joseph a picture of his father that could move the heart of a statue. As a prelude to the practical conclusion, Judah seeks to arouse the viceroy's compassion. At the same time, Judah subtly points out that, though he is de facto the viceroy's servant, his true and primary identity is as his father's son: in verse 24, Judah, for the first time, speaks not of "a father" or "his father," but of "my father." This personalization of the relationship almost certainly nudges Joseph also to think about "my father," especially because Judah refers to Jacob as "*thy* servant [but] *my* father." This father of Judah's, Joseph cannot help but feel, he is also my father, and not just my servant.[20]

Through Judah's speech, Joseph is also shown something of his father's attitudes toward his children, including his favoritism toward the children of Rachel and, most important, his attitude toward Joseph himself. Whereas Judah, in paraphrasing what *he* said to Jacob (43:3–5), has *all the brothers* speaking to Ja-

---

20. This formulation, "thy servant my father," repeated also in verses 27, 30, and 31, Judah will later divide and replace. In verses 32 and 34, at the end of the speech, Judah will refer to Jacob four times simply as "my father," silently denying that his father is Joseph's servant. Instead, "thy servant" in verses 32 and 33 refers to Judah himself.

cob about *"our youngest brother,"* Jacob in replying does not acknowledge the common brotherhood. Unlike Judah and his brothers, who in speaking to their father make no distinction between the sons of Leah and the sons of Rachel, Jacob is said to acknowledge only one wife and two sons: "Ye know that two did my wife bear me" (verse 27). With Jacob's "Ye know" now ringing in Joseph's ears, Joseph is reminded of his father's long-standing favoritism, in which he happily participated and which he had once exploited against his half brothers, giving rise to their enmity. Joseph also learns something else about his father, crucial for his feelings toward him; he learns that Jacob believes Joseph "went out," not that Jacob had sent him to his ill-fated meeting with the brothers: Jacob was not part of the conspiracy against him. Indeed, listening carefully, Joseph hears both that Jacob does not know that he was sold into Egypt but believes that he was torn to pieces, and that, hoping against hope, Jacob nonetheless harbors a faint thought that Joseph may yet be alive: "I have not seen him since."

Up until now, Joseph has had no clue about what Jacob thinks or knows or feels about his disappearance or about the state of family relations in his absence. He can only harbor the worst suspicions when he hears (on the brothers' first visit) that his beloved father is still living with his hateful brothers who sought to do him in. Thanks to Judah's account, Joseph may at last be able to understand why Jacob continues to live with his sons and why he has not come looking for him in Egypt. In addition to feeling pity for Jacob's lot, Joseph cannot but reconsider his unjust suspicion of his father and recognize how the cruelty of his theatrics now compounds mightily his father's anguish.

In a series of drawn-out yet carefully measured phrases, emphasizing the doings of each of the participants in the drama, Judah now draws the stark conclusion from his narrative of the past conversations (44:30–31; emphasis added):

> 30. Now, therefore, when *I* come to *thy servant my father,*
> and *the lad* is not with *us,*
> and seeing that *his life* [*or* his soul: *nafsho*] is bound up with *his life*
> [*nafsho*],
> 31. it will happen, when he seeth that *the lad* is not with us,
> that *he will die;*
> and *thy servants* will bring down the gray hairs of *thy servant our father*
> with sorrow to the grave.

Judah confirms, as an independent prophecy, Jacob's words of his horrible death, should Benjamin not return. And who will be responsible for his death? Why, we *thy servants,* we who are in this matter literally (and not merely politely) your slaves, acting utterly against our will and judgment but solely in obe-

THE BEGINNING OF WISDOM

dience to yours. Thy servants, acting on *your* insistence—in a word, *you*—will cause the death of another one of "thy servants," *"our father."* When Joseph hears "our father" roll off Judah's tongue, how can he not hear himself included in Judah's *"our"* father? Tactfully but firmly, Judah hammers home the conclusion in the form of a charge of incipient homicide. Judah enables Joseph to see himself as an incipient murderer; worse, as an incipient patricide, and as the patricide he has throughout the charade been willing to be.

Judah finishes off his speech with a second, more personal conclusion, in the process offering Joseph a practical alternative to the two plans that had hitherto been considered (44:32–34; emphasis added):

> 32. For *thy servant* [that is, I, Judah] became pledge for the lad unto *my father,* saying,
> "If I bring him not unto thee, then I shall bear the blame to *my father* forever."
> 33. Now therefore, please, let *thy servant* remain instead of the lad [*tachath hana'ar*] a slave to *my lord;* and let the lad go up with his brethren.
> 34. For how shall I go up to *my father,* if the lad be not with me?
> Let me not see the evil that would find out *my father.*

This is, without doubt, Judah's finest moment. Judah volunteers to be "the ram"—"instead of the lad" (*tachath hana'ar;* compare, in the story of the binding of Isaac, "instead of his son," *tachath beno;* 22:13). His magnanimous and self-sacrificing offer to remain as Joseph's slave in Benjamin's stead is unparalleled in the book of Genesis; in the Torah, it is surpassed only by Moses' plea to God to forgive Israel for the golden calf, asking to be erased from God's book should He refuse to forgive his people for their sin.

Commentators reviewing Judah's speech as a whole are impressed, quite appropriately, with Judah's turnaround from the man who had first devised the plan to sell Joseph into slavery and who had been willing "years before to watch his father writhe in anguish over Joseph's supposed death." Even those who recognize that Judah's speech is "at once a moving piece of rhetoric" no less than "the expression of a profound inner change" are inclined to emphasize Judah's (and the brothers') psychological transformation at Joseph's hand: "Joseph's 'testing' of his brothers is thus also a process that induces the recognition of guilt and leads to psychological transformation."

But such an assessment of Judah's speech catches only part of its grandeur. Judah is not newly converted to his prudent and protective outlook; he is rather exercising here the responsibility he assumed as a result of his education with Tamar. Robert Sacks has astutely made the connection, having noticed that Judah, in pledging himself to his father for Benjamin, had already made himself a replacement for the bracelet, staff, and signet ring he had once given to Tamar as a pledge:

> Judah's thoughts return to the *pledge* he gave to Tamar when he left his brothers, whose life he thought he could not share. He is now willing to accept the burden which he assumed in Canaan. His responsibility is that of a man. He makes no claim for any special relationship to God; he has no magic and handles himself in a purely human way.

Sacks is surely correct in his assessment. But a careful look at *how* Judah puts his concluding remarks (verses 32–34) shows how much further one may take Sacks's insight. In Judah's last three verses, the double expression "thy servant my father," used frequently at the start of the speech, has come apart: "thy servant" now means only Judah, while "my father" has been liberated in speech from subservience to the Egyptian overlord. In this subtle way, Judah in effect tells Joseph: "I may be your slave, and you, therefore, may be my master. But I belong first and most to my father, to whom I am pledged for my brother." Four times in these last three verses, and twice in the last one, does Judah utter the word *'avi*, "my father." It is, indeed, the last word he leaves ringing in Joseph's ear.

In addition to enunciating and defending with his freedom and honor the importance of filial piety and brotherly responsibility, Judah tacitly compels Joseph to think about his own guilt in betraying his familial and filial duty. He forces Joseph to think about the difference between the relation of master and slave and the ties between father and sons. In so doing, he obliges Joseph—and the reader—to ponder the difference between the Egyptian way of mastery, magic, and bureaucracy and the Israelite way of honoring one's father (and mother), between a way of life in which supreme obligations and obedience are to the god-king Pharaoh, channeled through his ministers ("thy servants"), and a way of life in which supreme obligations and obedience are to God, channeled through the father as the head of the clan. At least for a few moments, Joseph is being summoned to reacquire a concern for Judah's father, which is to say, also and especially for his own.

So perfect is Judah's speech—as a rhetorical and political speech, and as an expression of his own familial understanding and moral-political excellence—that one wonders how Judah could have produced and delivered it under the terrible circumstances in which he found himself. Even more to be wondered at, although Judah probably does not know (as far as we can tell) before whom he stands and to whom he speaks, he makes a speech perfectly suited to move and instruct his brother Joseph. Indeed, no one who *knew* that the viceroy *was Joseph* in disguise could have made a better or more powerful speech. Judah, though not speaking once about God, makes an inspired speech. What is it that enables Judah to speak better than he knows? Is there something about superior virtue that opens a man's heart and soul to inspired speech? Whatever the explanation, one comes away from Judah's speech feeling that it was providential. Judah's mother, at his birth, had named him well: Judah *(Yehudah)*—Praise *(hodah)* the Lord.

JOSEPH UNMASKS HIMSELF:
REVELATION, REUNION, AND RESERVE

Judah's speech finds its mark. Struck to the core, Joseph breaks down. The charade is over. The drama dissolves, as the star of the show is incapacitated.

> Then Joseph could not refrain himself before all them that stood firmly by him, and he cried, "Clear out every man around me!" And there stood no man with him while Joseph made himself known unto his brethren. And he gave his voice to weeping, and the Egyptians heard and the house of Pharaoh heard. (45:1–2)

Joseph is deeply moved by Judah's speech, and for the third time gives himself over to weeping. The first time, reminded by hearing Reuben's guilt-ridden memory of the crime committed against himself, Joseph had briefly turned aside from the brothers and wept, immediately returning to seize and bind Simeon and to command his servants (42:22–25). The second time, filled with compassion at the sight of Benjamin, Joseph had to remove himself temporarily to his chamber in order to weep in private; no one saw or heard him weeping, and he easily returned to his position of command (43:30–31). Here, his conscience stricken by Judah's heartrending portrait of "my father" and his stirring display of filial piety, Joseph completely loses control (even while desperately trying to retain it). He imperiously banishes his Egyptian retinue, so as to be alone with his brethren. There is no interpreter present: Joseph intends to speak to his brothers in Hebrew and, shedding his Egyptian disguise, to *"make himself known"* unto his brethren. (The text here employs the reflexive form of the verb "to know," a form that the Bible will use again only when God speaks of His own self-disclosure to His prophets; Numbers 12:6.) Yet before Joseph can speak even a word to his brothers, he cries and weeps aloud, so loudly that he is heard not only by his Egyptian retainers outside but all the way to the house of Pharaoh. Even before his verbal self-disclosure, Joseph the god-like involuntarily reveals himself through his weeping to be a vulnerable and humanly connected human being, on an equal footing with his brethren.

Restored to his human roots, but recovered from his sobbing, Joseph seeks to reestablish ties with his human family. But it will prove no easy task.

> And Joseph said unto his brethren, "I am Joseph; doth yet my father [*or* Father: *'avi*] live [*'ani Yosef ha'od 'avi chai*]?" But his brethren could not answer him, for they were dismayed [*or* terrified] before his presence. (45:3)

Joseph's five-word self-identification is deeply moving, not least because it shows the effect of Judah's great speech. Joseph's simple declaration of his identity *as Joseph* entails admitting that he comes from and still belongs to his father. Eight times Judah had put the word *'avi*, "my father," in Joseph's ears; Joseph poignantly now echoes it back to his brothers: the father you spoke of, he is *my* father too; we share the same origins. Indeed, *'avi* heard in its idiomatic and more familiar usage as "Father"—"Doth Father yet live?"—makes the claim of brotherly identity even more compelling.

But Joseph's immediate preoccupation with Jacob goes beyond his desire to prove to his brothers that he is one of them. His question, usually read as expressing either wonder that the old man is still alive after all these years or suspicion that his brothers had spoken falsely about their father when he stood over them in his viceroy's position, goes much deeper. For multiple reasons—ranging from his suspicion about Jacob's part in his own "disappearance" and his continued association with the hateful brothers, to guilt over his own recent "punishment" of his father through the "kidnapping" of Benjamin, to perhaps even some doubts about his father's reaction to his own Egyptianization—Joseph badly wants not just reunion but reconciliation with his father. "Doth my father yet live?" asks not only whether Jacob is physically alive. It also asks whether Father is alive *for me*, as *my* father. Whatever the answer, Joseph's question by itself constitutes the reconciliation of Joseph's heart with the man who once loved him above all others. Joseph, at least for the moment, has returned home. Does he, he desperately needs to know, still have a home in his father's heart?

Joseph's brothers are dumbstruck and terrified. Joseph speaks again, to explain and to give reassurance.

> And Joseph said unto his brethren, "Come near, please, to me," and they came near. And he said, "I am Joseph, your brother, whom ye sold into the land of Egypt. And now, be not grieved and be not angry with yourselves that ye sold me hither; for to preserve life God [*'elohim*] did send me be-

fore you. For these two years hath famine been in the land, and there are yet five years in which there shall be neither plowing nor harvest. And God [*'elohim*] sent me before you to preserve you a posterity in the earth, and to save you alive for a great deliverance. So now, it was not you who sent me hither but God [*'elohim*]; and He hath made me a father to Pharaoh, and lord over all his house, and ruler [*moshel*] over all the land of Egypt." (45:4–8)

It is difficult to know in what spirit Joseph is speaking. At least three different accounts of Joseph's state of mind all make sense. He may be trying simply to reconcile with his brothers, while at the same time explaining both to them *and to himself* the meaning of his own life, including especially why he has been promoted ahead of them. Or, second, he may be magnanimously trying to put his brothers at ease, by denying their guilt and having them believe that everything that has happened is part of God's plan. Or, third, Joseph may not be in full control: still overcome with passion, he wants both to give reassurance and to claim superiority, and he gets confused about which God is which or about the difference between human doings and God's.

Given that Joseph has surely seen that his brothers are disbelieving and frightened of him, he is almost certainly attempting to put them at their ease and to reassure them. He calls them near and, though reminding them of their misdeed against him, seeks to relieve their guilt and to remove their fear of his exacting retribution. But insofar as this magnanimous gesture intends to make reunion possible, it also introduces a new distance between his brothers and Joseph (as all acts of magnanimity tend to do). How could closeness be established between brothers, when one of them claims to be God's own instrument and appointed savior of the rest? Part of the difficulty of reconciliation lies, no doubt in the circumstances: Joseph is indeed in an exalted position, and they have been and are still at his mercy. And the brothers, having witnessed so many changes in this fellow's treatment of them, are going to be slow in accepting what he says at face value. But part of the difficulty lies also with Joseph's abiding character. Even when he tries to be brotherly, he cannot help but parade his superiority. A close reading of the motion of the speech makes this clear.

Joseph begins by asserting equality: "I am your brother." But you are morally beneath me, for you behaved unjustly and unbrotherly: "whom you sold into Egypt." Yet, never mind, do not feel guilty; for you are not really morally beneath me, as we are both, in this matter, equally instruments of God: "God sent me before you . . . to save you alive for a great deliverance." Here's proof that God is behind this: "He made me father to Pharaoh, lord over all his house, and ruler throughout all the land of Egypt." In sum: If you need proof that I am Joseph your brother, equally the son of our father, please know that God has made me superior to Pharaoh and the ruler over all Egypt.

Joseph honestly tries to reestablish brotherly relations. He calls himself their brother. He denies their responsibility for their unbrotherly act against him. He speaks (three times) of their God and invites them to see that both they and he are equally subject to God's plan. And he makes it clear that his great power can save them, because he is kindly disposed to do so.

At the same time, Joseph (partly, we suspect, *because* he is Joseph) cannot help but create distance. His largesse toward them, his self-proclaimed special relation to God, and his exaggerated description of his exalted status—"father to Pharaoh," and so forth—all emphasize how he stands over and apart. Joseph makes no apology for his deceptions or for the ordeal he has put them through. Indeed, in making answer to Judah's speech, Joseph says that, far from being a near patricide, I am the true savior. And why would or should Joseph apologize, exalted personage that he has become? For if Pharaoh is a demigod (the child of the sun god), then Joseph, "father to Pharaoh," presents himself as an (Egyptian) god. Joseph, in this speech of self-revelation, continues to display his characteristic and lifelong grandiosity.

In no place is this more evident than in his remarks about God. Joseph's interpretation of the events of his life as enacting a divine plan is usually taken as a sign of Joseph's superior intuition (not to say powers of divination) and superior piety. And to be sure, there is no evidence in the text that shows him to be mistaken: the Bible often presents events as doubly caused, the result simultaneously of human action and divine will. But there is equally no evidence to support Joseph's claim: indeed, at no point in his life does God speak to Joseph. Neither does Joseph pray to God or swear by His name. And the text, speaking in its own impartial voice, never corroborates Joseph's assertion—here and elsewhere—that his doings are the doings of God.[21] Thus we are in the dark about Joseph's claims about providence. We do not know whether this is a true moment of self-discovery and self-revelation. We do not know if this is a necessary or clever suggestion, indispensable for the purpose of reconciliation: would Joseph have been capable of forgoing revenge—and would the brothers have been willing to believe him—in the absence of the idea of the grand "divine plan"? We cannot be sure whether Joseph means by *'elohim* the God of Abraham, Isaac, and Jacob, or some other deity, or even something more general like providence or fate.[22] And though it may seem uncharitable to mention it, we do

---

21. We have touched on this matter earlier in the discussion of Joseph's interpretation of Egyptian dreams. See pp. 554, 564.

22. I owe this observation to Robert Alter, one of the few contemporary commentators who keeps an open mind about Joseph's piety. Commenting on Joseph's claim that "God has sent me before

not even know if Joseph believes what he is saying, or, perhaps, what he believes, since he all too often appears to us inclined to conflate himself with the deity.

But the most important question raised for Joseph's brothers—and for all of us readers—is not what (and why) Joseph believes about his being the instrument of God. It is rather whether he is right in his assertions of a providential plan. Those who know the future story of Israel in Egypt, and who also remember God's forecast to Abraham of four hundred years of servitude (15:13–14; the name of Egypt was not mentioned to Abraham), may well be inclined here to believe that Joseph is speaking truly, we know not how. But as in so many other places—in the text, and in life—where people claim to be enacting God's will or plan, the thoughtful auditor will want to know, "Is he right? How does he know? How can I be sure?" In the absence of direct corroboration of divine speech, we are wise to remain skeptical, keeping an open mind. When claims of divine dispensation come from someone like Joseph, this advice is supremely apt.

SUMMONING ISRAEL TO EGYPT

We return to Joseph's speech, which we interrupted in the middle, after his explanation to his brothers but before the main point, his instructions regarding his father:

> "Hasten ye, and go up to my father, and say ye unto him, 'Thus saith thy son Joseph: "God hath made me lord over all Egypt; come down unto me, and tarry not. And thou shalt dwell in the land of Goshen, and thou shalt be near unto me, thou, and thy children, and thy children's children, and thy flocks, and thy herds, and all that thou hast. And there I will sustain thee; for there are yet five years of famine; lest thou lose all, thou, and thy household, and all that thou hast." ' " (45:9–11)

Believing that he has reassured his brothers regarding his nonhostile intentions and impressed them with his great standing, he now commands them to tackle the more difficult yet, from his point of view, most important task: getting Jacob

---

you" (v. 5), Alter remarks: "Joseph's speech is a luminous illustration of the Bible's double system of causation, human and divine. Commentators have tended to tilt the balance to one side, making Joseph a mouthpiece of piety here. His recognition of a providential plan may well be admirable from the viewpoint of monotheistic faith, but there is no reason to assume that Joseph has lost the sense of his own brilliant initiative in all that he has accomplished, so that when he says 'God' ('elohim, which could also suggest something more general like 'providence' or 'fate'), he also means Joseph." My own reading of Joseph's character leads me to be even more suspicious than Alter regarding Joseph's piety.

to come to him in Egypt.[23] Ever since Judah finished speaking, reconciliation with his father, much more than with his brothers, is Joseph's preoccupation. But how shall he achieve it? Joseph here rejects the alternative of returning to his people in their native land. There is good practical reason for not doing so, as the famine remains great and in Egypt he can sustain his father and the entire clan. But there is no doubt another reason why Joseph would be unwilling to return to his father and his father's ways: he has too much to lose. A man who boasts of being father to Pharaoh and ruler of all Egypt is unlikely to be willing to sacrifice his lofty position and his great power in the world's leading nation in order to become again a lowly shepherd. However much Joseph has been—and remains—troubled about his divided identity, he here makes a self-defining choice: I will not rejoin my father, and he will not exactly rejoin me. Rather I will benefit him from on high. As I have become a father to Pharaoh, so I will become a father to my father, and a savior of the entire clan.

Joseph commands his brothers to carry his command to his father (he does not say "our father"). The speech he writes for them to make to Jacob reflects Joseph's awareness of his difficult rhetorical task. Jacob not only needs to be persuaded that Joseph is alive. He also needs to be shown why Joseph has not come to him, and especially why he and his entire clan should pick up and leave the Promised Land for the foreign ways of Egypt. And—an embarrassing point that Joseph in fact neglects—Jacob will no doubt want to know why Joseph has been tormenting him with his charades these past two years. The speech is only partly a success.

The brothers are told to begin by announcing *"Thy son Joseph* saith," but what he says first off is "God has made me [*that is,* I am] lord of all Egypt." Joseph wishes to impress Jacob with his great standing, so that Jacob will be more inclined to come to him. His high standing will also explain his ability and need to give commands and his refusal to come himself to his father. It will also attest to his ability to be Jacob's and the family's benefactor. For the core of the speech— providing the main inducement for Jacob to come—informs Jacob of Joseph's ability to save him and his clan, and it makes sure that Jacob is aware of his need to be saved by Joseph (five more years of famine).

But Joseph's speech suffers from his usual excess. He is not the lord of all Egypt, Pharaoh is. It is not up to him, but to Pharaoh, whether his people will be allowed to settle in the land of Goshen, or anywhere else—especially, as we learn later, because the Egyptians abominate shepherds. He fails to see—or perhaps deliberately hides from view—that his plan means permanent separation from

23. That he issues these commands regarding Jacob without having received an answer to his question "Doth my father yet live?" demonstrates that he did not really doubt the brothers' story about Jacob and supports our earlier suggestion that he did not mean the question literally.

his father and his brothers. Most important, Joseph is blind to the full meaning of his proposal that Israel come to Egypt. Joseph sees only five years of famine, not beyond. At the same time, he proposes long-term settlement, which risks Israelite assimilation or worse. He sees only his chance to be a benefactor, but not how that benefaction could inspire Egyptian enmity toward his people. He misunderstands God's plan (about which he so confidently speaks), which includes four hundred years of slavery for which his present proposal is the initiating cause. As Robert Sacks judiciously notes:

> To the reader there is something awkward and disturbing in Joseph's great claim that he will nourish his brothers during the five years of famine. His words seem honest and sincere, yet he appears to have wholly misunderstood the divine plan of which he is speaking. Joseph failed to understand that those five years of honor would drag on into four hundred years of slavery. Joseph was so caught up in his own magic that he was unable to see the toils and difficulties which would have to be endured before his brothers would return to their home. The author of Genesis shows his great sensitivity to men and their ways by forcing the reader to face Joseph's greatest weakness within the same speech that shows his strength. The reader must neither be beguiled by his humanity nor believe that humanity to be mere pretense.

Joseph concludes his speech appealing for their credulity and reiterating his wishes regarding Jacob:

> "And behold, your eyes see and the eyes of *my brother Benjamin,* that it is *my mouth* that speaketh unto you. And ye shall tell *my father* of all my glory in Egypt and of all that ye have seen. And ye shall make haste and bring down *my father* hither." (45:12–13; emphasis added)

As further evidence of his identity, Joseph points out to his astonished brothers, who in their distress may have overlooked the point, that he has been speaking to them directly, not through an interpreter (who might not be trustworthy), and speaking in their language (Hebrew). He also gains credibility by speaking Benjamin's name, though they had not told him the name of their youngest brother. Yet Joseph's plea for trust and closeness comes—once again—with provocations that imply continuing separation: he separates "your eyes" from those of "my brother Benjamin," rubbing the noses of his ten half brothers in the household's cleavage and in his willingness to call only Benjamin "my brother." He brings their eyes to witness that it is his mouth that speaks, that it is he alone that commands. He continues to speak of "my father," not "our father." And he commands his brothers to bear tidings of "all *my* glory." Unlike Judah, Joseph cannot forge the unity of the family, neither in speech nor, as we see in the sequel, in deed.

> And he fell upon his brother Benjamin's neck and wept; and Benjamin wept upon his neck. And he kissed all his brethren and wept upon them; and after that his brethren talked with him. (45:14–15)

Having finished speaking, Joseph proceeds first to embrace Benjamin and weep upon his neck, then to kiss his other brothers. The tension is released, the estrangement is over. The picture of Joseph and Benjamin, the sons of Rachel, reunited with mutual weeping each on the other's neck, is profoundly moving. They weep together for present joy as well as for past sorrows, and we weep with them. They weep because their deepest longings, long felt to be unfulfillable, are wondrously satisfied. A miracle has happened, and we participate in it. We rejoice also in Joseph's embrace of his other brothers, as there is no reason to doubt the sincerity of his expressed emotions.

But careful readers—and, no doubt, the observant brothers—notice the asymmetry of his approach to Benjamin and his approach to them. The difference is perfectly understandable: Joseph has many reasons for loving Benjamin more than the others. But it is a difference nonetheless, and it carries significance for future family relations. The difference in Joseph's conduct is reciprocated in the brothers' responses: Benjamin weeps upon Joseph's neck as Joseph weeps upon his; Joseph kisses and weeps upon his other brothers, but in response, they merely talk to him (though we are not told anything that they said). Despite his emotional frankness, Joseph leaves the brothers wary and disunited, even in this peak moment of reunion and reconciliation. True, the brothers may still be shell-shocked. True also, they are likely nonplussed by Joseph's mercurial changes, and they are unlikely to have forgotten both how he toyed with them and how much power he still wields over them. (To the end of Joseph's life, the brothers harbor fears that he will someday try to get revenge.) But this is not just the work of their fearful imaginations. Joseph keeps his superiority and his favoritism before them at all times. Even in his golden display of family feeling, we see Joseph's liabilities as a leader in Israel. Joseph, working from the outside, can serve and save life; but he cannot work from within to unify his people or preserve a way of life. He is a feudal servant, not a national leader.

A generation earlier, Joseph's father, returning home from Paddan-aram, encountered brother Esau coming toward him with what seemed to be fratricidal intentions. Like Joseph, Esau had become an outsider to the covenant of Abraham and a powerful prince in the region. Like Joseph facing his arriving brothers, Esau had a score to settle with his brother for past unbrotherly acts. Yet at the last moment, overcome with family feeling, Esau ran to meet Jacob, embraced him, *fell on his neck,* and *kissed* him; together *they wept* (33:4). Yet wary Jacob does not altogether trust the durability of Esau's change of heart; he won't forget that Esau still has grievances and that he had come against him with a war party; and he sees that Esau has adopted foreign ways.

Like Jacob reuniting with Esau, Joseph's brothers will remain wary of Joseph, and for similar reasons. They do not altogether trust his change of heart; they can't forget that he has cause to harm them and the power to do so with impunity; they feel acutely their inferior position; and everything about Joseph's appearance—from his clean-shaven face to his royal Egyptian garb—insists on his foreignness to their way of life. Sentimental readers, wishing to see only family reconciliation, overlook these matters. Joseph's brothers, and the way of Israel, cannot afford sentimentality.

As if intending to impress us with this fact, the text immediately broadens our vision of this more-than-familial event by reminding us of its Egyptian setting and context. We are forced to remember that not Joseph but Pharaoh is the ultimate authority.

> And the report thereof was heard in the house of Pharaoh, saying, "Joseph's brethren have come." And it was good in the eyes of Pharaoh and in the eyes of *his slaves* [*or* servants: *'avadim*].
>
> And Pharaoh said unto Joseph, "Say unto thy brethren, 'This do ye: Lade your beasts, and go, get you unto the land of Canaan. And take your father and your households and *come unto me;* and *I* will give you the good of the land of Egypt, and ye shall eat the fat of the land. Now thou art commanded, this do ye: Take your wagons out of the land of Egypt for your little ones and for your wives, and bring your father, and come. Also *regard not your stuff* [*literally,* your eyes shall not have pity on your stuff]; for the good things of all the land of Egypt are yours.'" (45:16–20; emphasis added)

Once again, the big picture looks very bright for the Children of Israel. Pharaoh, no doubt because of his regard for Joseph, is pleased with the news about Joseph's family and is even more magnanimous than his viceroy. On his own, and presumably not knowing that Joseph has already done so, Pharaoh invites the family to move to Egypt and offers them the best that Egypt has to offer, declaring with royal flair, "The good things of all the land of Egypt are yours." It sounds like an offer that only a fool would refuse, especially when the famine is severe at home and life is precarious.

But the fine print holds many clues that there are thorns among these proffered roses. Right away it reminds us of the existence of Egyptian slavery: Pharaoh is pleased, and so are his *slaves*.[24] Also, though Joseph may think that he is ruler of all Egypt, he—and we—are quickly reminded that Pharaoh is in charge. As Joseph dictated the speech for his brothers to make to Jacob, so Pharaoh dictates the speech that Joseph is to make to his brothers. Within that dictated speech, the command "Come to me" could mean either "Come to me, Joseph" or "Come to me, Pharaoh," and the "I" who is to be the benefactor is more likely Pharaoh than Joseph. Finally, when we compare Joseph's private offer to his father with Pharaoh's official offer to Joseph's family, one difference stands out: Pharaoh has in mind their assimilation into the land of Egypt, not their living apart in the land of Goshen. Three times Pharaoh mentions the land of Egypt, twice to offer up its goods. Whereas Joseph had urged his father to come with his flocks and his herds and *"all that thou hast,"* Pharaoh commands that only the people come, leaving their stuff behind. He pointedly tells them not to regret the abandonment of their own household goods ("your stuff" would include your pots and utensils, your clothing, and your instruments of worship), because they will be replaced by the best that Egypt can provide. Leave your ways behind, says Pharaoh. Become Egyptians, like Joseph.

Joseph does as he is told, and so do his brothers in turn. In describing what happens next, the text highlights the question of assimilation versus separation: it pointedly calls the men not "Joseph's brothers" (as they were moments ago called in the house of Pharaoh) but "the sons of Israel," a designation used only once before, at their first descent into Egypt to buy grain ("And the sons of Israel came to buy among those that came"; 42:5).

> And so the *sons of Israel* did; and Joseph gave them wagons, according to the commandment of Pharaoh, and gave them provisions for the way. To all of them he gave each man *changes of raiment;* but to Benjamin he gave three hundred shekels of silver, and five changes of raiment. And to his father he sent in like manner ten asses laden with the good things of Egypt,

24. The gentler translation of "servants" for *'avadim* would not decisively alter the point. What are today only Pharaoh's servants will soon enough become Pharaoh's slaves; in fact, as we shall see, Joseph himself will help institute widespread slavery in Egypt. Egypt is the place of masters and servants, where one man is the supreme master and, therefore, all others are in principle under his thumb. The Hebrew-speaking reader will hear in this remark about Pharaoh's servants the foreshadowing of Israel's future enslavement to Pharaoh, the one who knew not Joseph.

and ten she-asses laden with corn and bread and victual for his father by the way. So he sent his brethren away, and they departed; and he said unto them, "Do not be perturbed ['al-tirgezu] on the journey." (45:16–24; emphasis added)

We do not fail to notice that Joseph sends his brothers off with changes of clothing for the journey. If they make use of them, they will arrive back in Canaan and appear before Jacob as ambassadors bedecked in Egyptian dress, carrying the good things of Egypt to their father and an Egyptian invitation to move up in the world. The sons of Israel can hardly be confident of their father's favorable reception. This is not the least reason why Joseph might feel the need to encourage them "not to be perturbed on the journey."[25]

The brothers go up out of Egypt and return to Canaan and their father, Jacob. The account of their dramatic meeting is economically presented in but three verses:

And they told him, saying, "Joseph is yet alive, and he is the ruler over all the land of Egypt." And his heart stopped, for he believed them not. And they told him all the words of Joseph, which he had said unto them; and when he saw the wagons that Joseph had sent to carry him, the spirit of Jacob their father revived. And *Israel* said, "Enough! Joseph, my son, is yet alive. I will go and see him before I die." (45:26–28; emphasis added)

Forgetting the speech Joseph had "written" for them to make, the brothers blurt out the big news: Joseph is still alive; he is the ruler over all the land of Egypt! (The last phrase had been part of Joseph's self-description [45:8]; in repeating it, the brothers omit Joseph's claim that it was *God* who had made him ruler, as well as his claim that God had also made him "father of Pharaoh" and "lord of all his house.") Jacob, who Judah feared would die should Benjamin be lost to him, suffers transient cardiac arrest when he hears that Joseph still lives. There is no need for sophisticated explanations to account for the shock; the text tells us it is because he did not believe his sons' report.

But what exactly did Jacob not believe? Only that Joseph was indeed alive? Or

---

25. I follow Alter's translation of *'al-tirgezu* as "Do not be disturbed or perturbed" rather than the more common "Do not quarrel." "The primary meaning of the verb [r-g-z] is to quake or to shake, either physically (as a mountain in an earthquake) or emotionally (as a person trembling with fear), and it is the antonym of being tranquil or at peace. Joseph is reassuring his brothers that they need not fear any lurking residue of vengefulness on his part that would turn the journey homeward into a trap." Given the traps that Joseph had sprung on them twice before on homeward journeys, such reassurance is certainly called for.

also that he was ruler over all Egypt? Could these cruel sons, who long ago tricked me regarding Joseph's death, be tricking me again? There is another and more poignant possibility: Jacob may also have been unwilling to believe—or better, to accept—that it was his beloved Joseph who had played such a cruel joke on him, taking Simeon hostage and, especially, extracting Benjamin from him. "Could Joseph, my favorite son, torture me so? Impossible! Unthinkable!" Jacob cannot bear the thought that Joseph could bear him such ill will, not least because Jacob still feels responsible for Joseph's "disappearance."

Not the brothers' speech but the sight of the Egyptian wagons persuades Jacob to believe his sons' story. "Enough," he cries out: "Enough evidence, I now believe you; enough of this charade; enough that Joseph is alive, what do I care about his being the ruler?" The text indicates that when Jacob revives, he revives as "Israel," not as "Jacob." Nonetheless, he is not thinking in terms of the nation but, once again, purely as a father; and then, only of his favorite son. He will go to see not Joseph, prince of Egypt, but "Joseph, my son." Echoing, but at the same time answering, Joseph's opening query, "Doth *my father* yet live?" Jacob's closing reply, "Joseph, *my son*, is yet alive," makes clear that Joseph's father is still alive, *as a father*, to his departed son. Despite all that has happened, Jacob cannot help but love his son. No matter what Joseph may feel and do toward him, Jacob for his part has been and will continue to be alive as a father to his son. Israel will go to Egypt, not intending to become Egyptian, but simply to reknit the bond between father and son. That Israel may not be wise in doing so is suggested by one troubling fact: this is the first and only time in Genesis that a father follows after a son.

Old Israel goes to Egypt on his own terms. But will he like what he finds there? Will Israel and his people be able to preserve their identity and independence in Egypt? These are questions that, although he does not openly consider them, may soon cross Jacob's mind. They surely cross the mind of the reader.

CHAPTER TWENTY

ISRAEL IN EGYPT:
THE WAY NOT TAKEN

*T*he story of Joseph and his brothers has ended happily, at least for now. Joseph has stopped toying with his brothers and has ceased his dramaturgy. The brothers, repentant, are on good behavior, relieved and chastened. Fratricide has once again been avoided, as has death from famine. At last, family reunification of the generations of Jacob is a distinct possibility, under the leadership—or at least the protection—of Joseph. Israel, his aged father, will soon see for himself how his favorite son has risen to a position commensurate with his talents and boyhood dreams, wearing a mantle of rule more splendid than the ornamented tunic Jacob had once given him. Readers of Genesis who focus mainly on the family saga have ample reason to be cheerful.

But readers who are attuned to the larger meaning of the story know better than to expect a simply happy ending. For this particular "solution" to the intrafamilial problem poses a serious threat to the survival of this young nation *as* the people of God's covenant called to follow in His ways. The entrance of Israel into Egypt raises crucial questions—for the first, but hardly the last, time for this often exiled people—of assimilation or separation, under conditions of diaspora. How much must the Children of Israel become like their host nation in order to live securely and prosper under its rule? Will they be able to square the demands of survival, the attractions of worldly success, and the need to live in exile with the call to be a righteous and holy people, God's light unto the nations? Precisely because Egypt is civilization at its peak, careful readers of Genesis—tutored from the beginning to notice the unjust and unholy ways of cities and civilization—have every reason to be concerned about the fate of nascent Israel in its encounter with mighty and prosperous Egypt.

PRAYERFUL DESCENT, DIVINE REASSURANCE

Jacob, for his own personal reasons, is also apprehensive about going down to Egypt. It is not only that he is old and the journey is long and arduous. Joseph, even if he is alive, even if he is in command, rules not where Jacob had hoped, in God's Promised Land. What does this mean? What has happened to Joseph in Egypt? What will happen to me, to my generations, and to the divine covenant when we go down to Egypt? Who will watch over us and protect all that I care about against dilution, dissolution, and destruction?

Both eager and worried, Jacob sets out on his journey from Hebron, in the Promised Land, to Egypt. When he goes, he does not forget who he is. For one thing, he does not follow Pharaoh's instructions to leave behind his belongings; rather, he takes with him "all that he had." More important, he remembers the God of his ancestors:

> And Israel set out with all that he had and he came to Beer-sheba; and he offered sacrifices [*vayizbach zevachim*] unto the God of his father, Isaac. And God spake unto Israel in the visions of the night and said, "Jacob, Jacob"; and he said, "Here-am-I [*hineni*]." And He said, "I am the God, God of thy father. Fear not to go down into Egypt, for a great nation will I make of thee there. I Myself will go down with thee into Egypt and I Myself will surely also bring thee back up; and Joseph shall put his hand upon thine eyes." (46:1–4)

Jacob does not go directly to Egypt; he first makes a stop at Beer-sheba, a place in the south at the edge of the desert, a place rife with significance in the life of his ancestors Abraham and Isaac. Beer-sheba was the place where Abraham and Abimelech had sworn a covenant (21:32) and where Abraham went and stayed after the binding and wondrous deliverance of Isaac (22:19). It was at Beer-sheba that God had appeared to Isaac (26:23–24), who, in response, built there an altar and called upon the name of the Lord (26:25); there Isaac also had made a covenant with Abimelech and had wondrously found water (26:26–33). And when Jacob himself first went traveling into foreign lands, to Haran and Uncle Laban, he had set out from Beer-sheba (28:10). Now, probably once again fearful in anticipation of a risky foreign encounter, and surely filled with awe at the news both of Joseph's deliverance and of his Egyptianization, Jacob (as Israel) stops in Beer-sheba to offer sacrifice to the God of his father, Isaac.

This is only Jacob's second sacrifice reported in the Bible—the first since his covenant with Laban on his return from Haran (31:54)—and the only one said *explicitly* to be a sacrifice *to God*.[1] Perhaps in the spirit of thanksgiving, Jacob offers a sacrifice in place of Joseph, who he had believed to be dead (and whom he

---

1. As on that first occasion, the unusual character of this sacrifice is indicated in the Hebrew usage *vayizbach zevachim,* literally "He sacrificed sacrifices." We do not know what he offered. The word for burnt offering of an animal, *'olah,* is not used.

even thought he had sent to be "sacrificed"), but who has been wondrously "delivered." But Jacob may also be sacrificing in the spirit of petition, hoping that God will be moved to restore to him his "lost" (because Egyptianized) Joseph. In offering sacrifice, Jacob identifies himself here with his father, Isaac; perhaps he, like Isaac at his moment of great trembling (27:33), recognizes his own self-deception regarding his sons. Jacob had preferred Joseph and anointed him as the leader of the next generation in Israel; later, he had thought that Joseph was dead and that his other sons were his murderers. He was wrong, deeply wrong, about his preferences and about all his sons. As he heads for Egypt, Jacob may be even filled with foreboding that he is experiencing God's verdict on his preferential love of Rachel and especially of Joseph. He has no reason to know whether the God of his father, Isaac, holds any power in Egypt,[2] but he petitions Him nonetheless with sacrifices to protect his little family in its encounter with powerful Egypt, where his "found-but-lost" son, Joseph, holds sway.

God answers Jacob's appeal. For the first time since Joseph disappeared, twenty-two years ago—in fact, for the first time since Joseph was a boy[3]—God speaks to Jacob. This will be the last divine speech reported in Genesis. Indeed, it is God's last communication for four hundred years. When next we hear Him speak, He will call to Moses out of the burning bush (Exodus 3:2 ff.), summoning him to liberate the Children of Israel from Egyptian bondage. The opening exchange of the present encounter—"Jacob, Jacob" and "Here-I-am"—both anticipates that next conversation (*God:* "Moses, Moses"; *Moses:* "Here-I-am [*hineni*]") and echoes God's last exchange with Abraham, when He commanded him not to sacrifice Isaac (*the angel of the Lord:* "Abraham, Abraham"; *Abraham:* "Here-I-am [*hineni*]"; 22:11; compare 22:1). Jacob, like Abraham on Moriah and Moses at the call, announces himself as fully present to God; *hineni* is the last word that Jacob will ever speak to God, as it was for Abraham (22:11).

It seems significant that God, in responding to Jacob's sacrifice, speaks "unto Israel" but summons him as "Jacob, Jacob," not as Israel, and, moreover, does so through the mysterious vehicle of a dream. Though he answers *"hineni"* with full attentiveness, Jacob has not been thinking as a leader of the new way, but as a fearful old man in need of divine assistance, moved by a desire to see his favorite son. Thus, now that He has gained his complete attention, God not only offers precise answers to Jacob's fears and concerns. He also moves him to think

2. God had prevented Isaac from going down into Egypt (26:2).

3. The last time God spoke with Jacob was at Beth-El, on Jacob's return from Paddan-aram, after the episode with Dinah and Shechem (35:9–15). Joseph was then probably less than ten years old; Benjamin was not yet born.

about the nation and the divine promise: Do not be afraid that the encounter with Egypt will be deadly either to you or to your people. On the contrary, there you will become a great nation: I, the God of thy father, guarantee it. I am not powerless in Egypt; on the contrary, I Myself will go down with you. Do not be afraid about leaving the land and the ancestral place of burial: I Myself will surely bring you out again. And regarding Joseph, he is not altogether lost to you; Joseph himself will close your eyes.[4]

Jacob might well find the speech encouraging, but its message is hardly unambiguous. As often happens in dreams, only part of its truth is visible. Israel learns (for the first time) that his clan will become a great nation *in Egypt*,[5] but he does not know that it will happen only through being enslaved and losing its own identity. God will go down with Israel into Egypt, but He will keep silent and do nothing helpful for four hundred years. God will surely bring Jacob himself out again, but only as a corpse; God will surely bring the Children of Israel out again, but not for a long, long time. Joseph will literally close Jacob's eyes in death, but as Robert Sacks points out, he will also blind all of Israel to the fate of enslavement that awaits them: "When God says *Joseph shall put his hand upon thine eyes,* he is referring to Joseph's magic, which, as we saw in the last chapters, lulled the sons of Israel to sleep so that they could not see what would be in store for them in Egypt."[6] Paradoxically, we might say, in offering Jacob reassurance about his own fears, God is also telling Jacob precisely what to worry about: the danger of assimilation, the need for return, the promise and the danger of both Egypt and Joseph for the creation of God's great nation.

Suitably encouraged by God's message in his dream, Jacob now leaves Canaan and heads for Egypt. The text, though spare, allows us to imagine the procession.[7]

4. Our earlier exploration of Jacob's state of mind in offering sacrifice was influenced by reading backward from God's "response." On the generally sound assumption that God knows his "customers," and encouraged by previous instances where God's speech seems exactly fitting to His listener's concerns, we think that this exegetical tactic is permissible. When God says, "Fear not," we can reasonably assume that the addressee was afraid. (See, as a previous example, 15:1.)

5. The fact that it would be in *Egypt* that Israel would become a great nation was not told to anyone before.

6. Sacks argues, in my view quite powerfully, that such "going to sleep" is a necessary precondition of becoming God's new nation, since only slaves are empty enough of a way of their own to receive the new way. This would partly explain why the Children of Israel can become the people of Israel only in—and out of—Egypt.

7. The convoy bringing Jacob into Egypt is fruitfully compared with the funeral procession that brings his body back for burial (50:7–13). Jacob goes down into Egypt in Pharaoh's wagon, he comes up on the shoulders of his sons. (We shall discuss Jacob's funeral in Chapter Twenty-one.)

And Jacob rose up from Beersheba; and the sons of Israel conveyed Jacob, their father, and their little ones, and their wives, in the wagons that Pharaoh had sent to carry him. And they took their livestock, and their goods, which they had gotten in the land of Canaan, and they came into Egypt, Jacob and *all his seed with him.* His sons and the sons of his sons with him, his daughters and the daughters of his sons, and *all his seed,* he brought with him to Egypt. (46:5–7; emphasis added)

Though Israel enters Egypt conveyed in Pharaoh's wagons, he brings with him *everything* he has acquired in Canaan—livestock, goods, and especially all his seed—leaving nothing behind. Holding on to what belongs to them, Jacob's seed are transplanted into the fertile land. What will sprout there now becomes the crucial question.

THE DESCENDANTS INTO EGYPT

At this point in the narrative, the text offers a full and detailed census, naming names, of those who came into Egypt with Jacob. The insertion of this enumeration, at precisely this point in the account, not only serves to build dramatic tension by delaying the report of the reunion of Jacob and Joseph. It also focuses the reader's attention on the incipient nation, the Children of Israel. Perhaps Jacob himself, even while awaiting his reunion with Joseph, is also thinking more in terms of the nation, of his grandchildren ("all his seed . . . the sons of his sons . . . the daughters of his sons . . . all his seed") and not only of "Joseph, my son." In addition, by setting forth in concrete detail the Children of Israel at the start of Israel's encounter with Egypt, the census enables the reader to follow what will happen to them there. The phrase with which the census begins—"And these are the names [*ve'eleh shemoth*] of the Children of Israel that came into Egypt" (46:8)—is repeated verbatim at the very start of the book of Exodus (1:1),[8] in a chapter that tells how the individuated children of Israel (Jacob) and their descendants became the *people* of Israel.[9]

In one respect, the enumerated list of names is perplexing. The number of the enumerated names does not quite agree with the total head count given at the end of the census,[10] where—to complicate things further—two different numbers appear in the summing up:

8. The Hebrew name for this book is *Shemoth,* "Names."

9. The census of the named individuals also anticipates the postliberation census after forty years of wandering in the desert (Numbers 26), where the people are grouped according to their twelve tribes, named after Jacob's (and Joseph's) sons.

10. Verse 15 says that the number of Jacob's sons and daughters, born through Leah, was thirty-three, but counting Dinah, the last one named, thirty-four names have been mentioned. Two of

All the souls *that came with Jacob into Egypt,* sprung from his loins, besides the wives of Jacob's sons, all the souls were *threescore and six.* And the sons of Joseph, who were born to him in Egypt, were two souls; all the souls of the house of Jacob *that came into Egypt* were *threescore and ten.* (46:26–27; emphasis added)

Many interpreters have sought to solve the apparent contradictions and reconcile the numbers, while others think that sixty-six has been rounded to a symbolic approximation, one that conveys "fullness . . . ten times sacred seven." But readers alert to the problem that lurks beneath the cheerful surface of the impending family reunion will notice that the heart of the numerical difference concerns the proper place of Joseph and his Egyptian-born sons. Sixty-six souls *came with Jacob* into Egypt; counting Jacob, Joseph, and his two sons, there were seventy souls of the house of Jacob *now present* in Egypt. Will Joseph and his sons go with the sixty-six others? Or will the latter Egyptianize and go with Joseph? Will Jacob remain with the sixty-six who came with him? Or will he become most attached to Joseph, his favorite?

After the census naming the descendants of Israel that went down into Egypt, the text shows us a sequence of episodes that will enable us to answer these questions. Although Jacob has been reassured by God that he could go down to Egypt without worrying, Jacob does in fact worry. From the moment of his arrival, he seems very focused and concerned. Jacob, true to his character, does not simply take his dream with God's reassurance at face value. Perhaps sensing the dangers implicit in God's speech, Jacob sees that he must take action in order to avoid them. From the start, Jacob is on the alert regarding both Egypt and Joseph. In three stages, we watch Jacob gradually and reluctantly come to realize that Joseph is permanently lost to him and to the way of Israel and that his choice of Joseph as his replacement was a mistake. In the first episode, the reunion of Jacob and Joseph, we will see the first sign of Jacob's reserve toward his beloved but Egyptianized son and the prospective cultural antagonism of Egypt toward Israel.

---

them, Judah's sons Er and Onan, are said to have died in the land of Canaan; they would not figure in the count of those who accompanied Jacob to Egypt, leaving thirty-two who did. The enumerated children of Zilpah total sixteen (46:18); of Rachel, fourteen (counting Joseph and his sons, Manasseh and Ephraim; 46:22); and of Bilhah, seven (46:25). Thirty-two plus sixteen plus fourteen plus seven equals sixty-nine; subtracting Joseph and his sons, we get the sixty-six names that accompanied Jacob on his trip to Egypt. One further (albeit unrelated) fact deserves mention: young Benjamin, the "lad" who could not leave his father, has *ten* sons (!), three more than his next most prolific brother.

FATHER AND SON: THE SHEPHERD AND THE DEMIGOD

Jacob's concern for the problem of assimilation is apparent even on his arrival into Egypt, as the immediate sequel hints:

> And Judah he [Jacob] sent before him to Joseph, to show the way before him to Goshen; and they came unto the land of Goshen. And Joseph made ready his chariot and he went up to meet Israel, his father, in Goshen; and he [Joseph] appeared unto him [*vayera 'alayv*] and he fell on his neck and wept on his neck a long while. And Israel said unto Joseph, "Now let me die, after I have seen thy face, for thou art yet alive." (46:28–30)

Jacob does not go to Pharaoh or to Joseph at Pharaoh's court, though both had summoned him to them; instead, he goes to Goshen, sending Judah ahead to bring Joseph to him. Jacob preserves geographical distance from the heart of Egypt, prudently avoiding a perhaps risky encounter with Pharaoh and waiting also for Joseph to come and pay his respects. When Joseph, the self-proclaimed "father to Pharaoh," comes clean-shaven and in full royal Egyptian regalia, riding in his chariot of state, to meet *Israel,* his father, we have the long-awaited meeting not only of father and son but also of the two "cultures." Using an expression—"And he appeared unto him"—that the Bible uses only for the appearance of God before particular human beings, the text subtly proclaims the god-like manifestation of Joseph, descending to meet his earthly father.

We can only try to imagine what this "appearance" must seem like to Jacob, a man who has experienced the divine appearance of the God of his fathers, the God who only days before had spoken to him in a vision. Very likely, feelings of disbelief, joy, awe, repugnance, and sorrow trip over one another in his soul. Is this *really* Joseph? Look, how superbly he is bedecked and appointed! But where is his beard, where his hair, and what mean these foreign trappings? Have I found him, or have I lost him?

Yet Jacob remains outwardly composed in comparison to the god-like Joseph, who falls on his father's neck and weeps there a long while, not uttering a word. The scene of Joseph's tearful embrace of his father is deeply moving, especially for readers who have followed closely Joseph's softening regarding his father, brought about by Judah's speech in his ear. But as if to warn us against excessive sentimentality, the text silently announces that Jacob does not weep in turn on Joseph's neck, as Jacob had done when brother, Esau, had wept on his (33:4), or as Benjamin had done when Joseph had wept on his neck (45:14). Jacob holds back, perhaps preserving paternal dignity, more likely awestruck both that Joseph is indeed alive and that he is utterly transformed. Dry-eyed and collected, unmoved even by Joseph's weeping, Jacob makes but one remark, speaking not as Jacob but in his patriarchal name as *Israel:* Now I can die, for I have seen your face, you are still alive.

Jacob's economical speech, whatever else it is, is surely a speech of joy, relief, and contentment. Now that he has seen his beloved Joseph again, he is supremely content and has nothing more to live for. Joseph is alive. The brothers did not kill him. Nor did I. Joseph bears me no hard feelings for what had happened. The dreaded fratricide and "child sacrifice" have been avoided ("I have seen thy face," [yet] you [and I] are still alive).[11] My work as patriarch is now concluded. I may happily die.

But we also hear a less cheerful undercurrent in Jacob's brief speech, signaled by the fact that he does not even refer to him as "my son" (compare 46:30 with 45:28: "Joseph, *my son,* is yet alive. I will go and see him before I die"). Yes, I am glad that you are alive, but who are you to me and to Israel? Now that I have seen your Egyptian face, now that I have seen what has become of you, what is there left for me, both of you and of my hopes for you, my onetime favorite son? I am willing to die.[12]

Jacob does not die right away. He will live for seventeen years in Joseph's Egypt.[13] He discovers, in fact, that his work has not been concluded. As we shall see, Jacob has a few more important tasks to complete, tasks connected especially to Joseph's irreversible Egyptianization. For Joseph becomes even more Egyptian after Jacob comes down to Egypt; the presence of his father does not bring the son back within the covenant.

Joseph makes no response to his father Israel's speech. Instead he addresses his brothers and the problem of how to arrange with Pharaoh for their stay in Egypt:

> And Joseph said unto his brethren and unto his father's house, "I will go up and I will tell Pharaoh, and I will say unto him, 'My brethren and my father's house, who were in the land of Canaan, have come unto me. And the men are shepherds, for they have been keepers of livestock; and they

11. For a consideration of the connection between seeing the face of one's brother and seeing the face of God, and of both to the matter of fratricide, see 32:31 and 33:10 and my discussion of these passages in Chapter Fifteen.

12. Like Abraham at the binding of Isaac, Jacob has his favorite son restored to him only to lose him permanently. Unlike Abraham and Isaac, Jacob and Joseph will meet and speak again, under circumstances in which Jacob will fully confront the meaning of his erring heart and of Joseph's "disappearance" from Israel.

13. When we first met Joseph, he was seventeen years old. It seems to take Jacob seventeen years at the end of his life to correct the mistake he made during Joseph's first seventeen years: preferring Joseph and making him the de facto leader of his brothers. (I owe this observation to Yuval Levin.)

have brought their flocks and their herds and all that they have.' And it shall happen, when Pharaoh shall call for you and says, 'What is it you do?' that ye shall say, 'Keepers of livestock thy servants have been since our youth even until now, both we and our fathers'; that ye may dwell in the land of Goshen. For every shepherd is an abomination unto the Egyptians." (46:31–34)

The problem confronting Joseph is easy to state: how to obtain for his family a secure and honored place to live, despite the fact that the Egyptians abominate shepherds. Joseph lays out the strategy. He will tell Pharaoh the truth, and by making it clear not only that his family are shepherds but also that they have brought their flocks and all their ("shepherdly") goods with them, Pharaoh will see the need to sequester them apart from his own people. At the same time, the brothers themselves are not to explicitly mention shepherding, out of deference to Egyptian sensibilities. Rather, they are to speak generically about their long tradition of tending livestock, showing Pharaoh, in passing, their attachment to the ways of their fathers. Such tactful respect and display of filial devotion will make a good impression on Pharaoh and gain them acceptance, and will guarantee them a separate and treasured home in the fine pastureland of Goshen.[14] We shall soon see how well the brothers follow Joseph's advice. But it is already becoming clear what is at stake in this matter of separation.

THE ABOMINATIONS OF THE EGYPTIANS

We readers are granted an opportunity, before sitting in on the summit meeting of Israel (Jacob and his sons) and Egypt (Pharaoh), to consider the differences between the established way of Egypt and the nascent way of Israel, in the light of an important yet puzzling clue that we have just received: the Egyptians abominate shepherds. Why is this so, and what could this mean more generally about the Egyptians? Two reasons suggest themselves.

On the one hand, shepherds are mere animal keepers, lower-caste folk who hang out and live with animals. Unclean and uncivilized, these nomads lack settled habitation and a fixed relation to the land. Living artlessly and exposed, at the mercy of the elements, they represent a chaotic, natural element that threatens—at least symbolically—the high man-made order that is the work and goal of civilization. The sophisticated Egyptians may regard shepherds as abominable because they are "subhuman."

On the other hand, shepherds are not so much natural but "supernatural,"

---

14. I owe the insights of this and the following few paragraphs to Robert Sacks.

demonstrating human separation from and dominion over the animals (see 1:28: "Have dominion"). The shepherd does not confuse himself with his flock. And though he lives a rather artless life when compared with the life of agricultural city dwellers, he stands as a ruler—not merely a manager—over his charges. He is also clearly a meat eater and, very likely, a man who, when he is moved to sacrifice, will sacrifice "the firstlings of his flock" in a shared meal with the divine (see 4:4). Earlier we learned that the Egyptians also abominate eating with the Hebrews (43:32), perhaps because they eat lamb. And much later, Moses will refuse Pharaoh's permission to "sacrifice to your God in the land," because "we shall sacrifice *the abomination of the Egyptians* [most likely, sheep] to the Lord our God; lo, if we sacrifice the abomination of the Egyptians before their eyes, will they not stone us?" (Exodus 8:21–22). The Egyptians abominate what the Hebrews eat, how they gain their livelihood from animals, and what they choose to sacrifice to their God. From extrabiblical sources, we learn that the Egyptians are well known for their worship of certain animals. Accordingly, they may regard the Israelite assumption of human superiority over the animal world as an abomination, a deep violation of Egyptian belief in the unity (or at least the interchangeability) of man, nature, and the divine. The Egyptians, on this interpretation, abominate those who make too much of the difference of man.

This line of argument, as advanced by Robert Sacks, is supported by looking ahead to those things that will be declared abominations to the God of Israel (mentioned first in the laws of purity in Leviticus, especially chapter 18). Abominable or loathsome are those sexual practices said to be characteristic of the land of Egypt behind and the land of Canaan before: incest (Leviticus 18:6–18), male homosexuality (Leviticus 18:22; 20:13), and bestiality (Leviticus 18:23). Abominable too are child sacrifice (Leviticus 18:21; Deuteronomy 12:31 and 18:9–10) and, most especially, idolatry (Deuteronomy 7:25–26), as well as the related practices of divination, soothsaying, augury, and sorcery (Deuteronomy 18:10–12). In short, abominable in Israel are those activities that deny or efface the fundamental distinctions of creation: child sacrifice, which makes a child into an animal; bestiality, which makes an animal into a human being; homosexual sodomy, which makes a man into a woman; and idolatry, which makes an animal or a man or some other creature or object into a god. For the Israelite way, with its view that man—and man alone—carries the divine image, failure to see the superiority of man vis-à-vis the animals is necessarily connected with failure properly to apprehend what is truly divine. Setting itself in direct opposition to Egyptian (and Canaanite) ways, Israel eventually will separate itself by loathing the chaos-inducing denial of the importance of separation itself.

There is surely power in this interpretation, especially when the things found abominable by the Egyptians are set alongside the things that Israel will later be charged to find abominable. But one can argue that what characterizes Egypt is finally not so much worship of nature but efforts at mastery of nature. Revering the Nile, the sun, or the various sacred animals may hide, among the elite, a deeper and esoteric belief in the mastery (and divinity) of man. Egypt, via divination, magic, technology, and sophisticated administration, does not so much defer to nature as it seeks to control her—seeks to master change and time. Whether one looks at the change-denying practice of shaving the face and head, or at the dust-to-dust-denying practice of embalming and mummification of the dead (which we shall meet shortly), or at the practices of divination and magic practiced by Pharaoh's wise men (which we encounter in Exodus), one finds abundant evidence of the Egyptian efforts to smoke out and outsmart the ways of nature. In its highly successful efforts to make the world safe and comfortable for human life, Egypt places its trust in technology and administration; it pays scant attention to ruling the unruly hearts and minds of men. Accordingly, it produces a fake Eden, a lush and prosperous garden with no knowledge of God and with human relations that conduce not to human self-rule under law but, rather, to despotism and slavery, with one man promoted as a god over all the others. In Egypt, man is not just an image of God; man—or at least one man—is capable of crossing the line and becoming altogether a god.[15]

These general and admittedly speculative suggestions anticipate Israel's encounter with Pharaoh and, soon thereafter, the reader's encounter with Joseph's activity as Egyptian administrator par excellence (Genesis 47). It is here where the questions of the two cultures and the place of Joseph are most vividly addressed. It is here where Jacob will get his final two lessons in the problem of Egypt.

AT THE SUMMIT: ISRAEL BEFORE PHARAOH

Joseph returns home and tells Pharaoh about the arrival of his kin: "My father and my brethren, and their flocks and their herds, and all that they have, are come out of the land of Canaan; and behold, they are in the land of Goshen" (47:1). To Joseph's credit, he refuses to repudiate his family, and even lets Pharaoh know that they belong to the abominable class of shepherds ("their flocks"). From the pick of his brothers, Joseph takes five men and presents them to Pharaoh, who, as Joseph had predicted, immediately asks after their occupation: "What is it you do?" (47:3). The brothers, either forgetting or ignoring

15. In much of this description of Egypt, we again see how much Joseph resembles Egypt. As Yuval Levin has suggested to me, "Joseph is a one-man Egypt, containing its national character in himself."

Joseph's counsel, do not hide their non-Egyptian ways: "Shepherds are thy servants, both we and our fathers" (47:3).[16] And before Pharaoh can speak again, they explain their presence and make their request for his hospitality:

"To *sojourn* in the land we have come, for there is no pasture for thy servants' flocks because the famine is sore in the land of Canaan. And so, let *dwell*, please, thy servants in the land of Goshen." (47:4; emphasis added)

The brothers' speech conveys perhaps the confused state of their aspirations or perhaps their caution in asking too much from Pharaoh: they say that they have come "to sojourn," to live temporarily as resident aliens, but what they ask for is permission "to dwell," to settle.

Pharaoh gives his response to Joseph:

"Thy father and thy brethren are come unto thee. The land of Egypt, it is before thee; in the best of the land make thy father and thy brethren to dwell; let them dwell in the land of Goshen, and if thou knowest any able men among them, then make them rulers of my livestock." (47:5–6)

Pharaoh decides that Joseph's kin have come not to Egypt or to himself, but to Joseph ("unto thee"). Pleased with Joseph's service, and perhaps impressed also by the forthrightness and boldness of the brothers' reply, Pharaoh generously allows Joseph to pick out the best of Egypt as a dwelling place for his family, endorsing also the choice of Goshen that they have already made. Pharaoh apparently looks to a long-term arrangement (twice, Pharaoh speaks of their "dwelling" or "settling"; he does not mention "sojourning"), an arrangement from which he may profit should the men be as competent with livestock as their supremely gifted brother Joseph has been with agrarian policy. The careful reader notices that Pharaoh's welcome of the Israelites into Egypt depends entirely on his ties to Joseph; when this tie breaks, so will the welcome.[17]

Encouraged by Pharaoh's welcoming reply, Joseph next brings Jacob before Pharaoh. This singular meeting between the patriarch and the demigod is astonishing:

And Joseph brought in Jacob his father and set him before Pharaoh.

And Jacob blessed Pharaoh.

And Pharaoh said unto Jacob, "How many are the days of the years of thy life?"

16. The brothers no doubt speak Hebrew, and Joseph himself probably serves as their interpreter.

17. The account of Israelite slavery famously begins, "Now there arose a new king over Egypt who knew not Joseph" (Exodus 1:8).

And Jacob said unto Pharaoh, "The days of the years of my sojournings are one hundred and thirty years; few and evil have been the days of the years of my life, and they have not attained the days of the years of my fathers in the days of their sojournings."

And Jacob blessed Pharaoh, and Jacob went out from the presence of Pharaoh. (47:7–10)

Readers who have been taken in by Jacob's talk about his readiness to die, or who have written him off as a feeble old man no longer in command, should be amazed by his boldness in this scene. Even those who, despite his melancholy and sometimes pathetic outbursts, have continued to hold Jacob in high regard are unprepared for the way he stands up to Pharaoh.

Unlike Joseph, who only *talks* about being a "father to Pharaoh" but who acts as his inferior, Jacob plays the role of Pharaoh's superior. He twice blesses Pharaoh, does not bow down, never refers to himself as "thy servant," and takes his own leave (unaccompanied by his son, the viceroy, who had at the start of the scene "set him before Pharaoh"). True, Jacob's blessing of Pharaoh would be in keeping with a custom, seen later in the Bible, in which subjects wish the king long life (compare 2 Samuel 16:16; 1 Kings 1:31). It is also possible, as some have suggested, that Jacob is gratefully calling down God's blessing on the king who had favored and elevated his beloved son. But it is equally if not more likely that Jacob is not being deferential at all. Jacob, without being rude, has forgotten neither his special relation to the God of his fathers nor God's recent encouraging speech. Also, Jacob may have seen more than enough of Joseph's Egyptianization and subservience to Pharaoh, and he may therefore be deliberately holding himself aloof as an example to his son. Moreover, Pharaoh's question to Jacob shows him, despite his extraordinary worldly power, to be in need of a blessing.

For Pharaoh, the question of questions is the question of longevity, which is another way of saying the question of mortality. Jacob, as he is set before Pharaoh, appears as an old man; as we learned from his trip to Egypt, he was infirm enough to require conveyance in a wagon. But for Pharaoh, Jacob's longevity is a matter of wonder, perhaps even envy. The question "How old are you?" really asks, "Are you older than I am?"

Jacob, who catches on quickly, gives an answer that is at once honest and shrewd. It is true that he has had a troubled life. He surely carries with him the scars of his struggles (with Laban and Esau). He surely still feels the sorrows of his life (Dinah, Rachel, Joseph, and his many displacements.) Very likely, he is also deeply troubled by finding himself once more an alien, at the mercy of the Egyptian king and culturally estranged from his favorite son. But Jacob is also being prudent when he effectively tells the life-greedy Pharaoh, "There is no reason to envy me. I am a perpetual sojourner, always and everywhere a stranger, whose days these hundred and thirty years have been both few and evil. Why, I have even fallen short of the longevity achieved by my ancestors." [18]

But Jacob's answer goes beyond candor and shrewdness. It demonstrates strength of soul, born of remembering the truth about how things stand between man and God. Though he speaks about the troubles of his life, Jacob makes it clear that he stands in no need of pity or royal favor. It is rather Pharaoh who needs a blessing, who needs divine assistance. Jacob may be compelled by circumstances to live at the mercy of Pharaoh's generosity. But Jacob knows that he is answerable to a higher power. In his speech and his demeanor, he shows both Pharaoh and Joseph—and the reader—how a son of the covenant should conduct himself in exile and before pagan earthly power. It is a grand performance, one of Jacob's finest. There are yet a few more to come.

MINISTERING TO DESPOTISM: JOSEPH, FATHER OF PHARAOH

The meeting between Jacob and Pharaoh ended, the text turns its attention to Joseph's activities as manager of the Egyptian land during the final years of the famine. Here we see Joseph's administrative genius at work, but in ways that make clear why that genius is not and cannot be the guiding power in Israel. For Joseph's dealings in Egypt, and what these dealings show of his feelings about pagan earthly power, only confirm for the reader why Jacob feels little enthusiasm for both Egypt and his son's successes, and why, in the sequel, he will undertake measures to counteract the Egyptianization of his nation.

The account of Joseph's land management begins (and later ends) with remarks about Israel's settlement in Egypt:

> And Joseph *settled* his father and his brethren, and he gave them a *possession* [*'achuzah*] in the land of Egypt, in the best of the land, in the land of *Rameses*, as Pharaoh had commanded. And Joseph sustained his father and his brethren and all his father's house with bread, down to the mouths of the little ones. (47:11–12; emphasis added)

Joseph, though he remains apart from his family, more than cares for his own. He gives them possession of the best portion of the land; he sustains them in the

18. Abraham had lived to 175 ([5 x 5] x 7) and Isaac to 180 ([6 x 6] x 5). Jacob will live another seventeen years, to 147 ([7 x 7] x 3). (The sum of the factors in all three cases is 17; of what possible significance this is, I have no idea.) The full life span in Egypt is 110 years, the life span of Joseph (50:22); in Israel, 120 years, the life span of Moses (Deuteronomy 34:7).

THE BEGINNING OF WISDOM

midst of the famine, and even the least of them does not go hungry. But although he has secured their present, he has unwittingly endangered their future. They had come to sojourn, but he "settled" them and made them landowners. The land that is now the best will, the text subtly hints, soon become the worst. Lest the reader be inclined to celebrate Israel's good fortune in the award of land, the text calls it not by its current name of Goshen but by its future name of Rameses, the name of one of the cities that Israelite slaves will later build when there arises a Pharaoh "who knew not Joseph" (Exodus 1:11). In this way, the text lets us know that Joseph's present policy obtains Israel's survival at the cost of its future enslavement.

In fact, Israel is doubly cursed by Joseph's policies. Its prosperity, produced by Joseph's favoritism, will arouse the envy of the Egyptians, and even more important, Joseph's consolidation of Pharaoh's power will result in the practice of wholesale slavery. Thanks to Joseph's agrarian policies, Egypt is transformed into a nation of slaves and Pharaoh becomes Egypt's absolute master.

Immediately after we learn that Joseph sustained his entire family with bread (47:13), the text tells us, pointedly, "there was no bread in all the land," for the famine was most severe (47:14). Joseph now goes into action. For nine years, ever since Pharaoh appointed him to execute his plan for coping with the impending disaster, Joseph has been preparing for this moment, and he knows exactly what to do. To show the master administrator at work, we quote the entire passage:

And Joseph collected *all* the silver [*that is,* money] that was found in the land of Egypt and in the land of Canaan [in return] for the grain that they bought; and *Joseph brought the silver into Pharaoh's house.* And when the silver was all spent in the land of Egypt, and in the land of Canaan, *all* the Egyptians came unto Joseph, and said, "Give us bread; for why should we die opposite you? For the silver is gone." And Joseph said, "Give your livestock, and I will give you [bread] for your livestock, if the silver is gone." And they brought their livestock unto Joseph. And Joseph gave them bread in exchange for the horses, and for the flocks, and for the herds, and for the asses; and *he refreshed them* [*vayenahalem;* the verb *nahal* primarily means "lead or guide to a watering place"] with bread in exchange for *all* their livestock for that year. And when that year was ended, they came unto him the second year, and they said unto him, "We shall not hide from my lord that the silver is spent and the herds of cattle are *my lord's;* there is nothing left in the *sight of my lord* but our carcasses and our [farm]lands [*'admath-enu*]. Wherefore should we die before thy eyes, both we and our lands? *Buy us and our lands for bread;* and we with our lands will be slaves [*or* serfs] unto Pharaoh; give us seed, that we may live, and not die, and that the land become not desolate." So Joseph bought *all the land of Egypt for Pharaoh;* for the Egyptians sold each man his field, for harsh was the famine upon them; and *the land became Pharaoh's.* And as for the people, *he transferred them to cities* from one end of the borders of Egypt even to the other end thereof. Only the land of the priests bought he not; for the priests had a portion assigned them of Pharaoh, and did eat their portion that Pharaoh assigned them; wherefore they sold not their lands. Then Joseph said unto the people, "Behold, *I have bought you this day and your land for Pharaoh.* Behold, here is seed for you, and ye shall sow the land. And it shall happen at the harvests that ye shall *give a fifth unto Pharaoh,* and four parts shall be your own, for seed of the field, and for your food, and for them of your households, and for food for your little ones." And they said, "Thou hast saved our lives! Let us find grace in the eyes of my lord and we will be slaves to Pharaoh." And Joseph made it a statute concerning the land of Egypt unto this day, that Pharaoh should have the fifth; only the land of the priests alone became not Pharaoh's. (47:14–26; emphasis added)

The surface facts of the transactions are clear enough. As all Egypt comes before him facing starvation, Joseph sells the accumulated grain, first for money, then, when all the money is exhausted, for livestock. The following year, money and livestock both exhausted, Joseph sells grain in exchange for the Egyptians' lands and for their persons. By the end of two years (presumably the third and fourth or the fourth and fifth years of the famine), Joseph has gained possession for Pharaoh of all the money, livestock,[19] and farmland in Egypt (save that belonging to the priests), and he has allowed the entire population to sell itself into bondage to Pharaoh. In keeping with this centralization of all wealth and property, he removes all the people from their farmlands and concentrates them into the cities of Egypt (presumably where the grain stores are located). Finally, looking ahead to the end of the famine, Joseph institutes by statute a steep tithe on the harvest: fully one-fifth is to belong to Pharaoh (the priests, again, exempted). The Egyptians rejoice in their salvation at the hands of Joseph, willingly selling their lands and their independence in exchange for their survival. They speak to Joseph in the language reserved for speaking to a god ("Let us find grace in the eyes of my lord").

But if the facts are clear, what we are to make of them is not. Readers and scholars have disputed for centuries the wisdom and morality of Joseph's prac-

19. By giving Pharaoh sole ownership of all Egyptian livestock, Joseph is also serving the interests of his family, since they had been appointed custodians of Pharaoh's livestock (47:6).

tices, as they have disagreed also about how to judge the actions of the Egyptian people. What, for example, is responsible for the Egyptians' monetary shortfall that required them to sell their livestock, the lands, and themselves in order to survive? Did Joseph induce the crisis by buying low (during the years of plenty) but selling high? Or were the Egyptians to blame, by living too high during the fat years and squandering their surplus gains? Should Joseph be praised, as it seems the Egyptians praise him, for preserving life in dire circumstances, even at the cost of his subjects' freedom? Or should he be blamed for taking advantage of desperate people in order to enrich and consolidate the power of his master? Do the Egyptians owe their enslavement to their own servility (it was *they* who offered their own "carcasses" as payment for bread, and who were apparently pleased with the exchange)? Or do they owe it rather to Joseph's screwing them down so hard that they had no other choice (Joseph might have sold them grain on credit, especially if he knew that the famine would soon be over)? Is Joseph here the model administrator, managing things in difficult times to avoid catastrophe? Or is Joseph the amoral administrator who serves his master's good at everyone else's expense? Is Joseph strategically acting to benefit his own people, by impoverishing and disenfranchising the Egyptians in order to place them on an equal footing with his family? Or is he foolishly enlarging the power of a despotism that will later use its augmented powers to enslave his own people? Is Joseph the exemplar of how to act when God is silent, believing that God helps those who help themselves? Or is he impiously playing the part of a god, relishing the fulfillment of his grandiose dreams?[20]

Given the overall context, and following up certain textual clues, we are inclined to fault Joseph's conduct here, surely his deeds if not also his motives. The text starkly juxtaposes Pharaoh's extraordinarily generous welcome of the Israelite strangers (admittedly, a favor done to Joseph) with Joseph's extraordinarily ungenerous—not to say harsh—treatment of the native Egyptians (admittedly, in service to Pharaoh). To be sure, everything Joseph does he does not for his own gain but for Pharaoh's benefit. The money, the land, and the people

20. These and other opinions of Joseph's administrative handling of the famine are all considered in Aaron Wildavsky's penetrating account of "Joseph the Administrator," Chapter Six in his excellent study *Assimilation Versus Separation: Joseph the Administrator and the Politics of Religion in Biblical Israel.* Wildavsky regards Joseph's conduct as immoral, a view that I share—though not on exactly the same grounds. We both agree that Joseph is presented as an antihero in Israel and as a foil for Moses. His critique employs, anachronistically, the Mosaic Law—not yet given—to criticize Joseph's behavior and to support his contention that the Joseph story teaches that survival must not be gained through sin and that earthly powers may not be served unqualifiedly. I am more inclined to see Joseph's failings as emblematic of the administrative soul and the Egyptian way, in which the morally blind penchant for technical mastery over things and events logically implies the emergence of despotism and servitude.

themselves (also, later, the tithe), the text repeatedly tells us, all wind up in Pharaoh's hands (see 47:14, 20, 23, 24). But Joseph's zeal to benefit Pharaoh goes well beyond what a loyal administrator owes his ruler, unless the ruler is explicitly or implicitly bent on becoming a despot—in which case there is something deeply questionable in remaining his loyal administrator.

Joseph out-Pharaoh's Pharaoh, acting toward Pharaoh's people as the later tyrannical Pharaoh (who knew not Joseph) will act toward Joseph's people and, not incidentally, toward the Egyptians.[21] He appropriates all land and livestock, centralizes all ownership, institutes feudalism, enslaves or "enserfs" the entire population, and—in his cruelest move—destroys the farmers' attachment to their lands by uprooting them and removing them to the cities. In sum, Joseph acts to establish Pharaoh as the sole and supreme master of everything. To exaggerate but slightly, it is Joseph who introduces absolute overlordship into Egypt.

Joseph left the system into which he was elevated less humane than it was by making Pharaoh more powerful than he had been. In cultural terms, Joseph helped change an inclusive hierarchy, in which there was a place for a multitude of landowning farmers, into an exclusive hierarchy, narrow and steep, in which only a single hierarch rules. . . . Egyptian society became an exclusive hierarchy in which only a few were deemed worthy and the rest were subjugated.

Here, but not in the sense in which he meant it in his boast, we see Joseph as the "father to Pharaoh": he begets unqualified despotism.

This assessment, I hasten to add, need not imply that Joseph acts from malice or from other base motives—though one cannot escape the suspicion, acquired from remembering his dreams and from having watched him in action before, that Joseph rather enjoys the exercise of power and the subservient adulation of the multitudes. The adverse judgment of Joseph's conduct stands even if we grant him the best of intentions. It is a critique of his peculiar kind of "wisdom," a critique that goes to the heart of the difference between administration and statesmanship and therewith also of the difference between the wisdom and way of Egypt and the wisdom and way of Israel. For ruling the land and managing its produce is very far from governing the hearts and minds of men, who, from the Bible's point of view, are made miserable more because of their own evil imaginings than because of the stinginess of nature.

Joseph's sagacity is technical and managerial, not moral and political. He is

---

21. In his stubborn resistance to Moses' demands, Pharaoh brings down grievous plagues upon his own people, relenting only when the suffering reaches his own house in the tenth plague, the slaying of the firstborn. See Exodus 7:14–12:36.

long on forethought and planning but short on understanding the souls of men. He is shrewd about things, but dumb about the human heart. He is clairvoyantly intelligent but lacks both eros and *thymos* (and hence also deep longings for the divine or a strong sense of justice). He can serve a master, but he cannot lead men. He can preserve life, but only by destroying freedom and a way of life. The man he serves he elevates into a god, the people whose affairs he manages he reduces to serfdom. Joseph's Egyptian wisdom in action reveals the true meaning of Egypt: prosperity, idolatry, and in the end, despotism. Joseph takes the Egyptian principles of human mastery and rational administration in the service of life and longevity to their perverse conclusion: land, patrimony, and freedom are sacrificed to the goal of survival; and reverence only for human power (and remote cosmic gods) gives rise to despotism and servility.[22]

As a result of Joseph's doings, Egypt comes fully into its own. Pharaoh owns all the land, except that owned by the priests; the priests alone are autonomous, and the people are enslaved. Everyone double tithes (one fifth, rather than one tenth) to Pharaoh, a god among men. In Israel, things will be different—indeed, reversed. Reversal will require a Moses, in soul the antithesis of Joseph: a spirited and erotic man who is also capable of awe, a ruler, not an administrator. Moses will lead the Israelites into freedom, not only from Egyptian bondage but also from their own destructive tendencies, primarily by the supreme act of statesmanship, the giving of law, informed by reverence for God. In the Israelite society established under Mosaic Law, families will own the land and the priests will own none. People tithe to the priests, who are dependent on the people. There is no king or pharaoh; God and His law rule. Righteousness matters more than gain. All the people are summoned to be holy as the Lord their God is holy.

The Perils of Prosperity

In concluding its account of Joseph's agrarian policies, the text quietly casts a contrasting (one-sentence) sideward glance at the fate of the Israelites in Egypt:

> And Israel dwelt in the land of Egypt, in the land of Goshen; and they got themselves possessions there, and they were fruitful and they multiplied exceedingly. (47:27)

---

22. In the person of Joseph, grand vizier of Egypt, the biblical author anticipated, and as it were refuted, the dream of Karl Marx (and many others since Marx) that the rule over men would eventually be replaced by the administration of things, once human intelligence through technological mastery of nature and rationalized restructuring of society overcomes scarcity and class conflict. This apolitical dream becomes a political nightmare, yielding not liberation but despotism—and as the last century amply demonstrated, not only in Egypt.

While the Egyptians are being reduced to servitude, the Children of Israel, protected by Joseph's favoritism, are prospering and multiplying "exceedingly." A
complacent reader who is sympathetic with the fate of the Israelites will be delighted by this news and will praise Joseph for arranging it. But a reader who
knows what is coming later remembers that it is precisely the growth of Israel in
Egypt, described in almost exactly these terms, that triggers the Egyptian reaction against them and that leads to their enslavement.[23] There is also a more insidious internal danger, independent of future Egyptian envy and resentment.
All this prosperity and increase will make it very difficult for Israel to return as
intended to the Promised Land when the famine ends. Why will Israel want to
go back to the promises of the Promised Land from a place that already seems to
fulfill those promises?

A modern prosperous Jewish reader, comfortable in his own place of exile,
may not notice the difficulty. But as we learn in the next chapter, Jacob did. Genesis ends with an account of what he tried to do about it.

23. "And the Children of Israel were fruitful and increased abundantly and multiplied, and waxed
exceeding mighty and the land was filled with them. Now there arose a new king over Egypt, who
knew not Joseph. And he said unto the people, 'Behold, the people of the Children of Israel are too
many and too mighty for us. Come, let us deal craftily with them' " (Exodus 1:7–10).

CHAPTER TWENTY-ONE

LOSING JOSEPH, SAVING ISRAEL:

JACOB PRESERVES THE WAY

*T*he book of Genesis draws to a close, and with it the life of Jacob, the last of the patriarchs, and the story of his "generations." After his arrival from Canaan and his bold appearance before Pharaoh, Jacob lives seventeen years in Egypt (attaining the age of 147; 47:28), long enough to witness the increases in number and prosperity of his descendants. He has had enough time also to learn first-hand the ways and meaning of Egypt and to learn more than he wished to know about his Egyptianized son.[1] And he is frankly worried about the meaning of all this success for Israel's return to Canaan, especially if Joseph remains in charge of Israel's future. As he approaches the end of his life, Jacob does everything he can to point the way back and to keep the way alive. The first step is to arrange for his own burial.

"BURY ME NOT IN EGYPT"

And the days *of Israel* drew near to die; and he called his son Joseph and said unto him, "If, please, I have found grace in thy eyes, put, please, thy hand under my thigh, and deal kindly and truly: *do not, please, bury me in Egypt.* But when I sleep with my fathers, *thou* shalt *carry me* out of Egypt, and bury me in their burying place." And he said, "I will do as thou hast said." And he said, "*Swear unto me* [*hishav'ah li*]." And he swore unto him. And *Israel* bowed down at the head of the bed. (47:29–31; emphasis added)

It is difficult to exaggerate the importance Jacob attaches to this request about burial. That he demands an oath makes this plain. His reasons for insisting are no doubt multiple. Jacob, whatever may be the assimilationist inclinations of his

---

1. Although there is a time lapse of nearly seventeen years between Joseph's agrarian "reforms" and the episode now to be related, the fact that the text places them exactly side by side invites us to regard what Jacob does here as a response—a logical one, not a historical one—to what Joseph had done there.

sons or their descendants, still has a longing for the land where his fathers died. Resisting his own Egyptianization, he wants, at the end of his life, to sever his connection with Egypt and to lie with his ancestors. Only his "Egyptianized son," Joseph, can arrange it. But Jacob is concerned with more than where his own bones will lie. Acting here as *Israel* (not as Jacob), he is thinking also about how to effect a return of the Israelite clan to the Promised Land, away from the seductive but poisonous prosperity of Egypt. At the very least, he would like to keep the memory of the Promised Land alive in his descendants. A pilgrimage of his sons to the burial cave of the patriarchs would certainly produce the latter, and it might even prompt a desire for the former. Again, only Joseph can arrange it. Finally, Jacob may even have some hope that Joseph himself, by being compelled personally to carry his dead father back to the grave of the ancestors, might experience feelings for his lost home, and as a result, undergo a change of heart and return to the ways of his people. Joseph had once boasted that God had made him a "father to [god-like] Pharaoh"; now Jacob will compel him to acknowledge that he is in fact the (mortal) son of mortal Israel, obliged to attend to his wishes and his ways. As Robert Sacks observes,

> when the sons carry their father they do more than carry a dead body. Their *lifting* is the conscious human counterpart of God's act of *lifting*, which forms one of the major threads of the book. By taking the body of their father upon their backs they symbolically take onto themselves the responsibility of maintaining the tradition which their father had set up.

Jacob, acting as Israel, summons his life-giving son to teach him a lesson about death and burial, and therewith also about the ties and debts one has to those who have gone before. By insisting, "Not in Egypt but with my fathers," Jacob demonstrates to Joseph his own enduring attachments and loyalties. Appealing to Joseph in language used to supplicate a god, Jacob gets him to swear an oath[2] that he personally will carry Jacob out of Egypt and bury him in the family grave. This is the second time that Jacob has demanded an oath. Long ago, when we first met him, he made Esau swear that he would honor his agreement to sell Jacob the birthright (25:33). Now, at the end of his life, he makes Joseph swear that he will honor his promise not to bury him in Egypt—to give him his "death right."

Commentators friendly to Joseph see Jacob's demand for an oath as purely prudential: "Jacob exacts this solemn oath in addition to the promise in order to

---

2. It would be nice to know by what God or gods Joseph swears, but the text does not tell us. On the only occasion when we heard Joseph swearing, he swore "as Pharaoh liveth" (42:15–16).

strengthen Joseph's hand when he will request the royal authorization to fulfill the difficult assignment. Indeed, Pharaoh later refers to the oath in granting permission." But as with Esau earlier, Jacob has ample reason to doubt the trustworthiness of Joseph's words, especially about a matter that would involve his leaving Egypt, the land in which he is so effectively assimilated. After all, Joseph had, earlier, declined to leave Egypt even to get Jacob, demanding that Jacob, instead, come to him. Jacob's insistence that Joseph swear an oath addresses precisely Jacob's doubts about Joseph's resolution. Having taken an oath, Joseph will be obliged to keep his promise to his dead father, no matter the difficulty and no matter his true wishes. By this means, Jacob (called "Israel") arranges things so that he may continue to lead his sons toward the path of Israel even when he is dead.

> Not all traditions are maintained solely by the conscious effort of those who maintain them. According to our author, ideas and feelings can sleep underground for many years and yet their seeds remain in the ways of the people, from whom they rise again. Jacob knew that the New Way which the fathers had planted could grow only if the sons were willing to take on the burden. But he also knew that if the foundations were sufficiently well established they could outlast the insufficiencies of intervening generations.

> Thanks to Jacob's forethought, his funeral becomes the occasion for an enormous pilgrimage from Egypt to the Promised Land, described in the last chapter of Genesis—a prefiguring of the Exodus four hundred years later. Joseph has gotten Israel into Egypt and inadvertently taught Pharaoh how to keep them there. It will take Moses, with plenty of divine assistance, to get them out. Jacob will die trying. His final efforts, although insufficient to effect more than a temporary physical return, are not politically or spiritually fruitless.

REPLACING JOSEPH

The last deeds of Jacob occur on his deathbed, not long after his conversation with Joseph about burial. In the first episode (chapter 48), Jacob adopts Joseph's two sons, and in blessing them, corrects Joseph's preference for the firstborn. In the second episode (chapter 49), Jacob addresses all his sons together, prophesying their future and bestowing his final blessings and charges. Taken together, these final deeds reveal Jacob's final judgment of Joseph and his brothers as well as his assessment of his likely legacy. They constitute a refounding of the family in anticipation of its growth into a nation and a people.

And it happened after these things that [a man] said to Joseph, "Behold, thy father is sick"; and he took his two sons with him, Manasseh and Ephraim. And [a man] told *Jacob*, "Behold, thy son Joseph cometh unto thee"; and *Israel strengthened himself* and sat upon the bed. (48:1–2; emphasis added)

A mysterious "someone" informs Joseph that his father is ailing. A (different?) mysterious "someone" informs Jacob that his son Joseph has come. The text subtly contrasts Joseph's and Jacob's responses to the news. Rightly believing his father to be near death and very likely eager to get Jacob's final blessing of preeminence for his sons, Joseph, entirely on his own initiative, brings his boys with him, first Manasseh, the firstborn, then his younger brother, Ephraim. Jacob, though lying on his deathbed, still knows who he is and what he is about. Acting *as Israel*, he gathers his strength and sits up for the meeting. The scene that follows, the only full episode we are given of father and son alone,[3] is thus emblematic of the final meaning of their respective ways.

Although the text does not tell us that Joseph has brought his sons to receive a final blessing from their grandfather, it seems the likeliest explanation. Joseph would surely wish that Jacob, with final words, would ratify his preeminence in the line of descent, a primacy that he no doubt thinks he deserves. After all, his father had come to him rather than any of his brothers regarding the matter of burial. After all, he is the preeminent son, in the best position to care for his brothers' future well-being and that of their descendants. At the same time, Joseph would certainly be aware of the gulf between himself and his brethren, with whom his father has been living in Goshen these seventeen years. And he might have heard, in Jacob's recent plea for a non-Egyptian burial, something of a criticism of his own Egyptian ways. Joseph has every reason for arranging things so that his father should, at the end of his life, anoint him and his sons alone as the proper heirs apparent to the divine covenant.

Jacob has no intention of doing so. Indeed, he has formulated another plan entirely. Seated upright as Israel and clearheaded about his intentions, he begins his address to Joseph by reminding him of God Almighty:

"God Almighty appeared unto me at Luz in the land of Canaan, and He blessed me; and He said unto me, 'Behold, I will make thee fruitful and multiply thee and make thee a company of peoples, and I will give this land to thy seed after thee *for an everlasting possession* [*'achuzath 'olam*].'

3. Joseph's sons may be present, but as Jacob and Joseph speak to each other in Hebrew, the sons do not understand. Later, it becomes clear that if they were present, they were not initially evident to Jacob.

THE BEGINNING OF WISDOM

And now thy two sons, who were born unto thee *in the land of Egypt* before I came unto thee *in Egypt,* are mine; *Ephraim and Manasseh,* like Reuben and Simeon, shall be mine. And thy issue that thou begettest after them shall be thine; by their brothers' names they shall be called in their inheritance. And I, when I came from Paddan, Rachel died unto me in the land of Canaan in the way when there was still some way to come unto Ephrath; and I buried her there in the way to Ephrath—the same is Beth-lehem." (48:3–7; emphasis added)

God Almighty stands as the source of Jacob's self-understanding, and His blessing is the premise of the action he is about to take. Informing Joseph of his divinely sent dream at Beth-El (Luz is the local Canaanite name for the place; see 28:19), Jacob (Israel) summarizes God's two-part blessing: multitudinous progeny and possession of the Promised Land. Joseph, we recall, had given Jacob and his sons *a possession* [*'achuzah*] of land in the land of Egypt (47:11); but as Jacob pointedly informs Joseph, God has promised to Jacob's seed the entire land of Canaan for *an everlasting possession* [*'achuzath 'olam*]. Joseph is a benefactor, but only a temporary one and one inferior to God; in Egypt Joseph may give and take away, but contrary to appearances, Egypt is not the Promised Land.

But the more important point in the present encounter concerns progeny. God's promise to multiply Jacob's seed serves, somehow, as the justification for Jacob's declaration that the sons born to Joseph *in Egypt,* before Jacob came *to Egypt,* are not Joseph's but his. Any future sons Joseph may claim as his own, but these first two—we notice that Jacob, no doubt with conscious intent, names the younger, Ephraim, first—belong to Israel.[4] Joseph comes seeking a blessing on his Egyptian-born sons. Instead, he is told they are no longer his and, by implication, no longer Egyptian. Jacob has no doubt long been pondering and planning this capture or adoption of Joseph's sons for the tribe of Israel. He makes them his own even before he knows that they are present.

Most readers see, in this double adoption, Jacob's honoring his favorite son. Joseph, through his two sons, gets a double portion of Jacob's inheritance. And by indirectly being the father of two Israelite tribes, Joseph is again elevated above his brethren. But careful reading shows this to be, at best, only part of the truth. Yes, your sons, Joseph, are now my sons; but they will be to me like the less favored Reuben and Simeon—not like you, my once favored Joseph. Yes, there will be tribes of Ephraim and Manasseh, but there will be no tribe of Joseph.

4. Those who read this passage as signifying Jacob's adoption of Joseph's sons are not wrong to do so. But they do not realize what this means regarding the status of Joseph himself in the eyes of his father.

Even if you have more sons, they will not be called after your name, but after the name of these two who are now mine. In short: the name of Joseph will no longer live in Israel. Jacob here in effect "sacrifices" Joseph *as his son in Israel*, seeing as Joseph is already lost to Egypt, but he recovers two of his own to take Joseph's place. Having adopted the Egyptian way of combating change and mortality through technology and rational administration, Joseph, master of events, does not see himself as a mortal link in the covenantal chain. Jacob therefore elects to go directly to his sons, circumventing Joseph and reestablishing the continuity of the generations and tacitly reaffirming Israel's own response to the transience of life, the perpetuation of the way of the covenant. Unlike Noah, who once cursed his grandson Canaan (a brother of Egypt) for the impious ways of his son Ham, Jacob does not allow Joseph's sons to be abandoned to false gods despite Joseph's waywardness from the path of Israel.

Jacob's last remark, about Rachel, is surely puzzling, especially as part of a speech adopting Joseph's sons. Perhaps the name Ephraim reminds Jacob of Ephrath, the place of Rachel's burial. Perhaps, having just spoken of *Joseph's* future issue, he remembers his own days of fatherhood and the great loss he sustained when last he sired. Or perhaps, as Robert Alter suggests, Jacob on his deathbed "reverts obsessively to the loss of Rachel, who perished in childbirth leaving behind only two sons, and his impulse to adopt Rachel's two grandsons by her firstborn expresses a desire to compensate, symbolically and legally, for the additional sons she did not live to bear."

But perhaps, in keeping with the line of interpretation we have developed, Jacob is not so much wallowing in his grief as he is reminding himself—and Joseph—that Joseph is now lost to him, in the same way that his mother, Rachel, was lost to him long before. It is not just that, Rachel being gone, there is no other way Jacob can replace Joseph than by taking his sons in his stead. Rather, Jacob's emphasis on the place of Rachel's *burial* suggests something much more radical: Jacob may now understand the symbolic meaning of his decision not to bury Rachel with the other patriarchs and matriarchs (though she died not far from the cave at Machpelah). Rachel's burial "in the way to Ephrath" had left her on the outside of the new way. Now her preeminent son has chosen to assimilate himself to outside ways. Rachel had clung to her father's idols; Joseph now clings to the land of the idolaters. Jacob, who has only recently insisted on being buried with "his fathers" (please note: not with his beloved Rachel), sees that—like mother, like son—the beautiful Rachel and her beautiful Joseph are both detours on the way to the promise that God Almighty has made to him. Jacob revives and purifies the memory of Rachel, reclaiming her grandsons for himself, even as he recognizes that she and her son are both lost to the way of Israel. Ephraim and Manasseh are replacements for Joseph *and for Rachel.*

CORRECTING JOSEPH: THE WAY IS NOT YET SET

Having adopted Joseph's sons without even noticing their presence, Jacob (as Israel) suddenly sees them and asks, "Who are these?" (48:8). Joseph tells him that they are his sons, whom God has given him there. Jacob asks that they be brought forward for his blessing.

"Bring them, please, unto me and I will bless them."
Now the eyes of Israel were dim for age so that he could not see. And he [Joseph] brought them near unto him, and he [Israel] kissed them and he embraced them. And Israel said unto Joseph, "I had not thought to see thy face, and behold, God hath let me see thy seed also." And Joseph brought them out from between his knees and he fell down on his face to the earth. (48:9–12)

A generation earlier, Jacob's father, Isaac, was old and dim of sight when he was tricked into giving his blessing to Jacob instead of Esau, his firstborn. Jacob, though also unable to see, will not be fooled, for he has his wits fully about him. In bestowing his own blessing on his grandsons (now his adopted sons), he will once again overturn the natural preference for the firstborn.

And Joseph took both of them, Ephraim with his right hand to Israel's left and Manasseh with his left hand to Israel's right, and brought them near unto him. And Israel stretched out his right hand and laid it upon Ephraim's head, though he was the younger, and his left hand upon Manasseh's head, *crossing his hands,* for Manasseh was the firstborn.
And *he blessed Joseph* and said,
"The God before whom my fathers did walk, Abraham and Isaac,
the God who hath shepherded me as long as I have been, until this day,
the angel [*or* messenger] who hath redeemed me from all evil,
may He bless these lads;
and let my name be called in them and the name of my fathers
Abraham and Isaac;
and let them grow into a multitude in the midst of the earth."
(48:13–16; emphasis added)

Joseph places Manasseh, the firstborn, before Jacob's right hand, the hand that symbolizes power, action, and authority. Crossing his hands, Jacob knowingly extends those right-handed gifts to Ephraim, the younger—why, we shall discuss in a moment. And in what the text calls his blessing of *Joseph,* Jacob bestows the patriarchal and covenantal blessing upon Joseph's *sons.* Lest the point be lost on Joseph—or the reader—Jacob asks divine help so that his name and the names of patriarchs Abraham and Isaac may be carried on in the names of Joseph's sons, not of Joseph himself.

Joseph has good reason to be unhappy with what he sees and hears, and he attempts to interfere:

> And when Joseph saw that his father was laying his right hand upon Ephraim, *it displeased him,* and he held up his father's hand, to remove it from Ephraim's head unto Manasseh's head. And Joseph said, "Not so, my father, for this is the firstborn; put thy right hand upon his head." And his father *refused,* and he said, "I know it, my son, I know it; he also shall become a people, and he also shall be great; but his younger brother shall be greater than he, and his seed shall become a multitude of nations." And he blessed them that day, saying: "By thee shall Israel bless, saying, 'God make thee as Ephraim and Manasseh.' " And he set Ephraim before Manasseh. (48:17–20; emphasis added)

As Robert Sacks points out, Israel's decision has nothing to do with merit; he had decided to reverse the birth order even before he had met the boys. Neither is it tied to an irrational lifelong prejudice that Jacob, the second-born, has against all elder brothers. Rather, it reflects Jacob's sense that the stable and final condition of his people has yet to be achieved. When a society is well established and running smoothly, preferences are usually given to the firstborn, for the firstborn is the one who, naturally, guarantees a next generation; in arranging for perpetuation, custom follows and ratifies the natural order of succession. The automatic preference for firstborn sons, or primogeniture, bespeaks a community confident of its ways, which are regarded as permanent and steady as the ways of nature. Joseph, who has his own reasons for believing that the way of his native clan is now secure, sees himself as the last of the founding fathers and wants that way to be conserved through primogeniture. Jacob corrects Joseph's tacit belief that everything is now fully established and ripe for perpetuation in Egypt. And looking ahead, Jacob prophesies that the nation of Israel shall bless by Ephraim and Manasseh,[5] memorializing in such a blessing Jacob's inversion

---

5. This blessing, "God make thee as Ephraim and Manasseh," is used even today by fathers to bless their sons. For daughters the blessing is "God make thee as Sarah, Rebekah, Rachel, and Leah."

of the birth order, a deed that symbolizes Israel's rejection of both Joseph's offer to Egyptianize and his complacent belief that the new way was finally secure.

The son is displeased that the father is not following his wishes; the father refuses to obey his imperious son. The normal father-son relationship is reversed: "Joseph, the son, precisely because he considers himself the last founder, has suddenly become the conservative, whereas the old man has seen the necessity for renewal." In the previous generation, Jacob's mother, Rebekah, had seen the need to correct Isaac's conservative preference for Esau; and Jacob had helped her do so by guile. In Paddan-aram at Uncle Laban's, Jacob had challenged the local customary preference for the firstborn in his choice of Rachel, the younger sister.[6] Earlier, Jacob—in a conservative frame of mind—had anointed Joseph, the firstborn of his favorite wife, as heir apparent of the family. Now, however, when Joseph tries to enact that role, Jacob, having seen the error of his ways, reverts to the role of the critic and reformer—directly, knowingly, firmly, and utterly without guile.

Having crossed Joseph on the matter of his sons, Jacob concludes the private interview with some comforting and encouraging—if also puzzling—words:

And Israel said unto Joseph, "Behold, I die; but God will be with you and bring you back unto the land of your fathers. And I, I have given to thee one *shekhem* [portion?; shoulder?; Shechem the city?] above thy brethren, which I took out of the hand of the Amorite with my sword and with my bow." (48:21–22)

Israel expresses his wish for Joseph's return to the land and ways of his ancestors, even though he knows that he will not live to see it and can do nothing to bring it about. He places Joseph in God's hands, assuring him of providential assistance in his eventual return to the Promised Land. Then Israel tells him (in a phrase that continues to mystify commentators) he has already bestowed on him something[7] above his brethren—perhaps two portions in the land of Canaan, one each for Ephraim and Manasseh; perhaps also two shoulders, one Ephraim's, the other Manasseh's?—on which to carry Jacob to his grave; see below. Yet Jacob's bonus to Joseph carries also a dark shadow for readers who remember that Shechem was the city of violence and near fratricide to which

6. This antinomian preference of Jacob's was the result of love, not radicalism. But as we noted when this episode was discussed in Chapter Fourteen, the import of the choice is nonetheless radical.

7. *Shekhem* is usually translated "portion," but without the slightest philological support for such a rendering. The word means "shoulder," the part of the body that shoulders the burden. Shechem (in Hebrew, *Shekhem*), the location, eerily prefigures Joseph's final resting place.

Jacob had sent Joseph to meet his brothers and from which he did not return. As Sacks notes, Jacob concludes the interview in which he himself destroys the tribe of Joseph and removes Joseph from among his sons and inheritors "by presenting Joseph with a Shechem in connection with his brothers."[8] Jacob tacitly, and perhaps unwittingly, makes a deathbed confession of his own contribution to the "filiocide" of Joseph, both long ago and now in displacing him from the names of his sons.

REFOUNDING THE FAMILY

Having settled up with Joseph in private, Jacob now summons *all* his sons, Joseph among the twelve, for his last testament, "that I may tell you that which shall befall you in the end of days" (49:1). What follows is part blessing, part prophecy, part settling of scores, and part redirection of future family and tribal relations. The remarks are sometimes about the sons themselves, sometimes about the tribes in Israel to which they give their names: as the text says at the end of the testament, "All these are *the twelve tribes of Israel;* and this is it that their father spoke unto them and blessed them; every one according to his blessing he blessed them" (49:28; emphasis added).

As befits a deathbed prophecy, Jacob's testament is a highly poetic speech—the longest sustained poem in Genesis—with remarks addressed to (or about) each of the twelve sons (though in a somewhat strange order). For the first time, Jacob at least formally treats all the sons as equally his. The content of what is said is notoriously difficult to understand, not least because Jacob uses florid images, as well as many words that occur nowhere else in the Bible. Most commentators agree that this is the most difficult material in Genesis; as Robert Alter wryly comments, "Differences of interpretive opinion are such that in two instances there is no agreement about whether the language refers to animal, vegetable, or mineral!" Because even the simple meaning of the words is so elusive, we shall not here attempt a treatment of all that Jacob says. We shall focus only on those remarks of Jacob's that touch on leadership, transmission, and perpetuation of the covenantal way. It is here where we especially see the fruits of Jacob's education as patriarch of the covenantal way.

Regarding the question of leadership, some things are clear enough and deserve our attention. In terms of content, the bulk of Jacob's attention goes to Judah and Joseph, seventeen and nineteen statements respectively (five verses each); the sum for the other ten sons is only thirty-eight (fourteen verses alto-

---

8. Sacks also has some interesting speculations about the phrase "which I took out of the hand of the Amorite with my sword and with my bow," about which we shall say nothing here.

gether). Before attending to his remarks to Judah and Joseph, we notice that Jacob castigates his three eldest sons and dismisses them as candidates to lead.

Reuben, Jacob's firstborn—"my might, and the firstfruits of my manhood,
the excellency of dignity and the excellency of power"—is described as "unstable
as water" and denied supremacy because of his affair with Bilhah, Jacob's concubine (49:3–4). Reuben, who was naturally in line to take his father's place, did so
improperly and prematurely. We who have followed closely Reuben's ineptitude
in his several attempts to lead are not surprised that Jacob sets him aside as
"watery."

Simeon and Levi, dealt with as a pair and not addressed directly,[9] are described as men of violence and outrage. Jacob says nothing good about them,
dissociates himself from their company, and curses their anger: "Cursed be their
anger, for it was fierce, and their wrath, for it was cruel" (49:5–7). Many commentators see in Jacob's remarks his final judgment on the slaughter of the Shechemites; when it happened his concerns were strictly prudential and political
(34:30). "You've hurt my reputation among the Canaanites and Perizzites . . .
who may destroy me." Here his condemnation, cursing their anger, seems entirely moral.[10] But as the text hints, Jacob's moralism may itself be excessive, for
he appears to underestimate the importance of spiritedness. His last word
prophesies the future disappearance of both tribes: "I will divide them in Jacob
and scatter them in Israel" (49:7). But although the tribe of Simeon will in fact
lapse into obscurity, the tribe of Levi, though scattered in Israel and having no
territory of its own, becomes a most important tribe, the tribe of priests. Moses
and Aaron are both from the tribe of Levi; and it will be only the sons of Levi
who step forward when Moses asks those who are "on the Lord's side" to punish
the people for worshiping the golden calf (Exodus 32:25–29). The zeal shown in
the avenging of Dinah, once properly domesticated and subordinated to a higher
service, has a crucial part to play in the life of Israel—indeed, of any nation.[11]

His first three sons set to the side with harsh negative judgment, Jacob next
addresses Judah in highly favorable terms and unequivocally bestows on him the
blessing of rule. Here is the text in full:

> "Judah, thee shall thy brethren praise;
> thy hand shall be on the neck of thine enemies;

---

9. Only Reuben, Judah, and Joseph are addressed directly, with the use of the second person; all
the others are spoken of in the third person.

10. Because the commentators share this moral judgment, they uncritically accept it as representing the Torah's final judgment on the event. But we may not assume that Jacob speaks for the text or
that his final judgments should become ours, at least prior to careful consideration.

11. Sacks has an excellent discussion of the Levites in relation to Jacob's remarks here.

thy father's sons shall bow down before thee.
Judah is a lion's whelp;
from the prey, my son, thou art gone up.
He stooped down, he couched like a lion,
and as a lioness; who shall rouse him up?
The scepter shall not depart from Judah,
nor the ruler's staff from between his feet,
until Shiloh comes;
and unto him shall the obedience of the peoples be.
Binding his she-ass unto the vine,
and the son of his she-ass unto the choice vine;
he washes his garments in wine,
and his vestures in the blood of grapes.
His eyes shall be red with wine,
and his teeth white with milk." (49:8–12)

The political imagery abounds: Judah's brothers shall praise him and, as his father's sons, shall bow down to him. He shall have his enemies by the throat. He belongs to the royal family of the lion. The scepter and ruler's staff will be with him for a long time, and the people will obey him. His land will be blessed with an abundance of vines and wine, so much so that he will be able to wash his clothes in wine as if it were water.[12] In his final act, Jacob anoints Judah as first among equals, just as he had long ago anointed Joseph with the ornamented tunic. The complete fulfillment of the prophecy of Judah's supremacy will come only with the kingship of David.

Joseph, too, gets a bountiful blessing, filled with beautiful images:

"Joseph is a fruitful vine [*or* a wild ass],
a fruitful vine by a fountain [*or* a wild ass by a spring]
whose branches run over a wall [*or* wild colts on a hillside].
The archers have dealt bitterly with him,
and shot at him, and hated him.
But his bow abode firm,
and the arms of his hands were made supple.
By the hands of the Mighty One of Jacob,
from thence, from the Shepherd, the stone of Israel,
even by the God of thy father, who shall help thee,

---

12. Wildavsky, who has a less celebratory reading of Jacob's remarks to Judah, sees in this image a reminder of the staining of Joseph's coat of many colors.

and by the Almighty, who shall bless thee,
with blessings of heaven above,
blessings of the deep that coucheth beneath,
blessings of the breasts and of the womb.
The blessings of thy father
are mighty beyond the blessings of my progenitors
unto the utmost bound of the everlasting hills;
they shall be on the head of Joseph,
and on the crown of the head of the prince [*nazir*] among his brethren."
   (49:22–26)

Despite the uncertainty of the translation, there can be no doubt that Jacob has reserved a full and handsome blessing for his beloved Joseph. Yet notwithstanding the single final reference to Joseph as "the prince—the consecrated one; *nazir*—among his brethren," the entire blessing is more natural than political, a blessing for fertility and plenty, not for rule. Joseph is "a fruitful vine," not "a lion's whelp." Assailed by others, he endures but he does not conquer. His blessings are from the skies above and the deep below, from the breast and from the womb. They may crown his princely head, but they do not bring him praise or obedience from his brethren. He still has the love of his father, who backs his own blessing by calling down God's help for his naturally superior son, but not for supremacy in Israel. Joseph, master of the fertile place, gets the natural blessing; Judah, leader of his brothers, gets the national blessing. Joseph is blessed in the way of Egypt; but in the way of Israel, right is more important than beauty, justice more esteemed than natural gifts.

In this way, Jacob, at the end of his life—like his father, Isaac—confesses his error regarding his sons.[13] But unlike Isaac, Jacob does so in public, before all his sons. Everyone hears it from Jacob himself that Judah is to replace Joseph as the first among equals. Joseph, it appears, had only half understood his youthful "Egyptian" dream about the sheaves of wheat: his brothers did indeed bow down to him, but only in Egypt. In Israel, the brothers—including Joseph's sons—will be led by Judah.

THE DEATH AND FUNERAL OF JACOB

Having announced his prophetic blessings to each son, Jacob concludes by charging them all together regarding his burial. The earlier charge, given to

---

13. In doing so, Jacob, probably without knowing it, reveals the need for the institution of law. The inadequacy of a father's heart can be corrected only by adherence to principles that play no favorites. Patriarchy, the beginning of Israel's political wisdom, must be supplemented by and subordinated to the law.

Joseph alone and backed by an oath, emphasized Jacob's insistent wish not to be buried in Egypt. That charge is here supplemented—or is it replaced?—by a new one that does not mention Egypt at all but that speaks in detail (even somewhat redundantly) about the ancestral grave back in Canaan.[14]

> And he charged them and he said unto them,
> "I am to be gathered unto my people;
> bury me with my fathers
> in the cave that is in the field of Ephron the Hittite,
> in the cave that is in the field of Machpelah,
> which is before Mamre, in the land of Canaan,
> which Abraham bought with the field from Ephron the Hittite for a possession of a burying place.
> There they buried Abraham and Sarah, his wife;
> there they buried Isaac and Rebekah, his wife;
> and there I buried Leah.
> The purchase of the field and the cave that is therein was from the sons of Heth." (49:29–32)

Jacob's charge is a masterful combination of practical direction, legal instruction, and pious inspiration. With precision he specifies the cave geographically (in the field of Machpelah, which is before Mamre, in the land of Canaan) and legally (the cave within the field that Abraham bought from Ephron the Hittite as a possession for the purpose of a burial site). And he piously reminds his sons that this is the place of burial of Abraham and Sarah, his wife, and of Isaac and Rebekah, his wife, the place where, with his own hands, he buried Leah, anticipating his own later place beside her.[15]

Jacob concludes by again naming the field and the cave, this time as having been purchased not from Ephron the Hittite but from *the sons* (or *children*) of Heth. By speaking of the *sons* of Heth—"the sons [*or* children] of Heth [*beney Cheth*]" are literally Jacob's last words on earth—Jacob reminds his own sons of their filial duty of ancestral piety, and he gives them a charge that will unify them as the sons of Israel. He locates their personal filial relation to him in its larger context by recalling the memory of (nearly) all of the patriarchs and matriarchs.

14. These twofold instructions about his burial will be echoed in the account of the funeral itself, the first part of which is Egyptian in character and is engineered by Joseph, the second part of which is Israelite and involves all the brothers.

15. Strikingly, Jacob does not call Leah his wife. There is more than one possible reason for this glaring omission. But the important point is that, in death if not in life, Jacob links himself singularly to Leah. She is his "covenantal wife." He does not ask to be buried with Rachel.

For it is Israel's memory of these ancestors, preserved through burial in a specific memorialized site *purchased* for such purpose, that will constitute Israel's sole link to the Promised Land through the four hundred years of exile.

The funeral and burial of Jacob are the last great act of the book of Genesis, after which no Israelite will be found in Canaan until after the exodus and the giving of the Law. Ancestral piety, burial, and sacred memory prepare and keep the ground. But the return of these tribes *as a people* will be on the basis of divine redemption from slavery in Egypt and divine giving of law in the Sinai desert. Ancestral piety, the concluding theme of the book of "Beginning," *is* a beginning for the way of Israel, but *only* a beginning. Having done all he can, Jacob dies in peace; the rest will be up to God and Moses.

> And when Jacob made an end of charging his sons, he gathered up his feet into the bed, and he expired; and he was gathered unto his people.
>
> And Joseph *fell upon the face of his father,* and *he wept upon him* and *he kissed him.* Then Joseph commanded his servants the physicians to *embalm his father,* and the physicians *embalmed Israel.* And forty days were fulfilled for him, for so are fulfilled the days of embalming. And the Egyptians wept for him threescore and ten days. (49:33–50:3; emphasis added)

The report of the death of Jacob is remarkable in several ways, especially when compared with the reports of the deaths of Abraham and Isaac.[16] In the same forthright and unflinching way that he has been preparing for death in all the episodes discussed in this chapter, Jacob meets his end deliberately, gathering his body back into bed just before he breathes his last ("he expired"). Though his body lies "gathered" in the bed, Jacob *himself,* like Abraham and Isaac before him, is said to be "gathered unto his people"—meaning either that his soul or spirit has literally joined them elsewhere in some "afterlife" or, conversely, that he lives now, as they do, only in the realm of his people's memory. In contrast with the reports about the deaths of Abraham and Isaac, the text does not say that Jacob died "full (or sated) with years or days," or that he died in a "good old age." In fact, unlike with the other patriarchs, it does not explicitly use

---

16. "And these are the days of the years of Abraham's life which he lived, one hundred years and seventy years and five years. And Abraham expired, and died in a good old age, an old man, and full [of years], and was gathered unto his people. And Isaac and Ishmael, his sons, buried him in the cave at Machpelah, in the field of Ephron the son of Zohar the Hittite, which is before Mamre, the field which Abraham purchased of the children of Heth; there was Abraham buried and Sarah, his wife" (25:7–10). "And the days of Isaac were a hundred years and eighty years. And Isaac expired and died and was gathered unto his people, old and full of days; and Esau and Jacob, his sons, buried him" (35:28–29).

the expression, "and Jacob died." Perhaps we are meant to agree with Jacob's judgment, made to Pharaoh: "Few and evil have been the days of the years of my life, and they have not attained unto the days of the years of the life of my fathers in the days of their sojournings" (47:9). And perhaps, because we are now with Joseph in Egypt, we are meant to be less certain about what has happened to Jacob and, more important, what we are to do with and for him. The reader is told that Jacob has stopped breathing, but his body lies before us as before. What will the bystanders make of this? Will Joseph and his brothers react in the same way?

With Jacob expired, the text's spotlight falls again on Joseph, who once more occupies center stage. Joseph, alone among the brothers, falls upon "his father's face," weeping upon him (or "it") and kissing him (or "it"), treating the corpse as if it were still his father. Some say that this behavior shows that Joseph loved his father more than did his brothers, who, in any case, now that Jacob is gone, have other concerns (about Joseph's future conduct toward them) that prevent them from weeping. More radically, some claim that Joseph's behavior shows that he alone among the brothers truly cared for Jacob—a thesis belied by Judah's great speech and his standing as pledge to Jacob for Benjamin, and also by the example of Benjamin himself, now among the mourners. But it seems to us more likely that Joseph's emotional outburst and his embracing of the corpse reflects rather his own Egyptianized views of death and the dead body. Although he had brought his sons for a deathbed blessing, Joseph, alone among the brothers, seems utterly unprepared for his father's death. And in any case, he does not recognize the difference between his father—now "gathered to his people"—and his mortal remains. (Also, his weeping is in keeping with the protracted period the Egyptians set aside for wailing that we shall soon encounter.)

Rising from the dead body, Joseph summons his servants—not just any servants, but the physicians—and commands them to *embalm his father;* he does not summon priests, he does not move immediately to prepare for burial. Pious commentators rush to assure us that Joseph had Jacob's body embalmed "not in imitation of the custom of the Egyptians . . . [but] merely to preserve it from dissolution before it reached the cave at Machpelah." But who can be sure? The juxtaposition of Joseph's embracing the corpse and his tears of loss with his order to bring the healers certainly raises the possibility that Joseph, filled with grief, wanted the body preserved and, as the Egyptians believed, kept ready for reanimation. The countercultural nature of the deed of embalming is, in fact, subtly indicated: it was *Jacob* who expired and was gathered unto his people (49:33), and it was *his father* whom Joseph had commanded the physicians to embalm; but when the command is carried out, it is *Israel* whom the physicians mummify. Moreover, the death of Jacob is treated not just as a private matter for Joseph or a national matter for the Hebrews (it is taken completely out of the hands of Jacob's other sons). It is treated as a great calamity *for the Egyptians*, as the death of a great public figure—no doubt because of Joseph's high position, perhaps also because of Jacob's great age (147 years, well beyond the Egyptian ideal). The symbolically pregnant forty days of embalming are observed; and a tenfold complete number of days (seventy) are given over to weeping.[17] The Egyptians, with Joseph's active participation, claim Jacob in death as one of their exalted own.

Joseph has not forgotten his promise to his father. Yet keeping it requires Pharaoh's cooperation, not a sure thing. Whether because Joseph dare not approach his royal highness while in mourning, or because, fearing some loss of favor, he is worried about the answer he will receive, or because Joseph himself now feels some ambivalence about his Egyptianization or is afraid of calling attention to the cultural differences surrounding treatment of the dead—for whatever reason, Joseph addresses his request to Pharaoh indirectly.

> And when the days of weeping for him were past, Joseph spoke unto *the house* of Pharaoh, saying, "If, please, I have found grace in your eyes, speak, please, in the ears of Pharaoh, saying, 'My father made me swear, saying, "Behold, I die; in *my* grave *which I have digged for me* in the land of Canaan, there shalt thou bury me." Now, therefore, *let me go up*, please, and bury my father, and *I will come back*.' "
>
> And Pharaoh said, "Go up and bury thy father, as he made thee swear." (50:4–6; emphasis added)

Protected in the center of this indirect discourse, surrounded by layers of supplicating speech, is the alleged speech and command of Joseph's father, to which, Joseph wants Pharaoh to know, his father made him swear. But when we compare what Jacob actually said in charging Joseph with what Joseph tells Pharaoh, we notice that Joseph has tactfully altered the terms. He omits Jacob's insistence "not in Egypt," as well as his mention of the cave, the ancestors who are buried there, and the ownership of land in Canaan for just such purpose. In petitioning Pharaoh, Joseph plays down all ritual and cultural divergence, and points to a

---

17. Questions may be raised about the meaning of these Egyptian practices. Are they expressions of normal grief, or are they an attempt rationally to manage it and contain it? What view of mortality, or of our relation to the dead, is latent in a practice that puts a strict time limit on the fact that a person has died to us? How does it fit with the practice of embalming, seen as the alternative to burial? As we have seen and will soon see again, the Israelite approach to death and the dead body is poles apart from the way of Egypt. Later, in the elaboration of the so-called holiness code, the Israelite priests will be expressly forbidden to have anything to do with dead bodies.

merely personal request to be buried in a private grave that "I have digged for me"—words Jacob never used. And lest Pharaoh get the wrong idea, Joseph finishes by promising that he will return to Egypt. Any reader who knows what lies ahead will be struck by the contrast between Joseph's timid "Let me go up" and that of the next Israelite who stands before Pharaoh, Moses' bold demand "Let my people go." In the contrast between Moses (and earlier, Jacob) and Joseph we see the difference between the man who knows who he is and the man who is willing and able to be all things to all people, a difference that turns ultimately on how each man stands in relation to God.

Pharaoh readily gives his consent directly to Joseph, emphasizing the oath that Joseph has been forced to swear. Perhaps the oath alone persuaded Pharaoh to grant the request, perhaps Pharaoh is making Joseph—and the others— aware that nothing else could command permission to leave Egypt or perform burial. However this may be, once Pharaoh's permission is granted, a huge funeral party is assembled. We should do all we can to imagine the scene, following the text's abundant clues.

And Joseph went up to bury his father; and with him went *all the servants of Pharaoh, the elders of his house, and all the elders of the land of Egypt*; also all the house of Joseph, and his brethren, and his father's house. *Only their little ones and their flocks and their herds they left in the land of Goshen.* And there went up with him both chariots and horsemen; and it was a very great company. And they came to the threshing floor of Atad, which is *beyond the Jordan,* and there they wailed with a very great and sore wailing, and *he made a mourning* for his father for seven days. And when the inhabitants of the land, the Canaanites, saw the mourning in the floor of Atad, they said, "This is a grievous mourning *unto the Egyptians,*" wherefore the name of it was called 'Avel-mitsraim [mourning of Egypt], which is *beyond the Jordan.*

And *his sons* did unto him according as he commanded them. For *his sons carried him* into the land of Canaan, and *buried him* in the cave in the field of Machpelah, which Abraham bought with the field, for a possession of a burying place, of Ephron the Hittite, in front of Mamre.

And *Joseph* returned into Egypt, he, and his brethren, and all that went up with him to bury his father, *after he had buried* his father. (50:7–14; emphasis added)

Joseph leads a grand Egyptian funeral procession, complete with chariots and horsemen, and filled with the elite of the Egyptian court. The journey is long and difficult, with many miles across desert.[18] Eventually, when the entourage arrives in (or at the border of) Canaan—I have no idea about the possible significance of the threshing floor at Atad—Joseph produces yet another period of mourning, this time for seven days. The Canaanite witnesses see an enormous Egyptian party performing a clearly Egyptian rite of mourning; in this they are not mistaken.

But at this point (50:12) the text pointedly shifts from the Egyptian doings produced by Joseph to the deeds of all Jacob's sons. "His sons" did as he commanded them; that is, they carried him—not in a chariot, but on their shoulders—into the land of Canaan, and they buried him in the cave.[19] All specifications of the cave are given, once again, to demonstrate not only Jacob's place of final rest but also his sons' exact fidelity to Jacob's command. The funeral is, thus, a mixture. Its grand and noble Egyptian beginning gives way to the plain and austere Israelite journey to the cave. And who are "his sons" that buried Jacob? All his sons? All the sons other than Joseph? Or Joseph himself ("after *he* had buried his father" [50:14])? The text is ambiguous, leaving us to ponder how Joseph and his brothers will be related now that their father is gone. Much may depend on the experience they have just undergone.

I must confess that I get gooseflesh whenever I try to imagine Jacob's funeral. Whatever the route, the long, hot, arduous journey back to Canaan carrying their father's mummified body to the ancestral grave must surely have produced powerful feelings in the souls of the brothers, as it surely did to their bodies, es-

18. There appears to be something strange in the route that is taken. The direct way from Egypt to Hebron (the place of the cave at Machpelah) is straight northeast, the route going up the Mediterranean coast and then crossing the Negev desert and (probably) passing through Beer-sheba. But we are told (twice) that the procession entered Canaan from "beyond the Jordan," an expression that means "from the *east* of the river," that is, from trans-Jordan. It seems as if Joseph directed the procession to take a circuitous route across the Sinai and around the Dead Sea (a route, as it happens, not unlike the one the Israelites will take after the exodus), entering the land "from the rear," close to Hebron itself. Yuval Levin offers this highly plausible interpretation: "The route seems intentionally designed to avoid the [Promised] land, as if Joseph and his brothers are afraid of the effect that the land might have on them. Rather than travel through the Negev, perhaps passing through Beer-Sheva, which they all know and must remember (and where God spoke to their father when the family went down to Egypt), they have gone around and they enter the land directly near Hebron and then can exit it again, spending as little time as possible in it. Jacob, after all, didn't specify what route they should take, and so his attempt to remind them of the land might come up short." (Yuval Levin, personal communication.) My only amendment would be to insist that the decision to avoid the land of Canaan is entirely Joseph's doing (and not his brothers'), since he and he alone has the power to direct the Egyptian funeral procession. He also has the greatest motive to avoid remembering the life and ways he left behind in Canaan.

19. As noted in the last chapter, Jacob had gone down into Egypt in the Egyptian wagons provided by Pharaoh and Joseph; here, on his final return to rejoin his ancestors in burial, he sheds all Egyptian carriage.

pecially at the end. Lifting and carrying their father, six on each side, each leaning toward his load and all bending toward one another, the brothers would find
the walking cumbersome. Now stumbling, now bumping into the one in front
or behind, their individual gaits would be hampered as if by a limp, but they
would see that progress can be made together, each one now equally dependent
on ("curved toward") the others, all equally the sons of Israel. Meditating on
their current activity in light of their troubled past, it would be surprising if they
did not relive their turbulent saga and the vexed story of their father's dealings
with his sons. Although their little ones and livestock had been left behind, it
would be surprising if they felt no pull of return from and for the Promised
Land. It would be surprising if his brothers were not also thinking about Joseph
and how this journey would affect him and his subsequent conduct toward
them. And finally, it would be surprising if this journey did not stir Joseph's soul
most of all (despite his efforts to avoid such agitation), bringing the conflict between his "two cultures" into the open in his breast: Am I the Egyptian viceroy
in the chariot, or am I the dutiful son of the Israelite ancestors? What happens
next will depend in large measure on how Joseph handles the question of his
identity. How, we want to know, and in what spirit was it that "Joseph returned
to Egypt . . . after he had buried his father" (50:14)? We are not alone in focusing
on this question.

JOSEPH AND HIS BROTHERS:
SEPARATION, OR RECONCILIATION?

And when Joseph's brethren saw that their father was dead, they said, "It
may be that Joseph will hate us, and will fully requite us all the evil that we
did unto him." And they charged Joseph, saying, "Thy father did charge before he died, saying, 'Thus shall ye say unto Joseph: "Ah now, forgive [liter-
ally, lift; take away: nasa'] please the transgression of thy brethren, and
their sin, for that they did unto thee evil.' " So now, please, forgive [nasa']
the transgression of the servants ['avadiym] of the God of thy father." And
Joseph wept when they spoke unto him. And his brethren also went and
fell down before his face, and they said, "Behold, we be thy slaves
['avadiym]." (50:15–18)

Once they have returned to Egypt, the precariousness of their situation impresses itself on the brothers. The old guilt persists, coupled with the fact that
they have seen nothing so far in Joseph's behavior toward them—as opposed to
toward their father—that would encourage them to feel confident of his goodwill. They surely remember that Joseph had been forced to hear, in Jacob's final

testimony, that he was to be surpassed by Judah as ruler, and the brothers have reason to be concerned about how Joseph will react to this slight now that Jacob is gone. Had he not toyed with and threatened them before? Fearful but not without resources, they send a message to Joseph, using very indirect discourse—just as a fearful but resourceful Joseph had recently done when appealing to Pharaoh. Hiding behind yet also exploiting the authority of their dead father, they concoct a predeath speech for Jacob in which he commands them to ask Joseph, on Jacob's behalf, to forgive his brothers for their sins against him. In concord with their father's charge, they append to "Jacob's appeal" a petition of forgiveness for themselves, shrewdly identifying themselves not as "thy brethren" but, piously, as "servants of the God of thy father"—not "of *your* God" or "of *our* God," but of "*your father's* God." When they hear that Joseph is moved to tears by this message, these "servants [*'avadiym*] of the God of Joseph's father" come themselves and now offer themselves as servants/slaves [*'avadiym*] to Joseph. Once again, the brothers are bowing down before their brother Joseph, prince of Egypt.[20]

Joseph's response is remarkable:

> And Joseph said unto them: "Fear not; for am I in the place of God? And ye, although ye meant *evil* against me, *God* meant it for *good*, to bring to pass this day to save much people alive. So now, fear ye not; I, I will sustain you and your little ones." And he comforted them and spoke to their hearts. (50:19–21)

As has been true of Joseph's speeches and deeds from the start, his answer is highly ambiguous. He allays his brothers' fears and rejects their offer to become his slaves, but he does not offer them the begged forgiveness. Stirring the reader's memory of the forbidden tree in the Garden of Eden, Joseph implies that (only) God can make good come out of evil, yet Joseph himself presumes to god-like knowledge of good and evil, and he acts accordingly. Twice using a phrase, "Fear not," usually spoken only by God,[21] Joseph first denies that he is in

20. Bill Rosen comments, in a personal communication: "Since Judah is now, by parental fiat if nothing else, the de jure as well as de facto leader of the brothers, it seems to me that this speech has to be one for which he takes the greatest responsibility . . . and in its resourceful cleverness, reminds me of his speech back in chapter 44."

21. Once to Abraham after the war of the kings (15:1), once to Hagar after her banishment to the wilderness (21:17), once to Isaac in the dream at Beer-sheba after the quarrel with Abimelech's men about the wells of water (26:24), and once to Jacob in the vision at Beer-sheba, as he was apprehensive about going down into Egypt (46:3). The only two other uses in Genesis are by Rachel's midwife, telling her that she is giving birth to a son (she died in the process; 35:17) and by Joseph's steward (speaking for Joseph), who reassures the brothers after they are taken to Joseph's house on their return to Egypt with Benjamin (43:23).

God's place, capable of judging and forgiving sin, but he then insists that, like a god, he will sustain and succor them. Joseph manages at the same time to appear pious and hubristic: the ground of his generosity to his brothers is his interpretation that God has appointed him their savior—an interpretation for which, even if it is true, Joseph has absolutely no evidence. Perhaps most astonishing, Joseph ignores completely the brothers' appeal to their dead father; buried in a foreign land, Jacob no longer figures in Joseph's thought.

Joseph, as is often the case, functions on two levels, and in both capacities his response, albeit generous, is also alienating. Speaking as a human being, Joseph is unforgiving. Speaking as the self-appointed spokesman for God, Joseph insists that there is nothing to forgive. However much Joseph's speech succeeds in allaying his brothers' fears, he preserves his distant stance. There is no real reconciliation of Joseph and his brothers. Joseph, to the last, holds himself apart.

THE END OF JOSEPH: MUMMIFICATION AND MEMORY

Well, almost to the last. The book of Genesis ends with the end of Joseph:

And Joseph dwelt in Egypt, he and the house of his father; and Joseph lived a hundred and ten years. And Joseph saw Ephraim's children of the third generation; the children also of Machir, the son of Manasseh, were born upon Joseph's knees.

And Joseph said unto his brethren, "I die, but God will surely remember you and He will bring you up out of the land into the land that he swore to Abraham, to Isaac, and to Jacob." And Joseph took an oath of the Children of Israel, saying, "God will surely remember you, and ye shall carry up my bones from hence."

So Joseph died, being a hundred and ten years old. And they embalmed him and he was put into a coffin [ba'aron] in Egypt. (50:22–26)

Both Joseph and his father's house dwell in Egypt, but separately. Joseph lives more than fifty years after the death of his father and attains the blessed age for the Egyptians, 110 years. He lives to see the birth of great-grandchildren from both his sons. The text does not tell us anything about how Joseph felt in seeing his progeny increase. Yet he surely remembered Jacob's adoption of his sons and their descendants for the House of Israel, and he must have known that his progeny were, in the most important sense, no longer his. The text subtly conveys this message: Ephraim's children are mentioned before Manasseh's, after the practice and blessing of Jacob, and in neither case does the text call these sons and grandsons Joseph's. Whether because of sad longings related to the fate of his descendants, or from some other reason, Joseph at the very end of his life turns voluntarily back in the direction of Israel.

Joseph, though living a full life, acknowledges in the end that not he but God is the true savior of his father's house. God, remembering His promises, will lead the exodus "out of this land" and will bring them to the land promised to the patriarchs: in this penultimate speech, Joseph mentions the names of Abraham, Isaac, and Jacob for the first and only time in our hearing. But if God will remember the House of Israel, who will remember Joseph? And what place will he have in the world of the Promised Land? In his last act, Joseph gets his brothers to swear that *they* will remember him, when God remembers them, and that they will redeem his bones from "hence" (tellingly, Joseph in these last speeches, does not mention the name of Egypt). Joseph, the self-sufficient man and self-proclaimed savior of his people, must depend on his brothers and their children for a place within the orbit of the covenant. Joseph's mastery over life ends at the grave.

The Children of Israel remain true to their oath. Years later, during the exodus, "Moses took the bones of Joseph with him; for he had straitly sworn the Children of Israel, saying, 'God will surely remember you, and ye shall carry my bones hence with you' " (Exodus 13:19). And as we learn at the end of the book of Joshua, "the bones of Joseph, which the Children of Israel brought up out of Egypt, buried they in Shechem, in a parcel of ground that Jacob bought of the sons of Hamor, the father of Shechem, for a hundred pieces of silver; and it became the inheritance of the children of Joseph" (Joshua 24:32). Redeemed but never thoroughly, Joseph comes to rest in the fratricidal place, in a plot of land that his father had once purchased as a possession to live among the Canaanites.

When Joseph dies, he dies alone. There is no mourning for Joseph; there is no funeral of state described. Instead we are told that Joseph was embalmed and placed in a coffin or an ark *('aron)*: the same word will later be used for the repository of the Mosaic Law. Joseph, embalmed and resting in his ark, is the alternative to (and a foil for) the Torah resting in the Ark of the Covenant. The last word about Joseph is his mummification in Egypt. The very last word of Genesis is "in Egypt" *(bemitsrayim)*. Joseph is in all important respects a dead end.

The last chapter of Genesis begins with the burial of Jacob at Machpelah and ends with the mummification of Joseph in Egypt. The contrast between burial and embalming/mummification reveals a crucial difference between Israel and Egypt: the difference between the acceptance and the denial or defiance of death. Embalming the body is an attempt at human control after death. The putative beneficiary of this treatment is the deceased: embalming resists time and change, prevents decay, beautifies the body, and prepares for reanimation and continued life—not to say immortality. Burial accepts that we are "dust to dust."

It manifests a different attitude toward the body and its fragile beauty, toward time and finitude and memory, and toward the source of life and the (im)possibility of apotheosis. Burial, the Israelite way, lies between the extremes of revering the body and worshiping the dead, on the one hand, and contemning the body and ignoring the mortal remains, on the other. The way of Israel is the way of memory, keeping alive not the bodies of the dead but their ever-living legacy in relation to the ever-living God, who in the beginning created heaven and earth and made man alone in His own image, and who later summoned Father Abraham and his descendants to "walk before Me and be wholehearted."

Epilogue

The End of the Beginning

*W*e have arrived, at long last, at the end of the book about beginnings. We began by witnessing the creation and separation of light, sharing a god-like view of all Creation, ourselves included. We finished by attending the extinction of Joseph the brilliant, whose mortal remains lie embalmed in sun-worshiping and death-denying Egypt. It is impossible in few words to review the sights we have seen and the people(s) we have met, or to summarize what we may have learned along the way. Yet a brief return to the questions and concerns that were to guide our reading seems a fitting way to conclude.

As I suggested in the introduction, the book of Genesis is mainly concerned with this question: is it possible to find, institute, and preserve a way of life that accords with man's true standing in the world and that serves to perfect his god-like possibilities? A double-sided difficulty was revealed immediately. First, although he is the most god-like of the creatures, man, as he comes into being, is not yet complete, perfect, whole: man alone among the earthly creatures is not said to be "good." Because of his freedom, rooted in his reason and issuing in his pride, god-like man is most prone to waywardness, error, and unmitigated disaster. Second, as he seeks direction for his choices from his experience of the visible natural world, help is utterly unavailable. Even the splendidly shining and perfectly moving heavenly bodies are completely silent about better and worse, totally indifferent to human needs and purposes, and absolutely useless to anyone seeking guidance for how human beings are to live. How, then, can the human creature, whether alone or in community, be directed toward his completion and perfection? From where and from what can he take guidance? This has been the central human question from the beginning. It remains the central human question now and, very likely, forever.

Genesis, if read conventionally as an account of early human history and the beginning of the nation of Israel, offers a partial answer. Under God's own tutelage, a tiny sliver of humankind makes a precious if precarious beginning, against the uninstructed ways of mankind and in contrast with the ways of other nations. By the end of Genesis, a new way of life, charged with pursuing right-eousness and striving for holiness, has gained a toehold in the world. Springing from a single man separated out from all others, and growing from one house-hold into a flourishing tribe and incipient nation, the generations of the patri-archs succeed in establishing a new cultural, ethical, and political alternative, informed by and looking reverently to the divine. In doing so, they have demon-strated the ability, if not always the inclination, to avoid the manifest evils that universally bedevil human communities.

Unlike the city of Cain, this community is not founded in fratricide—al-though it barely escaped this outrage. Unlike the nations descended from Ham, this community does not begin with a revolt against paternal authority and filial piety. Unlike the Mesopotamian city of Babel, this community does not have its roots in human pride and the aspiration to rational autonomy, self-sufficiency, and human self-re-creation. Unlike the Canaanite cities of Sodom or Shechem, this community neither revels in sexual wildness nor preys upon strangers, and it does not ignore its own acts of injustice. And unlike the great civilization of Egypt, this nascent community seems to have accepted the given world and the limits of finitude, eschewing the quest for bodily immortality and apotheosis pursued through magic, technology, and administrative genius. Instead, this in-cipient nation is focused on transmitting a covenantal way of life that summons human beings to be wholehearted, to execute justice, and to walk deliberately and reverently before the divine.

The Israelite nation, with the help of divinely assisted instruction, has made an auspicious start in dealing with the perennial dangers that lurk in the hearts of human beings. Although it still harbors all the dangerous passions that make for family tragedy, the Israelite household has instituted an order based on awe and reverence—for wives and mothers, for husbands and fathers, and for the di-vine—that manifests itself in a proper and God-fearing patriarchy. Although set apart as a separate nation, the Israelites show a capacity for dealing with strangers not only justly but also generously, yet all the while escaping the temp-tation to assimilate. As the nation starts to grow, the divine becomes increasingly remote and noncommunicative; yet the children of the covenant cling to the new way, mainly because they remember God's solicitude and command as well as recall the inspiring merit of their ancestors. The fear of the Lord—the biblical "beginning of wisdom"—is alive and well in nascent Israel.

Yet at the end of Genesis success is at best only partial. Jacob, a.k.a. Israel, the last of the patriarchs, lies dead and buried in the cave with his forebears. Joseph, the leading light and onetime heir apparent, is a mummy entombed in Egypt awaiting reanimation yet also trusting that the descendants of his brethren will eventually provide him burial in the Promised Land. Even those whom Joseph served so ably will soon forget his brilliance and his devotion. Young Israel may be thriving, but in the wrong place; it will soon be enslaved by a new pharaoh who knows neither Joseph nor the fear-of-the-Lord. And young Israel suffers internal weaknesses as well. Although it has preserved its separated existence, the Israelite nation is not yet properly constituted to live on its own or in its own land. Patriarchy, the principle of familial authority, is necessary for perpetuating the way from fathers to sons. But it is hardly sufficient for governing a whole community or a political people. Regarding the survival and flourishing of the new way, Genesis gives us only the beginning and calls attention to the need for further and novel developments.

To turn a nation, linked largely by common lineage and descent, into a people with distinctive mores and a defined way of life, the Israelites must share not merely a set of ancestors but also a people-making history. Specifically, they must be collectively transformed by a special set of shared political and cultural experiences. They must first experience enslavement and loss of all worldly power. They must then be emancipated and liberated against all odds, yet in a manner that obliges the slaves to declare their willingness to be freed. And their former masters—the world's greatest civilization—must be brought to bear witness to the superiority of the God of Israel and the insufficiency of relying solely on human wisdom and power.

Yet, like the education of the patriarchs, those dramatic and transforming experiences are necessary but not sufficient. To enable the people to live justly and to pursue holiness in their own land, they will need comprehensive legislation touching on those aspects of human life where, left to their own devices, unregulated human beings will usually get it wrong—injuring their neighbors, defiling themselves, and worshiping idols. And they will need leadership of the sort that uses its power not to aggrandize the rule of (one) man, but to establish the rule of law in the service of God. In a word, familial principles and practices must be supplemented by and subordinated to legal, political, and priestly principles and practices. These necessary transformations are the subject of the following books, Exodus and Leviticus, for which Genesis is the proper prelude.

Yet gaining such an account of the happenings in the text is only part—and not the most important part—of what reading Genesis can achieve for the wisdom-seeking reader. As in any philosophical quest, the most significant accomplishments will have taken place in the mind and heart of the inquirer. As I hope my way of reading has shown, Genesis nurtures such soul-shaping activity. With its stories arranged more in pedagogical than chronological order, it has offered us revealing pictures of paradigmatic people, human beings recognizably "just like us," in the mirror of whose lives we can reflect on the complexities and moral ambiguities of our own. Thanks to the artfulness of the text, we acquire a stake in what happens to the characters in the stories, and we participate vicariously in their adventures. Yet also thanks to the artfulness of the text, we are encouraged to critically scrutinize and judge their deeds and speeches—and, by implication, also our own. Reflective participation—detached yet self-critical engagement—is the wisdom-seeking way of reading the book of Genesis that the text itself has invited and fostered.

The characters in the stories of Genesis did not have the benefit of reading a text that offers to make sense out of their lives. Indeed, they lacked the benefit of books altogether. Their education, such as it was, they acquired solely through their own experience. To be sure, according to the text the patriarchs occasionally benefited from divine assistance, including direct instruction given by God Himself. But what they learned was nonetheless rather circumscribed, limited to particular times and circumstances. Though some kind of accumulated understanding may have been handed down from Abraham to Isaac, and from Isaac (with Rebekah's help) to Jacob, each of the patriarchs (and Judah) needed to recapitulate for himself a similar educational journey. Although each was an indispensable protagonist in founding the new way, none of them knew it to be a new way or, more important, why it was necessary and desirable. Unlike the reader of Genesis, none of them had the benefit of reflecting on the human condition with the help of the pre-Abrahamic stories: of creation, the Garden of Eden, Cain and Abel, the age of heroes, Noah and the Flood, the rebellion of Ham, and the city and tower of Babel. None of them had access to the profound insights into human nature and human perversity that these stories make available to the philosophical reader.

Like the patriarchs and matriarchs in Genesis, we readers begin our search for wisdom and understanding firmly rooted in our time and place. Like them, we are blessed with the capacity to learn and remember what came before us. Whether we know it or not, most of us are heirs to an ethical, cultural, and spiritual tradition that they began. And to those of us who read the text from within a religious tradition, the accumulated treasures of Genesis are handed down to us along with the authoritative teachings of the community. But in every generation, all readers—even readers within a tradition—must find their own way both in the world and in the book, starting from where they are. Unlike the patriarchs and matriarchs, we have the advantage of a text that, if read carefully, obviates the need to recapitulate their experiences in order to acquire what they learned from them. If we have read in a wisdom-seeking spirit, the text will now be alive for us, as we dwell with its characters, probe its meanings, and feel its power to shape our thoughts, sentiments, and attitudes. Although God does not speak to us directly, as He did to the patriarchs, we have instead the stories that they lacked. We have learned from the great tales of the first eleven chapters the deeply troublesome elements of the human mind and heart. Suitably chastened and eager to find a superior human alternative, we willingly took a walk with Abraham when God called him to embark on a journey to found the new way. In the course of our travels, our prejudices have been challenged and our unexamined opinions have been called into question. Our perceptions of many things—among them, speech and reason, sexuality and shame, beauty and adornment, farming and sacrificing, pride and anger, man and woman, marriage and fatherhood, brotherhood and sisterhood, hospitality and piety, justice and punishment, tents and houses, cities and towers, dreaming and devising, envy and hatred, revenge and forgiveness, statesmanship and administration, gratitude and ingratitude, burial and embalming, time and memory, nature worship and the fear of God—are very likely no longer what they were. The thoughts and feelings aroused by my wrestlings with the text are spread throughout this book. I would not presume to say what you, my fellow reader, will have learned from your own readings and reflections. But regarding one crucial discovery, I trust we are in agreement.

In introducing this book on Genesis, I argued that the crisis in modern thought, as well as our personal and public need for wisdom, commends a serious examination of the Bible. Can this old book still have something important to say to us, as we confront our current version of the permanent human predicament? I trust that any wisdom-seeking reader, whether or not he agrees with any of my textual interpretations, will agree that there is wondrous much in this book from which he can still learn. I trust that he will see that the insights available with the help of the book of Genesis are in no way damaged by modern scientific discoveries or by other developments in modern thought or practice. Above all, I hope that the reader has discovered that the Bible can be a treasured companion in his quest to satisfy spiritual hunger and articulate love of wisdom.

The love of wisdom, according to the Greeks, begins in wonder. According to the Bible, wisdom begins in awe-fear-and-reverence for the Lord. Yet the text that has shown us the limits of reason has addressed itself precisely to our thoughtful minds. It has encouraged deeper understanding even as it has encouraged greater humility before that which is beyond our grasp. Addressing us as lovers of our own independence, it has shown how the enhancement of freedom might require the restrictions of law. Addressing us as lovers of our own cleverness, it has shown how the limitations of human reason corrupted by pride and vanity can be corrected by acknowledging our debt to powers beyond our control. By showing free and rational beings the necessary and desirable limitations of freedom and reason, it has, paradoxically, enhanced both our freedom and our understanding.

Long dwelling with the book of Genesis, and ever marveling at its beauty, its profundity, and, above all, its power to illuminate and lift the soul, this exhilarated reader of Genesis stands before it on his intellectual knees, filled with awe and gratitude for a text that makes such insights possible. I dare to hope that, with my book as a companion, other wisdom-seeking readers of Genesis may enjoy a similar experience.

ENDNOTES

xii   before it was published: Entitled "The Lion and the Ass: A Commentary on the Book of Genesis," it was first published serially in *Interpretation: A Journal of Political Philosophy,* beginning with vol. 8, nos. 2–3 (1980). It was later published as *Commentary on the Book of Genesis* (Edwin Mellen Press, 1991). My frequent citations of Sacks's commentary will be to the version published first.

xv   and Nahum M. Sarna: Robert Alter, *Genesis: Translation and Commentary* (New York: W. W. Norton, 1996). Umberto Cassuto, *A Commentary on the Book of Genesis* (Jerusalem: Magnes Press, 1964). *The Pentateuch and Haftorahs,* ed. Dr. J. H. Hertz (London: Soncino Press, 1967). *Pentateuch with Targum Onkelos, Haphtaroth, and Rashi's Commentary: Genesis,* trans. Rev. M. Rosenbaum and Dr. A. M. Silberman, in collaboration with A. Blashki and L. Joseph (New York: Hebrew Publishing Company, n.d.). Robert Sacks, "The Lion and the Ass: A Commentary on the Book of Genesis," published seriatim in *Interpretation,* vol. 8, nos. 2–3 (1980), through vol. 12, nos. 2–3 (1983). *The JPS Torah Commentary: Genesis;* traditional Hebrew text with new JPS translation; commentary by Nahum M. Sarna (Philadelphia: Jewish Publication Society, 1989).

INTRODUCTION

3   "not for anything useful": Aristotle, *Metaphysics* I:ii, 982b11–22. The translation is mine.

3   "reveals many distinctions": Ibid. I:i, 982a22–28.

3   "the sky proclaims His handiwork": Psalm 19:1.

3   "all who practice it": Psalm 119:10.

4   "in His commandments": Psalm 119:7–9, 120:1.

6   "which nature has provided us": René Descartes, *Discourse on Method,* in *The Philosophical Works of Descartes,* vol. I, ed. Elizabeth S. Haldane and G. R. T. Ross (Cambridge, Eng.: Cambridge University Press, 1981), 119–20. Emphasis added.

14   and names for God: For an extensive critique of the historicocritical approach, see Umberto Cassuto, *The Documentary Hypothesis and the Composition of the Pentateuch,* trans. Israel Abrahams (Jerusalem: Magnes Press, 1961).

CHAPTER ONE

28   "by subtle hint": Umberto Cassuto, *A Commentary on the Book of Genesis, Part One: From Adam to Noah* (Jerusalem: Magnes Press, 1964), 7.

33   "precede the sun": Strauss, "Interpretation," 12–13.

34   "what Plato calls *diaresis*": Ibid., 13.

51   "the man who does them": Strauss, ibid., 9.

53   *"to keep it holy":* Cassuto, *Commentary,* 64. Emphasis in original.

CHAPTER TWO

78   woman elicits poetry: See Rousseau's *Essay on the Origin of Languages,* chap. 3, in which Rousseau offers a profound discussion of his claim that man spoke poetry before he spoke prose.

81   counterpart for the human being: I owe this observation, and the third inference I draw from it, to Mark Schwehn.

83   addressee's desires and concerns: I owe this observation and some of the reflections in the following three paragraphs to an excellent paper, "The First Question and the Discovery of Autonomy in Genesis III:1–2," by Kirstin Wilcox, written in 1989 when she was an undergraduate student in my Genesis class.

85   hidden meaning and motive: I owe this insight to Yuval Levin.

86   the plural participle *yod'ey:* I owe this observation to Father Paul Mankowski. Rashi also translates *'elohim* in the plural, perhaps because of the plural participle. It is true, however, that the participle could refer back not to *'elohim,* "God" or "gods," but to the less proximate subject of the sentence, "ye."

86   "You will have insight": I owe this discovery to Father Paul Mankowski.

87   "gets itself into trouble": "And the Serpent was . . . : A Serpentine Reading of Genesis 3" (a paper Mr. Levin wrote for my most recent Genesis seminar, December 2000), 11–12. As my acknowledgments indicate, I have learned a great deal from this paper.

89   "tasted the latter": Immanuel Kant, "Conjectural Beginning of Human History," trans. Emil Fackenheim, in *Kant on History,* ed. Lewis White Beck (Indianapolis: Bobbs-Merrill, 1963), 55–56.

92   "and I did eat": The translation is Robert Alter's.

93   "lift anything up": Levin, "Serpentine Reading," 13.

CHAPTER THREE

103 cannot be restored: See p. 101 n. 4.

110 "spring from it": Immanuel Kant, "Conjectural Beginning of Human History," trans. Emil Fackenheim, in *Kant on History*, ed. Lewis White Beck (Indianapolis: Bobbs-Merrill, 1963), 57.

111 "happiness and innocence": Jean-Jacques Rousseau, *Discourse on the Origin and Foundations of Inequality Among Men*, trans. Roger D. and Judith R. Masters, in *The First and Second Discourses*, ed. Roger D. Masters (New York: St. Martin's Press, 1964), 148–49.

118 "its only bonds": Jean-Jacques Rousseau, ibid., 146–47; emphasis added.

119 "their common subsistence": Ibid., 147.

CHAPTER FOUR

127 "Abel barely exists": Robert Sacks, "The Lion and the Ass: A Commentary on the Book of Genesis (Chapters 1–10)," *Interpretation* 8, nos. 2–3 (1980), 68.

129 obtain a livelihood: Umberto Cassuto, *A Commentary on the Book of Genesis, Part One: From Adam to Noah* (Jerusalem: Magnes Press, 1964), 203.

130 "roam through the whole": Sacks, "The Lion and the Ass," 68.

137 "not necessarily the case": Sacks, ibid., 69.

137 He truly cares about: I owe this suggestion to Lisa Yountchi.

138 "they have received from him": *The Rhetoric of Aristotle* II.2, trans. Lane Cooper (Englewood Cliffs, New Jersey: Prentice-Hall, 1960), 93–95. Emphasis added.

139 "men bloodthirsty and cruel": Jean-Jacques Rousseau, *Discourse on the Origin and the Foundations of Inequality Among Men*, in *The First and Second Discourses and the Essay on the Origin of Languages*, trans. and ed. Victor Gourevitch (New York: Harper & Row, 1986), 175–76. Emphasis added.

147 for the sake of living well: Aristotle, *Politics* I.2 (1252b10–30).

148 "for that superiority": Sacks, "The Lion and the Ass," 75.

CHAPTER FIVE

152 what looked like mere genealogy: See Robert Sacks, "The Lion and the Ass: A Commentary on the Book of Genesis (Chapters 1–10)," *Interpretation* 8, nos. 2–3 (1980), 76–80.

155 "yield it to others": *The Iliad of Homer* XII.322–25, trans. Richmond Lattimore (Chicago: University of Chicago Press, 1951), 266–67.

157 "sacrifices of human blood": Jean-Jacques Rousseau, *Discourse on the Origin and the Foundations of Inequality Among Men*, in *The First and Second Discourses and the Essay on the Origin of Languages*, trans. and ed. Victor Goure-

vitch (New York: Harper & Row, 1986), 175; emphasis added. See also the last two paragraphs of chapter 9 of the *Essay on the Origin of Languages,* 271–72.

158 "generations of *Man ['adam]*": Sacks, "The Lion and the Ass," 76–80.

160 "God will choose": Sacks, ibid., 81. Emphasis in original.

164 "approximately 40 weeks": Ibid., 89.

165 this book as a whole: I rely heavily, in the following few paragraphs, on Umberto Cassuto's superb introduction to the Flood narrative in his *Commentary on the Book of Genesis, Part Two: From Noah to Abraham* (Jerusalem: Magnes Press, 1964), 3–46. (The direct quotations from the *Gilgamesh* epic are also taken from Cassuto's own summary translation of the Akkadian original.) Cassuto's analysis of the structure of the Flood story is also extremely helpful for convincing the reader that we are dealing with an integrated and very carefully contrived narrative.

CHAPTER SIX

173 "subjected to law": Jean-Jacques Rousseau, *Discourse on the Origin and Foundations of Inequality Among Men,* trans. Roger D. and Judith R. Masters, in *The First and Second Discourses,* ed. Roger D. Masters (New York: St. Martin's Press, 1964), 102.

177 opposite of wrong: See Chapter Two, p. 86.

178 "of earlier times": Robert Sacks, "The Lion and the Ass: A Commentary on the Book of Genesis (Chapters 1–10)," *Interpretation* 8, nos. 2–3 (1980), 96.

188 "external and explicit bonds": Sacks, ibid., 97.

190 "there is no covenant": Sacks, ibid., 97.

CHAPTER SEVEN

199 "dangerous to spell out": Robert Alter, *Genesis: Translation and Commentary* (New York: W. W. Norton, 1996), 40.

203 "something different": *Pentateuch with Targum Onkelos, Haphtaroth, and Rashi's Commentary: Genesis,* trans. Rev. M. Rosenbaum and Dr. A. M. Silberman, in collaboration with A. Blashki and L. Joseph (New York: Hebrew Publishing Company, n.d.), 39.

203 "by the Covenant": "The Lion and the Ass: A Commentary on the Book of Genesis (Chapters 1–10)," *Interpretation* 8, nos. 2–3 (1980), 98.

205 to cover up: See Chapter Three, p. 106ff.

206 precovenantal (or natural) origins: Sacks, "The Lion and the Ass," 98–99.

207 *aidoia,* "the awesome things": This discussion of *aidos* draws heavily on a profound essay by Kurt Riezler, "Comment on the Social Psychology of Shame," *American Journal of Sociology* 48 (January 1943), 457–65. See also my essay

"Looking Good: Nature and Nobility," in *Toward a More Natural Science: Biology and Human Affairs* (New York: Free Press, 1985).

207   Hebrew laws of purity: See especially Leviticus 18.

214   "all other virtues": Umberto Cassuto, *A Commentary on the Book of Genesis, Part Two: From Noah to Abraham* (Jerusalem: Magnes Press, 1964), 166.

CHAPTER EIGHT

222   every word with care: For a thorough and detailed literary analysis, see U. Cassuto, *A Commentary on the Book of Genesis, Part Two: From Noah to Abraham* (Jerusalem: Magnes Press, 1964), 225–38.

222   "game of mirrors": Robert Alter, *Genesis: Translation and Commentary* (New York: W. W. Norton, 1996), 47.

224   "essentially unchallengeable": Kristen Dietrich Balisi, "Creation and Evaluation: Human Speech and Relationality in the Garden and at Babel," a paper written for my Genesis seminar in 1997. It was Ms. Balisi who first called my attention to the way in which the constructivist character of human language is central to the constructivist character of the human city. She is responsible also for suggesting that the present uses of language constitute a culmination of the meaning of language implicit in Adam's naming of the animals. (See Chapter Two, pp. 73–76.)

225   equal to the speech: See Chapter One, p. 49.

228   "city of *burnt bricks*": Robert Sacks, "The Lion and the Ass: A Commentary on the Book of Genesis (Chapters 11–20)," *Interpretation* 9, no. 1 (1980), 2 (italics in original).

231   "all over the earth": Balisi, "Creation and Evaluation."

239   His multiplication of tongues: I owe this observation to Father Paul Mankowski.

CHAPTER NINE

255   higher than oneself: Hillel Fradkin, "God's Politics: Lessons from the Beginning," *This World*, winter 1983, 102–3. I have learned much from this fine essay.

CHAPTER TEN

280   "those of His emissaries": Robert Alter, *Genesis: Translation and Commentary* (New York: W. W. Norton, 1996), 69.

288   " 'as He had said' ": Alter, ibid., 96.

289   "evident in her language": Ibid., 97.

290   to be the legitimate heir: Ibid., 98.

293   "brother and sister": Jean-Jacques Rousseau, *Essay on the Origin of Languages,*

in *The First and Second Discourse and the Essay on the Origin of Languages,* trans. and ed. Victor Gourevitch (New York: Harper and Row, 1986), 272.

294   "destruction of mankind": Ibid. Emphasis added.

CHAPTER ELEVEN

301   the local inhabitants: Robert Sacks, "The Lion and the Ass: A Commentary on the Book of Genesis (Chapters 11–20)," *Interpretation* 9, no. 1 (1980), 11.

304   "the things they make": Ibid., 12.

306   to gain the land: Ibid., 21 ff.

312   "Abraham ceases to be Abraham": Hannah Hintze, "On the Testing of Abraham," a paper written for my Genesis class, autumn 2000. Ms. Hintze is a graduate student in the Committee on Social Thought.

315   "from God Himself": *The JPS Torah Commentary: Genesis;* traditional Hebrew text with new JPS translation; commentary by Nahum M. Sarna (Philadelphia: Jewish Publication Society, 1989), 127.

319   "characterize his descendants": Ibid., 132.

319   "over their doom": *The Pentateuch and Haftorahs,* ed. Dr. J. H. Hertz (London: Soncino Press, 1967), 65.

336   God says "please": Robert Sacks, "The Lion and the Ass: A Commentary on the Book of Genesis (Chapters 21–24)," *Interpretation* 10, no. 1 (1982), 76. Sacks adds: "To no other person aside from Abraham does God say *please* in the whole of the Bible."

336   "a one-sided dialogue": Robert Alter, *Genesis: Translation and Commentary* (New York: W. W. Norton, 1996), 103.

337   "be *tamim* (perfect)": Ibid., 76.

338   "Abraham's faith in God": Ibid., 77.

338   " 'God tried Abraham' ": *The Book of Legends; Sefer Ha-Aggadah: Legends from the Talmud and Midrash,* ed. Hayim Nahman Bialik and Yehoshua Hana Ravnitzky, trans. William G. Braude (New York: Schocken, 1992), 39. Readers are strongly encouraged to consult this spectacular midrash in its entirety; ibid., number 45, pp. 39–42. Reading it gives me gooseflesh.

342   "in postbiblical Hebrew": Alter, *Genesis,* 105, note to verse 22:7.

342   "so close together": Sacks, "The Lion and the Ass . . . (Chapters 21–24)," 80.

CHAPTER TWELVE

356   "evident in her language": Robert Alter, *Genesis: Translation and Commentary* (New York: W. W. Norton, 1996), 97.

358   "tradition set before him": Kristen Dietrich Balisi, "The Sacrifices of Isaac" (unpublished), 3.

358   "as to receive": Ibid., 6.

360 "but a beginning": Ibid., 9–10.

362 "and be killed": *The Book of Legends; Sefer Ha-Aggadah: Legends from the Talmud and Midrash,* ed. Hayim Nahman Bialik and Yehoshua Hana Ravnitzky, trans. William G. Braude (New York: Schocken, 1992), 41.

364 purchase and possession: Robert Sacks, "The Lion and the Ass: A Commentary on the Book of Genesis (Chapters 21–24)," *Interpretation* 10, no. 1 (1982), 97–102.

373 "I will go—at once": Maurice Samuel, "The Manager," *Certain People of the Book* (New York: Knopf, 1955), 139–40.

CHAPTER THIRTEEN

383 "Isaac's paternal favoritism": Robert Alter, *Genesis: Translation and Commentary* (New York: W. W. Norton, 1996), 128.

386 his people know not the Lord: Such an idea is implicit in Robert Sacks's discussions of the Abimelech episodes. See "The Lion and the Ass: A Commentary on the Book of Genesis (Chapters 11–20)," *Interpretation* 9, no. 1 (1980), 67–72; "The Lion and the Ass . . . (Chapters 21–24)," *Interpretation* 10, no. 1 (1982), 73–75; and "The Lion and the Ass . . . (Chapters 25–30)," *Interpretation* no. 10 nos. 2–3 (1982), 282–88.

386 "to be his sister": Alter, *Genesis,* 133.

388 "to die with him": Sacks, "The Lion and the Ass . . . (Chapters 25–30)," 287.

398 "unusual physical strength": Alter, *Genesis,* 144.

CHAPTER FOURTEEN

416 for the people: Robert Sacks, "The Lion and the Ass: A Commentary on the Book of Genesis (Chapters 25–30)," *Interpretation* 10, nos. 2–3 (1982), 301. Indeed, when Jacob returns to Beth-El, on God's command, Israel's future need for a king will be explicitly mentioned (35:11).

422 "respectful salutation" (Ibn Ezra): *The Pentateuch and Haftorahs,* 2nd ed., ed. J. H. Hertz (London: Soncino Press, 1967), 108.

422 " 'in his mouth' ": *Pentateuch with Targum Onkelos, Haphtaroth, and Rashi's Commentary: Genesis,* trans. Rev. M. Rosenbaum and Dr. A. M. Silberman, in collaboration with A. Blashki and L. Joseph (New York: Hebrew Publishing Company, n.d.), 136.

432 "the manumission of the slave": *The JPS Torah Commentary: Genesis,* commentary by Nahum M. Sarna (Philadelphia: Jewish Publication Society, 1989), 211. See also Exodus 21:2–4. Note that the word "serve" or "service" is thrice mentioned in this brief speech.

435 "beaten at his own game": Sarna, ibid., 216.

439 "any religious worth": Sarna, ibid., 219.

CHAPTER FIFTEEN

447   of being able to go to war: For a superb treatment of the unavoidably tragic character of family relations as these are revealed in Aeschylus's trilogy, the *Oresteia*, see Reeghan Raffals, "A House Divided: The Tragedy of Agamemnon" (doctoral diss., University of Chicago, 1997).

450   faking Esau's hairiness *(sa'ir)*: I owe this observation to Nahum Sarna, *The JPS Torah Commentary: Genesis* (Philadelphia: Jewish Publication Society, 1989), 224.

455   since the Garden of Eden: I owe this observation and several others in this paragraph to Robert Sacks, "The Lion and the Ass: A Commentary on the Book of Genesis (Chapters 31–34)," *Interpretation* 11, no. 1 (1983), 105.

459   1 Kings 12:25–30: Ibid., 106.

460   meaning "all and sundry": Sarna, *JPS Torah Commentary*, 227.

460   "of the verb in the name": Robert Alter, *Genesis: Translation and Commentary* (New York: W. W. Norton, 1996), 182.

469   " 'my soul has been preserved' ": Ibid., 230.

CHAPTER SIXTEEN

478   " 'Like mother, like daughter' ": *Pentateuch with Targum Onkelos, Haphtaroth, and Rashi's Commentary: Genesis,* trans. Rev. M. Rosenbaum and Dr. A. M. Silberman, in collaboration with A. Blashki and L. Joseph (New York: Hebrew Publishing Company, n.d.), 164–65.

481   "forcibly and against her will": William Blackstone, *Commentaries on the Law of England,* vol. IV, *Of Public Wrongs* (Boston: Beacon Press, 1962), chap. XV, sect. III, 235.

481   "the honour of the women": Ibid., 236.

481   "against the women's will": Ibid.

482   "that unlawful course of life": Ibid., 238.

482   "all its fields (Joma 77b)": Rashi, in *Pentateuch with Targum,* 165.

484   "Dinah's brothers to arrive": Robert Sacks, "The Lion and the Ass: A Commentary on the Book of Genesis (Chapters 31–34)," *Interpretation* 11, no. 1 (1983), 117.

485   "or to each other": Robert Alter, *Genesis: Translation and Commentary* (New York: W. W. Norton, 1996), 128.

486   "the Greek people as their foes": Herodotus, *The History* 1.4, trans. David Grene (Chicago: University of Chicago Press, 1987), 34.

490   male sexual self-restraint: See Chapter Eleven, pp. 313–14.

503   to his seed (compare 17:8): Nahum M. Sarna, *The JPS Torah Commentary: Genesis* (Philadelphia: Jewish Publication Society, 1989), 241–42.

504   Jacob's twelfth son, Benjamin: See the Coda of Chapter Fourteen.

CHAPTER SEVENTEEN

512 "of ancient *haute couture*": Robert Alter, *Genesis: Translation and Commentary* (New York: W. W. Norton, 1996), 209.

512 "*at his father's death*": *The Pentateuch and Haftorahs*, ed. Dr. J. H. Hertz (London: Soncino Press, 1967), 142.

513 "his father's wives": Robert Sacks, "The Lion and the Ass: A Commentary on the Book of Genesis (Chapters 35–37)," *Interpretation* 11, no. 2 (1983), 267 (emphasis added).

514 "cast her eyes upon him, etc.": *Pentateuch with Targum Onkelos, Haphtaroth, and Rashi's Commentary: Genesis*, trans. Rev. M. Rosenbaum and Dr. A. M. Silberman, in collaboration with A. Blashki and L. Joseph (New York: Hebrew Publishing Company, n.d.), 180.

517 "do you mean to rule us": Alter, *Genesis*, 210.

523 but beat him to it: Sacks, "The Lion and the Ass," 271–73.

525 "perhaps something histrionic": Alter, *Genesis*, 215.

525 "now believe their own lie": Sacks, "The Lion and the Ass," 274; emphasis in original.

533 "in a foreign land": Alter, *Genesis*, 220.

536 "duties of the firstborn": Robert Sacks, "The Lion and the Ass: A Commentary on the Book of Genesis (Chapters 38–39)," *Interpretation* 11, no. 3 (1983) 356–57; emphasis in original. Sacks is mistaken in one small detail: Joseph's coat was sent to Jacob through messengers.

543 "both men and women, was notorious": Nahum M. Sarna, *The JPS Torah Commentary: Genesis* (Philadelphia: Jewish Publication Society, 1989), 273. Hertz, ed., *The Pentateuch*, 148.

543 "lifted up her eyes, etc.": Rashi in *Pentateuch with Targum*, 191.

543 "gesture of discouraging it": Maurice Samuel, "The Brilliant Failure," in *Certain People of the Book* (New York: Knopf, 1955), 327–28.

544 " 'what is in the house' ": Ibid., 329–30.

545 "*and did not sin*": Rashi in *Pentateuch with Targum*, 192; emphasis in original.

546 "thrown into the pit": Samuel, "The Brilliant Failure," 330.

547 an insult to them all: I owe this observation to Robert Alter, *Genesis*, 226.

CHAPTER EIGHTEEN

550 only in a foreign land: I owe this observation to Yoram Hazony, *The Dawn: Political Teachings of the Book of Esther* (Jerusalem: Genesis Jerusalem Press, 1995), 278.

553 pursuit of sanctification: See Leon R. Kass, *The Hungry Soul: Eating and the Perfecting of Our Nature* (Chicago: University of Chicago Press, 1999), chap. 6.

556 very long time: Robert Sacks, "The Lion and the Ass: A Commentary on the Book of Genesis (Chapters 40–43)," *Interpretation* 12, no. 1 (1984), 52–53.

562 "separated by time": Sacks, ibid., 56.

562 could provide no remedy: Aaron Wildavsky, *Assimilation Versus Separation: Joseph the Administrator and the Politics of Religion in Biblical Israel* (New Brunswick, N.J.: Transaction Publishers, 1993), 85.

563 "will enhance Pharaoh's power": Ibid., 86.

564 regard it as impure: See Herodotus, *The History*, trans. David Grene (Chicago: University of Chicago Press, 1987), 2.35 ff. and 3.12.

565 "for the extended famine": Robert Alter, *Genesis: Translation and Commentary* (New York: W. W. Norton, 1996), 239.

570 "part of their efficacy": Wildavsky, *Assimilation*, 88.

572 "Facts are better than dreams": See Churchill's remarks on becoming prime minister after the fall of the Chamberlain government on May 10, 1940. Winston Churchill, *The Gathering Storm* (Boston: Houghton Mifflin, 1948), 667.

CHAPTER NINETEEN

575 "much more complicated": Robert Sacks, "The Lion and the Ass: A Commentary on the Book of Genesis (Chapters 40–43)," *Interpretation* 12, no. 1 (1984), 68.

577 awakened their memory of him: Sacks, ibid., 69.

586 "as a *pledge* (Genesis 38:18): Ibid., 76; italics in original.

586 "for their fraternal crime": Robert Alter, *Genesis: Translation and Commentary* (New York: W. W. Norton, 1996), 253.

590 what one thinks one is: For a discussion of this general point, see my book *The Hungry Soul: Eating and the Perfecting of Our Nature,* 2nd ed. (Chicago: University of Chicago Press, 1999), especially chap. 6, "Sanctified Eating: The Dietary Laws of Leviticus."

591 "he had acted before": Robert Sacks, "The Lion and the Ass: A Commentary on the Book of Genesis (Chapters 44–50)," *Interpretation* 12, nos. 2–3 (1984), 141.

594 "and its perpetrator": Alter, *Genesis*, 262.

599 "might be probable": Ibid., 264.

602 "over Joseph's supposed death": Ibid., 265.

602 "leads to psychological transformation": Ibid.

603 "in a purely human way": Sacks, "The Lion and the Ass . . . (Chapters 44–50)," 144; emphasis in original.

608 "he also means Joseph": Alter, *Genesis*, 267.

610   "to be mere pretense": Sacks, "The Lion and the Ass . . . (Chapters 44–50)," 147.

614   "into a trap": Alter, *Genesis*, 271.

CHAPTER TWENTY

619   "in store for them in Egypt": Robert Sacks, "The Lion and the Ass: A Commentary on the Book of Genesis (Chapters 44–50)," *Interpretation* 12, nos. 2–3 (1983), 152.

621   "ten times sacred seven": Robert Alter, *Genesis: Translation and Commentary* (New York: W. W. Norton, 1996), 276.

622   before particular human beings: See, for example, 12:7; 17:1; 18:1; 26:2, 4; 35:1, 9.

624   to Robert Sacks: See Sacks, "The Lion and the Ass," 155–57.

630   "but our carcasses": Translation following Alter. See his explanation, *Genesis*, 283.

632   Wildavsky: Aaron Wildavsky, *Assimilation Versus Separation: Joseph the Administrator and the Politics of Religion in Biblical Israel* (New Brunswick, N.J.: Transaction Publishers, 1993).

633   "and the rest were subjugated": Ibid., 143–45.

CHAPTER TWENTY-ONE

637   "which their father had set up": Robert Sacks, "The Lion and the Ass: A Commentary on the Book of Genesis (Chapters 44–50)," *Interpretation* 12, nos. 2–3 (1983), 164; emphasis in original.

638   "in granting permission": Nahum M. Sarna, *The JPS Torah Commentary: Genesis* (Philadelphia: Jewish Publication Society, 1989), 324.

638   "of intervening generations": Sacks, "The Lion and the Ass," 164.

641   "did not live to bear": Robert Alter, *Genesis: Translation and Commentary* (New York: W. W. Norton, 1996), 288.

643   even before he had met the boys: Sacks, "The Lion and the Ass," 167.

644   "the necessity for renewal": Ibid., 167.

645   "in connection with his brothers": Ibid., 169.

645   "animal, vegetable, or mineral": Alter, *Genesis*, 292.

645   of all that Jacob says: Interested readers may consult the following very different recent treatments of this material: Sarna, *The JPS Torah Commentary,* 331–47; Sacks, "The Lion and the Ass," 170–87; and Aaron Wildavsky, *Assimilation Versus Separation: Joseph the Administrator and the Politics of Religion in Biblical Israel* (New Brunswick, N.J.: Transaction Publishers, 1993), 163–89 (this last includes references to many earlier interpretations). Alter's notes to his translation are also helpful. Sarna believes the poem is a collection of frag-

ments from different sources and lacks an inner unity; nonetheless, he offers much helpful commentary on words and phrases and on the subsequent history of each of the twelve tribes. Sacks offers a more political reading, providing numerous helpful links to relevant later biblical episodes. In Wildavsky's interpretation, the so-called blessings are more like curses; he sees Jacob chastising his sons in a "negative collective portrait [that] helps explain why Israel's God seeks to make a new beginning with Moses" (187).

646 to Jacob's remarks here: Sacks, "The Lion and the Ass," 172–76.

651 "before it reached the cave at Machpelah": *The Pentateuch and Haftorahs,* 2nd ed., ed. J. H. Hertz (London: Soncino Press, 1967), 188.

655 the sons of Israel: I owe the insight about the hampered gait and the "limping" to Will Wilson.

INDEX

Animals (*cont.*)
  sacrifice of, 171, 194–195, 306n, 347n,
    564n
  talking, 81n
Answering discourse, 80–87
Anthropological beginnings, 10–11
Apotheosis, 86, 146, 148, 167
Appetites, 36, 49, 61–63, 66, 84,
    383–384
Arameans, 248, 377, 436
Aristotle, 1, 3, 43–43n, 96–97n, 138, 147,
    208, 215–215n, 227–228, 532n,
    556n
The Ark, 164, 166–170, 202, 214
Arts and crafts
  Babel, 217, 222, 225–227, 231,
    233
  Cain and Abel story, 123, 125
  fire, 226, 233, 331n, 341
  Garden of Eden story, 90, 94, 96,
    109
  generation of Lamech, 146, 148
Asenath, 569–570
Asher, 430, 505
Assimilation vs. separation
  Arameans/Mesopotamians, 436
  Canaanites/Hittites, 364–365, 489,
    649
  Egyptians, 538, 616–659
  Israel's challenges, 510
  Jacob and sons, 501, 609–610,
    613–614
  Joseph into Egypt, 575–576n
Assyrians, 52, 227
Astronomical observation, 43n, 229
Augury, 625
Authoritative speech, 345n
Authority, 82, 86–87, 113, 115, 197–216, 505,
    534
Autonomy. *See* Freedom

Awareness
  of divine providence, 171
  of God, 238
  living things and, 35
  of mortality, 96
  of nakedness, 106
  self-awareness, 76–80, 83–84, 238
  of time, 555–557
  See also Tree of knowledge of good
    and bad
Awe
  Abraham and, 258, 304–308, 324, 344,
    346
  animals toward man, 180
  Bible and, 3
  in creation stories, 53, 56, 419
  of Esau, 469
  Ham without, 206–207
  of Isaac, 395–396
  of Jacob, 416
  of Joseph's brothers, 581
  patriarchy and, 349
  principles of being and, 12, 91–92
  respect for life, 178–179
  See also Fear of God; Reverence;
    Wisdom

Babel, 10, 12, 20, 42, 217–243
Babylon/Babylonians, 13, 20, 28, 42,
    52, 218, 229–230, 240, 248, 253,
    302
Badness, knowledge of, 55, 62,
    66–67
Balisi, Kristen Dietrich, 71n, 78n–79n,
    191n, 231n, 333n, 357n, 475n,
    494n
Barrenness
  generative powers and, 117–118,
    270
  pride and, 148

Herding. *See* Shepherds

"Here-am-I [*hineni*]"

  Abraham, 334–335, 342, 344

  Esau, 390–391

  Isaac, 393

  Jacob, 617

  Joseph, 520n

  Moses, 345n, 618

Herodotus, 486, 564n

Heroes/heroism

  Abraham in war, 259–260, 301–304

  cities and, 228

  father/son relations, 198n

  flood stories and, 167

  Heroic Age, 12, 146–148, 161, 192, 218

  Jacob, 456

  masculine path to immortality, 155

  nobility of opponents and, 462

Hirah, 528, 531–533

Hittites, 248, 364–365, 389n, 649

Hobbes, Thomas, 162, 173

Holiness

  distinction as principle of, 52

  as Genesis topic, 20

  as goal, 3

  holiness code, 475, 553n, 652n

  human way and, 12

  Shem embodying, 215

  threat of politics, 249n

  See also Purity, simplicity, wholeheartedness

Homer, 59n, 114n, 146, 156, 198n

Homicide, 175–176, 181–187

Homosexuality, 329–330, 625

Hospitality

  of Abraham/Lot, 261, 263–264, 316–318, 326–329

  Israelite way, 475

  Joseph to brothers, 587–593

  of Laban, 371–373

  of Pharaoh, 626–629

  of Rebekah, 369–370

Human nature. *See* Man

Human reason. *See* Reason

Hunting, 222, 383–384, 390–391, 394, 408

Idolatry

  as abominable practice, 625

  Babel story and, 219, 237

  Jacob and sons, 501

  Jacob's worship of Rachel, 418–425, 432–436, 444

  Moses on, 42–43

Image of God

  in creation stories, 37–39, 55–56, 185

  filial piety and, 213–216

  longevity and, 160

  man and, 21, 34, 36

  Noahide law proscribing homicide, 175, 181, 184–187

Immortality, 21, 69, 148, 155, 557n, 658. *See also* Tree of life

Incest

  as abominable practice, 625

  exogamy vs., 293–296

  Ham's shameless looking, 206, 208

  Judah and Tamar, 533–535

  Lot's daughters, 207, 282, 327

  love of own flesh and, 104n

  Reuben's act of, 505

  sexuality and, 270

  taboo on, 268n

  wife of Cain, 144n

Independence

  aloneness and, 238

  Babel as symbol of, 230

  discourse and, 80–87

  farming and, 129

  as Genesis topic, 20

Leon R. Kass is the Addie Clark Harding Professor (on leave) in the Committee on Social Thought and the College at the University of Chicago and the Hertog Fellow at the American Enterprise Institute. Dr. Kass was educated at the University of Chicago, where he earned his B.S. and M.D. degrees, and at Harvard, where he took a Ph.D. in biochemistry. He taught at St. John's College in Annapolis, Maryland, and at Georgetown University, before returning to the University of Chicago, where he has been an award-winning teacher since 1976 and where he has, for twenty years, taught the seminar that resulted in this book. Currently chairman of the President's Council on Bioethics, he is the author of three books, most recently *Life, Liberty, and the Defense of Dignity: The Challenge for Bioethics,* and coauthor of two more. He lives in Washington, D.C., and Chicago.